Inside the Windows 95 Registry

Inside the Windows 95 Registry

Ron Petrusha

O'REILLY™

Cambridge · Köln · Paris · Sebastopol · Tokyo

Inside the Windows 95 Registry
by Ron Petrusha

Copyright © 1996 O'Reilly & Associates, Inc. All rights reserved.
Printed in the United States of America.

Published by O'Reilly & Associates, Inc., 101 Morris Street, Sebastopol, CA 95472.

Editor: Andrew Schulman

Production Editor: Jane Ellin

Printing History:

     August 1996:   First Edition

ISBN: 1-56592-170-4

Table of Contents

Preface

A single minute of user activity in Windows 95 can easily generate several thousand calls to the registry. Whenever you click on the "MyComputer" icon, on a typical computer over *five hundred* registry accesses are generated. Every time you open up a document in Microsoft Word for Windows, WinWord makes queries to the registry about two hundred times. Starting up the Netscape Navigator Gold 3.0, in Windows 95 or Windows NT, results in something like 1,400 calls to the registry—the Web browser is checking settings such as:

```
HKEY_ROOT\.html HKEY_ROOT\NetscapeMarkup\shell\open\command
HKEY_LOCAL_MACHINE\Software\Netscape\Netscape Navigator\Cache\
    Disk Cache SSL
HKEY_LOCAL_MACHINE\Software\Netscape\Netscape Navigator\Network\
    Warn Accepting Cookie
HKEY_LOCAL_MACHINE\Software\Netscape\Netscape Navigator\Java\
    Enable JavaScript
HKEY_LOCAL_MACHINE\Software\Netscape\Netscape Navigator\Security\
    Cipher Prefs
HKEY_LOCAL_MACHINE\System\CurrentControlSet\Services\Winsock\
    Autodial
```

In other words, the registry plays a crucial role in Windows 95 and Windows NT, and in the operation of important Windows applications such as WinWord and Netscape Navigator.

Yet, the registry is a source of mystery to many Windows 95 and NT programmers, system administrators, and users. Everyone seems to know that the registry is somehow important. But how or why it's important, what all those strange-looking settings mean, how these settings are used by applications or by

Windows itself, how one goes about using the registry to change the behavior of Windows—none of this is particularly well-understood.

For many users and developers of Windows 95 and NT, a fascination with the registry has been mingled with fear and dread. As a decidedly under-documented structure, the registry was and is a mysterious "black box" where information is somehow read and written. Frequently, as users, we're aware of the existence of the registry only when something goes wrong; and then, precisely because the registry is poorly documented, we often have no idea how to diagnose or fix the problem.

But along with interest in the registry as a reflection of our fascination with the unknown, the registry has attracted attention for another reason: it is an efficient structure for storing and retrieving a wide range of data that control Windows 95 and Windows NT. The registry is a central database that imposes a uniform structure and set of standards on applications, thereby removing some of the anarchy that plagued Windows 3.x. (If you're wondering whether "anarchy" is a fair description, and you have ever had Windows 3.1 installed on your system, it's instructive to search your system's hard drives for .INI files: on any heavily used system, you'll find about a hundred of them, but frequently you'll have no idea where they came from, why they're there, and whether they're actually still used by Windows or Windows applications.)

Inside the Windows 95 Registry addresses both areas of interest. In place of the view of the registry as a magical black box, it attempts to provide some solid documentation that helps you understand how the registry is organized and how it is used both by Windows 95 and by Windows NT. In the course of reading the book, hopefully you'll find that your own view of the registry has been transformed, and that instead of seeing the registry as inconvenient, mysterious, and troublesome, you'll instead see it as a practical database structure that you can use to store an almost unlimited range of data. The book's text is supplemented by several registry spying utilities, most notably *RegSpy95*, that you can use to actively explore how Windows and Windows applications use the registry.

Besides trying to demystify the registry, a second goal of the book is to help you actively use the registry in your applications. The book focuses in particular on C and Visual Basic programmers who are building 32-bit applications (although there's also a chapter for Win16 and DOS developers who would like to make their applications "registry-aware" when they're running under Windows 95). The book provides an in-depth examination of the registry API, and shows how to get particular kinds of data (like binary data) into and out of the registry under program control. It also examines what kinds of data you might want to have your application use the registry to store, as well as how you might best store that data.

Along with demystifying the registry and showing you how to use it, the book has a third goal: to *advocate* the use of the registry. Hopefully, in the course of reading the book, you'll come to view the registry as a robust, efficient, high-performance structure for reading and writing application configuration information. By using the registry, you can create applications that fall within the mainstream of Windows application development; by ignoring it, you may create applications that are somehow incomplete and idiosyncratic.

It's also important to stress what this book does not attempt to do. It does not attempt to provide a "complete" registry reference (although it does, of course, discuss some of what you'll find in the registry). Even assuming that it's possible to select a "typical" or "average" registry whose settings are to be documented (and that's a rather large assumption), documenting its settings in any way that is comprehensive and that does not raise more questions than it answers is quite likely an impossible undertaking.

A major stumbling block to this "documenting the registry" approach, for instance, is that frequently what matters is not what's in the registry, but what's *not* in the registry: an application, or Windows itself, queries the registry to see if it contains a certain item and, if the registry doesn't contain this item, Windows or the application takes some sort of action. The *RegSpy95* utility included with this book is superb at locating such "settings by absence." The best way to learn about how Windows and applications interact with the registry, then, is not to stare at some "complete registry reference," but to experiment with a utility such as *RegSpy95.*

Nor does the book attempt to provide more than a handful of the neat registry "tricks" that you can use to customize your system. If registry entries are fish, in other words, this book definitely gives you some fish, but more important it *teaches you how* to fish.

The Book's Audience

Although its collection of registry spying tools are of broad interest, and system administrators and power users who are experiencing difficulties with their registries may find individual chapters valuable, this is a book about developing applications that use the registry. It assumes that you're an intermediate to advanced programmer using a development tool that provides access to the Win32 API.

All of the book's sample code is written in either C or Visual Basic (VB). In some cases, we show the same operation once in C and again in Visual Basic: not only can C and VB programmers each find examples in their own preferred programming language, but this book may help VB programmers pick up a reading knowledge of C—and may give C programmers a chance to see what all the VB excitement is about.

The book's primary focus is the Windows 95 registry. But since any 32-bit application should be able to run on either Windows 95 or Windows NT, the book also devotes a considerable amount of attention to the registry under Windows NT. In particular, it emphasizes differences that you'll encounter when calling the registry API on the two platforms, and discusses some of the differences in policy (i.e., where particular kinds of information are stored) between the two implementations of the registry. If your major interest is the Windows NT rather than the Windows 95 registry, you'll still find enough substance in *Inside the Windows 95 Registry* to justify reading the book.

Organization of This Book

The book contains eleven chapters and two appendixes:

Chapter 1, *The Registry, or, What Was So Bad About .INI Files?*, examines how the registry evolved from the initialization files of Windows 3.0 and how the registry is organized under Windows 95 and Windows NT, and compares the performance of registry accesses with initialization file accesses.

Chapter 2, *Using the Registry Editor*, provides in-depth documentation of RegEdit, the registry editing tool included with Windows 95 (and Windows NT 4.0 as well). Although a number of registry editing tools are available, RegEdit remains the best general-purpose utility for viewing and modifying the contents of the registry.

Chapter 3, *Backing Up and Restoring the Registry*, offers a graduated set of techniques that you can use for backing up your registry and, in the event that your registry modifications (or the actions of some other program) damage some or all of your registry, for restoring your registry. You should definitely read this chapter before you begin testing your registry-enabled applications on your system.

Chapter 4, *The Win32 Registry API*, provides extensive coverage of the registry API, and includes some undocumented material and some little-known but important bugs in remote registry access. Although all of the chapter's examples are written in C, the material should be of interest to any programmer who accesses the registry API.

Chapter 5, *Win95 Registry Access from Win16, DOS, and VxDs*, shows how developers of DOS and 16-bit Windows applications can add registry "smarts" to their applications when they're running under Windows 95. The chapter includes a discussion of how the Win32 registry APIs are implemented in Win95. The bulk of material contained in this chapter is completely undocumented elsewhere.

Chapter 6, *The Registry and Visual Basic*, discusses the tools available to Visual Basic programmers who want their applications to use the registry. The chapter discusses VBA's intrinsic registry functions and their limitations, shows how to call the registry API directly from VB code, and covers some of the more common problems that Visual Basic programmers encounter when accessing the registry API.

Chapter 7, *The Desaware Registry Control*, provides documentation and some examples for Visual Basic programmers who are more comfortable using a custom control for registry access instead of direct calls to the registry API. A design-time version of the Desaware Registry Control is included on the diskette accompanying *Inside the Windows 95 Registry*.

Chapter 8, *What Goes in the Registry: System Settings*, examines the major system settings that you'll want your application to write to the registry so that it integrates with Windows 95 or the windows shells. Such apparently "built-in" features as drag-and-drop and context menus are actually the result of settings defined in the registry.

Chapter 9, *What Goes in the Registry: Application and User Settings*, discusses a range of settings that are unique to your application or to individual users of your application. It also examines how particular items of data can be stored in the registry most efficiently.

Chapter 10, *Spying on the Registry*, shows you how to use *RegSpy95* and *APISpy32*, two utilities included on the *Inside the Windows 95 Registry* diskette, to intercept registry accesses. Using these tools, you can see how Windows itself (in the case of *RegSpy95*) or individual applications (in the case of both *RegSpy95* and *APISpy32*) actually use the registry.

Chapter 11, *Migrating from .INI Files to the Registry* examines the process of converting an initialization file-based application to a registry-aware application. The chapter also includes a small utility, *Ini2Reg*, that you can use to convert your initialization files to registry entries.

Appendix A, *Where Am I Running?*, examines how to determine the platform on which either a 16-bit or a 32-bit application is running. Determining the platform or the version of the operating system has been a traditional stumbling block for developers; the number of applications that check version or platform incorrectly is astounding. Given the differences between the Win95 and WinNT registries, knowing which platform you're running on is, unfortunately, usually important.

Appendix B, *The Inside the Windows 95 Registry Diskette*, details the organization of sample programs and software on the accompanying diskette and provides installation instructions. In addition, the *README.TXT* file in the diskette's root directory contains information on the software and code samples that did not make it into the book.

Conventions in this Book

Throughout this book, we've used the following typographic conventions:

`Constant width`

> indicates a language construct such as a data type, a data structure, or a code example. Text in constant width also indicates registry key and value names. In syntax statements, text in constant width indicates such elements as a function or procedure's name and its return value.

Italic

> in command syntax indicates parameter names. Italicized words in the text also represent variable and parameter names, API functions, and user-defined functions, as well as system elements like filenames and directory names.

The complete path to a registry key can frequently become quite long, and not uncommonly can span more than one line. To save space, we've used the following abbreviations throughout the book for top-level registry keys:

HKCR	HKEY_CLASSES_ROOT
HKCU	HKEY_CURRENT_USER
HKLM	HKEY_LOCAL_MACHINE
HKU	HKEY_USERS
HKCC	HKEY_CURRENT_CONFIG
HKDD	HKEY_DYN_DATA

Obtaining Updated Information

All sample programs presented in the book, as well as the software discussed in the book, are included on the accompanying diskette; for details, see Appendix B, *The Inside the Windows 95 Registry Diskette*. Updates to the material contained in the book, along with other registry-related developments, are available from our Web site at *http://www.ora.com/pub/examples/windows/win95.update/registry.html.*

We'd Like to Hear From You!

We have tested and verified all of the information in this book to the best of our ability, but you may find that features have changed (or even that we have made mistakes!). Please let us know about any errors you find, as well as your suggestions for future editions, by writing:

O'Reilly & Associates, Inc.
101 Morris Street
Sebastopol, CA 95472
1-800-998-9938 (in the U.S. or Canada)
1-707-829-0515 (international/local)
1-707-829-0104 (FAX)

You can also send us messages electronically. To be put on the mailing list or request a catalog, send email to:

nuts@oreilly.com

To ask technical questions or comment on the book, send email to:

bookquestions@oreilly.com

Acknowledgments

Almost all computer books, as they move from their initial, conceptual stage to finally appear in printed form, undergo a certain process of evolution. This is true of *Inside the Windows 95 Registry*. In fact, in many ways, the finished book bears only a superficial resemblance to the original plan. Originally, this was going to be a registry book for anyone even remotely interested in the registry, from developers to system administrators to "power users"—a kind of *Everyman's Guide to the Windows 95 Registry*. But it quickly became clear that this kind of broad, general book on the Windows registry would be impossible to do properly. Maintaining a consistent quality and comprehensiveness throughout would have resulted in a work several thousand pages long. And a handy alternative—to focus on the registry-related "tricks" and techniques that are very popular in many computer magazines—seemed superficial; if a user doesn't fully understand why a trick works, he or she is often powerless to restore Windows 95 to its original state when that registry modification has unintended side effects. So instead, the everyman's primer to the registry gradually evolved into a book that focuses on developing applications that make use of the Windows registry.

Recasting a book so dramatically ultimately requires an enormous commitment in time. An inevitable consequence is that, for the past six months or so, I've really been an absentee husband and father. So I want to thank my wife, Vanessa, and son, Sean, for their support and understanding while I've been working on this book; certainly their commitment to this book has been as great as my own. I also want to thank Dakota, my Alaskan Malamute, for the regular bonding sessions (my neighbors probably call it hellacious howling) that reminded me how much my presence was missed.

In more ways than I can name, this book was the result of a collaboration between myself and my editor, Andrew Schulman. In working on this book, Andrew went far beyond the call of duty; he wrote the chapter on registry access from Win16, DOS, and VxDs, and contributed many of the book's coding examples. His boundless enthusiasm for the book also constantly pushed me to explore the undocumented aspects of the registry at the same time that he kept me focused and more or less on schedule.

Although an author usually gets all the credit (or blame, as the case may be) for a finished work, there are always a large number of people who help to shape a computer book in ways ranging from the obvious to the subtle. Tracy van Hoof of Microsoft Corporation invariably responded to all my questions—regardless of how stupid many of them were—with her characteristic patience, efficiency, and good humor. Nagarajan Subramaniyan, formerly of Microsoft, readily answered our many registry-related questions. Kent Daniel Bentkowski wrote a number of chapters for the "other" registry book that, unfortunately, we were unable to include after the book's focus changed. Alex Shmidt, the developer of *FootPrnt* and *RegSpy95*, wrote a portion of the chapter on spying on the registry, responded with amazing competence and speed while we were testing his software, and was a real pleasure to work with. Dan Appleman, Stjepan Pejic, and Roan Bear of Desaware provided the Desaware Registry Control for the book, responded to my many questions about its operation, and reviewed several chapters of the book. Matt Pietrek of Nu-Mega Technologies graciously allowed us to include his spying utility, *APISpy32*, in the book. Fred Hewett of Vireo Software contributed his very interesting sample VxD, RegFSD, to the software accompanying the book. And Mark Russinovich (also of Nu-Mega) and Bryce Cogswell provided their graphical registry spying utility, *RegMon*.

Lastly, I'd like to thank my colleagues and coworkers at O'Reilly & Associates. Tim O'Reilly and Frank Willison allowed me to suspend my editorial duties while I tried my hand at authoring. Troy Mott did an excellent job of keeping both Andrew and myself organized, and in handling all of those little details that are critical to a book, but that authors and editors tend to overlook. The production staff at ORA did an incredibly great job of producing this book in a very short time. Special thanks to Jane Ellin, who managed the production process, Sheryl Avruch, Mike Sierra, Chris Reilley, Seth Maislin, Nancy Priest, Mary Jane Walsh, Michael Deutsch, Clairemarie Fisher O'Leary, Kismet McDonough-Chan, Eden Reiner, Hanna Dyer, Sue Willing, and, of course, to Edie Freedman for her cover (which, I'm convinced, is really a thinly disguised photograph of my dog Dakota).

1

The Registry, or, What Was So Bad About .INI Files?

As if the movement from 16-bit to 32-bit applications, from a familiar user interface to a brand new one, and from File Manager and Program Manager to the Windows 95 Explorer were not enough, Windows 95 (Win95) brings yet another innovation to Windows: the registry. The registry is, in brief, a centralized site for storing system-wide and application-specific settings and configuration information. It is a sort of storage house for data that Windows uses to make sure that the proper device drivers are loaded, that the services required by applications are made available, that the proper application is loaded to open a file when you double-click on the file in the Explorer, that an application window appears in the proper place on your screen when you first launch it, and so on. In fact, many of the features that appear to be "built in" to Win95 are actually just the result of settings in the registry. These settings can be changed by the user or by an application.

Unlike the initialization (.INI) files that it replaces, the registry is not directly readable or accessible. While initialization files can be read (and therefore modified) by any text editor or can even be displayed by using the standard *DOS TYPE* command, special utilities are needed to access and display the registry. That, combined with the fact that major components of the registry are either underdocumented or wholly undocumented, lends an aura of mystery to the registry that causes users, system administrators, and developers alike to shy away from exploring or using the registry.

As we'll see, one of the goals that led to the decision to replace the Windows 3.x initialization files with a centralized registry was a desire to make configuration information *less* accessible. But for many developers, the registry instead becomes *inaccessible*. This failure to take advantage of the registry has several implications:

- Since Win32 applications are supposed to write to the registry rather than to initialization files, developers who fail to use the registry can produce applications that are not completely compliant with the Win95 software design guidelines.

- Ignoring the registry continues the "every application is an island unto itself" philosophy that Win95, with its emphasis on integration in general and on OLE (object linking and embedding) in particular, was supposed to break down.

- Since users are coming to expect many of the services that are defined by the registry, non-compliant applications appear to be idiosyncratic, quirky, amateurish, poorly designed, and unfriendly.

Producing quality 32-bit software for Win95, in short, requires that the registry be used. In this book, we'll explore both how and why you'd want to do that.

This chapter will begin to remove some of the mystery that surrounds the registry by examining how and why the registry evolved from the initialization files of Windows 3.x, why the registry offers an improvement over Windows 3.x's system of initialization files, and how the registry is organized. While this book focuses on the registry under Win95, this chapter will also briefly compare the Win95 registry with the registry in Windows NT (WinNT).

Windows 3.x and Initialization Files

When Windows 3.0 was introduced in the first half of 1990, it became an overnight success that far exceeded Microsoft's wildest expectations. In addition to the ease of use that its graphical interface offered inexperienced users, part of its success was attributable to its overwhelming acceptance by "power users," or experienced computer users. The appeal of Windows 3.0 to more experienced users was in part due to the fact that Windows was easily customizable. Most of Windows' basic settings were stored in a series of initialization files that could be viewed and modified by using any text editor. (In fact, Windows was preconfigured so that, if a user double-clicked on any file with an .INI extension in a File Manager window, Windows would automatically load Notepad, the standard Windows text editor, which in turn would open the file for editing.) As a result, "tweaking" initialization files rapidly became a favorite (if not always sensible) pastime of power users.

Windows supported two different kinds of initialization files: in Windows 3.1, five *system initialization files (SYSTEM.INI, WIN.INI, CONTROL.INI, PROGMAN.INI,* and *WINFILE.INI*, as well as *PROTOCOL.INI* in Windows for Workgroups 3.1x) were responsible for loading the device drivers that Windows needed to access its hardware resources, for determining how the Windows environment would appear and how Windows as a system would behave, and for controlling the operation of two of Windows' major components, Program Manager and File Manager. In addition, *private initialization files* could be created by any application to store its individual settings, like its position on the screen when it is loaded, the last few data files opened by the program, or the state of checkable menu items.[*]

Figure 1-1. A portion of a sample initialization file

The format of an initialization file, as shown in Figure 1-1, which depicts a portion of a *WIN.INI* file, is quite simple. Any initialization file consists of one or more sections, which start with a section name inside square brackets, such as [windows] in Figure 1-1. A particular section can be located anywhere within an initialization file; sections don't need to appear in any predefined order. *Section names* basically serve as labels that allow the individual entries of an initialization file to be organized or categorized. Figure 1-1, for instance, contains a section

---

[*] Properly speaking, only *WIN.INI* and *SYSTEM.INI* were system initialization files, while all other *.INI files were *private* initialization files. This is because *SYSTEM.INI* was used for Windows' hardware configuration, and developers used *GetProfileString* and *WriteProfileString* to read and write *WIN.INI* software configuration information. All other initialization files had to be accessed using the *GetPrivateProfileString* and *WritePrivateProfileString* APIs, which read from and write to private initialization files.

named [windows]. Each entry within a section in turn consist of a keyname, an equals sign, and the keyname's corresponding value. In Figure 1-1, for example, the first line of the [windows] section is spooler=yes. This value indicates that Print Manager should spool output sent to a system printer. Windows or an application could retrieve this value using the following code fragment:

```
#define BUF_SIZE 256

char szBuffer[BUF_SIZE] ;

GetProfileString("windows", "spooler", "no", szBuffer, BUF_SIZE) ;
if (stricmp(szBuffer, "yes") == 0)
  // do something appropriate
```

A value can consist of any combination of any printable ASCII characters, including embedded spaces, backslashes, and equal signs. While a keyname can have embedded spaces, it cannot include either backslash characters or an equal sign. Leading spaces are significant only in values (they are ignored in keynames), while trailing spaces are never significant.

So far, so good. However, as Windows became the platform of choice for PC compatibles, and as more and more software became available for Windows, it quickly became apparent that initialization files were severely flawed for controlling the configuration and operation of the Windows environment. There were several reasons why:

- *Simplicity and accessibility.* The simple format of and easy access to initialization files were both a strength and an enormous weakness. Because of their simple organization and the ease of browsing and modifying them, initialization files made it easy to customize the appearance or behavior of Windows, and to correct problems in Windows' operation. But incorrect or inadvertent modifications to initialization files frequently changed the behavior of either individual applications or of Windows as a whole, resulting in confusion and disorientation for users. In extreme cases, changes to initialization files rendered entire applications, entire Windows components (like its printing subsystem), or even Windows as a whole inoperable. Despite these potentially disastrous consequences, the fact that the files were so readily accessible encouraged tinkering (and obsessive-compulsive over-tinkering) by experienced users at the same time that it made inadvertent modification or even deletion by inexperienced users more likely.

- *Size and performance.* Windows 3.x imposed an arbitrary limit of 64K on the size of initialization files, and ignored any portion of an initialization file that exceeded this limit. On systems with large numbers of programs installed, however, the system initialization files, and particularly *WIN.INI*, became a favorite dumping ground for all kinds of information. The result? Bloated file sizes. And although it might have been possible to raise this limit, considerations of Windows' overall performance prevented it. The basically free-form format of an initialization file, and the absence of any order among sections, meant that Windows performed a *linear* search whenever it was asked to retrieve information from the file. Therefore, the longer the file, the longer it took to access an item or a section near the end of the file.

- *Lack of conformance to standards.* Although the original *Microsoft Windows Programmer's Reference* for Windows 3.0 had clearly stated that the system initialization files should be used only to record information that affected either the Windows environment as a whole or multiple applications within Windows, developers frequently chose to ignore this injunctive and instead wrote application-specific settings to *WIN.INI*. In addition to causing bloated file sizes, it was common for one application to overwrite the values written by other applications or even by Windows itself. The result was erratic behavior and frequent technical support problems. For example, some third-party replacements for Program Manager frequently defined themselves as the default Windows shell (i.e., changed the value of the *SHELL=* keyword in the [boot] section of *SYSTEM.INI*) without notifying users. As a result, instead of Program Manager, users would unexpectedly be confronted by a new Windows shell that they didn't know how to use. (By the way, we're talking as if all this is in the past, but as we'll see, Win95 *still* relies on *SHELL=* and other *SYSTEM.INI* settings.)

- *Absence of unique key names.* Although the Windows initialization files occasionally included duplicate key names within a single section (the most notable example is *DEVICE=* in *SYSTEM.INI*), the initialization file functions within the Windows 3.x application programming interface (API) could locate and modify only the first occurrence of the keyname, a fact not explicitly noted in the Windows documentation.[*] The result was sometimes an inadvertent change to the wrong entry in cases where duplicate key names existed.

- *Absence of system-level standards.* Aside from the most general criteria (i.e., system initialization files are for storing system-level or multi-application information), there was no real indication of what kinds of information should be stored in what ways in initialization files. As a result, initialization files on many computers rather quickly became indiscriminate collections of incongru-

---

[*] How then, you might ask, could anyone access multiple keys with the same name such as `device=`? With the *Get_Profile_String* and *Get_Next_Profile_String* functions documented in the Windows 3.1 Device Driver Kit (DDK), a device driver could read the values belonging to multiple keys with the same name from *SYSTEM.INI*. This could not be done, though, with the old Win16 Profile API. Under Win32, you can use *GetProfileSection*, which reads all of the keynames and values, in one go, from a designated section of *WIN.INI*. *GetProfileSection* is just one of several enhanced initialization file functions that were added to the Win32 API (*GetProfileSection* is also exported by the Win16 kernel in Windows 95).

ous data. Moreover, the loose degree of integration within the Windows environment, the lack of firm guidelines for what kinds of events initialization files should record, and the failure to incorporate significant events (like the removal of an installed program) into Windows at a system level meant that the Windows initialization files, and particularly *WIN.INI*, did not necessarily reflect the state of the system as a whole. For instance, if you deleted an application, its entries in *WIN.INI* would be unaffected, and its private initialization files might continue to survive as well. Incredibly, "uninstaller" applications, whose job is to *remove* other applications, became some of the hottest-selling software items.

- *Numerous fragmented initialization files.* With the release of Windows 3.1, developers were urged to rely on private initialization files rather than *WIN.INI* to hold any configuration data that did not relate to OLE or File Manager's support for their application. This led to a proliferation of initialization files throughout the user's file system. On systems with large numbers of applications, their sheer number made it almost inevitable that, sooner or later, an initialization file would be deleted or modified, often with disastrous consequences. Frequently these initialization files contained information that, because they were of concern to other applications, should have been stored in *WIN.INI*. Meanwhile, *WIN.INI*, as noted earlier, contained settings belonging to some application the user had deleted six months earlier.

- *No uniform storage location for private initialization files.* Although the initialization file functions looked in the Windows directory for a private initialization file unless instructed otherwise, there were no explicit standards for where to store private .INI files. So not only did they proliferate in number, they also proliferated throughout the directories of a user's hard disk, as some applications used the Windows directory while others used an application directory to store them. In some cases, users ended up with two or more private initialization files for the same application, each with different settings.

- *Inappropriate use of initialization files to avoid Windows services.* Sometimes, applications used private initialization files to store system-level information that they should have retrieved from elsewhere. For example, several word processors and desktop publishers relied on font information that they stored in private initialization files. If these fonts became unavailable, the application crashed. Microsoft Publisher is a good example.

- *Unsuitability for networked computer environments.* Windows' dependence on initialization files began during a period when PCs were primarily stand-alone, single-user systems. It quickly became clear, however, that the trend was for systems to be networked, and that it was not uncommon for a single user to have access to any of several corporate computers. The simple format of an initialization file, in which sections and entries could appear in any order and sections could not be nested, made it all but impossible to store individual users' configuration data or to easily move blocks of configuration data from one networked machine to another on which a particular user might work. Windows' reliance on text files, such as *AUTOEXEC.BAT* and *CONFIG.SYS* as well as *SYSTEM.INI*, *WIN.INI*, and the now proliferating private initialization files, created a bewildering array of files that made configuration management in a network environment a nightmare.

.INI Files and Win-CGI

Still, .INI files are simple, and have their place. Temporary private initialization files are an important part of the Win-CGI (Common Gateway Interface for Windows) standard for writing Windows applications that produce dynamic, "on the fly," hypertext pages for the World Wide Web (see *http://website.ora.com/wsdocs/32demo/windows-cgi.html*). For example, a Win-CGI program can retrieve the name of a user's Web browser (such as "Mozilla/2.01Gold" for Netscape Navigator Gold 2.01) with the code below; Windows Web servers pass the name of a temporary private .INI file to Win-CGI applications on their command line (`lpszCmdLine`):

```
char user_agent[256];
GetPrivateProfileString("CGI", "User Agent", "unknown",
    user_agent, 256, lpszCmdLine);
```

Similarly, a Win-CGI application can find out about a user-supplied query (such as from the FORM section of a Web page) with the following code:

```
char query_string[256];
GetPrivateProfileString("CGI", "Query String", "",
    query_string, 256, lpszCmdLine);
if (*query_string)
    // process user's query
else
    // no query — send back default initial web page
```

Of course, in the event that a Web form allows the user to send more than 64K of data to a server, *or* if a query string is too long, or contains non-text characters that are unsuitable for inclusion in an .INI file, Win-CGI can't put the data in an .INI file. Win-CGI must then use an external file, whose filename alone appears in the [`Form External`] or [`Form Huge`] section of the .INI file.

The Win-CGI application mentioned here is discussed in more detail in Chapter 11, *Migrating from .INI Files to the Registry*. For more information on Win-CGI itself, see the O'Reilly book, *CGI for Windows*, by Linda Mui and Bob Denny (available late 1996) and *http://devl.ora.com/andrew/wincgi*.

It's also crucial to realize that .INI files are *not* completely a thing of the past. As one example, Win95 relies totally on the `shell=` setting in the `[boot]` section of *SYSTEM.INI*. By default, this setting reads `shell=Explorer.exe` because the standard user interface to Win95 is the Explorer. However, change this to `shell=ProgMan.exe` or even `shell=c:\command.com`, and Win95 will take on a totally different "look and feel." Change this to the name of a non-existent file, and Windows refuses to load, informing you that you need to reinstall Windows. We even know one user who, taking seriously the notion that Windows isn't really used for anything but playing Solitaire anyway, actually put `shell=Sol.exe` in the `[boot]` section of his *SYSTEM.INI*. The point is that the registry does not replace, but *supplements*, the old *SYSTEM.INI* and *WIN.INI* files from Windows 3.x.

Windows 3.1 and REG.DAT

With the limitations of initialization files becoming more apparent, Windows 3.1 for the first time included a registration database, which was an alternate form of storing certain kinds of configuration information. The Windows 3.1 registration database, or registry, which resided in a single file named *REG.DAT*, was used for OLE, for drag-and-drop operations, and for establishing associations between data files and the programs capable of handling them based on their data file extension.

Unlike the initialization files, which were loosely structured ASCII files, *REG.DAT* was a binary file that end-users could browse and modify only with a special utility program, the Registration Info Editor (*REGEDIT.EXE*) bundled with Windows 3.1. Figure 1-2 shows the Registration Editor in its advanced mode displaying a portion of a Windows 3.1 registration database file.

As Figure 1-2 shows, in addition to its relative inaccessibility, the registration database featured an organization different from the linear, more or less free-form structure typical of initialization files. The registration database was organized as a hierarchical inverse tree-like structure, very much like the DOS/Windows file system. Starting from a single root (called `HKEY_CLASSES_ROOT`), the registration database featured a variable number of keys, each identified by a key name. For instance, in Figure 1-2, `ExcelChart` is the name of a key directly off the root. Each key in turn could have one or more subkeys; in other words, the Windows 3.1 registration database supported *nested keys*. For instance, `protocol` is a subkey of `ExcelChart`, while `StdFileEditing` is a subkey of `protocol`. Just as in the case of the file system, the backslash character ("\") was used as the path separator to delimit a key and its subkey (e.g., `HKEY_CLASSES_ROOT\ExcelChart\protocol\StdFileEditing`). Each subkey required a unique name with respect to its parent key. In other words, a single

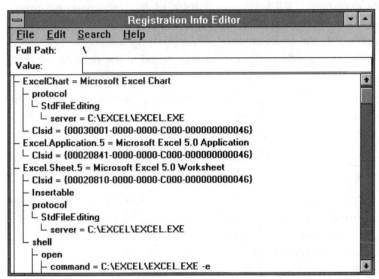

Figure 1-2. RegEdit in advanced mode displaying the Windows 3.1 registration database

key could not contain two identically named subkeys, but as long as a given key could be identified by a unique path, duplicate names were valid.

Besides having one or more subordinate keys, a key could be assigned an optional text string to define its value. For instance, the key `HKEY_CLASSES_ROOT\ExcelChart\protocol\StdFileEditing` has no value, while the value of one of its subkeys, `server`, is "C:\EXCEL\EXCEL.EXE."

The Windows 3.1 registration database was used as a system integration tool in four major ways:

- *Integration with File Manager*. File Manager allowed the user to choose the File Open and File Print menu options after selecting a data file in a directory list window. Based on the file's extension and the information it obtained from the registration database, File Manager would "know" how to display or to print the file.

- *Drag-and-drop*. Windows 3.1 allowed the user to print a file by dragging its icon from File Manager onto Print Manager, or to embed a file in a compound document by dragging its icon from File Manager into the target application (the one in which it was to be embedded). The information that allowed Windows to handle a file based on its file extension was contained within the registration database. Previously, this file-association information was found in the `[Extensions]` section of *WIN.INI*; for example, the entry `txt=notepad.exe ^.txt` established *notepad.exe* as the handler for *.txt files. Not surprisingly though (given the requirements of backwards compatibility), this [Extensions] section *still* exists in Windows 3.1 and Win95.

- *Dynamic data exchange (DDE)*. DDE is a form of interprocess communication that allows one application to link to data contained within another running application. The information needed for an application to conduct a DDE conversation with another application was stored in the registration database.

- *Object linking and embedding (OLE)*. The information needed to create compound documents and to open the application responsible for editing embedded objects was stored in the registration database.

Developers were given two methods for taking the information that Windows needed about their applications and storing it in *REG.DAT*:

- *A new set of API functions*. The *RegCreateKey*, *RegOpenKey*, *RegDeleteKey*, *RegCloseKey*, *RegEnumKey* (to list the subkeys of a particular key), *RegSetValue* (to define a particular key's value), *RegQueryValue* (to retrieve a key's value), and *FindExecutable* (to identify the application associated with a given file extension) functions were added to the Windows 3.1 application programming interface to allow applications to directly access and manipulate the registration database.

- *Registration (.REG) files*. A specially formatted registration text file (resembling in many ways an .INI file) could be included as a part of an application's installation routine. During installation, the Registration Editor could be invoked by using the command *REGEDIT /s <regfilename>*. This would launch the Registration Editor as a background process and merge the registration file into the registration database. This action corresponds to a `reg=regedit.exe /s ^.reg` setting in WIN.INI.

There were several limitations and problems with Windows 3.1's use of a registration database to store configuration. First, as with initialization files, Windows imposed a 64K limit on the file size of *REG.DAT*. Second, upgrades to Windows 3.1 did not properly update *REG.DAT* to reflect information on any OLE-compliant applications that ran under Windows 3.0; to correct it, the user had to manually run REGEDIT and merge the application's .REG file. Third, the registration database was a special purpose structure whose functionality was partially duplicated by other portions of the system, most notably *WIN.INI*. This created the possibility that the registration database and *WIN.INI* might become out of synch, although in this case Windows 3.1 assumed that the information in the registration database was correct.

Despite the rather specialized character of the registration database, it was central to Windows 3.1's support for both OLE and drag-and-drop. These were, after all, the newest and most significant features incorporated into Windows 3.1; Microsoft was trying to position OLE as the centerpiece of its "vision" for "information at your fingertips." This gave a clear indication that, in future versions of its graphical operating systems, Microsoft was leaning toward using something akin to the Windows 3.1 registration database as a centralized repository for storing a system's configuration information. So too did Microsoft's high-end operating system, Windows NT, which from its initial release included a very different registry as the central repository for all information relating to a computer system's hardware and software configuration. See the section later in this chapter on differences between the Win95 and NT registries.

The Registry in Win95

In place of *SYSTEM.INI* for hardware configuration, *WIN.INI* for system software configuration, *REG.DAT* for file associations and object linking and embedding, and its miscellaneous assortment of private initialization files for configuring individual applications, Win95 features a single repository for hardware, system software, and application configuration information known as *the registry*. At the same time that the registry offers centralized storage of configuration information, it also uses several techniques to make itself relatively inaccessible to users.

Limiting Access to the Registry

In designing the Win95 registry, Microsoft clearly aimed at restricting access to a system's configuration information. As we noted earlier, unlike the initialization files of Windows 3.x, which stored their data in plain ASCII files that could be read by any text editor or word processor, the registry stores its data in a proprietary binary format.

Rather than storing this binary data in a single file, the registry is actually stored in three different locations:

- The bulk of the registry's data is stored in a file named *SYSTEM.DAT*. A copy of *SYSTEM.DAT* from the last successful Windows session is stored in *SYSTEM.DAO*.

- User configuration data is stored in a file named *USER.DAT*. A backup copy from the last session is stored in *USER.DAO*.

- Some of the registry's configuration data is built by Win95 on the fly at system start up, and resides only in memory. It is not stored in a file on the hard disk. The same goes for "dynamic" registry information maintained by virtual device drivers (VxDs) which install registry handlers with the *_RegCreateDynKey* service. These dynamic registry settings are generally used by performance-monitoring tools such as *PVIEW.EXE*.

This is the simple view. It is therefore not really accurate. We'll see as we go along that there are actually many more files than just *SYSTEM.DAT* and *USER.DAT* that Win95 may use in constructing the registry on a particular machine.

Besides fragmenting its data and storing it in a special format, the two permanent registry files are also stored as hidden, read-only system files, thus making their examination, modification, or accidental deletion by inexperienced users much more difficult.

Why, one might ask, did Microsoft go to such pains to "hide" the basic details of a system's configuration from its users? The answer lies in the central role of the registry in the operation of Win95: the registry contains virtually every item of data that Windows needs to start and run the system, rather than just information for such special-purpose operations as associating files, supporting drag-and-drop, or handling object linking and embedding. The size of the two files that compose the registry on single-user systems has consequently swelled to somewhere in the neighborhood of a megabyte on most machines. By modifying the registry in inappropriate ways or by providing invalid values for particular keys, it is possible to cripple individual applications, Windows' interprocess communications, or even the operation of Windows as a whole. In some cases (which are, unfortunately, surprisingly easy to achieve), the result can transform a computer system into a rather expensive paperweight: Windows cannot find the information that it needs to load.

The Importance of the Registry

Many developers wish to rely on initialization files rather than use the registry. There are several reasons why:

- *Compatibility.* Programmers writing applications for both 16- and 32-bit Windows platforms who decide to use the registry must create separate platform-specific code modules to write to initialization files under Windows 3.x and to the registry under Win95 and Windows NT. It's much easier not to support the registry, which allows the same code to run on both platforms. Microsoft, in fact, made this alternative much more appealing by enhancing the initialization file functions in the latest versions of the Win32 API.

- *Newness of the registry.* As software has increased in complexity, the demands made on developers have increased geometrically, even with the development of powerful, easy-to-use development tools and the emphasis on component-based programming. Using the registry is one of those new demands, though one that seems secondary to migrating applications to 32 bits or supporting OLE.

- *Intimidation.* Because it is comparatively inaccessible and underdocumented, the registry is frequently viewed with fear, loathing, and intimidation by developers no less than by users. There is some basis for this—incorrect registry entries can partially or wholly disable a system. And no developer wants to write the application that, instead of increasing the user's productivity, puts his or her computer out of commission (though arguably this might increase their true productivity).

However, avoiding the registry is a mistake. Quite simply, the registry is the glue that holds Windows together. By failing to take full advantage of the registry, developers risk creating applications that are outside of the mainstream of Windows software development. The result is almost invariably an application that quickly becomes irrelevant: from the viewpoint of users, such software appears idiosyncratic, quirky, difficult to learn and use, and underpowered.

Performance and the Registry

If you're skeptical about the advantages of a centralized registry and continue to prefer initialization files to store application information, a comparison of Windows' performance when accessing the registry and initialization files may change your mind. Whether you're reading or writing data, registry accesses are *significantly* faster under almost any circumstance.

Example 1-1 displays a relatively straightforward console mode benchmark that measures the time required to write about 60K of string data to the [tmp] section of a private initialization file, *TMP.INI*, and to a registry key named HKCU\Software\Test. The program writes a roughly equivalent number of bytes to both the initialization file and the registry; the precise number of bytes written to the registry is determined by how many complete entries (measured by the value of *numkey*) the *WritePrivateProfileString* function is able to write before failing because it had exceeded the approximately 64K (in practice, about 60K) limit on .INI file size.

The final portion of the benchmark measures the time taken by a *RegExportBranch* function to write the new registry entries to a .REG file. Note the use of the *STRINGIZE(x)* preprocessor directive, which uses the C stringize operator to convert the constant HKEY_CURRENT_USER to a string. This string in turn is used by the *sprintf* function to form a command line that includes the complete registry path. Once it builds a valid command line, the *RegExportBranch* function calls the *WinExec* function to run *RegEdit*. Incidentally, *RegExportBranch* only works with the Win95 and Win NT 4.0 registry editors; for the reason why this function doesn't work as expected under Win NT 3.x, see "Registry Compatibility: Policy vs. Mechanism" later in this chapter.

Example 1-1. An .INI file/registry benchmark

```c
// inireg.c — simple INI vs. REG performance test
// cl inireg.c advapi32.lib

#include <stdio.h>
#include <time.h>
#include <windows.h>

int RegExportBranch(char *keystr1, char *keystr2, char *filename)
{
    char cmd[256];
    sprintf(cmd, "regedit /E %s %s\\%s", filename, keystr1, keystr2);
    return WinExec(cmd, SW_HIDE);
}

main()
{
    HKEY hkey;
    char *keystr = "Software\\Test";
    int i, numkey, bytes;
    time_t t1, t2;

    // first test .INI file access
    time(&t1);
    for (i=0, bytes=0; ; i++)
    {
        char key[256];
        char value[256];
        bytes += sprintf(key, "key_number_%u", i);
        time(&t2);
        bytes += sprintf(value, "value_number_%u (%lu)", i, t2);
        if (! WritePrivateProfileString("tmp", key, value, "TMP.INI"))
            break;   // probably exceeded 60-64k limit
    }
    time(&t2);
    numkey = i;
    printf("Private INI file:\n");
    printf("Wrote %u bytes in %u key/values\n", bytes, numkey);
    printf("%lu seconds\n\n", t2 - t1);

    // now test registry access
    time(&t1);
    if (RegCreateKey(HKEY_CURRENT_USER, keystr, &hkey) != ERROR_SUCCESS)
        return 1;
    for (i=0, bytes=0; i<numkey; i++)
    {
        char keystr2[256], value[256];
        int valuelen;
        bytes += sprintf(keystr2, "key_number_%u", i);
        time(&t2);
        valuelen = sprintf(value, "value_number_%u (%lu)", i, t2);
        bytes += valuelen;
        if (RegSetValue(hkey, keystr2, REG_SZ, value, valuelen) !=
```

Example 1-1. An .INI file/registry benchmark (continued)

```
                ERROR_SUCCESS)
                break;
    }
    RegCloseKey(hkey);
    time(&t2);
    printf("Registry:\n");
    printf("Wrote %u bytes in %u key/values\n", bytes, i);
    printf("%lu seconds\n\n", t2 - t1);

    // now test writing the whole 60-64k registry data to a .REG file
    time(&t1);
    #define STRINGIZE(x)    #x
    RegExportBranch(STRINGIZE(HKEY_CURRENT_USER), keystr, "TEST.REG");
    time(&t2);
    printf("%lu seconds to run REGEDIT to export branch\n", t2 - t1);

    return 0;
}
```

The results of the test are fairly dramatic: on two different Pentium computers, it took between 10 and 16 seconds to write 61,184 bytes to 1,440 initialization file key/value entries, but only 2 to 5 seconds to write 61,140 bytes to 1,440 registry keys and their default values. It took an additional 1 to 3 seconds for *RegEdit* to export the HKCU\Software\Test branch. In other words, writing to the registry is from two to eight times faster than equivalent writes to a private initialization file.

Any benchmark, of course, should be viewed with skepticism. Nevertheless, this particular benchmark is just one in a series that we developed for comparing the performance of the registry with that of initialization files. In each case, using the registry offered vastly superior performance over initialization files. This was true even in a "worst case" scenario, where hundreds of registry accesses were required to retrieve the same data gathered by a single initialization file access with the new *GetProfileSection* function.

These results amount to an even more compelling endorsement of the registry when you consider two of the "fringe benefits" the registry offers:

- *No limitation on file size.* The actual number of write operations that our benchmark times is determined by the restriction on the size of initialization files; once the size of an initialization file reaches its upward limit of about 60K, the *WriteProfileString* or *WritePrivateProfileString* functions fail. It is very easy for an .INI file, and particularly a system initialization file, to become this large. In contrast, you don't have to be particularly concerned that writes to the registry will fail because the registry has become too large; it has no practical size limitation, as long as free disk space is available.

- *Flexibility and ease of data handling.* Our benchmark measured the time taken to write string data to a private initialization file and the registry. Initialization files, though, are able to handle *only* string data. (Actually, you can also write integer data to an initialization file using the *WriteProfileInt* or *WritePrivateProfileInt* functions, but, since it's stored as a string, you must retrieve it as string data; there are no "GetProfileInt" or "GetPrivateProfileInt" functions.) The registry, on the other hand, handles a diversity of data types, including structured data, with equal ease. This means that, when you use the registry, entirely apart from the actual time consumed by the read and write operations, processing data in order to write it or after reading it generally takes far less time and requires far less effort and coding on your part. In other words, there are additional and potentially very significant performance benefits involved when using the registry to handle "real world" data.

If this last point seems somewhat murky, consider the simple case of retrieving a window's coordinates from an initialization file. Typically, the coordinates are stored as four separate values (like Left=92, Top=88, Height=692, Width=499) or as a single string (Window=92 88 692 499). In the first case, four read operations are required to retrieve what amounts to one piece of data. In the second, the string has to be parsed and each of its members extracted to pass to a window management function. In both cases, since this is plain text that any user can modify, a good deal of validation should also be performed to insure that the coordinates are sensible ones (e.g., the window isn't positioned well off the screen); most programs, of course, don't bother with this. In contrast, these coordinates can be stored as members of a single binary data structure in the registry; they can be retrieved with a single read operation, stored to a program-defined structured data type, and passed to an API function with no further processing.

The registry, then, offers real advantages both in terms of organizing the user's computing environment and of performance. For many developers, this is likely to come as a major shock, not so much because initialization files are so popular as because the registry remains a Windows system structure that is cloaked in obscurity. The first step in removing the veil of secrecy (or at least the veil of confusion) that surrounds the registry involves understanding how it is organized.

The Basic Structure of the Windows 95 Registry

As mentioned earlier, the Win95 registry is not a single physical file. Instead, when Win95 is installed using its default configuration (i.e., it has not been configured to support multiple users; see below), the registry consists of the files *SYSTEM.DAT* and *USER.DAT*, along with a non-file "dynamic" portion maintained by VxDs. However, in working with the registry, you don't have to concern yourself with the physical files in which particular kinds of data are stored. Nor do

What Are User Profiles?

In large measure as a legacy of DOS, previous versions of Windows equated the user with the computer system; Windows stored one set of application state information, which supposedly belonged to that user. Windows 95, on the other hand, recognizes that more than one person might be using a system at various times, and allows each of their settings to be preserved based on their login name. That way, the next time that they log on to a system, many of the features of their Windows environment are preserved. On systems configured to support multiple users, Windows saves each user's configuration settings to the subkey of `HKEY_USERS` that corresponds to their user name.

The *system settings* that Windows saves on a per-user basis include such things as the sounds assigned to particular system events, the share names of persistent network connections, most options that can be configured from the Control Panel, the names of recent documents that appear on the Start menu, and the most recent file specifications used in the Explorer's Find: All Files dialog.

Application settings from individual 32-bit Windows applications can also be saved on a per-user basis. For this to happen, though, each application must explicitly write particular user settings to subkeys of `HKEY_CURRENT_USER`. Microsoft Excel, for instance, saves such items as the names of the four most recently used files, the default directory for storing files, the preferred x-y coordinates for displaying dialog boxes, and the default font for new worksheets.

Aside from the convenience of having your own settings saved from session to session, you can also configure individual applications in creative ways, depending on which settings they save on a per-user basis. You could, for example, create three different user profiles for yourself (e.g., "home," "office," and "road") and configure your email program so that a particular email configuration corresponds to a particular user profile. Once again, this depends on the application's having been written to support the necessary configuration options on a per-user basis. For example, Microsoft Exchange stores settings in `HKEY_CURRENT_USER\Software\Microsoft\Windows Messaging Subsystem\Profiles\MS Exchange Settings`.

you need to know how registry data within these files or within memory are formatted; this is officially undocumented (though, if you're interested, in Win95 an HKEY is usually a pointer to a RGKN data structure). This is to say that the registry, very much like your computer's file system, is a *logical* rather than a physical entity. The translation between the registry's physical data in files and memory and the logical view of the registry is handled automatically by the registry functions in the Win32 API, which together with *RegEdit* constitute the only "official" way to access the registry.

On Win95 systems that have been configured to support multiple users, or on Win95 systems that are clients on NT or Novell NetWare networks, the way that Win95 assembles the registry can be yet more complicated. Depending on how a system's administrators have chosen to configure the system, the registry can be assembled in one of the following ways:

- *User profiles.* Windows 95 supports user profiles: it can be configured to save a variety of basic settings for individual users based on their user names. On a Windows 95 system with separate user profiles, Windows pieces the registry together from *SYSTEM.DAT*, a memory-only component, the system-wide *USER.DAT* file (which is usually, although not always, stored in the Windows directory), and the individual user's *USER.DAT* file (which is usually, although again not always, stored in *WINDOWS\PROFILE\<user name>\USER.DAT*).

Configuring Windows 95 for Multiple Users

Since by default Windows 95 supports a single user, it must be configured beforehand to save profiles for multiple users. To do this, double-click on the Passwords icon in the Control Panel to open the Passwords Properties dialog, then select the User Profiles property sheet shown in Figure 1-3. When the `Users can customize...` button is selected, Windows 95 is configured to save user profiles.

When Windows 95 boots and displays a logon dialog like the one shown in Figure 1-4 and a new user logs on, Windows next displays the new user dialog shown in Figure 1-5. If the user selects the `Yes` button, Windows displays another dialog that prompts the user to confirm his or her password. Windows then configures the system to support the new user and saves the user name and password in a .PWL file in the Windows directory. Observe that passwords are *not* stored in the registry; the .PWL file is, of course, encrypted (though apparently not very well; according to a December 1995 Web posting by Frank Stevenson, .PWL files are "well suited for a known plaintext attack as the 20 first bytes are completely predictable").

- *Mandatory user profiles.* On a Windows 95 system that is configured to support multiple users and that belongs to a domain on a Windows NT or Novell NetWare network, system administrators can define a "mandatory" user profile for each user by creating a copy of *USER.DAT*, renaming it *USER.MAN*, and storing it in the user's home directory (on a Windows NT network) or the user's mail directory (on a Novell NetWare network). In this case, Windows 95 creates the registry in the same way as it does on systems with user profiles, except that the *USER.MAN* file is loaded last and therefore takes precedence over an individual's *USER.DAT* file. Changes to a user's individual settings that are made in the course of a session are stored in the registry, but are lost the next time the user logs on.

- *Policy settings.* Windows 95 includes a utility named System Policy Editor (*POLEDIT.EXE*) that system administrators can use to modify a particular computer's registry directly, or to generate a policy (.POL) file. On Windows NT and Novell NetWare networks, Windows 95 can be configured to automatically download this file if it is named *CONFIG.POL.* In other cases, including single-user systems or Windows 95 peer-to-peer networks, it is possible to configure Windows 95 to download a particular policy file whenever Windows 95 loads. In either case, when a .POL file is used, its contents are downloaded into the registry whenever a user logs on to Windows 95.

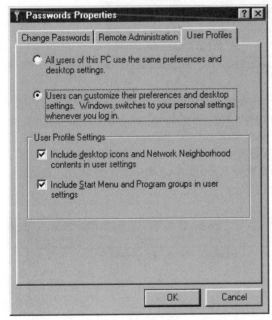

Figure 1-3. The User Profiles property sheet of the Passwords Properties dialog

Thus, to the simple picture presented initially, in which the registry equals *SYSTEM.DAT* plus *USER.DAT* plus dynamic keys maintained by VxDs, we must now add files such as *PROFILE\<user name>\USER.DAT, USER.MAN,* and *CONFIG.POL.*

Like directories in the DOS/Windows file system, the Win95 registry is an inverse tree-like structure that contains nested keys (which correspond to the file system's directories) and data (which correspond to files). The file system on a particular drive, though, consists of a single top-level or root directory. Similarly, *REG.DAT,* the Windows 3.1 registration database which is the precursor to the Win95

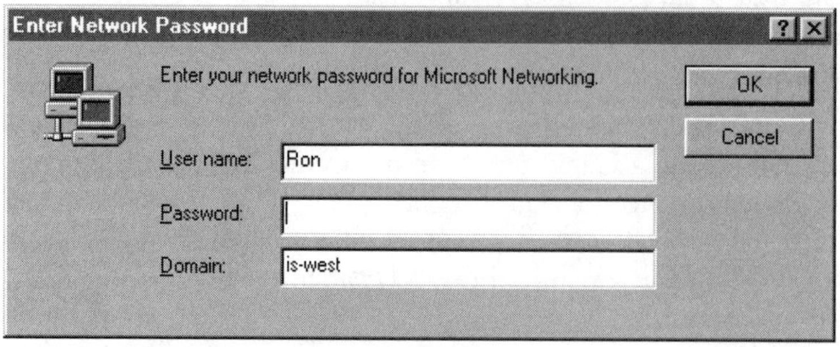

Figure 1-4. The Windows logon dialog

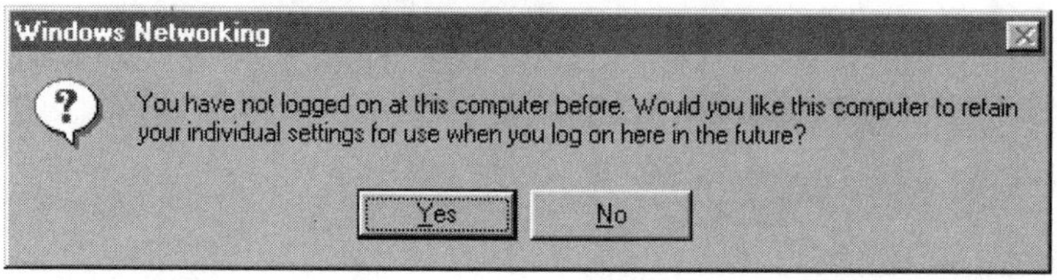

Figure 1-5. The new user dialog

registry, consists of a single top-level key, `HKEY_CLASSES_ROOT`. The Win95 registry, on the other hand, consists of six top-level keys, which you can think of as somewhat analogous to six different disk drives. Figure 1-6 shows how these six keys are presented using the Registry Editor, the standard registry browser Microsoft includes with Win95; you'll find a complete discussion of the Registry Editor in Chapter 2, *Using the Registry Editor.*

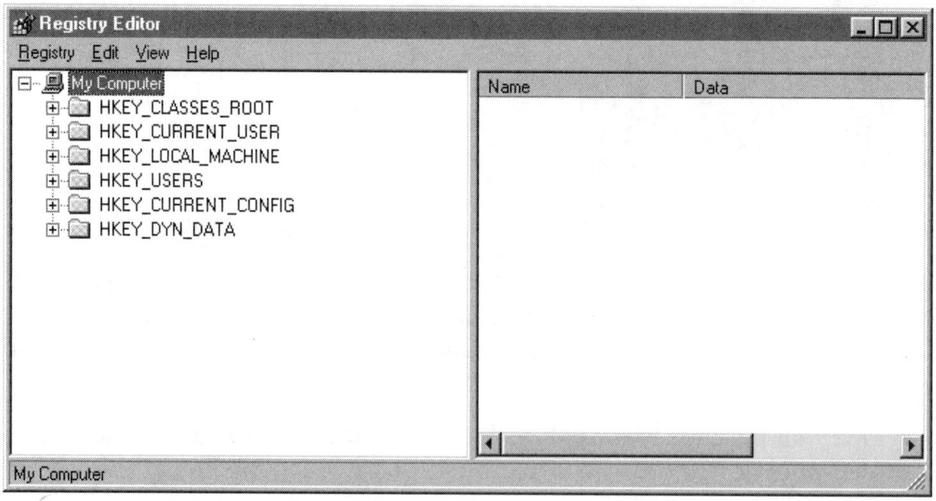

Figure 1-6. The registry's six top-level keys

Each of these top-level keys is automatically defined by Win95. They are always open. In source code, they are always referred to by their handles rather than by their names, as the following line of code, which retrieves the names of a subkey of `HKEY_CLASSES_ROOT`, shows:

```
RegEnumKeyEx(HKEY_CLASSES_ROOT, dwIndex, lpName, cbName) ;
```

All other keys within the Win95 registry must be defined as named subkeys of one of these six keys or of their subkeys. The Win95 registry does not support additional developer-created or user-created top-level keys.

Like the Windows 3.1 registration database, the registry supports nested keys—that is, individual keys can contain additional keys. For instance, the Registry Editor in Figure 1-7 shows that the top-level key `HKEY_LOCAL_MACHINE` has seven subkeys (`Config`, `Enum`, `hardware`, `Network`, `Security`, `SOFTWARE`, and `System`). `CurrentControlSet`, the single subkey of `HKEY_LOCAL_MACHINE\System`, is also shown, as are its subkeys, `Control` and `Services`. These latter subkeys in turn contain subkeys, although they are not visible in the Registry Editor view shown in Figure 1-7.

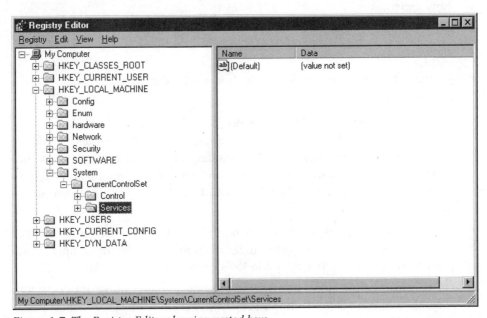

Figure 1-7. The Registry Editor showing nested keys

As the Registry Editor's graphical presentation suggests, you can traverse the registry much as you would your computer's file system: starting at the top of the registry, you can describe a path from the top-level key to the current key by separating each key from its parent key by a backslash. For instance, in Figure 1-7, the subkey named `Services` is the current key, as indicated both by the highlight and by the open folder icon. Its complete path can be described as HKEY_LOCAL_MACHINE\System\CurrentControlSet\Services.

Note that the Registry Editor in Figure 1-7 also prefixes the complete registry path with the string "My Computer" in the status bar. This is primarily to identify the computer whose registry is being displayed, since, if Microsoft Remote Registry Service is installed, Win95 supports remote registry access; the local computer can browse and modify the registry on a remote machine. In this case, the remote computer name is displayed in place of "My Computer." For example, if you're connected to a machine named PC100, the status bar displays the complete path as PC100\HKEY_LOCAL_MACHINE\System\CurrentControlSet\Services.

The six top-level Registry keys, in the order in which they appear in the Registry Editor, are:

- HKEY_CLASSES_ROOT

- HKEY_CURRENT_USER

- HKEY_LOCAL_MACHINE

- HKEY_USERS

- HKEY_CURRENT_CONFIG

- HKEY_DYN_DATA

Win95 uses each of its six top-level keys for a different purpose and to store a different kind of data:

- **HKEY_LOCAL_MACHINE.** By size, HKEY_LOCAL_MACHINE is the largest key, and contains the bulk of information relating to a system's basic hardware configuration, its peripheral devices (including PnP devices), its installed software, OLE, and software configuration, including the configuration of Windows itself. The data found in HKEY_LOCAL_MACHINE are physically stored in *SYSTEM.DAT.*

- **HKEY_USERS.** Whereas Windows 3.x tacitly assumed that there was one user per computer, Windows 95 can handle multiple users sharing a single computer, each with his or her own Windows environment.

  On systems that are not configured to support multiple users, HKEY_USERS contains a single subkey, .Default, which defines the user settings for a user logging on to that system. Physically, these data are stored in the *USER.DAT* file, which is usually located in the computer's Windows directory.

  On systems with "user profiles" enabled, settings for individual users are usually stored in subdirectories of the *\WINDOWS\PROFILES* directory. When a new user logs on, Windows 95 uses the default user settings in the system-wide user registry file (usually *\WINDOWS\USER.DAT*) to create HKEY_

USERS\.Default, while it uses the current user's registry file (usually *WIN-DOWS\PROFILES\<user name>\USER.DAT*) to create the HKEY_USERS\ <user name> subkey. Interestingly, the user profiles of users other than the current user are not included in the registry. For instance, if a particular Windows 95 system has user profiles for two users, John and Jane, when John logs on to the system, HKEY_USERS consists of two subkeys: HKEY_USERS\ .Default and HKEY_USERS\John. HKEY_USERS\Jane is present in memory only when Jane is logged on to the system. This means John can't change or view Jane's settings without first logging on as Jane (which requires knowing her password).

- **HKEY_CLASSES_ROOT**. This "key" is actually a link to HKEY_LOCAL_ MACHINE\SOFTWARE\Classes. That is, HKEY_CLASSES_ROOT is not a physical key, but instead merely points to a subkey of HKEY_LOCAL_ MACHINE. The primary reason for its existence is compatibility with Windows 3.1 and 16-bit applications: HKEY_CLASSES_ROOT was the single top-level key in the Windows 3.1 registration database, which was the antecedent of the Windows 95 registry. HKEY_CLASSES_ROOT is used to store information on OLE, DDE, and shell integration (i.e., file associations and drag-and-drop operations).

- **HKEY_CURRENT_USER**. Like HKEY_CLASSES_ROOT, this is a link rather than a physical key. It points to the key in HKEY_USERS that belongs to the user who is currently logged on. (Windows determines who the current user is based on the user name that they enter in the logon dialog shown earlier in Figure 1-4.) HKEY_CURRENT_USER was implemented in Windows 95 in order to preserve compatibility with applications using the Windows NT registry.

- **HKEY_CURRENT_CONFIG**. Much as Windows 95 can handle multiple users on a single machine, and therefore preserves individual users' settings within the registry, so too does it support multiple hardware configurations, which are also preserved within the registry. This "key" is yet another link, in this case pointing to HKEY_LOCAL_MACHINE\Config\xxxx, where *xxxx* is a subkey representing the numeric value of the hardware configuration currently being used by Windows 95. For instance, on a system with only a single configuration, its value is 0001. The name of the configuration that is current—and therefore the subkey of HKEY_LOCAL_MACHINE\Config to which this key points—is stored to the CurrentConfig value entry of the HKEY_LOCAL_MACHINE\System\CurrentControlSet\control\IDConfigDB key.

- **HKEY_DYN_DATA**. The data maintained by the previous five top-level registry keys are *static*—that is, they are relatively constant, and therefore can

Windows 95 and Multiple Hardware Configurations

To see what hardware configurations are in use, or to create new ones, double-click on the System icon in the Control Panel, then select the Hardware Profiles property sheet in the System Properties dialog. Windows displays the Hardware Profiles property sheet shown in Figure 1-8.

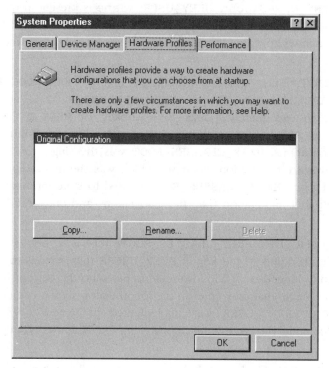

Figure 1-8. The Hardware Profiles property sheet

safely be stored on disk. HKEY_DYN_DATA, on the other hand, maintains *dynamic* data. This portion of the registry is used for Plug and Play (PnP) hardware information maintained by the Windows 95 Configuration Manager (CONFIGMG), for performance statistics, and also as a data area for Windows virtual device drivers (VxDs). Because this information changes constantly, it cannot be stored on disk; instead, this registry tree is entirely memory-resident. Its specific contents are defined by various virtual device drivers loaded by the system, usually at system start up. Since much of these data are time-sensitive, HKEY_DYN_DATA does not actually store the data values; instead, it stores pointers to functions that generate data "on the fly." (VxDs install these function pointers with a service called _RegCreateDynKey). When an application attempts to retrieve a particular value, the registry actually calls the function and provides its return value as the value of the entry. This "on the fly" character of dynamic keys, however, is transparent to applications: keys and values in `HKEY_DYN_DATA` appear like "normal" registry keys and value entries, except that they are read-only.

As you've no doubt gathered from Figure 1-7, unlike the Windows 3.1 registration database, where nesting rarely, if ever, exceeded two or three levels, the Win95 registry seems to support, and commonly takes advantage of, almost infinite levels of nesting. As a result, the complete path to a particular registry subkey can become quite long. No doubt, part of the reason that the registry is often viewed with a glazed-over expression is that the complete path and key name can frequently exceed a line of text, as it does in `HKEY_LOCAL_MACHINE\System\CurrentControlSet\Control\MediaResources\MediaExtensions\shellex\AdvancedProperties\MCI`. And actually, since Win95 provides remote registry access, the full pathname of a registry key includes the computer name (the local computer has the silly-sounding but nonetheless official name `My Computer`). So the "pathname from hell" above should actually be `My Computer\HKEY_LOCAL_MACHINE\...\MCI` or `Tim\HKEY_LOCAL_MACHINE\...\MCI` or whatever. To save space, we also won't include "My Computer" as part of the complete registry path; unless otherwise noted, assume that all references to registry paths refer to the registry on the local machine.

To save trees, we'll also use the following abbreviations for the six top-level keys throughout the book:

HKCR	HKEY_CLASSES_ROOT
HKCU	HKEY_CURRENT_USER
HKLM	HKEY_LOCAL_MACHINE
HKU	HKEY_USERS
HKCC	HKEY_CURRENT_CONFIG
HKDD	HKEY_DYN_DATA

For convenience, these abbreviations also appear on the bookmark included with *Inside the Windows 95 Registry*.

So far, we've focused on the registry as a collection of keys and their subkeys. Each registry key, though, can have multiple values assigned to it, something that the Windows 3.1 registration database did not support. In *REG.DAT*, each key other than the HKCR could have one optional value (called its *default value*). This value had to be a string. In the Win95 registry, it is still possible to assign a single value directly to a key in this way, in which case the value must also be a string. But the Win95 registry also allows multiple values to be assigned to a single key. Each value entry (other than the optional single value that is assigned directly to a key) consists of three parts: a *value name*, a *data type indicator*, and a *value*. The value of a complete value entry need not be a string; it can also be one of several string, numeric, and binary data types.[*] The Win95 registry can support single value entries whose data is up to 16,364 bytes in size (in WinNT, this size limit is approximately 64K, which was, incidentally, the maximum allowable size of the *entire* Windows 3.1 registration database). Because of the poor performance that would result from reading and writing such a large quantity of data, though, developers are urged not to store values to the registry that exceed approximately 2K. Larger amounts of data should be stored in a separate file, using the registry only to store the filename.

This is confusing, so let's look at an example. Figure 1-9, which shows the value entries of HKCU\Control Panel\Desktop\WindowMetrics, a subkey containing settings that control the appearance of icons, fonts, captions, and menus, uses the Registry Editor (which is discussed in Chapter 2) to illustrate the various kinds of values and value entries that can be stored to a key. The first entry in the value pane reads "(Default)", and represents the single string value that can be assigned directly to the key. In this case, a value has not been assigned ("value not set"); this absence of an optional default value is very common in the registry as a whole. All the remaining items in the value pane are complete value entries for this subkey. For instance, the value name of the second entry is "Border-Width". The "ab" icon to the left of its name indicates that the entry contains string data (REG_SZ); in this case, its value is "-15". The value name of the third entry is "CaptionFont". Its icon indicates that it contains binary data (08 00 00, etc.).

The Registry in Windows 95 and Windows NT

As we mentioned earlier, the registry as a central repository for system-wide data first appeared in WinNT 3.1 (which, oddly, was actually the first, 1.0, release of WinNT). But although the registry in WinNT 3.x serves as the model on which the Win95 registry is based, the two implementations are completely different. In most cases, these differences are completely transparent to the user, administrator, or developer, and are reflections of the different architectures of the two operating systems; in other cases, however, they are not. This section contains a high-level survey of the differences between the registries on the two platforms.

---

[*] For details on the data types supported by the Windows 95 Registry, see Chapter 4, *The Win32 Registry API*.

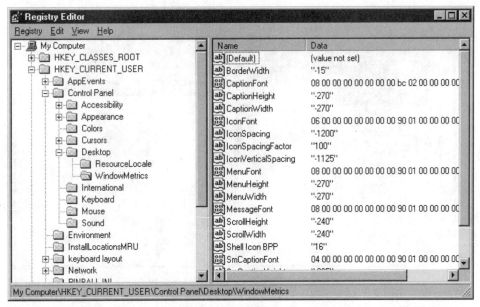

Figure 1-9. Sample value entries in the Registry Editor

Like Win95, WinNT has a Registry Editor (named *REGEDT32.EXE* in WinNT 3.x and *REGEDIT.EXE* in WinNT 4.0) that allows you to browse and modify the NT registry. When you launch it, its WinNT 3.x version appears as in Figure 1-10. Although the Registry Editor offers a completely different interface than the Win95 Registry Editor by creating a child window for each top-level key, it is also clear that the difference in appearance between the two Registries is due to more than the difference in the interface between the two utilities.

The most crucial difference is the one most likely to go unnoticed: whereas the bulk of the Win95 registry is stored in *SYSTEM.DAT* and *USER.DAT*, the WinNT registry consists of a series of logical units called hives[*] defined by value entries in the `HKLM\System\CurrentControlSet\Control\hivelist` key. Each hive contains the first subkey of a top-level key, along with all its accompanying subkeys (e.g., `HKLM\Software` and its subkeys).

Except for the Hardware hive, which is volatile and therefore resident in memory only, each hive is stored in a separate file that has no file extension. Typically, the hive files are stored in the `\WINNT\SYSTEM32\CONFIG` directory. (Since user hives can be located anywhere on a network, though, the value assigned to the hive entry for the current user and the default user in the registry indicates the

---

[*] Although the "plain vanilla" Windows 95 Registry does not contain hives, it is possible, although not very common, to temporarily add a hive to it. For details, see the discussion of the *RegLoadKey* function in Chapter 4.

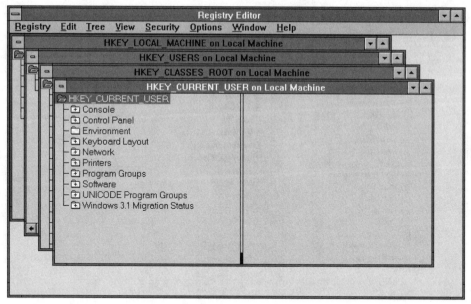

Figure 1-10. The Registry Editor in WinNT 3.51

physical location of those hives; in WinNT 3.x, the value entries for the other hives typically have no values assigned to them.)

For each physical hive except the system hive (that is, `HKEY_LOCAL_MACHINE\ System`), there is also a .LOG file that records transactions to the hive. Because the system hive cannot be effectively restored from a transaction log, WinNT basically mirrors the system hive in a file named *SYSTEM.ALT*.

Table 1-1 lists the files that compose the WinNT registry and shows how they relate to the registry's structure. However, the names of the files and their contents are officially undefined; that is, Microsoft does not guarantee that the organization or the physical implementation of the WinNT registry will be compatible from one version of the operating system to the next. Therefore, applications or utilities should not attempt to access registry files directly, but instead should access the registry only through the Win32 API, which handles the details of the physical structure and organization of the registry.

Table 1-1. The files of the WinNT registry

Key	Files
`HKEY_LOCAL_MACHINE\SYSTEM`	*SYSTEM, SYSTEM.ALT*
`HKEY_LOCAL_MACHINE\SOFTWARE`	*SOFTWARE, SOFTWARE.LOG*
`HKEY_LOCAL_MACHINE\SECURITY`	*SECURITY* and *SECURITY.LOG*
`HKEY_LOCAL_MACHINE\SAM`	*SAM, SAM.LOG*

Table 1-1. The files of the WinNT registry (continued)

Key	Files
HKEY_CURRENT_USER	*USER###, USER###.LOG* or *ADMIN###* and *ADMIN###.LOG*
HKEY_USERS\.DEFAULT	*DEFAULT, DEFAULT.LOG*

Figure 1-10 also reflects another crucial difference between the Win95 and the WinNT registries: whereas the Win95 registry consists of six top-level keys, there are only four in WinNT 3.x and five in WinNT 4.0. These are:

- **HKEY_LOCAL_MACHINE**. This key contains the machine-specific data on hardware and software configuration. It is broadly similar to HKEY_LOCAL_ MACHINE in Windows 95, except for the inclusion of two security-related sub- keys, SECURITY and SAM (Security Account Manager). These latter subkeys, though, cannot be accessed through the registry functions in the Win32 API, but instead must be accessed through its security or Security Account Man- ager functions. Windows 95, on the other hand, does not support security. As a result, this difference between the two operating systems should have a min- imal impact on developers. The major subkey used by developers, HKLM\ SOFTWARE, is compatible in the two operating systems.

- **HKEY_USERS**. This key contains user-specific configuration information. As in the Windows 95 registry, it contains a .Default subkey and a subkey belonging to the current user. The name of the current user's subkey, though, is the user's Security ID string rather than his or her user name, as in Win- dows 95.

- **HKEY_CLASSES_ROOT**. Like the corresponding Windows 95 key, this is actu- ally a link to HKLM\SOFTWARE\Classes.

- **HKEY_CURRENT_USER**. Again like the Windows 95 key, this is a link to the current user's key in HKEY_USERS. Unlike Windows 95, Windows NT creates user configurations by default.

- **HKEY_CURRENT_CONFIG**. First introduced in Win95, this top-level Key was added to the winNT 4.0 registry as part of its support for Plug and Play.

As the list indicates, the WinNT registry lacks the HKEY_DYN_DATA key that is present in Win95. The WinNT registry contains only static, disk-resident data. HKEY_DYN_DATA, on the other hand, holds dynamic, memory-resident data. It was first introduced in Win95, and is used primarily for performance monitoring. (In NT, the registry API has performance-monitoring features that were hacked in at the last minute when developers complained about the use of undocumented NT functions by utilities such as PVIEW. These entries don't correspond to actual registry entries; they are merely accessed via the registry API. See the book *Optimizing WinNT* by Russ Blake for further details.)

Similarly, because they don't support Plug and Play (PnP), WinNT 3.1 and 3.5 do not support multiple hardware configurations, and therefore do not contain an HKEY_CURRENT_CONFIG registry key. But in Win95, HKEY_CURRENT_CONFIG is merely a link to the subkey of HKEY_LOCAL_MACHINE\Config that represents the current configuration.

The differences between the WinNT and Win95 registries apply not only to the files and number of keys that compose the registry, but also to the items of information stored in both keys and values. In WinNT, keys other than the top-level keys contain not only a key name, but a class name (which, in the current version of the Win32 API, is an arbitrary string that is otherwise unused), a security descriptor, and the date and time of the last write to the key. WinNT value entries are broadly comparable to their Win95 counterparts, except that WinNT supports several data types not found in the Win95 registry; for details, see Chapter 4, *The Win32 Registry API*.

One of NT's more interesting features—and one absent from Win95—is its support for *initialization file mapping*, which allows WinNT to place information in, or retrieve information from, the registry when a program attempts to access either a system or a private initialization file using the initialization file functions in the Win32 API. WinNT's support for system initialization file mapping, though, has been a frequent area of confusion: contrary to much of what has been written, reads and writes by 32-bit applications to *WIN.INI* using API functions like *GetProfileInt* or *GetProfileString* are not automatically remapped to the registry, but instead continue to access *WIN.INI*. Remapping occurs only when there is an entry in the registry's HKLM\Software\Microsoft\Windows NT\CurrentVersion\IniFileMapping\WIN.INI key that equates a section of *WIN.INI* to a particular key within the registry. The value entry's name must be the name of the section in *WIN.INI* whose entries are to be remapped; the entry's value is a string containing the name of the registry key to which initialization file data is to be stored.

It is also possible to remap private initialization files so that the initialization file functions operate on either the registry or both the registry and the initialization file, rather than on the initialization file alone. For this to occur, there must be a subkey of HKEY_LOCAL_MACHINE\Software\Microsoft\Windows NT\CurrentVersion\IniFileMapping whose name is the same as that of the full filename of the initialization file to be remapped. For example, the presence of a subkey named system.ini means that at least part of a file named *SYSTEM.INI* is mapped to the registry. The name of each value entry belonging to this subkey

Registry Compatibility: Policy vs. Mechanism

While Microsoft has done a remarkably good job of making the registry API compatible between Windows 95 and Windows NT—it's remarkable because these are really, after all, totally different operating systems—compatibility at the API level does not automatically turn into actual registry compatibility. Indeed, Microsoft itself has explained that when "upgrading" from Windows 95 to NT (as if switching from one operating system to a different operating system can really be called an "upgrade"), your Win32 applications such as WinWord will have to be *reinstalled*, because of registry differences (*InformationWeek*, April 15, 1996).

But if the registry API is compatible between Windows 95 and NT, why would a user need to reinstall WinWord when switching from one to the other? Quite simply, because of the difference between mechanism and policy. *Mechanism* is an underlying system, like the registry API. *Policy* is how that underlying system is actually used. Just because roughly the same registry API is available on Win95 and NT does not necessarily mean that the operating system and applications will use this underlying system in the same way.

To take a concrete example, let's say you've written an application that uses two Win32 API functions, *RegOpenKey* and *RegQueryValueEx*, to access the Windows 95 `IconSpacingFactor` value of `HKEY_CURRENT_USER\Control Panel\desktop\WindowMetrics`.

Now you want to move this application to WinNT. The good news is that the program runs as is, without any changes, without even recompiling. The bad news, though, is that the program does not do what you expect. Why? Because of the difference between mechanism and policy. Sure, WinNT supports the same registry API that your program relied upon under Win95. But there's one problem: the WinNT registry does not keep the `IconSpacingFactor` value in the same place as it's kept in Win95! Instead, it's called `IconSpacing` and its kept in `HKEY_LOCAL_MACHINE\Control Panel\Desktop`.

For that matter, even the Registry Editor in WinNT 3.x doesn't have the same name as the Registry Editor in Windows 95. In Win95 (and in WinNT 4.0), it's *REGEDIT.EXE*, but in WinNT 3.x it's *REGEDT32.EXE*. So even the simple-looking *RegExportBranch* function shown back in Example 1-1 is not portable, even though it relies entirely upon a portable API, *WinExec*, because it embeds the non-portable name of the Registry Editor.

Now, you might consider making a version of *RegExportBranch* that's portable between Win95 and WinNT, perhaps by looking for the name of the Registry Editor in `HKEY_CLASSES_ROOT\regfile\shell\open\command`.

—Continued—

> There's just one problem: in WinNT 3.x, there is no HKEY_CLASSES_ROOT\
> regfile. It's called HKEY_CLASSES_ROOT\regedit, and it turns out to
> point, not to *REGEDT32.EXE*, but to *REGEDIT.EXE*, with which WinNT handles
> old Win31-style .REG files! Files exported from *REGEDT32.EXE* don't have
> .REG extensions. So, even for a simple matter like this, genuine portability be-
> tween the two systems is difficult to achieve.

indicates the section of the private initialization file that is to be remapped, while
its value provides the remapped registry key. For instance, the value entry

```
KEYBOARD:REG_SZ: SYS:Microsoft\Windows NT\CurrentVersion\WOW\keyboard
```

indicates that the [keyboard] section of *SYSTEM.INI* maps to HKLM\Software\
Microsoft\Windows NT\CurrentVersion\WOW\keyboard. (WinNT uses
the symbols and abbreviations shown in Table 1-2 for initialization file mapping.)
If a default value is provided for the subkey, it indicates that all of the sections of
the private initialization file other than those having their own value entries in the
registry are to be remapped to the key corresponding to the default value. For
instance, if the default value of the Clock.ini subkey is

```
<No Name>:REG_SZ: #USR:Software\Microsoft\Clock
```

all sections of *CLOCK.INI* that don't have their own value entries are mapped to
HKCU\Software\Microsoft\Clock.

Table 1-2. Symbols used by Windows NT in initialization file mapping

Symbol	Description
SYS	The HKLM\Software key
USR	The HKCU key
!	Writes data to both the registry and the .INI file
#	Sets the registry value to the value contained in the initialization file when a new user first logs in

Another important difference between WinNT 3.x and Win95, which in turn is
related to a number of the differences in the organization of the registry, is that
WinNT 3.x does not currently support PnP. WinNT fills the HKLM\Hardware key
and its subkeys with information on the system's current hardware configuration
at system start up. This registry hive consists entirely of *volatile* keys and value
entries that are not preserved from session to session. In contrast, Win95 does not
support volatile registry keys; rather than filling HKLM\Hardware with information on the system's current hardware configuration, it leaves the branch mostly
empty. Instead, Win95 uses its Plug and Play functions to gather information on

the current hardware configuration dynamically, while the subkeys of the HKLM\ Enum key are used to store information on all the hardware that has *ever* been available on the system; this latter key, however, does not exist on WinNT systems.

Where is HKEY_PERFORMANCE_DATA?

Windows NT supports a feature called *performance monitoring* that allows applications to collect performance data. While the details of performance monitoring (the application whose performance can be monitored, the DLL containing monitoring functions, and the names of its exported functions) are defined in the registry, the actual data are not stored there. Despite that, collecting performance data is implemented through calls to the registry API, using the HKEY_PERFORMANCE_DATA handle. Like its roughly corresponding HKEY_DYN_DATA key in Windows 95, HKEY_PERFORMANCE_DATA is not a physical registry tree. Both HKEY_DYN_DATA and HKEY_PERFORMANCE_ DATA indicate to the system that it should query the components responsible for monitoring performance, and collect the data they return.

Finally, the registry functions in the Win32 API are slightly different for the two platforms:

- The Windows 95 "Configuration Manager" (CONFIGMG) supports several PnP functions that allow virtual device drivers (VxDs) to access the registry; these are not supported by Windows NT.

- Windows 95 supports one registry access function, *RegQueryMultipleValues*, that Windows NT does not implement.

- Several Windows NT registry functions, like *RegGetKeySecurity*, *RegSetKeySecurity*, *RegSaveKey*, and *RegReplaceKey*, do not work under Windows 95 because of differences in the structure of the two Registries.

For a more detailed discussion of differences in the organization and structure of the Win95 and WinNT registries for programmers developing for both platforms, see Chapter 4.

Summary

This chapter has aimed not only at providing an introduction to the structure and organization of the Win95 registry, but also at placing it in a broader historical perspective: at understanding why the registry evolved into its current form. The following points are particularly worth noting:

- Initialization files are a relic of the past. Initialization files offer poor performance, provide only limited storage because of their 64K size limitation, and, as a result of their linear character, are incapable of reflecting the complexity of modern computing environments, where multiple users share a single computer, the same user can use multiple computers on a network, and processes and components interact with one another in various "interesting" ways.

- The registry evolved from and developed in response to the limitations and shortcomings of initialization files. In comparison to initialization files, the registry is a *structured* storage facility that offers high *performance* and a *multidimensional* organization that is capable of reflecting both the diversity and the complexity of modern computing environments. Since in many ways OLE is the driving force behind its implementation, a fundamental principle of the registry is that control of the system should be centralized at a system level, and that no application should be an island unto itself. Whereas initialization files offer chaos, the registry offers structure and a rigorous organization.

- The registry offers major performance benefits when compared to accessing information in initialization files.

- The Windows 95 registry consists of six *trees*, or top-level keys, to each of which can belong a virtually unlimited number of nested keys. Each key can have one or more *value entries*, which are a combination of a value name and the data assigned to it. This structure distinguishes it from the registration database under Windows 3.1, which consisted of a single top-level tree and an optional default value that might be assigned to any key. It also distinguishes it from Windows NT, which has only four top-level keys.

Hopefully, this chapter has left you with a new sense of the importance of the registry, a renewed commitment to use the registry as a repository for configuration information for your applications, and a basic sense of how the Win95 registry is structured. In the next chapter, we'll examine the major tool provided by Win95 to browse and modify the registry, the Registry Editor.

2

Using the Registry Editor

As we saw in "Limiting Access to the Registry" in Chapter 1, *The Registry, or, What Was So Bad About .INI Files?,* one of the motivations behind replacing the Windows 3.x system of initialization files with a binary, multifile configuration database is the desire to make critical system information less accessible to users. And in fact, the Win95 documentation encourages users and administrators to make modifications by using the standard Windows configuration tools (like the applets available in the Control Panel) rather than mucking with the registry directly. This is generally good advice.

Interestingly, despite Microsoft's position that changes to the registry should not be made directly, and despite the apparent refusal of Microsoft technical support to offer support for systems on which the user has directly modified the registry, Microsoft *has* bundled a utility program for browsing and editing the registry with Win95. This program, the Registry Editor (*REGEDIT.EXE*), is the focus of this chapter.

Typically, users, system administrators, and even many developers approach using *RegEdit* in both its Windows NT (WinNT) and Windows 95 (Win95) versions with considerable trepidation. This is partly because the registry itself seems intimidating: its enormous size, deeply nested trees, and wide diversity of data all make it difficult to wrap one's mind around the registry.

There is some confusion between the registry itself and the Registry Editor (*RegEdit*). The registry is a specialized database that's used to store hardware and software configuration information. It is accessible, at least officially, exclusively through a collection of registry functions in the Win32 API that allow access to what might be called the registry's database engine. *RegEdit*, on the other hand, is only one of any number of possible front-end tools which use this API to access this particular database. It offers a particular view of the registry (and in fact, as we saw in the previous chapter, the WinNT Registry Editor, with its multiple document interface, presents a rather different view than the Win95 Registry Editor), but by no means the only possible view.

In fact, a wide range of software to supplement or replace the operation of RegEdit either has been or is being developed. Still, RegEdit remains the best general-purpose tool for browsing and modifying the registry. For developers, it is an invaluable debugging tool: it allows you to examine particular registry keys immediately before and after your application modifies them, and to modify the registry to examine your application's behavior under particular circumstances. For this reason, a detailed look at RegEdit is well worth while.

Launching RegEdit

In keeping with the general goal of making the registry relatively inaccessible, Microsoft has also made RegEdit relatively difficult to find. When Win95 is installed, RegEdit (*REGEDIT.EXE*) is automatically copied to the Windows directory. However, the setup routine does not create an icon for RegEdit in any menu or program group, or on the desktop. So unless you know to look for a file named *REGEDIT.EXE*, it's likely you'll miss it.

There are several ways to launch RegEdit, depending on how important you think it is and how frequently you use it. You can choose from the following options; our own preference is to place a shortcut to RegEdit on the desktop:

- *Adding a shortcut to RegEdit on your desktop.* This method makes RegEdit most accessible. Click on the desktop with the *right* mouse button, then select New | Shortcut from the context menu. When Windows displays the Create Shortcut dialog, enter `regedit` in the Command Line text box and click the Next button. Then enter `Registry Editor` or any other name you'd like to identify the shortcut in the "Select a Title for the Program" dialog and click the Finish button. If you prefer using drag and drop, you can simply select *REGEDIT* in the Explorer window and drag it onto your desktop.

- *Running RegEdit from the command line.* Select the Run option from the Start menu, and type `regedit` in the Open drop-down combo box. Since Win95 maintains a list of the programs most recently executed by using the Run menu option, you should be able to run RegEdit subsequently by simply selecting it from the drop-down list. This is an efficient way to run RegEdit in two cases: first, if you don't do it very often; and second, if you want to run RegEdit with one of its command-line options. (RegEdit supports a number of command-line options that are available even when running RegEdit as a Windows rather than a DOS program; see "Running RegEdit from MS-DOS" later in this chapter, and the sidebar "Working with .REG Files" in Chapter 4, *The Win32 Registry API*.

- *Adding RegEdit to your Programs menu.* Select the Settings option from the Start menu, then select the Taskbar option. When Win95 opens the Taskbar Properties dialog, select the Start Menu Programs property sheet and click the Add button. Windows opens the Create Shortcut dialog; enter `regedit` in the Command Line text box and click the Next button. When Windows opens the Select Program Folder dialog, select the folder in which you'd like the RegEdit icon to appear.

It is possible, though, that when you actually try to run RegEdit, you'll instead see the dialog box shown in Figure 2-1, and Windows will not allow you to access the registry. That's because someone (most likely your system administrator) has used the Microsoft System Policy Editor (*POLEDIT.EXE*), which is shown in Figure 2-2, to disable the standard registry tools.

Figure 2-1. No access to RegEdit

Here's how this works: when you attempt to launch RegEdit, it first attempts to open the `HKCU\Software\Microsoft\Windows\CurrentVersion\Poli-cies\System` key. If it finds the key present, it checks the value of its `DisableRegistryTools` entry. If its value is 1, RegEdit displays the dialog shown in Figure 2-1 and refuses to load.

Although this may seem like an effective security measure, it has a major flaw: it is not implemented at a system (or API) level, and instead depends on "well-behaved" utilities *checking* for this registry setting before allowing a user access to the registry. At least at the time this book was written, however, Microsoft has not documented the presence of the `DisableRegistryTools` entry. This means that most third-party registry editing utilities will permit users to edit the registry even if a system administrator has explicitly denied those users access to the registry. As long as `DisableRegistryTools` remains undocumented, all third-party registry utilities are likely to remain "ill-behaved." And even if it is documented, a programmer can deliberately choose to ignore this setting and give unauthorized users access to the computer's registry. It is fair to say that `DisableRegistry-Tools` only establishes a *false* sense of security.

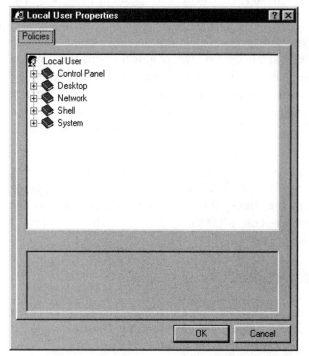

Figure 2-2. The Policy Editor's Local User Properties dialog

Browsing the Registry with RegEdit

Once you launch RegEdit, it displays the registry's six top-level keys, as shown in Figure 2-3. Notice that RegEdit presents you with a familiar Explorer-style interface, which likens the registry to your computer's file system.

RegEdit's User Interface

The left-hand pane of RegEdit is the *key pane*; it displays registry keys and subkeys. A plus sign next to a particular key's icon indicates that that key contains subkeys that are not currently visible. You can expand the key to display the names of its subkeys by double-clicking it, or by clicking the right mouse button and selecting the Expand option from the context menu. A minus sign next to a key's icon indicates that that key has been fully expanded; all of its subkeys are visible. To contract it so that none of its subkeys is visible, double-click it, or click the right mouse button and select the Collapse option from the context menu.

On the right side of the RegEdit window is the *value pane*; it displays the value names (described on the label bar as "Name") and values (described on the label

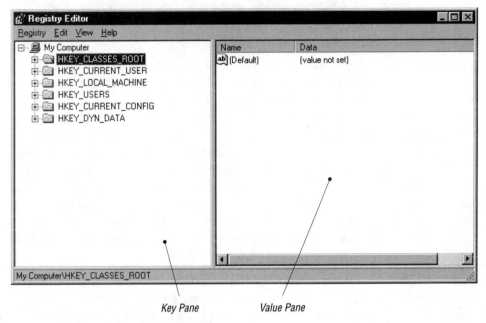

Key Pane   Value Pane

Figure 2-3. The Windows 95 Registry Editor

bar as "Data") of the current key (that is, the one that is highlighted or represented by an open directory icon) in the key pane. In addition, the Name field displays one of the two icons shown in Table 2-1 to represent the value's data type.

Table 2-1. Data type icons used by RegEdit

Icon	Description
![binary icon]	Binary data type
![text icon]	Text data type

RegEdit's user interface comes from several Win32 "common controls": SysTreeView32, SysListView32, and SysHeader32. The Win95 Explorer uses the same common controls (which are provided by *COMCTL32.DLL*), so if you know how to use Explorer, you know how to use RegEdit. The two RegEdit panes are sizable, as are the Name and Data fields in the value pane. To move the bar separating the two panes with the keyboard, select the Split option from the View menu, then use the right and left cursor keys to position the vertical separator bar where you'd like it. When you're finished, press Enter. With the mouse, simply position the mouse cursor over the vertical separator bar. When the mouse cursor changes to a double arrow, drag it to the separator bar's new position and release. The relative size of the Name and Data files can only be modified with the mouse. To resize the fields, position the mouse cursor between the Name and Data field labels. When the cursor changes to a double arrow, drag it to the field separator's new position and release.

Sometimes, even though you resize the value pane, RegEdit still is unable to display the entire value for an entry. This is generally the case when a long string or a large amount of binary data has been stored to a particular entry. In this case, RegEdit displays as much of the value as it can, then uses ellipses (...) to indicate that all of the entry's data is not visible in the value pane. If you want to view the entire value, you can either double-click the entry's value name or select the Modify option from the Edit menu. RegEdit then opens either the Edit Binary Value dialog or the Edit String dialog, depending on the data type of the value entry. If you've opened the dialog solely to view the complete dialog, be careful not to make any changes to the value; and just to be sure that you don't inadvertently change some registry data, always exit the dialog by pressing the Cancel button.

Overall, RegEdit presents you with a familiar interface that allows you to navigate the registry in the same way that you navigate your file system. When you move through the registry in this way, you are simply browsing it; there is no danger of making any modifications.

For performance reasons, RegEdit's display of data is static rather than dynamic. That is, the contents of the RegEdit window are accurate as of the time the window is first painted, and the RegEdit window accurately reflects all changes to the registry that you've made using RegEdit. But changes made to the registry by other applications or by Windows itself after the registry window has first been painted may not be reflected in RegEdit's display. This is important to keep in mind when you use RegEdit as a debugging tool, when you want to see the effect of your code by examining some portion of the Registry both before and after your program has run. When you want to be sure that you're viewing accurate data, you can have RegEdit reread the registry and update its display by selecting the Refresh option from the View menu, or by pressing the F5 key.

Searching the Registry

While you can use the standard RegEdit interface to navigate through the registry, moving to deeply nested keys can be time consuming. It also presumes that you know more or less precisely where you want to go. If you want to move directly to a particular key or value in the registry, or to see if a particular key or value exists, you can instead search for it by selecting the Find option from the Edit menu, or by clicking the right mouse button on any key in the key pane and selecting the Find option from the pop-up menu. RegEdit opens the Find dialog shown in Figure 2-4.

Figure 2-4. RegEdit's Find dialog

One of the more convenient features of the Find dialog is that it allows you to designate whether you want to search for keys, value names (which the dialog terms "values"), or values ("data") by selecting one or more of the appropriate check boxes. RegEdit's ability to locate particular values, though, has one major limitation: although values can be string or binary data, RegEdit's search module is capable of searching only for what it considers to be string values (that is, to anticipate the discussion of registry data types in Chapter 4, values of type REG_ SZ only). Searches are *not* case sensitive, and you can enter strings with embedded spaces into the Find What text box without having to delimit them with quotation marks.

RegEdit will attempt to locate the first occurrence of the string that you specify beginning with the currently selected key to the end of the registry. Since RegEdit's search module performs a relatively slow sequential search of the entire registry, you can significantly reduce its search time by first selecting a top-level key or a subkey from which RegEdit can begin searching. Conversely, if you're not sure where a particular string is stored, you'll want to be sure to select a key at or near the beginning of the registry; otherwise, you may have to begin the search over again. If you want to locate subsequent occurrences of the string, you can select the Find Next option from the Edit menu or press the F3 key. Actually, the phrase "relatively slow" above isn't right: in truth, while handy, a RegEdit search can be *incredibly* slow. As discussed later, it can be faster to export the entire registry to a .REG file, pull up the .REG file in your favorite text editor or word processor, and search that way. Amazing.

The registry and clipboard support

Although RegEdit's menu does not contain an Edit Copy or Edit Paste menu option, it nevertheless does offer almost full Clipboard support. That means that, when you identify a particular key that interests you and you want to find additional occurrences of its name or value in the registry, you can use the Clipboard to enter text into the Find dialog's "Find what" text box. This saves you from having to type in relatively error-prone entries like {00020D75-0000-0000-C000-000000000046}. (See "The Class Identifier, or CLSID," in Chapter 8, *What Goes in the Registry: System Settings*, for a discussion of what these {x-y-z-a-b} things are.)

To use the Clipboard, begin by selecting the data you'd like to place on the Clipboard. This can be done as follows, depending on what kind of registry element you'd like to search for:

- For a *key name*, highlight the key, select the Rename option from the Edit menu, then press Ctrl-C. You can then press Esc to keep from accidentally renaming the key.

- For a *value name*, highlight the value name, select the Rename option from the Edit menu, then press Ctrl-C. You can then press Esc to keep from accidentally renaming the entry.

- For a *string value* or a *DWORD value*, highlight the value name, select the Modify option from the Edit menu, then highlight the data you'd like to copy to the Clipboard and press Ctrl-C. You cannot use the Clipboard to paste a DWORD value into the Find What text box (RegEdit incorrectly interprets it as a string), nor can you use the Clipboard to copy and paste binary data at all.

Once the data you'd like to search for is on the Clipboard, you can paste it into the "Find what" Text box by opening the Find dialog and pressing either Ctrl-V or Shift-Ins.

Working with .REG Files

Along with displaying a Win95 system's registry, RegEdit allows you to import and export .REG files. These are specially formatted ASCII files that contain information on registry keys and value entries. Figure 2-5, for instance, shows a portion of a .REG file. They look somewhat like .INI files! (In fact, as you'll see in Chapter 4, the Win32 initialization file functions can be used to read and write entries to .REG files.)

Creating a .REG File

RegEdit allows you to generate a .REG file based on the entire contents of the registry or on a particular key and all of its subkeys. This is useful in four different situations:

- *Backing up the registry.* If you're planning on using RegEdit to make direct modifications to the registry, it's a good idea to generate a .REG file that contains information on the keys whose names or values you intend to modify. In that case, the .REG file serves as a backup copy; you can use it to restore

Figure 2-5. A sample .REG file

the registry to its original state should your modifications not work as expected.

- *Installing new applications.* If you're a developer whose application writes default values to the registry during installation, you can generate a .REG file to include with your installation routine instead of writing code to call the registry functions in the Win32 API. You'd begin by using RegEdit to enter the keys and values that your application requires, then save them to a .REG file that you could distribute with each copy of your application.

- *Modifying the registry.* Once you export a .REG file, you can modify it with any text editor and then merge it back into the registry (see the following section, "Importing a .REG File"). Most commonly, this is done to generate a .REG file for an installation program.

- *Investigating the registry.* If you'd like to see how changes in Windows' system configuration affect the registry, you can create two .REG files containing the relevant registry sections, one generated before the change and the other after. You can then determine how they differ (i.e., find out what registry changes occurred) with a file comparison utility like *diff* from the superb MKS

Toolkit (*http://www.mks.com/solution/tk/*), or with *WinDiff*, which is included with both Microsoft Visual C++ and the Win32 SDK.

- *Searching the registry.* Since .REG files are ASCII files, they can be opened by any word processor or text editor. This means that you can generate a .REG file, open it with a word processor and text editor, and then use the editor's search facilities to search the registry. Although you lose the benefits of Reg-Edit's graphical presentation of the registry, there are two major advantages to searching the registry in this way:

The first is speed: RegEdit's search function is amazingly slow. This is perhaps because RegEdit stores very little of the registry's contents in memory at any given time. Table 2-2, for instance, shows the times required to locate the first occurrence of two strings, "ComputerName" and "WindowMetrics", using RegEdit and WordPad (which, having been written in C++ with MFC, is itself not blazingly fast) on a 66MHz 486. Even with the overhead involved in generating a .REG file containing the *entire* registry (on a typical machine, this .REG file might be about a megabyte in size), WordPad is over twice as fast as RegEdit in locating the two strings.

In addition to major performance gains, a second advantage of searching a .REG file is that you can search for numeric and binary data. Binary data in .REG files are represented in hexadecimal format, with each byte of data separated by a comma (e.g., `hex:95,00,00,00`), while numeric (long integer, or DWORD) values are represented as four-byte hexadecimal values (e.g., `dword:00000000`).

Table 2-2. Time (in seconds) required to search for strings

	RegEdit	.REG File
Overhead[a]	n/a	16
Find "ComputerName"	62	8
Find "WindowMetrics"	5	3
Total Time	67	27

[a] Overhead includes the time required to generate a .REG file of the entire registry, to load WordPad, and to open the .REG file.

To create a .REG file, select the "Export Registry File" option from the File menu. When RegEdit opens the Export Registry File dialog shown in Figure 2-6, select the directory and filename of the .REG file you'd like to create. By selecting the All button in the Export range group box, you can save your entire registry to a .REG file. By selecting the Selected Branch button, you can save the current key along with all of its subkeys to a .REG file. Or you can enter the name of the key that you'd like to save (along with its subkeys) into the Selected Branch text box.

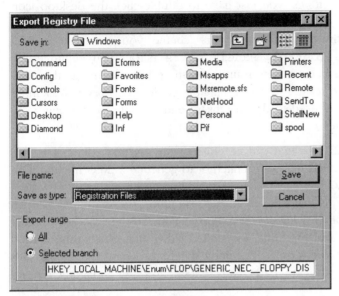

Figure 2-6. RegEdit's Export Registry File dialog

Importing a .REG File

.REG files can be thought of as "RegEdit macros" that allow RegEdit to write information to the registry and instruct it where to make the appropriate changes. So along with generating .REG files that contain all or part of the registry, RegEdit provides several ways to import (or merge, to use Microsoft's terminology from RegEdit's context menu) existing .REG files. This ability to import a .REG file is crucial in three situations:

- *Restoring the registry.* If you've generated a .REG file as a backup before making changes to the registry, you can import that .REG file to restore the registry to its condition before the changes if your modifications didn't work as expected.

- *Installing new software.* A .REG file can be included as part of a software program's installation routine to enter the information in the user's registry that is necessary for that program to run. In most cases, the program's installation routine makes the process of merging the .REG file with the registry transparent to the user. The installer just "runs" the .REG file with a Win32 API such as *ShellExecuteEx*, and the Win95 file association for .REG files takes care of running RegEdit to merge the .REG file's contents into the registry.

- *Testing software.* You can use a .REG file to easily "roll back" changes you've made to the registry and return it to its original condition. Place either a .REG file or a shortcut/link to a .REG file on the desktop. Then, when you want to restore your registry settings, you just have to double-click the desktop icon for the .REG file. For example, if you're developing a utility that makes it easier for users to modify the Windows colors scheme, you can create a .REG file containing `HKCU\Control Panel\Colors` before you begin testing the utility. When you begin a new round of testing, you can merge the .REG file into the registry to restore it to its original condition. (However, remember that .REG files can't be used to delete registry entries, only to add new ones or modify existing ones.)

Since .REG files are ASCII files that can be edited with any text editor, it is also possible to create a new .REG file from scratch or to generate a .REG file and then modify it. (And since .REG files have such a simple format, it's also easy to write a program whose output is a .REG file; for example, see Example 11-4 in Chapter 11, *Migrating from .INI Files to the Registry.*) You can then modify a particular computer's registry by importing the edited .REG file. Since this method provides even less error checking than editing the registry directly, though, it's best reserved for those who are particularly experienced with making registry modifications.

You can merge a .REG file with your existing registry in any of the following five ways:

- *Using the RegEdit menu.* Select the Import Registry File option from the File menu. When RegEdit displays the Import Registry File common dialog, just select the .REG file that you'd like to import. RegEdit will import the file and display a dialog box informing you of its successful completion.

- *Double-clicking on a .REG file.* If you double-click on a .REG file in an Explorer window, Win95 will launch RegEdit as a background process and import the .REG file. Windows will not actually open the RegEdit window, but it will display a dialog box informing you that the .REG file has been successfully incorporated into the registry once the process has completed. (This works, incidentally, because .REG files are associated with *REGEDIT.EXE* in the registry. For details on how the registry is used to handle file associations, see "Launching Your Application" in Chapter 8.)

- *Using drag and drop.* When you drag a .REG file from the Explorer window and drop it on a RegEdit icon or in the RegEdit window, Windows will import the .REG file. If RegEdit is not open on the desktop when you drop the file, Windows will launch the Editor as a background process.

- *Using the command line.* If you select the Run option from the Start menu and enter the name of the .REG file you'd like to import in the Open drop-down combo box, RegEdit will import the .REG file in the background. If the path and filename of the .REG file uses long filenames containing embedded spaces, the complete path and filename should be delimited with quotation marks, as in the following example:

```
regedit "c:\REG files\User settings.reg"
```

Since Windows associates .REG files with RegEdit, you can simply enter the name of the .REG file, as follows:

```
"c:\REG files\User settings.reg"
```

- *Running RegEdit in MS-DOS mode.* This is a method that's best reserved for coping with a badly damaged registry. Given its importance, it is discussed in the section "Running RegEdit from MS-DOS."

If you are using .REG files as a means of backing up your registry, it is important to recognize just what the process of restoring from a .REG file does and does not do. In importing a .REG file, RegEdit looks for exact matches between the keys and the value names stored in the registry and those contained in the .REG file. When it finds an exact match, RegEdit replaces all values with the values that it finds in the .REG file. If it does not find a match, RegEdit adds any unmatched keys, default values, or value entries in the .REG file to the registry. In other words, restoring all or part of the registry from a .REG file *overwrites* values and *adds* values. When you restore from a .REG file, RegEdit does *not* delete registry keys and values that have no equivalents in the .REG file.

This is important: it means that, if you've modified the registry by adding new subkeys, making new value entries, or adding a default value to replace an undefined one—which RegEdit describes as "(value not set)"—RegEdit will leave these intact when importing a .REG file.

It is also worth repeating that RegEdit replaces keys and values for which it finds *exact* matches. This means that if you generate a .REG file and then modify a registry key or value by (probably inadvertently) adding a *trailing space*, RegEdit will fail to find an exact match and will add a new key or value entry. Similarly, if you add a trailing space to a key or value name in a .REG file, RegEdit will add keys or values, rather than replace them, when it imports the .REG file. Yes, spaces (even trailing spaces) are significant.

Printing the Registry

Instead of saving all or a part of your computer's registry to a .REG file, you can print it by selecting the Print option from the File menu. When RegEdit opens the Print common dialog, you can designate the printer to which you'd like your output sent, or you can have RegEdit send its output to a .PRN file that you can print later. Example 2-1, for instance, shows a portion of a .PRN file that RegEdit has generated using the Generic/Text Only printer driver.

Example 2-1. A .PRN file generated by RegEdit

```
[HKEY_LOCAL_MACHINE\SOFTWARE\Description]
[HKEY_LOCAL_MACHINE\SOFTWARE\Description\Microsoft]
[HKEY_LOCAL_MACHINE\SOFTWARE\Description\Microsoft\Rpc]
[HKEY_LOCAL_MACHINE\SOFTWARE\Description\Microsoft\Rpc\UuidPersistentData]
ClockSequence=81,0c,00,00
LastTimeAllocated=60,1f,d7,3f,17,f0,ce,01
[HKEY_LOCAL_MACHINE\SOFTWARE\Description\Microsoft\Rpc\UuidTemporaryData]
NetworkAddress=00,aa,00,21,51,25
NetworkAddressLocal=00,00,00,00
```

If you do want printed output of registry keys and values, keep in mind that the registry as a whole and some of its top-level keys (particularly HKCR and HKLM) store an enormous amount of data, so that printed output quickly becomes voluminous. In most cases, generating a .REG file that can be examined with a word processor or text editor is a far better alternative to printed output.

Running RegEdit from MS-DOS

REGEDIT.EXE is really two programs in one. When run from Win95, it is a graphical registry viewer. When run from MS-DOS mode (or real mode), it is a command-line utility for importing and exporting .REG files. As a Windows program, it is an all-purpose tool for examining, editing, backing up, and restoring the registry. As a real mode utility, it is useful to correct a seriously damaged or corrupted registry that prevents Windows from starting. For this reason, Win95 includes a copy of RegEdit on the startup disk that is created during installation.

When run in real mode, RegEdit has no real interface. Instead, its operation is controlled by the switches and arguments that are passed to it on the command line. These are listed in Table 2-3.

Table 2-3. Command-line switches for RegEdit in real mode

Switch	Description
/?	Display RegEdit command-line syntax
/L:system	Path and filename of SYSTEM.DAT
/R:user	Path and filename of USER.DAT
/E *filename* <regpath>	Generate a .REG file
filename	Import or merge a .REG file
/C *filename*	Replace the entire registry with the contents of *filename*

While the Windows version of RegEdit is a "smart" program that knows where to find the files that compose the registry, RegEdit in real mode needs to know the location of *SYSTEM.DAT* and *USER.DAT* if they are stored somewhere other than in the Windows directory. The two optional command-line switches, /L: and /R:, can be used to provide their location to RegEdit. If either switch is used, the complete path and filename are required.

They're Not Just for DOS

Although the documentation leads one to believe that these command-line switches work only in real mode, all of them with the exception of /? are available when RegEdit is run as a Windows application. For example, you can export HKLM to a .REG file by typing a command such as `regedit /E c:\ hklm.reg HKEY_LOCAL_MACHINE` in the Explorer's Start | Run box. Because this is mostly of use when developing programs, it is discussed in more detail in the sidebar "Working with .REG Files" in Chapter 4.

Information on the command-line switches and parameters supported by RegEdit in real mode is available when you enter either of the following command lines:

```
REGEDIT
REGEDIT /?
```

You can use RegEdit in real mode to generate a .REG file that contains all or part of the registry. This file can then be edited to repair incorrect entries and imported. To generate a .REG file, use the following syntax:

```
REGEDIT [/L:system] [/R:user] /E filename [regpath]
```

where *filename* is the complete path and filename of the .REG file to be generated, and *regpath* is the highest-level registry key to be exported. An explicit file extension should be provided as part of *filename*. *regpath* is an optional parameter; if not present, RegEdit will export the entire contents of the registry.

The following syntax is used to import a .REG file:

```
REGEDIT [/L:system] [/R:user] filename
```

where *filename* is the complete path and filename, including an explicit file extension, of the .REG file you'd like to import. Using RegEdit in this way is identical to importing a .REG file in the Windows environment.

Finally, RegEdit in real mode allows you to *replace* the existing registry with the contents of a .REG file. To do this, use the following syntax:

```
REGEDIT [/L:system] [/R:user] /C filename
```

This option should be reserved for systems that are disabled because of a corrupted registry. In fact, if only because it executes extremely slowly (on an average 486 system, it takes somewhere between 12 and 18 hours to restore the registry from a .REG file that contains a complete backup of the registry), you'll want to use it only as a last resort, in those cases in which no other technique to restore a damaged registry works. Clearly, it's much better, if the option is available to you, to use some other means of restoring your registry; for a discussion of techniques for restoring the registry, see Chapter 3, *Backing Up and Restoring the Registry.*

Modifying the Registry with RegEdit

So far, we've used RegEdit as a tool for browsing registry keys and examining their values. RegEdit, though, is more than a read-only tool for examining the registry; it also allows you to create and modify both keys and their values. At the same time (and for understandable reasons), the registry is a rather bare-bones utility: it does not let you perform such operations as dragging and dropping a registry key or value entry, nor does it allow you to cut, copy, or paste portions of the registry. Less understandable, given the destructive potential of changes to the registry, is the absence of an Edit Undo option.

Although this section covers using RegEdit to modify registry keys and values, you should not feel that it gives you the license to make wholesale changes. Some modifications may have no effect on the system; others may cripple or disable it. Changes require planning and forethought. In addition, never modify the registry without being sure that you have a working backup copy. For a discussion of registry backup techniques, see Chapter 3.

Adding Keys

To create a new key, begin by clicking the right mouse button on the parent key of the subkey that you want to create, then select the New option from the pop-up menu. Alternatively, you can click on the new key's parent, then select the New option from the Edit menu. In either case, RegEdit will open a submenu that allows you to indicate whether you want to create a key or one of several values; select the Key option. RegEdit will position the new key after the last existing key, and assign it a temporary name of **New Key #x**, where **x** is the new key's ordinal position among the new subkeys you've added to a particular parent. You can then modify the name.

Windows 95 is quite flexible in allowing you to assign key names. Valid characters in key names include the printable ANSI characters (whose codes range from 32 to 127) and spaces. However, backslashes are not allowed (they serve as separator characters), nor are the wildcard characters * and ?. Finally, you should not assign key names that begin with a period (.), since these are reserved by the system.

There are two major restrictions on adding keys:

- You cannot add a top-level key (i.e., a key at the same level as the pre-defined keys HKEY_LOCAL_MACHINE or HKEY_USERS). If you attempt to do so, the Key option on the New menu should be disabled. Occasionally, though, you may find that it is enabled; in that case, if you still attempt to create a new top-level key, RegEdit displays the error message, "Cannot create key. Error while opening the key My Computer."

- Each subkey of a particular parent key must have a unique name. If you try to assign the same name to two subkeys of a single parent, RegEdit displays the error message, "Cannot rename New Key #*x*: The specified key name already exists. Type another name and try again." Duplicate names are allowed, though, as long as their keys do not share the same parent; such duplicate key names abound throughout the registry.

Although in most cases *adding* a key to the registry is probably the most innocuous change that you can make, it is worth considering beforehand whether there is any advantage to adding a particular key. Windows itself and Windows applications software look for keys with particular paths and names when they access the registry. If a particular key is present but Windows or an application does not look for or does not recognize its name, the information it contains is useless. It only makes sense to add a key if you know that Windows or an application actually read it (or, of course, if you're developing the application that reads it).

If you use .REG files as your primary means of backup, these added keys can also be problematic when they have undesirable effects and you have to restore the registry. As noted earlier, restoring a registry branch from a .REG file will restore the values of all keys that were in existence at the time the .REG file was created, but it will leave intact all keys and their values that were added subsequently. This makes it necessary to maintain a separate list of added keys.

Renaming Keys

RegEdit also permits you to rename existing keys. To do this, click on the key in the key pane with the right mouse button, then select the Rename option from the context menu. Alternatively, you can click on the key you'd like to rename in the key pane to highlight it, then select the Rename option from the Edit menu. Windows will place a box around the key's name and allow you to edit it in place.

The same restrictions that apply to adding a key apply to renaming it: you cannot rename any of the six top-level keys, nor can you rename a key so that it has the same name as another key belonging to its parent.

How Do You Know if it Makes Sense to Add a Key or Value Entry?

Our advice that you should only add a key if you know that Windows or an application looks for it appears at first glance to be nonsensical. After all, if the key or value doesn't exist, obviously it therefore can't be used. And unless it's used, you have no way of knowing what effect it has, right?

But consider this example: it takes only a second to create a new key such as HKEY_CURRENT_USER\Software\Magic\TimeToMakeLunch, and to assign this key a value giving the time at which Win95 should make your lunch each day. This will not, however, result in the production of soup and sandwiches. To repeat: it only makes sense to add a key if you know that Windows or an application actually read it (or, of course, if you're developing the application that reads it). Shakespeare actually commented on just this situation in *Henry IV, Part 1*: When Glendower brags that he can "call spirits from the vasty deep," Hotspur responds, "So can I, or so can any man, but do they come when you call for them?" (Interestingly, Glendower rather than Hotspur is the sympathetic character here, but Shakespeare's complex attitude to magic is another story.) So, yes, you can put any keys or values you please in the registry, but this does not automatically mean that the keys and values will actually function as proper settings or incantations.

If you want to find out what keys and values Windows and applications *attempt* to access, independently of whether they actually find them, you can use *RegSpy95*, a utility included on the accompanying diskette. It is documented in Chapter 8.

It is somewhat surprising that RegEdit supports renaming keys at all. The registry functions in the Win32 API, for instance, don't support renaming keys directly, largely because this is not seen as a useful feature. So make sure that you have a good reason for renaming a key before you actually do change its name. Since both applications and Windows use key names as a kind of shorthand that allows them to identify particular settings and data values, renaming a key usually serves to make its data inaccessible to the program that requires it. An application or a system that is wholly or partially disabled can be a very real side effect of renaming a key.

Although these cautions should always be observed, renaming a key can be of real advantage to a developer precisely because it makes it *inaccessible* without deleting it. For instance, imagine that you've finished testing an installation program for your application; among other things, it writes a complete set of user settings for your application to the subkeys of HKCU\MyCompany\MyApp in the registry. When you return to debugging your application, though, you want to make sure that it is able to function regardless of whether it is able to find settings for the current user or not. In that case, one option is to delete MyApp and all of its subkeys. But a better option would be to rename it to something similar, like MyAppInstall. Then it's always available to be examined (which can be especially useful if it contains valid data), and can at some point be renamed to MyApp once again.

Deleting Keys

The final operation that you can perform on a registry key is to delete it. The easiest way to do this is with the keyboard: select the key you'd like to delete, then press the Del key. With the mouse, begin by clicking the right mouse button on the key that you'd like to delete, then select the Delete option from the context menu. Alternatively, you can highlight the key you'd like to delete, then select the Delete option from the Edit menu. In either case, RegEdit will open a dialog box that prompts you to confirm that you want to delete the key. The dialog, unfortunately, does not display the name of the key that you've selected. So before clicking on the Yes button to confirm the deletion, reexamine the key pane to make sure that you're about to delete the correct key; it is the only key that is displayed with the open folder icon that is shown in Table 2-4. If the key you'd like to delete has a closed folder (also shown in Table 2-4) beside it, don't do it; you're about to delete the wrong key.

Table 2-4. Folder icons used by RegEdit

Icon	Description
	The open folder icon
	The closed folder icon

RegEdit will allow you to delete any key other than the six top-level keys. When you delete a key, RegEdit deletes not only the key and all of its values, but all of the subkeys that belong to it, along with their values. Since you cannot conveniently reverse these changes, and, unless you're very careful, your deletions can become rather extensive, you should take the following precautions before you even begin to think of deleting a key:

- Make a backup copy that contains the key you're thinking of deleting, along with all of its subkeys

- Visually check all of the subkeys of a particular key, along with their values, before deleting that key

- Carefully consider whether you have a good reason for deleting the key

Adding Values

Along with allowing you to add new keys, RegEdit allows you to add new value entries to existing keys. You cannot add a new default value to a key, though; that's because every key automatically has a default (or unnamed) value, whether it is present or not. Instead, you can only add complete value entries to a particular key.

To add a new value entry, select the key to which the value will be added in the key pane. You can click the right mouse button on the key, then select the New option from the context menu. Alternatively, you can highlight the key, then select the New option from the Edit menu. Next, from the context menu, select one of the following value types to add:

- *String*. RegEdit inserts a new value entry at the bottom of the value pane. This includes a default value name of "New Value #*x*", where *x* is the number of new value entries that you've added, the string icon, and an empty string ("") value. A rectangle is shown around the value name, allowing you to enter the name that you'd like to assign to the value entry; if you want to add several value entries at the same time, though, you can rename it later. However, to actually assign a value to the new entry, you have to modify the value.

- *Binary*. A binary value is a numeric value of unspecified length; the Win95 registry can hold binary values of up to approximately 64K. In adding the value entry, RegEdit displays the binary icon and the default value name. In addition, it assigns a zero-length value to the entry. You can modify the value name immediately, but you'll have to select the Modify menu option to change the entry's value.

- *DWORD*. A DWORD value is a double-word, or 4-byte binary value. In adding the value entry, RegEdit displays the binary icon and the default value name. In addition, it assigns value of zero (0x00000000) to the entry. You can modify the value name immediately, but you'll have to select the Modify menu option to change the entry's value.

In some cases, depending on the data type of a particular value, RegEdit may not be the appropriate tool to use for adding a new value. The registry supports several different data types, as Table 4-7 in Chapter 4 shows. However, RegEdit allows you to add only three of them:

- String values corresponding to the REG_SZ data type, the most common form of string data. However, RegEdit should not be used to add other string data types, like strings that are to be macro-expanded (the `REG_EXPAND_SZ` data type) and arrays of strings (the `REG_MULTI_SZ` data type).

- Double word values corresponding to the `REG_DWORD` or `REG_DWORD_LITTLE_ENDIAN` data type. (The two data types are synonymous.) Values of type `REG_DWORD_BIG_ENDIAN`, though, cannot be added with RegEdit.

- Binary data corresponding to the `REG_BINARY` data type.

In addition, before adding value entries, it might be useful to read the cautions discussed earlier in the section "Adding Keys." Above all, applications must actually *use* value entries that you add to the registry. For instance, if you're dissatisfied with the way that the Explorer window positions itself on your desktop when it runs, you might add a `WindowPos` entry to `HKCU\Software\Microsoft\Windows\CurrentVersion\Explorer` and assign it a string value containing the coordinates at which you'd like the Explorer to load. You then can select your favorite reason for why this didn't work from among many available:

- The Explorer does not expect to find its window position in `HKCU\Software\Microsoft\Windows\CurrentVersion\Explorer`, and looks elsewhere for it.

- The Explorer does not expect to retrieve its window position from an entry named `WindowPos`, and therefore doesn't read it.

- The Explorer is not prepared to parse its window coordinates from string data; instead, it expects them to be members of a binary data structure. As a result, it doesn't read the data.

It's important not only that an application read data from the registry, but that the right module read it. For example, some documentation for Win95 mentions that support for long filenames can be disabled by assigning the `REG_DWORD` value 1 to the `Win31FileSystem` value entry in `HKLM\System\CurrentControlSet\Control\FileSystem`. And in fact, *RegSpy95* shows that this setting is read during system initialization:

```
_RegOpenKey        VREDIR    HKLM      C116ED88
                             'System\CurrentControlSet\Control\FileSystem'
_RegQueryValueEx   VREDIR    C116ED88  BIN  1    'Win31FileSystem'  '00'
_RegCloseKey       VREDIR    C116ED88
```

RegSpy95 also shows that `Win31FileSystem` is read only by *VREDIR.VXD*, the Client for Microsoft Networks virtual redirector; it is not read by the Installable File System (IFS) Manager or by the Virtual File Allocation Table (VFAT) driver. These are the two VxDs, though, that are directly responsible for implementing the local file system. In other words, without IFS Manager or VFAT reading the setting, it has no effect. (Indeed, it's hard to imagine how Win95 could work without long filename support.)

Very much like adding a key that's not accessed, adding unread value entries (such as `HKCU\Software\Magic\TimeToMakeLunch`) is fairly innocuous. It is possible, though, to add value entries that aren't so innocuous. To take one example that we mentioned earlier, if you add a value entry named `DisableReg-istryTools` to the `HKCU\Software\Microsoft\Windows\CurrentVersion\Policies\System` key, assign it a `REG_DWORD` value of 1, and then close RegEdit, you'll prevent yourself from running RegEdit again. In order to restore registry access, you'll have to run Microsoft System Policy Editor or write a short program that changes this setting.

Renaming Values

You can rename any value name other than the one described as "(Default)"; this is because the latter consists of a value only and is not a complete value entry. To rename a value, click the right mouse button on the value name and select the Rename option from the context menu. Alternatively, select the value entry in the value pane, then select the Rename option from the Edit menu. RegEdit displays a rectangle around the value name and positions the cursor at the end of the string, allowing you to edit it.

Before renaming existing value entries, it might be useful to read the cautions discussed earlier in the section, "Renaming Keys."

Modifying Values

To modify the value component of a value entry, you can either double-click on its value name or click the right mouse button on the value name, then select the Modify option from the context menu. You can also select the value entry, then select the Modify option from the Edit menu. RegEdit opens one of three editing dialogs, depending on the value's data type:

*   *String.* RegEdit opens the Edit String dialog shown in Figure 2-7, which allows you to enter the string value. You do not have to include quotation marks.

*   *Binary.* RegEdit opens the Edit Binary Value dialog shown in Figure 2-8 and allows you to enter any valid sequence of hexadecimal digits.

*   *DWORD.* RegEdit opens the Edit DWORD Value dialog shown in Figure 2-9. You can decide whether you want to enter the value as an unsigned decimal number (the valid range is 0 to 4,294,967,295) or a hexadecimal number (with a range of 00000000-FFFFFFFF) by selecting the appropriate button in the Base group box.

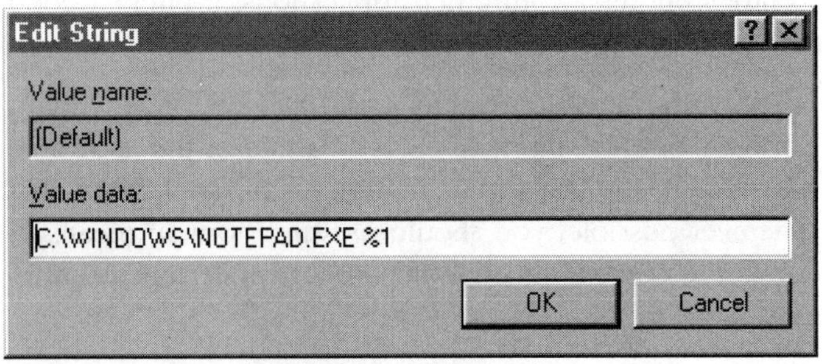

Figure 2-7. The Edit String dialog

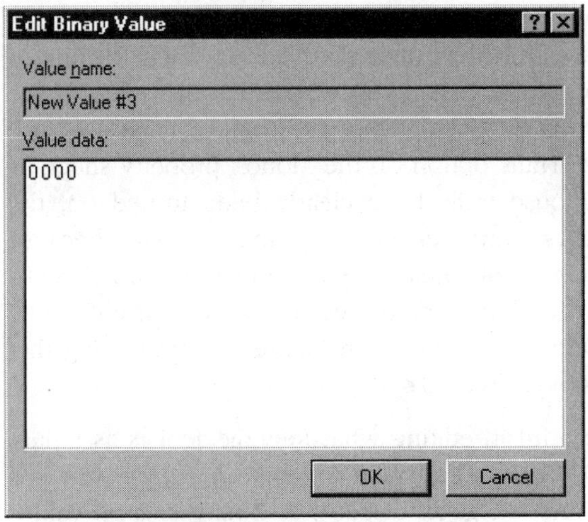

Figure 2-8. The Edit Binary Value dialog

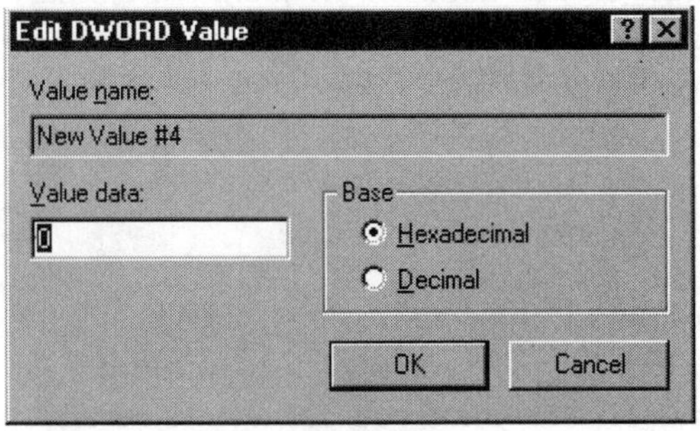

Figure 2-9. The Edit DWORD Value dialog

If you click the right mouse button inside of the Value Data text box, you can undo any changes, as well as cut and copy to, and paste from, the Windows Clipboard. (Note, however, that clipboard operations are not supported in the Edit Binary Value dialog.) Since Clipboard support allows you to copy data not only from other registry value entries but also from other applications, it offers a good method for accurately importing data into the registry.

Although the edit dialogs perform very rudimentary type checking (you cannot enter invalid characters or digits, or enter numeric values outside of the allowable range), it is nevertheless easy to enter data that is invalid to the application that will read it. As a result, wherever possible, you should use the "normal" means of modifying the registry through the Control Panel applets or an application's configuration options facilities.

Control Panel in particular is essentially a RegEdit "wizard" that allows you to change registry settings without having to interface directly with RegEdit. To single out just one example, let's see how enabling and disabling mouse trails using the Control Panel's Mouse applet affects the registry. First, open RegEdit to display the value entries of HKCC\Display\Settings; note that the value of the MouseTrails entry, if it's present, is "0". Next, open the Control Panel's Mouse applet and check the Show Pointer Trails option on the Motion property sheet, as shown in Figure 2-10. Although mouse trails have clearly been turned on, the value of the registry's MouseTrails entry remains unchanged. That's because RegEdit displays static data, and it has not reread the value of the MouseTrails entry after you used Control Panel to change it. To see the entry's current value, press F5; RegEdit will update its window as shown in Figure 2-11, indicating that Control Panel changed the value of MouseTrails to "1".

It is particularly important to be careful in editing what RegEdit depicts as binary data. Whereas string and DWORD values correspond to single registry data types (REG_SZ and REG_DWORD, respectively), RegEdit displays as binary data all values that belong to all other data types, including strings containing macros (REG_EXPAND_SZ) and string arrays (REG_MULTI_SZ). In addition, frequently the binary data is actually a structured data type that an application has stored in the registry, so be careful above all not to reduce or increase the number of bytes of binary data belonging to a value entry.

Deleting Values

To delete a value, click the right mouse button on its value entry, then select the Delete option from the context menu. RegEdit will prompt you to confirm your deletion. Amazingly, RegEdit has no undo feature; once you delete a value entry, you cannot restore it.

RegEdit allows you to delete complete value entries only. Although RegEdit fails to disable the Delete menu option when you select a key's default value, the attempt to delete it will produce an error message that reads, "Unable to delete all specified values."

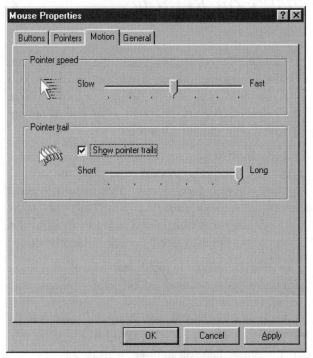

Figure 2-10. The Mouse Property dialog's Motion property sheet

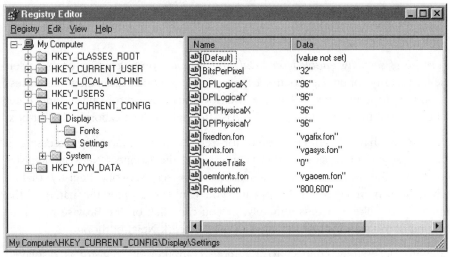

Figure 2-11. The MouseTrails value entry after pressing F5

RegEdit permits you to delete multiple value entries at a single time. To do this, simply hold down the Ctrl key while selecting the value entries to be deleted. Be careful!

Accessing the Registry on Remote Computers

In addition to using RegEdit to examine the registry on your own computer, you may also be able to use it to examine the registry on a remote computer. This makes RegEdit useful for system administrators, or as a debugging tool if you're developing an application that modifies a registry remotely, or if you're debugging an application that is being tested on a remote computer.

Accessing a remote registry does require that you set up some additional components after Win95 has been installed on your system, and that the remote computer be configured to support remote registry access. This in turn requires that both computers be members of the same domain on a WinNT network or be clients on a Novell NetWare network, and that both share at least one common network protocol. If this is the case, remote registry access requires the following:

- *Microsoft Remote Registry Services installed on local and remote machines.* Microsoft Remote Registry Services must be installed on your computer and on any computers whose registries you'd like to access remotely. It is included as an optional component on the Win95 CD-ROM, and can be installed at any time after Win95 itself has been installed; for step-by-step instructions, see the sidebar "Installing Microsoft Remote Registry Services."

- *Remote administration enabled on remote computers.* To enable remote administration, open the Control Panel's Passwords applet, select the Remote Administration property sheet, and check the Enable Remote Administration of this server box.

- *User-level security enabled on local and remote computers.* To enable user-level security, open the Control Panel's Network applet and select the Access Control property sheet. Select the user-level access control button, and enter the name of the server that provides pass-through authentication in the list box.

Once systems have been configured for remote access, actually accessing a remote registry is quite simple: you simply select the Connect Network Registry option from the Registry menu. When the Connect Network Registry dialog, which is shown in Figure 2-12, appears, you can either enter the name of the computer you'd like to access remotely, or you can click on the Browse button to select one of the systems that belongs in your Network Neighborhood.

Once you successfully connect to a remote computer, its registry is displayed immediately beneath your own, as Figure 2-13 illustrates. Except for the difference in performance caused by network traffic, you can navigate, browse registry keys and values, and make changes to registry keys and values on the remote registry just as if it were the registry on your local computer.

Installing Microsoft Remote Registry Services

Microsoft Remote Registry Services should be installed on all remote computers, as well as on your computer. On remote computers, *REGSERV.EXE* is the RPC server that you connect to when you access a remote registry; on your computer, *WINREG.DLL* is an RPC client that routes registry access requests onto the network. For an illustration depicting how remote and local registry access works, see Figure 4-1 in Chapter 4.

Installing Microsoft Remote Registry Services involves the following steps:

1. Open the Control Panel Network applet and click the Add button. The Select Network Component Type dialog opens.

2. Double-click on Service in the list box. The Select Network Service dialog opens.

3. Click the Have Disk button. The Install from Disk dialog opens.

4. Enter the path to the `ADMIN\NETTOOLS\REMOTREG` directory on the Win95 CD-ROM, then click OK. The Select Network Service dialog opens.

5. Make sure that Microsoft Remote Registry is highlighted in the Models list box, then click OK.

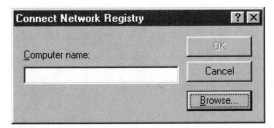

Figure 2-12. The Connect Network Registry dialog

Once you're finished working with the remote registry, you should disconnect from it by selecting the Disconnect Network Registry option from the Registry menu.

The Registry Editor and the Registry

As we mentioned earlier, the Registry Editor and the registry are by no means synonymous: the registry is a configuration database, while RegEdit is just a particular utility to access the registry. Very much like any other application, RegEdit depends on the registry functions within the Win32 API to gather information

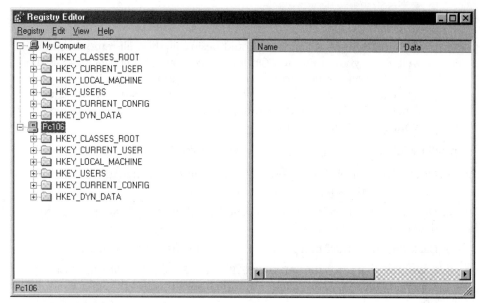

Figure 2-13. RegEdit connected to a remote registry

about the registry. To illustrate this point, Example 2-2 displays the output
produced by a modified version of APISpy32, a utility developed by Matt Pietrek
and included on the accompanying diskette. APISpy32 was used to intercept the
calls to the registry API that RegEdit makes before displaying its initial window.

Example 2-2. The output produced by APISpy32 when launching RegEdit

```
RegOpenKeyA(HND: HKCU,
            "Software\Microsoft\Windows\CurrentVersion\Policies\System",)
RegOpenKeyA ret 0
RegQueryValueExA(HND:C3410FBCh,"DisableRegistryTools",,,,)
RegQueryValueExA ret 2
RegCloseKey(HND:C3410FBCh)
RegCloseKey ret 0
RegOpenKeyA(HND: HKCU,
            "Software\Microsoft\Windows\CurrentVersion\Applets\Regedit",)
RegOpenKeyA ret 0
RegQueryValueExA(HND:C3410FBCh,"FindFlags",,,,)
RegQueryValueExA ret 0
RegQueryValueExA(HND:C3410FBCh,"View",,,,)
RegQueryValueExA ret 0
RegCloseKey(HND:C3410FBCh)
RegCloseKey ret 0
RegEnumKeyA(HND: HKCR,DW:0h,"e_f R~",DW:100h)
RegEnumKeyA ret 0
RegEnumKeyA(HND: HKCU,DW:0h,"CLSID",DW:100h)
RegEnumKeyA ret 0
RegEnumKeyA(HND: HKLM,DW:0h,"Control Panel",DW:100h)
RegEnumKeyA ret 0
```

Example 2-2. The output produced by APISpy32 when launching RegEdit (continued)

```
RegEnumKeyA(HND: HKU,DW:0h,"Network",DW:100h)
RegEnumKeyA ret 0
RegEnumKeyA(HND: HKCC,DW:0h,".Default",DW:100h)
RegEnumKeyA ret 0
RegEnumKeyA(HND: HKDD,DW:0h,"Display",DW:100h)
RegEnumKeyA ret 0
RegCreateKeyA(HND: HKCU,
             "Software\Microsoft\Windows\CurrentVersion\Applets\Regedit",)
RegCreateKeyA ret 0
RegSetValueExA(HND:C11C0064h,"View",DW:0h,DW:3h,,DW:3Ch)
RegSetValueExA ret 0
RegSetValueExA(HND:C11C0064h,"FindFlags",DW:0h,DW:4h,,DW:4h)
RegSetValueExA ret 0
RegCloseKey(HND:C11C0064h)
RegCloseKey ret 0
```

When it's launched, RegEdit begins by attempting to open a key named HKCR\
Software\Microsoft\Windows\CurrentVersion\Policies\System; its purpose here is to determine whether RegEdit should continue to load itself. If the
key exists and contains an entry named DisableRegistryTools whose value is
1 (yes, this sophisticated-sounding "System Policy" is nothing more than a registry
setting), RegEdit refuses to load.

If user access to the registry is not prohibited, RegEdit opens the HKCR\Software\
Microsoft\Windows\CurrentVersion\Applets\Regedit key in order to
retrieve the values of the FindFlags and View entries, which it uses to restore
the RegEdit window. So, RegEdit itself relies upon the registry. In particular, the
value of the View entry is a structured REG_BINARY data type that determines
where the RegEdit window should be positioned, while the lower four bits of the
FindFlags REG_DWORD value are used to store the state of the four check boxes
in RegEdit's Find dialog, as Table 2-5 shows.

Table 2-5. Bit values of the FindFlags value entry

Bit	Setting
0	Match whole string only
1	Search key name
2	Search value name
3	Search value

Finally, RegEdit uses the *RegEnumKeyEx* function to retrieve the name of the first
ordinal key belonging to each of the registry's six top-level keys. This very clearly
indicates that RegEdit has no "knowledge" of the registry aside from what's made
available through the Win32 API: the program here is checking to make sure that
each of the top-level keys has at least one subkey, so that RegEdit's TreeView

common control (which is used to form RegEdit's key pane) knows what kind of button (a plus sign, a minus sign, or no button) to assign to each top-level key.

That RegEdit is simply a utility program that, like any other registry utility, depends on the registry functions in the Win32 API means that creating a RegEdit clone is well within the reach of virtually any programmer. For example, Figure 2-14 shows a RegEdit clone created using the Professional Edition of Microsoft Visual Basic 4.0.

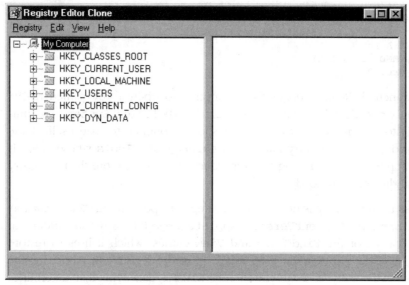

Figure 2-14. A RegEdit clone

The code to display the initial view of the registry shown in Figure 2-14 is contained in the main form's *Form_Load* event procedure and is shown in Example 2-3. (For non-Visual Basic programmers, the *Form_Load* event procedure contains a form's initialization code, and is executed automatically when a form loads.) Since all of the objects—My Computer, as well as the six top-level keys—shown in the key pane when the editor first opens are predefined, they are simply added to the editor's TreeView control as node objects without the program's having to access the registry API.

However, the key pane has to do more than simply display visible keys; it also must let the user know which keys have unexpanded children (which it indicates by a plus sign), which have expanded children that are fully visible in the pane (indicated by a minus sign), or which terminate their branch and have no children (indicated by no sign). So for the TreeView control to reflect the presence or absence of subkeys, we have to add at least one node object as a child of each top-level key; that way, the user can see that the key has subkeys which can be made visible by clicking on the key. To do this, for each of the six top-level keys, *RegQueryInfoKey* determines the length of that key's longest subkey name; this prevents the program from allocating too small a buffer to retrieve subkey names. Next, the *RegEnumKeyEx* function retrieves the name of the first subkey belonging to each top-level key. This subkey is then added to the TreeView control. This is exactly how the the registry API calls during RegEdit's initialization work; the result, as shown in Figure 2-14, is a TreeView control that both displays the registry's predefined top-level keys and indicates that they can be expanded because each contains hidden subkeys.

Example 2-3. The RegEdit clone's Form_Load event procedure

```
Private Sub Form_Load()
Dim intCtr As Integer, intHdrWidth As Integer
Dim hKey As Long
Dim lngLenSubkeyName As Long
Dim strSubkeyName As String
Dim strNode As String
Dim nodRegTree As Node
' Create ListView column headers
intHdrWidth = (ListView1,Width)/2*0.84
Dim objHeader As Column Header
SetobjHeader = ListView1.ColumnHeaders.Add(, , "Value Name", intHdrWidth)
SetobjHeader = ListView1.ColumnHeaders.Add(, , "Data", intHdrWidth)
' Add "My Computer" as top-level node
Set nodRegTree = TreeView1.Nodes.Add(, , "home", "My Computer", "comp")
nodRegTree.Tag = 1                          ' Mark as fully expanded
' Add six top-level keys as nodes of "My Computer"
Set nodRegTree = TreeView1.Nodes.Add("home", tvwChild, "HKCR", _ "HKEY_
CLASSES_ROOT", "closed", "open")
Set nodRegTree = TreeView1.Nodes.Add("home", tvwChild, "HKCU", _
                       "HKEY_CURRENT_USER", "closed", "open")
Set nodRegTree = TreeView1.Nodes.Add("home", tvwChild, "HKLM", _
                       "HKEY_LOCAL_MACHINE", "closed", "open")
Set nodRegTree = TreeView1.Nodes.Add("home", tvwChild, "HKU", _
                       "HKEY_USERS", "closed", "open")
Set nodRegTree = TreeView1.Nodes.Add("home", tvwChild, "HKCC", _
                       "HKEY_CURRENT_CONFIG", "closed", "open")
Set nodRegTree = TreeView1.Nodes.Add("home", tvwChild, "HKDD", _
                       "HKEY_DYN_DATA", "closed", "open")
' Display tree view up to this point
nodRegTree.Sorted = True
nodRegTree.EnsureVisible
' Check that each root key has at least 1 subkey
For intCtr = 1 To TreeView1.Nodes.Count
   strNode = TreeView1.Nodes.Item(intCtr).Key
   If strNode <> "home" Then
' Convert node abbreviation to handle
      Select Case strNode
         Case "HKCR"
            hKey = HKEY_CLASSES_ROOT
         Case "HKCU"
```

Example 2-3. The RegEdit clone's Form_Load event procedure (continued)

```
            hKey = HKEY_CURRENT_USER
        Case "HKLM"
            hKey = HKEY_LOCAL_MACHINE
        Case "HKU"
            hKey = HKEY_USERS
        Case "HKCC"
            hKey = HKEY_CURRENT_CONFIG
        Case "HKDD"
            hKey = HKEY_DYN_DATA
    End Select
' Get size of each key's longest name to allocate buffer
    Call RegQueryInfoKey(hKey, 0, 0, 0, 0, lngLenSubkeyName, _
                    0, 0, 0, 0, 0, 0)
    strSubkeyName = String(lngLenSubkeyName + 1, 0)
' Retrieve one subkey
    If RegEnumKeyEx(hKey, 0&, strSubkeyName, lngLenSubkeyName, 0&, _
                0&, 0&, 0) = ERROR_SUCCESS Then
        strSubkeyName = Left(strSubkeyName, lngLenSubkeyName)
'Add node to top-level key so icon appears with a "+"
        Set nodRegTree = TreeView1.Nodes.Add(strNode, tvwChild, _
                        , strSubkeyName, "closed", "open")
    End If
  End If
Next
End Sub
```

Instead of displaying the top-level keys and adding one subkey for each of them, the program's initialization code could instead have read the entire registry and organized the TreeView control accordingly. This produces a program that performs incredibly poorly at startup (it takes a long time to read all of those keys) and wastes memory (the overwhelming majority of registry keys are never viewed or accessed during a single editing session). As a result, this RegEdit clone, like RegEdit itself, aims at minimizing memory consumption by reading only the absolute minimum amount of information necessary. The TreeView control automatically handles the process of graphically expanding and collapsing the subkeys of the selected key. But because of its design, the program has to provide the node objects to be expanded and unexpanded on the fly. The code to do this is stored in the TreeView control's Expand event procedure, and is shown in Example 2-4.

Example 2-4. The RegEdit clone's TreeView1_Expand event procedure

```
Private Sub TreeView1_Expand(ByVal Node As Node)
' My Computer is constant - nothing to do other than expand
If Node.Text = "My Computer" Then Exit Sub
Dim intCtr As Integer
Dim hKey As Long, hRootKey As Long, hChildKey As Long
Dim lngSubkeys As Long, lngValues As Long
Dim lngLenSubkeyName As Long, lngLenValueName As Long
```

Example 2-4. The RegEdit clone's TreeView1_Expand event procedure (continued)

```
Dim lngLenValueData As Long, lngLenSubkey As Long
Dim lngIndex As Long, lngSubSubkeys As Long
Dim lngChildren As Long, lngNodeIndex As Long
Dim strSubkey As String, strRoot As String
Dim strTemp As String
Dim blnKeyOpen As Boolean
Dim nodRegTree As Node
' Parse node name
strTemp = Node.FullPath
strTemp = Mid(strTemp, InStr(1, strTemp, "\") + 1)
If InStr(1, strTemp, "\") > 0 Then
    strRoot = Left(strTemp, InStr(1, strTemp, "\") - 1)
    strSubkey = Mid(strTemp, InStr(1, strTemp, "\") + 1)
Else
    strRoot = strTemp
End If
Select Case strRoot
    Case "HKEY_CLASSES_ROOT"
        hRootKey = HKEY_CLASSES_ROOT
    Case "HKEY_CURRENT_USER"
        hRootKey = HKEY_CURRENT_USER
    Case "HKEY_LOCAL_MACHINE"
        hRootKey = HKEY_LOCAL_MACHINE
    Case "HKEY_USERS"
        hRootKey = HKEY_USERS
    Case "HKEY_CURRENT_CONFIG"
        hRootKey = HKEY_CURRENT_CONFIG
    Case "HKEY_DYN_DATA"
        hRootKey = HKEY_DYN_DATA
End Select
' Gather subkey information
If Len(Trim(strSubkey)) > 0 Then
    Call RegOpenKey(hRootKey, strSubkey, hKey)
    blnKeyOpen = True
Else
    hKey = hRootKey
End If
Call RegQueryInfoKey(hKey, 0, 0, 0, lngSubkeys, lngLenSubkeyName, _
                    0, lngValues, lngLenValueName, lngLenValueData, 0, 0)
' See if node is fully expanded
If (Val(Node.Tag)) <> 1 Or (Node.Children <> lngSubkeys) Then
' Delete existing nodes
    lngChildren = Node.Children
    For intCtr = 1 To lngChildren
        TreeView1.Nodes.Remove Node.Child.Index
    Next
' Enumerate subkeys
    For lngIndex = 0 To lngSubkeys - 1
        lngLenSubkey = lngLenSubkeyName + 1
        strSubkey = String(lngLenSubkey, 0)
        Call RegEnumKeyEx(hKey, lngIndex, strSubkey, lngLenSubkey, 0, _
                        0, 0, 0)
```

Example 2-4. The RegEdit clone's TreeView1_Expand event procedure (continued)

```
        strSubkey = Left(strSubkey, lngLenSubkey)
' Add node
        Set nodRegTree = TreeView1.Nodes.Add(Node.Index, tvwChild, , _
                                        strSubkey, "closed", "open")
' Determine if new node has subkeys
        Call RegOpenKey(hKey, strSubkey, hChildKey)
        Call RegQueryInfoKey(hChildKey, 0, 0, 0, lngSubSubkeys, _
                        lngLenSubkey, 0, 0, 0, 0, 0, 0)
        If lngSubSubkeys > 0 Then
           lngLenSubkey = lngLenSubkey + 1
           strSubkey = String(lngLenSubkey, 0)
           Call RegEnumKeyEx(hChildKey, 0, strSubkey, lngLenSubkey, 0, _
                        0, 0, 0)
           Call RegCloseKey(hChildKey)
' Add to most recent key
           lngNodeIndex = nodRegTree.Index
           Set nodRegTree = TreeView1.Nodes.Add(lngNodeIndex, tvwChild, _
                        , strSubkey, "closed", "open")
        End If
    Next
    Node.Tag = 1
End If
Node.Sorted = True
' Close Registry key
If blnKeyOpen Then Call RegCloseKey(hKey)
End Sub
```

When the user attempts to expand a key, the program first checks the node's Tag
property to determine whether the key's subkey information has already been
collected; a value of 1 indicates that all of a key's subkeys have been enumerated.
The program also compares the number of subkey nodes (which is returned by
the Nodes.Children property) with the number of subkeys reported by the
RegQueryInfoKey function. If the program has not yet gathered subkey information, or if the number of subkey nodes does not equal the number of registry
subkeys (indicating that subkey information has changed since the program last
read the registry), it deletes all child nodes, enumerates the subkeys, and adds
them as nodes to the TreeView control. It also determines whether each subkey
added to the TreeView control in turn has child keys, in which case it adds one
child node to that subkey's node in the control; this permits the TreeView control
to indicate whether the user can expand the subkey by clicking on it.

Summary

Despite the growing availability of registry-related software, RegEdit, Microsoft's
Registry Editor, remains the most significant general-purpose registry utility for
Win95. Some of the central points we covered in this chapter are:

- There is nothing magical about RegEdit, nor does it have a special relationship to the registry. RegEdit is just an ordinary Win32 application, very much like any application that anyone might write. It uses common controls as its interface components, and accesses the registry through the registry API.

- Its ability to generate .REG files makes RegEdit a critical utility for backing up some or all of the registry.

- Its ability to operate both under Windows and in real mode, as well as its ability to import .REG files, makes RegEdit one of the best available utilities for restoring some or all of the registry.

- RegEdit supports remote registry access, which allows the user to connect to another registry, as well as to navigate and modify its keys and values as if they were his or her local registry.

- Its graphical depiction of the Win95 registry makes RegEdit an excellent tool for debugging code modules that call the registry API. It does, however, offer a static, rather than dynamic, view of registry data, which makes it necessary to manually refresh the registry window by pressing F5.

- The Registry Editor offers a limited representation of the diverse data types found in the registry. It is able to handle `REG_SZ` (string) data, `REG_DWORD` (integer) data, and `REG_BINARY` (binary) data. All other data types are represented as `REG_BINARY`. This means that the developer has to be very careful about using RegEdit to add values to the registry.

3

Backing Up and Restoring the Registry

Much of the mystification that surrounds the registry, and the trepidation with which users, system administrators, and developers alike sometimes approach the registry, has arisen for a very good reason: it's easy to thoroughly trash your system when you muck with the registry. Sometimes, a few features suddenly stop working. More seriously, entire software components mysteriously become inoperative. In extreme cases, Windows itself is unable to load, and your computer system is crippled until you reinstall Windows 95.

Users who muck with the registry run a great enough risk of trashing their system. But for developers, the risk is even greater. As you begin to incorporate calls to the registry API into your applications, those portions of your code that write to the registry are sure to include an occasional bug. In most of these cases, *something* is being written *somewhere* in the registry, although in a way and possibly in a place rather different than you intended. The result can be a partially or wholly corrupted registry.

If you're the kind of developer who likes to go spelunking—who is concerned with exploring and experimenting with the registry, seeing how it works, and developing for the registry in ways that go beyond Microsoft's standard guidelines on how developers should store their applications' state information in the registry—that danger is even greater. If you think, for instance, that *RegSpy95*, the registry spying utility included with this book, is outstanding because it lets you see how other applications use the registry at the same time as it sheds light on how Win95 operates, then you fall into this category.

Sooner or later, if you play with the registry enough, you're going to run into problems. In this chapter, we'll examine what you can do *beforehand* to back up the registry so that, when a problem does occur, you can deal with it with a minimum of disruption to yourself, your computer system, and your work. This is, as you've probably surmised from the title, a chapter about making backups. But rather than simply dispensing the usual pointless advice that you should back up everything as often as possible, we've tried to show how you can make various kinds of backups in various ways for various circumstances. And we've also tried to examine how you might go about restoring the registry once you begin to run into problems.

Backing Up the Registry in a Stable System

After you've installed Win95 and your major software applications and your system appears to be stable, but before you begin experimenting with the registry, it's a good idea to make several copies of the registry. By doing this, you prepare yourself to deal with two different kinds of disasters:

- *The registry is clearly damaged but Windows loads*. If Windows begins to behave erratically and the other techniques that you use to repair the registry don't work, you can "roll back" the registry to a point at which you're fairly certain the registry was not damaged. You'll lose some system and application state information, depending on how many backups you have and how old the backup copy that you use is. But your system won't be a complete loss.

- *Windows refuses to load, or is so crippled that it might as well not load*. If Windows is completely incapacitated, you can replace the existing damaged version with one that you believe to be stable. You should then be able to load Windows.

Actually, by making a good backup copy of the registry, you're doing much more than protecting yourself from the unintended consequences of your own registry modifications; you're also protecting yourself from the accidental side effects of any installation program and any application that writes to the registry. If the behavior of most Windows 3.x applications, and the amazing popularity of commercial "uninstaller" products, are any indication, these can easily be far more problematic than the damage inflicted by your own code.

Backing up the registry just one time, though, is of relatively little value. Most major application packages, like Microsoft Office, Microsoft Visual C++, or Microsoft Visual Basic, write to the registry extensively during installation. If their registry settings are lost, in most cases you'll have to reinstall the applications to get them working again. In other words, you should be sure to back up the entire registry at several critical junctures:

- When you're reasonably certain that the system is stable

- Immediately before you install a major piece of software

- Immediately before you install any piece of software that you're not completely certain is a "well-behaved" Windows application

If you run into difficulties later, you can restore the registry from the latest complete backup copy. If that still doesn't correct the problem, you can restore from progressively older backups until the problem that you're trying to correct is resolved.

WinDiff and Backups

If you're concerned not only with safeguarding your system but also with figuring out how applications modify the registry, you'll want to generate a .REG file not only before installing a software package, but also after it. You can then compare the two versions with a file comparison utility like *WinDiff*, which is included in both Microsoft Visual C++ and the Microsoft Win32 SDK. This allows you to see what modifications an installation program has made to the registry, which in turn gives you some sense of how its application uses the registry.

Similarly, if you're interested in determining how the data in some portion of the registry is organized, you can generate a .REG file before performing some operation that modifies the data, generate a .REG file after the operation, and then use *WinDiff* to compare them. For instance, if you're interested in how the Explorer uses its `Streams` and `StreamsMRU` subkeys to organize the Windows desktop, you can generate a .REG file containing `HKCU/Software/Microsoft/Windows/CurrentVersion/Explorer`, reposition an application window or an icon, then generate a second .REG file. Once you open them both in *WinDiff,* you can rapidly identify differences in the two .REG files—and therefore discover how the registry has been modified—by selecting the Next Change option from WinDiff's View menu.

So far, we've exhorted you to back up the registry. It's time, however, to focus on the tools that you can use to create the backups.

A basic tool for backing up the registry—and, as an added bonus, one that requires no effort on your part—is Windows itself. At the beginning of each session, immediately after it discovers that it is able to boot, Windows makes a copy of each of the files that it is using to form the registry and assigns them a .DA0 file extension. They are your first line of defense against registry failure. Later in this chapter, in "Using Windows' Own Backups," we'll see how to restore the registry using this copy. But when problems arise, Windows' own backups sometimes form a rather weak line of first defense; it's best to supplement them with a set of backups that you create. We'll begin by examining some of the ways of doing this.

Microsoft Configuration Backup

The best tool for the first kind of backup is named Microsoft Configuration Backup (*CFGBACK.EXE*), and it's included on both the Windows 95 CD-ROM and on the *Microsoft Windows 95 Resource Kit* CD-ROM.[*] The utility, which is shown in Figure 3-1, allows you to save up to nine backup copies of the registry. Each backup copy is stored in the Windows directory and is assigned a filename *REGBACKx.RBK*,[†] where x is a number from one to nine that indicates the ordinal number of the backup. Much like the registry files themselves, .RBK files are stored in a proprietary, undocumented format; .RBK files are readable only by Microsoft Configuration Backup.

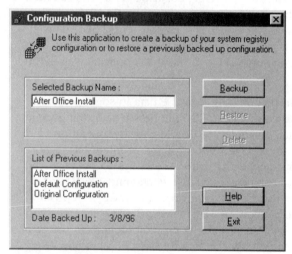

Figure 3-1. Microsoft Configuration Backup

A major problem with backing up the registry is that the backup files can consume enormous amounts of disk space. On most machines, *SYSTEM.DAT* and *USER.DAT*, the two files that compose the registry, together exceed a megabyte. If you make frequent backup copies by simply making copies of these files (as well as individual *USER.DAT* files, if your system is configured to support multiple

---

[*] It's easy to overlook the Microsoft Configuration Backup utility. On the Windows 95 CD-ROM, it's stored in the \OTHER\MISC\CFGBACK directory. And it's one of the components that's installed if you select the PSS Support tools for Windows 95 option when installing the *Microsoft Windows 95 Resource Kit* software.

[†] Interestingly, Microsoft Configuration Backup does not register the .RBK file type in the registry.

users), they quickly eat up all of your hard disk space. If you make backup copies by using RegEdit to generate .REG files, they consume even more disk space. And although you can compress these files to save disk space, they are, for all intents and purposes, inaccessible until you uncompress them again.

In contrast, a nice feature of Microsoft Configuration Backup is that it automatically generates compressed registry backup (.RBK) files and, if you restore the registry from a backup, automatically uncompresses them as well. Although the file sizes are slightly larger than similar .ZIP files, they are always accessible to the utility as long as they continue to be stored in the Windows directory.

Although *CFGBACK.EXE* supports just nine backup copies, you can easily work around this limitation by storing older registry backups somewhere other than the Windows directory, as long as you're careful not to overwrite a later backup copy if you move it back to the Windows directory. If you do store .RBK files elsewhere to save more than nine backup copies, it's probably also a good idea to assign a long filename to the older copies to help you identify them. That's because the name that you assign to the backup when you generate it is stored within the file, and is not part of the file's name.

There is one significant limitation of *CFGBACK.EXE*: according to the documentation, on systems configured to support multiple users, it saves user information in its .RBK files, but will not restore them to the registry. But in fact, because of a program bug (which is discussed in the section "APISpy32" in Chapter 10, *Spying on the Registry*), *CFGBACK.EXE* does not save any user settings in its backup files independently of whether a system is configured to support multiple users or not. So it cannot restore any user settings, since they're not included in the .RBK file. This means that all of the ways that you've customized both your Windows environment (such things as persistent network connections, system colors, video display resolution, custom cursors and sounds, and screen saver behavior) as well as the environment of your applications are lost if you have to restore an older version of the registry. Since this prospect is not exactly enticing, you'll have to use *CFGBACK.EXE* along with some other backup method if you want to preserve user information.

In addition, when used as the sole tool for backing up the registry, *CFGBACK.EXE* is completely inadequate in one major case: since it is a Windows application that generates proprietary .RBK files, its backup copies are worse than useless if Windows itself cannot run because of a damaged registry. That means that, at a minimum, when you use Microsoft Configuration Backup to generate your very first stable backup copy, you should also use RegEdit to make a second backup copy. If you do need to restore the registry completely, you can use the .REG file generated by RegEdit as your starting point, and then restore a later, hopefully good version of the registry using Microsoft Configuration Backup.

The Emergency Recovery Utility

If you're dissatisfied with or don't own Configuration Backup, you can also use the Emergency Recovery Utility (*ERU.EXE*), although, as you'll see shortly, we wouldn't recommend it. The Emergency Recovery Utility is a little-known utility which is included in the \OTHER\MISC\ERU directory of the CD-ROM edition of Windows 95. As a backup and recovery tool, the Emergency Recovery Utility has several advantages over both Configuration Backup and backups using .REG files:

- *It backs up all essential system configuration files.* By default, backups generated by ERU include not only the registry files, but also several other system configuration files listed in Table 3-1. These files should probably be considered as effectively part of the Win95 registry.

- *It runs in real mode.* ERU stores a real mode recovery utility, *ERD.EXE*, along with the backed up system files. This makes it easy to restore one or more damaged components.

Table 3-1. Files backed up by the Emergency Recovery Utility

AUTOEXEC.BAT

COMMAND.COM

CONFIG.SYS

IO.SYS

MSDOS.SYS

PROTOCOL.INI

SYSTEM.DAT

SYSTEM.INI

USER.DAT

WIN.INI

When you run ERU, it first prompts you for the destination drive or directory where the backup files should be stored; the default is a floppy disk drive, although you can override this to store your backups on a network or a local drive. Next, a dialog lists the files that are to be backed up; by clicking its Custom button, you can control which files are included in the backup. ERU then performs the backup.

To restore backed up files, enter real mode or Safe Mode real mode, make the directory or the floppy disk that contains the backed up files your current directory, and run *ERD.EXE*. You can then choose the components you'd like to restore.

It is important to note that, as a backup/restore utility, Emergency Recovery Utility has several major limitations that, on balance, are far more serious than those of Configuration Backup Utility:

- *Exclusion of critical files.* ERU begins by determining how much disk space is available to backed up files, and then determines which files fit in the available space. If you're backing up your files to a floppy disk or a hard disk that has too little free space, ERU arbitrarily discards files that it can't fit on the disk or in the directory. (If you're backing up to a floppy, ERU works only with a single diskette; it cannot create backups spanning multiple floppy disks.) Most commonly, it does not back up *SYSTEM.DAT,* the file that contains the HKEY_LOCAL_MACHINE registry tree. Although ERU displays a dialog that accurately lists the files it will include in the backup set, as Figure 3-2 shows, you're likely not to notice critical files that are missing unless you actually look for them.[*] If you haven't noticed, for instance, *SYSTEM.DAT* is rather inconspicuously absent from Figure 3-2.

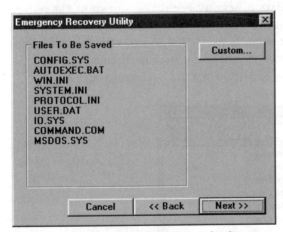

Figure 3-2. The list of files the ERU is to back up

- *Exclusion of some user information.* ERU backs up the system-wide *USER.DAT* registry file. However, on systems configured to support multiple users, it does not back up the *USER.DAT* file belonging to the current user, which is usually stored in the Windows PROFILES\<username> subdirectory.

- *Lack of robustness.* ERU tends to hang if it cannot find any of the files that it is expecting to back up. When this happens, it generally does not produce an error message indicating the cause of the problem.

---

[*] This is also a good example of poor interface design. The dialog shown in Figure 3-2 puts the burden on the user to make sure that all the relevant files are included; but many users don't even have a clue as to what the relevant files might be. At a minimum, a series of check boxes that allow the user to see at a glance what files are and are not included in the backup would have been a vast improvement.

Given these problems, if you feel uncomfortable about the integrity of backups created with either Configuration Backup or Emergency Recovery Utility, you may want to simply use .REG files as your major means of backing up the registry. You could also write a simple batch file to back up all of the necessary system files to a drive or directory of your choice. Another option, of course, is to buy a commercial utility that backs up the registry, but while several products were reputed to be in development at the time of this writing, none, so far as we know, has yet made it to market.

.REG Files Containing the Entire Registry

As you may recall from Chapter 2, *Using the Registry Editor*, RegEdit can generate .REG files, which are specially formatted ASCII files that contain the contents of the disk-based portions of the registry. RegEdit in turn is capable of reading these files and importing their contents either from a Windows session or from a Win95 real mode ("DOS") session. If you select the Export Registry File option from the Registry menu, RegEdit opens the Export Registry File dialog shown in Figure 3-3. If you select the All option button in the Export Range group box, RegEdit will generate a .REG file containing the entire registry. You should take full advantage of Win95's support for long filenames to assign the backup a name that immediately indicates to you the state of the registry when the backup was made.

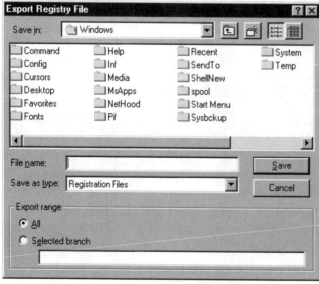

Figure 3-3. RegEdit's Export Registry File dialog

When you generate a .REG file containing the entire registry, it's a good idea to compress it and save it on a floppy disk, as well as to leave a compressed version of the original copy on your hard disk.

Where's the Rest of My Registry?

If you examine a .REG file supposedly containing the entire registry, you'll notice that RegEdit "forgot" to include most of the registry. Of the six keys, the file includes the contents of only two: HKEY_LOCAL_MACHINE and HKEY_ USERS. As noted in "The Basic Structure of the Windows 95 Registry" in Chapter 1, *The Registry, or, What Was So Bad About .INI Files?*, three of the other keys (HKEY_CLASSES_ROOT, HKEY_CURRENT_USER, and HKEY_ CURRENT_CONFIG) are really just pointers to locations within these two keys, which means that their contents are duplicated within these two keys.

The sixth key, HKEY_DYN_DATA, is memory resident; its contents are produced dynamically by virtual device drivers (VxDs). Since these data are, at least in theory, completely variable from session to session (or even from minute to minute), it would be meaningless to import them into the registry. If for some reason you're interested in looking at a .REG file of your system's HKEY_DYN_DATA (in addition to the performance-monitoring data mentioned in Chapter 1, it also contains Plug and Play [PnP] hardware information maintained by the Win95 Configuration Manager), you must explicitly ask RegEdit to export that selected "branch" of the registry. The resulting file will generally be several times larger than a .REG file supposedly containing "all" of the registry. However, most of the HKEY_DYN_DATA will almost always be runs of zeroes. You're better off looking at HKEY_DYN_DATA with tools such as PVIEW for the performance-monitoring data, and Control Panel | System for the PnP hardware information.

A .REG file that backs up the entire registry also overcomes one major limitation of Microsoft Configuration Backup: on systems configured to support multiple users, it contains user information. More precisely, it includes registry information from those user components that were included in the registry at the time the .REG file was generated. This means that it does *not* contain all user information, but only information on settings for the current user (presumably yourself) and the default user; information about other user preferences is excluded. As long as you've adequately backed up the non-user portions of the registry, your changes should not affect them.

We've been discussing safeguarding your system against a corrupted or damaged registry, but, very frequently, what appear to be registry problems are actually problems that arise from erroneous entries in either *WIN.INI* or *SYSTEM.INI.* Although the documentation for Win95 indicates that it does not "need" these files, it in fact relies on them for several critical settings, like the program that is to serve as the Windows shell, the name of the system screen saver, and, in a perverse way, the default printer (as you'll see in "System Printers and the Default Printer" in Chapter 8, *What Goes in the Registry: System Settings*). In addition, *SYSTEM.INI* continues to load some device drivers. So along with your stable backup of the complete registry, it's a good idea to include a stable copy of *WIN.INI* and *SYSTEM.INI* as well.

SYSTEM.INI and the Windows Shell

Despite the emphasis on the registry, *SYSTEM.INI* continues to be a central Windows component; at least, if Windows is unable to locate *SYSTEM.INI*, it refuses to load, and informs you that Windows needs to be reinstalled. The most critical setting stored in *SYSTEM.INI* is the name of the Windows shell, which is defined by the `shell=` keyword in the [boot] section. The program used as the Windows shell determines exactly how the basic Windows interface appears. By default, the Windows Explorer (*EXPLORER.EXE*) is the Windows shell; so if there is no `shell=` keyword, Windows can load successfully by using the Explorer as its shell. If `shell=` designates a file that doesn't exist, though, Windows again refuses to load and displays a message that Windows must be reinstalled.

Making Partial Backups

Once you've created backups of the registry that you can use to restore the registry in the event of a system-wide failure, you can focus on creating partial backups of those portions of the registry that your application will modify.

Typically, the settings that your application changes are fairly localized: most of your application's registry activity, assuming that you follow Microsoft's interface guidelines, should focus on HKCU\Software\<*YourCompany*>\<*YourApplication*> and HKLM\Software\<*YourCompany*>\<*YourApplication*>. (For details on Microsoft's interface guidelines, see Chapter 9, *What Goes in the Registry: Application and User Settings.*) Your installation program, although it will write to a more diverse array of keys, will similarly focus most of its activity on one or two major keys. This, coincidentally, makes it very easy to back up those portions of the registry that your application writes to extensively.

Before you actually begin testing code that modifies an existing portion of the registry, use RegEdit to generate one or more .REG files that contain the highest-level parent key of the keys to which your application will write. For instance, if you've written a 32-bit replacement for the now-defunct Microsoft Windows Write and are working on its installation program, your program should probably modify the following keys, among others:[*]

- `HKCR\wrifile\CLSID`
- `HKCR\wrifile\DefaultIcon`
- `HKCR\wrifile\shell\new\command`
- `HKCR\wrifile\shell\open\command`
- `HKCR\wrifile\shell\print\command`
- `HKCR\wrifile\shell\printto\command`
- `HKCR\CLSID\<CLSID of OLE server>`
- `HKCR\CLSID\<CLSID>\InProcServer32`

So you'd want to make two partial backups: one of `HKCR\wrifile`, the other of `HKCR\CLSID`. To do this, you select the Selected Branch option button in the Export Registry File dialog's Export Range group box, and indicate what portion of the registry you'd like to back up. You can do this either by typing its complete path in the text box or by highlighting it in RegEdit's tree view pane before you open the dialog.

Frequently, the registry modifications that your application makes are to your application's own subkeys. For instance, an application named MyApp that you've developed for MyCompany writes extensively to `HKCR\Software\MyCompany\MyApp` and `HKLM\Software\MyCompany\MyApp` and their subkeys. In this case, if the project is a relatively small one that involves only yourself or a small development team, you may choose not to back up `MyApp` and its subkeys. If you experience a problem with these registry keys, the best thing to do is simply delete them using RegEdit; when you rerun your application, it should be able to recreate them. (If it doesn't do this, in most cases you need to rethink the way that your application uses the registry.) By restoring good keys and values from a backup after your application has thoroughly trashed them, you run the risk of hiding bugs, thereby making the debugging process much more difficult.

Ordinarily, these partial backup files are comparatively small, and your interest in them is fairly short-lived: you want to keep a good copy when you're testing and debugging particular portions of code. When you're certain that that code works,

---

[*] By the way, if you're wondering where these key names come from, these are the registry entries you would make if your Write clone handles a particular kind of file or files and therefore registers its application identifier, *wrifile*. (For details, see "Registering a File Association" in Chapter 8.) It also assumes that your Write clone supports OLE and is capable of being an OLE server.

you'll want to generate a new partial backup. Generally, it's not even worth the investment of time to compress them. It is a good idea, though, to delete older copies fairly quickly. If you use the registry at all intensively in your applications (and you should), they quickly proliferate. Even with long filenames, it becomes difficult to remember what a particular partial .REG file contains and what state the registry was in when it was made.

With this system of backing up the registry in place, you can be more or less confident that, should you run into problems, you can handle them with minimal disruption to your system.

Restoring the Registry

If you have complete and partial backups of your registry, you have a wide range of options for correcting registry problems, depending on the exact severity of the problem and how quickly you think you detected it. In this section, we'll outline a series of steps that you can use in attempting to restore your registry to a stable state.

Restoring from a Partial Backup

Ordinarily, if the modifications that you've made to the registry during testing and debugging are the culprit, you know this almost immediately. You can then restore from your most recent partial backup by clicking on its filename in the Explorer window or by selecting the Import Registry File option from RegEdit's Registry menu. In either case, RegEdit will import the contents of the .REG file.

Testing and "Rolling Back" Registry Changes

You can also generate a .REG file containing the registry keys with which you're working and place either the file itself or a link to the file on your desktop. Then you just have to double-click to "roll back" the registry to its original state. If you use this method, though, remember that a .REG file can add new keys and values and replace existing ones, but cannot *delete* keys and values already present in the registry.

When you do this, though, you're not precisely restoring from a "backup" copy in the strict sense. RegEdit does not identify the highest-level key contained in the backup and replace all of its subkeys and value entries with those contained in your .REG file. Instead, as Chapter 2 explained, RegEdit adds new keys and values contained in the .REG file to the registry, and replaces existing keys and values that are common to both the registry and the .REG file. It does not delete keys and value entries in the registry that are not found in the .REG file. This leaves open the possibility that importing the .REG file won't repair your registry problem, since it stems from a key that you've added during testing.

To guard against this possibility, you should use RegEdit to delete the lowest-level subkey possible before importing the .REG file. To use the example of the Windows Write clone again, if your modifications have corrupted one or more subkeys of HKCR\wrifile\shell, you should delete the shell subkey rather than the wrifile subkey. (You can't, of course, delete any of the top-level keys, such as HKEY_CLASSES_ROOT.)

All of this assumes that your modifications somehow haven't thoroughly hosed the subkeys of HKCR. If they have, Win95 won't know what to do when you double-click on a .REG file (that's defined by the .reg subkey) or when you double-click on an .EXE file or on a link to *REGEDIT.EXE* (that's defined by the .exe subkey); instead, it presents you with the Open With dialog, which allows you to choose the application used to open either the .REG file or RegEdit itself. Although RegEdit appears in the dialog's list box, selecting it merely causes Win95 to redisplay the Open With dialog. Instead, to run RegEdit, you'll have to launch it from a DOS window. You can then repair the registry by importing your partial backup.

Restoring a portion of the registry from a partial backup is by far the easiest way to solve a registry problem. Sometimes, though, you don't have a backup of the affected portions of the registry or importing the .REG file doesn't help to solve the problem. In this case, there are still several things that you can do to restore your registry.

Letting Windows Do the Work: The Registry Problem Dialog

Occasionally, even though your registry is damaged or corrupted, you may not have to take any measures to restore it. Instead, Windows will detect the problem and attempt to restore the registry automatically. Typically, this happens at start up when Windows is either unable to find one or both of the files that compose the registry or is unable to read from them, although occasionally it happens in the middle of a session when Windows attempts to access the registry and its registry API call returns a read or write error. In that case, Windows greets you with the Registry Problem dialog shown in Figure 3-4, which asks whether you want to restore the registry from a system backup copy and restart the system. Actually, the dialog really leaves you with no choice: you either have to click on the Restore button or turn off your computer—something the dialog explicitly

Why Does RegEdit Exhibit Dual Behavior?

Possibly you're wondering why damage to HKCR should prevent RegEdit from running, or perhaps you've been struck by RegEdit's dual behavior: if you double-click on the RegEdit icon, you launch RegEdit as a registry browser and editor, but if you double-click on a .REG file, you run RegEdit as a background process (with no user interface) that imports the .REG file you've selected into the registry.

The explanation is found in the file associations defined in the registry's HKEY_CLASSES_ROOT key.

When you double-click on *REGEDIT.EXE*, or on any .EXE file, the Windows shell looks in the registry to see how it should handle a file whose extension is .EXE by retrieving the default value of HKCR\.exe. Its value, which is exefile, is an application identifier; it tells the shell where to look for information about the application that can handle double-clicks on .EXE files. So the Windows shell next retrieves the default value of HKCR\exefile\shell\open\command, which provides it with the command line that it passes to the *ShellExecute* function. This value, "%1" %*, indicates that the command line is to consist of the name of the file on which the user clicked—in this case, *REGEDIT.EXE*—followed by any command-line options.

When you double-click on a .REG file, on the other hand, the Windows shell finds that .REG files are handled by the regfile application identifier key. It then retrieves the value of HKCR\regfile\shell\open\command, which is *regedit.exe %1*. This indicates that *ShellExecute* should call *REGEDIT.EXE* and pass it the name of the .REG file on which the user clicked. As you may recall from the discussion of RegEdit in real mode, this is the syntax required by RegEdit to import a registration file.

In other words, RegEdit exhibits this dual behavior because of registry settings.

warns against. When you select the Restore button, Windows attempts to restore your registry and, if it succeeds, asks whether you want to restart your computer.

This is able to work because, at the start of each Windows session, Windows makes a backup copy of *SYSTEM.DAT*, the system-wide *USER.DAT*, and, on a machine configured to support multiple users, the current user's *USER.DAT* file, and names the system file *SYSTEM.DA0* and the user files *USER.DA0*. Like *SYSTEM.DAT* and *USER.DAT*, these are hidden, read-only system files.

If Windows is able to find the system backup files *SYSTEM.DA0* and *USER.DA0*, when you click the Restore button it simply copies them and names them *SYSTEM.DAT* and *USER.DAT*. Since this is the registry from the beginning of your

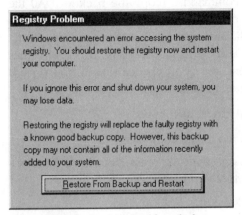

Figure 3-4. The Registry Problem dialog

last session, any changes that you made in the course of your previous session are lost. If you have a backup from sometime during your previous session, you can try using it to restore the registry so that you'll lose as little information as possible.

If it is unable to restore the registry, Windows informs you that registry services are unavailable and starts in Safe Mode. Windows then displays another message that allows you to restore the registry, although the message is meaningless; since the first attempt to restore the registry failed either because the backup files did not exist or they were unreadable, the second attempt must necessarily fail as well. And without registry access in Safe Mode, there's very little that you can do with your computer. At this point, it's best to begin trying to restore the registry using the techniques discussion from the section "Restoring the Registry Using Your Backups" onward.

Using Windows' Own Backups

You may suspect that you're experiencing problems with the registry even though Windows hasn't displayed a Registry Problem dialog like the one shown in Figure 3-4. If you suspect that these problems were introduced in the course of your current Windows session, you may be able to use Windows' own backup copies of the registry files to fix the problem. If these backup copies are good, you can use them to restore the registry to its state at the beginning of your Windows session. Of the system-wide restore procedures, this is the preferable method, since in most cases (depending on when you made your last complete backup of the registry) it involves the least loss of configuration information: you lose only the changes that were made to the registry during your session.

Although you can simply use the *COPY* command to copy the backup .DA0 file to the registry's .DAT file, in the process overwriting the original .DAT file, this is a bad idea. Both Windows and any application that you are using are constantly reading from and writing to the registry, and changes to registry keys and values are not immediately flushed to disk. There is a good chance that, if you do use this method to copy the backup registry file, it will also become corrupted.

A better method involves using Win95 real mode, as follows:

1. Terminate your Windows session and restart the computer.

2. When the "Starting Windows 95" message appears, press F8 to have Windows display the Microsoft Windows 95 Startup Menu.

3. Select option 7 to begin a safe mode real mode session.

4. Change to the Windows directory and use the ATTRIB command to make the .DAT and .DA0 files visible:

```
ATTRIB -r -h -s SYSTEM.DA?
ATTRIB -r -h -s USER.DA?
```

5. Use the *COPY* command to replace the two registry .DAT files with the backup .DA0 files.

6. Restart your computer to begin your Windows session.

Although this method sometimes works in restoring registry problems, its success rate is fairly low. It's usually most appropriate in cases of serious registry corruption; but, as we saw in the previous section, "Letting Windows Do the Work: The Registry Problem Dialog," Windows itself is capable of detecting this at start up and during a session if it detects a damaged registry.

In most cases, though, the registry isn't completely corrupted and unusable; only individual parts of it are. And unless Windows or an application tries to read those corrupted portions of the registry, there may be absolutely no indication that there is a problem. As a result, once a portion of the registry becomes corrupted, it may be days or even weeks before you notice. In the meantime, the backup registry file will also become partially corrupted, and your attempt to repair the registry by restoring the backup file will fail.

Restoring the Registry Using Your Backups

If your attempt to repair the registry by restoring the .DA0 files fails, or if you decide that there's no real point in attempting to use the .DA0 files, the next best thing to do is to restore the registry using your most recent .RBK file. Microsoft Configuration Backup makes this very easy and convenient: you simply select the particular registry backup that you'd like to restore from a list of your previous backups and click the Restore button. Configuration Backup responds with a

---

What if You Can't Press F8 in Time?

To get Win95 to display the Startup Menu, you have to press F8 before the "Starting Windows" message disappears, but sometimes the message disappears before you have a chance to do that. You can do several things to make sure that your normal Windows session doesn't start:

- Insert a PAUSE statement as the last line of your *AUTOEXEC.BAT* file. (If you don't have an *AUTOEXEC.BAT* file, create one that contains only the PAUSE statement.) When your system boots, you should press F8 twice, once in response to the "Press any key" prompt and once to display the Startup Menu. Or you can just hit ^C to break out of *AUTOEXEC.BAT* and leave yourself at a real-mode C:\> prompt.

- If there is an entry in the [options] section of *MSDOS.SYS* that reads BootKeys=0 (which disables the use of the function keys), change its value to 1. Otherwise, increase the value of the BootDelay keyword in the [options] section to increase the time that the "Starting Windows" message is displayed. If there is no BootDelay key, add one, and give it a value of 3 or greater (the default value is 2).

- Create an entry in the [options] section of *MSDOS.SYS* that reads BootMenu=1. Instead of loading the Win95 graphical user interface, your system will automatically display the Startup Menu.

---

completely misleading warning message ("You are about to backup over a previous backup. Do you want to proceed?"), which you can safely ignore by clicking the OK button. Microsoft Configuration Backup then replaces the current contents of the registry with the backup copy you select and asks you to reboot the computer so that your changes can take effect.

Before you do this, though, it's best to make a backup of the current registry, even though you suspect that something is seriously wrong with it. If restoring the registry from backups doesn't fix the problem, you can restore this latest version of the registry, then see if RegEdit can repair the damage, a technique discussed in the following section, "Using RegEdit to Repair the Registry."

If you restore from an .RBK backup, all registry changes that occurred since the backup are lost. In most cases, this means that you'll need to reinstall any 32-bit applications that you've installed since the backup. In addition, if your system is configured to support multiple users, no user information will be restored from the backup; Configuration Backup leaves the user branches of the registry exactly as they were before the restore.

However, if you've used RegEdit to create a .REG file that backs up the entire registry at the same time that you backed up the registry using Microsoft Configuration Backup, you can edit it so that it contains only the user branches of the registry. (Remember, a .REG file can represent as much as the entire non-dynamic registry, or as little as a single key.) You can then use it to restore user settings. To do this, do the following:

1. Make a copy of the .REG file that you'll use to restore user settings. Since you'll be modifying a .REG file, this allows you to preserve your original backup.

2. Use your text editor to open the .REG file that you'll use to restore the registry's user settings. Then delete everything from the third line (which should read "[HKEY_LOCAL_MACHINE]") to the last line that refers to the HKEY_LOCAL_MACHINE key before saving the file. The beginning portion of your .REG file should then resemble the one shown in Figure 3-5, and the file itself should contain information only about the HKEY_USERS registry tree.

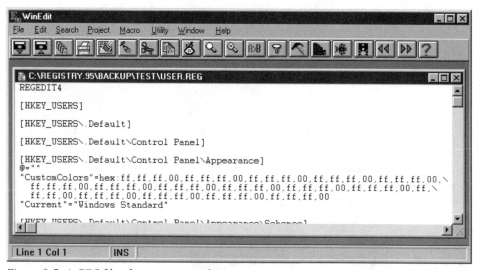

Figure 3-5. A .REG file after removing references to HKEY_LOCAL_MACHINE

3. Using RegEdit, delete each subkey of HKEY_USERS\.Default and of HKEY_USERS\<your username> in the current registry.

4. Import the modified .REG file by selecting the Export Registry File option from RegEdit's Registry menu, or double-click on the .REG file in an Explorer window.

If you find that *this* version of the registry is also wholly or partially corrupted, you can a begin to restore the registry from progressively older .RBK files. The basic problem in doing this is that the older the file, the more configuration information is lost. If you continue to experience problems with the restored registries, at some point you may decide to either abandon the process of restoring the registry from .RBK files or to interrupt it to see if RegEdit can repair the most recent version of the registry.

Using RegEdit to Repair the Registry

Sometimes, you can use RegEdit to "repair" a damaged registry. RegEdit can do this because, when you use RegEdit to generate a .REG file, it includes entries only for valid, undamaged keys and values. This means that the damaged portions of the registry are not included in the .REG file. If you then replace the existing registry with the contents of the .REG file, the new version of the registry should not contain the damaged keys or value entries. As long as the missing information is not critical to the system's operation, this technique can succeed in repairing the registry.

To generate the .REG file, you should begin by restoring the most recent version of the registry, if the current version of the registry is one of the restored registries. Then you use the Export Registry File option on RegEdit's Registry menu to create the .REG file. Once you've created the .REG file, you can replace the current registry with it, as described in the next section, "Restoring the Registry from a Backup in Real Mode."

If the damage to the registry is so extensive that Win95 refuses to load, you can still try to generate the .REG file by running RegEdit in real mode. To do this, either press F5 to restart the computer in real mode or press F8 to display the Microsoft Win95 Startup Menu, then select option 7 to start a safe mode real mode session. You can then launch RegEdit and provide it with the parameters that it needs to generate the .REG file:

```
REGEDIT /L:<path to SYSTEM.DAT> /e <path to .REG file>
```

For instance, if your Windows directory is `C:\WINDOWS` and your .REG file is named `CURRENT.REG` and is located in a directory called `REG FILES`, the complete command line to run the real mode version of RegEdit and create the .REG file in a directory called `C:\REG FILES` is:

```
REGEDIT /L:C:\Windows\System.DAT /e "c:\reg files\current.reg"
```

RegEdit generates a .REG file that serves as a complete backup copy of the entire registry. The next section describes how to use it to restore the registry.

Restoring the Registry from a Backup in Real Mode

Whether you've just exported the current version of your registry and are now hoping to import it again or you're hoping to restore an older version of the registry that's stored in a .REG file, the method that you use to attempt to repair the registry is the same.

A basic problem with using RegEdit is that, when it reads a .REG file, it imports registry keys and values, but does not delete unique keys or values contained in the current version of the registry. As a result, a certain proportion of what's currently in the registry is likely to remain there; if this is the portion of the registry that's causing problems, then restoring the registry from a .REG file is unlikely to resolve them. You can, of course, delete registry subkeys before importing a .REG file, but this is a very labor-intensive process.

In other cases, you may be unable to load the Windows version of RegEdit at all. As a Windows application, of course, RegEdit's user interface requires that your computer be running Win95 before it can load. But sometimes your system's configuration information is so badly damaged and confused that Windows is unable to start.

When Windows Won't Start

If Windows won't load, read the next section, "Where Did My Registry Go?", before using the real mode component of RegEdit to restore the registry from a .REG file. Windows is sometimes unable to find the registry when the *MS-DOS.SYS* file is missing or damaged; the source of the problem is not the registry at all.

The solution to both of these problems is to run RegEdit in real mode. On the one hand, RegEdit in real mode is accessible even if the Windows Registry Editor is not. On the other hand, RegEdit in real mode allows you to restore, rather than to import, the registry from a .REG file; this is to say that the existing version of the registry is deleted, and the contents of the .REG file substituted for it. This avoids the problems that result from merging the registry with a .REG file.

Depending on the capabilities of the your system and how severely damaged it is, there are several ways that you can access RegEdit:

* In real mode, by restarting your computer and pressing F5.

* In safe mode real mode, by restarting your computer and pressing F8. When the Microsoft Windows 95 Startup Menu appears, select option 7.

* By starting your system using the Emergency Startup Disk that you created during Win95 installation. A copy of *REGEDIT.EXE* is included on the startup disk.

Once you're sitting at the real mode command prompt (such as C:\>), you can run RegEdit and restore the registry from a .REG file by entering the following:

```
REGEDIT /L:<path to SYSTEM.DAT> /R:<path to USER.DAT> /C <.REG filename>
```

The /C switch instructs RegEdit to restore the .REG file, rather than merge it with the existing contents of the registry. In order for this to be effective, the .REG file must contain a backup of the complete registry.

For the most part, you'll want to try this method of restoring the registry using RegEdit in real mode just once, so it's best to select what you think is the most reliable full backup of the registry or to plan on working with the .REG file that you've just generated. The major reason for this is that the operation of RegEdit in real mode when it is deleting and importing keys is extremely slow; the procedure on a relatively slow (486/66) machine can take almost 24 hours. You're probably better off reinstalling Win95.

There is one serious problem that you may encounter in using RegEdit in real mode. Since RegEdit is running in real mode, only 640K of memory is available to it. If more than 640K is required to maintain a registry tree in memory, the program will report either that it cannot open the registry or that there is an error in accessing the registry. If this happens and your computer is still capable of running Windows, it's best to try to run RegEdit in Windows mode, delete the necessary keys, and import the .REG file. Otherwise, you can try the last technique to restore a damaged registry, which involves using the *SYSTEM.DAT* file that the Win95 setup program generated when Win95 was first installed on the system. This is discussed in a later section, "Restoring Your System's Original Registry."

Where Did My Registry Go?

Sometimes, what appears to be a very serious registry problem that prevents Windows from starting is actually completely unrelated to the registry. Instead, it's caused by a missing or damaged real-mode initialization file, *MSDOS.SYS,* whose absence can prevent Win95 from knowing where to look for the registry and other critical system files. This is a serious possibility if, instead of loading, Windows displays the error messages, "Registry File Was Not Found" or "Invalid Vxd dynamic link call from IFSMGR (03)."

Figure 3-6 shows a more or less typical *MSDOS.SYS* file, which in Win95 is a more or less standard ASCII initialization file that contains section names, keywords, and values (*MSDOS.SYS* used to be the file containing the MS-DOS operating system; in the MS-DOS 7.0 component of Win95, that has been merged into *IO.SYS*). It is stored as a hidden, read-only system file in the root directory of the system's boot drive. As you can see in Figure 3-6, the end of the file is padded with meaningless text to pad its size to over 1K; this is necessary because some Windows 3.x applications, like virus checking programs, expect any file named *MSDOS.SYS* to be over 1K in size. Each of these meaningless lines begins with a semicolon, which is used to indicate comment lines in initialization files.

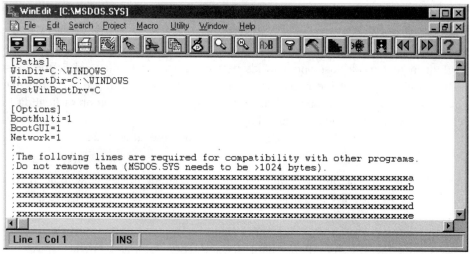

Figure 3-6. A typical MSDOS.SYS file

If *MSDOS.SYS* is missing, it can be restored by copying it from the Win95 Emergency Startup Disk, which you should have created during setup. If it is damaged, the following entries in the [Paths] section are used to find Win95 system files and to locate the registry:

HostWinBootDrv
> The name of the system's boot drive (e.g., C)

WinBootDir
> The directory containing the files necessary to boot windows (e.g., C:\WINDOWS)

WinDir
> The location of Win95's main directory (e.g., C:\WINDOWS)

If any of these values are missing, Windows will refuse to load, and, because it can't identify the location of its system files, will frequently complain that it is unable to find the registry. You can use a real mode text edit, like *EDIT.COM*, the ASCII editor that is included with Win95, to add the necessary keywords and assign them the appropriate values.

Restoring Your System's Original Registry

If you're still experiencing difficulties with the Win95 registry after trying to restore it using the techniques discussed above, there's one final thing you can do before you actually have to reinstall Windows: you can restore the original registry that Win95 created during installation.

When Win95 is first installed on a computer, it builds *SYSTEM.DAT* in the root directory of the system's boot drive. It later copies this file to the Windows directory and renames the original file stored in the root directory *SYSTEM.1ST*. Like *SYSTEM.DAT*, *SYSTEM.1ST* is a hidden, read-only system file.

To do this, using either the Emergency Startup Disk or the safe mode real mode, change the attributes of both *SYSTEM.DAT* and *SYSTEM.1ST* so that they are no longer hidden, read-only system files. Then use the COPY command to overwrite *SYSTEM.DAT* with *SYSTEM.1ST*. You can then try to launch Windows.

In many ways, restoring the registry is very much like reinstalling Win95, except that it saves you the time and effort required by the installation itself. When you restore the registry using *SYSTEM.1ST*, you lose every item of information about software, hardware, and user preferences added after Windows was installed on the system. In most cases, to get them to function at all, you'll have to reinstall all of your 32-bit applications. In addition, if you've added any new hardware since Windows was installed, you should probably have Windows scan for it.

Restoring *SYSTEM.1ST* is the last-ditch measure to try before reinstalling Windows (or before concluding that what seems to be a registry problem is really a hardware problem).

Summary

In this chapter, we've tried to develop a sensible strategy for backing up the registry to minimize data loss if and when the registry becomes corrupted. We've also reviewed what may seem like a bewildering array of graduated steps that you might try if you want to restore a wholly or partially damaged registry. To summarize, to increase the chance that you can successfully deal with a damaged registry without having to reinstall Windows, you should make periodic backups as follows:

- After you've installed Windows and your system is stable, as well as before you install any major new software program, you should back up your registry completely.

- In between complete backups, you can make partial backups of keys that you work with or change particularly often.

- Although you can use several utilities (like the Configuration Backup Utility and the Emergency Recovery Utility) to back up the registry, generating .REG files remains the most flexible and reliable method; in addition, .REG files provide the only reliable means of restoring a registry that is so severely damaged that Windows is unable to load.

With a backup strategy in place, you have more options for dealing with registry problems if and when they occur:

- You can repair limited damage to a portion of the registry with which you've been working by restoring from a partial backup.

- If the damage is more extensive, and if Windows doesn't try to fix the problem automatically, you should first see if Windows' own backup files, *SYS-TEM.DA0* and *USER.DA0*, can be used to replace the registry files.

- If Windows' backup files are unable to repair the registry, you can restore the registry using your own backups.

- In cases of extreme damage, you can use RegEdit in real mode to completely replace your current registry with the contents of a .REG file backup.

- If you don't have backups or they're too old, you can try generating a .REG file from the damaged registry and then replacing the registry with the contents of the .REG file.

- If nothing else works, you can restore the original registry that was created when Win95 was first installed on your computer.

4

The Win32 Registry API

The Windows 95 registry, as we've already noted, can be accessed only by a selected set of functions in the Win32 API that we might collectively term the *registry API*. Or it requires a utility such as RegEdit that, in turn, relies upon this registry API. But despite the clear value of the registry as a centralized database of configuration information, programmers frequently avoid using it. For example, developers targeting both the Windows 3.x (Win3x) and Win95 platforms often don't want to do the additional coding needed to store application information in initialization files on the first platform and in the registry on the other.

This chapter aims at making the registry API accessible by thoroughly examining and documenting its functions. It does this by offering a step-by-step approach to accessing the registry and by examining the suitability of particular registry functions for particular tasks.

Much of this material is targeted at the C programmer; as a result, almost all coding examples use C. But the bulk of this chapter is also of interest to a broader audience of developers; although the examples happen to be in C, the basic syntax and operation of the registry API remain the same independent of the programming language used. Since this chapter aims at offering complete documentation for the registry API and at covering some of the general programming issues that arise when using the registry functions, like developing for multiple platforms, we've tried to make it accessible to any programmer who might be able to take advantage of the registry API, regardless of their programming language.

The Win32 Registry API?

The Win32 API is also considerably broader that the 32-bit API for Windows 95. Win32 also targets the Windows NT and (via Win32s) the Windows 3.1 environments. In focusing on "the Win32 registry API," we primarily mean the Windows 95 version of the Win32 registry API, which is, of course, the focus of this book. We also try to pay enough attention to the 32-bit registry API for Windows NT to allow you to avoid some obvious traps and pitfalls if you want to develop an application that runs under both Windows 95 and Windows NT. But in any case, our assumption is that you're focusing your development efforts on 32-bit applications for Windows 95 and secondarily for Windows NT. For the most part, we ignore Win32s, except for showing you how to check for its presence on 32-bit platforms in Appendix A, *Where Am I Running?*

Actually, our reference to the Win32 registry API is, literally speaking, not quite correct on an additional count. In the next chapter, we'll see how to access the Win95 registry from Win16, from DOS programs running under Win95, and from VxDs. In fact, we'll see that the "true" Windows 95 registry API isn't in Win32; it's in the Win95 Virtual Machine Manager (VMM), and Win32 is just one of several available "wrappers" for this API provided by VMM. In focusing on the Windows 95 registry, we also try to show you how to access the registry API regardless of the platform that you're developing for, so long as Windows 95 can run applications developed for that platform, and so long as the application itself is running under Win95. So in that sense, this chapter really covers the Win95 API, which is not completely synonymous with the Win32 API.

Finally, we'll refer periodically to the Win31 registry API, which is the 16-bit registry API as it's implemented on Windows 3.1 to allow access to the registration database. This set of registry functions are not quite synonymous with the Win16 registry API, since, as we'll see in the next chapter, the latter can be extended under Win95 to support the Win95 registry.

In Windows 3.1 (Win31), all registration database functions resided in *SHELL.DLL*, one of the supplemental Windows libraries; in the Win31 SDK, functions for working with the registration database were defined by the *SHELLAPI.H* header file. In the Win32 API, on the other hand, all registry functions have been moved to *ADVAPI32.DLL*, a supplemental library that, in Win95, also includes a variety of "dummy" security and audit control functions that are supported by WinNT but not by Win95; and in the Win32 SDK, registry-related constants and functions are defined by the *WINREG.H* header file.

For anyone familiar with Windows (or even DOS) programming, using the registry functions follows a very simple and familiar model based on file I/O: you open a registry key, you perform the needed operations either to the key or to its subkeys, and, when you're finished, you close the key. For example:

```
if (RegOpenKey(HKEY_CURRENT_USER, "Control Panel\\Colors", &hKey)
    == ERROR_SUCCESS)
{
    // … Perform some operation using hKey …

    RegCloseKey(hKey) ;
}
```

The point of opening a key is that you get back an item of data called an HKEY—the handle to a registry key. You then use that handle to indicate the key on which you want an operation performed, and you use it again to close the key. But notice that, in order to get back an HKEY, you need to provide an HKEY. This seems like a chicken-and-egg kind of problem. Fortunately, it's not, because the top-level keys (like **HKEY_CURRENT_USER**, the one used in our example) are predefined.

ANSI and Unicode

Like the Win32 API as a whole, the Registry API actually has two functions for each documented function that requires a string parameter. *RegEnumKey*, for instance, does not actually exist in *ADVAPI32.DLL*. Instead, each call to *RegEnumKey* is translated into a call to either *RegEnumKeyA* or *RegEnumKeyW*. The first is the ANSI version of the function, which is capable of handling single-byte, null-terminated strings. The second is the unicode (wide character set) version, in which a single character occupies two bytes. Windows NT supports both ANSI and unicode strings, and strings in the WinNT registry itself are stored as unicode strings. Win95, on the other hand, does not support unicode.

We'll examine each of these steps involved in accessing the registry (and provide considerably greater content to that vague phrase "needed operations") in the following sections.

Opening a Registry Key

Windows programmers rarely work with objects directly, but instead work with a variety of *handles*, or integers that serve as identifiers of objects. For example, when a program creates an instance of a window, Windows assigns that new window a window handle; subsequent operations that affect that window generally must make use of this window handle (or HWND), rather than the window's name or some other attribute that might identify it. Before painting a window, a program must first obtain a handle to a device context; this handle (or HDC) is then used for subsequent paint operations. Similarly, to perform file operations, a program can first open a file by obtaining a file handle (HFILE); by using the file handle, the application can then read from or write to the file. In each of these three cases, once all operations affecting the window, the device context, or the file have completed, the object should be closed, again by using its handle.

Accessing the registry works in much the same way. Before you can examine the subkeys of a particular registry key or retrieve its values, you must first open that key; then, when you're finished performing the necessary operations, you close it. When you open the key, Windows provides a handle to the registry key (HKEY) that is used instead of the key's name in all subsequent operations affecting the key. This handle is an unsigned long (4-byte) integer.

In Win95, it just so happens that this long integer is usually a pointer to an in-memory internal data structure called a RGKN: in other words, `typedef struct RGKN *HKEY`. Yes, applications are usually handed "live" read/write pointers into the registry. ("Usually," because the top-level HKEYs such as `HKEY_LOCAL_MACHINE` are numeric identifiers rather than pointers, and because HKEYs to remote machines are obfuscated pointers to memory on the remote machine.) In Win95, any application has total control over the registry and its integrity. But while this tells you that Win95 is not a secure operating system, and that damage to the registry by errant programs is more of a possibility than one would like, you should not rely on this unfortunate implementation detail. It presumably does not work that way on WinNT, and hopefully will not work that way in future releases of Win95. You should use an HKEY as a "magic cookie," that is, as a handle whose numeric value is unimportant.

The Win32 API provides five functions that can open a registry key. In brief, they are:

- *RegOpenKey*, a "compatibility" function (i.e., one that also exists in the Win16 API) that opens an existing registry key

- *RegOpenKeyEx*, the new Win32 function that opens an existing registry file

- *RegCreateKey*, a "compatibility" function that opens an existing key or creates a new key if that key cannot be found

- *RegCreateKeyEx*, the new Win32 function that opens an existing key or creates a new key if that key cannot be found

- *RegConnectRegistry*, which opens a top-level key on a remote system

Before examining the syntax and usage of these functions, it is worthwhile to survey some of the common features of this set of registry functions. In each case, the function returns an error code indicating whether or not it has executed successfully. Some of the possible values are shown in Table 4-1. Also see Table 4-5 for status codes returned by the registry operation functions.

Table 4-1. Status codes returned by the open registry key functions

Constant	Value	Explanation
ERROR_SUCCESS	0	The registry key was opened or created.
ERROR_FILE_NOT_FOUND	2	The registry key does not exist or is read-only.
ERROR_ACCESS_DENIED	5	Security access mask insufficient to open key (WinNT only), or not authorized to access network resource (*RegConnectRegistry*), or value entry is read-only.
ERROR_INVALID_HANDLE	6	The handle for an open registry key is invalid.
ERROR_BAD_NETPATH	53	The network path is invalid (*RegConnectRegistry* only).
ERROR_BAD_PATHNAME	161	Invalid registry path.
ERROR_LOCK_FAILED	167	The registry's internal read/write locking scheme failed.
ERROR_BADKEY	1010	Key is invalid. If returned by *RegConnectRegistry*, it indicates a failure to connect to the remote computer.
ERROR_REGISTRY_CORRUPT	1015	Unable to access information in registry.
ERROR_DLL_INIT_FAILED	1114	Unable to establish RPC connection (*RegConnectRegistry* only); usually, this indicates that *WINREG.DLL*, the remote registry client library, could not be found.

Notice that none of these functions actually returns a handle to a registry key; instead, each returns an error code that indicates whether the function succeeded in opening or creating the key. A variable to hold the handle is passed to the function "by reference" (i.e., a *pointer* to the handle variable is passed as a parameter). If a function returns a value of ERROR_SUCCESS, that variable will contain the valid handle to the registry key; otherwise, its value is undefined. Again, the variable to which Windows is to store the registry key's handle must be a pointer to an HKEY (which happens to be a four-byte unsigned long); the failure to pass a pointer (or to pass this variable by reference) is *the most common error* that both C and Visual Basic programmers make when attempting to use the open registry key functions.

Finally, each of these functions requires that it be passed a valid handle of a registry key as a parameter. This may seem somewhat circular: if the purpose of opening a key is to retrieve a valid handle to the key, why is a valid handle to a key required to open a new key? The reason is that, to open a new key, its name

Variables and Pointers

At the expense of being repetitive, we should note again that the most common reason for the registry's open key functions to fail or to behave unpredictably is that the handle to the registry key is passed incorrectly. Most commonly, the programmer passes the function the handle itself rather than a *pointer* to the handle. For example:

```
HKEY hDefaultKey ;
nResult = RegOpenKey(HKEY_USERS, ".Default",
   hDefaultKey) ;   // WRONG! -- missing &
```

or

```
PHKEY phDefaultKey ;
nResult = RegOpenKey(HKEY_USERS, ".Default",
   phDefaultKey) ; // WRONG! -- doesn't point anywhere!
```

When a handle is passed to an API function, that handle is passed by value; that is, the API function is receiving a *copy* of the handle; any modifications that the function may make to the handle's value have no effect on the original value of the handle.

When a pointer to a handle is passed to an API function, that handle is passed by reference. The API function is actually receiving the address at which the handle is stored, and consequently any modifications that it makes to the value of the handle will be reflected in its value once control returns to the calling program. All registry functions that open keys expect the handle of the key to be opened to be passed to them by reference, which allows them to supply the calling program with the correct value for the handle; the data type of these handles is indicated as **PHKEY**. For example, the following code fragment successfully opens the HKEY_USERS\.Default key:

```
HKEY hDefaultKey;
nResult = RegOpenKey(HKEY_USERS, ".Default",
   &hDefaultKey) ; // CORRECT - notice &
```

Assuming that the function returns **ERROR_SUCCESS**, *hDefaultKey* contains the handle of the newly opened key.

All currently open handles are passed by value in the registry API; their data type is indicated as **HKEY** in the template for each registry function. For instance, the following code fragment passes a pointer to the *RegOpenKey* function to retrieve a registry handle, then uses that handle to retrieve a value from the registry and then to close the key:

```
if (RegOpenKey(HKEY_LOCAL_MACHINE,
            "System\CurrentControlSet\control", &hKey)
   {
   RegQueryValueEx(hKey, "Current User", NULL, &dwType,
                szBuffer, &cbszBuffer) ;
   RegCloseKey(hKey) ;
   }
```

must be expressed as a path with some starting point; that starting point is designated by the handle of an open registry key, and the termination point (the key to be opened) must be a subkey of the open key.

The way out of this "chicken and egg" problem is simple: in any series of calls to the registry open functions, one of the registry's built-in top-level keys (such as HKEY_USERS or HKEY_LOCAL_MACHINE) must serve as the initial starting point for registry access. All top-level keys are always open, and can be accessed by using predefined handles represented by the constants shown in Table 4-2.

Table 4-2. Predefined handles of the top-level registry keys

Constant	Value
HKEY_CLASSES_ROOT	0x80000000
HKEY_CURRENT_USER	0x80000001
HKEY_LOCAL_MACHINE	0x80000002
HKEY_USERS	0x80000003
HKEY_CURRENT_CONFIG	0x80000005
HKEY_DYN_DATA	0x80000006

This means that, once you've opened a particular registry key, you can always open any of its subkeys in either of two ways. For instance, if your application has opened and retrieved a valid handle of HKCR\txtfile, you can open one of its subkeys, HKCR\txtfile\shell\open\command by one of two ways:

- Supplying the handle of the top-level key, along with the complete path to the subkey you'd like to open (e.g., txtfile\shell\open\command)

- Supplying the handle of HKCR\txtfile, along with the relative path to the subkey you'd like to open (e.g., shell\open\command)

Open and Unopened Keys

Although we've implied that you must open a key before working with either its subkeys or its values, this isn't completely true. Several "compatibility" functions inherited from the Win16 API, notably *RegSetValue* and *RegQueryValue*, allow you to work with a key other than the open key. However, each of these functions has a recommended equivalent in the Win32 API that allows you to work only with objects belonging to the open key.

This support for relative paths makes it easier to navigate what can be a deeply nested registry tree without having to be concerned with the complete path from the top-level key to the key you'd like to open. Regardless of which method you use, though, note that the key name *never* begins with the path delimiter character (e.g., `shell\open\command` *not* `\shell\open\command`). The latter form causes each of the registry open key functions to fail.

The names of registry keys are *not* case sensitive. Win95 will reflect the case you've used in the function that created the registry key. But the open key functions in the registry API will successfully open a key whether or not the case of the key's name in the function matches that in the registry.[*]

Finally, remember from Chapter 1, *The Registry, or, What Was So Bad About .INI Files?*, that trailing spaces are considered part of a key's name. That means that, if you attempt to open a key whose name includes trailing spaces and you fail to match those spaces in the key name parameter to the registry open function, Windows will not be able to open the key. Conversely, if your key name argument to the registry open function has trailing spaces while the actual key name has none, your attempt to open the key will fail. This means that you should always be sure to trim key names that are based on data supplied by the user at run-time.

RegOpenKey

While each of the open key functions performs the same basic operation, and despite their commonalties, the situations in which each might be used are, for the most part, different. The simplest of these functions is *RegOpenKey*:

```
LONG RegOpenKey( hKey, lpSubKey, phkResult ) ;
```

which has the following parameters:

HKEY	*hKey*	Handle of an open key to serve as the point of origin of *lpSubKey;* it can be one of the predefined keys listed in Table 4-2, or the handle of a key opened previously using one of the registry's open key functions.
LPCTSTR	*lpSubKey*	A pointer to the string containing the path and name of the registry key to open. If *lpSubKey* is NULL or a pointer to an empty string, the function increments the key's usage counter and returns in *pkhResult* the same handle passed in to it as *hKey*.
PHKEY	*phkResult*	A pointer to an HKEY that contains the handle of the newly opened key if the function succeeds.

---

[*] This is not true, of course, of the top-level keys' names (like HKEY_USERS or HKEY_LOCAL_MACHINE). These are actually symbolic constants that represent handles to registry keys, and must always appear in upper case. Although this may seem obvious to most programmers, forgetting it is an occasional cause of error. If you want, you can create new lower-case symbolic constants, such as `#define hkey_local_machine HKEY_LOCAL_MACHINE`. You can also create abbreviations, such as `#define HKLM HKEY_LOCAL_MACHINE`.

RegOpenKey requires that the key specified by *lpSubKey* actually exist. The function merely checks for the existence of the key and, if it is able to find it, opens it, stores its handle at the address indicated by *phkResult* and returns ERROR_SUCCESS. Otherwise, if it is unable to open the key, the function returns an error code, usually ERROR_FILE_NOT_FOUND. (Yes, ERROR_ FILE_NOT_FOUND is the error code when a registry key can't be found! If you dislike having to talk about files when you mean to talk about keys, you might want to #define ERROR_KEY_NOT_FOUND ERROR_FILE_NOT_FOUND.) This makes the function useful in either of the following instances:

- To check for the existence of a key. If the function returns ERROR_SUCCESS, you know that the key exists; otherwise, you know that it does not exist, and can act accordingly.

- To open an existing key without creating a new one if the key doesn't exist.

The major strength of *RegOpenKey* is its simplicity. Example 4-1, for instance, illustrates the use of *RegOpenKey*. The program uses the *RegEnumKey* function (which is discussed later in the section "Performing Operations on the Registry") to store the name of each subkey of HKEY_LOCAL_MACHINE to the *lpName* character array. (The program is able to retrieve the names of these registry keys without having to open HKEY_LOCAL_MACHINE first because each of the registry's top-level keys is constantly open and its handle predefined.) *RegOpenKey* then uses *lpName* to open each of these subkeys. If the call to the function is successful (i.e., its return value is ERROR_SUCCESS), *hkResult* contains the handle to the open registry key; in calling *RegOpenKey*, we are actually passing a pointer to *hkResult*, which allows the function to modify its value. Before closing each open key, the program displays a dialog box containing the key's name.

Example 4-1. OPENKEY1.C, a program using RegOpenKey

```
// openkey1.c
// runs on Win95 and NT; not Win32s

#include <windows.h>

int APIENTRY WinMain(HANDLE hInstance, HANDLE hPrevInstance,
    LPSTR lpszCmdLine, int nCmdShow)
    {
    char lpName[MAX_PATH] ;
    HKEY hkResult, hKey = HKEY_LOCAL_MACHINE ;
    DWORD dwIndex = 0 ;
    LONG nResult = ERROR_SUCCESS ;

    // loop until enumeration is finished
    while (nResult == ERROR_SUCCESS)
        {
```

Example 4-1. OPENKEY1.C, a program using RegOpenKey (continued)

```
    nResult = RegEnumKey(hKey, dwIndex++, lpName, sizeof(lpName)) ;
    // if enumeration successful, open key
    if (nResult == ERROR_SUCCESS)
        {
        RegOpenKey(hKey, lpName, &hkResult) ;
        // Display key name if successful
        MessageBox( NULL, lpName, "Key Opened", MB_OK) ;
        // Close open key
        RegCloseKey(hkResult) ;
        }
    }
  return 0 ;
  }
```

Along with this simplicity, *RegOpenKey* has the advantage of working on both the 16-bit and 32-bit Windows platforms and on WinNT. This appears to make it, at least on the surface, one of the most portable of the registry APIs, and therefore one of the most useful functions for multiplatform development. In practice, however, its portability is strictly limited.

As a 16-bit function, *RegOpenKey* has a dual character, depending on the platform on which it's running. Under Windows 95, it can function just like its 32-bit equivalent. (For details on how to get it to do this, see Chapter 5, *Win95 Registry Access from Win16, DOS, and VxDs.*) Under Win31, however, it is capable only of accessing the limited registration database. The differences between it and the Win95 registry require that code for Win31 be "massaged" much more than most developers would prefer. In particular, the call to *RegOpenKey* for Win95 in most cases must be supplemented by code that allows the Win31 version of the application to read *WIN.INI* or a private initialization file. In other words, while *RegOpenKey* is "compatible" across the two platforms, its presence in 16-bit Win31 applications is largely superfluous.

The incompatibilities between Win95 and WinNT are less severe, but still significant. In WinNT, when a key is created, it is assigned a security descriptor that determines what privileges particular users must have in order to open that key (e.g., if it is read-only, if its value entries can be edited, if new subkeys can be created, etc.). Internally, the *RegOpenKey* function under WinNT calls the Win32 *AccessCheck* function, but it uses a default security access mask to define the kind of access desired. If a different mask is required to open the key, the function fails and returns ERROR_ACCESS_DENIED.

In addition, it is possible to assign another handle to the same key by passing a NULL as the value of *lpSubKey*. However, the meaning of this extra handle differs under the two platforms. Internally, the Win95 registry maintains a usage counter that indicates how many threads are accessing a particular key. All threads share a single handle with a single value. The handle is closed only when the key's usage counter is decremented to zero. (This behavior, incidentally, is also true of *RegOpenKeyEx*, discussed below.) In WinNT, this form of the function also returns the same handle. However, WinNT lacks a usage counter to indicate how many threads are sharing the same handle. Consequently, the following code fragment, which works under Win95, fails under WinNT. Under Windows 95, assigning the same handle to *hReadKey* increments the usage counter to two; when *hKey* is closed, the usage counter is decremented to one, which leaves the key open. Since Windows NT returns the same handle when *hReadKey* is opened, and since there is no usage counter, closing *hKey* closes both *hKey* and *hReadKey*, since they are the same key. *RegQueryValueEx* attempts to access a handle that's been closed by the previous function call:

```
RegOpenKey( hKey, NULL, &hReadKey ) ;
RegCloseKey( hKey ) ;
RegQueryValueEx(hReadKey,"WindowState", NULL, &dwType, lpData, &cbData );
RegCloseKey(hReadKey) ;
```

In short, *RegOpenKey* is not a particularly portable function. In addition, as a "compatibility" function, Microsoft is not necessarily committed to retaining it in future versions of the Windows API, and developers are urged instead to use the *RegOpenKeyEx* function, which is discussed below. Despite this, the simplicity of *RegOpenKey* makes the function rather appealing, and accounts for its continued use. In fact, *REGEDIT.EXE*, Microsoft's Registry Editor, consistently uses *RegOpenKey* rather than the officially approved *RegOpenKeyEx* to open registry keys. 'Nuff said.

RegOpenKeyEx

Like *RegOpenKey*, *RegOpenKeyEx* opens an existing registry key. Unlike *RegOpenKey*, it is the recommended function for opening a registry key using the Win32 API; as just noted, Microsoft's own RegEdit doesn't use it. In addition, it is not implemented in *KRNL386.EXE*, the 16-bit Windows kernel that contains the enhanced versions of the 16-bit registry API for Windows 95. The syntax of *RegOpenKeyEx* is:

```
LONG RegOpenKeyEx( hKey, lpSubKey, ulOptions, samDesired, phkResult ) ;
```

Its parameters are:

HKEY	*hKey*	Handle of the open key that serves as the point of origin of *lpSubKey*; it can be one of the predefined keys listed in Table 4-2, or the handle of a key opened previously using one of the registry's open key functions.
LPCTSTR	*lpSubKey*	A pointer to the string containing the path and name of the registry key to open. If *lpSubKey* is NULL or a pointer to a null string, the function returns an additional handle to the key whose handle is *hKey*.

DWORD	*ulOptions*	Reserved; must be 0.
REGSAM (LONG)	*samDesired*	Security access mask indicating the permissions required to open the key; it consists of one or more of the values shown in Table 4-3. Multiple values should be logically ORed.
PHKEY	*phkResult*	A pointer to an HKEY that will contain the handle of the newly opened key if the function succeeds.

Table 4-3. Possible values for the samDesired parameter

Constant	Value	Explanation
KEY_ALL_ACCESS	0xF003F	Combination of KEY_QUERY_VALUE, KEY_ENUMERATE_SUB_KEYS, KEY_NOTIFY, KEY_CREATE_SUB_KEY, KEY_CREATE_LINK, and KEY_SET_VALUE access.
KEY_CREATE_LINK	0x0020	Permission to create a symbolic link, which WinNT uses to manage and identify devices. It creates an association between a logical name and the device's object name.
KEY_CREATE_SUB_KEY	0x0004	Permission to create subkeys.
KEY_ENUMERATE_SUB_KEYS	0x0008	Permission to enumerate subkeys.
KEY_EXECUTE	0x20019	Permission for read access; same as KEY_READ.
KEY_NOTIFY	0x0010	Permission for change notification.
KEY_QUERY_VALUE	0x0001	Permission to query subkey data.
KEY_READ	0x20019	Combination of KEY_QUERY_VALUE, KEY_ENUMERATE_SUB_KEYS, and KEY_NOTIFY access.
KEY_SET_VALUE	0x0002	Permission to set subkey data.
KEY_WRITE	0x20006	Combination of KEY_SET_VALUE and KEY_CREATE_SUB_KEY access.

Basically, *RegOpenKeyEx* is identical to *RegOpenKey*, except for the addition of an unused parameter and the security access mask. This latter value, however, is not read by Win95. This means that, if an application runs under Win95, samDesired can be any long integer, and not necessarily a combination of the values shown in Table 4-3. However, if the program runs under WinNT, an invalid value for samDesired causes the function to return ERROR_ ACCESS_DENIED. Consequently, the value assigned to samDesired by an application should *always* accurately reflect the operations that will be performed on the key while it is open.

Example 4-2, which is a Windows console program that accepts a filename as a parameter and then launches the application capable of handling that file, illustrates the use of the *RegOpenKeyEx* function. After the program extracts the file extension from the command line, *RegOpenKeyEx* is used to determine whether the specified file extension is "registered"—i.e., whether it has a file association key in the registry. This use of *RegOpenKeyEx* (or of *RegOpenKey*) to check for the existence of a particular key is very common. If the file association key is not present, a message box informs the user that the file extension is not registered. On the other hand, if one is present, the *RegQueryValueEx* function, which retrieves a particular value entry belonging to the open registry key and will be discussed later, finds the application identifier. The *RegOpenKeyEx* function checks that the application identifier key exists. If it does, another call to *RegOpen-KeyEx* opens its `shell\open\command` subkey. The *RegQueryValueEx* function retrieves the subkey's default value, which is the name of the program, along with any parameters, that Windows ordinarily passes to the *ShellExecute* function. The program substitutes the command line for the "%1" parameters, and passes this string as the first argument to the *WinExec* function. This loads the program that is associated with the file type that was entered on the command line, and (depending on how the action of the "open" verb is defined in the registry) usually loads the program.

Notice the use of the dual backslashes in defining the key to be opened (e.g., "\\shell\\open\\command", instead of "\shell\open\command"). Forgetting them is a frequent cause of error in C programs. A pair of backslashes, rather than a single one, is needed because a backslash character, when it's contained in a string, marks the beginning of an escape sequence—a series of characters that represents a single special character, like \n (the newline character) or \0 (the null-terminator). Because of this, the escape sequence needed to include a back-slash in a string is a dual backslash; two backslashes are then represented as "\\\\".

Example 4-2. OPENKYX1.C, a program using RegOpenKeyEx

```
#include <windows.h>
#include <string.h>

int APIENTRY WinMain(HANDLE hInstance, HANDLE hPrevInstance,
                LPSTR lpszCmdLine, int nCmdShow)
    {
    int ch = '.', CharPos ;
    HKEY hKey ;
    LONG cbBuffer ;
    char lpAppID[50], lpPgmName[MAX_PATH], lpAppIDKey[MAX_PATH] ;
    char lpCmdEx[MAX_PATH], lpExten[10], *lpStrPtr ;

    // Test for no command line
    if (strlen(lpszCmdLine) == 0)
        {
            MessageBox(NULL, "Syntax: OPENKYX1 <filename>", "OPENKYX1 Error",
                MB_OK) ;
        exit (0) ;
        }
    // extract extension from filename
```

Example 4-2. OPENKYX1.C, a program using RegOpenKeyEx (continued)

```
if (lpStrPtr = strchr(lpszCmdLine, ch))
    strcpy(lpExten, lpStrPtr) ;
else
    {
    printf("The filename does not include a file extension.") ;
    exit (0) ;
    }
// Determine if file extension is registered
if (RegOpenKeyEx(HKEY_CLASSES_ROOT, lpExten, 0, KEY_READ, &hKey)
        == ERROR_SUCCESS )
    {
    // Retrieve application identifier
    cbBuffer = sizeof(lpAppID) ;
    RegQueryValue(hKey, NULL, (LPTSTR)lpAppID, &cbBuffer) ;
    RegCloseKey(hKey) ;
    // Form subkey path
    strcpy(lpAppIDKey, lpAppID) ;
    strcat(lpAppIDKey, "\\shell\\open\\command") ;
    // Retrieve name of associated program
    if (RegOpenKeyEx(HKEY_CLASSES_ROOT, (LPCTSTR)lpAppIDKey, 0,
                    KEY_READ, &hKey) == ERROR_SUCCESS)
        {
        cbBuffer = sizeof(lpPgmName) ;
        RegQueryValue( hKey, NULL, (LPTSTR)lpPgmName, &cbBuffer ) ;
        RegCloseKey(hKey) ;
        // Replace first parameter to program
        // todo: deal with %*
        CharPos = strcspn(lpPgmName,"%1") ;
        if (CharPos > 0)
            {
            strncpy(lpCmdEx, lpPgmName, CharPos - 1) ;
            strcat(lpCmdEx, " ") ;
            strcat(lpCmdEx, lpszCmdLine) ;
            }
        else
            strcpy( lpCmdEx, lpPgmName ) ;
        // Execute Program
        if (WinExec(lpCmdEx, SW_SHOWNORMAL ) < 32 )
    MessageBox(NULL, "Unable to launch associated program...",
                lpPgmName,MB_OK) ;
        }
    else
        MessageBox(NULL, "The file type is not associated with a
            particular program!", lpszCmdLine, MB_OK) ;
    }
else
    MessageBox(NULL, "Unregistered file extension", lpszCmdLine,
        MB_OK) ;

return 0 ;
}
```

Using *RegOpenKeyEx*, it is possible to open the same key multiple times by passing a NULL as the value of *lpSubkey*. However, the behavior of the function differs significantly under Win95 and WinNT. In Win95, the same key is always assigned the same handle unless it is one of the top-level keys. That's because, internally, Win95 maintains a counter for each open registry key. Each time a handle is requested, Win95 increments a usage counter, and each time a request to close the key is made, it decrements the counter. When the counter reaches 0, the key is finally closed. Under WinNT, on the other hand, there is no counter. And, except in the case of the top-level keys, attempts to open the same key produce unique handles. Consequently, a code fragment like the following does not execute successfully under WinNT but does work under Win95, since the values of *hKey* and *hNewKey* are the same, and both handles refer to the same key:

```
RegOpenKeyEx( hKey, NULL, 0, KEY_READ, &hNewKey ) ;
RegCloseKey( hNewKey ) ;
RegQueryValueEx(hNewKey,"WindowState", NULL, &dwType, lpData, &cbData );
RegCloseKey( hNewKey) ;
```

RegCreateKey

"*RegCreateKey*" is something of a misnomer. It is true that this function creates a new registry key. But in fact, that isn't necessarily its sole purpose. Instead, like *RegOpenKey*, its major use is to provide a handle to a registry key. *RegOpenKey*, though, returns an ERROR_FILE_NOT_FOUND message if the specified key does not exist; *RegCreateKey*, on the other hand, will create a key that it is unable to find, and then provide a handle to it. This is surprisingly handy.

The syntax of *RegCreateKey* is fairly straightforward, and is basically identical to that of *RegOpenKey*:

```
LONG RegCreateKey( hKey, lpSubKey, phkResult ) ;
```

Its parameters are:

HKEY	*hKey*	Handle of the open key that serves as the point of origin of *lpSubKey*; it can be one of the predefined keys listed in Table 4-2, or the handle of a key opened previously using one of the registry's open key functions.
LPCTSTR	*lpSubKey*	A pointer to the string containing the path and name of the registry key to open. If *hKey* is HKEY_DYN_DATA or one of its subkeys, *lpSubKey* must be an existing key; the function can open an existing key, but it cannot create a new one in this registry tree. (New keys in HKEY_DYN_DATA must be created by a VxD calling the VMM _RegCreateDynKey service.)
PHKEY	*phkResult*	A pointer to a long integer that will contain the handle of the newly opened key if the function succeeds.

If *lpSubkey* is a complete registry path that includes more than one subkey, *RegCreateKey* creates all of the missing keys needed to create the subkey. Assuming that the file extension `.tst`, for example, is not registered in HKEY_CLASSES_ROOT, the code fragment:

```
LPCTSTR lpszSubkey = ".tst\\shell\\open\\command" ;
HKEY hkResult = 0 ;
RegCreateKey(HKEY_CLASSES_ROOT, lpszSubkey, &hkResult) ;
```

creates the following subkeys of HKEY_CLASSES_ROOT:

- `HKEY_CLASSES_ROOT\.tst`

- `HKEY_CLASSES_ROOT\.tst\shell`

- `HKEY_CLASSES_ROOT\.tst\shell\open`

- `HKEY_CLASSES_ROOT\.tst\shell\open\command`

On the other hand, the behavior of the *RegCreateKey* function (as well as that of the *RegCreateKeyEx* function, which is discussed in the following section) varies somewhat when the function is used to open a dynamic key. HKEY_DYN_DATA and its subkeys are read-only; because they are virtual keys that store function pointers and actually retrieve their data on demand, these two functions can open existing keys, but they cannot create new keys. If you attempt to use either of these two functions to open a dynamic key, it returns ERROR_FILE_NOT_FOUND.

Like *RegOpenKey*, *RegCreateKey* is a "compatibility" function that is inherited from the Win16 API. Developers writing Win32 applications are urged instead to use the *RegCreateKeyEx* function. (The developers of RegEdit at Microsoft, though, have evidently chosen not to follow this exhortation: *REGEDIT.EXE* creates new subkeys with *RegCreateKey* rather than *RegCreateKeyEx*.)

Despite its continued use, though, *RegCreateKey* does have some significant drawbacks. First, when the function executes successfully, it gives no indication of whether it has found an existing key to open, or created a new key. This, however, can be an important item of information, particularly in installation routines and initialization code. Consequently, *RegCreateKey* is frequently used in combination with *RegOpenKey* only after *RegOpenKey* has failed to find a particular key, as the following code fragment illustrates:

```
#define ERROR_KEY_NOT_FOUND ERROR_FILE_NOT_FOUND
if (RegOpenKey(hKey, lpName, &hkResult ) == ERROR_KEY_NOT_FOUND )
    RegCreateKey(hKey, lpName, &hkResult) ;
else
    // the key already exists
```

This, however, requires calls to two separate functions for what amounts to a single operation. Second, like *RegOpenKey*, *RegCreateKey* (or a subsequent operation on an open key) is likely to fail under WinNT because it does not support

---

Naming Registry Keys

In choosing names for registry keys that you create, you can use any printable ANSI character *except* for the following:

- *Backslashes.* They're used as the path delimiter character.

- *Asterisks.* They can be interpreted by the Windows shell as applying to every object in a collection.

- *Periods at the beginning of the name.* In some cases, these keys are interpreted by the registry as containing default settings.

These last two exceptions are not really hard and fast rules; you should just avoid using these characters to make sure that their meaning isn't misinterpreted by Windows.

Initialization file key names cannot include the equal sign ("="), since they serve to delimit key names from their values. They are, however, valid in registry key names. Information on registry key names that have an equal sign can also be successfully written to a .REG file or merged from a .REG file into the registry.

Key names can also include embedded spaces. They can even include leading and trailing spaces, although this is not advisable, since it needlessly complicates attempts to open the key.

---

security parameters, instead relying on the system's default value for the security access mask. In addition, regardless of whether *RegCreateKey* is being used to create a new key or to open an existing one, the function will succeed only if the key designated by *hKey* has been opened with `KEY_CREATE_SUB_KEY` or `KEY_WRITE` access.

The limitations of *RegCreateKey* probably outweigh any advantages gained by the function's simplicity. It is indeed best used as a "compatibility" function, in those relatively few instances in which the same code must run on both the Win16 and Win32 platforms.

RegCreateKeyEx

Like *RegCreateKey*, *RegCreateKeyEx* opens an existing key or creates and opens a new key, and provides the key's handle. Since it is the "official" Win32 function for creating a registry key on both the Win95 and WinNT platforms, its syntax is considerably more complicated.

```
LONG RegCreateKeyEx( hKey, lpSubKey, Reserved, lpClass, dwOptions,
samDesired, lpSecurityAttributes, phkResult, lpdwDisposition ) ;
```

Its parameters are:

HKEY	*hKey*	Handle of the open key that serves as the point of origin of *lpSubKey*; it can be one of the predefined keys listed in Table 4-2, or the handle of a key opened previously using one of the registry's open key functions. For the function to succeed if the application is run under WinNT, this key must have been opened using KEY_CREATE_SUB_KEY (or KEY_WRITE) as the value of the *samDesired* parameter to the *RegOpenKeyEx* or *RegCreateKeyEx* functions.
LPCTSTR	*lpSubKey*	A pointer to the string containing the path and name of the registry key to open. If *hKey* is HKEY_DYN_DATA or one of its subkeys, *lpSubKey* must be an existing key; the function can open an existing key, but it cannot create a new one in this registry tree.
DWORD	*Reserved*	Reserved; must be 0.
LPTSTR	*lpClass*	Pointer to a string containing the key's class name; Win95 does not store class names as part of a key's information.
DWORD	*dwOptions*	Special options flag. In Win95, only one option is supported: REG_OPTION_NON_VOLATILE, which creates a key in one of the physical files that compose the registry.
REGSAM	*samDesired*	The minimum security access for the new key; this consists of one or more of the values listed earlier in Table 4-3; since Win95 is not secure, it ignores the value of this parameter.
LPSECURITY ATTRIBUTES	*lpSecurityAttributes*	A NULL, or a pointer to a security structure that defines security attributes for a new key; the security structure is described in Table 4-4. Since Win95 does not support security, this parameter is ignored.
PHKEY	*phkResult*	A pointer to an HKEY that will contain the handle of the newly opened key if the function succeeds.
LPDWORD	*lpdwDisposition*	Pointer to a DWORD buffer that, if the function returns ERROR_SUCCESS, indicates whether a new key was created (REG_CREATED_NEW_KEY) or an existing one was opened (REG_OPENED_EXISTING_KEY).

Table 4-4. The SECURITY_ATTRIBUTES Structure

Data Type	Parameter	Description
DWORD	nLength	The size, in bytes, of the data structure.
LPVOID	lpSecurity-Descriptor	A pointer to the key's security descriptor, a data structure that controls access to the key and that is created and maintained by using a specialized set of Win32 security functions.
BOOL	bInheritHandle	A Boolean value that indicates whether the handle to the registry key can be inherited by a child process.

Like *RegOpenKeyEx*, *RegCreateKeyEx* includes several parameters that provide information necessary for the function's proper operation under WinNT, but that are not actually used by Win95:

- *The key's class name.* Since class names are not included with keys in the Win95 registry, the function will return successfully if `lpClass` is assigned a null string.

- *The options flag.* Win95 only supports a single options flag, `REG_OPTION_NON_VOLATILE`, whose value happens to be 0. But in fact Win95 completely disregards the value of this parameter.

- *The security access mask.* Since Win95 does not support security, this parameter is ignored. It can be any value, including a 0. If the application is run under WinNT, the system's default security access mask is substituted for any invalid values.

- *The security descriptor.* Win95 does not store a security descriptor with a registry key; therefore, this parameter may be a NULL. If the application is run under WinNT, the system substitutes its default security descriptor if one is not specified.

Under WinNT, each of these parameters except for `samDesired` is ignored as well if the function opens an existing key; they are used only if a new key is created.

Along with its support for these NT-specific features, the *RegCreateKeyEx* function also addresses an important limitation of *RegCreateKey*: it indicates whether an existing key has been opened, or whether the function has instead created a new key. This requires, of course, that the `lpdwDisposition` parameter be correctly passed as a *pointer* to a DWORD.

RegCreateKeyEx is implemented exclusively under Win32; it is not one of the enhanced registry functions exported by *KRNL386.EXE*, the 16-bit Windows kernel for Win95.

Like *RegCreateKey*, a single *RegCreateKeyEx* function can create multiple keys, as
Example 4-3 illustrates. In this code fragment, the program checks to see whether
an application identification key named "Dual Associate" is present by calling
RegCreateKeyEx. If the value of `dwDisposition` after the function returns is
`REG_OPENED_EXISTING_KEY` (that is, if it is not `REG_CREATED_NEW_KEY`), the
application is already defined, so the program closes the open registry key and
exits. On the other hand, if its value is `REG_CREATED_NEW_KEY`, the program must
add all of the information needed to define the application. It first uses *RegSetValueEx* to add the application identifier description, which is the default value of
the application identifier's key. It next calls *RegCreateKeyEx* after setting the value
of `lpszKeyName` to "shell\\open\\command". This adds all three keys
(`DualAssociate\shell`, `DualAssociate\shell\open`, and `DualAsso-
ciate\shell\open\command`), while opening the last one. Finally, it writes
the path and filename of Dual Associate to the default value of this key.

Example 4-3. Using RegCreateKeyEx

```
#include <windows.h>
#include <string.h>

int APIENTRY WinMain(HANDLE hInstance, HANDLE hPrevInstance,
                     LPSTR lpszCmdLine, int nCmdShow)
   {
   HKEY hKey, hSubkey ;
   DWORD dwDisposition, dwCharWritten ;
   CHAR lpszKeyName[] = "DualAssociate" ;
       CHAR lpszDftValue[] = "Dual File Association" ;
   CHAR szPath[MAX_PATH], lpszPathValue[MAX_PATH] ;

   // Open DualAssociate application identification key
   RegCreateKeyEx(HKEY_CLASSES_ROOT, lpszKeyName, 0, NULL,
                  REG_OPTION_NON_VOLATILE, KEY_ALL_ACCESS,
                  NULL, &hKey, &dwDisposition) ;
   // If the key is new, add application identification information
   if (dwDisposition == REG_CREATED_NEW_KEY)
      {
      // Add the application description to the key's default value
      RegSetValueEx(hKey, NULL, 0, REG_SZ, lpszDftValue,
                    sizeof(lpszDftValue)) ;
      // Add the remaining keys
      strcpy( lpszKeyName, "shell\\open\\command") ;
      RegCreateKeyEx(hKey, lpszKeyName, 0, NULL,
                     REG_OPTION_NON_VOLATILE, KEY_ALL_ACCESS,
                     NULL, &hSubkey, &dwDisposition) ;
      // Add the command string
      dwCharWritten = GetCurrentDirectory( sizeof(szPath), szPath ) ;
      if (dwCharWritten > 0 )
         {
         strcpy(lpszPathValue, szPath ) ;
         strcat(lpszPathValue, "\\" ) ;
```

Example 4-3. Using RegCreateKeyEx (continued)

```
        strcat(lpszPathValue, "DualAssn.Exe %1" ) ;
        }
    else
        strcpy(lpszPathValue, "DualAssn.Exe %1" ) ;
    // Write command string to Registry
    RegSetValueEx(hSubkey, NULL, 0, REG_SZ, lpszPathValue,
                strlen(lpszPathValue)+1) ;
    // Close "shell\command\open" subkey
    RegCloseKey (hSubkey) ;
    }
// Close HKCR\DualAssociate
RegCloseKey(hKey) ;
return 0 ;
}
```

Also like *RegCreateKey*, *RegCreateKeyEx* can open but can't create dynamic keys. If the *hKey* parameter designates a handle to HKEY_DYN_DATA or any of its subkeys, that key must exist in order for *RegCreateKeyEx* to succeed.

Although the function *RegCreateKeyEx* makes it easy to create new registry keys, a certain degree of caution should be exercised in using the function under Win95. Because of its security system, WinNT will prevent a program from adding some particularly nonsensical or dangerous keys, like direct subkeys of HKEY_USERS or HKEY_LOCAL_MACHINE. Win95, however, lacks this safeguard.

It's also important to resist the temptation to view both *RegCreateKey* and *RegCreateKeyEx* as "safer" variations of *RegOpenKey* and *RegOpenKeyEx*. Since the key creation functions create a key if they cannot find it, you don't have to concern yourself with handling the ERROR_FILE_NOT_FOUND error if you use the key creation functions instead of the key open functions.

But in fact, the functions aren't always direct equivalents. In some instances, keys are used as flags or as Boolean values; that is, Windows or an application uses the mere presence or absence of a key, rather than any value assigned to it, to control its behavior. For instance, if you click your right mouse button on any file system object, Windows displays a context-sensitive menu that includes either an Open or an Open With... menu option. To determine which to display, the Windows shell looks for the presence of a key named HKCR\<AppIdentifier>\shell\open: if it's present, the shell displays the text "Open" on the menu; otherwise, it displays "Open With..." Only if it displays the Open option and you select it does the shell check for the presence of a command subkey whose default value tells it what to do. In cases such as these, adding a key simply because you don't want to handle an ERROR_FILE_NOT_FOUND message can substantially modify Windows or an application's behavior.

RegConnectRegistry

The four open registry key functions that we've examined so far all provide what is in effect a single point of origin: any open key must either be a top-level key or a subkey of a top-level key on the user's computer. In contrast, the *RegConnectRegistry* function establishes a connection to the registry on a remote computer by providing a handle to one of its top-level keys. Its syntax is:

```
LONG RegConnectRegistry( lpMachineName, hKey, phKey ) ;
```

where the parameters are:

LPTSTR	*lpMachine-Name*	Pointer to a string containing the UNC computer name. (UNC stands for *universal naming convention*; it allows you to specify an absolute path to identify a network resource.) This takes the general format *computername* (that's "\\\\\\\" in a C string). However, the function still succeeds under Win95 if the two initial backslashes are omitted. If the parameter is NULL, its default value is the name of the local computer.
HKEY	*hKey*	Predefined handle of one of the top-level registry keys on the remote computer. It can be any of the six top-level keys found in the Win95 registry. When connecting to a WinNT machine, it must either be HKEY_LOCAL_MACHINE or HKEY_USERS.
PHKEY	*phkResult*	A pointer to an HKEY that will contain the handle of the remote computer's top-level key if the function succeeds.

When working with the registry on a remote computer, you first use *RegConnectRegistry* to establish the connection to a top-level key. In essence, *RegConnectRegistry* returns a duplicate handle to one of the remote computer's top-level keys, thereby removing any potential confusion between the handles to registry keys on the local computer and on the remote computer. Once the connection is successfully established, an application can successfully enumerate subkeys of the top-level key by using this handle; or it can use *RegOpenKey*, *RegOpenKeyEx*, *RegCreateKey*, and *RegCreateKeyEx* to navigate the remote computer's hierarchy of keys and to open subkeys of the top-level key. From this point on, everything else works the same as local access.

You can use *RegConnectRegistry* to connect to any of the Win95 registry's top-level keys. This is in contrast to the function's documentation, which says that *hKey* must be either **HKEY_LOCAL_MACHINE** or **HKEY_USERS**.

Interestingly, when you connect to a remote computer using *RegConnectRegistry* and perform registry operations remotely, you are actually using a completely different set of functions residing in a separate library from when you open a handle to a local registry key. That's because, when you're accessing the registry

---

Requirements for Remote Registry Access

RegConnectRegistry will invariably fail to connect to remote registries on Win95 systems in their default configuration. It requires, among other things, user-level security relying on a WinNT or Novell NetWare server for pass-through authentication and the installation of Microsoft Remote Registry Services. For a more detailed discussion of these requirements, see "Accessing the Registry on Remote Computers" in Chapter 2, *Using the Registry Editor.*

---

on a local computer, the individual functions in the registry API are really wrappers that call their corresponding routines in the Win95 Virtual Machine Manager (VMM). Remote registry access, on the other hand, is implemented through the Win32 API as a client/server application using Microsoft Remote Procedure Calls (RPC).* In this case, the *server* is the computer whose registry is being examined, while the *client* is the computer that is being used for remote access and on which *RegConnectRegistry* has been called. RPC permits the client to execute functions and initiate processes on the server. When you use a registry function with a remote handle, the function calls its corresponding *Remote_* routine (e.g., *RegCreateKeyEx* calls *Remote_RegCreateKeyEx*) located in *WINREG.DLL*, a dynamic link library that serves as the client for Microsoft Remote Registry Services. *WINREG.DLL* contains the RPC code that sends registry requests to, and receives information back from, a server application, *REGSERV.EXE*, running on the remote machine. REGSERV.EXE, not surprisingly, calls its local VMM to access the registry. This difference between local registry access and remote registry access is illustrated in Figure 4-1.

WINREG.DLL and REGSERV.EXE

WINREG.DLL, the remote registry services client library, and *REGSERV.EXE*, the remote registry server, are automatically copied to your computer when you install Microsoft Remote Registry Service; for details, see the sidebar "Installing Microsoft Remote Registry Services" in Chapter 2, *Using the Registry Editor.*

This method of implementing local and remote registry access has implications in two major areas: robustness and performance.

---

* For a full-length treatment of writing client/server applications with Microsoft Remote Procedure Calls, see John Shirley and Ward Rosenberry, *Microsoft RPC Programming Guide*, published by O'Reilly & Associates.

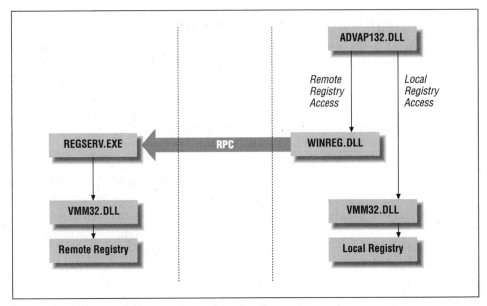

Figure 4-1. Local and remote registry access

Remote registry access and robustness

If you use the *RegOpenKeyEx* function on a local computer, Windows executes the *_RegOpenKey* function in the VMM. If you use *RegOpenKeyEx* on a remote computer, Windows executes the *Remote_RegOpenKey* function, which in turn calls *REGSERV.EXE* on the remote computer. In other words, even though the high-level function may be the same, a completely different set of code is executed for remote registry access and for local registry access. If only because local registry access is more common than remote registry access, the registry API for local access has been tested extensively and is very robust. This is not true, though, of the registry API for remote access. Consequently, the behavior of the registry API during remote registry access at times appears very idiosyncratic or even outright buggy. In covering the individual registry functions, we'll discuss the bugs in remote registry access that we know about and their workarounds; all can be corrected with relatively easy code modifications. It's a good idea, though, to plan spending some extra time in testing and debugging applications that rely on remote registry access.

RegConnectRegistry and performance

Since *RegConnectRegistry* involves two computers on the network "talking" to one another, the function can sometimes fail. When it does, the length of time that it takes to return an error code can at times be considerable (e.g., up to several minutes). This is particularly true in cases where `lpMachineName` designates a computer that does not exist or is not currently on the network, and where TCP/IP is used as the major network protocol as well as for dial-up networking. During this time, it is very likely that a user will assume the application has crashed and will take some undesirable action. To prevent this, you might want to use multiple threads to implement remote registry access; the main thread could display a dialog box or a message informing the user of the progress of the connect operation and include a Cancel button, while a "worker" thread handles the remote registry connection. In Example 4-4, for instance, a worker thread attempts to make the remote registry connection, while the main thread is free to accept user input. If the user presses the C key before a connection is established, the main thread calls the *TerminateThread* function to abort the attempt to make the connection and kill the thread.

Although *RegConnectRegistry* is primarily intended for remote registry access, it also can access the local computer's registry. If *lpMachineName* is NULL, the function substitutes the local computer's name. It then calls the Win32 *GetComputerName* function to retrieve the name of the local computer and compares it with the value of *lpMachineName*. If they are the same, indicating that this parameter designates the local computer, *RegConnectRegistry* provides a handle to a registry key without invoking Microsoft Remote Procedure Calls or the Remote_ functions in *WINREG.DLL*. In fact, if the function returns successfully, *phkResult* is one of the predefined registry handles listed earlier in Table 4-2; the function returns a handle to a key that is already open. There is a slight performance penalty, though, for using *RegConnectRegistry* to accomplish what the local registry functions do for "free."

If your system is configured for remote registry access and you're interested in assessing the performance of *RegConnectRegistry*, you can use a program like *REGCONN.C*, a multithreaded console mode utility which is shown in Example 4-4. It simply reports the number of seconds that elapse before the function returns a valid registry handle or an error message, then immediately closes any open handles to a remote registry key. It is particularly useful for seeing how much time is consumed by waiting for the function to return an error code.

Example 4-4. Evaluating the performance of RegConnectRegistry

```
// regconn.c
// cl -DUSE_THREAD regconn.c advapi32.lib
// About 15 seconds to get access denied
// About 45 seconds to get bad net path

#include <stdio.h>
#include <time.h>
#include <conio.h>
#include <ctype.h>
#include <windows.h>
```

Example 4-4. Evaluating the performance of RegConnectRegistry (continued)

```
#define OK ERROR_SUCCESS

BOOL IsHkeyRemote(HKEY hkey)
{
    DWORD dw = (DWORD) hkey;
    if ((hkey >= HKEY_CLASSES_ROOT) && (hkey <= HKEY_DYN_DATA))
        return 0;    // local
    return ! (((~dw) & 1));
}


#ifdef USE_THREAD
typedef struct {
    int done;
    LPSTR lpMachineName;
    HKEY hKey;
    PHKEY phkResult;
    LONG err;
    } REGCONN;

DWORD WINAPI RegConnectRegistryThread(LPVOID param)
{
    REGCONN *p = (REGCONN *) param;
    p->err = RegConnectRegistry(p->lpMachineName, p->hKey,
        p->phkResult);
    p->done = 1;
    return p->err;
}


LONG ThreadedRegConnectRegistry(LPSTR lpMachineName, HKEY hKey,
    PHKEY phkResult)
{
    HANDLE hthread;
    REGCONN p;
    DWORD id;

    p.done = 0;
    p.lpMachineName = lpMachineName;
    p.hKey = hKey;
    p.phkResult = phkResult;

    if (! ((hthread = CreateThread(NULL, 4096, RegConnectRegistryThread,
        (void *) &p, 0, &id))))
        return ERROR_OPERATION_ABORTED;

    printf("Started thread to connect to remote registry\n"
           "Press C to cancel... ");

    for (;;)
    {
        if (p.done)
        {
```

Example 4-4. Evaluating the performance of RegConnectRegistry (continued)

```
                putchar('\r');
                return p.err;
            }
            else if (kbhit() && (toupper(getch()) == 'C'))
            {
                TerminateThread(hthread, 0);
                putchar('\r');
                return ERROR_OPERATION_ABORTED;
            }
            else
                Sleep(50);
        }
        /*NOTREACHED*/
}
#endif

main(int argc, char *argv[])
{
    HKEY hkey, hkey2;
    int err;
    time_t t1, t2;
    char *name = (argc < 2) ? "" : argv[1];
    time(&t1);
#ifdef USE_THREAD
    if ((err = ThreadedRegConnectRegistry(name, HKEY_CLASSES_ROOT,
        &hkey)) == OK)
#else
    if ((err = RegConnectRegistry(name, HKEY_CLASSES_ROOT,
        &hkey)) == OK)
#endif
    {
        time(&t2);
        if (! *name) name = "local registry";
        printf("%lu seconds to connect to %s\n", t2 - t1, name);
        if (RegOpenKey(hkey, ".txt", &hkey2) == OK)
        {
            printf("hkey for HKCR\\.txt on %s ==> %08lXh\n",
                name, hkey2);
            printf("hkey is %s\n",
                IsHkeyRemote(hkey2) ? "remote" : "local");
            RegCloseKey(hkey2);
        }
        RegCloseKey(hkey);
    }
    else if (err == ERROR_DLL_INIT_FAILED)
        printf("You have to install WINREG.DLL to do this!\n");
    else
    {
        time(&t2);
        switch (err)
        {
            #define MSG(x) case x : printf("%s\t\t\t\n", #x)
```

Example 4-4. Evaluating the performance of RegConnectRegistry (continued)

```
                MSG(ERROR_OPERATION_ABORTED); break;
                MSG(ERROR_BAD_NETPATH); break;
                MSG(ERROR_ACCESS_DENIED); break;
                default: printf("Error #%u (look in WINERROR.H)\n", err);
                break;
            }
        printf("%lu seconds before failed to connect to %s\n",
                t2 - t1,
                (*name) ? name : "local registry");
        }
    printf("bye!\n");
    return 0;
}
```

RegConnectRegistry is not a "bad" function, but clearly it can take a long time to connect to a registry on a remote machine—or even more to find that you *can't*. This means that your program should try to qualify the user's choices of remote computer names. Some ways of doing this are:

- *Retrieving the local computer's name.* Before calling *RegConnectRegistry*, the program should check if **lpMachineName** is NULL or contains the name of the local computer. If so, omit the call to *RegConnectRegistry!* The local computer name is stored as the value of the **ComputerName** entry in HKLM\System\CurrentControlSet\Control\ComputerName\ComputerName. An *IsLocal* function that retrieves this value might look something like Example 4-5.[*]

Example 4-5. SLOCAL.C, a function to check whether a computer name is local

```
#include <windows.h>
#include <string.h>

BOOL IsLocal(LPSTR lpszName)
    {
    static char lpszComputerName[128] ;
    static BOOL blnInitialized ;
    HKEY hNetKey ;
    DWORD lenComputerName ;
    BOOL blnRetVal ;

    // Retrieve computer name if lpszComputerName has no value
    if (!blnInitialized)
        {
```

---

[*] If you want to use this function to run under Windows NT as well, you'll have to check for the platform on which your application is running (see Appendix A) and, if it's Windows NT, retrieve the REG_SZ value of HKLM\System\CurrentControlSet\Control\ComputerName\ActiveComputerName. Although Windows NT has a ComputerName key, it's value will not be the current name of the computer if the user has changed it in the course of the current session. ActiveComputerName, on the other hand, *always* reflects the local computer's name.

Example 4-5. SLOCAL.C, a function to check whether a computer name is local (continued)

```
RegOpenKey(HKEY_LOCAL_MACHINE,
  "System\\CurrentControlSet\\Control\\ComputerName\\ComputerName",
            &hNetKey) ;
lenComputerName = sizeof(lpszComputerName) ;
RegQueryValueEx(hNetKey, "ComputerName", 0, 0,
                (LPTSTR)lpszComputerName, &lenComputerName) ;
blnInitialized = TRUE ;
}
// Check if parameter is empty
if (strlen(lpszName) == 0 )
   return TRUE ;

// Check if strings are different sizes
if (strlen(lpszName) != strlen(lpszComputerName))
   return FALSE ;

// Compare strings that have not failed the previous comparisons
return (_strnicmp(lpszName,
   lpszComputerName, strlen(lpszName)) ==
}
```

- *Listing remote computers in a list box.* Rather than letting the user type in the name of a remote computer (an extremely error-prone process), it's best for the program to gather the names of remote computers and to allow the user to choose one from a list box. One way to do this is by parsing the names of the subkeys of HKCU\Network\Recent and the values of the RemotePath entry for each subkey of HKCU\Network\Persistent; each of these contains the UNC name of a shared network drive. This, however, only provides the names of computers to which the user connects regularly or has connected recently. On a large Win95 network, this could be a very small subset of the computers to which the user might need to connect. The names of computers on the network, however, are readily available—in fact, it's part of the desktop's namespace, and is displayed whenever the user clicks on the Network Neighborhood icon on the desktop or in an Explorer window.[*] To retrieve them, it is first necessary to call the *SHGetSpecialFolderLocation* function to retrieve a pointer to the Network Neighborhood's item identifier list, or *pidl*. This can then be passed to the *SHBrowseForFolder* function, which displays network computers in a tree control. *GetRemoteComputer*, a function that does this, is shown in Example 4-6. It takes two parameters: the handle of the calling application's window, and a string buffer that is assumed to be *MAX_PATH* bytes to hold the name of the selected computer. It returns a Boolean value indicating whether or not *lpRemoteComputer* is valid, i.e.,

---

[*] Note that, because it relies on the Windows 95 shell, this discussion does not apply to Windows NT 3.x. Another way to list computers on the network is with the *WNetEnumResource* and *WNetOpenEnum* Win32 APIs.

whether the user has exited the "Select a Remote Computer" dialog by selecting a computer.

Example 4-6. GETREM.C, a function to retrieve the name of a remote computer

```
#include <shlobj.h>

BOOL GetRemoteComputer( HWND hWnd, LPSTR lpRemoteComputer)
  {
  LPITEMIDLIST pidlNetwork ;
  BROWSEINFO biComputer ;

  SHGetSpecialFolderLocation(hWnd, CSIDL_NETWORK, &pidlNetwork) ;

  biComputer.hwndOwner = hWnd ;
  biComputer.pidlRoot = pidlNetwork ;
  biComputer.pszDisplayName = lpRemoteComputer ;
  biComputer.lpszTitle = "Select the Remote Computer" ;
  biComputer.ulFlags = 0 ;
  biComputer.lpfn = NULL ;
  biComputer.lParam = 0 ;

  return (SHBrowseForFolder(&biComputer) != NULL) ;
  }
```

Even after your application successfully connects to a remote computer, performance is an issue. This is particularly the case because operations such as enumerating all of the subkeys or all of the values of a key can be time-consuming on a network that's experiencing bottlenecks. To optimize performance in remote registry applications, you might try any of the following:

- If possible, avoid enumerating subkeys or values. This, of course, isn't possible if you don't know the names of keys or values. But if you do, look for them directly.

- Don't use *RegFlushKey* (described later in this chapter). It's slow on a local computer, and even slower on a remote one.

- Try to "batch" the data that you retrieve by using the *RegQueryMultipleValues* function. See the section "Retrieving Multiple Values: RegQueryMultipleValues" later in this chapter.

Performing Operations on the Registry

Once your program has opened a registry key by retrieving its handle, you can reference that handle to perform registry operations using the registry API. These operations include:

- Gathering information about a key

- Retrieving the names of all subkeys or the value entries belonging to a key

- Getting a particular value or multiple values

- Modifying a value

- Immediately committing changes to the registry's physical files

- Loading and unloading a WinNT registry hive

- Deleting a key or a value

The functions that operate on the registry share a common set of return values, which indicate the presence of an error condition. Some of the more common values are listed in Table 4-5. Also see Table 4-1 for status codes returned by the open registry key functions.

Table 4-5. Status codes returned by the registry operation functions

Constant	Value	Explanation
ERROR_SUCCESS	0	The registry operation completed successfully.
ERROR_FILE_NOT_FOUND	2	The named value or key does not exist.
ERROR_ACCESS_DENIED	5	Security access mask insufficient for operation (WinNT only), or operation not permitted on key.
ERROR_INVALID_HANDLE	6	The handle passed to the function is invalid. This can occur under a variety of circumstances: the earlier attempt to open the key failed; the open key has since been closed; or the handle is a remote handle, but the function does not support remote registry access.
ERROR_INVALID_PARAMETER	87	An extra parameter, a missing parameter, or a parameter that doesn't correspond to its declared length, its expected data type, or its expected value.
ERROR_CALL_NOT_IMPLEMENTED	120	Function not implemented for Win95 in the Win32 API.
ERROR_INSUFFICIENT_BUFFER	122	The value written by the function during remote registry access exceeds the size of the buffer.
ERROR_LOCK_FAILED	167	The registry's internal read/write locking scheme failed.
ERROR_TRANSFER_TOO_LONG	222	The length of the requested data exceeds the system's limit of one megabyte; used by *RegQueryMultipleValues*.
ERROR_MORE_DATA	234	The value written by the function to a buffer exceeds the size of the buffer.
ERROR_NO_MORE_ITEMS	259	There are no additional items to enumerate.
ERROR_BADDB	1009	The registry is damaged.

Table 4-5. Status codes returned by the registry operation functions (continued)

Constant	Value	Explanation
ERROR_BADKEY	1010	Invalid handle to a registry key.
ERROR_CANTOPEN	1011	Unable to open a registry key.
ERROR_CANTREAD	1012	Unable to access a dynamic key.
ERROR_CANTWRITE	1013	Unable to write to a dynamic registry key.
ERROR_REGISTRY_RECOVERED	1014	One of the registry's files had to be recovered by using an alternate copy.
ERROR_REGISTRY_CORRUPT	1015	Unable to access some portion of the registry.
ERROR_REGISTRY_IO_FAILED	1016	Unsuccessful attempt to read from or write to an external file.
ERROR_NOT_REGISTRY_FILE	1017	Unable to recognize format of file to be loaded or imported.
ERROR_KEY_DELETED	1018	The open key has been deleted.

The most interesting of these error codes (inasmuch as an error code can be said to be interesting) is ERROR_MORE_DATA, which may be returned by any of the functions that retrieve information from the registry. In order for these functions to provide information about registry keys and value entries, variables must be passed to them as parameters by reference; the parameter points to a buffer—or a block of memory—that is to receive the value retrieved by a function. For key name, value name, and data values, the newer registry functions (that is, those functions that are not also found in Win16 API) also include a second parameter, a pointer to a DWORD that indicates the number of bytes in the buffer. When the buffer is too small to hold all the data that the registry function attempts to write to it, the function returns ERROR_MORE_DATA. In the case of some functions, like *RegQueryValueEx*, which retrieves the data belonging to a particular value entry, the pointer points to a DWORD value that contains the correct length of the string. Because of this, functions that use *RegQueryValueEx* to retrieve registry data and are likely to return an ERROR_MORE_DATA error code can be made self-correcting; when the function fails, the required amount of memory can be reallocated and the function called once again. For an example, see "Retrieving a Specific Value: RegQueryValue and RegQueryValueEx" later in this chapter.

Gathering Information About a Key: *RegQueryInfoKey*

Any application's attempts to access registry information fall into two broad categories: *top-down* and *bottom-up.*

The top-down approach is appropriate when the information stored in the registry is finite and known in advance. For instance, an application may store all

of the registry information it needs to one key, `HKCU\Software\`
`NextMicroSquish\KillerApp\Settings`. From this key, perhaps it needs
to retrieve two values whose format is known in advance. The first is the value of
`WindowPos`, which is a string that consists of four integers; the second is the
value of `ShowState`, which is a DWORD whose value can range from 0 to 4. In
other words, an application uses the top-down approach when the names of
keys, the names of value entries, and the range of values for each entry are all
known in advance; all you need back are the current values.

The top-down approach, though, quickly breaks down when large amounts of
registry data are to be retrieved, when the precise format of the data is not clearly
known in advance, or when the data by its nature are stored as a set, making it
difficult to know the precise quantity and format of the data. For instance, an
application may have to retrieve the names of its most recently used documents
from the registry to display at the bottom of the File menu. It does not know in
advance, though, how many document filenames are stored in the registry, nor
does it know how long the combined paths and filenames of these documents
may be. The application can, of course, make assumptions about the number of
values and the size of strings to be retrieved. But generally, this either wastes
resources, fails to handle particular instances of data, or, worse, does both at once.

Rather than making assumptions about registry data, the *RegQueryInfoKey* function can retrieve a broad array of information about an open registry key. Its
syntax is:

```
LONG RegQueryInfoKey( Hkey, lpClass, lpcbClass, lpReserved, lpcSubKeys,
    lpcbMaxSubKeyLen, lpcbMaxClassLen, lpcValues,
    lpcbMaxValueNameLen, lpcbMaxValueLen,
    lpcbSecurityDescriptor, lpftLastWriteTime ) ;
```

with the following parameters:

HKEY	*hKey*	Handle of the key about which you wish to gather information. It can be either one of the predefined keys listed in Table 4-2 or a handle returned by one of the registry open key functions. Under WinNT, it should have been opened with KEY_QUERY_VALUE access.
LPTSTR	*lpClass*	Pointer to the key's class name. Since Win95 does not store class names with registry keys, its value is always a null string ("") when the function completes successfully.
LPDWORD	*lpcbClass*	Pointer to the length of the class name string, excluding the terminating null character; under Win95, this value is always 0 when the function returns.
LPDWORD	*lpReserved*	Reserved; must be NULL.

LPDWORD	*lpcSubKeys*	Pointer to the number of subkeys of the open key.
LPDWORD	*lpcbMaxSubKeyLen*	Pointer to the length of the longest name of a subkey belonging to the open key. According to the documentation, the terminating null character is not included in the count when the function returns; in fact, it is included.
LPDWORD	*lpcbMaxClassLen*	Pointer to the length of the longest class name of the open key's subkeys; since the Win95 registry does not contain class names, this value is always 0 after the function completes successfully.
LPDWORD	*lpcValues*	Pointer to the number of value entries belonging to the open key.
LPDWORD	*lpcbMaxValueNameLen*	Pointer to the number of characters in the longest value name belonging to the open key, excluding its terminating null character.
LPDWORD	*lpcbMaxValueLen*	Pointer to the length of the longest value belonging to the open key, excluding its terminating null character.
LPDWORD	*lpcbSecurityDescriptor*	Pointer to the length of the open key's security descriptor. Under Win95, this variable always equals 0 after the function returns.
LPDWORD	*lpftLastWriteTime*	Pointer to a **FILETIME** data structure containing the date and time a write to the key last occurred; since the Win95 registry does not store date and time information with its keys, this variable is always 0 after the function completes successfully. The **FILETIME** data structure is listed in Table 4-6.

Table 4-6. The FILETIME[a] data structure

DWORD	*dwLowDateTime*	The low-order four bytes of the time.
DWORD	*dwHighDateTime*	The high-order four bytes of the time.

[a] **FILETIME** is an 8-byte (64-bit) data structure whose value represents the number of 100-nanosecond intervals since January 1, 1601. *dwHighDateTime* contains the four high-order bytes, while *dwLowDateTime* contains the four low-order bytes.

In using *RegQueryInfoKey*, in most cases you're interested in just one or two items of information, rather than in each piece of data gathered by the function. Fortunately, you can pass a NULL in place of any parameter in which you're not interested. The only parameter for which the function expects a valid variable is *hkey*, the handle of the registry key about which the function is reporting information.

RegQueryInfoKey and OREGLIB.DLL

As you can see, the syntax of *RegQueryInfoKey* is needlessly complex, particularly if you're using it to extract just one or a few items of information. You may find it far more convenient to use some of the utility functions (like *RegGetMaxValueLen*, *RegGetNumSubKeys*, or *RegGetValueInfo*) available in *OREGLIB.DLL*, a 32-bit DLL on the accompanying diskette. A number of its functions simply call *RegQueryInfoKey* to extract specific items of information, and work under both Win95 and WinNT. For details, see Appendix B, *The Inside the Windows 95 Registry Diskette.*

Most of these parameters are intended for WinNT and are completely disregarded under Win95. This makes it possible to make some rather dramatic programming errors, like providing a constant as a parameter when *RegQueryInfoKey* is expecting a pointer to a DWORD, or declaring the size of a buffer to be different than the actual buffer, and still have the function return ERROR_SUCCESS. In these cases, though, the function will fail if the application is run under WinNT. If your application is likely to run under WinNT, this makes it important to be particularly careful about those unused and seemingly uninteresting parameters, and to test the application under WinNT as well as Win95.

Under Win95, the major use of *RegQueryInfoKey*, then, is to retrieve the following five items of information:

- The number of subkeys belonging to the open key
- The number of characters in the longest name of these subkeys
- The number of value entries belonging to the open key
- The number of characters in the key's longest value name
- The number of bytes used by the key's longest data value

Each of these items of information is important primarily because it makes enumerating (or retrieving) the names of the subkeys and the value entries belonging to the open key easier, and it allows you to allocate a sufficiently large buffer to hold registry data. Consequently, under Win95, *RegQueryInfoKey* usually is issued before *RegEnumKey, RegEnumKeyEx, RegEnumValue,* and *RegQueryValueEx* to provide information used by those functions.

If you're using *RegQueryInfoKey* on a remote registry, though, you'll find that the function supplies inaccurate values for both the *lpcbMaxSubKeyLen* and *lpcbMaxValueNameLen* parameters. This is probably due to a problem of ANSI/Unicode conversion; in any case, the function reports values that are about

---

Can *RegQueryInfoKey* Be "Wrong"?

In (hopefully) isolated cases, you may find that you've correctly retrieved and handled such information as the maximum length of a subkey name or the maximum length of a value entry, but that your application nevertheless fails. In this case (assuming that, if you're using remote registry access, you've made an adjustment for the *RegQueryInfoKey* bug that's discussed below), the problem may not be *RegQueryInfoKey*, but Win95's registry locking. The *RegQueryInfoKey* function is atomic; the accuracy of the data it collects is assured by the registry mutex at the time the function executes. But there is no guarantee that some other application (or even your own) has not written to the registry, in the process invalidating your data, before you complete a series of *multiple* API calls that you used *RegQueryInfoKey* to begin. For details, see "Registry Locking" later in this chapter.

---

half of the correct values.[*] So if you use *RegQueryInfoKey* to determine how much memory to allocate for subkey names from remote machines, you should make the following correction after you call the function:

```
cbMaxSubKeyLen = cbMaxSubKeyLen * 2 + 2 ;
cbMaxValueNameLen = cbMaxValueNameLen * 2 + 2 ;
```

Since these lengths are integer values whose remainders are lost when they are divided by two, we have to double the value name length or subkey name length variable and add one, in the event that the original integer was an odd number. In addition, *RegQueryInfoKey* counts only the actual number of characters in the longest subkey or value name, and does not add a byte for the terminating null character. To allocate space for it in our buffer, we have to add an extra byte to each of these values. That's why our correction adds two bytes instead of just one.

In addition, if you're using the *RegQueryInfoKey* function when accessing a remote registry, it's important to pay particular attention to the `lpReserved` parameter, since the function's handling of this parameter is considerably different in remote registry access than in local registry access. For local registry access, Win95 completely ignores the parameter. Although the documentation indicates that its value must be NULL, you can also provide a value of zero or a pointer to a DWORD without affecting the function's return value. For remote registry access, on the other hand, `lpReserved` must be either NULL or 0; if it is a pointer to a DWORD (even a DWORD that equals zero), the function returns `ERROR_INVALID_PARAMETER`. If you're programming in Visual Basic, this means

---

[*] More precisely, the correct value is either twice the number of characters reported or one more than twice the number reported, depending on whether the correct value is even or odd.

that you must pass a zero by value, using the BYVAL keyword, when you call the function, as the following example shows:

```
Call RegQueryInfoKey(hKey, 0, 0, BYVAL 0, lngSubkeys, lngSubkeyNameLen,
                     0, 0, 0, 0, 0, udtFiletime) ;
```

Enumerating Keys: RegEnumKey and RegEnumKeyEx

Enumeration involves cycling through either the subkeys or the values of an open key to retrieve information about them. This is done either because the application does not know in advance all of the keys or values that may be present, or because the application is interested in some or all of the open key's subkeys or values.

For example, a program may need to retrieve the names of all registered file extensions. These file extensions are stored as the names of *some* of the direct subkeys of HKEY_CLASSES_ROOT. But because subkeys are organized in no particular order (or, more precisely, because they're stored in the order in which they were written to the key), the program has to enumerate each subkey of HKEY_CLASSES_ROOT to find out what keys are present.

The Win32 API provides two functions for this purpose. The first, a "compatibility" function inherited from the Win16 API, is *RegEnumKey*. Its syntax is:

```
LONG RegEnumKey( hKey, dwIndex, lpName, cbName ) ;
```

Its parameters are:

HKEY	*hKey*	Handle of the key whose subkeys are being enumerated. It can be either one of the predefined keys listed earlier in Table 4-2 or a handle returned by one of the registry open key functions. Under WinNT, it should have been opened with KEY_ENUMERATE_SUB_KEYS access.
DWORD	*dwIndex*	Index of the subkey to query.
LPTSTR	*lpName*	Pointer to a string buffer in which *RegEnumKey* will write the subkey name if the function succeeds.
DWORD	*cbName*	Length of the *lpName* buffer, which must include space for the terminating NULL character. Note that, in contrast to *RegEnumKeyEx*, the parameter is passed by value (*cbName*) rather than by reference (*lpcbName*).

RegEnumKeyEx, the "official" Win32 function, provides access to some NT-specific information about each key, namely its class name and when the last write to the key occurred. Its syntax and parameters are:

```
LONG RegEnumKeyEx( hKey, dwIndex, lpName, lpcbName, lpReserved, lpClass,
lpcbClass, lpftLastWriteTime ) ;
```

HKEY	*hKey*	Handle of the key whose subkeys are being enumerated. It can be either one of the predefined keys listed earlier in Table 4-2 or a handle returned by one of the registry open key functions. Under WinNT, it should have been opened with KEY_ENUMERATE_SUB_KEYS access.
DWORD	*dwIndex*	Index of the subkey to query.
LPTSTR	*lpName*	Pointer to a string buffer in which *RegEnumKeyEx* will write the subkey name if the function succeeds.
LPDWORD	*lpcbName*	Pointer to a variable indicating the size of the *lpName* string buffer, which must include space for the terminating NULL character. When the function returns, its value represents the number of bytes written to the buffer, *not* including the terminating null.
LPDWORD	*lpReserved*	Reserved; must be NULL.
LPTSTR	*lpClass*	Pointer to a string buffer in which the function will write the subkey's class name. Its value can be NULL if the function should not retrieve the subkey's class name. Under Win95, this parameter is not used.
LPDWORD	*lpcbClass*	Pointer to a DWORD value that indicates the size of *lpClass*. When the function returns, its value indicates the number of bytes written to the *lpClass* buffer, *excluding* the terminating NULL character. Its value can be NULL if the function should not retrieve the subkey's class name. Under Win95, this parameter is not used.
PFILETIME	*lpftLast-WriteTime*	Pointer to a FILETIME structure that receives the time the subkey was last written to; *RegEnumKeyEx* uses this parameter only when running under WinNT. The FILETIME structure is listed in Table 4-6.

RegEnumKeyEx differs from *RegEnumKey*, in other words, by the addition of some WinNT-specific information on the subkey's class name and the time that a write to the subkey last occurred, and by the inclusion of a reserved parameter. None of these is particularly significant, at least for local registry access. Of greater interest is the *lpcbName* parameter, which corresponds to the *cbName* parameter in *RegEnumKey*. In *RegEnumKey*, *cbName* is passed by value; that is, it can be a variable or a constant that represents the length of the string buffer passed to the function, but *RegEnumKey* will not update it to reflect the number of bytes that the function writes to the buffer. In contrast, *cbName* is passed by reference to *RegEnumKeyEx*, and its value, once the function terminates, represents the number of bytes written to the string buffer, excluding a terminating null character. This information is useful whenever you need to know how many characters have been written to the buffer. It is particularly useful, though, if you program in a language like Visual Basic; knowing the actual length of the string eliminates the need to parse the string buffer to extract the null-terminated string written by the function.

Table 4-7. The registry API and the terminating null character

Function/Parameter	Status of Terminating Null When:			
	Calling Function		Function Returns	
	Included	Excluded	Included	Excluded
RegQueryInfoKey				
Subkey Name	N/A		X	
Value Name	N/A			X
Value	N/A		X	
RegEnumKey				
Subkey Name	X		N/A	
RegEnumKeyEx				
Subkey Name	X			X
RegEnumValue				
Value Name	X			X
Data Value	X		X	
RegQueryValue				
Data Value	X		X	
RegQueryValueEx				
Data Value	X		X	
RegSetValue				
Data Value		X	N/A	
RegSetValueEx				
Data Value	X		N/A	

Although this indicator of the number of characters actually written to `lpName`, in our opinion, makes *RegEnumKeyEx* a more convenient function to use than *RegEnumKey*, it is also important to keep in mind that `lpcbName` is not a "self-correcting" parameter. That is, if the fun ction returns `ERROR_MORE_DATA` to indicate that the buffer is too small to hold the name of a particular subkey, `lpcbName` is not updated to reflect the actual number of characters in the current subkey's name. This makes it particularly important to make sure that your application allocates in advance a sufficiently large buffer to accommodate the largest subkey name (available from *RegQueryInfoKey*, described earlier in this chapter) *plus* the terminating null character.

Each call to either the *RegEnumKey* or *RegEnumKeyEx* function retrieves the name of one subkey. Hence, enumerating subkeys involves placing the function call inside a loop and using `dwIndex` as the loop counter for each call to the function. There are three ways to do this:

- Use the `while` statement to enumerate the subkeys until the return value of the function no longer equals `ERROR_SUCCESS`. This method eliminates the

Those Cursed Terminating Nulls...

One of the things that developers don't like about the registry API is its inconsistent inclusion of the terminating null in character counts. In some cases, variables that indicate the number of characters written to a buffer include it; in other cases, they don't. Figuring out when they do and when they don't seems hopelessly confusing, particularly if you look at the use of the terminating null on a function-by-function basis. This makes the functions difficult to commit to memory, and requires that either an online or a printed reference guide to the Win32 SDK always be kept handy.

Either you need to supply the number of bytes when calling a registry function or a function returns with a byte count in three particular cases:

- When you are retrieving a key's name
- When you are retrieving a value entry name
- When you are retrieving a value entry's data

We haven't discussed all of the functions that do these things yet, but quickly introducing some regularity into the registry API seems sufficiently important to mention them at this point. If you examine Table 4-7, which shows how individual functions in the registry API handle the terminating null character, a pattern *almost* emerges, which may make it easier to remember and to use the functions.

- When you initialize a buffer that a function uses to write a string value, you should always include room for the terminating null character.

- When you declare the size of a buffer in which the function will write a string value, you should always include a null character in the count. (The sole exception to this is *RegSetValue*, a "compatibility" function that is superseded by *RegSetValueEx*.)

- If you are retrieving a key name or a value name, the terminating null is excluded from the byte count returned by the function. (The sole exception to this is *RegQueryInfoKey*, which includes the terminating null in the byte count for the longest subkey name; this is probably unintentional behavior, though.)

- When you are reading a value entry's data, the registry function always includes the terminating null in the character count if the data is string data.

need to use *RegQueryInfo* key to determine the number of subkeys. But since it involves executing the statements inside the `while` loop at least once, the loop should include some conditional logic to handle keys that have no subkeys.

- Use the `for` statement to initialize the loop counter to 0, then increment it for each iteration until it becomes one less than the value of the *lpcSubKey* variable returned by the *RegQueryInfoKey* function.

- Use the `for` statement to initialize the loop counter to one less than the value of the *lpcSubKey* variable returned by the *RegQueryInfoKey* function, then decrement it until it reaches 0.

In each of the last two cases, the loop will not execute if the key contains no subkeys.

Officially, the ordering of subkeys within the registry is undefined. Actually, subkeys are retrieved in the order in which they were first written to a key. But since this order is, in most cases, beyond your application's control, your application generally should make no assumptions about the order in which particular subkeys occur when it enumerates subkeys.

The *FillList* function in Example 4-7 uses the second method of enumeration to retrieve the names of the subkeys of HKEY_CURRENT_USER\AppEvents\ EventLabels in order to extract the names of system sound events and display them in a list box. (For a discussion of the organization of the registry to handle sounds, see Chapter 9, *What Goes in the Registry: Application and User Settings.*) The call to *RegQueryInfoKey* determines both how many subkeys there are (which *FillList* stores to the *nSubkeys* variable) and how many characters are in the longest subkey name (stored to *nSubkeyNameLen*). This latter variable is incremented by one to accommodate each name's terminating null character, and is then used to allocate a buffer (*lpBuffer)* that is large enough to hold the longest subkey name. The `for` loop then iterates *nSubkeys* times. Within the `for` loop, the *dwBufSize* variable is updated at each pass of the loop to reflect the correct buffer size, since it is passed by reference to *RegEnumKeyEx*, which modifies it to reflect the number of characters actually written to the buffer. *FillList* must reset `dwBufSize` each time to the correct buffer size; otherwise, its value would diminish, causing the function to return an ERROR_MORE_DATA error. *RegEnumKeyEx* then places the name of each subkey in *lpBuffer*, and its contents are added to the list box by the *SendMessage* function.

Example 4-7. Building a list box containing the names of system sound events

```
#include <windows.h>

VOID FillList(HWND hWnd)
    {
    HKEY hKey ;
    HANDLE hHeap ;
    DWORD dwIndex, dwBufSize, nSubkeys, nSubkeyNameLen ;
    LPTSTR lpBuffer ;
    // Open sound event labels key
```

Example 4-7. Building a list box containing the names of system sound events (continued)

```
if (RegOpenKey(HKEY_CURRENT_USER,"AppEvents\\EventLabels",
               &hKey ) == ERROR_SUCCESS )
   {
   // Determine number of keys to enumerate
   RegQueryInfoKey(hKey, NULL, NULL, NULL, &nSubkeys,
                   &nSubkeyNameLen, NULL, NULL, NULL,
                   NULL, NULL, NULL ) ;
   // Allocate memory
   hHeap = GetProcessHeap() ;
   lpBuffer = HeapAlloc(hHeap, 0, ++nSubkeyNameLen) ;

   // Retrieve Registry values
   for (dwIndex = 0 ; dwIndex < nSubkeys; dwIndex++)
      {
      dwBufSize = nSubkeyNameLen ;
      RegEnumKeyEx(hKey, dwIndex, lpBuffer, &dwBufSize,
                   NULL, NULL, NULL, NULL) ;
      // Add sound event to list box
      SendMessage(hWnd, LB_ADDSTRING, 0, (LPARAM)(LPCTSTR) lpBuffer);
      }
   RegCloseKey(hKey) ;
   HeapFree(hHeap, 0, lpBuffer) ;
   }
return ;
}
```

System Sound Events and Windows NT

This program in Example 4-7 runs under Windows 95 only, since the organization of sound information in the Windows NT registry is considerably different. Windows NT 3.x stores the names of sound events, as well as their associated sound files, as value entries in HKCU\Control Panel\Sounds. This is a problem of registry "policy vs. mechanism," as discussed in Chapter 1.

If you're enumerating keys on a remote registry, it's important to note an anomaly in the behavior of *RegEnumKeyEx*. For local registry access, the *lpReserved* parameter is ignored by *WINAPI32.DLL*; provided that the remaining parameters are all correct, the function still returns ERROR_SUCCESS if you provide a value of NULL, 0, or a pointer to a DWORD as the value of *lpReserved*. It is not ignored, though, for remote registry access; *RegEnumKeyEx* returns ERROR_INVALID_PARAMETER if the value of *lpReserved* is not NULL or 0. If you're programming in Visual Basic, this means that you want to be sure to pass the *lpReserved* parameter by value, as in the following line of code:

```
Call RegEnumKeyEx(hKey, lngIndex, strBuffer, lngBufSize, BYVAL 0,
          0, 0, udtFiletime)
```

Finally, the process of enumerating all of a key's subkeys is not atomic—that is, Windows 95 does not guarantee that all of the keys will be in the same state when you finish your enumeration as when you begin it. This means that you should not make changes to keys while you are enumerating them. It also means that your application should be prepared to handle unexpected changes (made by other applications) to the keys that it is iterating. For details, see "Registry Locking" later in this chapter.

Enumerating a Key's Values: RegEnumValue

Besides enumerating the subkeys of a key, you can also enumerate its values. Because the Win31 registry supported only a single value per key, there is no "compatibility" function to enumerate values: there are no values to enumerate in Win31. Instead, there is only a single function in the Win32 API, *RegEnumValue*:

```
LONG RegEnumValue( hKey, dwIndex, lpValueName, lpcbValueName,
                lpReserved, lpdwType, lpData, lpcbData ) ;
```

HKEY	*hKey*	Handle of the key whose values are being enumerated. It can be either one of the predefined keys listed earlier in Table 4-2 or a handle returned by one of the registry open key functions. Under WinNT, it should have been opened with KEY_QUERY_VALUE access.
DWORD	*dwIndex*	Index of the subkey to query.
LPTSTR	*lpValueName*	Pointer to a string buffer in which *RegEnumValue* will write the name of the value entry if the function succeeds.
LPDWORD	*lpcbValueName*	Pointer to a variable indicating the length of the *lpVal-ueName* buffer passed to the function, including its terminating null character. When the function returns, its value represents the number of bytes written to the buffer, not including the terminating null. This is not a "self-correcting" parameter. That is, if the function succeeds, *lpcbValueName* indicates the number of bytes written to *lpValueName*; if it fails, though, *lpcb-ValueName* is unchanged.
LPDWORD	*lpReserved*	Reserved; must be NULL.
LPDWORD	*lpdwType*	Pointer to a DWORD that the function uses to indicate the type of data stored to the value entry; otherwise, if the data type is not needed by the application, this parameter can be NULL. The data types supported by the Win95 registry are listed in Table 4-7.
LPBYTE	*lpData*	Pointer to a buffer in which the function will store the value entry's data. If the value is not required, this parameter can be NULL.

LPDWORD *lpcbData*   Pointer to a DWORD value indicating the size (length in
                                   bytes) of the buffer for value data. If the function
                                   completes successfully, *cbData* contains the number of
                                   bytes written to the buffer. If *lpData* is NULL, this
                                   parameter must also be NULL.

Table 4-8. Win95 and WinNT registry data types

Constant	Value	Explanation
REG_BINARY	3	Binary data in any form. Although a single binary value in the Win95 registry can occupy as many as 16,364 bytes, Microsoft recommends that, for performance reasons, 2K serve as a practical limit on the size of binary data; larger data structures should be stored in separate files, with the registry used to point to these. In practice, the largest binary values rarely exceed 1K; most entries are four bytes, while the average size of large entries larger than 4 bytes is typically about 150 bytes.
REG_DWORD	4	A 32-bit (or 4-byte) number stored in REG_DWORD_LITTLE_ENDIAN format.
REG_DWORD_LITTLE_ ENDIAN	4	A 32-bit number in little-endian format (same as REG_DWORD). In little-endian format, the most significant byte of a word is the high-order byte, and the most significant word of a long integer is the high-order word. This is the most common format for computers running WinNT and Win95.
REG_DWORD_BIG_ENDIAN	5	A 32-bit number in big-endian format. In big-endian format, the most significant byte of a word is the low-order byte, and the most significant word of a long integer is the low-order word.
REG_EXPAND_SZ	2	A null-terminated string that contains unexpanded references to environment variables (for example, "%PATH%") that should be replaced with their values.
REG_FULL_RESOURCE_ DESCRIPTOR	9	In WinNT only, a list of hardware resources actually used by a physical device. These data are written to the subkeys of HKLM\HARDWARE\Description by the operating system during initialization and are reserved for use by the system.
REG_LINK	6	A *symbolic link* under WinNT. WinNT uses symbolic links, which create an association between a logical name and a device's object name, to manage and identify devices. Symbolic links are defined by the Windows I/O Manager *IoCreateSymbolicLink* function.
REG_MULTI_SZ	7	An array of null-terminated strings, terminated by an additional null character to mark the end of the array.

Table 4-8. Win95 and WinNT registry data types (continued)

Constant	Value	Explanation
REG_NONE	0	No defined value type. This does not mean that the data is of a type the registry API cannot recognize. Instead, the value of `lpData` is generally REG_NONE when the registry function fails.
REG_RESOURCE_ REQUIREMENTS_LIST	10	In WinNT only, a list of possible hardware resources a device driver or one of the physical devices it controls can use. It is written to the subkeys of HKLM\Hardware\ResourceMap during initialization when a device driver calls the Hardware Abstraction Layer's *HalAssignSlotResources* function or the I/O Manager's *IoAssignResources* function.
REG_RESOURCE_LIST	8	In WinNT only, a list of the hardware resources used by a device driver or the physical devices it controls. It is written to the subkeys of HKLM\Hardware\ResourceMap during initialization when a device driver successfully calls the HAL *HalAssignSlotResources* function or the IO/Manager *IoAssignResources* or *IoReportResourceUsage* functions.
REG_SZ	1	A null-terminated string.

Enumerating a key's value entries is virtually identical to enumerating its subkeys. The function returns information about a single value entry at a time. Therefore, to gather information about all of a key's value entries, you must use one of the three kinds of looping structures discussed above in "Enumerating Keys: RegEnumKey and RegEnumKeyEx."

Like enumerating keys, the process of enumerating a key's value entries is not atomic; Win95 makes no guarantees that the value entries and their data will be the same when you finish your enumeration as when you begin it. Consequently, you should not modify value entries as you enumerate them. Of course, some other application is free to modify them as you enumerate, so your application should be prepared to handle unexpected changes to the value entries that it is enumerating. For details, see "Registry Locking" later in this chapter.

As you may recall from the discussion of the Win95 registry's structure in Chapter 1, a key can have two different kinds of value entries: the default value, which must be a string (REG_SZ) data type; or a complete value entry that consists of a value name and its associated value, which can be any valid data type supported by the Win95 registry, as shown in Table 4-8. If a default value is present, it is always located in the first ordinal position; that is, it is the value retrieved when *dwIndex* equals zero. If there is no default value, however, a complete value entry, if one is present, is stored in the first ordinal position. It is also possible for a key to have *no* values to enumerate; the loop that repeatedly executes *RegEnumValue* must also be capable of dealing with such value-less (but not necessarily valueless) keys.

According to the *Microsoft Windows 95 Resource Kit*, there is a limit of about 64K on the number of bytes in a single value entry. In fact, however, we've found that the actual limit applies not to the data entry as a whole (that is, not to the total amount of space consumed by the structure of the value entry and its data), but to the number of bytes of data assigned to that value entry. (This applies, really, to value entries whose data types support variable amounts of data, like the various string data types and the REG_BINARY data type; REG_DWORD and REG_DWORD_BIG_ENDIAN data always occupy four bytes.) That limit, moreover, is actually 16K bytes—considerably lower than the 64K limit mentioned in the Resource Kit, but more than adequate for holding the kinds of data that you might store in the registry.

The diverse data types supported by the registry frequently require special handling. The following points are worth keeping in mind when working with particular data types:

REG_EXPAND_SZ

Like MS-DOS, Win95 supports environment variables, such as TEMP (the location in which Windows stores temporary files), WINDIR (the location of the Windows directory), or, for C/C++ programmers, INCLUDE (the location of C/C++ header files). Actually, environment variables are of two kinds: *system-level environment variables* that are typically defined by Win95 automatically or by statements in the *MSDOS.SYS* and *AUTOEXEC.BAT* files; and *registry-defined environment variables* that are stored as value entries of the HKCU\Environment and possibly the HKLM\System\CurrentControlSet\Control\SessionManager\Environment keys. The REG_EXPAND_SZ data type allows you to make use of these variables. Within a registry value, unexpanded environment variable names are delimited by two % characters (e.g., %WINDIR%). However, *RegEnumValue* does not expand these automatically when it writes a value to the *lpData* buffer. Instead, the system-level environment variable names can be expanded by passing *lpData* as a parameter to the *ExpandEnvironmentStrings* function. Its syntax is:

```
DWORD ExpandEnvironmentStrings(lpSrc, lpDst, nSize);
```

where *lpSrc* is a pointer to the original unexpanded (REG_EXPAND_SZ) string, *lpDst* is a pointer to the buffer to which the function writes the expanded string, and *nSize* is the total size of *lpDst*. If the function is unable to expand *lpSrc*, it simply copies the original string to *lpDst*. The function returns the number of characters written to *lpDst*. If you need to determine whether *ExpandEnvironmentStrings* has expanded *lpStr*, you should compare the strings themselves, not the lengths of the two strings, since it is possible for an expanded string to be the same length as or even shorter than an unexpanded string. Registry-defined environment variables are not expanded by *ExpandEnvironmentStrings*; if you want to expand them, you'll have to retrieve the variable's value from the registry, extract the environment variable name, and replace it with its value.

REG_SZ

In theory, the difference between the REG_SZ and REG_EXPAND_SZ strings is that the latter contain "macros" (environment variables that are to be replaced with their values), whereas the former do not. In practice, the Win95 registry contains several REG_SZ value entries that contain unexpanded environment variable names; this is true in particular of many of the value entries stored in the subkeys of HKLM\SOFTWARE\Microsoft\Windows\CurrentVersion\MS-DOSOptions. This means that, if you use *RegEnumValue* to retrieve a value that contains a pathname, you cannot assume that it is fully expanded just because its data type is REG_SZ. Instead, potential pathnames should be passed as parameters to the *ExpandEnvironmentStrings* function, as the following code fragment illustrates:

```
RegQueryValue( hKey, dwIndex, (LPTR)lpValueName, &cbValueName, NULL,
               &lpType, (LPTR)lpData, &cbData ) ;
if (lpType == REG_SZ )
   {
   nStrSize = ExpandEnvironmentStrings(lpData,(LPTR)lpDest, 256) ;
   if (strncmp( lpDest, lpData, nStrSize) != 0 ) // if expanded…
      strcpy(lpData, lpDest) ;                   // …copy it back
   }
```

Unfortunately, this works only for system-level environment variables; it does not expand environment variables that are defined in the registry. If you're certain that a REG_SZ value still contains unexpanded strings after you've called *ExpandEnvironmentStrings* or you know in advance that an unexpanded string is defined in the registry, you'll have to expand it yourself.

REG_DWORD_BIG_ENDIAN

REG_DWORD (or REG_DWORD_LITTLE_ENDIAN) values are standard Intel-format long integers. That is, they are stored as 4-byte values with the lower-order bytes sequentially preceding the higher-order bytes in memory. (They're called "little-endian" because the little end of the number is stored first; for further details, see Jonathan Swift, *Gulliver's Travels*.) REG_DWORD_BIG_ENDIAN values reverse this order: they are stored as 4-byte values with the higher-order bytes sequentially preceding the lower-order bytes. Intel x86-based computers support little-endian architecture exclusively, though big-endian architecture is used extensively in networking protocols (most notably in TCP/IP), on the Motorola family of processors, and on many RISC systems. REG_DWORD_BIG_ENDIAN data in the registry is extremely rare; however, if you do encounter it, *RegEnumValue* seamlessly handles its conversion to a little-endian value if you assign the data to a long integer.

REG_BINARY

Typically, binary data has no inherent interpretation, and instead has meaning primarily to the application that stored it in the registry in the first place. There are, however, two kinds of binary data: *structured binary data*, in which a value corresponds to a system or application-defined data structure (like the Win32 WINDOWPOS structure, for example); and *free-form binary data*, in which a value consists of a series of bytes that are to be manipulated individually (like a string of flags) or in their totality (like a patch to be applied to an executable file). If the number of bytes of REG_BINARY data is 4 or less (which it very typically is), you can *possibly* interpret it as a DWORD, as shown in the following code fragment from a character-mode registry dumper:

```
void printvalue(DWORD type, char *data, DWORD cb) {
    switch (type) {
        // ...
        case REG_BINARY:
            printf("BIN (%d bytes) ", cb);
            switch (cb) {
                case 1: printf("[%02Xh] ", *((BYTE *) data)); break;
                case 2: printf("[%04Xh] ", *((WORD *) data)); break;
                case 4: printf("[%081Xh] ", *((DWORD *) data)); break;
                default:
                    putchar('\n');
                    dump(data, cb, "%04X", 0, 16);
                    break;
            }
            break;
        // ...
    }
}
```

The basic problem of *RegEnumValue* is that it writes a collection of bytes to lpData. Interpreting that sequence of bytes in a meaningful way—as a DWORD, as a string, or as a structured data type stored in binary format—is frequently challenging, particularly since you often don't know in advance precisely what data type lpData represents. As a result, exactly how you use *RegEnumValue* depends on the particular values that you want to enumerate and on the programming language that you're using. Because it returns a wealth of information about the value entries belonging to the open key, *RegEnumValue* can be used in three different ways:

- *To gather all available information about a collection of similar value entries.* Frequently, the value entries belonging to a subkey form a coherent collection, like the value entries of HKLM\System\CurrentControlSet\Control\VMM32Files, which list the component virtual device drivers (VxDs) contained within the 32-bit Virtual Machine Manager, *VMM32.VXD*. In addition, the data type of each value is generally the same, and most often it is string (REG_SZ or REG_EXPAND_SZ) data. In this case, you can use *RegEnumValue* to gather all available information about each value entry, then process the data as needed.

- *To gather information about value names and data types.* If you're interested in only some subset of the value entries, or are not completely sure of the value names and their data types, you can use *RegEnumValue* to retrieve this information while leaving the lpData and lpcbData parameters NULL. Once you know the name of a particular value entry and its data type, you can then use *RegQueryValue* or *RegQueryValueEx* (both of which are discussed later) to retrieve its value. This approach is the easiest, since it makes handling the varied data types stored as registry values significantly easier; it also represents the "official" way to use *RegEnumValue*.

- *To gather all available information about a value entry.* Frequently, you're interested in all of the values belonging to a particular subkey, but you may not know the precise names of the value entries, and their data may be of disparate types. In this case, if you're programming in C or C++, the most efficient approach is to define a union that can accommodate each of the data types found in the registry and to use it as the value of the lpData parameter to the *RegEnumValue* function.

Example 4-8, which enumerates all the value entries of HKEY_CURRENT_USER\Software\Microsoft\Windows\CurrentVersion\Policies\Explorer, shows how this might be done using C. (Incidentally, because it relies on registry settings created by the Explorer and the Windows shell, the program does not run under WinNT 3.x.)

Example 4-8. Defining a union to hold registry values

```c
#include <windows.h>
#include <stdlib.h>
#include <stdio.h>
#include <string.h>

int APIENTRY WinMain(HANDLE hInstance, HANDLE hPrevInstance,
                LPSTR lpszCmdLine, int nCmdShow)
    {
    // define union for Registry data types
    union ventry {
        DWORD dw ;          // REG_DWORD, REG_DWORD_LITTLE_ENDIAN
        CHAR sz[256] ;      // REG_SZ
        CHAR esz[256] ;     // REG_EXPAND_SZ
        CHAR bin[1024] ;    // REG_BINARY
        CHAR dwbig[4] ;     // REG_DWORD_BIG_ENDIAN
        CHAR msz[2048] ;    // REG_MULTI_SZ
    } ventry1;
```

Example 4-8. Defining a union to hold registry values (continued)

```
// define variables
unsigned int i ;
signed int ctr ;
LONG lngRegError = ERROR_SUCCESS ;
HKEY hOpenKey ;
DWORD dwIndex = 0, cbValueName, dwType, cbValue, nStrSize ;
CHAR lpTemp[20], lpValueName[32], msg[512] ;

// Open a Registry key
RegOpenKey(HKEY_LOCAL_MACHINE,
    "Software\\Microsoft\\Windows\\CurrentVersion",
    &hOpenKey) ;
// Enumerate key's values
while (lngRegError == ERROR_SUCCESS)
    {
    memset(msg, 0, sizeof(msg)) ;
    cbValueName = 32 ;
    cbValue = sizeof(ventry1) ;
    if ((lngRegError = RegEnumValue( hOpenKey, dwIndex++,
                lpValueName, &cbValueName, NULL, &dwType,
                (LPBYTE) &ventry1, &cbValue )) == ERROR_SUCCESS)
        {
        // Display the data type in a message box
        switch (dwType)
            {
            case REG_SZ:
                // We actually should use ExpandEnvironmentStrings
                // here, but we won't
                MessageBox(NULL, ventry1.sz, lpValueName, MB_OK ) ;
                break ;
            case REG_EXPAND_SZ:
                nStrSize = ExpandEnvironmentStrings(ventry1.esz,
                            msg, 256) ;
                MessageBox(NULL, msg, lpValueName, MB_OK ) ;
                break ;
            case REG_MULTI_SZ:
                strcpy(msg, "String Array: \n    ") ;
                for (i = 0; i < cbValue - 1; i++)
                    {
                    if ((BYTE)ventry1.bin[i] != 0)
                        sprintf(lpTemp, "%c", (BYTE)ventry1.bin[i]) ;
                    else
                        sprintf(lpTemp,"\n    ", (BYTE)ventry1.bin[i]) ;
                    strcat(msg, lpTemp) ;
                    }
                MessageBox(NULL, msg, lpValueName, MB_OK ) ;
                break ;
            case REG_DWORD:
                sprintf(msg, "Long: %ld", ventry1.dw) ;
                MessageBox(NULL, msg, lpValueName, MB_OK ) ;
                break ;
            case REG_DWORD_BIG_ENDIAN:
                strcpy(msg, "Big Endian: ") ;
```

Example 4-8. Defining a union to hold registry values (continued)

```
                    for (ctr = 3; ctr >= 0; ctr--)
                        {
                        sprintf(lpTemp, "%02X ", (BYTE)ventry1.dwbig[ctr]) ;
                        strcat(msg, lpTemp) ;
                        }
                    MessageBox(NULL, msg, lpValueName, MB_OK) ;
                    break ;
                case REG_BINARY:
                    strcpy(msg, "Binary: ") ;
                    for (i = 0; i < cbValue; i++)
                        {
                        sprintf(lpTemp, "%02X ", (BYTE)ventry1.bin[i]) ;
                        strcat( msg, lpTemp) ;
                        }
                    MessageBox(NULL, msg, lpValueName, MB_OK ) ;
                    break ;
                default:
                    MessageBox(NULL, "Unknown data value", lpValueName, MB_OK )
;
                }
            }
        }
    return 0 ;
    }
```

If you're enumerating value entries on a remote registry, *RegEnumValue* shares the same anomaly as the *RegEnumKeyEx* function discussed earlier: `lpReserved` must always be NULL. In addition, if the value entry that the function enumerates contains REG_SZ data, the value of `lpcbData` is one greater than the actual size of the buffer required to retrieve the data or than the number of bytes actually written to the buffer. For instance, if *RegEnumValue* retrieves the value of the `ProductType` entry in `HKLM\Software\Microsoft\Windows\Current-Version` and its value is the string "2", *RegEnumKey* returns with a value of 3 for the buffer size.[*] If you're using *RegEnumValue* to allocate the proper buffer before calling *RegQueryValueEx* to retrieve the value, this isn't a problem. If you're using it to retrieve the data as well, it can be, particularly if you're using a language like Visual Basic and use the value of `lpcbData` to "trim" the string; the final, unnecessary byte typically contains garbage.

Retrieving a Specific Value: RegQueryValue and RegQueryValueEx

Generally, you'll want to enumerate a key's values if you want to retrieve a collection of data, or if you're uncertain about the values belonging to that key. In the

---

[*] The correct value in this example would be two: one byte to hold the "2", and a second byte for the null character.

latter case, you can use the values that the *RegEnumValue* function stores to the *lpValueName* and *lpType* variables to retrieve the data belonging to a specific value entry. In addition, much of the time, you don't want to cycle through the value entries belonging to a particular key, since you know in advance which ones interest you. In these two cases, you can use either the *RegQueryValue* or *RegQueryValueEx* functions to access a particular value.

RegQueryValue is the "compatibility" function found in the Win16 API; it is capable of retrieving only the default (or unnamed) string value of a particular key. Its syntax is:

```
LONG RegQueryValue( hKey, lpszSubkey, lpszValue, pcbValue ) ;
```

HKEY	*hKey*	A valid handle to a registry key. It can be either one of the predefined keys listed earlier in Table 4-2 or a handle returned by one of the registry open key functions. Under WinNT, it should have been opened with KEY_QUERY_VALUE access.
LPCTSTR	*lpszSubKey*	Pointer to a string containing the name of a subkey whose (unnamed) default value is to be retrieved. If the value of this parameter is NULL, the function retrieves the default value of the open key.
LPTSTR	*lpszValue*	Pointer to a buffer in which the function will store the string data assigned to the subkey's default value. The buffer should be large enough to include the terminating null. If this parameter is NULL, the function will merely update *pcbValue* to reflect the total length of the string data.
PLONG	*pcbValue*	Pointer to a LONG value indicating the size (length in bytes) of the buffer for the default string value. When the function returns, *pcbValue* contains the number of bytes written to the buffer, *including* the terminating null character. If *lpszValue* is NULL, *pcbValue* indicates the size of the buffer needed to successfully retrieve *lpszValue*.

Although it's a "compatibility" function, *RegQueryValue* is not completely compatible with its Win16 equivalent. In particular, the following code fragment under Win32 allows you to determine the size of a buffer before you actually retrieve a registry value:

```
if (RegOpenKey(HKEY_CLASSES_ROOT, lpSubkey, &hKey)==ERROR_SUCCESS) ;
   {
   RegQueryValue(hKey, NULL, NULL, &cbValue) ;
   hHeap = GetProcessHeap() ;
   lpValue = HeapAlloc(hHeap, 0, cbValue) ;

   RegQueryValue(hKey, "", lpValue, &cbValue ) ;
   MessageBox(NULL, lpValue, lpSubkey, MB_OK) ;

   RegCloseKey(hKey) ;
   HeapFree(hHeap, 0, lpValue) ;
   }
```

Under Win31, this first variation of the call to the *RegQueryValue* function is not supported.

But also because it's a compatibility function, *RegQueryValue* has one major idiosyncrasy that distinguishes it from the "standard" Win32 registry API: it does not require that the key whose value is being queried be open. Unlike most of the registry functions, which operate only on objects (keys or values) belonging to the open key, *RegQueryValue* works either on a value belonging to the open key or on a value belonging to any subkey of the open key. If the value of `lpsz-SubKey` is NULL, the function behaves as expected by retrieving the default value of the open key designated by `hKey`. On the other hand, if `lpszSubKey` is not NULL and is a valid path to a subkey of `hKey`, the function retrieves the default value of that subkey, even though it isn't open. For example, both of the following code fragments retrieve the default value of the `HKEY_CLASSES_ROOT\CLSID` key:

```
RegOpenKey(HKEY_CLASSES_ROOT, "CLSID", &hKey) ;
RegQueryValue(hKey, NULL, lpszValue, &cbValue) ;
RegCloseKey(hKey) ;

RegQueryValue( HKEY_CLASSES_ROOT, "CLSID", lpszValue, &cbValue ) ;
```

This somewhat confusing (though convenient) ability to operate on an unopened key has led to an error in the documentation for *RegQueryValue*. The documentation states that, if `lpszValue` is NULL or a pointer to an empty string, the function retrieves the default value "set by the *RegSetValue* function for the key identified by `hKey`." In fact, its operation is unrelated to *RegSetValue*, the "compatibility" function that can be used for assigning a default value to a particular key. Instead, if `lpszValue` is NULL, the function behaves like a "conventional" member of the registry API by retrieving the default value of the registry key whose handle is `hKey`.

RegQueryValue shares an additional peculiarity with *RegQueryValueEx*, the "official" Win32 value retrieval function: both can return `ERROR_SUCCESS` even though they fail. This is covered in greater depth in the discussion of *RegQueryValueEx*.

Finally, there is an additional error in some of the documentation on *RegQuery-Value*. According to the overview of the registry API in the *Win32 Programmer's Reference*, if *RegQueryValue* encounters an unexpanded environment variable name in a key's default value, it expands it into its value when it writes to the `szValue` buffer. But this seems unusual: since the *RegQueryValue* function cannot handle any data type other than `REG_SZ`, the function would either have to parse every value for an unexpanded variable name or simply pass every value to the *ExpandEnvironmentStrings* function—a fairly substantial amount of overhead for what is actually a relatively simple function. And in fact, the documentation is incorrect: *RegQueryValue* does not expand environment variable names. (Neither does *RegQueryValueEx*, as the documentation in this case correctly notes.)

In contrast to *RegQueryValue*, the operation of *RegQueryValueEx* is more in keeping with the spirit of the current registry functions. Its syntax is:

```
LONG RegQueryValueEx( hKey, lpszValueName, lpdwReserved, lpdwType,
                      lpbData, lpcbData ) ;
```

HKEY	*hKey*	Handle of the key whose value is being queried. It can be either one of the predefined keys listed earlier in Table 4-2 or a handle returned by one of the registry open key functions. Under WinNT, it should have been opened with KEY_QUERY_VALUE access.
LPTSTR	*lpszValueName*	Pointer to a string containing the name of the value to query. If this parameter is NULL or a pointer to a null string, the function retrieves the key's default value.
LPDWORD	*lpdwReserved*	Reserved; must be NULL.
LPDWORD	*lpdwType*	Pointer to a DWORD value that the function uses to indicate the type of data stored to the value entry; otherwise, if the data type is not needed by the application, this parameter can be NULL. The data types supported by the Win95 registry are listed in Table 4-7.
LPBYTE	*lpbData*	Pointer to a buffer in which the function will store the value entry's data. If the value is not required, this parameter can be NULL.
LPDWORD	*lpcbData*	Pointer to a DWORD value indicating the size (length in bytes) of *lpbData*. When the function returns, *cbData* contains the number of bytes written to the buffer. If *lpbData* is one of the string value types (REG_SZ, REG_EXPAND_SZ, or REG_MULTI_SZ), *lpcbData* *includes* the string's terminating null. If *lpData* is NULL, *lpcbData* can also be NULL. If it is not NULL, its value when the function returns indicates the size of the buffer necessary to hold the complete value, including its terminating null character if it is a string data type.

Like *RegQueryValue*, *RegQueryValueEx* can, when the function is retrieving the value of the open key's default (or unnamed) value, return ERROR_SUCCESS even when the function fails. If *szValueName* is NULL and the open key's default value is absent, the function returns ERROR_SUCCESS, modifies the value of *bData* so that it is a null string, and changes the value of *cbData* to 1. In contrast, when enumerating a key that has no complete value entries and no default value, *RegQueryValue* returns ERROR_NO_MORE_ITEMS.

To see how *RegQueryValueEx* might work, consider the case of an MRU list, which is usually implemented as follows: a value—usually named MRUList—contains "pointers" to either the value names or the subkeys that contain information on most recently used objects. For instance, an MRUList value of *baefc* indicates that information on the most recently used object is stored in a subkey or value entry whose name is b; the second most recently used object is stored in a subkey or value named a; and so on. Example 4-9[*] examines the registry's most recently used document list (which is stored in HKCU\Software\Microsoft\Windows\CurrentVersion\Explorer\RecentDocs) and adds their names to a window's File menu.

Example 4-9. An MRU menu list application using RegQueryValueEx

```
// Build an MRU list using RegQueryValueEx
#include <windows.h>
#include <stdlib.h>
#include <string.h>
#include <memory.h>
#include "mrumenu.h"

LRESULT CALLBACK WndProc (HWND hWnd, UINT uMsg, WPARAM wParam , LPARAM
    lParam) ;

int APIENTRY WinMain(HANDLE hInstance, HANDLE hPrevInstance,
    LPSTR lpszCmdLine, int nCmdShow)
    {
    unsigned int nMenuItem = 1 , nMenuID = 51 ;
    unsigned long nMRUCounter ;

    char bMRUList[25], bMRUPointer[5], bMenuItem[40] ;
    char bTemp[38], bMenuPos[5] ;
    char szClassName[] = "MRUMenu", *bMRUInfo ;
    HMENU hMenu, hFileMenu ;
    HANDLE hHeap ;
    HWND hWnd ;
    HKEY hKey ;
    LONG cbMaxValueLen, cbMRUList = 25, cbMRUInfo ;
    DWORD dwData ;
    MSG msg ;
    WNDCLASS wndclass ;

    // Define window class
    wndclass.style = CS_HREDRAW | CS_VREDRAW ;
    wndclass.lpfnWndProc = WndProc ;
    wndclass.cbClsExtra = 0 ;
    wndclass.cbWndExtra = 0 ;
    wndclass.hInstance = hInstance ;
    wndclass.hIcon = LoadIcon (NULL, IDI_APPLICATION) ;
    wndclass.hCursor = LoadCursor (NULL, IDC_ARROW) ;
    wndclass.hbrBackground = (HBRUSH) (COLOR_WINDOW + 1) ;
    wndclass.lpszMenuName = NULL ;
    wndclass.lpszClassName = szClassName ;
```

---

[*] Because it relies on registry settings created and maintained by the Windows 95 shell, this program does not work under WinNT 3.x.

Example 4-9. An MRU menu list application using RegQueryValueEx (continued)

```
RegisterClass (&wndclass) ;
// Define File menu
hMenu = CreateMenu() ;
hFileMenu = CreateMenu() ;

AppendMenu( hFileMenu, MF_STRING, IDM_NEW, "&New") ;
AppendMenu( hFileMenu, MF_STRING, IDM_OPEN, "&Open...") ;
AppendMenu( hFileMenu, MF_STRING, IDM_SAVE, "&Save") ;
AppendMenu( hFileMenu, MF_STRING, IDM_SAVEAS, "Save &As...") ;
AppendMenu( hFileMenu, MF_SEPARATOR, 0, NULL) ;
// Add MRU List
if (RegOpenKey(HKEY_CURRENT_USER,
"Software\\Microsoft\\Windows\\CurrentVersion\\Explorer\\RecentDocs",
            &hKey) == ERROR_SUCCESS )
   {
   // Determine maximum size of a value entry to set buffer size
   RegQueryInfoKey(hKey, NULL, NULL, NULL, NULL, NULL, NULL, NULL,
                 NULL, &cbMaxValueLen, NULL, NULL ) ;
   // Allocate buffer to MRU object information
   hHeap = GetProcessHeap() ;
   bMRUInfo = HeapAlloc(hHeap, 0, cbMaxValueLen ) ;
   // Get MRUList value
   RegQueryValueEx(hKey, "MRUList", NULL, NULL, bMRUList,
                  &cbMRUList) ;
   // Cycle through MRU objects
   for (nMRUCounter = 0; nMRUCounter < 5 && nMRUCounter + 1 <
       cbMRUList ;
       nMRUCounter++ )
     {
     // Get first through fifth pointer
     memcpy(bMRUPointer, bMRUList + nMRUCounter, 1 ) ;
     memcpy(bMRUPointer + 1, "\0", 1) ;
     cbMRUInfo = cbMaxValueLen ;
     // Retrieve MRU object information
     RegQueryValueEx(hKey, bMRUPointer, NULL, &dwData, bMRUInfo,
                  &cbMRUInfo) ;
     // Extract name of file from structure
     _memccpy(bTemp, bMRUInfo, '\0', cbMRUInfo) ;
     // Form menu item
     sprintf(bMenuItem, "&%d. %s", nMenuItem++, bTemp) ;
     AppendMenu( hFileMenu, MF_STRING, nMenuID++, bMenuItem) ;
     }
   // Close registry key
   RegCloseKey(hKey) ;
   // Free allocated memory
   HeapFree(hHeap, 0, bMRUInfo) ;
   }
if (nMenuID > 51) AppendMenu( hFileMenu, MF_SEPARATOR, 0, NULL ) ;
AppendMenu( hFileMenu, MF_STRING, IDM_EXIT, "E&xit") ;

AppendMenu (hMenu, MF_POPUP, (UINT) hFileMenu, "&File") ;
```

Example 4-9. An MRU menu list application using RegQueryValueEx (continued)

```
    // Create and display window
    hWnd = CreateWindow (szClassName, "Querying a Registry Value",
            WS_OVERLAPPEDWINDOW, CW_USEDEFAULT, CW_USEDEFAULT,
            CW_USEDEFAULT, CW_USEDEFAULT, NULL, hMenu, hInstance, NULL) ;
    ShowWindow (hWnd, nCmdShow) ;
    UpdateWindow (hWnd) ;
    // Message processing loop
    while (GetMessage (&msg, NULL, 0, 0))
        {
        TranslateMessage (&msg) ;
        DispatchMessage (&msg) ;
        }
    return msg.wParam ;
    }

// Message handler
LRESULT CALLBACK WndProc (HWND hWnd, UINT uMsg, WPARAM wParam ,
                    LPARAM lParam)
    {
    switch (uMsg)
        {
        case WM_CREATE: return 0 ;
        case WM_SETFOCUS: SetFocus (hWnd); return 0 ;
        case WM_DESTROY: PostQuitMessage (0) ; return 0 ;
        }
    return DefWindowProc (hWnd, uMsg, wParam, lParam) ;
    }
```

The program uses a header file, *MRUMENU.H*, to store the menu item identifiers for the *AppendMenu* function. It contains the following **#define** statements:

```
#define IDM_NEW        10
#define IDM_OPEN       20
#define IDM_SAVE       30
#define IDM_SAVEAS     40
#define IDM_EXIT       99

#define IDM_MRU1       51
#define IDM_MRU2       52
#define IDM_MRU3       53
#define IDM_MRU4       54
#define IDM_MRU5       55
```

Since the basic structure of the registry keys and the specific kinds of data that the application needs to retrieve are known in advance, the application can simply use *ReqQueryValueEx* to retrieve each value entry's data. The value of the only real unknown—the size of the buffer needed to store information about each file in the MRU list—is determined by the initial call to the *RegQueryInfoKey* function. Note that the function updates the value of a single parameter, *cbMaxValueLen*, while all the remaining parameters are NULL, since our program does not need the information that they provide. This value, in turn, is used to dynamically assign the size of the buffer for retrieving information on MRU objects by calling the *HeapAlloc* function.

Once this basic information is retrieved, the application can retrieve the value of `MRUList` and extract each character in turn. These characters serve as pointers to the value entries that contain information on a recently used file.

In this example, we've used *RegQueryInfoKey* to determine the size of the buffer needed for storing information; then we've used *HeapAlloc* to dynamically allocate memory for it. *RegQueryValue* and *RegQueryValueEx*, however, support an additional method of dynamically sizing a buffer. If either function is called with its `lpbData` parameter as NULL and `lpcbData` parameter as non-NULL, the function returns the number of bytes needed to store the value. Similarly, if the function is called with non-NULL values for both `lpbData` and `lpcbData` but the buffer is too small, the function returns `ERROR_MORE_DATA` and stores the total number of characters needed in the buffer to `lpcbData`.

This makes it possible to create self-correcting routines that allocate additional memory for themselves when needed. To take a very corny example, imagine that in building our MRU list we didn't want to call the *RegQueryInfoKey* to determine how many bytes should be allocated for MRU filenames; instead, we could just assume that all files have standard 8+3 names, and allocate 13 bytes for `bMRUInfo`. (Incidentally, quite independently of the probability that our application will encounter a long filename in the MRU list, our attempt to retrieve file information will fail because *RegQueryValueEx* here is actually retrieving a structured data type that contains more than a single filename.) However, just in case this doesn't work, we can examine the return value of *RegQueryValueEx* and, if it returns `ERROR_MORE_DATA`, reallocate memory for the `bMRUInfo` buffer. The `for` loop that is responsible for retrieving each MRU filename, and adding it to our application's File menu, then appears as follows:

```
// Cycle through MRU objects
for (nMRUCounter = 0; nMRUCounter < 5 && nMRUCounter + 1 <
    cbMRUList ; nMRUCounter++ )
  {
  // Get first through fifth pointer
  memcpy( bMRUPointer, bMRUList + nMRUCounter, 1 ) ;
  memcpy( bMRUPointer + 1, "\0", 1) ;
  cbMRUInfo = cbMaxValueLen ;
  // Retrieve MRU object information
  nRegErr = RegQueryValueEx(hKey, bMRUPointer, NULL, &dwData,
                        bMRUInfo, &cbMRUInfo ) ;
  if (nRegErr == ERROR_MORE_DATA)
     // Reallocate memory if buffer too small
     {
     cbMaxValueLen = cbMRUInfo ;
     HeapFree(hHeap, 0, bMRUInfo) ;
     hHeap = GetProcessHeap() ;
     bMRUInfo = HeapAlloc(hHeap, 0, cbMaxValueLen) ;
```

```
            nMRUCounter-- ;
            }
        else
            {
            // Extract name of file
            _memccpy(bTemp, bMRUInfo, '\0', cbMRUInfo ) ;
            // Form menu item
            sprintf(bMenuItem, "&%d. %s", nMenuItem++, bTemp) ;
            AppendMenu( hFileMenu, MF_STRING, nMenuID++, bMenuItem) ;
            }
        }
```

If you're using *RegQueryValueEx* to retrieve data from a remote registry, it's important that `lpdwReserved` be a null (or, if you're using Visual Basic, that a 0 be passed to the function using the BYVAL keyword); otherwise, the function returns ERROR_INVALID_PARAMETER. Unlike *RegEnumValue*, though, the value of `lpcbData` is correct when the function returns.

Retrieving Multiple Values: RegQueryMultipleValues

Although it is most common to retrieve a single registry value at a time, the Win32 API for Win95 also allows you to retrieve multiple values from a single open key with a single function, *RegQueryMultipleValues*. The function, though, is not currently supported by WinNT as of Version 3.51. It was implemented to support performance monitoring (when large amounts of related data must be gathered nearly simultaneously in order to be meaningful) and to facilitate remote registry access (it minimizes the performance bottlenecks involved in making multiple separate requests and data transfers over the network).

The major obstacle to using *RegQueryMultipleValues* is its lack of documentation: as a relatively late addition to the Win32 API, it is under-documented, and lacks a code sample in Microsoft Visual C++, the Win32 Software Development Kit, and the Win95 Device Driver Kit.

The syntax of *RegQueryMultipleValues* is:

```
LONG RegQueryMultipleValues(hKey, val_list, num_vals, lpValueBuff,
                            ldwTotsize ) ;
```

HKEY	*hKey*	Handle of the key whose values are to be retrieved. It can be either one of the predefined keys listed earlier in Table 4-2 or a handle returned by one of the registry open key functions.
PVALENT	*val_list*	Pointer to an array of **VALENT** structures, each element of which contains information on a single value entry. The structure is described in Table 4-7. When the function is called, the *ve_valuename* member of each structure must contain a pointer to the name of a value to retrieve. If the function returns successfully, the remaining members of each structure are updated to reflect the value entry.

DWORD	*num_vals*	Number of elements in the *val_list* array.
LPTSTR	*lpValueBuf*	Pointer to the buffer to which the function is to write each entry's value. The size of the buffer can be determined by first calling the function with *lpValueBuf* set to NULL; in that case, if the function returns ERROR_SUCCESS, *ldwTotsize* will contain the required size of the buffer.
LPDWORD	*ldwTotsize*	Pointer to a value that specifies the size, in bytes, of the buffer pointed to by the *lpValueBuf* parameter. If the function succeeds, *ldwTotsize* contains the number of bytes copied to the buffer, or, if *lpValueBuf* is NULL, the number of bytes required to successfully accommodate all values. If the function fails because the buffer is too small, *ldwTotsize* also contains the required size of the buffer.

Table 4-9. The VALENT data structure

Data Type	Parameter	Description
LPTSTR	*ve_valuename*	Pointer to a null-terminated string containing the name of the value entry which the function is to query. To retrieve the default (or unnamed) value of an entry, set *ve_valuename* to a null string.
DWORD	*ve_valuelen*	When the function returns, specifies the number of bytes written to the buffer containing the entry's value data.
DWORD	*ve_valueptr*	When the function returns, contains a pointer to the buffer where the entry's value data was written. Its value points to a location somewhere within the buffer defined by *lpValueBuf*, the fourth parameter to the *RegQuery-MultipleValues* function.
DWORD	*ve_type*	Indicates the value entry's data type. This value is represented by one of the constants listed earlier in Table 4-7.

In the event that you're somewhat confused about the relationship between the *ve_valueptr* member of the VALENT structure and the *lpValueBuf* parameter to the *RegQueryMultipleValues* function, Figure 4-2 should provide some clarification. *lpValueBuf* is a pointer to the beginning of a block of memory that you've allocated to hold all of the values that you want to retrieve; when you call the function, it automatically provides each element's member with the starting address to which it had written its value data. *ve_valueptr*, then, points to a smaller buffer within the larger buffer beginning at the address *lpValueBuf*.

In other words, you're responsible for providing the function with three items of information:

- The value entries whose data you wish to retrieve (their names are stored as members of a larger, mostly empty, data structure)

- The starting address of a block of memory where the function is to write each entry's value

- The total number of bytes available to the function to write all values

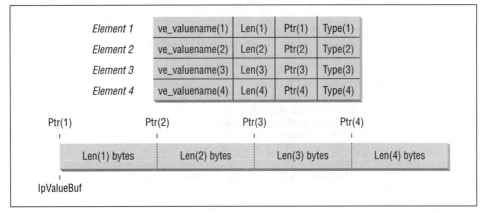

Figure 4-2. Using lpValBuf in RegQueryMultipleValues

All remaining items of information are filled in by the function when it concludes.

The major challenge posed by the function, then, is to allocate a block of memory large enough to hold all of the values whose entries the function queries. Example 4-10, a simple example that retrieves two color values from the HKCU\ Control Panel\Colors key, shows one way of allocating memory for the function at the same time that it illustrates how *RegQueryMultipleValues* might be used. If the function is called initially with NULL as the value of *lpValueBuf*, it will determine how large a buffer is needed to hold all of the values and return this number in the *dwTotSize* parameter. After a buffer of *dwTotSize* bytes has been allocated, the function can then be called again to retrieve data on each value entry.

Example 4-10. Using RegQueryMultipleValues to retrieve multiple values

```
#include <windows.h>

int APIENTRY WinMain(HANDLE hInstance, HANDLE hPrevInstance,
                LPSTR lpszCmdLine, int nCmdShow)
    {
    unsigned int iCtr ;
    HKEY hKey ;
    HANDLE hHeap ;
    DWORD num_vals = 2, dwTotsize ;
    LPTSTR lpValueBuf ;
    VALENT pValueData[2] ;

    // Define value entries to query
    pValueData[0].ve_valuename = "AppWorkspace" ;
    pValueData[1].ve_valuename = "Background" ;

    // Open Registry key
    if (RegOpenKey(HKEY_CURRENT_USER,"Control Panel\\Colors", &hKey )
                == ERROR_SUCCESS)
```

Example 4-10. Using RegQueryMultipleValues to retrieve multiple values (continued)

```
        {
        // Determine size of buffer
        RegQueryMultipleValues(hKey, pValueData, num_vals, NULL,
                                 &dwTotsize) ;
        // Allocate memory
        hHeap = GetProcessHeap() ;
        lpValueBuf = HeapAlloc(hHeap, 0, dwTotsize) ;
        // Retrieve Registry values
        RegQueryMultipleValues(hKey,pValueData,num_vals,lpValueBuf,
                                 &dwTotsize) ;
        for ( iCtr = 0; iCtr <= 1; iCtr++ )
           MessageBox(NULL, (LPCSTR) pValueData[iCtr].ve_valueptr,
                      pValueData[iCtr].ve_valuename, MB_OK) ;

        RegCloseKey(hKey) ;
        HeapFree(hHeap, 0, lpValueBuf) ;
        }
    return 0 ;
    }
```

There is one major caveat involved in using *RegQueryMultipleValues*: It's an all or nothing proposition. If Windows can locate and retrieve information about every key specified by the `ve_valuename` member of the PVALENT array, the function returns ERROR_SUCCESS; otherwise, it returns one of the error codes shown earlier in Table 4-5. This, combined with its inability to function under WinNT, means that, for "ordinary" applications that do not involve performance monitoring or the transfer of large amounts of data across the network, the overhead involved in insuring that *RegQueryMultipleValues* functions reliably may be more trouble than it's worth.

Creating and Modifying Registry Values: RegSetValue and RegSetValueEx

Much as the *RegCreateKey* and *RegCreateKeyEx* functions open an existing key and, if the key does not exist, create it, so the *RegSetValue* and *RegSetValueEx* functions modify an existing value and, if the value does not exist, create it.

RegSetValue is the "compatibility" function that works on both the Windows 16- and 32-bit platforms and that can create or modify a key's default (or unnamed) value. Its syntax is:

```
LONG RegSetValue( hKey, lpSubKey, dwType, lpData, cbData );
```

HKEY	*hKey*	A valid handle to a registry key. It can be either any of the first five predefined keys listed earlier in Table 4-2 or a handle to a subkey in one of the five registry trees returned by one of the registry open key functions. The function cannot modify HKEY_DYN_DATA and its subkeys, since they are read-only. Under WinNT, the registry key should have been opened with KEY_SET_VALUE access.
LPCTSTR	*lpSubKey*	Pointer to a string containing the name of the subkey whose default value is to be set. If the value of this parameter is NULL or an empty string, the function sets the default value of the open key whose handle is *hKey*.
DWORD	*dwType*	The value's data type. The value of this parameter must always be REG_SZ, which indicates a "normal" string value; otherwise, the function returns ERROR_INVALID_PARAMETER.
LPCTSTR	*lpData*	Pointer to a null-terminated string containing the default value that is to be assigned to the key. If the key has no default value, the function creates one; otherwise, it modifies the key's existing default value. While *lpData* can be an empty string (*lpData* = ""), it cannot be a NULL (*lpData* = (char *) 0).
DWORD	*cbData*	Specifies the size in bytes, excluding the terminating null character, of the string designated by the *lpData* parameter.

Like *RegQueryValue*, *RegSetValue* does not require that a key be open in order to modify its default value. The function operates on either the open key whose handle is *hKey* or on any of its subkeys. The function operates on the open key if *lpSubKey* is NULL, and operates on a subkey of *hKey* if it is not.

Null Strings and Null Pointers

We mentioned that the *lpData* parameter to *RegSetValueEx* can be a null string (*lpData* = " "), but it can't be a NULL (*lpData* = (char *) 0). Surprisingly, programmers often miss the difference between these two. When you define a null string, that string has a valid pointer; the pointer references a single byte of memory whose value is "\0" (the null character). A NULL, on the other hand, is a null pointer—a pointer whose value is 0; in a protected-memory system such as Win95 or WinNT, attempting to dereference this pointer (*lpData* or *lpData[0]*) is an error. If you pass a NULL in place of a null string to an API function that is expecting a null string, the API's parameter-validation code will return ERROR_INVALID_ADDRESS (487).

It is worth emphasizing that, if the *lpSubKey* parameter designates a path to a key's default value from an open registry key and that path is invalid, *RegSetValue* will create all the necessary keys before writing the final key's default value. Let's assume, for instance, that in the following code fragment the value of *hKey* is HKEY_CURRENT_USER, and that all keys from MyCompany onward are not present:

```
RegSetValue( hKey, "MyCompany\\MyApp\\CurrentVersion\\WindowState",
   REG_SZ,"1",1)
```

In this case, the function creates each of the following keys:

• HKCU\MyCompany

• HKCU\MyCompany\MyApp

• HKCU\MyCompany\MyApp\CurrentVersion

• HKCU\MyCompany\MyApp\CurrentVersion\WindowState

It's sort of as if the DOS command

```
MKDIR c:\foo\bar\baz
```

created not only \foo\bar\baz, but, if necessary, \foo\bar and \foo as well.

However, other than returning ERROR_SUCCESS, the function does nothing to indicate what it has done. This makes it, on the whole, a rather dangerous function to use.

Naming Registry Value Entries

In choosing names for registry value entries that your application creates, you can use any printable ANSI character. The equal sign is permitted, as is the backslash; three of the subkeys of HKEY_DYN_DATA\PerfStats, in fact, make extensive use of it. For instance, HKDD\PerfStats\StartData has value entries with names like KERNEL\CPUUsage, VFAT\DirtyData, and VMM\cPageFaults. While embedded spaces are perfectly acceptable, leading and trailing spaces, though legal, are a bad idea: an occasional cause of difficulty in retrieving and writing registry settings stems from a function's inability to match the leading or trailing spaces that were placed in a key name or a value name either inadvertently or by design.

The "official" Win32 registry value modification function, *RegSetValueEx*, on the other hand, can only work on either the default value or a complete value entry belonging to an open key:

```
LONG RegSetValueEx(hKey, lpValueName, Reserved, dwType, lpData, cbData );
```

HKEY	*hKey*	Handle of the key whose value is being created or modified. It can be either one of the first five predefined keys listed earlier in Table 4-2 or a handle to a subkey in one of these five registry trees returned by one of the registry open key functions. The sixth registry tree, HKEY_DYN_DATA, and its subkeys are read-only, since their "data" as such doesn't actually exist; these are virtual keys provided by VxDs that supply the data on demand. As a result, the function can't be used on them. If the program is running under WinNT, the registry key should have been opened with KEY_SET_VALUE access.
LPCTSTR	*lpValueName*	Pointer to a string containing the name of the value to set. If a value with this name does not already exist, the function creates it; otherwise, the function modifies an existing value. If this parameter is NULL or a pointer to a null string and the value of *dwType* is REG_SZ, the function sets the key's default value.
DWORD	*Reserved*	Reserved; must be zero.
DWORD	*dwType*	A value that indicates the type of data to be stored to the value entry; the data types supported by the Win95 registry are listed in Table 4-7.
CONST BYTE	**lpData*	The address of a buffer containing the data to be assigned to the designated value entry. Notice that this must be a pointer.
DWORD	*cbData*	Size (in bytes) of *lpbData*. If *cbData* is one of the string data types (REG_SZ, REG_EXPAND_SZ, or REG_MULTI_SZ), it should include the string's terminating null character. If *cbData* is greater than 16,364, the amount of data your application is attempting to store to the registry exceeds the allowable size of a single value, and the function returns ERROR_INVALID_PARAMETER.

Committing Changes to Disk: RegFlushKey

In order to improve performance, large portions of the registry are cached in memory. In fact, as far as your application is concerned, it's best to assume that the entire registry is in memory (actually, in virtual memory) at all times. All file input and output is handled by the page swapper, which automatically takes care of bringing pages in from disk and saving pages out to disk whenever it wants. This entire process of bringing the registry into memory and updating the registry files from the in-memory registry is completely transparent to you, your application, and its users.

This means, though, that changes to registry keys and values are neither written to disk as soon as they are made, nor immediately when a key is closed. Since Win95 does not implement the logging features that are present in WinNT to prevent data loss, there is a chance that configuration data could be lost between the time the user or the application changes it and the time that Win95 actually flushes it to disk. And since this entire process is transparent to you, you have no idea of what registry data has been committed to disk and what hasn't. When it is critical that an important piece of configuration information be accurately saved to the registry, you can make the registry's caching scheme less transparent by using the *RegFlushKey* function to force Windows to flush its cache to the registry files. The function's syntax is:

```
LONG RegFlushKey( hKey ) ;
```

    HKEY   *hKey*   Handle of the open key whose data is to be flushed to disk. It can also be any of Win95's six predefined top-level keys (although flushing **HKEY_DYN_DATA** is, of course, meaningless).

Before you add the function to your programming repertoire, though, it's important to understand precisely what the function does and how it works. Although you specify the handle of the key whose data you'd like flushed to disk, the function may flush data belonging to any or all other open keys. *RegFlushKey* then returns control to its calling application only when all data has been written to disk; a return value of **ERROR_SUCCESS** is really a guarantee that the key's data has been recorded in the registry.

As a result, there is an enormous performance penalty for using this function. Although the documentation advises that the *RegFlushKey* be used rarely, it does not indicate precisely how much the function degrades an application's performance. The effect is far more dramatic than one might think. On a 486/66 computer, a sample program that used *RegSetValueEx* to write an 8-character (**REG_SZ**) string value to a key 1,000 times took approximately 2 seconds to complete if *RegFlushKey* was not used, and almost four minutes (236 seconds) to complete if *RegFlushKey* was called after every write. The message is clear: except for insuring the integrity of *extremely* critical data that can't be replaced by default values and whose absence would completely cripple an application, *RegFlushKey* should *never* be used.

Deleting Keys and Values: RegDeleteKey and RegDeleteValue

While *RegSetValue* and *RegSetValueEx* allow you to create and modify a key's value entry, neither function allows you to delete an unwanted value entry. Instead, the registry API has two functions for deleting registry objects: *RegDeleteValue*, which removes both unnamed values and named value entries, and *RegDeleteKey*, which deletes unwanted keys.

The syntax of *RegDeleteValue* is very straightforward:

```
LONG RegDeleteValue( hKey, lpValueName ) ;
```

HKEY	*hKey*	Handle of the key containing a value to be deleted. It can be either one of the predefined keys listed earlier in Table 4-2 or a handle returned by one of the registry open key functions. Under WinNT, it should have been opened with `KEY_SET_VALUE` access.
LPCTSTR	*lpValueName*	Pointer to a string containing the name of the value to delete. If *lpValueName* is NULL or a pointer to a null string, the function deletes the key's unnamed or default value.

In contrast, since you have to specify the subkey of the current key that you want to delete, the syntax of *RegDeleteKey* recalls that of the "compatibility" functions *RegQueryValue* and *RegSetValue*. Its syntax is:

```
LONG RegDeleteKey( hKey, lpSubKey ) ;
```

HKEY	*hKey*	Handle of the key whose subkey is to be deleted. *hKey* can be either one of the predefined keys listed in Table 4-2 or a handle returned by one of the registry open key functions. Under WinNT, it should have been opened with `KEY_CREATE_SUB_KEY` access; in most cases, this probably precludes opening a key with either the *RegOpenKey* or *RegCreateKey* functions.
LPCTSTR	*lpSubkey*	Pointer to a string containing the name of the subkey of *hKey* that's to be deleted. If its value is NULL or if it is a pointer to an empty string, *RegDeleteKey* will delete the current key.

Interestingly, if you don't provide a value for *lpSubkey*—that is, if this parameter is a NULL or a pointer to an empty string—Win95 deletes the key that is currently open. This is how the *RegDeleteKey* function behaves under WinNT as well.

Earlier, we noted that Win95 and WinNT differ in their handling of open registry keys: internally, Win95 maintains a usage counter and assigns identical numbers to duplicate handles, making it possible to manipulate an otherwise closed registry key. However, *RegDeleteKey* does not consider a key's usage count. That is, *RegDeleteKey* will immediately remove a key, even if it is opened multiple times, or if it has been opened by other applications. Subsequent attempts to perform operations on the key (other than closing it) produce an `ERROR_KEY_DELETED` return value.

In contrast to *RegDeleteValue*, which is elegant in its simplicity, *RegDeleteKey* has two major cross-platform differences:

- *Deleting the subkey of a top-level key.* Although neither operating system allows you to delete a top-level key (like HKCU), Win95 allows you to delete any other key. You can, for instance, delete a subkey of the top-level key (like `HKLM\Enum`). WinNT, on the other hand, does not allow you to delete a subkey of the top-level key, although it does allow you to delete any of its subkeys. So, for example, you cannot delete `HKLM\System`, but you can delete `HKLM\System\Select`. This difference should not cause a major problem, though, since there is little need to ever delete a subkey of a top-level key.

- *Deleting all subkeys*. If the key to be deleted itself has subkeys, Win95 will delete the key along with all of its subkeys. WinNT, on the other hand, will only delete a key if it has no subkeys (very much like the DOS `RD` command). That means that, if your want your application to run under WinNT as well as Win95 and your application deletes keys that may contain subkeys, your application should do a "cascading delete" by using the *RegQueryInfoKey* function to determine if a key has subkeys, then using the *RegEnumKeyEx* function to determine their names.

Since deleting a registry key is ordinarily an irreversible action, in cases where your application is deleting system-level data or critical application-specific data, you might want to consider backing up the key and its subkeys before actually deleting the key. That allows your application to restore it if necessary. To do this, you can either invoke RegEdit as a background process to generate a .REG file containing the key that you'd like to delete, or you can use the *RegSaveKey* function which, conveniently enough, is discussed in the following section.

Backing Up and Restoring the Registry

The most accessible and readable format for storing backup information from the Windows registry, and in many ways one of the most comprehensible, is the .REG file. .REG files are just plain ASCII files that are arranged in a relatively simple format. Unfortunately, though, the registry API does not support the generation and merging of .REG files.

Nevertheless, the registry API does allow you to create backups of portions of the registry. Its major drawback, though, is that, unlike .REG files, which can be exported and then modified as needed, these files are not accessible or comprehensible: they are stored in a binary format.

On the other hand, using the registry API to back up registry data offers some advantages over .REG files. One of these is performance: if *RegSaveKey* is used to save a particularly large branch of the registry, like the entire `HKEY_LOCAL_MACHINE` key, its performance is slightly superior to that of RegEdit. (On a relatively slow machine, it still takes a comparatively long time for the function to complete execution; notifying the user of that fact is important so that he or she doesn't think that the application has crashed.) Second, it consumes less hard disk space: the files generated by *RegSaveKey* tend to be about 15% smaller than the corresponding .REG files generated by RegEdit.

Working with .REG Files

Just because the registry API doesn't support .REG files does not mean that you can't use them in your application. The easiest way to generate a .REG file containing all or part of the Windows 95 Registry is to have RegEdit do it. Although the documentation implies that RegEdit accepts command-line switches only when run in real mode, it also recognizes the /E switch, which instructs it to create a .REG file containing all or part of the registry, when running under Windows; its syntax is:

```
REGEDIT /E <filename> [<Registry path>]
```

If the registry path is omitted, RegEdit generates a .REG file containing the entire registry. This means that you can use *ShellExecute* to generate the .REG file in the background while your application is running. You can also use *ShellExecute* to run RegEdit if you want to import a .REG file from within your application.

Interestingly, the Windows API also provides a set of tools for working with .REG files: the initialization file functions. A registry key corresponds to an initialization file section; a registry value name is similar to an initialization file key name; and a registry value is an initialization file value. By using the *GetPrivateProfileSectionNames*, *GetPrivateProfileSection*, *GetPrivateProfileInt*, and *GetPrivateProfileString* functions, you can retrieve data from existing .REG files, massage it slightly, and write it to the registry.

It is also relatively trivial for a program to create new .REG files from scratch. See Example 11-4 in Chapter 11, *Migrating from .INI Files to the Registry*.

Most important, though, using the registry API offers enhanced flexibility. .REG files are an all-or-nothing proposition: unless you directly modify the .REG file or do the programming necessary to parse a .REG file, you have to import its entire contents. Nor can you control the destination of the data. The result is that the data in the .REG file overwrites duplicate data in the registry, but that unique data in the registry remains intact. If you want to *replace* the data in the registry with data in a .REG file, you have use RegEdit in real mode and, on a 486 computer, spend as much as a day importing a .REG file. The backup and restore functions in the registry API, on the other hand, give you the flexibility of deciding what portion of a file you'd like to import and how you would like to incorporate it into the existing registry.

Its backup and restore functions are probably the most under-documented component of the registry API. In fact, some of the documentation even says that these functions are not supported by Win95, and instead are targeted exclusively at

WinNT. Much of this confusion surrounding the operation of these functions, though, probably stems from the fact that their intent is unclear.

To understand what the backup and restore functions do, it is important to remember that the Win32 API's registry export functions, like the entire registry API, were originally developed for WinNT. The WinNT registry, as we saw in Chapter 1, consists of several *hives,* or files that contain either a top-level key and all its subkeys or a subkey of a top-level key and all its subkeys. Although the structure of the Win95 registry and the terminology used to describe it are considerably different, it nevertheless consists of two or more physical files (depending on whether a system supports multiple users) that are functionally equivalent to WinNT hives. The operating system itself assembles the registry from these components without requiring that either the developer or the user knows what the files are or where they fit into the registry as a whole.

Basically, the registry API's backup and restore functions are nothing more than methods for creating a detached hive out of some portion of the current registry and for later incorporating it back into the registry. To put it another way, *RegSaveKey* writes some part of the registry to a separate physical file which is really a detached hive of the registry's native format. To be meaningful, it either has to be attached to the registry or imported into the registry again. These, however, are two very different procedures: when the detached file is attached to the registry, the file itself becomes one of the registry's components, just like the files *SYSTEM.DAT* and *USER.DAT* are two central components of the registry. Changes to registry keys and values that are attached in this manner are reflected in the detached file. Conversely, when a detached file is imported into the registry, its contents are copied into the registry and assume an existence independent of the original file. Changes to imported keys and values are not reflected in the detached file.

The registry restore functions support both attaching and importing files. The *RegLoadKey* function attaches a registry hive. It remains attached until the *RegUnLoad* function is used to detach it. *RegReplaceKey* and *RegRestoreKey,* on the other hand, both import data from a detached registry file into the registry.

Creating a detached registry hive: RegSaveKey

The syntax of *RegSaveKey,* the sole function in the registry API that is capable of exporting registry data to a detached registry file, is:

```
LONG RegSaveKey( hKey, lpFile, lpSecurityAttributes ) ;
```

HKEY	hKey	Handle of the key from which the save operation is to begin; the file will contain information on all of its values, as well as all of its child keys and their values. *HKey* can be either one of the predefined keys listed in Table 4-2 (although it makes little sense to write HKEY_DYN_DATA to a file) or a handle returned by one of the registry open key functions. To run under WinNT, the user must have the SeBackupPrivilege security privilege.
LPCTSTR	lpFile	Pointer to a string containing the optional path and name of the file to be generated by the function. The file should not have a file extension; if it does, the import functions in the registry API cannot read it successfully on MS-DOS (FAT) file systems. For maximum portability, long filenames should also be avoided. If *hKey* is an open registry key on a remote computer, the path is relative to the remote computer. *RegSaveKey* does not overwrite or replace an existing file; if a file named *lpFile* already exists, the function returns ERROR_REGISTRY_IO_FAILED. If the function succeeds, it creates a hidden, read-only system file.
LPSECURITY	lpSecurity-Attributes	A pointer to a security attributes structure, which is described earlier in Table 4-4. This structure is of concern to WinNT only. Since Win95 does not support security, this parameter can be a NULL, since it is ignored in any case. If the application runs under WinNT and *lpSecurityAttributes* is NULL, the file receives a default security descriptor.

Attaching a detached registry hive: RegLoadKey

Once your application has created a detached registry file, you can attach it to the registry using the *RegLoadKey* function; this means, once again, that the file whose name is passed as a parameter to *RegLoadKey* physically becomes a part of the registry, although only temporarily; in many ways, it resembles a file system mount. The function's syntax is:

```
LONG RegLoadKey( hKey, lpSubKey, lpFile );
```

HKEY	hKey	Handle to one of the two non-volatile predefined keys, HKEY_LOCAL_MACHINE or HKEY_USERS, or a handle to one of these two predefined keys on a remote computer, as provided by the *RegConnectRegistry* function. *hKey* defines the top-level key whose registry tree will be affected by the process of attaching a registry hive; the registry hive is attached as its direct subkey. To execute successfully under WinNT, the calling process must have the SE_RESTORE_PRIVILEGE privilege.
LPCTSTR	lpSubKey	Pointer to a null-terminated string that designates the name to be assigned to the file's top-level key.

LPCTSTR   *lpFile*   A pointer to the string containing the path and name of the file
                          containing registry data. The file must have been created with
                          the *RegSaveKey* function. For the function to execute success-
                          fully under the FAT system, the file cannot have a file exten-
                          sion. If *hKey* is the handle to a remote key returned by the
                          RegConnectRegistry function, the path contained in *lpFile* is
                          relative to the remote computer.

RegLoadKey requires that you indicate the static top-level key to which the
registry file is to be attached. If the function executes successfully, it attaches the
contents of the registry file as a direct subkey of the top-level key. For this reason,
it is important that *lpSubKey* not be a fully qualified registry path (like `Enum\`
`AttachedFile`), and that it not contain the path delimiter character. Since the
function provides minimal error checking, it will actually attach the registry file
and assign it a keyname that includes the path delimiter. For instance, the
following line of code

```
RegLoadKey( HKEY_LOCAL_MACHINE, "c:\\windows\\regfile1",
          "Network\\Internet")
```

executes successfully. But rather than creating the key `HKLM\Network\`
`Internet`, it creates a key whose name is `Network\Internet` that is a direct
child of `HKLM`. The backslash, though, is an invalid character in a key name
(although it's legal in a value name). Since the registry's open key functions all
interpret the backslash as a path separator, any subkeys and values in the
attached registry file are inaccessible.

lpSubKey also need not be the name of the highest-level key from which the
registry file was created using the *RegSaveKey* function. In fact, there does not
have to be any correspondence between these two key names. You can, for
instance, use *RegSaveKey* to generate a detached registry file containing `HKLM\`
`SOFTWARE\Classes\CLSID` and its subkeys, then use *RegLoadKey* to attach it
as a key named `HKLM\OLE`.

While the registry file is attached, your application can access its contents just as it
would any registry key, with a single exception. If you attempt to use
RegDeleteKey   to   delete   the   key,   the   function   fails,   returning
`ERROR_ACCESS_DENIED`. You can, though, modify the values of *lpSubKey* and
any of its subkeys, as well as delete existing subkeys or add new ones. All modifications that you make to the *lpSubKey* tree are permanent; the detached registry
file is updated to reflect them.

Detaching an attached hive: RegUnloadKey

Attached registry files, though, are not a permanent part of the registry. They
become detached in either of two ways. The first is under user control: when the
user either shuts down or restarts the computer, the registry files are not reloaded

when the computer next reboots; they can then be reloaded only under program control. (Logging off and logging back on doesn't affect registry files loaded with *RegLoadKey*; they continue to be attached, even if they are subkeys of HKEY_USERS.) The second is under program control: the *RegUnLoadKey* function can detach an attached registry file. Its syntax is:

```
LONG RegUnLoadKey( hKey, lpSubKey ) ;
```

HKEY	*hKey*	Predefined handle of the non-volatile top-level key that contains an attached registry file. Its value can be HKEY_LOCAL_MACHINE, HKEY_USERS, or a handle to one of these two predefined keys on a remote computer, as provided by the *RegConnectRegistry* function.
LPCTSTR	*lpSubKey*	Pointer to a null-terminated string that designates the name of the subkey to unload. It must have been defined by the *RegLoadKey* function. In addition, for the function to succeed under WinNT, the process must have the SE_RESTORE_NAME privilege.

Since *RegLoadKey* does not add a permanent component to the registry and does not import the contents of a detached registry file into the permanent portion of the registry, it is not suitable for restoring the registry from a backup copy. However, this ability to attach and detach subkeys to a top-level registry key has several applications:

- *Temporary storage.* Some applications, like installation programs, frequently run only once or, at most, a couple of times. Attaching a registry hive allows the application to use the registry but to efficiently remove all traces of itself after the routine has ended.

- *Security.* Although *RegLoadKey* is not intended as a security feature, there are situations in which security is enhanced by simply storing configuration data in a separate hidden file that is functionally inaccessible when its application is not running.

- *Performance.* During installation or when it is first run, an application that makes extensive use of the registry could spend an excessive amount of time writing registry settings. Instead, putting all of the settings in a registry file and attaching it when the application is run helps to improve the program's perceived performance.

Restoring the registry from a hive: RegReplaceKey

Although it is not appropriate to use *RegLoadKey* for restoring the registry, the *RegReplaceKey* function is ideal, since it not only replaces the current contents of the registry with data contained in a file, but even saves the discarded portions of the registry to a backup file. Its syntax is:

```
LONG RegReplaceKey( hKey, lpSubKey, lpNewFile, lpOldFile )
```

HKEY	hKey	The handle of an open registry key, or one of the predefined static registry keys (HKCC, HKCR, HKCU, HKLM, or HKU). If *hKey* is a handle other than a predefined registry key or a handle returned by the *RegConnectRegistry* function, it must be the handle to a key that is a direct subkey of a top-level key, and the value of *lpSubKey* must be NULL.
LPCTSTR	lpSubKey	Pointer to a null-terminated string that designates the key whose subkeys and values are to be replaced by the function. The key must be an existing subkey of the key whose handle is *hKey*; *RegReplaceKey* will not create a new subkey. For the function to complete successfully under WinNT, its process must have the SE_RESTORE_NAME privilege. If *hKey* is not a top-level key, *lpSubKey* must be NULL.
LPCTSTR	lpNewFile	Pointer to a null-terminated string with the name of the file that contains the registry data to import. This must be a registry file created by the *RegSaveKey* function. For compatibility with MS-DOS (FAT) file systems, the filename should not have an extension. If *hKey* is a handle on a remote computer, the file's path is relative to the remote computer. The file remains open until the computer is restarted.
LPCTSTR	lpOldFile	Pointer to a null-terminated string containing the name of the file to which the function will write the current contents of the keys that are being replaced. If the file does not exist, *RegReplaceKey* creates it. For compatibility with MS-DOS file systems, the filename should not have an extension. If *hKey* is a handle on a remote computer, the file's path is relative to the remote computer.

RegSaveKey, then, can generate a backup file; and not only can *RegReplaceKey* restore a single subkey of a top-level key of some portion of the registry from a backup file, it can also save the information replaced by the restored copy. This makes it easy to "undo" a restore if it has undesirable effects.

Unlike *RegLoadKey*, *RegReplaceKey* does not attach a new registry hive to the existing registry. Instead, *RegReplaceKey* is an import function: it operates by saving the current contents of *lpSubKey* and all of its subkeys to a file, deleting *lpSubKey* and all of its subkeys, and then importing the subkeys and values from *lpNewFile* to *lpSubKey*. But this doesn't happen immediately: the function takes effect when the system is next booted. (Logging off and logging back on doesn't cause Win95 to import the file defined by *RegReplaceKey*.)

It is important to remember that *RegReplaceKey*, like *RegLoadKey*, only works at the "hive" level. That is, *RegReplaceKey* requires that the initial key whose information is to be replaced must be a direct subkey of one of the static top-level keys. In addition, this initial key must exist; *RegReplaceKey* does not create the key whose data it is to overwrite.

Who Is the Current User? RegRemapPreDefKey

Device drivers frequently require access to the registry as much as applications do, but device drivers access the registry directly through the services provides by the Win95 Virtual Machine Manager. The Win95 Device Driver Kit, which documents these low-level functions, includes a little-used function called *_RegRemapPreDefKey* that can change the registry key to which the two top-level keys HKEY_CURRENT_USER and HKEY_CURRENT_CONFIG point. The function, according to the documentation, is "intended for use by the system" and should not be used by device drivers.

It is surprising that *_RegRemapPreDefKey* is an exported function that is available to device drivers. As a low-level function intended primarily for system use, it would be even more surprising if it were exported by a higher-level API, like the one provided by *ADVAPI32.DLL*. But an examination of the DLL's export table shows that, indeed, a function named *RegRemapPreDefKey* is included. *RegRemapPreDefKey* is an undocumented function that probably should not have been exported, but that actually works more or less as advertised. Its syntax is:

```
LONG RegRemapPreDefKey( hKey, hRootKey ) ;
```

HKEY   *hKey*   Handle of the key that is to be remapped to *hRootKey*.

HKEY   *hRootKey*   Handle to either of two predefined top-level keys:
                       HKEY_CURRENT_USER or HKEY_CURRENT_CONFIG.

Unless the function attempts to access a corrupted registry, it appears to invariably return ERROR_SUCCESS whether it actually succeeds or not. This does not, however, indicate an underlying lack of robustness. *RegRemapPreDefKey* allows you to change only the key to which either HKCU or HKCC point; you cannot change the key to which HKCR points, nor can you replace a physical or memory-resident key (like HKLM or HKDD) with a pointer. The function also does not allow you to arbitrarily define which key will become HKCU or HKCC. Instead, if a computer is configured for multiple users, only either of the two direct subkeys of HKU can be remapped to HKCU. Similarly, if a machine has multiple hardware configurations, the function allows you to remap HKCC to any direct subkey of HKLM\Config. All other attempts to remap keys fail even though they return ERROR_SUCCESS.

According to the documentation, in order to prevent read and write operations that other applications intend to perform on one set of keys from being arbitrarily rerouted to another, *_RegRemapPreDefKey* invalidates all open handles from the previous HKCU or HKCC. This, however, is not how *RegRemapPreDefKey* works. Instead, all open handles remain open after the remapping; however, the handles operate on the *physical* keys, rather than on *pointers* to the physical keys. This means that the read and write operations performed by applications that obtained registry handles before the remapping continue to operate on the intended keys.

Applications that open either HKCU or HKCC after the remapping, on the other hand, obtain handles to the newly remapped registry keys.

This makes *RegRemapPreDefKey* a much safer function that one would expect, and one that can be useful in several mostly specialized situations. For example, in installation programs on computers configured to support multiple users, the location of per-user settings can sometimes be problematic. Your installation program, though, can ask the user whether your application will be used by other users or whether it is for the sole use of the current user. If the former, you can use *RegRemapPreDefKey* to define HKU\.Default as HKCU and write the settings there; then, when the program is run, it can copy default settings from HKCU\.Default to each user's registry subtree. If the former, you can leave HKCU intact and write the per-user settings to it; when the application is run, they apply only to the user who installed your application. Using *RegRemapPreDefKey* allows you to use the same code to handle both situations.

At the same time, although it appears to be robust, *RegRemapPreDefKey* is both undocumented and rarely used. If you choose to call it in your application, be sure to test that portion of your program especially thoroughly. In particular, you should be on the lookout for unintended side effects of using the function, and for undesirable consequences of remapping HKLM or HKCU, particularly in other applications that may be running at the same time as your own.

Closing an Open Registry Key: RegCloseKey

After you're finished using any registry key other than one of the six top-level keys, you should close it by using the *RegCloseKey* function. Its syntax is:

```
LONG RegCloseKey( hKey ) ;
```

    HKEY   *hKey*   Handle of any open key other than one of the registry's six top-level keys.

If *hKey* is the handle to a top-level registry key, *RegCloseKey* returns ERROR_SUCCESS, although of course the key remains open. This is a useful feature: it means that, if you're developing a utility that allows the user to open any registry key, you don't have to go through the trouble of determining which handles belong to top-level keys and which don't so that your call to *RegCloseKey* won't generate an error; you can simply call *RegCloseKey* with no real overhead.

Much as it's important to close all open files, it's important to close all open registry keys as soon as you're finished accessing their contents. The major reason for this is data integrity: if you're writing data to the registry, you can't be sure that your modifications have been committed to disk until as much as several seconds after the key has been closed; if the system crashes in the meantime, your changes could be lost or the key corrupted. You can use the *RegFlushKey* function to make certain that changes have been committed to disk, but it involves an enormous performance penalty. The best solution is to close open keys as quickly as possible.

Registry Locking

The registry, as we've mentioned, is really a centralized database of system settings and application state information. In Chapter 1, we characterized it as "the glue that holds Windows together"—i.e., a critical structure in Windows' and its applications' operation. Windows itself is a very capable multitasking operating system. An examination of the voluminous output produced by *RegSpy95* (which is discussed in Chapter 10, *Spying on the Registry*) shows that Windows and Windows applications access information in the registry hundreds or even thousands of times per second.

Put all this together, and it's probably already occurred to you that, just as in any database application that is used intensively and that supports multiple processes, collisions are inevitable. At some point, one process is sure to attempt to read data that another process is busily writing. Or two processes eventually will attempt to update the same value, thereby thoroughly confusing and corrupting it. Recognizing this, you may even be reviewing the Win32 API to refresh your memory about functions like *CreateMutex* and *ReleaseMutex*.[*]

Good news: internally, Windows 95 (or, more precisely, the Win95 Virtual Machine Manager) implements what appears to be robust locking to insure the integrity of registry data. A single mutex is used to guard the entire registry. Whenever Windows or an application writes, and in most cases when it reads, a registry key or a value entry, the VMM calls an ENTRY_LOCK procedure that includes a call to the VMM's *_EnterMutex* service. If the mutex is unowned when *_EnterMutex* is invoked, the calling thread takes ownership of it, and can access a particular registry resource. If the mutex is already owned, the calling thread is blocked until the owning thread calls an EXIT_UNLOCK procedure, which in turn calls the VMM *_LeaveMutex* service. If this locking fails during registry access, the registry function returns ERROR_LOCK_FAILED.

The following functions invoke the ENTRY_LOCK procedure:

- *RegCreateKey* and *RegCreateKeyEx*, which create or open a registry key
- *RegOpenKey* and *RegOpenKeyEx*, which open a registry key

---

[*] In the event that you're unfamiliar with mutexes, they are objects used to protect a shared resource from simultaneous access by multiple threads or processes. Only one thread or process can have ownership of the mutex at any point, and only the thread or process with ownership of the mutex is allowed to access the resource guarded by the mutex.

- *RegEnumKey*, which retrieves information about a registry key

- *RegQueryInfoKey*, which retrieves a variety of information about a registry key and its value entries

- *RegDeleteKey*, which removes a registry key

- *RegSetValue* and *RegSetValueEx*, which write data to a value entry and (optionally) create one or more keys

- *RegDeleteValue*, which deletes a value entry from the registry

- *RegEnumValue*, which retrieves information about a value entry

- *RegQueryValue*, *RegQueryValueEx*, and *RegQueryMultipleValues*, which retrieve data from registry value entries

- *RegFlushKey*, which commits the in-memory registry to disk

To test the effectiveness of this scheme, we created two programs, the first a simple registry "writer" and the second a simple registry "reader." The writer program continuously wrote 16,364 bytes of REG_BINARY data (the maximum amount of data that can be stored to a single value) to a value entry. During each iteration of the loop, the *memset* function was used to assign each of these bytes the same value. After each iteration of the loop, that value was incremented by one. (Once the value of each byte reached 255, of course, it was reinitialized to 0.) The reader program meanwhile continuously retrieved the entry's REG_BINARY value, read its first byte, then reported if the value of any subsequent byte differed from the value of the first byte. In repeated tests, including one in which three instances of the writer and two instances of the reader application were running simultaneously, the reader application did not report a single divergent byte of data.

This suggests that read and write operations performed on a single registry key or a single value entry are atomic, very much like those in Windows NT. That is, barring some catastrophic failure (like a loss of power), the locking scheme insures that a particular operation is completed before some other operation on that key or value entry—indeed, on *any* part of the registry—is permitted.

However, it's important to recognize that a single thread owns the registry mutex only for the duration of its call to a particular registry API function; before each registry function exits, it calls an EXIT_UNLOCK procedure. For instance, the thread that calls *RegOpenKey* or *RegOpenKeyEx* takes ownership of the mutex, but only for the period that the function executes; the thread does not retain ownership of the registry mutex for the entire period that the key is open. (Otherwise, failing to call *RegCloseKey* would completely disable the entire system.)

The Registry Mutex and RegConnectRegistry

You might be wondering how the multithreaded *REGCONN* program is able to kill a thread while it's attempting to access a remote registry when this locking scheme is in place. The answer is that locking is implemented by the local VMM, but *RegConnectRegistry* is not implemented by calling down to the Virtual Machine Manager; instead, it calls *WINREG.DLL*, which does a remote procedure call (RPC) to *REGSERV.EXE* running on the remote machine, which calls down to *its* VMM (see Figure 4-1).

Multiple operations, thus, are not atomic. For instance, if your application uses *RegEnumValue* to enumerate all the values belonging to a particular key, a mutex is used to insure the integrity of the individual read operation. But the integrity of the enumeration as a whole cannot be guaranteed; that is, there is no guarantee that the properties of the value entries and the values themselves will be the same when you finish your enumeration as they were when you began your enumeration. In fact, since the registry's locking scheme is implemented at a system level by the Virtual Machine Manager, it is not possible to apply it to multiple operations, since the system has no way of knowing how many operations you intend to perform. Attempting to apply it to multiple operations would inevitably block other applications' access to the registry and bring the system to a crawl. Consequently, the documentation for *RegEnumKey*, *RegEnumKeyEx*, and *RegEnumValue* in the Win32 SDK warns that, while enumerating keys or values, your application should not modify any of the objects being enumerated.

So it is quite possible, when you're in the middle of a series of registry operations, that some other application can change either the data itself or information about the data (like the number of value entries belonging to a subkey or the number of bytes in the longest data value). For instance, before using *RegEnumValue* to enumerate a series of values, you call *RegQueryInfoKey* to determine both the number of value entries and the length of the longest data item. As you're enumerating the values, another application deletes a value that you haven't yet enumerated, and writes new data to another value entry that you haven't enumerated that is significantly longer than *RegQueryInfoKey* reported. As you'll see in the next section, "I Was Shocked to Discover That It's a Whole New Registry...," the absence of registry change notification messages or services means that you'll never be informed that anything has changed. Yet, your application undoubtedly is prepared to loop x times, until all keys have been read, and to store their data in a buffer of y bytes, which is just enough to accommodate the largest value entry. This means that your application will probably fail.

Given this potential problem, what can you do to insure that your application continues to function reliably? You have two alternatives:

- You can create a mutex to insure the integrity of a series of write operations. Sample code for doing this is contained in Ron Murray's article, "How to Use the Windows NT Registry in Your Application," on the Microsoft Developer Network CD-ROM.

- You can rely on a combination of your error handling and the values returned by the registry API to correct problems and keep your application running. For instance, if the size of a value entry's data expands to become larger than the buffer you've allocated for it, the *RegQueryValueEx* function returns ERROR_MORE_DATA. The function's *lpcbData* parameter, though, indicates how many bytes are needed to store the entry's data.

I Was Shocked to Discover That It's a Whole New Registry...

The registry is a very dynamic structure. Both Windows itself and individual applications use it to store user information, application state information, system information, and interapplication information, among other things. As a result, the registry is continually changing. Typically, though, applications read most of the basic registry settings that they need just once, when the application is loading. And, of course, they are aware of changes to registry settings that they themselves make. But from the time that an application last retrieves data from the registry, any other application can also modify the settings that it has read. How, then, do Windows applications learn that a registry setting on which they're depending has changed?

In Win31, with its system of initialization files, the Windows messaging system was responsible for notifying running applications of changes to *WIN.INI*, the major software configuration file. If Windows or an application changed *WIN.INI*, it could use either the *SendMessage* or the *PostMessage* function to send a WM_WININICHANGE message to selected windows or to all windows. The syntax of both functions in the Win32 API is:

```
BOOL PostMessage( hWnd, Msg, wParam, lParam ) ;
BOOL SendMessage( hWnd, Msg, wParam, lParam ) ;
```

HWND	*hWnd*	Handle of the window to which the message is to be sent; if the message is intended for all open windows, its value should be HWND_BROADCAST (0xFFFF).
UINT	*Msg*	Code number for the message to post, in this case WM_WININICHANGE (0x1A).

| WPARAM | *wParam* | The first message parameter; for WM_WININICHANGE, this parameter is not used and must be 0. |
| LPARAM | *lParam* | The second message parameter; for WM_WININICHANGE, it should be a pointer to a null-terminated string containing the name of the section in *WIN.INI* that was modified. A NULL value indicates that multiple sections of *WIN.INI* have changed. |

In addition, the WM_WININICHANGE message could automatically be sent by the *SystemParametersInfo* function if it was used to modify the value of one of its predefined system settings in *WIN.INI*.

Notification and Atomic Operations

In the previous section, "Registry Locking," we saw that only the operation of single registry functions are automatically protected by the registry mutex; multiple operations are not automatically protected. So even when accessing the registry for a series of operations (like enumerating a key's subkeys or value entries), Windows cannot guarantee that the information you're accessing differs from the state of the registry when you began your operation. That makes it important that Windows provide some mechanism to let you know that the registry has changed, and that those changes may affect the integrity of your series of operations. Once you've accessed information in the registry, this same mechanism should inform you that settings have changed, and that you need to read the original information once more. This section explores Win95's failure to implement such a mechanism.

In short, applications that modified *WIN.INI* were supposed to send a message indicating which section of *WIN.INI* they had modified. Conversely, all applications that depended on settings in *WIN.INI* were supposed to include an option for handling the WM_WININICHANGE message in their window procedures. This involved determining whether the application relied on any entries in the modified section and, if it did, rereading the section's values. Finally, a window procedure that processed the WM_WININICHANGE message was to return a 0, indicating that it had successfully handled the message.

Unfortunately, though, this was more of an ideal than a reality. While generally applications did send messages notifying other applications that *WIN.INI* had changed, most applications failed to include the code to handle WM_WININICHANGE messages in their standard window procedures.

This lack of compliance with the standards for Win31 may have inspired the current state, in which there is no standard way (and, in most cases, no meaningful way at all) to let other applications know that particular values or a particular area of the registry has changed. One would expect, of course, that since Win95 has moved the bulk of configuration information from initialization files to the registry, the Win32 API *should* include a new message, like WM_REGCHANGE, whose parameters indicate which key and possibly which value entry has changed. But instead, the Win32 API does not include a message that indicates the registry has changed.

Rather than supporting a message to notify of registry changes, WinNT offers a function, *RegNotifyChangeKeyValue*. Its major purpose, though, is to allow for thread synchronization in multithreaded applications. And it is not implemented on Win95.

Instead, Win95 adds a new message, WM_SETTINGCHANGE, to the Win32 API. According to the Win32 SDK documentation, it completely supplants WM_WININICHANGE, which is no longer supported by Win95.

In contrast to WM_WININICHANGE, which was used to indicate any change to *WIN.INI* that might interest an application, WM_SETTINGCHANGE has a much more limited role: it indicates that one of the basic system parameters set by the *SystemParametersInfo*[*] function has changed. This function both retrieves the state of individual system settings and allows a myriad of basic system options to be set, such as the dimensions of icons, whether a screen saver is enabled, or whether fast task switching (the use of Alt-Tab to navigate among tasks) is allowed. The last parameter of *SystemParametersInfo* defines the character of the changes: according to the documentation, a value of SPIF_UPDATEINIFILE makes the new value permanent by modifying the registry, while a value of SPIF_SENDWININICHANGE (sic) under Win95 presumably causes the function to send a WM_SETTINGCHANGE message. Since this message is implemented exclusively on Win95, WinNT continues to send the more traditional WM_WININICHANGE message.

When the WM_SETTINGCHANGE message is sent, the *wParam* and *lParam* parameters to the *SendMessage* and the *PostMessage* functions are:

WPARAM *wFlag*	Indicates which system parameter has been changed by the *SystemParametersInfo* function. This value is the same as the value supplied to the *uiAction* parameter of *SystemParametersInfo*.

---

[*] The general syntax of *SystemParametersInfo* is:

```
BOOL SystemParametersInfo( UINT uiAction, UINT uiParam, PVOID pvParam,
UINT fWinINI );
```

where: *uiAction* indicates the system parameter to query or set, and is generally represented by one of a vast array of constants; *uiParam* and *pvParam* provide additional information needed to change the setting indicated by *uiAction*; and *fWinIni* indicates whether modifications are to be made to the registry or to *WIN.INI*.

LPARAM   *pszMetrics*   Points to a buffer containing the string "WindowMetrics" if the value of *wFlag* is SPI_SETANIMATION, SPI_SETNONCLIENTMETRICS, SPI_SETICONMETRICS, or SPI_SETMINIMIZEDMETRICS. Otherwise, its value is NULL.

An application that processes the WM_SETTINGCHANGE message should return 0 as the value of its window procedure.

SystemParametersInfo and MisInfo

Aside from the fact that its terminology (SPIF_UPDATEINIFILE and SPIF_SENDWININICHANGE) hasn't been updated, the behavior of the Win95 implementation of *SystemParametersInfo* differs from the behavior described in the documentation in two ways:

- According to the documentation, the *fWinIni* parameter, which determines whether changes are written to the registry and a WM_SETTINGCHANGE message sent, can be 0 or one of the two constants. In fact, if the program is to both update the registry and send a message, the two constants must be ORed.

- But in any case, if you specify SPIF_SENDWININICHANGE, the function sends neither a WM_SETTINGCHANGE or a WM_WININICHANGE message. If you want to notify other applications of the change, you'll have to send the message yourself.

Interestingly, if we examine *WINUSER.H*, the header file that contains the definitions of Windows messages, we find the following lines:

```
#define WM_WININICHANGE     0x1A
#define WM_SETTINGCHANGE    WM_WININICHANGE
```

So in fact, Windows does continue to support WM_WININICHANGE. WM_SETTINGCHANGE is simply a syntactical variation on the standard version of WM_WININICHANGE: *wParam*, instead of being 0, now indicates the specific system setting modified by *SystemParametersInfo*. Given the value of *wParam*, it is very easy for the application that processes the WM_SETTINGCHANGE message to use the *SystemParametersInfo* function to retrieve the new setting by calling the constant used to retrieve a setting instead of the constant used to modify it. For example, if an application has modified the width of windows' sizing borders, the following code fragment in the application's window procedure retrieves the new value:

```
// Check for change using SystemParametersInfo
case WM_SETTINGCHANGE:
```

```
switch (wParam)
   {
   case (SPI_SETBORDER):
      SystemParametersInfo( SPI_GETBORDER, &uintBorderSize, 0, 0 ) ;
      … etc. …
```

The more conventional variation of WM_WININICHANGE, on the other hand, indicates which section of *WIN.INI* has changed. Given the very different structures of the registry and initialization files, in most cases this is of very little value in indicating which section of the registry has changed.[*]

Despite its lack of apparent utility, and despite the documentation's claim that WM_WININICHANGE is not implemented on Win95, Microsoft recommends that the WM_WININICHANGE message be used to indicate particular kinds of changes to the registry or to *WIN.INI.* Two of these special-purpose uses of WM_WININICHANGE include:

- *The default printer.* After an application modifies the default printer in *WIN.INI*, it should send a WM_WININICHANGE message to all open windows. The message's major recipient, though, is Windows itself; when it learns that the [Windows] section has been modified, it copies the default printer's information from WIN.INI to the Win95 registry.

- *Environment variables.* The Win32 SDK Knowledge Base recommends that the following WM_WININICHANGE message be sent under both Win95 and WinNT whenever the modification of an environment variable should take effect immediately, without requiring the user to log off and then log back on:

  SendMessage(HWND_BROADCAST, WM_WININICHANGE, 0, (LPARAM) "Environment")

  Since there is ordinarily no Environment section in *WIN.INI*, the message provides a very focused reference that the environment table should be examined and the environment variables defined in the registry enumerated. (User-specific environment variables are stored in HKEY_CURRENT_USER\Environment, while system environment variables are stored in HKEY_LOCAL_MACHINE\System\CurrentControlSet\Control\SessionManager\Environment.) However, Win95 appears to ignore the message completely. Registry-defined environment variables remain unknown to the system, while environment table variables that are defined using the *_putenv* function become visible immediately.

---

[*] This is not completely true of the message under Windows NT if it applies to an initialization file setting that has been relocated to the registry. Since Windows NT supports initialization file mapping, the *Get-ProfileString* and *GetProfileInt* functions, which can be used to retrieve initialization file settings, will instead retrieve information from the registry.

This lack of a standardized method of notifying applications of changes to system-wide settings—and frequently the lack of *any* method of notifying applications of changes—is a real shortcoming in Win95. There is a certain irony in this situation: On the one hand, Win95 aims at putting an end to the anarchy of Win3x, where far too many applications behaved as if they were the only programs on the user's desktop; on the other hand, one excellent means of doing this, which complements the other methods—like a reliance on OLE and the extensive use of the registry—would involve further developing the Windows messaging system. In failing to do this, Win95 in some sense represents a step backwards from the viewpoint of one application letting other applications know what it is doing to the system as a whole.

Windows NT Registry Functions Not Supported by Windows 95

Several functions in the Win32 API either were developed to take advantage of a distinctive feature of WinNT (like its support for security) or relied heavily on its architecture. As a result, although each of these functions can run under Win95, they do not really work. A worthwhile design goal for unsupported functions, however, is that they "degrade gracefully"—which is another way of saying that, while they may not do anything good because they're not supported, they at least shouldn't do anything bad. And in fact, each unsupported registry function that runs under Win95 returns the error code ERROR_CALL_NOT_IMPLEMENTED.

The Win32 registry functions that are not supported under Win95 are:

- *RegRestoreKey*
- *RegGetKeySecurity*
- *RegSetKeySecurity*
- *RegNotifyChangeKeyValue*

Under WinNT, *RegRestoreKey* is one of the functions used to import data from an external registry file generated by the *RegSaveKey* function. *RegRestoreKey* is similar to *RegReplaceKey*, except that it does not impose the limitation that the key whose values and subkeys are to be replaced be a direct subkey of one of the top-level keys. In addition, *RegRestoreKey* can save WinNT's volatile data.

In addition, WinNT provides two functions, *RegGetKeySecurity* and *RegSetKeySecurity*, to define or retrieve a registry key's security descriptor. Since Win95 is not a secure operating system, the functions are clearly out of place.

Finally, under WinNT, *RegNotifyChangeKeyValue* is used to notify an application that a change has occurred to the registry. The function in turn requires that the

---

The Profile API and the Registry

Because Windows NT supports initialization file mapping, which allows functions like *GetProfileString* or *WritePrivateProfileString* to operate on the registry along with or instead of initialization files, the Win32 initialization file functions can be considered a legitimate part of the Windows NT registry API. (For details on initialization file mapping, see "The Registry in Windows 95 and Windows NT" in Chapter 1, *The Registry, or, What Was So Bad About .INI Files?*) Windows 95, however, does not support initialization file mapping. Nonetheless, .INI files remain an important part of Win95 configuration, and hence should perhaps be considered "conceptually" part of the registry.

CreateEvent function be used to define an event, which in turn is assigned an event handle; this makes the function suitable primarily for inter-thread synchronization. Under Win95, however, the function is not supported.

Summary

At various points in this book, we've focused on the difference between registry policy and registry mechanism. This chapter has focused on documenting the mechanism—that is, on how you go about putting information in and getting information out of the registry, regardless of its content, by using the registry API. Several points are worth emphasizing:

- Accessing the registry follows a pattern familiar to most Windows (and DOS) programmers: you open a registry key, you perform one or more operations, then you close the key. A crucial difference, however, is that to open an HKEY, you first need an HKEY. This seeming "chicken and egg" problem is solved with top-level, always-open HKEYs such as HKEY_LOCAL_MACHINE.

- If you don't know the precise structure of the registry or the character of the data that you want to retrieve, you should use the *RegQueryInfoKey* function to collect information about the open key's subkeys and values.

- The *RegEnumKey* and *RegEnumValue* functions can be used for situations in which you don't know what keys or values exist, or in which you need to read all of a key's subkeys and value entries.

- When you do have a precise idea of what data you want to retrieve from the registry, you can use the *RegQueryValue* or *RegQueryValueEx* functions.

- The registry relies on a single mutex to implement locking and to insure the integrity of registry operations. However, only single registry function calls are   atomic   operations;   multiple   function-call   sequences   (such   as open/query/close or open/enum.../close) are not.

- Both because multiple registry function calls are not atomic and because Windows 95 lacks a method for notifying a process of modifications to the registry, you should make sure that your application is prepared to handle unexpected changes that other applications make to the registry.

5

Win95 Registry Access from Win16, DOS, and VxDs

While we've been focusing on accessing the registry from Win32 programs, it's important to remember that Win16 and DOS programs also run under Windows 95. While it's unlikely that anyone is writing brand new programs for these platforms, many developers do have "legacy" Win16 and DOS programs. They may want to give these Win16 and DOS programs some Windows 95 "smarts"—such as registry access—but can't afford right now to port the entire program to Win32. So it's worth taking a few moments to look at accessing the Windows 95 registry from Win16 and DOS programs.

To see how to access the registry from a Win16 or a DOS application, we need to understand a little of how the registry APIs are implemented under Windows 95. So this chapter will also provide an "inside" look at the Win16 and Win32 kernels and at the Windows 95 Virtual Machine Manager (VMM), which among its many other duties provides the actual registry access code that the higher-level APIs rely upon.

Win16 Registry Access

The Win16 API, of course, supports a subset of the registry API (the "compatibility" functions that we discussed in the last chapter) to permit access to the Windows 3.x registration database. For this purpose, developers for the Win16 platform can tap into the Win16 API's registry support by using the *SHELLAPI.H* header file, included with 16-bit C compilers and Windows SDKs:

```
#include "windows.h"
#include "shellapi.h"
```

But since *SHELLAPI.H* was designed for the limited Win31 registration database described in Chapter 1, *The Registry, or, What Was So Bad About .INI Files?*, it is missing some features required to fully access the Windows 95 registry. For example, the only data type it defines is REG_SZ, and it defines only a single top-level key, HKEY_CLASSES_ROOT, as follows:

```
#define REG_SZ              1
// ...
#define HKEY_CLASSES_ROOT   1
```

This definition, though, is incorrect for Windows 95. So we need to define all the data types and top-level keys (and undefine those that *SHELLAPI.H* already defines). Let's start a WIN16REG.H header file (the complete file is located on the disk accompanying this book):

```
#ifdef REG_SZ
#undef REG_SZ
#endif
#define REG_SZ                         ( 1 )
#define REG_EXPAND_SZ                  ( 2 )
#define REG_BINARY                     ( 3 )
#define REG_DWORD                      ( 4 )
#define REG_DWORD_BIG_ENDIAN           ( 5 )
#define REG_LINK                       ( 6 )
#define REG_MULTI_SZ                   ( 7 )
#define REG_RESOURCE_LIST              ( 8 )
#define REG_FULL_RESOURCE_DESCRIPTOR   ( 9 )
#define REG_RESOURCE_REQUIREMENTS_LIST ( 10 )

// Win16 shellapi.h does HKEY_CLASSES_ROOT, but wrong (1, not 80000000h)
#ifndef HKEY_CURRENT_USER
#undef HKEY_CLASSES_ROOT
#endif
#define HKEY_CLASSES_ROOT         (( HKEY ) 0x80000000 )
#define HKEY_CURRENT_USER         (( HKEY ) 0x80000001 )
#define HKEY_LOCAL_MACHINE        (( HKEY ) 0x80000002 )
#define HKEY_USERS                (( HKEY ) 0x80000003 )
#define HKEY_PERFORMANCE_DATA     (( HKEY ) 0x80000004 )
#define HKEY_CURRENT_CONFIG       (( HKEY ) 0x80000005 )
#define HKEY_DYN_DATA             (( HKEY ) 0x80000006 )
```

For convenience, we can also add the following constants (I really hate typing ERROR_FILE_NOT_FOUND when what I mean is that a registry key wasn't found):

```
// for convenience
#define OKAY        ERROR_SUCCESS
#define ERR_NO_KEY  ERROR_FILE_NOT_FOUND
#define HKCR        HKEY_CLASSES_ROOT
#define HKLM        HKEY_LOCAL_MACHINE
```

Since the registration database supports only a single unnamed (default) value per key, the Win16 *SHELLAPI.H* is missing a #define for *RegEnumValue*, of course.

You also won't find it among the functions exported by *SHELL.DLL*, the 16-bit shell library under Windows 95 that at first glance appears to contain the actual code for the functions declared in *SHELLAPI.H*. However, do not despair, because as Table 5-1 shows, a 16-bit version of *RegEnumValue* is provided by the 16-bit Windows 95 kernel, *KRNL386.EXE* (in addition, all the Win16 registry functions under Windows 95 are exported by *KRNL386.EXE*).

Table 5-1. Registry functions exported by KRNL386.EXE

Ordinal #	Name
216	*REGENUMKEY*
217	*REGOPENKEY*
218	*REGCREATEKEY*
219	*REGDELETEKEY*
220	*REGCLOSEKEY*
221	*REGSETVALUE*
222	*REGDELETEVALUE*
223	*REGENUMVALUE*
224	*REGQUERYVALUE*
225	*REGQUERYVALUEEX*
226	*REGSETVALUEEX*
227	*REGFLUSHKEY*

The equivalent functions in the 16-bit *SHELL.DLL* are just wrappers around calls to the KERNEL versions.

One would hope that the Windows 95 16-bit version of *RegEnumValue* found in *KRNL386.EXE* works the same as the documented Win32 version in *ADVAPI32.DLL*. And fortunately, it does. Of course, it has no declaration in *SHELLAPI.H*, and it's unlikely that your import library contains a reference to it. So here's a Win16 *RegEnumValue* function that links to the function at run-time, using the *GetProcAddress* and *GetModuleHandle* APIs:

```
#if (sizeof(int) != 4) // only needed for Win16
LONG RegEnumValue (HKEY hKey, DWORD dwIndex, LPSTR lpValueName,
    LPDWORD lpcbValueName, LPDWORD lpReserved, LPDWORD lpType,
    LPBYTE lpData, LPDWORD lpcbData)
{
    // RegEnumValue is KERNEL.223
    static LONG (WINAPI *pRegEnumValue)(HKEY,DWORD,LPSTR,LPDWORD,
        LPDWORD,LPDWORD,LPBYTE,LPDWORD);
    static int did_init = 0;
    if (! did_init)
    {
        // you ought to test for Win95 in here
        #define GET_PROC(mod,func) \
```

```
              (GetProcAddress(GetModuleHandle(mod), (func)))
        if (! (pRegEnumValue = (LONG (WINAPI*)()
              GET_PROC("KERNEL", "REGENUMVALUE")))
              fail("Can't link to RegEnumValue");
        did_init = 1;
    }
    return (*pRegEnumValue)(hKey,dwIndex,lpValueName,lpcbValueName,
        lpReserved,lpType,lpData,lpcbData);
}
#endif
```

`#if (sizeof(int) == 4)` is just a silly way of testing at compile-time whether you're building a 16-bit or 32-bit program; more likely, you'll define something on the command line that you can test for with `#ifdef WIN32_APP` or `#ifdef WIN16_APP` or whatever. In Visual Basic, you can use the `#If…Then…#Else` conditional compiler directive to test the value of the Win16 or Win32 compiler constants.

If you're using Visual Basic, you don't have to retrieve the address of the 16-bit registry function you'd like to call; instead, you can call it as you would any external function, using the standard Visual Basic **DECLARE** statement. The statement required to define *RegEnumValue* in a Visual Basic 4.0 code module, for instance, is:

```
// don't need Alias "REGENUMVALUE" here because Win16
// GetProcAddress is case-insensitive
Public Declare Function RegEnumValue Lib "Kernel" _
      (ByVal hKey As Long, ByVal dwIndex As Long, _
      ByVal lpValueName As String, lpcbValueName As Long, _
      lpReserved As Long, lpdwType As Long, lpByte As Byte, _
      lpcbByte As Long) As Long
```

Regardless of whether you're using C or Visual Basic, this is 16-bit code that uses the Win16 API, but it requires Windows 95 to run. So you probably want to check for the presence of Windows 95. The easiest way to do this is by examining the DWORD value returned by the Win16 *GetVersion* function. (For a complete discussion of testing for the different flavors of Windows, see Appendix A, *Where Am I Running?*) As Figure 5-1 shows, the low-order byte of its low-order word is the major Windows version number, while the high-order byte of its low-order word is the minor version number. Under Win16, Windows 95 returns a version number of 3.95 (i.e., the major version is 3 and the minor is 95). The *IsWindows 95* function shown in Example 5-1 illustrates how to check for the presence of Windows 95. It returns a Boolean value which, if the platform is something other than Windows 95, allows you either to display a message box and terminate your application or to use some method other than the registry to store application state information. A comparable *IsWindows 95* function for Visual Basic programmers is shown in Example 5-2.

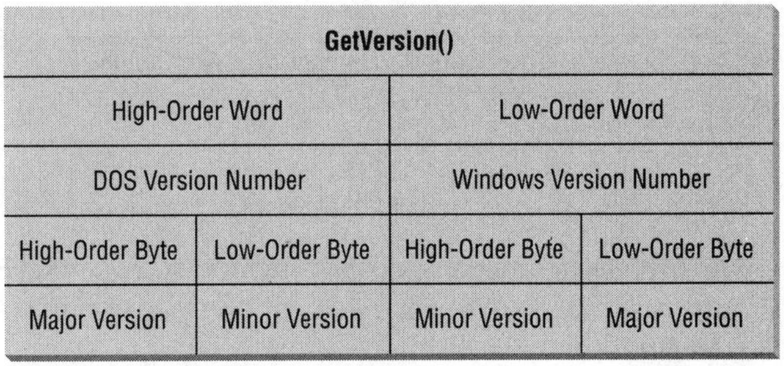

GetVersion()			
High-Order Word		Low-Order Word	
DOS Version Number		Windows Version Number	
High-Order Byte	Low-Order Byte	High-Order Byte	Low-Order Byte
Major Version	Minor Version	Minor Version	Major Version

Figure 5-1. The return value of GetVersion

Example 5-1. Win16 code to test for the presence of Windows 95

```
BOOL PASCAL IsWindows95() // Win16 only!!
    {
    DWORD dwVersion = GetVersion() ;
    return ((LOBYTE(LOWORD(dwVersion)) == 3) &&
            (HIBYTE(LOWORD(dwVersion)) == 95)) ;
    }
```

Example 5-2. Testing for the presence of Windows 95 with Visual Basic

```
Public Function IsWindows95() As Boolean

Dim intWinVersion As Integer

IsWindows95 = False
intVersion = GetVersion() Mod 65536

If (intVersion Mod 256 = 3) And (intVersion \ 256 = 95) Then
    IsWindows95 = True
End If

End Function
```

There are some limitations on Win16 registry access. First, a number of the functions implemented in the 32-bit API—most of them minor—are not found in *KRNL386.EXE*; they are listed in Table 5-2. You can't, for instance, do remote registry access from a Win16 application. More important, there isn't a Win16 version of *RegQueryInfoKey*.

Table 5-2. Registry functions not implemented in the Win95 Win16 API

Function	Comments
RegConnectRegistry	
RegCreateKeyEx	The "extended" version of *RegCreateKey*
RegEnumKeyEx	The "extended" version of *RegEnumKey*

Table 5-2. Registry functions not implemented in the Win95 Win16 API (continued)

Function	Comments
RegOpenKeyEx	The "extended" version of *RegOpenKey*
RegQueryInfoKey	
RegQueryMultipleValues	
RegReplaceKey	

Similarly, the Win16 registry functions do not include *RegOpenKeyEx* or *RegCreateKeyEx*. So those calls need to be changed to *RegOpenKey* and *RegCreateKey*, respectively. For example:

```
#if (sizeof(int) == 4)
    if (RegOpenKeyEx(hkey, name, 0,
        KEY_QUERY_VALUE | KEY_ENUMERATE_SUB_KEYS | KEY_READ,
        &hkey2) == OKAY)
#else
    if (RegOpenKey(hkey, name, &hkey2) == OKAY)
#endif
```

Finally, all of the 32-bit registry API functions that are not implemented under Windows 95[*] return `ERROR_CALL_NOT_IMPLEMENTED`; they are completely absent, however, from *KRNL386.EXE*. So you'll have to be careful not to call them from 16-bit code.

That's about it. Mostly, Win16 registry code can look just like the Win32 code we looked at in Chapter 4, *The Win32 Registry API*. The same goes for DOS registry code, but to see how to implement this, we need to take a short detour to look at how the Win16 registry code is implemented in Windows 95.

How Is Win16 Registry Access Implemented in Windows 95?

To figure out how to access the registry from a DOS program running under Windows 95, it's useful to first look at how Win16 support is implemented. Let's look at *RegOpenKey*. *SHELLAPI.H* has the following declaration:

```
LONG WINAPI RegOpenKey(HKEY, LPCSTR, HKEY FAR*);
```

In *SHELL.DLL*, this function is just a wrapper around a call to KERNEL.217. That, as shown in Table 5-1, is *RegOpenKey*. Here's a disassembly from the Windows 95 version of *KRNL386.EXE*, the Win16 kernel:[†]

---

[*] These are *RegGetKeySecurity*, *RegNotifyChangeKeyValue*, *RegRestoreKey*, *RegReplaceKey*, and *RegSetKeySecurity*.

[†] The raw disassembly was generated using Windows Source from V Communications (*http://webmill.com/vcom/winsrc*), a product written by this book's editor.

```
2.0530    REGOPENKEY    proc   far
2.0530        push   bp
2.0531        mov    bp,sp
2.0533        push   offset PARAM_ERROR ; (0553)
2.0536        mov    ax,[bp+0Ah]
2.0539        mov    cx,[bp+0Ch]
2.053C        mov    bx,1
2.053F        call   PARAM_VALIDATION
2.0542        mov    ax,[bp+6]
2.0545        mov    cx,[bp+8]
2.0548        mov    bx,1
2.054B        call   PARAM_VALIDATION
2.054E        pop    cx
2.054F        pop    bp
2.0550        jmp    IREGOPENKEY        ; (6ADC)
2.0553    PARAM_ERROR:
              mov    ax, ERROR_INVALID_PARAMETER ; (57h)
              retf   0Ch
          REGOPENKEY    endp
```

So the *RegOpenKey* function in *KRNL386.EXE* simply performs some validation on
the parameters passed to it and jumps to **IREGOPENKEY**. The Win16 kernel also
has some inline calls to **IREGOPENKEY** that may make it easier to see what's going
on. For example:

```
1.C1CB    push   8000h      ; 80000002h = HKEY_LOCAL_MACHINE
1.C1CE    push   2
1.C1D0    push   ds         ; ds:24DEh  -> "Software\..." (see below)
1.C1D1    push   24DEh
1.C1D4    push   ds         ; ds:24DAh  -> hkey (see below)
1.C1D5    push   24DAh
1.C1D8    call   far ptr IREGOPENKEY   ; (2.6ADC)
1.C1DD    cmp    ax,0
1.C1E0    jne    short ERROR
1.C1E2    cmp    dx,0
1.C1E5    jne    short ERROR

4.24DA    dd     0
4.24DE    db     'Software\Microsoft\Windows\CurrentVersion', 0
```

What, then, is **IREGOPENKEY**? It's the Win16 kernel's "internal," no-parameter-vali-
dation version of *RegOpenKey*:

```
2.6ADC    IREGOPENKEY    proc    far
2.6ADC        push   bp
2.6ADD        mov    bp,sp
2.6ADF        push   ds
2.6AE0        mov    ax,DGROUP
2.6AE3        mov    ds,ax
2.6AE5        mov    ax,word ptr VMM_API+2 ; (4.12AA)
2.6AE8        or     ax,VMM_API            ; (4.12A8)
2.6AEC        jnz    short CALL_VMM_API    ; (2.6AF4)
2.6AEE        mov    ax, ERROR_CANTOPEN    ; (3F3h)
2.6AF1        cwd
2.6AF2        jmp    short DONE ; (2.6AFB)
```

```
2.6AF4    CALL_VMM_API:
2.6AF4         mov    ax,100h
2.6AF7         call   dword ptr VMM_API    ; (4.12A8)
2.6AFB    DONE:
2.6AFB         pop    ds
2.6AFC         leave
2.6AFD         retf   0Ch
          IREGOPENKEY  endp
```

In other words, the 16-bit *RegOpenKey* pushes its parameters onto the stack, moves the value 100h into the AX register (we'll see the significance of the value 100h in a few moments; basically, it is the "magic number" for *RegOpenKey*), and invokes something called VMM_API:

```
push hkey+2
push hkey
push lpstr+2
push lpstr
push phkey+2
push phkey
mov ax, 100h
call dword ptr VMM_API
```

So what, you must be asking, is VMM_API? It's a function pointer created during kernel initialization with a call to INT 2Fh function 1684h, the Windows "Get VxD API" entry point (for more details, see Andrew Schulman, *Unauthorized Windows 95*, published by IDG Books):

```
1.B7AA    mov    ax,1684h
1.B7AD    mov    bx,1               ;;; 1 = VMM VxD ID
1.B7B0    xor    di,di
1.B7B2    mov    es,di
1.B7B4    int    2Fh                ; Get device API entry point for
                                    ;  ID bx, returns ptr in es:di
1.B7B6    mov    word ptr VMM_API+2,es    ; (4.12AA=0)
1.B7BA    mov    VMM_API,di         ; (4.12A8=0)
```

In other words, the Win95 Win16 kernel calls INT 2Fh function 1684h to get a function pointer to the API that VMM provides for protected-mode 16-bit callers.

Now, if you run some VxD listing utility (such as *VXDLIST* from *Unauthorized Windows 95*), you'll see that VMM provides both a V86 (Virtual-8086 mode) and PM (protected mode) API—and uses the same block of code (here, located at C0002C09h) to handle both:

Name	Vers	ID	DDB	Control	V86 API	PM API	#Srvc
VMM	4.00	0001h	C000E990	C00024F8	C0002C09	C0002C09*	402 ! 41

Because the same piece of code in VMM handles both V86 and PM callers, once you know how Windows 95 implements the Win16 registry API, you also know how to provide DOS access.

DOS Registry Access

To access the registry from a DOS program running under Win95, you simply need to do what the Win16 kernel does: maybe some parameter validation, then push parameters on the stack, move the function number (such as 100h for *RegOpenKey*) into AX, and call the VMM.

The function numbers that go into AX are listed in the *REGDEF.H* header file included with the Windows 95 Device Driver Kit (DDK; *ddk**inc32**regdef.h*):

```
#define RegOpenKey_Idx          0x100
#define RegCreateKey_Idx        0x101
#define RegCloseKey_Idx         0x102
#define RegDeleteKey_Idx        0x103
#define RegSetValue_Idx         0x104
#define RegQueryValue_Idx       0x105
#define RegEnumKey_Idx          0x106
#define RegDeleteValue_Idx      0x107
#define RegEnumValue_Idx        0x108
#define RegQueryValueEx_Idx     0x109
#define RegSetValueEx_Idx       0x10A
#define RegFlushKey_Idx         0x10B
#define RegLoadKey_Idx          0x10C
#define RegUnLoadKey_Idx        0x10D
#define RegSaveKey_Idx          0x10E
#define RegRestore_Idx          0x10F
#define RegRemapPreDefKey_Idx   0x110
```

These are the "magic numbers" for the 16-bit (both DOS and Win16) registry API provided by VMM in Win95.

Any one of these functions can be implemented for DOS (or, for that matter, for Win16, if the implementation didn't already exist in *KRNL386.EXE*) like so:

```
static FUNCPTR vmm = (FUNCPTR) 0;

LONG pascal far <SomeRegistryFunction>(<params...>)
{
    if (! vmm)
    {
        // one-time initialization
        if (! (vmm = GetVxDAPI(VMM_VXD_ID)))
            fail("This program requires the VMM API");
    }
    _asm mov ax, <appropriate idx number from regdef.h>
    _asm call dword ptr vmm
}
```

where:

```
#define VMM_VXD_ID      1

// call the Windows "Get Device Entry Point Address" function
```

```
// Interrupt 2Fh Function 1684h
FUNCPTR GetDeviceAPI(WORD vxd_id)
{
    _asm {
        push di
        push es
        xor di, di
        mov es, di
        mov ax, 1684h
        mov bx, vxd_id
        int 2fh
        mov ax, di
        mov dx, es
        pop es
        pop di
        }
    // return value in DX:AX
}
```

For example:

```
LONG pascal far RegOpenKey(HKEY, LPCSTR, HKEY far*)
{
    if (! vmm)
    {
        // one-time initialization
        if (! (vmm = GetVxDAPI(VMM_VXD_ID)))
            fail("This program requires the VMM API");
    }
    _asm mov ax, RegOpenKey_Idx
    _asm call dword ptr vmm

}
```

Rather than create each of these by hand, or rely on a text editor to copy and paste, we can let the C preprocessor do it with macros, as shown in the program *DOSREG.C* in Example 5-3.

Example 5-3. Implementing the Win95 registry API for DOS programs

```
/*
DOSREG.C -- Registry access for DOS apps running under Win95
See also DOSREG.H
Andrew Schulman (andrew@ora.com)
May 1996
*/

#include <stdlib.h>
#include <dos.h>
#include "dosreg.h"

// GetDeviceAPI is shown above

// from ddk\inc32\regdef.h
#define RegOpenKey_Idx          0x100
```

Example 5-3. Implementing the Win95 registry API for DOS programs (continued)

```
#define RegCreateKey_Idx       0x101
#define RegCloseKey_Idx        0x102
#define RegDeleteKey_Idx       0x103
#define RegSetValue_Idx        0x104
#define RegQueryValue_Idx      0x105
#define RegEnumKey_Idx         0x106
#define RegDeleteValue_Idx     0x107
#define RegEnumValue_Idx       0x108
#define RegQueryValueEx_Idx    0x109
#define RegSetValueEx_Idx      0x10A
#define RegFlushKey_Idx        0x10B
#define RegLoadKey_Idx         0x10C
#define RegUnLoadKey_Idx       0x10D
#define RegSaveKey_Idx         0x10E
#define RegRestore_Idx         0x10F
#define RegRemapPreDefKey_Idx 0x110

static FUNCPTR vmm = (FUNCPTR) 0;

#define REG_FUNC(idx) { \
    if (! vmm) { InitRegAPI(); if (! vmm) return -1; } \
    _asm mov ax, idx; \
    _asm call dword ptr vmm; \
    }

// "parameter not used" errors in here are expected

LONG pascal far RegOpenKey(HKEY a, LPCSTR b, HKEY far* c) \
    REG_FUNC(RegOpenKey_Idx)
LONG pascal far RegCreateKey(HKEY a, LPCSTR b, HKEY far* c) \
    REG_FUNC(RegCreateKey_Idx)
LONG pascal far RegCloseKey(HKEY a) REG_FUNC(RegCloseKey_Idx)
LONG pascal far RegDeleteKey(HKEY a, LPCSTR b) REG_FUNC(RegDeleteKey_Idx)
LONG pascal far RegSetValue(HKEY a, LPCSTR b, DWORD c, LPCSTR d, DWORD e) \
    REG_FUNC(RegSetValue_Idx)
LONG pascal far RegQueryValue(HKEY a, LPCSTR b, LPSTR c, LONG far* d) \
    REG_FUNC(RegQueryValue_Idx)
LONG pascal far RegEnumKey(HKEY a, DWORD b, LPSTR c, DWORD d) \
    REG_FUNC(RegEnumKey_Idx)
LONG pascal far RegEnumValue(HKEY a, DWORD b, LPSTR c, LPDWORD d,
    LPDWORD e, LPDWORD f, LPBYTE g, LPDWORD h) REG_FUNC(RegEnumValue_Idx)

#define VMM_VXD_ID       1

int InitRegAPI(void) { return ((vmm = GetDeviceAPI(VMM_VXD_ID)) != 0); }
```

Example 5-4 shows the *DOSREG.H* include file.

Example 5-4. Implementing the registry API under DOS

```
/*
DOSREG.H -- Registry access for DOS apps running under Win95
See also DOSREG.C
Andrew Schulman (andrew@ora.com)
```

Example 5-4. Implementing the registry API under DOS (continued)

```
May 1996
*/

typedef unsigned char BYTE;
typedef unsigned short WORD;
typedef long LONG;
typedef unsigned long DWORD;
typedef LONG (far *FUNCPTR)(void);
typedef DWORD HKEY; // not WORD!
typedef char far *LPCSTR;
typedef char far *LPSTR;
typedef DWORD far *LPDWORD;
typedef BYTE far *LPBYTE;

int InitRegAPI(void);

// from include\shellapi.h
LONG pascal far RegOpenKey(HKEY a, LPCSTR b, HKEY far*c);
LONG pascal far RegCreateKey(HKEY a, LPCSTR b, HKEY far*c);
LONG pascal far RegCloseKey(HKEY a);
LONG pascal far RegDeleteKey(HKEY a, LPCSTR b);
LONG pascal far RegSetValue(HKEY a, LPCSTR b, DWORD c, LPCSTR d, DWORD e);
LONG pascal far RegQueryValue(HKEY a, LPCSTR b, LPSTR c, LONG far* d);
LONG pascal far RegEnumKey(HKEY a, DWORD b, LPSTR c, DWORD d);
LONG pascal far RegEnumValue(HKEY a, DWORD b, LPSTR c, LPDWORD d,
    LPDWORD e, LPDWORD f, LPBYTE g, LPDWORD h);

#define REG_SZ                         ( 1 )
#define REG_EXPAND_SZ                  ( 2 )
#define REG_BINARY                     ( 3 )
#define REG_DWORD                      ( 4 )
#define REG_DWORD_BIG_ENDIAN           ( 5 )
#define REG_LINK                       ( 6 )
#define REG_MULTI_SZ                   ( 7 )
#define REG_RESOURCE_LIST              ( 8 )
#define REG_FULL_RESOURCE_DESCRIPTOR   ( 9 )
#define REG_RESOURCE_REQUIREMENTS_LIST ( 10 )

#define HKEY_CLASSES_ROOT              (( HKEY ) 0x80000000 )
#define HKEY_CURRENT_USER              (( HKEY ) 0x80000001 )
#define HKEY_LOCAL_MACHINE             (( HKEY ) 0x80000002 )
#define HKEY_USERS                     (( HKEY ) 0x80000003 )
#define HKEY_PERFORMANCE_DATA          (( HKEY ) 0x80000004 )
#define HKEY_CURRENT_CONFIG            (( HKEY ) 0x80000005 )
#define HKEY_DYN_DATA                  (( HKEY ) 0x80000006 )

// for convenience
#define ERROR_SUCCESS    0
#define OKAY             ERROR_SUCCESS
#define ERR_NO_KEY       ERROR_FILE_NOT_FOUND
#define HKCR             HKEY_CLASSES_ROOT
#define HKCU             HKEY_CURRENT_USER
#define HKLM             HKEY_LOCAL_MACHINE
```

It's important to emphasize that this applies only to DOS programs running under Windows 95. This is *not* access under real-mode DOS; the Windows Virtual Machine Manager must be running. (You may be wondering, then, how *REGEDIT.EXE* manages to work in real mode. The answer is that it has its own copy of Microsoft's registry code, the same code that's in the VMM.)

An Example of Portable Registry Access: REGDUMP

Armed with *DOSREG.C* and *DOSREG.H*, it's quite easy to create DOS applications that access the Win95 registry—or to make DOS versions of existing Win32 applications that access the registry. Similarly, with the *WIN16REG.C* and *WIN16REG.H* files on the disk accompanying this book (these files incorporate the Win16 code shown earlier in this chapter), it's easy to produce Win16 applications that access the Win95 registry.

For example, *REGDUMP.C* below is a program that dumps out the entire contents of the Win95 registry. The program can be built as a Win32 Console (character-mode) program, a DOS program, or a Win16 "stdio" program (using something like Borland's EasyWin library, Microsoft's QuickWin library, or the WINIO library from the book *Undocumented Windows*). When built as a Win16 program, most of *REGDUMP*'s output scrolls away immediately, but at least you can see that it's a Win16 program that accesses the Win95 registry. For what it's worth, the DOS version is about twice as fast as the Win32 version.

REGDUMP attempts to reduce the number of lines of output required to display the registry. For example, whereas *REGEDIT* export produces output such as:

```
[HKEY_LOCAL_MACHINE\SOFTWARE\Classes\CLSID\{BD84B381-8CA2-1069-AB1D-
08000948F534}]
@="PANOSE Core Mapper"

[HKEY_LOCAL_MACHINE\SOFTWARE\Classes\CLSID\{BD84B381-8CA2-1069-AB1D-
08000948F534}\InprocServer32]
@="panmap.dll"

"ThreadingModel"="Apartment"
```

REGDUMP would represent this as:

```
HKEY_LOCAL_MACHINE
  SOFTWARE
    Classes
      CLSID -> ""
        {BD84B381-8CA2-1069-AB1D-08000948F534} -> "PANOSE Core Mapper"
          InprocServer32 -> "panmap.dll"
            ThreadingModel="Apartment"
```

REGDUMP shows default (unnamed) values on the same line as the key, as "`keyname -> default value`". Named values are shown as "`name=value`".

REGDUMP also tries to convert values (not keys) with those confusing-looking {x-y-z-a-b} CLSIDs into readable names. For example, assuming that the registry (HKCR\CLSID, HKCR\Interface, or HKCR\TypeLib) contains a definition such as:

```
{00020420-0000-0000-C000-000000000046} -> "PSDispatch"
```

then, rather than:

```
ProxyStubClsid -> {00020420-0000-0000-C000-000000000046}
```

REGDUMP will instead show:

```
ProxyStubClsid -> {PSDispatch}
```

Typically *REGDUMP* output is about 15,000 lines, representing over 7,000 keys and over 12,000 values.

```
/*
REGDUMP.C -- Win95 registry dumper for Win32, Win16, and DOS
Andrew Schulman (andrew@ora.com)
August 1995, revised May 1996

Win32 version: cl regdump.c advapi32.lib
DOS version: bcc -DDOS_VERSION regdump.c dosreg.c
Win16 version: bcc -W -DWIN16_VERSION regdump.c win16reg.c
*/

#include <stdlib.h>
#include <stdio.h>
#include <string.h>
#include <ctype.h>

#ifdef DOS_VERSION
#include "dosreg.h"
#else
#ifdef WIN16_VERSION
#include "win16reg.h"            // includes shellapi.h
#else
#define WIN32_LEAN_AND_MEAN
#include "windows.h"             // includes winnt.h and winreg.h
#endif
#endif

#define OKAY ERROR_SUCCESS

void indent(int level)
{
    int i;
    for (i=0; i<level; i++)
        fputs("  ", stdout);
}
```

```
void dump(unsigned char *fp, unsigned bytes,
    char *mask, unsigned long addr, int width)
{
    unsigned char *p;
    unsigned i, j, c;

    for (i=0; i<bytes; i += width)
    {
        c = ((bytes-i) > width) ? width : bytes-i;
        printf(mask, addr+i);
        putchar(' '); putchar('|'); putchar(' ');
        for (j=c, p=fp+i; j--; p++)  printf("%02X ", *p);
        for (j=width-c; j--; )  fputs("   ", stdout); // pad out last line
        putchar('|'); putchar(' ');
        for (j=c, p=fp+i; j--; p++) putchar( isprint(*p) ? *p : '.' );
        putchar('\n');
    }
}


static int do_dump = 0;

void printdword(DWORD dw, int brackets)
{
    if (brackets)    putchar('[');
    if (dw < 10)     printf("%d", dw);
    else             printf("%0Xh", dw);
    if (brackets)    putchar(']');
}

// key: "CLSID" or "Interface" or "TypeLib"
char *get_clsid_name(char *data, int len, char *key)
{
    static char buf[256];
    char buf2[256];
    long buflen = 256;
    HKEY clsid;
    if ((data[0] != '{') || (data[len] != '}'))
        return data; // unchanged
    if (RegOpenKey(HKEY_CLASSES_ROOT, key, &clsid) != OKAY)
        return data; // can't open
    strcpy(buf2, data);
    if (strcmp(key, "TypeLib") == 0)
        strcat(buf2, "\\1.0"); // todo: modify hard-wired version number
    if (RegQueryValue(clsid, buf2, buf, &buflen) != OKAY)
        strcpy(buf, data); // unchanged
    if (! *buf)
        strcpy(buf, data); // name was blank
    RegCloseKey(clsid);
    return buf; // static -- must use immediately
}

void printvalue(DWORD type, char *data, DWORD cb)
{
    switch (type)
```

```c
        {
        case REG_EXPAND_SZ:
            // todo: expand environment variables
        case REG_SZ:
            if ((data[0] == '{') && (data[cb-2] == '}'))
            {
                char *s = get_clsid_name(data, cb-2, "CLSID");
                if (*s == '{') s = get_clsid_name(data, cb-2, "Interface");
                if (*s == '{') s = get_clsid_name(data, cb-2, "TypeLib");
                if (*s == '{') printf("%s", s);  // unchanged
                else           printf("{%s}", s);  // converted CLSID to name
            }
            else
            {
                char c = (strchr(data, '\"')) ? '\'' : '\"';
                printf("%c%s%c", c, data, c);
            }
            break;
        case REG_DWORD:
            printdword(*((DWORD *) data), 0);
            break;
        case REG_BINARY:
            printf("BIN (%d bytes) ", cb);
            switch (cb)
            {
                case 1: printdword(*((BYTE *) data), 1); break;
                case 2: printdword(*((WORD *) data), 1); break;
                case 4: printdword(*((DWORD *) data), 1); break;
                default:
                    if (do_dump)
                    {
                        putchar('\n');
                        dump(data, cb, "%04X", 0, 16);
                    }
                    break;
            }
            break;
        default:
            printf("<type %d>", type);
            break;
        }
}

static DWORD numvalue = 0, numkey = 0;

void enumvalue(int level, HKEY hkey)
{
    char name[256], data[1024];
    DWORD size, cb, type, iValue;
    for (iValue=0; ;iValue++)
    {
        size = 256;
        cb = 1024;
        if (RegEnumValue(hkey, iValue, name, &size, 0, &type, data, &cb) !=
```

```
                OKAY)
                break;
        if (size && *name)
        {
            putchar('\n');
            indent(level);
            printf("%s=", name);
        }
        else    // display default value with -> on same line
            printf(" -> ");
        printvalue(type, data, cb);
        numvalue++;
    }
}

void enumkey(int level, HKEY hkey, char *str)
{
    char name[256];
    HKEY hkey2;
    DWORD iSubKey = 0;
    putchar('\n');
    indent(level);
    fputs(str, stdout);
    enumvalue(level+1, hkey);
    while (RegEnumKey(hkey, iSubKey, name, 256) == OKAY)
    {
        if (RegOpenKey(hkey, name, &hkey2) == OKAY)
        {
            enumkey(level+1, hkey2, name);  // recursive call!!
            RegCloseKey(hkey2);
        }
        iSubKey++;
        numkey++;
    }
}

void fail(const char *s) { puts(s); exit(1); }

main(int argc, char *argv[])
{
    int i;
    int did_enum = 0;
    char *s;

#ifdef DOS_VERSION
    // Explicitly calling InitRegAPI is not required, but it lets us
    // put up an error message if we're not running under Win95
    if (! InitRegAPI())
        fail("This is a DOS program, but it requires Windows 95");
#endif

    for (i=1; i<argc; i++)
    {
        s = argv[i];
```

```
        if (*s == '-' || *s == '/')
        {
            if (strcmp(strupr(s+1), "DUMP") == 0)
                do_dump++;
            else
                fail("usage: regdump [-dump] [key#]");
        }
        else
        {
            enumkey(0, (HKEY) ((DWORD) HKEY_CLASSES_ROOT + atoi(s)),
                "??");
            did_enum++;
        }
    }

    if (! did_enum)
    {
        // don't show HKCR: same as HKLM\SOFTWARE\Classes
        // enumkey(0, HKEY_CLASSES_ROOT, "HKEY_CLASSES_ROOT");

        // don't show HKCU: same as HKEY_USERS\<user>
        // enumkey(0, HKEY_CURRENT_USER, "HKEY_CURRENT_USER");

        enumkey(0, HKEY_LOCAL_MACHINE, "HKEY_LOCAL_MACHINE");
        enumkey(0, HKEY_USERS, "HKEY_USERS");

        #ifndef HKEY_CURRENT_CONFIG
        #define HKEY_CURRENT_CONFIG     (HKEY) ((DWORD)HKEY_CLASSES_ROOT+5)
        #define HKEY_DYN_DATA           (HKEY) ((DWORD)HKEY_CLASSES_ROOT+6)
        #endif

        enumkey(0, HKEY_PERFORMANCE_DATA, "HKEY_PERFORMANCE_DATA");
        enumkey(0, HKEY_CURRENT_CONFIG, "HKEY_CURRENT_CONFIG");
        enumkey(0, HKEY_DYN_DATA, "HKEY_DYN_DATA");
    }

    printf("\n\nKeys: %u\n", numkey);
    printf("Values: %u\n", numvalue);
    return 0;
}
```

Note how little the source code differs between the Win32, Win16, and DOS versions. At the top, *REGDUMP.C* includes *WINDOWS.H*, *DOSREG.H*, or *WIN16REG.H* (which in turn includes *SHELLAPI.H*). Of course, the Win16 and DOS versions really ought to check for the presence of Win95: the DOS version of *REGDUMP* won't work under real-mode DOS, and the Win16 version won't work under Win31. But then, even the Win32 version really ought to be checking for Win95 too, since Win32 apps might find themselves running under Win31, courtesy of Microsoft's Win32s add-in. See Appendix A for complete details on checking for the presence of Win95.

The Implementation of Win32 Registry Access

We've seen how Win16 registry access is implemented under Windows 95, and we've seen how this implementation can easily be imitated to implement DOS registry access.

Since both Win16 and DOS registry access work by creating wrappers around calls to VMM, it's worth asking how Win32 access is implemented. It turns out that this, too, is a wrapper around a call to the VMM—but a wrapper with an important twist.

Again, let's use the example of *RegOpenKey*. In *WINREG.H*, there are two versions of *RegOpenKey*:

```
WINADVAPI LONG APIENTRY RegOpenKeyA (HKEY hKey, LPCSTR lpSubKey,
    PHKEY phkResult);

WINADVAPI LONG APIENTRY RegOpenKeyW (HKEY hKey, LPCWSTR lpSubKey,
    PHKEY phkResult);

#ifdef UNICODE
#define RegOpenKey   RegOpenKeyW
#else
#define RegOpenKey   RegOpenKeyA
#endif // !UNICODE
```

In Windows 95, the unicode version of the function, *RegOpenKeyW* (the "W" stands for "wide" or "wide character set," indicating unicode) is not implemented. So let's look at *RegOpenKeyA* in *ADVAPI32.DLL*:[*]

```
RegOpenKeyA:
    BFED17CD:       push    esi
    BFED17CE:       push    edi
    BFED17CF:       mov     esi,dword ptr [esp+14]
    BFED17D3:       push    04
    BFED17D5:       push    esi
    BFED17D6:       call    dword ptr ds:[IsBadWritePtr]
    BFED17DC:       test    eax,eax
    BFED17DE:       je      loc_17E7
    BFED17E0:       mov     eax,00000057
    BFED17E5:       jmp     loc_1825
```

---

[*] The disassembly was generated using the /DUMPBIN option of Microsoft's *LINK* utility, which in turn has /DISASM and /EXPORTS options. The command line that produces this output is:

`link /dumpbin /disasm /exports \windows\system\advapi32.dll`

The output was then massaged with an AWK script. (By the time you read this, the "Windows Source" product from V Communications should have been updated to support the Win32 "portable executable" (PE) file format.)

```
loc_17E7:
  BFED17E7:      mov      edi,dword ptr [esp+0C]
  BFED17EB:      push     edi
  BFED17EC:      call     IS_REMOTE?
  BFED17F1:      test     eax,eax
  BFED17F3:      je       Remote_RegOpenKey
  BFED17F5:      push     esi
  BFED17F6:      push     dword ptr [esp+14]
  BFED17FA:      push     edi
  BFED17FB:      push     00010011
  BFED1800:      call     dword ptr ds:[VxDCall]      ; KERNEL32.4
  BFED1806:      jmp      loc_1825
```

Notice that *VxDCall* with the number 10011h pushed on the stack. (Also notice the *Remote_RegOpenKey* and *IS_REMOTE*. We'll get to those in a minute—that's the important twist mentioned earlier.)

VxDCall is an API provided by *KERNEL32.DLL* that allows Win32 programs to make selected calls into VMM and other VxDs. *VxDCall* is crucial to the internal operation of Win95. (For full details, see Schulman, *Unauthorized Windows 95*; Pietrek, *Windows 95 System Programming Secrets*, published by IDG Books; and sample programs on ORA's Web site: *http://www.ora.com/pub/examples/windows/win95.update/ unauthw.html*.)

A specific Win32 service is specified by pushing its magic number on the stack before calling *VxDCall*. Here is a list of the registry-related services, from Matt Pietrek's *Windows 95 System Programming Secrets*, (p. 439):

```
RegOpenKey/Ex                10011
RegCreateKey                 10012
RegCloseKey                  10013
RegDeleteKey                 10014
RegSetValue                  10015
RegDeleteValue               10016
RegQueryValue                10017
RegEnumKey/Ex                10018
RegEnumValue                 10019
RegQueryValueEx              1001A
RegSetValueEx                1001B
RegFlushKey                  1001C
RegQueryInfoKey              1001D
// 1E, 1F, 20 are unrelated to registry
RegLoadKey                   10021
RegUnloadKey                 10022
RegSaveKey                   10023
RegRemapPreDefKey            10024
// 25 is unrelated to registry
RegQueryMultipleValues       10026
RegReplaceKey                10027
```

(These are the VMM function numbers for the 32-bit registry API. Do not confuse these with the VMM function numbers for the 16-bit registry API, shown earlier in this chapter.)

For example, here's a simple function call. The following code snippet comes from *ADVAPI32.DLL*:

```
RegRemapPreDefKey:
   BFED1D8E:   push   dword ptr [esp+08]
   BFED1D92:   push   dword ptr [esp+08]
   BFED1D96:   push   00010024
   BFED1D9B:   call   dword ptr ds:[VxDCall]
   BFED1DA1:   ret    0008
```

So that's how the Win32 registry APIs work: some parameters are pushed onto the stack, a VMM service number is pushed on the stack, and the *VxDCall* function is called.

More precisely, that's how the registry APIs work under certain common conditions. The *RegConnectRegistry* function is not implemented this way. And, for a particular registry function to be "forwarded" to the VMM, the handle passed as an argument to the function must be *local*; remote registry access is implemented completely differently, and does not rely on the local VMM. Instead, remote registry access from one machine uses Remote Procedure Call (RPC) to do a "Vulcan mind meld" with VMM on another machine. How? Read on.

Implementing Remote Registry Access

Recall that earlier in the disassembly of *RegOpenKey*, we encountered the following:

```
BFED17EC:   call   IS_REMOTE?
BFED17F1:   test   eax,eax
BFED17F3:   je     Remote_RegOpenKey
```

Let's now look at the two missing pieces, **IS_REMOTE?** and *Remote_RegOpenKey*.

IS_REMOTE? is too boring to show. It first checks whether the handle of the registry key passed to it as an argument is one of the built-in top-level keys 80000000h through 80000006h (and it uses some rather silly code to perform this simple test). If it's not, **IS_REMOTE?** next does the following test on the handle:

```
BFED1129:   not   eax
BFED112B:   and   eax,01
```

In other words:

```
BOOL IsHkeyRemote(HKEY hkey)
{
    DWORD dw = (DWORD) hkey;
    if ((hkey >= HKEY_CLASSES_ROOT) && (hkey <= HKEY_DYN_DATA))
```

```
        return 0;   // local
    return ! (((~dw) & 1));
}
```

Now for *Remote_RegOpenKey*. Again, the code itself is not that interesting. It basically links to and then calls a function called *Remote_RegOpenKey* in a dynamic link library called *WINREG.DLL*. The link is performed at run-time, using Windows' ability to turn string module.function names into executable function pointers:

```
HANDLE winreg;
WINADVAPI (LONG APIENTRY *Remote_RegOpenKey)(HKEY hKey,
    LPCSTR lpSubKey, PHKEY phkResult);
winreg = LoadLibrary("WINREG.DLL");
Remote_RegOpenKey = GetProcAddress(winreg, "Remote_RegOpenKey");
(*Remote_RegOpenKey)(hKey, lpSubKey, phkResult);
```

Or, using the GET_PROC macro shown earlier in our Win16 definition for *RegEnumValue* (and assuming that *WINREG.DLL* is already loaded into memory):

```
#define GET_PROC(mod,func) \
    (GetProcAddress(GetModuleHandle(mod), (func)))

WINADVAPI (LONG APIENTRY *Remote_RegOpenKey)(HKEY hKey,
    LPCSTR lpSubKey, PHKEY phkResult);
Remote_RegOpenKey = GET_PROC("WINREG", "Remote_RegOpenKey");
(*Remote_RegOpenKey)(hKey, lpSubKey, phkResult);
```

Naturally, we know want to know how *Remote_RegOpenKey* in *WINREG.DLL* is implemented. This would take us rather far afield, into the realm of Remote Procedure Calls (RPC; see John Bloomer, *Power Programming with RPC*; Ward Rosenberry and Jim Teague, *Distributing Applications Across DCE and Windows NT*; and John Shirley and Ward Rosenberry, *Microsoft RPC Programming Guide*, all published by O'Reilly & Associates). For our purposes, we can just note that the *Remote_RegXXX* functions in *WINREG.DLL* rely on RPC APIs such as *NdrSendReceive*, *NdrPointerMarshall*, etc., provided by *RPCRT4.DLL* (RPC run-time). These functions are declared in *RPCNDR.H* (NDR = "Network Data Representation").

What happens on the other end? There's a Windows 95 service, *REGSERV.EXE*, which calls the same VMM services, using *VxDCall*, that are called for local registry access.

VMM Registry Services and Dynamic Keys

So Win32, Win16, and DOS registry access are all based on calls to the VMM. Not surprisingly, then, there are VxD-based registry calls (VMM is really just a VxD,

---

REGSERV.EXE

When Microsoft Remote Registry Service is installed on a computer, the `HKLM\Software\Microsoft\Windows\CurrentVersion\RunSer-vices` key is created if it doesn't exist, and a `REG_SZ` entry whose name is `regserv` is added. Its value is *regserv.exe*. This means that the remote registry server is launched as a Windows 95 service at system start up, before a user logs on. The server runs as a background process with no interface; however, if you run *PView95* or another process viewer, you'll find it present. For details on defining Windows 95 services, see "Automatically Launching a Service" in Chapter 8, *What Goes in the Registry: System Settings*.

---

albeit the most important one in Win95). For example, here's a call that VMM itself makes to its own registry services:

```
48518    dd     00000h                    ;  xref 4198C, 19F2, 1BA6, 1BE2

4863C    db     'System\CurrentControlSet\Services\'
4865E    db     'Arbitrators\IOArb'
4866F    db     0

41926    push   48518h
4192B    push   4863Ch
41930    push   80000002h
41935    VMMcall _RegOpenKey          ; Win-VMM function    fn=10148h
4193B    add    esp,0Ch
4193E    cmp    eax,0
41941    jne    ERROR

; ...

419F2    push   48518
419F8    VMMcall _RegCloseKey         ; Win-VMM function    fn=10149h
```

The VMM registry services are documented in the Windows 95 device driver kit (DDK). Also see the following header files included with the DDK:

REGDEF.H, REGDEF.INC
VMM.H, VMM.INC
VMMREG.H, VMMREG.INC
VXDWRAPS.H

Notice that creating a dynamic registry key requires a VxD, which calls the *_RegCreateDynKey* service provided by VMM. This service is passed by several function pointers (callbacks) in your VxD; whenever your dynamic key is queried, VMM will call your VxD to produce the dynamic data. See `\DDK\DOCS\`

DYNKEYS.DOC, which describes *_RegCreateDynKey*, and a "provider" data structure, and the *DYNKEY.C* sample program included with the DDK. Also see *VMMREG.H*:

```
VMM_RegCreateDynKey(PCHAR lpszSubKey, PVOID pvKeyContext,
    PVOID pprovHandlerInfo, PVOID ppvalueValueInfo,
    DWORD cpvalueValueInfo, PVMMHKEY phkResult);
```

The provider data structure must be filled in with a function pointer to *RegKeyHandler*. This is the code that VMM will call whenever the "dynamic" (essentially, fictitious) key is accessed:

```
VMMREGRET __cdecl RegKeyHandler(PVOID pvKeyContext,
    PVALCONTEXT pValueContext, DWORD cValueContext,
    PBYTE pbBuffer, DWORD *pcbBuffer, DWORD fFlags);
```

Vireo's Registry File System Device

An old adage tells us that if you encounter something unfamiliar, the best way to respond to it is to turn it into something that you already know how to handle. A very interesting example of this is the Registry File System Device (Reg-FSD), a virtual devide driver (VxD) developed by Fred Hewitt at Vireo Software. RegFSD, which is found on the accompanying diskette, transforms the Win95 registry into a file system. Registry keys and value entries can then be accessed—from both 16-bit and 32-bit code—just as you would access any directory and file. RegFSD is one of the sample VxDs that is included with Vireo's VToolsD for Windows 95; for additional information, see Vireo Software's Web site at *http://www.vireo.com.*

Summary

A few key points were discussed in this chapter:

- Win32 is not synonymous with Win95, and Win16 is not synonymous with Win31. Win16 programs can access the Win95 registry, and Win32 programs attempting to access the Win95 registry must ensure that they are really and truly running under Win95, not Win32s (and, often, not WinNT either).

- DOS programs can also access the Win95 registry, so long, of course, as they are actually running under Win95.

- All local Win95 registry access is handled by VMM. All remote Win95 registry access is handled by *WINREG.DLL*, which RPCs to *REGSERV.EXE* on the remote machine, which then calls down to its VMM.

- Virtual device drivers (VxDs) can also access the Win95 registry. Dynamic registry keys can only be created and maintained by a VxD.

6

The Registry and Visual Basic

While C has a reputation for difficulty, most Visual Basic (VB) programmers find accessing the registry through the Win32 API far more challenging than their C counterparts. VB is an extensible development tool that provides a variety of ways to tap into the Windows API, but its major objective is to *shield* the developer from many of the complexities of Windows programming. And because VB programmers are insulated from most low-level details of Windows' operation and from the conventions of the Windows software development kits, extending VB to incorporate the registry (or any other enhanced Windows feature) can be a rather vexing process of trial and error.

There is another reason for this difficulty. Whereas C programmers, at least until recently, had to rely on the Win32 Software Development Kit (or a comparable substitute) to develop their applications, VB programmers suffer from an embarrassment of riches—almost an over-abundance of tools from which to choose:

- *VBA intrinsic functions.* Version 4.0 of VB (VB4) includes four functions that allow registry values to be created, modified, retrieved, and deleted. The functions are designed as a broad, cross-platform solution: they will work with private initialization files in the 16-bit version of VB, and with the registry under Win95 and WinNT in the 32-bit version of VB.

- *The registry API.* Through the DECLARE statement, which defines an external routine to a VB application, programmers can extend VB to call almost all routines in the Windows API. When a particular routine is correctly defined, it is called in code just as if it were a built-in part of VB.

- *Third-party dynamic link libraries.* One area in which VB is most extensible is in its support for external and third-party dynamic link libraries. The entire Windows API consists of calls to over 1,000 routines located in external DLLs. Third-party libraries usually aim at providing a higher level, and therefore a more accessible, interface to the API, or to offer a less function-oriented, more object-oriented form of access to the Windows API.

- *Custom OLE (.OCX) controls.* The complexity of the registry, and the difficulty that programmers often face in navigating it, makes it a perfect candidate for an OLE custom control. Like VB itself, registry controls offer relatively full access to the registry at the same time as they shield programmers from many of the intricacies of the registry API.

This chapter focuses on the first two of these options. VB's intrinsic support for the registry is examined in detail. In our judgment, though, the major issue that these functions raise is not *how* to use them, but *why*. As we shall see, they offer limited registry access in a way that violates Microsoft's own guidelines for how the registry should be used.

In discussing the registry API, this chapter does not provide a review of its individual functions. Although Chapter 4, *The Win32 Registry API*, focuses primarily on C programming, we assume you've read it carefully enough to get a sense of the registry API's individual functions and what they do. Instead, this chapter focuses on particular problems that VB programmers face when they are extending VB by accessing the registry API.

If you need to access the registry in your VB application but are intimidated by the registry API, another solution is available: an OLE custom control. The diskette accompanying *Inside the Windows 95 Registry* includes a design-time version of the Desaware Registry Control; it is discussed at length in Chapter 7, *The Desaware Registry Control.*

The VBA Registry Functions

Under Win31, accessing the initialization file functions within the Win16 API was something of a "black art" to many VB programmers. In view of this, it was not surprising that, when VB4 appeared, it included four functions that offered built-in registry access, thus freeing VB programmers from the need to make direct calls to the registry API.

Unfortunately, in implementing these functions, Microsoft decided that providing a method for flexible registry access was far less important than achieving compatibility across Windows versions and platforms. That means that the VBA registry functions access initialization files under Win3x and the registry under Win95 and WinNT, and that the same code can run without modification on all three platforms.

For many programmers, this compatibility promises to eliminate the need for separate platform-specific code fragments. For instance, the three lines of code below can replace the relatively lengthy code fragment shown in Example 6-1:

```
Dim strDefault As String, strWindowPos As String
strDefault = Str(Form1.Left) & Str(Form1.Top) & _
             Str(Form1.Width) & Str(Form1.Height)
strWindowPos = GetSetting("MyApp", "Settings", "WindowPos", strDefault)
```

Example 6-1. Coding for 16- and 32-bit versions of Windows

```
Function WinPos() As String

Dim lngLenValue As Long
Dim strDefault As String, strWindowPos As String

' Determine default window position
strDefault = Trim(Str(Form1.Left)) + " " + Trim(Str(Form1.Top)) + _
         " " + Trim(Str(Form1.Width)) + " " + Trim(Str(Form1.Height))

#If Win32 Then
   Dim lngRegError As Long, hKey As Long, lngDataType As Long
   Dim strValue As String

   ' Retrieve string value
   If RegOpenKey(HKEY_CURRENT_USER, _
           "Software\VB and VBA Program Settings\MyApp\Settings", _
           hKey) = ERROR_SUCCESS Then
      lngLenValue = 25
      strWindowPos = String(lngLenValue, 0)
      If RegQueryValueEx(hKey, "WindowPos", 0&, lngDataType, _
                         strWindowPos, lngLenValue) = ERROR_SUCCESS Then
         ' Extract string from buffer if it's found
         strWindowPos = Left(strWindowPos, lngLenValue - 1)
      Else
         strWindowPos = strDefault
      End If
      Call RegCloseKey(hKey)
   End If
   ' If string is absent, substitute default
   If Len(Trim(strWindowPos)) = 0 Then strWindowPos = strDefault

#Else
   strWindowPos = String(25, 0)
   lngLenValue = GetPrivateProfileString("Settings", "WindowPos", _
                       strDefault, strWindowPos, 25, "myapp.ini")
   If lngLenValue > 0 Then strWindowPos = Left(strWindowPos, lngLenValue)
#End If

WinPos = strWindowPos

End Function
```

Although VB's built-in registry functions enormously reduce both coding and debugging time, compatibility generally implies the need to adapt to a lowest common denominator. We'll begin our coverage of the VBA functions by examining the implications of this broad compatibility.

VBA's Built-in Support: Is It for You?

The four VBA registry functions or statements—*GetSetting, GetAllSettings, SaveSetting,* and *DeleteSetting*—all have two major syntactical and operational features in common. Understanding them, and the reasons for their implementation, is important for deciding whether or not you'll benefit from using them.

First, the major design goal in implementing VBA's support for the registry was that it work on all Windows platforms, whether they be 16-bit or 32-bit. This allows the same VB code to run on all platforms, from Win31 (or, presumably, even Win30) to WinNT, without modification, even if the way the functions actually work on each platform is different.

It is possible, of course, that the functions could be implemented in the same way on the 32-bit platforms and on Win31 if the registry were to be used in the first case and the registration database (*REG.DAT*) were to be used in the other. However, given the specialized character of the Win31 registration database as a repository of information about file associations and OLE, as well as its 64K size restriction, this expansion of the role of the registration database is a spectacularly bad idea. This means that the implementation of the common set of functions and statements in VBA had to differ by platform, and in particular that the Win3x implementation had to support private initialization files. (The only other alternative, using *WIN.INI*, is also problematic because of its 64K size limitation.)

Initialization files, of course, organize their information in sections. A section contains a variable number of entries, each of which consists of a keyword and its associated value. To put this another way, while the tree-like structure of the registry offers the possibility of a multidimensional approach to storing information, initialization files offer an organization that is inherently linear and one-dimensional. The two can only be made compatible by assuming a structure like that of the Win31 registration database, *REG.DAT.* And in fact, in attempting to find a common format for information in the registry and in private initialization files, this is precisely what the VBA registry functions assume.

The VBA commands and syntax share a common set of parameters:

`appname`   The name of the application or project, which is stored as a registry key under Win32.

`section`   The name of the key containing the value entry; it is a subkey of **appname** under Win32.

`key`   A misnomer under Win32, this is actually a value name.

For instance, the following statement stores a "1" to the value entry `Toolbar`, which is found in a key named `MyApp\Settings`:

```
SaveSetting "MyApp", "Settings", "Toolbar", "1"
```

Its value can then be retrieved by the following statement:

```
strValue = GetSetting("MyApp", "Settings", "Toolbar", "0")
```

If the function cannot find the `Toolbar` entry, it substitutes a value of "0" for the setting.

If the VBA registry functions seem like throwbacks to 16-bit Windows and its initialization files, that's because in many ways they are. In particular:

- They allow you to store only string values, since this is the only data type supported by initialization files. You cannot store numeric or binary data.[*]

- They allow you to assign complete initialization file entries (`keyword=value`). These are stored in the registry as complete value entries consisting of a value name and its associated value, but the language used to describe this in the documentation ("a key") applies to initialization files.

- They can't support the unrestricted nesting typical of the registry, since they are limited by the level of nesting (initialization file name, section name, key name) supported by initialization files.

This last limitation is particularly important, since it means that the VBA registry functions have to offer a very restricted form of access to the Win95 and WinNT registries. Basically, they can allow you to navigate only as many levels of the registry as the syntax of an initialization file function allows. So, starting from some arbitrary point in the registry, you can only work with value entries belonging to a key that is the subkey of another key.

Second, since the VBA registry functions offer what amounts to a window into the registry, that arbitrary starting point becomes quite important in defining what part of the registry you can access and, therefore, how you can use the registry. In implementing these functions, it was decided that they would write values to subkeys of `HKCU\Software\VB and VBA Program Settings`.

It is worth noting that, although an arbitrary starting point is imposed by the need for compatibility, this particular starting point is not. Microsoft's current software interface guidelines suggest that application software settings be stored in subkeys of *<company name>\<application name>\<version number>*; for

---

[*] There is a pair of initialization file functions, *GetProfileInt* or *GetPrivateProfileInt*, which retrieve integer data. They do this, though, by automatically converting the string value in an initialization file to an integer. The only way to write a value to an initialization file is with the *WriteProfileString* or *WritePrivateProfileString* functions.

instance, Microsoft stores most Win95 settings in either `HKCU\Software\`
`Microsoft\Windows\CurrentVersion` or in `HKLM\Software\Micro-`
`soft\Windows\CurrentVersion`. The VBA registry functions, on the other
hand, offer a different typology for classifying our applications based on the tool
used to create them. Perhaps, in a future version of Windows, this will serve as a
model for reorganizing the registry along more rational (?) lines. Then we can find
Windows user-specific settings in either `HKCU\Software\Visual C++`
`Program Settings\16-Bit`, `HKCU\Software\Visual C++ Program`
`Settings\32-Bit`, or `HKCU\Software\MASM Program Settings`,
depending on which tool was used to create the code that accesses a particular
item of data. That's very sensible. Not.

But quite independently of the absurdity of this naming convention, it is important to note that the VBA registry functions read from and write to a subkey of
HKCU. In other words, they are suitable for storing user settings only. This is
more than a semantic distinction: if the system registry supports multiple users, a
single user installs the application, and the VBA registry functions are used to
store critical application-specific information, that information will be unavailable
to other users, since it won't have been stored in their particular registry tree. Similarly, system-level information does not belong here. For instance, if your
application handles a special file type, you cannot define the file association using
the VBA registry functions; since this must be visible to Windows and to all other
applications, it must be in a location where they automatically look for them.

In short, although the idea of encapsulating the functionality of the registry API
into a handful of very practical functions is certainly worthwhile, this particular
implementation leaves a good deal to be desired. In particular, the requirement
that the functions be compatible across the Windows platforms undermines their
utility to the extent that we would recommend them only for relatively inexperienced VB programmers who feel uncomfortable with accessing the Win32 API. If
you're in this category, we will, however, briefly show you how to use them, and
provide sample code fragments.

Retrieving Registry Values: GetSetting and GetAllSettings

VB has two functions that allow you to retrieve information from the registry,
depending on whether you want to access a single value or multiple values. To
retrieve the default value of a single key, you use the *GetSetting* function; its
syntax is:

```
GetSetting( appname, section, key [, default] )
```

appname	String	Name of the application or project; it must be a subkey of `HKCU\Software\VB and VBA Program Settings`.
section	String	Name of the section; it must be a subkey of *appname*.
key	String	Name of the entry whose value is to be retrieved.
default	String	Return value if the function is unable to retrieve a value from the registry.

The function returns a string that contains the key's default value. If the key does not exist or does not have an assigned default value, it returns *default*.

For instance, users typically expect that, when they open an application, it will be positioned in the same place as when they last closed it. The `Form_Load` routine in Example 6-2 illustrates how to do this by using the *GetSetting* function to retrieve a value named `WindowPos` from the key `HKCU\Software\VB and VBA Program Settings\VBRegF\Settings`. To show the relationship between the *GetSetting* function and the registry, here's a .REG file that contains information from the relevant portion of the registry:

```
REGEDIT4

[HKEY_CURRENT_USER\Software\VB and VBA Program Settings\VBRegF]

[HKEY_CURRENT_USER\Software\VB and VBA Program Settings\VBRegF\Settings]
"WindowPos"="720 3390 6810 4770"
"SaveSettings"="1"
```

Since *GetSetting* retrieves a single string that holds all four window coordinates (left, top, height, and width), it is parsed and its individual values are converted to integers before being assigned to each window-coordinate property.

Example 6-2. Using GetSetting to retrieve a window's screen coordinates

```
Private Sub Form_Load()

Dim intPos As Integer          ' Position within WindowPos string
Dim intCtr As Integer          ' Array counter
Dim strWindowPos As String     ' Window coordinates from registry
Dim strDefault As String       ' Default value of window coordinates
Dim lngWindowPos(3) As Long    ' Array of values extracted from string

' Form default string from form's current values
strDefault =Trim(Str(Form1.Left)) & " " & Trim(Str(Form1.Top)) & " " & _
          Trim(Str(Form1.Width)) & " " & Trim(Str(Form1.Height))
strWindowPos = GetSetting("VBRegF", "Settings", "WindowPos", strDefault)
' Parse string for integers and store them in an array
intPos = 1
intCtr = 0
Do While intPos <> 0
   intPos = InStr(strWindowPos, " ")
   If intPos > 0 Then
      lngWindowPos(intCtr) = Val(Left(strWindowPos, intPos - 1))
```

Example 6-2. Using GetSetting to retrieve a window's screen coordinates (continued)

```
        strWindowPos = Mid(strWindowPos, intPos + 1)
        intCtr = intCtr + 1
    Else
        lngWindowPos(intCtr) = Val(strWindowPos)
    End If
Loop
' Store array values to window properties
Form1.Left = lngWindowPos(0)
Form1.Top = lngWindowPos(1)
Form1.Width = lngWindowPos(2)
Form1.Height = lngWindowPos(3)

End Sub'
```

The *GetAllSettings* function retrieves the name and value of each entry belonging to a key. Its syntax is:

appname   String   Name of the application or project; it is a subkey of `HKCU\Soft-ware\VB and VBA Program Settings`.

section   String   Name of the section; it must be a subkey of *appname*.

The function returns a variant containing a two-dimensional array. (The array is dynamically resized by the function itself.) Its first dimension represents the value entry's ordinal position. Registry entries, incidentally, are stored in the order in which the entry was created. The first element in the second dimension (at ordinal position 0) represents the value name, while the element in the second position of the second dimension represents the entry's value. If there is no data to retrieve, either because *appname* or *section* are incorrect, or because there are no value entries stored in the registry key, the function returns an uninitialized variant; it returns **vbEmpty** if tested with the *VarType* function and **True** if tested with the *IsEmpty* function.

Example 6-3 displays a *Form_Load* event procedure that uses the *GetAllSettings* function to add the most recently used documents to a window's File menu. Rather than having the value entry's name indicating the order of the document, the value of an entry named "MRU" indicates the position of a particular value entry's document in the MRU list. For instance, if the value of MRU is 3124, the document stored to the value entry whose name is 3 is the most recently used, followed by the document whose value entry is 1, etc.

Example 6-3. Using GetAllSettings to retrieve an MRU list

```
Private Sub Form_Load()

Dim intCtr As Integer              ' Loop counter
Dim intMRUCtr As Integer           ' Loop counter for MRU value
Dim intMenuPos As Integer          ' Current menu item to fill
Dim strMRU As String               ' MRU list
```

Example 6-3. Using GetAllSettings to retrieve an MRU list (continued)

```
Dim strValueName As String        ' MRU value name
Dim objMenu As Object             ' Item in menu array
Dim varFileInfo As Variant        ' Array of value entry information

intMenuPos = 0

' Retrieve registry information
varFileInfo = GetAllSettings("VBRegF", "MRU")
If IsEmpty(varFileInfo) Then Exit Sub
' Get value of MRU entry
For intCtr = 0 To UBound(varFileInfo, 1)
   If UCase(varFileInfo(intCtr, 0)) = "MRU" Then
       strMRU = varFileInfo(intCtr, 1)
       Exit For
   End If
Next
' Use MRU value to position MRU files
For intMRUCtr = 1 To Len(strMRU)
   strValueName = Mid(strMRU, intMRUCtr, 1)
   For intCtr = 0 To UBound(varFileInfo, 1)
       If varFileInfo(intCtr, 0) = strValueName Then
           If intMenuPos > 0 Then Load mnuFile_MRU(intMenuPos)
           mnuFile_MRU(intMenuPos).Caption = varFileInfo(intCtr, 1)
           intMenuPos = intMenuPos + 1
           Exit For
       End If
   Next
Next
' Display menu items
For Each objMenu In mnuFile_MRU
   objMenu.Visible = True
Next
mnuFile_Sep3.Visible = True

End Sub
```

Saving Registry Values: SaveSetting

The *SaveSetting* statement writes a single value entry to the registry. Its syntax is:

```
Call SaveSetting( appname, section, key, setting )
```

appname	String	Key indicating the name of the application or project; it is a subkey of HKCU\Software\VB and VBA Program Settings. If the key doesn't exist, the function creates it.
section	String	Name of the section; it is a subkey of *appname*. If the key doesn't exist, the function creates it.
key	String	Name of the value entry.
setting	String	The value to be assigned to the value entry.

For example, Example 6-4 displays an application's `Form_Unload` event procedure. It uses the *SaveSetting* command to save the state of its Save Settings on Exit
menu item. (Even if settings are not being saved, this is the single item that
always must be saved for the option to make any sense.) It then checks the value
of the Save Settings on Exit option to determine whether it should save the application window's coordinates as well.

Example 6-4. Using SaveSetting to save application state information

```
Private Sub Form_Unload(Cancel As Integer)

Dim strSaveSettings As String
Dim strWindowPos As String

If mnuOptions_Settings.Checked Then
   strSaveSettings = "1"
Else
   strSaveSettings = "0"
End If
Call SaveSetting("VBRegF", "Settings", "SaveSettings", strSaveSettings)
If mnuOptions_Settings.Checked Then
   strWindowPos = Trim(Str(Form1.Left)) & " " & _
            Trim(Str(Form1.Top)) & " " & _
            Trim(Str(Form1.Width)) & " " & Trim(Str(Form1.Height))
   Call SaveSetting("VBRegF", "Settings", "WindowPos", strWindowPos)
End If

End Sub
```

Deleting Registry Keys and Values: DeleteSetting

You can use the *DeleteSetting* statement to delete either a single value or an entire
key, along with all of its associated value entries or a single value. Its syntax is:

```
Call DeleteSetting( appname, section[, key] )
```

appname	String	Key indicating the name of the application or project; it is a subkey of HKCU\Software\VB and VBA Program Settings.
section	String	Name of the section; it is a subkey of *appname*.
key	String	Optional name of the value entry to delete. If *key* is present, the statement deletes a single value entry with that name. If this parameter is absent and both *appname* and *section* are provided, the statement deletes the key named *section* and all of its value entries.

If you delete a key using the statement *Call DeleteSetting(appname, section)*, VB
also deletes any subkeys belonging to that key under Win95; under WinNT, it
deletes the key only if it has no subkeys. Although it isn't mentioned in the documentation, you can also use the *DeleteSetting* statement to delete the application's
top-level key, *appname*. The syntax for this form of the statement is quite simply
Call DeleteSetting(appname).

Windows NT and DeleteSetting

Ordinarily, WinNT requires that a registry key have no subkeys in order to successfully delete it. This also applies to the *DeleteSetting* statement: if you attempt to delete a key using the statement `CallDeleteSetting(`*appname*`,` *section*`)` and *section* has subkeys, the procedure fails and generates runtime error 5, "Invalid procedure call." (Subkeys of *section*, though, can't be created by VB's intrinsic registry functions.) Interestingly, though, if you attempt to delete an application key with the statement `CallDeleteSetting(`*appname*`)`, the operation succeeds whether or not *appname* has subkeys.

Accessing the Win32 API

Given their severe limitations, it is fortunate that the VBA registry functions are not the sole tool that VB developers can use to registry-enable their applications. Instead, all but one of the registry API functions that we discussed in Chapter 4 can be called directly from VB. (The reason for this single exception, *RegQuery-MultipleValues*, is discussed later in this chapter.) Since the previous chapter provided an in-depth treatment of the API functions themselves, in this section we'll focus on specific issues that arise when calling the registry API from VB. Before examining the functions themselves, we'll begin with a review of what you need to call Windows API functions (or, for that matter, any function that resides in an external dynamic link library) from VB. Then we'll examine the two major difficulties that programmers have in using the registry API: retrieving data from the registry, and writing data to the registry.

One feature of VB that has generated both the most excitement and the most pain for programmers is its ability to access external routines in dynamic link libraries and to make them appear as if they are a part of the core VB language. Particularly for programmers who are just beginning to extend VB with calls to external library routines, it is common for programs to continually fail when they call an API function. But this is an area where experience, and a bit of knowledge, rapidly increase the programmer's comfort level and decrease the number of programming errors that occur when calling API functions.[*]

---

[*] And a good book doesn't hurt, either. We highly recommend Dan Appleman's *Visual Basic Programmer's Guide to the Win32 API*, published by Ziff-Davis Press, for its comprehensive coverage of the Win32 API for Visual Basic programmers. See *http://www.desaware.com/desaware/vbpgw32a.htm*. Dan, incidentally, is the president of Desaware, whose custom registry control is included with this book.

This section aims at providing the basic knowledge needed to access the registry functions by examining the three steps involved in calling a routine in a dynamic link library:

- Defining the routine to be called

- Defining any constants used by the function

- Calling the function in your program

The first step involves using one DECLARE statement to define each external routine that your program calls. For instance, the following DECLARE statement allows you to call the *RegOpenKey* function from your Visual Basic program:

```
Declare Function RegOpenKey Lib "advapi32.dll" Alias "RegOpenKeyA" _
        (ByVal hKey As Long, ByVal lpctstr As String, phkey As Long) _
        As Long
```

Defining the Routine: The DECLARE Statement

Because a library routine is external, VB knows nothing about it. VB doesn't know where to find external routines, it doesn't know what kinds of data they return, and it doesn't know how many parameters they expect or what kinds of data they require. In fact, it doesn't even really know the names of external routines. Think of it this way: the external routine could have been written *after* VB itself was written, so it is impossible for VB to know anything about it—unless you tell it. In order to communicate with the external routine, VB requires a kind of template that provides it with these necessary items of information. The DECLARE statement is that template.

VB4 includes a new utility, *API Viewer*, shown in Figure 6-1, that allows you to paste DECLARE statements, constant definitions, and TYPE statements into you application. This is an extremely useful tool that can save you a good deal of time. The *Inside the Windows 95 Registry* diskette also includes a VB code module, *WINREG.BAS*, that you can include in your projects. At the same time, neither is a substitute for understanding the issues involved in how VB calls DLL routines. If you rely solely on the *API Viewer* or *WINREG.BAS*, at some point you're sure to have difficulty calling a DLL routine. And without having a good sense of how VB communicates with external routines, the chance of your finding a rapid solution is rather small.

Almost all routines in the registry API should be defined as functions (that is, as code which returns some value to its caller, as opposed to subroutines, which are code which produces some effect, but which returns no value). The general syntax of the DECLARE statement when it defines a function is:

```
[Public | Private] Declare Function <globalname> Lib <libname> _
   [Alias <aliasname> ] [(([ByVal | ByRef ] <variable> [ As <type>] _
   [,[ByVal | ByRef] <variable> [ As <type>] ] . . .])] [As <type>]
```

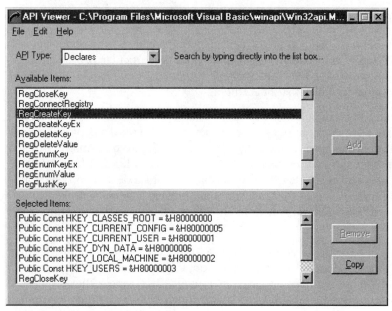

Figure 6-1. The API Viewer

Whew! Here's a simple example, the DECLARE statement for the *RegCloseKey* function. Notice that most syntax parts aren't used:

```
Declare Function RegCloseKey Lib "advapi32.dll" _
    (ByVal hKey As Long) As Long
```

Since a sizable number of errors in accessing the Windows API are caused by errors in the DECLARE statement, we'll examine this syntax in some detail before discussing constants and the actual function call.

Visibility: The PUBLIC and PRIVATE keywords

The optional PUBLIC and PRIVATE keywords are new to the DECLARE statement in VB4, and are used to define the *visibility* of a DLL routine (i.e., the locations in a program's source code from which the routine can be called). If you don't specify either token, it will default to PUBLIC if you place the routine in a code module; this means that the routine can be called from code anywhere in the application. This is the most common form of DECLARE statement.

Specifying the PRIVATE keyword in a code module means that the routine is only visible and can only be called from within that code module. You would do that if you were calling the routine from procedures and functions that are also stored in the code module, and you want to make sure that routines in other modules or in individual forms do not call the DLL routine directly.

How Do Visual Basic Components "Fit" Together?

Beginning Visual Basic programmers typically have a difficult time understanding how VB code fits together, and where to place particular programming constructs—like variables, DECLARE statements, and subroutines—so that they are visible to code modules that need them.

The key to understanding all this is the Visual Basic project (or .VBP) file, which is created for every application you develop. A typical VB project file, *TSTPROJ1.VBP*, is shown in a text editor window in Figure 6-2. Among other things, the project file defines each code module (.BAS file) and form (.FRM file) that is part of a project. Each code module contains a declarations section and optional functions and subroutines; a form contains a general declarations section, general user-defined functions and procedures, and application-defined event procedures.

At run-time, VB begins by reading each code module included in a project. It first reads a code module's declarations section; the constants, variables, user-defined types, and definitions of external routines that appear there, unless they are defined using the PRIVATE keyword, are visible throughout the application. Then it reads any functions and subroutines stored in the code module. These are also visible throughout the application unless they are defined as PRIVATE; however, any variables they define are visible only to that procedure.

When VB loads a form at run-time, it first reads that form's general declarations section followed by its functions, subroutines, and event procedures. Variables defined in the form's general declarations section are always private; they are only visible to the functions and procedures defined in the form. As long as a form is loaded, though, its event procedures, subroutines, and functions can be visible to other forms and code modules if they are defined as PUBLIC. By default, functions and procedures stored in a form are defined as PUBLIC; event procedures, though, are created as PRIVATE by default.

What all of this means is that, if you're calling API functions from only a single form, you can define the functions, as well as their associated constants and structured data types, in the form's general declarations section. But this does make them invisible to other forms, as well as to routines stored in code modules. If you want them to be visible to more than one form, you have to store them in a code module's declarations section, which is where they appear in most programs.

However, whenever you place a DECLARE statement in a form's declarations section rather than in a code module, you must declare it as PRIVATE, which means that the routine can be called only from code stored in the form itself.

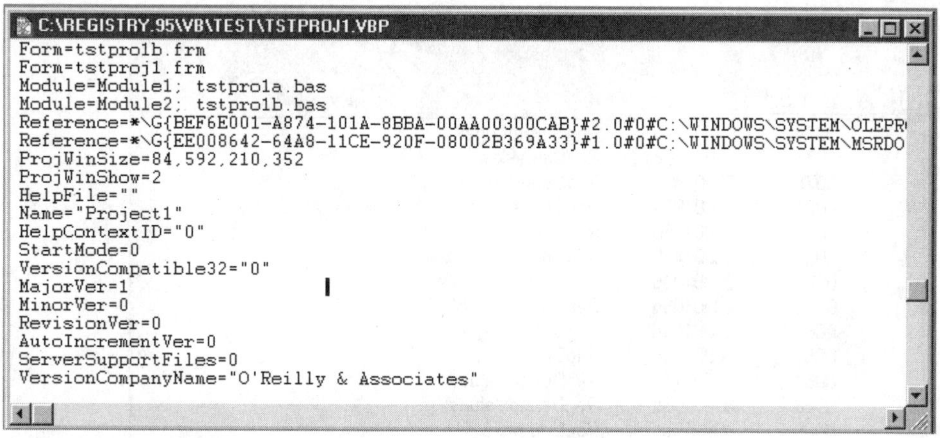

```
C:\REGISTRY.95\VB\TEST\TSTPROJ1.VBP                                    _ □ ×
Form=tstpro1b.frm
Form=tstproj1.frm
Module=Module1; tstpro1a.bas
Module=Module2; tstpro1b.bas
Reference=*\G{BEF6E001-A874-101A-8BBA-00AA00300CAB}#2.0#0#C:\WINDOWS\SYSTEM\OLEPR
Reference=*\G{EE008642-64A8-11CE-920F-08002B369A33}#1.0#0#C:\WINDOWS\SYSTEM\MSRDO
ProjWinSize=84,592,210,352
ProjWinShow=2
HelpFile=""
Name="Project1"
HelpContextID="0"
StartMode=0
VersionCompatible32="0"
MajorVer=1                           I
MinorVer=0
RevisionVer=0
AutoIncrementVer=0
ServerSupportFiles=0
VersionCompanyName="O'Reilly & Associates"
```

Figure 6-2. A Visual Basic project (.VBP) file in a text editor window

Attempting to DECLARE a routine as PUBLIC or omitting the PRIVATE keyword in a form's declarations section results in the syntax error, "Constants, fixed-length strings, and arrays not allowed as Public members of class or form modules."

The routine's name

globalname is the name of the routine as it will appear when you call it in your programs (e.g., *RegOpenKey*). If you do not use the ALIAS clause (which is described in "Aliasing DLL Routines" later in this chapter), that must also be the name of the routine as it is found in the dynamic link library. If the ALIAS clause is not used, *globalname* is case-sensitive. That is, if you fail to specify the routine's name in the same combination of upper- and lowercase characters as it appears in the dynamic link library itself, VB will be unable to locate the routine when you call it, and will display the message, "Run-time error '453:' Specified DLL function not found."

Finding the Correct Case of DLL Routines

The name of each function in the documentation for the Win32 API accurately reflects the combination of upper- and lowercase characters in its name. You can also use QuickView, if you've installed it, to examine a DLL's Export Table in order to find the precise format of a routine's name. In Figure 6-3, a Quick-View file viewer is displaying the part of the export table from *ADVAPI32.DLL* that lists the registry functions. If you're developing 16-bit applications using the 16-bit version of VB, the documentation does not accurately reflect the case of API functions as they appear in DLLs; but the names of functions in the Win16 API are *not* case sensitive.

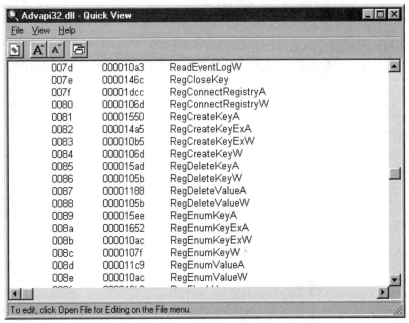

Figure 6-3. QuickView listing the registry functions in ADVAPI32.DLL

For instance, the attempt to define *RegCloseKey* in the following DECLARE statement will produce a run-time error when the function is actually called:

```
' WRONG!
Declare Function REGCloseKey Lib "advapi32.dll" _
(ByVal hkey As Long) As Long
```

The name of the function in *ADVAPI32.DLL* is actually *RegCloseKey*, not *REGCloseKey*.

The library name

libname is the name of the dynamic link library in which the routine resides, along with its optional path. In this case, since we're only interested in the registry API, all of whose routines reside in a single library, the value of *libname* in our DECLARE statements should be *ADVAPI32.DLL*.

Because *ADVAPI32.DLL* is one of the major system libraries used by Windows, it is not necessary to include an optional path along with the filename. In fact, since Windows "knows" about the file and where it is, it is not even necessary to include its file extension. The following DECLARE statement, for example, is also fine:

```
Declare Function RegFlushKey Lib "advapi32" (ByVal hkey As Long) As Long
```

Aliasing DLL routines

Ordinarily, the DECLARE statement's *globalname* parameter provides the name of the routine as it exists in a dynamic link library and as you will refer to it in your program. The ALIAS clause, however, allows you to assign a name to a DLL routine that is different from the routine's actual name in the DLL. *aliasname* then contains the name of the routine as defined in its dynamic link library, while *globalname* is the name by which the routine is identified in your program when it is called. *aliasname* must be enclosed in quotation marks, and its case must exactly match the case of the function's name in *libname*.

Why would you want to do that? Although the use of an alias may seem fairly esoteric, all but two of the DECLARE statements for the registry API provided by *API Viewer* uses the ALIAS clause. That's because the Windows system libraries contain two versions of every routine that accepts a string parameter; one is the ANSI version, while the other is the unicode (wide-character) version to support long character sets. For example, while Microsoft documents the function *RegOpenKey*, it turns out that such a function does not actually exist in *ADVAPI32.DLL*; instead, the C header file *WINREG.H* translates all references to *RegOpenKey* into calls to either of two internal functions, *RegOpenKeyA* and *RegOpenKeyW*, when the application is compiled. In the case of Windows 95, which doesn't support Unicode, *RegOpenKey* is translated into *RegOpenKeyA*. Since *RegOpenKey* is documented and its name corresponds more closely to the function's purpose, it is best to use that as the function name in calls to the function.

An alias can also be important in enhancing the readability of your code, and even in helping you remember a function's name. For instance, if you've decided that you would always prefer to use *RegQueryValueEx* instead of *RegQueryValue*, but never remember to include the "Ex" in the function call when you're coding, you could simply take advantage of the ALIAS clause:

```
Declare Function RegQueryValue Lib "advapi32.dll" _
            Alias "RegQueryValueExA" _
            (ByVal hkey As Long, ByVal lpszValueName As String, _
            lpdwReserved As Long, lpdwType As Long, _
            ByVal lpbData As String, lpcbData As Long) As Long
```

You can also use aliases to differentiate between different variations of a single function. For instance, *RegSetValueEx* assigns a particular value to a value entry. The standard version of the DECLARE statement allows you to supply any data type for the *lpData* parameter:

```
Declare Function RegSetValueEx Lib "advapi32.dll" _
            Alias "RegSetValueExA" _
            (ByVal hkey As Long, ByVal lpValueName As String, _
            ByVal Reserved As Long, ByVal dwType As Long, _
            lpData As Any, ByVal cbData As Long) As Long
```

For a variety of reasons (which we'll discuss in the section on passing parameters), you may find this undesirable. Instead, you can create three aliases for the same function, depending on whether you want to write binary, string, or numeric data. The template for writing string data to the registry might be:

```
Declare Function RegSetStringValue Lib "advapi32" _
                Alias "RegSetValueExA" _
                (ByVal hkey As Long, ByVal lpValueName As String, _
                ByVal Reserved As Long, ByVal dwType As Long, _
                ByVal lpData As String, ByVal cbData As Long) As Long
```

So while it may seem arcane, aliasing is extremely useful.

The function's return value

When you define a function, you must also indicate the data type of the function's return value. There are two ways to do this:

- By specifying the data type in the statement's final AS <TYPE> clause. For instance, the statement

  ```
  Declare Function RegCloseKey Lib "advapi32.dll" _
  (ByVal hkey As Long) As Long
  ```

  indicates that the *RegCloseKey* function returns a long (32-bit) integer.

- By appending a type specifier to the name of the function, `globalname`. Since all registry functions return a long integer, you can append an ampersand ("&"), the long integer's type specifier, to the function name. For example,

  ```
  Declare Function RegCloseKey& Lib "advapi32.dll" _
  (ByVal hkey As Long)
  ```

Formal parameters

The remaining portion of the DECLARE statement lists the parameters to be passed to the dynamic link library routine using the standard calling convention.[*] The parameter name, `variable`, is an arbitrary name; it really serves as a placeholder for the parameter when the routine is actually called. You do not have to

---

[*] The *calling convention* defines how parameters are exchanged between the calling program and the called routine (which might or might not reside in the same program). In particular, the calling convention determines the order in which parameters are placed on and removed from the stack (from right to left or from left to right as they appear in source code) and whether the calling program or the callee is responsible for stack cleanup (i.e., popping parameters from the stack). Both Visual Basic and the Win32 API use the "standard" calling convention, which specifies that parameters are pushed onto the stack from right to left (in the reverse order in which they appear in the function call) and that the function called is responsible for stack clean-up. The 16-bit Windows API and previous versions of VB used the so-called "Pascal" calling convention; Microsoft's 32-bit development tools, on the other hand, don't support the Pascal calling convention. (Attempts to use the Pascal calling convention in Visual C++ are translated into the standard calling convention by *WINDEF.H*.) The change from the Pascal to standard calling convention, incidentally, is one of the factors that allows Visual Basic to support named arguments.

use *variable* as the variable name when you call the DLL routine, nor does *variable* have to be an actual variable that is defined and initialized within your VB code. For instance, in the DECLARE statement for *RegCreateKey*:

```
Declare Function RegCreateKey Lib "advapi32.dll" Alias "RegCreateKeyA" _
    (ByVal hKey As Long, ByVal lpctstr As String, phkey As Long) _
    As Long
```

hKey, *lpctstr*, and *phkey* represent parameters that are passed to the function when it is called. They do not have to exist as variables in your program; they simply tell Visual Basic what kind of data to expect and how much stack space to allocate to each item. They are replaced by variables or literal values at the point that the function is actually called in your program.

Along with a placeholder for the variable or value that will be passed when the routine is actually called, two additional items are needed for each parameter:

- Whether the parameter is passed by value (in which cased it should be preceded by the BYVAL keyword) or by reference (which, since it is the default when calling external libraries, can be indicated by not providing a keyword or by specifying the BYREF keyword). The meaning of the BYVAL and BYREF keywords is explored in detail in the next section, "Passing parameters: The BYREF and BYVAL keywords."

- The correct VB data type.

One of the most common reasons that attempts to access the Windows API from VB go astray is that parameters that should be passed by value are passed by reference, and vice versa. In order to make accessing the Windows API less painful, we'll examine how parameters are passed to DLL routines.

Passing parameters: The BYREF and BYVAL keywords

When you invoke a DLL routine from VB, you're accessing code that almost invariably was written in some other programming language; most of the routines in the Win32 API, for instance, were written in C or assembly language. In many cases, the routines in the dynamic link library manage their own memory, and they format their data in ways significantly different from VB. Clearly, for calls to external routines to work, there has to be some convention about how your program and the library routine should communicate with one another. And in fact, there is: a calling and a called routine communicate through parameters that the calling routine places on "the stack."

When you call any external DLL routine, VB places the parameters that you specify on the application's stack and passes control to the dynamic link library, which then retrieves the parameters from the stack and adjusts the position of the stack pointer. Since the dynamic link library has no knowledge of the operation of the VB routine, it is important that the VB program place the kind of data on the stack that the dynamic link library is expecting. For any particular data type, VB allows you to put either of two items on the stack:

- The data itself. This is known as passing a parameter *by value.*

- A pointer to the data (i.e., the address in memory at which the data resides). This is known as passing a parameter *by reference.*

Passing a parameter by value or by reference determines what is placed on the parameter stack and what the dynamic link library can do with it. In the case of a variable that is passed by value to a routine, the value of the variable is placed on the stack. This is illustrated in Figure 6-4, which depicts the stack when VB passes a long integer variable by value to a DLL. The memory location at &H00ACF25C contains a long integer (a 32-bit value), 3. When it is passed by value to the dynamic link library, VB places the 32-bit value on the stack. When control returns to VB, any changes that the external routine may have made to the integer value are irrelevant, since the integer value on the stack is in no way tied to the integer value at memory location &H00ACF25C. In other words, passing a variable by value involves passing a copy of the variable, which then becomes completely unrelated to and independent of the original.

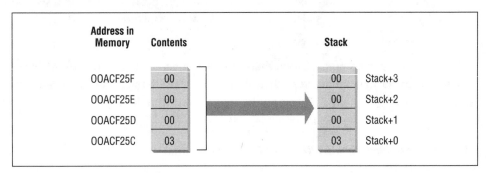

Figure 6-4. Passing a parameter by value

On the other hand, when a variable is passed by reference to a routine, a 32-bit pointer containing its address is placed on the stack. This is illustrated in Figure 6-5, which depicts the stack when VB passes a long integer variable by reference to a DLL. The memory location at &H00ACF25C contains a long integer (a 32-bit value), 3. When it is passed by reference to the dynamic link library, VB places the 32-bit address, &H00ACF25C, on the stack. When control returns to VB, any changes that the external routine may have made to the integer are reflected in its value, since the routine, by having its address, had access to the variable itself. In other words, passing a variable by reference, because it involves passing a pointer to the variable, means that both the calling and the called routine are accessing a single variable at a single location in memory.

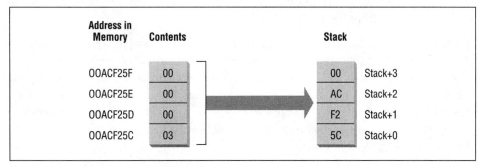

Figure 6-5. Passing a parameter by reference

When you pass a parameter to an external library routine, it expects to find a particular kind of value on the stack. If we look again at Figure 1-1 and Figure 1-2, it becomes clear what happens when a parameter that should have been passed by value is passed by reference, or vice versa. Taking the data in these figures as an example, if the C language DLL routine is expecting to find a long integer value (&H03) on the stack (C routines, incidentally, by default pass their parameters by value), but you instead pass that long integer by reference (which VB does by default), the routine will read the integer &00ACF25C and move the stack pointer downward by four bytes. So you've provided the routine with a wildly incorrect value.

Passing a parameter by value rather than by reference has even more serious consequences. Here, the external routine expects that the calling routine will pass it a 32-bit pointer, in this case &H00ACF25C. Instead, it receives the value &H00000003, which it interprets as a pointer. So it may attempt to retrieve the value at memory location &H00000003, and it may even attempt to write to that location. This block of memory, though, may be used by the application to store another variable's data; or, more likely, it may not even belong to the application at all. Since this compromises the integrity of your application, VB should display an error message and terminate your application.

To put this another way, if you expect an API routine to modify the value of one of the parameters passed to it, then that parameter must be passed by reference; what VB must actually pass to the routine is a pointer that contains the data's address in memory. On the other hand, if the API routine simply reads the value of the parameter without modifying it, the parameter should be passed by value.

A function can have only a single return value; that is, an external routine can return a single value to the calling program by using the CPU's registers. In the case of a C program, there is a further restriction on return values: the value returned by a function cannot be a string. But what happens if a function has to "return" multiple items of information, or if the data that the calling program needs to retrieve from the external routine is a string?

If you've looked at Chapter 4, you already know that examples of this abound in the registry API. The functions that compose the registry API have a consistent set of return values; each of the registry functions returns an error code indicating whether the function has succeeded or why it has failed. In most cases, though, this return value is of no real interest to you: you've called the function not to receive an error code, but to extract some necessary item of information about a registry key or value. For instance:

- You need a handle (*hKey*) in order to work with a registry key.

- You used *RegCreateKeyEx* to open a registry key, but now you need to know whether the function found an existing key or whether it had to create a new key.

- You want to know how many subkeys a key has so that you can enumerate them.

- You want to retrieve the name of a registry key.

- You want to retrieve the name of the program that's associated with a particular file type.

Despite the limitation of one return value per function and no returned strings, you can retrieve each of these items of information by passing the respective parameter by reference. The registry API routine then updates the variable passed as a parameter with the correct value.

There is one very confusing exception to the subject of passing parameters by value and by reference: in VB (as in C), you can only pass strings by reference to DLL routines; that is, your application can only put a 32-bit pointer to a string, rather than the string itself, on the stack. However, you can pass a string by reference in either of two ways:

- *As a VB string.* If you use the BYREF keyword or don't include a keyword with the parameter, VB passes the string by reference in its proprietary format. But unless the DLL has been developed specially to work with VB, it cannot understand this format. This is true of all of the routines in the Win32 API that expect string values: none can handle VB strings.

- *As a null-terminated C string.* If you use the BYVAL keyword, VB transparently copies the string to a buffer, adds a null character—that is, CHR(0)—to mark the end of the string, and passes the C routine the string buffer's starting address. This is called an ASCIIZ string (zero-terminated ASCII) and is the way that C conventionally handles its strings. When control returns to VB, it translates the C string back into VB's native format.

In other words, to borrow from the language of object oriented programming, VB *overloads* the BYVAL keyword—it gives it multiple meanings, the precise one of which is determined by the character of its data. Practically, this means that, in calling the registry API or the Win32 API in general, the definition of a string parameter in a DECLARE statement should always be prefaced by the BYVAL keyword.

The type declaration: AS ANY

Ordinarily, VB uses strong typing in calls to external DLLs; that is, VB expects you to explicitly define in advance the type of data that will be passed as a parameter to an external routine. Some DLL routines, though, are capable of accepting more than one data type as a single parameter. For instance, both the *RegQueryInfoKey* and *RegEnumKeyEx* functions have an *lpftLastWriteTime* parameter that takes a FILETIME structure as a parameter. If you're not interested in the date and time the last write to the key occurred (and, of course, you're not likely to be, since Win95 does not save this information), you can pass a NULL as an argument. The conventional DECLARE statement does not allow this, though, since FILETIME and NULL are two very different data types. To handle these situations, VB provides you with a workaround: rather than requiring you to always specify the precise type of data that your program passes to a DLL routine, VB allows you to use the AS ANY type declaration for those cases in which you're not certain in advance what kind of data will be passed to a function. For example, since you can write any of a variety of data types to the registry, the standard DECLARE statement provided for *RegSetValueEx* by the API viewer makes use of the AS ANY type definition:

```
Declare Function RegSetValueEx Lib "advapi32.dll" _
            Alias "RegSetValueExA" _
            (ByVal hkey As Long, ByVal lpValueName As String, _
            ByVal Reserved As Long, ByVal dwType As Long, _
            lpData As Any, ByVal cbData As Long) As Long
```

Although it offers a certain amount of flexibility, the AS ANY type definition has a major liability: it suspends the type checking that VB ordinarily performs on any parameter that it passes to a routine, and allows any data type to be passed to the external function. In the case of *RegSetValueEx*, this allows a program to pass a string, a long integer, or an array of byte data as the value of *lpData*. Unfortunately, though, it also allows VB to pass a value that's clearly inappropriate, like a date value, a floating point number, or a Visual Basic variant. This places the responsibility for rigorous type checking on the developer rather than on the VB interpreter, and makes the process of calling external library routines just a little more complicated and a little more error-prone.

One of the peculiarities of the AS ANY type declaration is that, if you remove type restrictions, the DECLARE statement assumes that the parameter is passed *by reference* to the external routine. A type declaration in the form

```
ByVal anyVar as Any
```

generates a syntax error. This means that, when you actually call the API function (a topic discussed in greater detail in "Calling the Function" later in this chapter), you must explicitly indicate whether you're passing by value an argument whose type checking is suspended. But when calling this function, you have to remember this detail, and it's precisely this kind of detail that many developers overlook.

The use of AS ANY causes run-time errors in two cases in particular:

- When the function accepts a range of data types, including strings, all of which are passed to it by reference. In this case, in order to pass a C string by reference, you have to remember to include the BYVAL keyword along with the actual function call to pass a C-style string, rather than a Visual Basic string, by reference.

- When arguments are passed to the function by reference, or a NULL can be passed if you're not interested in a particular parameter. Visual Basic has no data type that corresponds to the C language's NULL;[*] ordinarily, you pass a NULL to an API routine by passing it a 0 value. When the AS ANY declaration is used, though, the 0 has to be explicitly passed by value; otherwise, you end up passing a pointer to a NULL (that is, a pointer to a memory location whose value is null), rather than the NULL pointer (a pointer that doesn't point to anything) required by the function.

For a more detailed discussion of the problems that arise from the use of the AS ANY type declaration, along with some examples, see "Is AS ANY used in the DECLARE statement?" later in this chapter.

You can use the ALIAS clause to place the responsibility for type checking back on the VB interpreter. Instead of using AS ANY to describe the data type of a parameter, you can assign a meaningful name to a particular API routine that describes the specialized function it performs. You can also specify the exact data types that that variation of the external routine expects. For example, in "Aliasing DLL routines," we defined a special-purpose function, *RegSetStringValue*, as a replacement for the general-purpose *RegSetValueEx* using the AS ANY type definition.

---

[*] Visual Basic does support a NULL data type, but it is not the same as a C language NULL. The Visual Basic NULL is a variant data type that has not been assigned a value.

Defining Constants

In earlier versions of VB, there were very few system-level constants. In VB 1.0, for instance, even the TRUE and FALSE constants had to be defined in a code module, while the values of the *MsgBox* constants, like vbOKCancel or VBNo, also had to be defined in code. As the number of system (or built-in) constants has increased from version to version, many developers have forgotten that Windows API constants are not automatically recognized by VB; they have to be defined (preferably) as public constants in a code module. When this detail is overlooked, the attempt to access the registry inevitably fails when an application attempts to open a registry key and to retrieve its handle. That's because the handles of all top-level keys, like HKEY_LOCAL_MACHINE, are unknown to VB unless you explicitly define them.

Constants and Variable Declaration

The failure to define registry-related constants to VB is very easy to detect if your projects use the "require variable declaration" option. In that case, as soon as VB encounters an undefined constant (which, of course, it interprets as an undefined variable), it displays a "Variable not defined" error message. If you don't require variable definition, though, it interprets your undefined constant as an uninitialized variant. In that case, when you call any of the registry open functions, the constant representing the handle to the top-level registry key is assigned a value of 0. This, of course, is not a valid handle, so the function fails.

This alone is a strong argument in favor of requiring variable declaration; it's more than worth the extra work involved. To require variable declaration in all your projects, select the Options option from the Tools menu, then check the Require Variable Declaration box in the Environment property sheet.

Virtually all API constants, including most of the registry-related constants, can be added to your VB programs by using the *API Viewer*. In addition, the accompanying diskette includes *WINREG.BAS*, a code module that defines all registry-related constants, structures, and functions.

A second problem that arises if you want your application to run under WinNT and are including the registry security constants, like KEY_READ, KEY_WRITE, and KEY_ALL_ACCESS, is related to the way that VB interprets constants. At compile-time (as well as when code is interpreted in the design-time environment), VB simply replaces each constant name with its value. However, in doing this, VB does not handle forward references particularly well; it's best that each constant already be defined when VB encounters its first use in code. Since you can define constants in terms of other constants (something that the registry security constants do), this means that the constants used to define other constants should be defined first in a code module.

For example, the following code fragment produces a "Constant expression required" syntax error when you attempt to use the value of the constant conVALUE in your code:

```
' WRONG
Public Const conVALUE = conONE And conTWO And conFOUR
Public Const conTHREE = (conONE Or conTWO)
Public Const conONE = 1
Public Const conTWO = 2
Public Const conFOUR = 4
```

This can be fixed by simply rearranging the order in which the constants are declared:

```
' CORRECT
Public Const conONE = 1
Public Const conTWO = 2
Public Const conFOUR = 4
Public Const conTHREE = (conONE Or conTWO)
Public Const conVALUE = conONE And conTWO And conFOUR
```

Calling the Registry API

We've spent what seems like an interminable amount of time covering the intricacies of the DECLARE statement and the declaration of constants. At this point, you're no doubt wondering when we're ever going to get around to actually *calling* a declared API.

The good news, though, is that once you've successfully defined an external routine using the DECLARE statement and have included all necessary constants, you call it in your code just as if it were an intrinsic part of the VB language. Using the DECLARE statement as your template, you simply replace its placeholders with the actual variables or values that are to be passed as parameters to the routine. For example, the DECLARE statement for *RegOpenKey*:

```
Declare Function RegOpenKey Lib "advapi32.dll" Alias "RegOpenKeyA" _
    (ByVal hKey As Long, ByVal lpctstr As String, phkey As Long) _
    As Long
```

allows you to call the function as follows:

```
strKeyName = ".txt"
lngRegError = RegOpenKey(HKEY_CLASSES_ROOT, strKeyName, hKey)
```

If you're completely uninterested in the function's return value (What?! If you're wondering how you can be completely uninterested in an error code, see

"Handling Errors" later in this chapter), you can also invoke the function using the CALL statement.[*] Various ways to call a declared function are illustrated using the *RegOpenKey* function in Table 6-1.

Table 6-1. Calling API functions from VB programs

Type	Statement
Assigned to variable	`lngRegError = RegOpenKey(HKEY_CLASSES_ROOT,".vbp", hKey)`
Evaluate expression	`if RegOpenKey(HKEY_CLASSES_ROOT, ".vbp", hKey) _` `                <> ERROR_SUCCESS)`
Discard return value	`Call RegOpenKey(HKEY_CLASSES_ROOT, ".vbp", hKey)`

When Things Go Wrong ...

But although you *should* be able to call API routines seamlessly as if they were part of the VB language, problems frequently arise. Some of the more common errors—but ones which are sometimes difficult to track down—include:

- Failing to pass a parameter correctly, particularly when the AS ANY type definition is used in a function declaration
- Failing to initialize variables properly before passing them to the routine
- Inadvertently changing the size of a buffer in successive calls to the routine
- Using a constant for economy when a variable is required
- Failing to trim a string that is used in a comparison
- Failing to pass a NULL correctly

These errors in calling routines in external DLLs, in fact, are so common that they're worth exploring in some detail.

Is AS ANY used in the DECLARE statement?

When a DECLARE statement includes a parameter whose type definition is AS ANY, that parameter is frequently passed incorrectly in the function call. Consider the following DECLARE statement and its corresponding function call:

---

[*] If you're consistently uninterested in a function's return value, you can also define it as a procedure (procedures have no return value) instead of a function. For instance, you could define *RegCloseKey* as a procedure:

```
Declare Sub RegCloseProc Lib "advapi32.dll" Alias "RegCloseKey" _
        (ByVal hKey As Long)
```

and call it as follows (note that parentheses can even be left off, making the function call look exactly like a built-in Basic statement):

```
RegCloseProc hKey
```

```
Declare Function RegSetValueEx Lib "advapi32.dll" _
Alias "RegSetValueExA" _
(ByVal hKey As Long, ByVal lpValueName As String, _
ByVal Reserved As Long, ByVal dwType As Long, _
lpData As Any, ByVal cbData As Long) As Long

' WRONG
strData = "c:\windows\notepad.exe"
lngLenData = len(strData) + 1           ' Add 1 for chr(0) at end
lngRegError = RegSetValueEx(hKey, "", 0&, REG_SZ, _
                              strData, lngLenData)
```

According to the DECLARE statement, *lpData* is to be passed by reference to the *RegSetValueEx* function. The call to the function uses the variable *strData*, which is a string data type; strings are always passed by reference to DLL routines. In the actual call to the function, though, *strData* is passed by reference as a VB string. Instead, for the function to actually store the string "c:\windows\ notepad.exe" to the open key's default value, the string should be passed by reference as a null-terminated C string. In this case, the call to the function appears to succeed (that is, it returns ERROR_SUCCESS), but the function actually writes garbage to the key's default value.

In cases such as these, you must override the method used to pass a parameter that's defined by the DECLARE statement. To do this, you just include the BYREF or BYVAL keyword along with the variable whose method you're changing. So a successful call to *RegSetValueEx* which both returns ERROR_SUCCESS and works as we expect would look like the following:

```
' CORRECT
   lngRegError = RegSetValueEx(hKey, "", 0&, REG_SZ, _
                              ByVal strData, lngLenData)
```

An even harder error to detect occurs when you intend to pass a NULL (or a null pointer) as a parameter whose type definition is AS ANY; it's difficult to identify because you pass a NULL when you don't want to retrieve the particular value, and you don't expect what is from your point of view an "unused" parameter to cause you problems. What you don't care about can hurt you.

In VB, you can pass a C language NULL as an argument by passing *by value* a long integer whose value is zero, or by passing an uninitialized string by value. For example, the following statement initializes a null pointer (this support for null pointers is new to Visual Basic 4.0):

```
Private pNull As String
```

Frequently you know the name of a string or binary value entry, but don't know how large a buffer is needed to retrieve its data. In that case, you can use the *RegQueryValueEx* function to determine the size of the value entry's data before you make a second call to *RegQueryValueEx* to actually retrieve it. The typical definition of *RegQueryValueEx* (including the one provided by the *API Viewer*) is:

```
Declare Function RegQueryValueEx Lib "advapi32.dll" _
     Alias "RegQueryValueExA" _
     (ByVal hKey As Long, ByVal lpValueName As String, _
     ByVal lpReserved As Long, lpType As Long, lpData As Any, _
     lpcbData As Long) As Long
```

The following call, then, seems as though it should determine how large a buffer to allocate for the value entry's data, without actually retrieving the data:

```
' WRONG
Call RegQueryValueEx(hKey, "StringValue", 0, lngDataType, 0, _
                lngLenValue)
```

Unfortunately, though, this call to the function returns ERROR_MORE_DATA, indicating that one of the string buffers is too short. The culprit turns out to be the *lpData* parameter, which you've chosen to ignore. Because parameters defined using the AS ANY type declaration are passed by reference, Visual Basic interprets this zero as a pointer to a NULL. Instead, we want to pass the function a null pointer, which requires that the function be called in either of the following two ways:

```
' Correct
Call RegQueryValueEx(hKey, "StringValue", 0, 0, ByVal 0, _
                lngLenValue)
```

```
' Correct
dim pNull as string
Call RegQueryValueEx(hKey, "StringValue", 0, 0, ByVal pNull, _
                lngLenValue)
```

Are strings properly initialized?

When a Win32 function is communicating with your program by means of a buffer—that is, when you've passed a variable by reference to the function and the function is placing some value in the buffer that your program will eventually retrieve—the buffer must be properly initialized. For instance, if you're using the *RegEnumKey* function to retrieve the names of the subkeys of the open key, you might call the function as follows:

```
lngRegError = RegEnumKey(HKEY_CLASSES_ROOT, lngIndex, _
                strKeyName, lngLenKeyName )
```

RegEnumKey, though, knows nothing of your variables or your program. From its point of view, *strKeyName* is an area of memory that your program has allocated for it in which to write a sequence of bytes. All it knows about this area of memory is its starting address (this is what it receives as the value of the *strKeyName* parameter) and its size (indicated by the *lngLenKeyName* variable).

For the function to work, you have to be sure that you've actually allocated the necessary memory by initializing the variable to the proper size (in the case of string variables) or value. The failure to do this happens most often when passing string parameters, but sometimes it applies as well to numeric parameters. For example, the following code fragment probably reflects the most common error in calling API routines from VB:

```
' WRONG
Dim strKeyName as String
Dim lngResult as Long, lngIndex as Long, lngLenKeyName as Long

lngLenKeyName = 32
lngResult = RegEnumKey(HKEY_CLASSES_ROOT, lngIndex, _
                    strKeyName, lngLenKeyName )
```

We've told the *RegEnumKey* function that it has a 32-byte buffer (the value of *lngLenKeyName*) to which it can write the name of the key. However, the actual buffer that we've created for the function only has one byte; since it has been declared but has not been initialized, *strKeyName* is a null string (""), and VB terminates it with a null character. Since the API routine writes a null-terminated string to the buffer, we've provided it with a zero-length buffer. This means that, if *RegEnumKey* were to place the name of the subkey in memory, it would store it in an area of memory that probably has been allocated for some other use either by your program or another program. Fortunately, when confronted with an inadequate buffer, the registry functions usually return either ERROR_INVALID_PARAMETER or ERROR_MORE_DATA.

You can correct this error by properly initializing *strKeyName* and making *lngLenKeyName* dependent on the actual size of *strKeyName*, as the following code fragment shows:

```
Dim strKeyName as String
Dim lngResult as Long, lngIndex as Long, lngLenKeyName as Long

strKeyName = string(32,0)
lngLenKeyName = len(strKeyName)

lngResult = RegEnumKey(HKEY_CLASSES_ROOT, lngIndex, _
                    strKeyName, lngLenKeyName+1 )
```

In this case, *strKeyName* is a variable length string whose size is set to 32 bytes by the *String* function. It's also possible to define it as a 32-byte fixed-length string when you declare the variable:

```
Dim strKeyName as String * 32
```

This allows you to omit the line containing the *String* function entirely. In either case, remember that, in defining the buffer size, you have to add one to the length of the buffer to account for the extra null character that VB appends when it converts a VB string to a null-terminated C string.

Is your buffer more dynamic than you intended?

Since the enumeration functions are usually called within a loop, a difficult error to detect occurs when you properly initialize the buffer variables outside of the loop rather than inside of it. Consider the following example, which uses *Reg-EnumKeyEx*. The function is declared as follows:

```
Declare Function RegEnumKeyEx Lib "advapi32.dll" _
                Alias "RegEnumKeyExA" _
                (ByVal hKey As Long, ByVal dwIndex As Long, _
                ByVal lpName As String, lpcbName As Long, _
                lpReserved As Long, ByVal lpClass As String, _
                lpcbClass As Long, lpftLastWriteTime As FILETIME) As Long
```

It is then called in the following code fragment:

```
' WRONG
Dim lngRegError As Long, lngIndex As Long
Dim lngBufferSize As Long, lngClassLen As Long
Dim strBuffer As String * 50
Dim strClass As String
Dim udfFileTime As FILETIME

lngIndex = 0
lngRegError = ERROR_SUCCESS
lngBufferSize = Len(strBuffer)

Do While lngRegError = ERROR_SUCCESS
    lngRegError = RegEnumKeyEx(HKEY_CLASSES_ROOT, lngIndex, _
                        strBuffer, lngBufferSize, 0&, strClass, _
                        lngClassLen, udfFileTime)
    If lngRegError = ERROR_SUCCESS Then
        List1.AddItem left(strBuffer, lngBufferSize)
        lngIndex = lngIndex + 1
    End If
Loop
```

The code fragment should enumerate all the subkeys of HKCR; we intend for it to loop until the call to *RegEnumKeyEx* returns an error, hopefully ERROR_NO_MORE_ITEMS, which causes the loop to terminate. Although in some cases this code fragment might successfully enumerate all a key's subkeys, its success is actually dependent on the name of each subkey having the same number of or fewer characters than the preceding subkey enumerated by the function. In the case of keys with a large number of subkeys, it will almost certainly enumerate only a few subkeys before returning ERROR_MORE_DATA.

The problem here is clearly not our string variable: since we've initialized it as a fixed-length string, regardless of the value of the string at any time, a fixed

number of bytes has been allocated for it. If we look at the long integer that indicates the size of the string buffer, *lngBufferSize*, it quickly becomes clear
what the problem is: we've initialized the variable outside of the loop under the
assumption (evidently) that its value would remained unchanged. After all, we're
not changing it, so who else would be? The tooth fairy? But since it is passed by
reference to *RegEnumKeyEx*, that API function updates it on each pass through
the loop to reflect the actual number of characters that *RegEnumKeyEx* has
written to the string buffer. That means that the value of *lngBufferSize* is
likely to diminish more or less quickly as the program loops, until the size of the
buffer reported to *RegEnumKeyEx* becomes inadequate to hold a string.

Fixing this bug simply involves reinitializing *lngBufferSize* at the beginning of
each pass through the loop, as the following code fragment shows:

```
Dim lngRegError As Long, lngIndex As Long
Dim lngBufferSize As Long, lngClassLen As Long
Dim strBuffer As String * 50
Dim strClass As String
Dim udfFileTime As FILETIME

lngIndex = 0
lngRegError = ERROR_SUCCESS

Do While lngRegError = ERROR_SUCCESS
   lngBufferSize = Len(strBuffer)     ' REINITIALIZE lngBufferSize HERE
   lngRegError = RegEnumKeyEx(HKEY_CLASSES_ROOT, lngIndex, _
               strBuffer, lngBufferSize, 0&, strClass, _
               lngClassLen, udfFileTime)
   If lngRegError = ERROR_SUCCESS Then
      List1.AddItem left(strBuffer, lngBufferSize)
      lngIndex = lngIndex + 1
   End If
Loop
```

The false economy of constants

Everyone knows that constants are more efficient to use, and offer better performance, than variables. But if we are passing a parameter by reference, it is
important that the parameter be a variable, since the API function must be able to
modify its value. It's common to forget this, though, and to create code like the
following fragment, which retrieves the path and name of the program associated
with text (.TXT) files:

```
Dim lngRegError As Long, hKey As Long, lngDataType As Long
Dim strFileAssn As String, strPgmName As String

strFileAssn = "txtfile\shell\open\command"  ' single backslash; VB
                          ' doesn't have escape char
lngRegError = RegOpenKey(HKEY_CLASSES_ROOT, strFileAssn, _
                hKey)
```

```
If lngRegError = ERROR_SUCCESS Then
   strPgmName = String(MAX_PATH + 1, 0)
   lngRegError = RegQueryValueEx(hKey, "", 0, lngDataType, _
                                 strPgmName, MAX_PATH + 1)
End If
```

The major problem with this code fragment isn't that it doesn't work; in fact, it returns ERROR_SUCCESS and writes the appropriate value to the *strPgmName* buffer. The problem is that the value of *strPgmName* after the function call is a string whose length is MAX_PATH characters. Ordinarily, that string could be shortened as follows if *lngLenPgmName* were used instead of MAX_PATH as a parameter:

```
lngLenPgmName = MAX_PATH  + 1
strPgmName = string(lngLenPgmName, 0)
lngRegError = RegQueryValueEx(hKey, "", 0, lngDataType, _
                             strPgmName, lngLenPgmName)
strPgmName = left(strPgmName,lngLenPgmName)
```

Instead, eliminating "white space" from the string requires that we use the more costly (in terms of performance) *InStr* function to locate the first null character in *strPgmName*:

```
strPgmName = Left(strPgmName, Instr(strPgmName, Chr(0))-1)
```

So although we've saved ourselves a few bytes of memory by using MAX_PATH instead of a variable, we've consumed far more memory and resources in dealing with the consequences of our choice.

Are your strings lean and mean?

The discussion of the false economy of constants suggests that you have a choice in manipulating the string values that the registry API stores to buffers—that if you're not concerned about wasting memory (and, after all, we're probably only talking about a few hundred bytes in most applications at the most), there's no real need to "trim" string variables by removing everything from the null character to the end of the string buffer. The failure to do this, however, can easily derail an application.

This is particularly the case when the string retrieved from a buffer is compared to another string variable. For instance, consider the following code fragment, which retrieves a string (presumably either "0" or "1") from the StatusBar value entry of HKCU\Software\MyCompany\MyApp\Settings:

```
Dim hKey As Long
Dim lngToolbar As Long
Dim strToolbar As String

lngToolbar = 10
strToolbar = String(lngToolbar, 0)
```

```
Call RegOpenKey(HKEY_CURRENT_USER, _
               "Software\MyCompany\MyApp\Settings", hKey)
Call RegQueryValueEx(hKey, "Toolbar", 0, 0, ByVal strToolbar, _
                     lngToolbar)
If strToolbar = "1" Then _
   StatusBar1.Visible = True
```

Although this is a contrived example, it does illustrate a problem. In this example, the length of the string buffer *strToolbar* is 10. Even though *RegQueryValueEx* presumably writes only a single byte to the buffer, its length continues to be 10 bytes. This means that, when *strToolbar* is compared to the string constant "1", the comparison *always* fails, and the form's status bar is never displayed. They're different strings, even though both start with "1". Fixing the problem is very easy: *strToolbar* must be trimmed to remove all characters from the null character to the end of the buffer, as the following **IF** statement illustrates:

```
If Left(strToolbar, lngToolbar - 1) = "1" Then
```

Are your NULLs really NULL?

A number of API functions require that a parameter ordinarily passed by reference to a function be left NULL if you don't want to retrieve its value, or if it is unused (reserved). For instance, each of the "extended" registry functions in the Win32 API include either an *lpReserved* or a *Reserved* parameter. The C syntax for these functions indicate that the value of this parameter is supposed to be either NULL (for *lpReserved*) or 0 (for *Reserved*).

To pass a function a NULL (which is the same thing as a *null pointer*) in Visual Basic, you pass it a zero-value long integer *by value*. The pointer is null because its value is 0, so it doesn't point to a valid memory location in protected mode. If you mistakenly pass the zero-value long integer by reference, you're actually passing a *pointer to a null*. Before calling the function, Visual Basic stores your zero to a location somewhere in memory and passes the DLL routine its starting address; so the routine has a valid starting address that points to some area of memory.

The point of all of this is that it's very common to pass a pointer to a null rather than null pointer. It happens whenever a parameter is defined using the **AS ANY** type definition and you pass it a zero without specifying the BYVAL keyword; this problem was discussed earlier, in the section "Is AS ANY used in the DECLARE statement?" But the problem is somewhat broader than that; it also occurs in two other situations:

- Whenever you pass a 0 by reference to a function that's expecting byte data. This is true of the *lpByte* parameter to both *RegEnumValue* and *RegQuery-ValueEx*.

- When you pass a 0 by reference to a registry function whose reserved parameter is a pointer (lpDWORD).

For example, the *API Viewer* provides the following definition for *RegEnumValue*:

```
Declare Function RegEnumValue Lib "advapi32.dll" _
    Alias "RegEnumValueA" _
    (ByVal hKey As Long, ByVal dwIndex As Long, _
    ByVal lpValueName As String, lpcbValueName As Long, _
    lpReserved As Long, lpType As Long, lpData As Byte, _
    lpcbData As Long) As Long
```

The following call to *RegEnumValue* neatly succeeds in passing two pointers to nulls to the function:

```
' WRONG!
if RegEnumValue(hKey, lngIndex, strValName, lngLenValName, 0, _
            lngDataType, 0, lngDataLen)
```

Because of the second pointer to a null that's supplied as an argument to the `lpData` parameter, the function necessarily fails, and returns `ERROR_MORE_ DATA`. The error can be fixed as follows:

```
' STILL WRONG, BUT IT WORKS FOR LOCAL REGISTRY ACCESS UNDER WIN95!
if RegEnumValue(hKey, lngIndex, strValName, lngLenValName, 0, _
            lngDataType, ByVal 0, lngDataLen)
```

If your application is accessing a local registry under Win95, this version of the function returns `ERROR_SUCCESS` and properly updates the value of `lngDataLen` to reflect the size of the buffer needed to retrieve the value entry's data. However, if you run it under WinNT, or if you attempt to enumerate a value entry on a remote computer, the function once again fails, and returns `ERROR_ INVALID_PARAMETER`. To fix it, you need to correctly pass the `lpReserved` parameter:

```
' FINALLY CORRECT
 if RegEnumValue(hKey, lngIndex, strValName, lngLenValName, ByVal 0, _
            lngDataType, ByVal 0, lngDataLen)
```

Now you're passing two null pointers, rather than two pointers to nulls, when you call the function. But why was the second version of the function call able to work under Win95, while it failed under WinNT? The reason is that Win95 (or, more precisely, *ADVAPI32.DLL*) does not validate unused parameters in calls to the registry API. It simply discards them and calls down to the Virtual Machine Manager. (Interestingly, what it discards are usually the "extended" parameters that are new to the Win32 API; what it ends up calling for the most part are the "compatibility" functions within the VMM.) On the other hand, both WinNT and *WINREG.DLL* (if you're doing remote registry access under Win95) validate all of their parameters, whether they're used or not.

Handling Errors

Typically, you trap run-time errors in your code by providing an error handler that is activated by the ON ERROR statement. For example, the following code fragment attempts to open the HKCR\.tlt key. The programmer might expect that, if the operation fails, the error handler should be invoked. This means that, if the error occurred because the key didn't exist, the *RegCreateKey* function should create it and return control to the line following the call to *RegOpenKey*.

```
' WRONG
Dim hKey As Long, lngRegError As Long

On Error GoTo Error_Handler

lngRegError = RegOpenKey(HKEY_CLASSES_ROOT, ".tlt", hKey)
' do something
Call RegCloseKey(hKey)

Exit Sub

Error_Handler:

Select Case lngRegError
    Case ERROR_FILE_NOT_FOUND
        Call RegCreateKey(HKEY_CLASSES_ROOT, ".tlt", hKey)
        Resume Next
    Case Else
        MsgBox "Registry access error " & lngRegError
End Select

End Sub
```

Unfortunately, though, if the *RegOpenKey* function cannot open the key and instead returns ERROR_FILE_NOT_FOUND, the error handler is never invoked, and the VB Err object is never updated to reflect the registry access error. That's because calls to external dynamic link libraries are outside the scope of VB's error handling subsystem. VB knows only that *RegOpenKey*, in the case of our example, is to return a long integer that should be assigned to the *lngRegError* variable. It has no idea of what possible return values are error codes and which ones aren't, nor does it know what any of the error codes mean. In fact, to be accurate, it doesn't even know that the function's return value is an error code.

Under VB4, the Err object features a new property, LastDLLError, which should contain the system error code for the last call to a dynamic link library. VB, though, does not generate an exception when it updates the value of Last-DLLError, which in turn means that the enabled error handler is not activated. Finally, and most importantly, the dynamic link library returning the error code must support the LastDLLError property; the registry API does not.

VB's limited support for error handling in calls to the Win32 API poses something of a challenge for the VB programmer. So too do the error codes returned by the registry API themselves: in many cases, they are *contextual*, rather than *absolute*, errors. For instance, the attempt to open a key with *RegOpenKey* in most cases returns either ERROR_SUCCESS or ERROR_FILE_NOT_FOUND. Whether the latter return value is really an error depends on the program's assumptions: if the program expects to open the key, its inability to open it is an error; but if the program is merely testing whether the key exists, the failure to open it is information, not an error. Similarly, we've seen that, when enumerating values, it's common to loop until the registry enumeration function returns ERROR_NO_ MORE_ITEMS. In this case, the proper execution of the program depends on a call to the function returning an "error code"; without it, the program would loop endlessly.

Clearly, one of the disadvantages of stepping outside of the relatively "safe" confines of the VB environment by accessing external libraries is that error handling necessarily requires a good deal more attention and planning. At the same time, though, three methods for handling errors are available:

- No error handling

- Inline error handling

- Creating user-defined errors and activating an error handler

We'll briefly survey these three alternatives, assess the strengths and weaknesses of each, and provide a few examples. As we'll see, though, these three methods are not mutually exclusive: effective error handling involves selecting the method that's most suitable for each function call.

No error handling

At first glance, it might appear that this is some kind of joke—after all, how can the absence of error handling be considered a method of error handling? In fact, though, the deliberate omission of error handling is a fairly common form of error handling. It is used whenever a programmer decides to use the Call statement to invoke an external function, thereby discarding the function's return value. (It is also used whenever a programmer fails to think about what might go wrong, and therefore does not provide adequate error handling as an error of oversight.)

Choosing to omit error handling generally involves balancing probabilities. For example, consider the case of *RegOpenKey* once again. Almost invariably, it returns either ERROR_SUCCESS or ERROR_FILE_NOT_FOUND. But if a program is attempting to retrieve a duplicate handle to a top-level key, for instance, the function should always return ERROR_SUCCESS. If it doesn't, something is so seriously wrong with the registry—and therefore with Windows as a system—that it seems unlikely that the application can execute in the first place, or that, if it does, any error handling that the application might do will not noticeably improve the user's computing session. In other words, the decision to omit error handling is a deliberate one, based in part on the belief that the cost of handling errors exceeds the benefits it might return, and in part on the probability that the errors that would otherwise be handled will never occur.

This is not to say that a decision to forgo error handling in an application is acceptable. Rather, in the case of some calls to particular functions, there may be a legitimate basis to decide not to trap errors, and to assume that the code is sufficiently robust that error handling is not required. In short, not handling errors is not an error handling strategy by itself, but rather one that works effectively in combination with one or both of the other methods.

Portability and No Error Handling

If you want your program to run under WinNT as well as Win95, you have to be much more careful about error handling, and the situations in which you can deliberately choose to not trap errors are considerably restricted. That's because, as a secure operating system, WinNT can deny your application access to the registry because its user doesn't have the necessary authority to perform certain kinds of operations.

Inline error handling

Inline error handling involves placing the error handling code for a function immediately after the call to that function. In the case of the registry API, the value returned by each function must be stored to a variable, and then the value of that variable must be evaluated. Some type of conditional statement—either an `IF/END IF` statement or a `SELECT CASE` statement—located immediately beneath the function call is executed if the function call returns an error. Example 6-5 provides a fairly typical example of inline error handling in an application's startup code. The code fragment attempts to open a key. If the attempt fails because the key does not exist, the module creates the key, initializes the application's screen coordinates to their default value, and adds a value entry containing the screen coordinates. Once this initialization code within the `IF/END IF` statement executes, the application can be confident that the default values of all of its configuration settings have been written to the registry.

The chief advantage of inline error handling is its flexibility: it allows the error handling code to be modified and adapted on a function-by-function basis,

Example 6-5. An example of inline error handling

```
Private Sub Form_Load()

Dim hKey As Long, lngRegError As Long, lngPosLen As Long
Dim strSubkey As String
Dim udfPosition As WinPosition

lngPosLen = Len(udfPosition)
' Open registry key
strSubkey = "Software\MyCompany\MyApp\Settings"
lngRegError = RegOpenKey(HKEY_CURRENT_USER, strSubkey, hKey)
' If successful, retrieve window position
If lngRegError = ERROR_SUCCESS Then
    Call RegQueryValueEx(hKey, "WindowPos", 0, 0, udfPosition, lngPosLen)
    Call RegCloseKey(hKey)
' Inline error handling
Else
    ' Do if key does not exist
    If lngRegError = ERROR_FILE_NOT_FOUND Then
        udfPosition.x = Form1.Left
        udfPosition.y = Form1.Top
        udfPosition.w = Form1.Width
        udfPosition.h = Form1.Height

        Call RegCreateKey(HKEY_CURRENT_USER, strSubkey, hKey)
        Call RegSetValueEx(hKey, "WindowPos", 0&, REG_BINARY, _
                            udfPosition, Len(udfPosition))
    ' Any other error is fatal
    Else
        MsgBox "Fatal error " & lngRegError
        Exit Sub
    End If
End If

End Sub
```

depending on the requirements of a particular function call. Because the error handling code is located immediately after the function, it can be written to reflect the requirements of that particular function call. This in turn tends to make inline code cleaner and more readable: whereas general error handlers have to rely on a multiplicity of flags being set to reflect special conditions, special conditions can be incorporated into the code for inline error handlers in a very straightforward manner.

Inline error handling also has substantial disadvantages, though. First, where external functions are called with some frequency (as the registry API should be), it causes duplicate code to proliferate throughout an application. When this duplicate code contains some errors, locating and correcting each occurrence of it can easily become a nightmare. Second, it makes the logic of a program difficult to follow. Someone examining the code (including the programmer who wrote it in the first place) might be excused for thinking that the program's actual purpose is to test for errors.

Its flexibility makes inline error handling most suitable for handling special cases. Given the nature of the registry API, whose return values frequently provide information to a far greater degree than they indicate an error condition, these special cases abound. But for the "regular" cases of errors, enabling an error handler that is activated when an error occurs—which is what the ON ERROR statement does— seems ideal. In the next section, we'll see how to enable and activate an error handler when calling routines in the Win32 API.

Enabling and activating an error handler

The basic reason that the enabled error handler cannot be activated when calling a DLL routine stems from the lack of integration between VB and the dynamic link library, and particularly with the external routine's failure to update the VB Err object with the results of the function. However, with a little bit of work, it is possible to provide this integration in code.

The VB Err object is at the center of an error-handling system that is at least partially customizable. In particular, the Err object supports user-defined errors. The Err object stores error codes to its **Number** property, which is a long integer; that is, if it is interpreted as a signed long integer, its value can range from -2,147,483,648 to 2,147,483,647. The range from 0 to 65,535 and from -2,147,221,504 to -2,147,220,992 is reserved for VB system errors and for error codes that VB remaps into system errors.

Even with over 4 billion error codes to choose from, there is always some possibility of an overlap with VB's own error codes. To avoid this, Microsoft recommends that user- or application-defined error codes be added to the value of the vbObjectError constant. Since the value of vbObjectError is -2,147,221,504, there is room for somewhat over 2 billion application-defined errors before there is a serious danger of overlap with VB's own error codes.[*]

Once a user-defined error code is defined, the enabled error handler can be activated by using the `Err.Raise` method to generate a designated run-time error. The `Raise` method also updates the various properties of the Err object with the values passed to it as parameters:

```
Err.Raise(Number, [Source], [Description], [HelpFile], [HelpContext])
```

---

[*] The major intent of the vbObjectError constant is to assist in debugging and handling run-time errors from OLE automation servers. If your application uses an OLE automation server, you should also be sure that you remap registry API errors to a range that doesn't overlap with error codes generated by the OLE server. In addition, the error codes vbErrorObject through vbErrorObject + 512 are reserved for use by Visual Basic, and should not be used either for registry error codes or for OLE server error codes.

Number	A longer integer containing the error code.
Source	An optional string indicating the name of the object or application that generated the error. If this parameter is omitted, its value defaults to the programmatic ID of the current VB project.
Description	An optional string describing the error. If this parameter is omitted and *Number* is not a standard VB error, its value defaults to "Application-defined or object-defined error."
HelpFile	An optional fully qualified path to the Help file containing information about the error. If this parameter is omitted, its value defaults to the path and filename of the standard VB Help file.
HelpContext	An optional string containing the context ID of a topic within the Help file that provides help for the error. If this parameter is omitted and *Number* is a system-defined error, it defaults to the VB Help file context ID for that error; otherwise, it is null.

Notice that all parameters are optional except for the first. So the method can simply be invoked by supplying it an error number, as follows:

```
Err.Raise(errno)
```

Enabling an error handler that takes advantage of user-defined errors requires the following steps:

1. *Define an alternate set of errors that don't overlap VB's own.* The code in Example 6-6, which is stored in a code module, defines a unique error constant for each error value returned by the registry API.

Example 6-6. User-defined error constants

```
Public Const vbREG_ERROR = vbObjectError + 2048

Public Const regERROR_SUCCESS = vbREG_ERROR + ERROR_SUCCESS
Public Const regERROR_ACCESS_DENIED = vbREG_ERROR + ERROR_ACCESS_DENIED
Public Const regERROR_FILE_NOT_FOUND = vbREG_ERROR + _
                                ERROR_FILE_NOT_FOUND
Public Const regERROR_CALL_NOT_IMPLEMENTED = vbREG_ERROR + _
                                ERROR_CALL_NOT_IMPLEMENTED
Public Const regERROR_INVALID_HANDLE = vbREG_ERROR + _
                                ERROR_INVALID_HANDLE
Public Const regERROR_INVALID_PARAMETER = vbREG_ERROR + _
                                ERROR_INVALID_PARAMETER
Public Const regERROR_NO_MORE_ITEMS = vbREG_ERROR + ERROR_NO_MORE_ITEMS
Public Const regERROR_MORE_DATA = vbREG_ERROR + ERROR_MORE_DATA
Public Const regERROR_CANTOPEN = vbREG_ERROR + ERROR_CANTOPEN
Public Const regERROR_CANTREAD = vbREG_ERROR + ERROR_CANTREAD
Public Const regERROR_CANTWRITE = vbREG_ERROR + ERROR_CANTWRITE
Public Const regERROR_REGISTRY_CORRUPT = vbREG_ERROR + _
                                ERROR_REGISTRY_CORRUPT
Public Const regERROR_REGISTRY_IO_FAILED = vbREG_ERROR + _
                                ERROR_REGISTRY_IO_FAILED
Public Const regERROR_REGISTRY_RECOVERED = vbREG_ERROR + _
                                ERROR_REGISTRY_RECOVERED
```

Example 6-6. User-defined error constants (continued)

```
Public Const regERROR_KEY_DELETED = vbREG_ERROR + ERROR_KEY_DELETED
Public Const regERROR_NOT_REGISTRY_FILE = vbREG_ERROR + _
                                          ERROR_NOT_REGISTRY_FILE
```

2. *Write the error handler.* Usually, an error handler processes one or more of the possible error constants defined in Example 6-6 within a SELECT CASE statement. Ordinarily, you would not include regERROR_SUCCESS in your error handler, since it's not really an error code. However, given the way that this error handler will be activated, it's particularly important that this error code be adequately handled. Example 6-7 illustrates what a primitive error handler might look like.

Example 6-7. A rudimentary error handler

```
Error_Handler:

Dim strWarning As String

Select Case Err.Number
    Case regERROR_SUCCESS
        Resume Next
    Case regERROR_FILE_NOT_FOUND
        Call RegCreateKey(hKey, strSubkey, hNewKey)
        Resume Next
    Case regERROR_MORE_DATA
        strBuffer = String(lngLenData, 0)
        Resume
    Case regERROR_REGISTRY_CORRUPT
        strWarning = "MyApp has detected serious corruption in the "
        strWarning = strWarning & "Registry and cannot continue."
        MsgBox strWarning
        If blnKeyOpen Then Call RegCloseKey(hNewKey)
        End
End Select

End Sub
```

3. Enable the error handler with the ON ERROR GOTO Error_Handler statement.

4. Use the Err.Raise method whenever you call a registry API function and you'd like to activate the error handler if an error occurs. The *number* parameter should be set equal to vbObjectError plus the return value of the function. Example 6-8 illustrates the use of the Err.Raise method in two registry API calls.

Example 6-8. Using the Err.Raise method

```
Dim hKey As Long, hNewKey As Long, lngLenData As Long
Dim strSubkey As String
```

Example 6-8. Using the Err.Raise method (continued)

```
Dim strValueName As String, strBuffer As String
Dim blnKeyOpen As Boolean

On Error GoTo Error_Handler

' Open Key
hKey = HKEY_CURRENT_USER
strSubkey = "Software\MyCompany\MyApp\Settings"
Err.Raise (vbREG_ERROR + RegOpenKey(hKey, strSubkey, hNewKey))
blnKeyOpen = True

' Get MRU list
lngLenData = 4
strBuffer = String(lngLenData, 0)
strValueName = "MRUList"
Err.Raise (vbREG_ERROR + RegQueryValueEx(hKey, strValueName, 0&, 0&,
strBuffer, lngLenData))
Call RegCloseKey(hNewKey)

Exit Sub
```

There are several alternate ways of implementing an error-handling system and activating the error handler. One of the most common, for instance, involves converting the Win32 API error code to a VB error code, like the following code fragment does:

```
lngRegError = RegOpenKey(HKEY_CLASSES_ROOT, _
                         "Software\MyCompany\MyApp\Settings", hKey)
' Convert to VB File Not Found error (53)
If lngRegError = ERROR_FILE_NOT_FOUND Then Err.Raise(53)
```

The major problem with this approach to error handling is that the **RESUME** or **RESUME 0** statement, which the error handler ordinarily uses to return control to the line on which the error occurred, cannot be used in any meaningful way, since it returns control to the line on which the API routine's return value was modified, and not the line on which the function call failed. This means that, instead of the relatively elegant and unambiguous **RESUME 0** statement, the programmer has to resort to some combination of labels, flag variables, and loops in order to direct program flow, which in turn makes code difficult to understand, debug, and maintain, and program flow hard to follow.

In contrast, implementing a system of user-defined errors and calling the **Err.Raise** method produces code that is much cleaner and more readable, as well as much easier to debug. It does, however, have one major drawback: a performance penalty results from invoking the error handler each time a registry API function is called, even if it returns **ERROR_SUCCESS**. Any attempt to avoid this, though, requires that the exception be signaled on a line other than the function call, which in turn tends to produce "spaghetti" code.

Reading Registry Data

For the most part, the operation of functions like *RegOpenKeyEx*, *RegEnumKey*, or *RegQueryInfoKey* are very clear, and any remaining difficulties can usually be resolved by examining a C code fragment, even for programmers who do not use or are not really familiar with C. This is not true, though, of *RegEnumValue* or *RegQueryValueEx*, which extract information about the values assigned to particular value entries.

The basic problem here is that the value retrieval functions return a variety of data types. (You might want to review these by taking a look at Table 4-7 in Chapter 4.) How to extract some of these, like REG_SZ (the VB string data type) or REG_DWORD (the VB long data type) is fairly clear, provided that you know the data type in advance. How to handle other data whose types are known in advance (like REG_BINARY, which doesn't immediately correspond to a VB data type, or REG_DWORD_BIG_ENDIAN, which is a "backward" Motorola-style long integer) is not so apparent. Nor is it apparent how to retrieve structured data types that might be stored in the registry.

Furthermore, when your application is cycling through the values belonging to a particular subkey with the *RegEnumValue* function, the data type of each registry value entry is not known in advance, which makes retrieving its value difficult. Although you can use *RegEnumValue* not only to retrieve general information about each value entry (like its name and data type), but also to write the value of each value entry to a buffer, your application must handle the individual bytes in the buffer in a way that makes sense. Consequently, the registry API provides two methods for extracting a value from a value entry:

- A difficult method that, because it handles the byte data returned by *RegEnumValue* directly, presupposes that you're comfortable working with buffers of byte data. At first glance, it seems like the more efficient method, since it "saves" an API call to *RegQueryValueEx*. The additional coding required to coerce raw binary data into a meaningful VB data type, though, involves far more effort than making an additional API call. This approach is discussed very briefly in the section "Retrieving Unknown Data Types."

- An "easy" way that involves making an additional registry API call for each value entry that is enumerated. *RegEnumValue* is used merely to get the value name and its data type. These are then used to call a specific variant of the *RegQueryValueEx* function to retrieve the actual data. This method, which really retrieves an unknown data type by turning it into a known data type, is included in the section "Retrieving Known Data Types." It is also the method that we recommend, and that the Win32 documentation recommends.

Retrieving Known Data Types

In some cases, you can be reasonably sure of the data type of a registry value entry in advance. For instance, if your application reads an entry named Location in HKLM\Software\MyCompany\MyApp\Settings, you can be certain that, unless someone has mucked with the registry (which is entirely possible, of course), it contains string data whose value is the full path and filename to *MYAPP.EXE*. In other cases, though, you may not be sure of a value entry's data type, either because it might be one of several kinds of data, or because your application uses a general routine to read a large number of registry keys.

The recommended method of dealing with this second situation is to use the *RegEnumValue* function to turn the unknown data type into a known one. For instance, the code fragment in Example 6-9 enumerates each value entry of HKLM\Software\Microsoft\Windows\CurrentVersion\Network to determine the entry's name and data type. The *RegQueryValueEx* function can then retrieve the entry's data.

Before calling *RegEnumValue* to retrieve information about each value entry, the code module calls *RegQueryInfoKey* to determine the number of value entries belonging to the open key (stored to lngValueCount) and the number of characters in its longest value name (stored to lngNameLength). These two values determine the number of times that the module needs to enumerate the values of the open key and the size of the string buffer to be passed to the *RegQueryValue* function. This in turn allows us to use the Call statement to call the function and discard its return value, since we can be reasonably certain that, unless the registry is corrupted (in which case all bets are off, and error handling in our application is unlikely to help matters), the function will return ERROR_SUCCESS. All other parameters are left null. (In the declaration of *RegQueryInfoKey*, we've changed the data type of the lpftLastWriteTime parameter to AS ANY to allow us to pass a null value, rather than a FILETIME structure.)

The module calls the *RegEnumValue* function lngValueCount times in a do while loop. In each pass of the loop, it uses lngNameLength to initialize lngActualNameLength, which indicates the number of characters in the string buffer when the function is called and the number of characters written to the buffer when the function returns. lngActualNameLength is one greater than lngNameLength to accommodate the terminating null character that *RegEnumValue* adds to the value name string. The string buffer, strValueName, is then initialized within the loop using the *String* function.

In the call to *RegEnumValue* itself, we're only concerned with three items of information: the name of the value entry, the number of characters in the value entry's name, and the value entry's data type; for the moment, we're not interested in the data itself or its length, the two other items of information provided by the function. So in their place, the code fragment passes null values to the function. To do this, the second to the last parameter, defined as *lpData* in the function's DECLARE statement, has to be passed by value. This is because *lpData* is byte data that is ordinarily passed by reference to the function. If we assign this parameter a value of 0 and still pass it by reference, what VB actually passes to the function is the address of our zero value. To use terminology from the C language, what we're actually passing is a pointer to a null ("*"), rather than the null pointer ((char *) 0) that we intend to pass. The function will attempt to write its data to the *lpData* buffer. But since we've defined its length as 0 (the value of the final parameter), the function fails and returns ERROR_MORE_DATA.

Example 6-9. Determining the data type of a value entry

```
Dim hKey As Long
Dim lngIndex As Long
Dim lngValueCount As Long
Dim lngNameLength As Long
Dim lngActualNameLength As Long
Dim lngDataType As Long
Dim strValueName As String

lngIndex = 0

' Open key and gather information about its values
If RegOpenKey(HKEY_LOCAL_MACHINE, _
        "Software\Microsoft\Windows\CurrentVersion\Network", _
        hKey) = ERROR_SUCCESS Then
    Call RegQueryInfoKey(hKey, "", 0, 0, 0, 0, 0, lngValueCount, _
            lngNameLength, 0, 0, 0)
    Do While lngIndex <= lngValueCount - 1
        lngActualNameLength = lngNameLength + 1
        strValueName = String(lngActualNameLength, 0)
        Call RegEnumValue(hKey, lngIndex, strValueName, _
                lngActualNameLength, 0, lngDataType, ByVal 0, 0)

        Select Case lngDataType
            ' Handle each returned data type within SELECT CASE statement
            Case REG_SZ
                ' do something
            Case REG_DWORD
                ' do something
            ' handle other data types
        End Select
        lngIndex = lngIndex + 1
    Loop
    Call RegCloseKey(hKey)
End If
```

Once the data type is known, you can use the *RegQueryValueEx* function to retrieve a particular entry's data. The most common kinds of data found in the registry are strings (data types REG_SZ and occasionally REG_EXPAND_SZ), long integers (REG_DWORD), and binary values (REG_BINARY). We'll examine retrieving each of these in turn.

String values: REG_SZ and REG_EXPAND_SZ

At least in theory, the Win95 registry contains two major kinds of string data, "ordinary" strings (REG_SZ) and strings containing an unexpanded variable name (REG_EXPAND_SZ). Variable names are any of several environment variables that Win95 recognizes automatically or that are defined by value entries of HKCU\ Environment. Unexpanded variable names that are embedded within strings are usually delimited by percentage signs (e.g., %PATH%). In practice, there's no real assurance that REG_SZ data does not contain an unexpanded variable name and that REG_EXPAND_SZ data contains an unexpanded variable name. (For more information on dealing with environment variable names in REG_SZ and REG_ EXPAND_SZ data, see the discussion of the individual data types in "Enumerating a Key's Values: *RegEnumValue*," in Chapter 4.)

To retrieve this string data, your program simply needs to define a string variable of the necessary size to hold the data and to pass it to the function by reference (using the BYVAL keyword in order to pass it by reference as a C string, rather than using the BYREF keyword to pass it by reference as a VB string). There are several ways to determine the appropriate size of the string buffer variable that you pass to *RegQueryValueEx*:

- Use the *lpcbMaxValueLen* parameter of the *RegQueryInfoKey* function to determine the length of the open key's longest data value. If the longest value entry contains string data, this value includes the terminating null character.

- Call the *RegEnumValue* function, passing 0 by value in place of the *lpData* parameter and a long integer variable passed by reference in place of the *lpcbData* parameter. If the function can enumerate a value, it returns ERROR_SUCCESS and updates the long integer variable to reflect the size of the value entry's data. The updated value includes the terminating null character. This method is illustrated in Example 6-12. It is useful when you know neither the name of the value entry you'd like to retrieve nor the size of the string buffer to allocate to hold its data.

- Call the *RegQueryValueEx* function twice, the first time passing a null as the value of the *lpData* parameter and a long integer variable for the *lpcb-Data* parameter. If the function can retrieve the specified value entry, it returns ERROR_SUCCESS and updates the long integer variable to reflect the size of the entry's data, in this case *including* the null character used to terminate string data. After properly initializing the string buffer, the second call to the function can then retrieve the entry's data. This method is useful when you know the name of the value entry in advance, but aren't sure about the length of its string data.

- Arbitrarily create a string buffer variable whose size you feel is sufficient to handle the value's data. In this case, though, your program should be prepared to handle an ERROR_MORE_DATA error if the buffer turns out to be too small.

After the *RegQueryValueEx* function returns, you should "trim" the string variable to remove any characters not written to the buffer by the function. You can do this using the VB *Left* function, as follows:

```
strValue = Left(strValue, lngValueLen - 1)
```

where **strValue** is the string buffer passed to the function and **lngValueLen** is the variable used in place of the **lpcbData** parameter that indicates the number of characters that the function writes to the buffer. Since **lngValueLen** includes the terminating null character, be sure to subtract one from it.

When Is the Terminating Null Counted?

At this point, you're probably having a hard time remembering when the terminating null is included in the count returned by parameters that indicate how many characters a registry API function wrote to a string buffer. You might want to review "Those Cursed Terminating Nulls…" in the section "Enumerating Keys: RegEnumKey and RegEnumKeyEx" in Chapter 4.

Finally, whether the program has retrieved a string of type REG_SZ or type REG_EXPAND_SZ, you should decide whether you want to expand any environment variable names within it. Typically, environment variable names are used in registry value entries that contain path and filename information. By definition, of course, REG_EXPAND_SZ data *should* contain unexpanded variable names, although none of the instances of it in a typical Win95 registry seem to.

If you want to determine whether a string value may contain an unexpanded variable name, you can use the *InStr* function to determine whether it contains a percentage sign. If it does, you can call the Win32 API *ExpandEnvironmentStrings* function, which replaces the variable name with its value. The percentage sign occurs relatively rarely in the registry except to delimit a variable name. *ExpandEnvironmentStrings* simply returns the original string if it does not contain a variable name; it does not "damage" the original string.

```
intCharPos = InStr( strBuffer, "%")
If intCharPos > 0 Then
```

```
      strtemp = String(128, 0)
      lngChars = ExpandEnvironmentStrings( strBuffer, strTemp, len(strTemp))
      strBuffer = Left(strTemp, lngChars - 1)
End If
```

In calling the *ExpandEnvironmentStrings* function, you have to initialize the destination buffer (indicated in our code fragment by the **strTemp** variable) to the
proper size. You can do this either arbitrarily, as in the preceding code fragment,
or by making an extra call to *ExpandEnvironmentStrings*. As long as a valid destination buffer (that is, one that contains at least one byte of memory) is passed to
the function, it returns the required buffer size, including the terminating null character. So an alternative, and more robust, version of the preceding code fragment is:

```
intCharPos = Instr( strBuffer, "%")
if intCharPos > 0 then
    strTemp = string(1, 0)
    lngChars = ExpandEnvironmentStrings( strBuffer, strTemp, len(strTemp))
    strTemp = string(lngChars,0)
    Call ExpandEnvironmentStrings( strBuffer, strTemp, len(strTemp))
    strBuffer = left(strTemp, lngChars - 1)
endif
```

Example 6-10 contains the *Form_Load* procedure of a VB program that reads the
value entries of the HKCU\\Environment key and displays the names of the
user's environment variables (represented by each entry's value name) in a
combo box. The value of the selected environment variable is displayed in a list
box.

Example 6-10. Retrieving string data from the registry

```
Private Sub Form_Load()

Dim hKey As Long                   ' Handle of open Registry key
Dim lngIndex As Long               ' Index of value entry
Dim lngValueCount As Long          ' Number of value entries in open key
Dim lngNameLength As Long          ' Length of longest value entry name
Dim lngNameLen As Long             ' Length of individual value entry's name
Dim lngDataType As Long            ' Value entry's data type
Dim lngBufferLen As Long           ' Length of buffer for entry's data
Dim lngCharCount As Long           ' Number of characters in expanded string
Dim strValueName As String         ' Name of value entry
Dim strValue As String             ' Value entry's string data
Dim strTemp As String              ' Temporary expanded string

Dim lngregerror As Long

' Open key and gather information about its values
If RegOpenKey(HKEY_CURRENT_USER, "Environment", hKey) = _
            ERROR_SUCCESS Then
    Call RegQueryInfoKey(hKey, 0, 0, ByVal 0, 0, 0, 0, lngValueCount, _
         lngNameLength, 0, 0, 0)
    lngIndex = 0
```

Example 6-10. Retrieving string data from the registry (continued)

```
    If lngValueCount > 0 Then ReDim strEnvValues(lngValueCount - 1)
    ' Retrieve value name and data length
    Do While lngIndex <= lngValueCount - 1
        lngNameLen = lngNameLength + 1
        strValueName = String(lngNameLen, 0)
        Call RegEnumValue(hKey, lngIndex, strValueName, _
                lngNameLen, ByVal 0, lngDataType, ByVal 0, lngBufferLen)
        ' Retrieve entry's data
        strValueName = Left(strValueName, lngNameLen)
        strValue = String(lngBufferLen, 0)
        Call RegQueryValueEx(hKey, strValueName, 0, lngDataType, _
                          ByVal strValue, lngBufferLen)
        Select Case lngDataType
            ' Handle regular string data
            Case REG_SZ
                ' We should check to see if we need to expand the string,
                ' but we won't
                strEnvValues(lngIndex) = Left(strValue, lngBufferLen - 1)
            ' Handle unexpanded strings
            Case REG_EXPAND_SZ
                strValue = Left(strValue, lngBufferLen - 1)
                strTemp = String(1, 0)
                ' Determine size of buffer
                lngCharCount = ExpandEnvironmentStrings(strValue, _
                              strTemp, Len(strTemp))
                ' Expand string if it needs expansion
                If lngCharCount - 1 > Len(strValue) Then
                    strTemp = String(lngCharCount, 0)
                    lngCharCount = ExpandEnvironmentStrings(strValue, _
                        strTemp, Len(strTemp))
                    strValue = Left(strTemp, lngCharCount - 1)
                End If
                ' Add value to array of environment values
                strEnvValues(lngIndex) = strValue
        End Select
        ' Add environment variable name to combo box
        Combo1.AddItem strValueName
        lngIndex = lngIndex + 1
    Loop
    ' Close registry key
    Call RegCloseKey(hKey)
End If
' Check if there are any entries
If Combo1.ListCount = 0 Then
    Combo1.AddItem "< None >"
    ReDim strEnvValues(0)
    strEnvValues(0) = "< None >"
Else
    Text1.Text = strEnvValues(0)
End If
Combo1.ListIndex = 0

End Sub
```

In Example 6-10, we use the *RegQueryInfoKey* function to determine how many user environment variables are present (indicated by the `lngValueCount` variable) and to determine how large a buffer is needed to store their names (indicated by `lngNameLength`). Within the `do while` loop, the *RegEnumValue* function retrieves the name of each entry (`strValueName`), its data type (`lngDataType`), and the size of the buffer needed to hold the data (`lngBufferLen`). *RegQueryValue* then retrieves the entry's data. Note that, since the `DECLARE` statement for *RegQueryValue* declares the data type of the `lpData` parameter as `Any`, the `strValue` variable must be passed explicitly by reference to the function using the BYVAL keyword. When each value is retrieved, it can be trimmed and, if its data type is `REG_EXPAND_SZ`, expanded by calling the *ExpandEnvironmentStrings* function.

Interestingly, if you use the VB debugger to see which set of `Case` statements are executed when the program reads these string values, you'll see that the data type of each entry of the `HKCU\Environment` key is `REG_EXPAND_SZ`. None of the values, though, actually contain unexpanded variable names, nor would you expect that they should; instead, these value entries contain the values that are used to replace environment variables that appear in other `REG_EXPAND_SZ` entries.

String arrays: REG_MULTI_SZ

Although string array (`REG_MULTI_SZ`) data is comparatively rare in the Win95 registry, it is still possible that you might encounter it on rare occasions. You retrieve it in the same way that you would retrieve any string data type. Once you retrieve it, however, your program has to parse the string buffer and assign each string to an array.

Registry string array data is stored as sequential null-terminated strings. In addition, the array as a whole is terminated with a null character (so it ends with two nulls). All information that registry functions like *RegQueryInfoKey*, *RegEnumValue*, and *RegQueryValueEx* collect from `REG_MULTI_SZ` value entries is based on the array as a whole. This means that the array adds one to the count of value entries belonging to the open key, and that the size of the entry's data is calculated using the entire length of the array, including all of its null characters.

Retrieving a string array from the registry, then, involves the following steps:

- Writing the array to a string buffer using the techniques discussed earlier in "String Data: `REG_SZ` and `REG_EXPAND_SZ`"
- Determining the number of elements in the string array
- Parsing the string buffer to assign each string to an array element

These are illustrated in the following code fragment, which retrieves some hypo-thetical REG_MULTI_SZ data from the registry and assigns it to a string array named *strArray*:

```
' Retrieve registry value
lngRegError = RegQueryValueEx(hKey, "StringArray", 0, _
             lngDataType, ByVal strValue, lngValueLen)
Call RegCloseKey(hKey)

If lngRegError = ERROR_SUCCESS Then
' Trim string, removing final null
   strValue = Left(strValue, lngValueLen - 1)
' Determine number of elements
   For intCtr = 1 To Len(strValue)
      If Mid(strValue, intCtr, 1) = Chr(0) Then _
         intElements = intElements + 1
   Next
   ReDim strArray(intElements - 1)

' Store individual strings to array
   strTemp = ""
   For intCtr = 1 To Len(strValue)
      If Mid(strValue, intCtr, 1) = Chr(0) Then
         strArray(intArrayCtr) = strTemp
         intArrayCtr = intArrayCtr + 1
         strTemp = ""
      Else
         strTemp = strTemp + Mid(strValue, intCtr, 1)
      End If
   Next
End If
```

Note that, when the *strValue* variable is trimmed, its terminating null character, which indicates the end of the array, is removed. Because of this, counting the remaining number of CHR(0)'s in the string yields the number of elements in the string array. The C string can then be parsed once more and its components assigned to a VB string array.

Long integers: REG_DWORD and REG_DWORD_BIG_ENDIAN

The registry supports two types of long integer data: REG_DWORD_LITTLE_ENDIAN and REG_DWORD_BIG_ENDIAN. "Endian" indicates which end of the data—the bytes containing the large numbers or the bytes with the small ones—are stored first. In the little-endian format, which is used on Intel x86 systems, the low-order byte of each word precedes the high-order byte. So the long integer value 102Fh, for instance, would be stored in four consecutive bytes of memory as shown in Figure 6-6, while it would be stored in big-endian format as shown in Figure 6-7. Because both WinNT and Win95 use the little-endian format, the REG_DWORD_LITTLE_ENDIAN data type is the same as REG_DWORD.

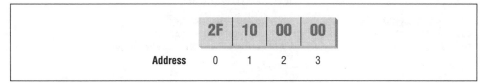

Figure 6-6. Long integer 102Fh in little-endian format

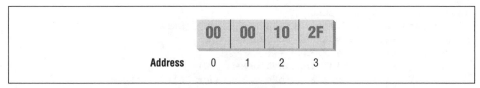

Figure 6-7. Long integer 102Fh in big-endian format

Although neither Win95 nor WinNT (or, more precisely, their Intel processor) actually is able to interpret big-endian data correctly, the registry nevertheless supports it as a data type, probably because it allows network data (like data for TCP/IP networks) to be stored without conversion. In any case, REG_BIG_ENDIAN data does not appear by default in the Win95 registry. But the registry enumeration, retrieval, and modification functions all handle the conversion of the big-endian format to the little-endian format without your having to do anything. If your application does encounter big-endian data in the Win95 registry, you just have to make sure that you specify the proper data type as a parameter to the registry API call that you're using. So aside from that, working with big-endian long integers is the same as working with "normal" ones.

In comparison with retrieving string data, reading long integers (the REG_DWORD data type) from the registry is comparatively easy: since a VB long integer necessarily occupies four bytes of memory, just as a REG_DWORD value does, you just initialize a long integer variable and pass it by reference as a parameter to the *RegQueryValueEx* function. This is illustrated in Example 6-11, a procedure that lists the dynamic link libraries registered with Win95 (i.e., the shared DLLs stored as value entries in HKLM\Software\Microsoft\Windows\CurrentVersion\SharedDLLs) and displays a count of the number of applications that access them.

Example 6-11. Retrieving REG_DWORD data

```
Private Sub Form_Load()

Dim intCtr As Integer          ' Index to value name string
Dim hKey As Long               ' Handle to SharedDLLs key
Dim lngRegError As Long        ' registry API return value
Dim lngIndex As Long           ' Index of registry value
Dim lngLenValueName As Long    ' Length of value name
```

Example 6-11. Retrieving REG_DWORD data (continued)

```
Dim lngSharedDLL As Long      ' Shared DLL count
Dim strValueName As String    ' Name of value entry
Dim strDLLName As String      ' Filename of DLL without path

' Open SharedDLLs key
Call RegOpenKey(HKEY_LOCAL_MACHINE, _
            "Software\Microsoft\Windows\CurrentVersion\SharedDLLs", _
            hKey)
lngRegError = ERROR_SUCCESS
' Enumerate value entries until ERROR_NO_MORE_DATA
Do While lngRegError = ERROR_SUCCESS
   lngLenValueName = MAX_PATH + 1
   strValueName = String(lngLenValueName, 0)
   lngRegError = RegEnumValue(hKey, lngIndex, strValueName, _
                         lngLenValueName, 0, 0, ByVal 0, 0)
   If lngRegError = ERROR_SUCCESS Then
' Trim value name string
      strValueName = Left(strValueName, lngLenValueName)
' Retrieve entry's value
      Call RegQueryValueEx(hKey, strValueName, 0, 0, lngSharedDLL, 4)
' Extract filename
      strDLLName = ""
      For intCtr = Len(strValueName) To 0 Step -1
         If Mid(strValueName, intCtr, 1) = "\" Then
            strDLLName = Right(strValueName, Len(strValueName) - intCtr)
            Exit For
         End If
      Next
      If Len(Trim(strDLLName)) = 0 Then strDLLName = strValueName
         List1.AddItem strDLLName + Space(30 - Len(strDLLName)) + _
                     Str(lngSharedDLL)
         lngIndex = lngIndex + 1
      End If
   Loop

End Sub
```

Since the `SharedDLLs` key is a system-generated key, we can be reasonably sure that it exists in any uncorrupted Win95 registry.[*] Therefore, rather than using the *RegQueryInfoKey* function to gather information about the key's values, the program simply enumerates the key's value entries until *RegQueryValue* no longer returns ERROR_SUCCESS.

Binary data: REG_BINARY

The exact meaning of the registry's "binary data" is extremely varied. In some cases, a binary value means nothing at all, but represents a means of creating a

---

[*] Surprisingly, it's also generated by default on WinNT systems, so this program runs without modification on WinNT 3.x.

value entry while allocating just a single byte to its data. For instance, in `HKLM\System\CurrentControlSet\control\VMM32Files`, each value entry contains one byte of binary data with a value of 0. The value names indicate the virtual device drivers that form the individual components of the Win95 virtual machine, *VMM32.DLL*. In other cases, the binary values are free-form data that the system uses in seemingly arbitrary ways. `HKCU\Software\Microsoft\Windows\CurrentVersion\Policies\Explorer`, for instance, contains an entry named `NoDriveTypeAutoRun`; its four-byte binary value is interpreted as a series of bits that determine whether the autoplay feature[*] is enabled or disabled on particular drives. The free-form binary data can also be interpreted or used in its entirety, as are the `Change` value entries belonging to the subkeys of `HKLM\System\CurrentControlSet\control\SessionManager\AppPatches`, which contain patches that Win95 applies to executable code. Finally, binary data can be any of a variety of standard or application-defined structured data types. We'll first examine how to extract structured data from the registry, and then how to retrieve binary data using the standard Visual Basic data types.

In most cases, retrieving structured binary data from the registry is almost as easy as retrieving long integer values—provided, of course, that the complete definition of the structure is known in advance, and that it has been initialized by a `TYPE` statement in an application code module. To retrieve structured data types, you merely have to pass a properly defined and initialized structure by reference to *RegQueryValueEx*.

For instance, one of the user settings that you'll probably want to store in the registry is the position and state (minimized, maximized, restored) of the window when the user last closed it. Typically, this value is stored as a string, but this requires that your program parse it to extract four long integers. A more efficient approach is to make use of either the Win32 `WINDOWPOS` structure or a data structure of your own creation, like the following:

```
Type WinPosition
    lngLeft As Long
    lngTop As Long
    lngWidth As Long
    lngHeight As Long
    lngState As Long
End Type
```

---

[*] Autoplay is an ease-of-use feature designed to allow Windows to automatically execute a designated program on a particular CD-ROM drive or other removable medium when it is first inserted. When Windows detects a change event (like the insertion of a new CD-ROM), it searches the new medium for an initialization file named *AUTORUN.INF* and executes the program defined by the open= keyword in its [autorun] section. However, autoplay can be enabled on any storage medium, including network drives and floppy disks, by setting its bit in `NoDriveTypeAutoRun`.

The resulting data structure from the registry is shown in RegEdit's Edit Binary Value dialog in Figure 6-8. Notice that there is a perfect correspondence between the WinPosition data structure and this REG_BINARY. Since the members of the data structure are long integers, each occupies four bytes and is stored from left to right, in the same order that they appear in the data structure.

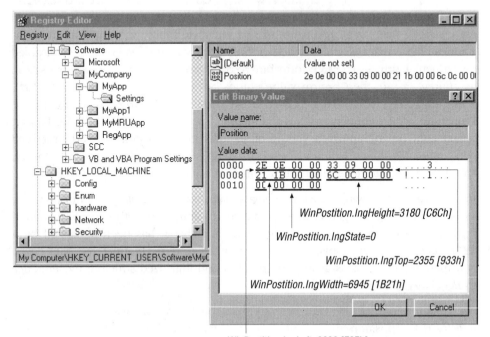

Figure 6-8. A data structure in the RegEdit Edit Binary Value dialog

You can then position the window by including the code fragment shown in Example 6-12 in the window's *Form_Load* event procedure, which reads the structure from the Position value entry in HKCU\Software\MyCompany\MyApp\Settings.

Example 6-12. Retrieving structured data from the registry

```
Dim hKey As Long                    ' Handle to Registry key
Dim lngRegError As Long             ' Error code
Dim lenPosition As Long             ' Length of WinPosition structure
Dim lngType As Long                 ' Registry data type
Dim udfPosition As WinPosition      ' Structured window position data

' Open Registry key, or create it if not found
If RegOpenKey(HKEY_CURRENT_USER, "Software\MyCompany\MyApp\Settings", _
          hKey) <> ERROR_SUCCESS Then _
          Call RegCreateKey(HKEY_CURRENT_USER, _
          "Software\MyCompany\MyApp\Settings", hKey)
```

Example 6-12. Retrieving structured data from the registry (continued)

```
' Extract WinPosition structure
lenPosition = Len(udfPosition)              ' equivalent to C sizeof()
lngRegError = RegQueryValueEx(hKey, "Position", 0, lngType, udfPosition,
lenPosition)
' If value entry does not exist, add it using defaults
If lngRegError <> ERROR_SUCCESS Then
    udfPosition.lngLeft = Form1.Left
    udfPosition.lngTop = Form1.Top
    udfPosition.lngWidth = Form1.Width
    udfPosition.lngHeight = Form1.Height
    Call RegSetValueEx(hKey, "Position", 0, REG_BINARY, udfPosition,
lenPosition)
Else
    ' Position window based on stored registry settings
    Form1.Left = udfPosition.lngLeft
    Form1.Top = udfPosition.lngTop
    Form1.Width = udfPosition.lngWidth
    Form1.Height = udfPosition.lngHeight
    Form1.WindowState = udfPosition.lngState
End If

' Close registry key
Call RegCloseKey(hKey)
```

If the structure contains any strings, though, these must be defined in the TYPE
statement as fixed-length strings, rather than the variable-length strings that VB
programmers use most frequently. For instance, if an application also allows the
user to customize the window caption, the *WinPosition* structure could be
modified to store this information as well; this places all of the information
needed to open the window in a single data structure, defined as follows:

```
Type InitInfo
    lngLeft As Long
    lngTop As Long
    lngWidth As Long
    lngHeight As Long
    lngState As Long
    strCaption As String * 32
End Type
```

The structure can then be accessed, and the window initialized, by the code fragment shown in Example 6-13, which is a straightforward extension of
Example 6-12.

Example 6-13. Retrieving a data structure containing a string

```
Dim hKey As Long                ' Handle to Registry key
Dim lngRegError As Long         ' Error code
Dim lenPosition As Long         ' Length of WinPosition structure
Dim lngType As Long             ' Registry data type
```

Example 6-13. Retrieving a data structure containing a string (continued)

```
Dim udtInit As InitInfo              ' Structured window position data

' Open Registry key
Call RegCreateKey(HKEY_CURRENT_USER, _
                "Software\MyCompany\MyApp\Settings", hKey)
' Extract InitInfo structure
lenPosition = Len(udtInit)           ' equivalent to C sizeof()
lngRegError = RegQueryValueEx(hKey, "WindowInfo", 0, lngType, udfInit,
lenPosition)
If lngRegError <> ERROR_SUCCESS Then
   ' handle exceptions here
Else
   ' Position window based on stored registry settings
   Form1.Left = udtInit.lngLeft
   Form1.Top = udtInit.lngTop
   Form1.Width = udtInit.lngWidth
   Form1.Height = udtInit.lngHeight
   Form1.WindowState = udtInit.lngState
   Form1.Caption = udtInit.strCaption
End If

' Close registry key
Call RegCloseKey(hKey)
```

To some degree, the registry data type that you use to store particular kinds of data in your programs is arbitrary. For instance, an application-defined byte array with four or fewer elements can be stored in the registry as either a REG_SZ or a REG_DWORD value, although most commonly it's stored as REG_BINARY data. More frequently, values stored as REG_BINARY in the registry correspond to long integers or standard C strings. In these cases, where you know that REG_BINARY data corresponds to a particular Visual Basic data type (or, more precisely, to a particular Visual Basic data type that's equivalent to a C data type), you can simply use a variable of type to store the value retrieved by *RegQueryValueEx*.

For example, one of the Win95 registry's top-level keys, HKEY_DYN_DATA, stores pointers to VxD routines that can collect dynamic information on system perfor-mance in one of its subkeys, HKDD\PerfStats\StatData. Each value entry represents a particular item of data that Win95 is collecting, and each contains four bytes of REG_BINARY data, as Figure 6-9 shows. That each item is stored in four bytes, combined with the prevalence of zeroes in the high-order word, suggests that these are actually long integer values stored in the registry as REG_BINARY data. In this case, we can retrieve them by using *RegQueryValueEx* and storing them to a long integer variable.

With this knowledge, we can construct a very simple utility to display a variety of system statistics by reading selected values in by HKDD\PerfStats\StatData at a regular interval, whenever a Timer control's Timer event is fired.

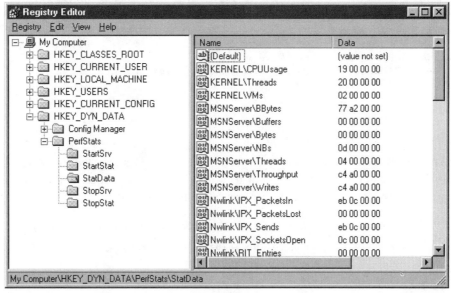

Figure 6-9. Performance statistics in HKDD\PerfStats\StatData

Example 6-14 shows the program's *Timer_Timer* event procedure, which collects five items of information from the registry: the number of threads in the system, the number of active virtual machines, the number of reads per second by the file system, the number of writes per second by the file system, and the number of defective bytes in the swap file.* (Notice, incidentally, that the name of the value entries used to retrieve each of these items includes a backslash.) To collect the data and display it in text boxes, the *Timer* event procedure calls the *GetBinDW* subroutine and passes it the registry key handle, value entry name, and name of the text box control to display the data.

Example 6-14. The Timer_Timer event procedure for a system reporting utility

```
Private Sub Timer1_Timer()

Dim hKey As Long

' Open key
Call RegOpenKey(HKEY_DYN_DATA, "PerfStats\StatData", hKey)

' Get number of threads
Call GetBinDW(hKey, "Kernel\Threads", Text1)
' Get number of virtual machines
Call GetBinDW(hKey, "Kernel\VMs", Text2)
' Get reads per second
```

---

* Because it relies on settings in **HKEY_DYN_DATA**, a top-level key that is unique to Win95, this program does not run under Windows NT.

Example 6-14. The Timer_Timer event procedure for a system reporting utility (continued)

```
Call GetBinDW(hKey, "VFAT\ReadsSec", Text3)
' Get writes per second
Call GetBinDW(hKey, "VFAT\WritesSec", Text4)
' Get defective bytes in swap file
Call GetBinDW(hKey, "VMM\cpgSwapFileDefective", Text5)

' Close key
Call RegCloseKey(hKey)

End Sub
```

The *GetBinDW* subroutine is shown in Example 6-15. It calls *RegQueryValueEx* to retrieve the dynamic data and stores it to a text box's Text property; if for some reason it fails to retrieve a value, it displays "n/a" in the text box.

Example 6-15. Retrieving REG_BINARY data that corresponds to a basic data type

```
Public Sub GetBinDW(hKey As Long, strValueName As String, _
                    objTextBox As Object)

Static lngDWLength As Long
Dim lngValue As Long
Dim blnInit As Boolean

' Once-time initialization of DWORD length
If Not blnInit Then
   lngDWLength = Len(lngValue)
   blnInit = True
End If
' Get dynamic data item
If RegQueryValueEx(hKey, strValueName, 0, 0, lngValue, _
                   lngDWLength) = ERROR_SUCCESS Then
   objTextBox.Text = Format(lngValue, "###,###,##0")
Else
   objTextBox.Text = "n/a"
End If

End Sub
```

Retrieving Unknown Data Types

So far, we've emphasized using *RegQueryValueEx* to retrieve known data types from the registry. If you don't know the data type of a value entry, we've recommended that you use *RegEnumValue* to determine the value entry's data type, then call *RegQueryValueEx* to retrieve it.

It's probably occurred to you, though, that *RegEnumValue* also can be used to write a value entry's data to a buffer; as long as you initialize a buffer of the proper size and pass it in place of the `lpByte` parameter, `lpData` contains the value entry's data when the function returns. You may suspect that, by doing this,

Retrieving Multiple Values with *RegQueryMultipleValues*

We've focused exclusively on using *RegQueryValueEx*, which allows you to read a single value entry at a time, to retrieve data from the registry. The registry API actually contains an additional data retrieval function, *RegQueryMultipleValues*, that allows you to access multiple values with a single function call. However, the function cannot be called from a VB program. That's because the function requires that it be passed an array of VALENT data structures, one for each value entry whose data the function is responsible for retrieving. One of the members of this data structure is a pointer to a string which is stored outside of the data structure itself; *RegQueryMultipleValues* supplies the address within a larger buffer to indicate where a particular value entry's data begins. VB, however, can't access strings whose pointers are stored in a data structure.

you can save yourself a function call, in the process improving your application's performance.

An earlier draft of this book took precisely that approach, and showed in laborious detail how to handle the data written to the `lpData` buffer by *RegEnumValue*. So *RegEnumValue* is certainly usable as a function that retrieves your registry data. However, retrieving registry data in this way imposes two requirements:

- You have to be comfortable working with low-level binary data. When *RegEnumValue* enumerates registry value entries and retrieves their data, the function stores the data to a byte array. (It is also possible, although considerably more unwieldy, to store it to a string variable.) This is raw binary data. You have to manipulate it on a byte-by-byte basis in order to transform it into something meaningful. For example, if the data you retrieve is a REG_DWORD value, you have to be able to assemble a long integer from its component four bytes. Some programmers are comfortable doing this (although most of them are using languages like C or assembly language, which are far more suited for this sort of thing); most programmers aren't.

- You have to enjoy coding, because you'll be doing a lot of it. If you use this approach, you have to be prepared to handle any type of registry data whenever you call *RegEnumValue*. For each data type, you generally have to iterate each element of the byte array and coerce it into some other data type that VB can handle.

The original justification for using *RegEnumValue* to retrieve registry data is that it eliminates an unnecessary function call, thus improving an application's performance whenever registry data is accessed. Ironically, in almost all cases, the additional processing required to transform the byte array retrieved by *RegEnum-Value* into something manageable more than offsets any performance gains that result from not calling *RegQueryValueEx*; and in applications that make intensive use of the registry, or that rely on the registry to store a lot of structured binary data (which can be converted from a byte array only with enormous difficulty), the implications of the decision to "save" by eliminating the call to *RegQueryValueEx*—and instead to convert binary data—severely degrade performance.

In short, unless you have a very compelling reason, you should use *RegEnumValue* to enumerate value entries, in the process collecting information about them, and *RegQueryValueEx* to retrieve them.

Writing Registry Data

To write data to the registry, you use the *RegSetValueEx* function. The value that you want to store in the registry is represented by the `lpData` parameter, which is passed by reference to the function. If you use the standard `DECLARE` statement provided by the *API Viewer*, the data type of this parameter is defined as `AS ANY`, which allows you to pass any value or variable to the function.

In those cases where VB and C data types closely correspond to one another, writing data to the registry is fairly straightforward. This is true, in particular, of long integer (`REG_DWORD` or `REG_DWORD_BIG_ENDIAN`) values and of string (`REG_SZ` and `REG_EXPAND_SZ`) values.

For instance, the following code fragment writes the value of a form's `WindowState` property to the `WindowState` value entry of the `HKCU\Software\MyCompany\MyApp\Settings` key:

```
Dim hKey As Long
Dim lngWindowState As Long

lngWindowState = Form1.WindowState

Call RegCreateKey(HKEY_CURRENT_USER, _
                Software\MyCompany\MyApp\Settings", hKey)
If RegSetValueEx(hKey, "WindowPosition", 0, REG_DWORD, lngWindowState, _
                4) <> ERROR_SUCCESS Then _
                MsgBox "Error writing registry value"
Call RegCloseKey(hKey)
```

Writing string data to the registry is just as easy, except that, if you use the standard `DECLARE` statement that defines the data type of the `lpData` parameter as

ANY, you have to remember to use the BYVAL keyword when calling the function. The following code fragment, for instance, writes the filename stored to the variable *strFileName* to a value entry in HKCU\Software\MyCompany\MyApp\MRU:

```
Dim hKey As Long
Call RegCreateKey(HKEY_CURRENT_USER, _
                "Software\MyCompany\MyApp\MRU", hKey)
If RegSetValueEx(hKey, "a", 0, REG_SZ, ByVal strFileName, _
                Len(strFileName) + 1) <> ERROR_SUCCESS Then _
                MsgBox "Error writing registry value"
Call RegCloseKey(hKey)
```

In addition to passing *strFileName* by reference with the BYVAL keyword, the function's final parameter, *cbData*, which indicates the size of the string to be written to the registry, should be one greater than the string's actual length in order to include its terminating null character.

The REG_EXPAND_SZ data type, incidentally, is an ordinary string variable that contains an environment variable name in place of its value; environment variable names are delimited by percentage signs (e.g., *%PATH%*). For instance, if your application uses temporary files but you don't want to "hard code" or make any assumptions about their location, you can use an environment variable instead. The following code fragment illustrates this by using the *TEMP* environment variable:

```
Dim hKey As Long
Dim strTempDir As String

strTempDir = "%temp%"
Call RegCreateKey(HKEY_CURRENT_USER, _
                "Software\MyCompany\MyApp\Settings", hKey)
If RegSetValueEx(hKey, "TempFileLocation", 0, REG_EXPAND_SZ, _
                ByVal strTempDir, Len(strTempDir) + 1) _
                <> ERROR_SUCCESS Then _
    MsgBox "Error writing registry value"
Call RegCloseKey(hKey)
```

User-specific environment variables are defined by value entries contained in the HKCU\Environment key. In addition, Win95 automatically recognizes the environment variables listed in Table 6-2. The names of environment variables, incidentally, are not case sensitive.

Table 6-2. Environment variables automatically recognized by Win95

Variable	Explanation	Comments
comspec	Name and location of the command processor	
path	Locations to search for executables and DLLs	
prompt	Meta symbols defining the command prompt	

Table 6-2. Environment variables automatically recognized by Win95 (continued)

Variable	Explanation	Comments
temp	Location of the directory for temporary files	
tmp	Location of the directory for temporary files	
WinBootDir	Directory from which Windows was booted	Defined in *MSDOS.SYS*
WinDir	Windows directory	Defined in *MSDOS.SYS*

Writing other data types to the registry, however, is somewhat more complicated. We'll first look at writing REG_MULTI_SZ and REG_BINARY values, then examine how the *RegSetValueEx* function can store other VB data types not supported by the registry API.

String Arrays: REG_MULTI_SZ

Although you can pass arrays of numeric data to Win32 API functions by passing the first element of the array by reference, you cannot reliably pass string arrays. This does not mean, however, that you cannot use VB to store a string array in the registry; it merely means that you have to massage the data to create a valid C string array before passing it to *RegSetValueEx*.

Each element of a C string array is terminated by a null character (i.e., CHR(0)). In addition, the array itself must be terminated by an additional null character. Once you iterate the elements of the VB string array and store them to an appropriately formatted string variable, you can call *RegSetValueEx* in the same way that you would call it to write an ordinary string value. This is illustrated in Example 6-16, which writes an array of four color strings to the Colors value entry of HKCU\Software\MyCompany\MyApp\Settings.

Example 6-16. Writing REG_MULTI_SZ data to the registry

```
Dim intCtr As Integer
Dim hkey As Long
Dim strStringArray As String

For intCtr = 0 To UBound(strColors)
   strStringArray = strStringArray + strColors(intCtr) + Chr(0)
Next

strStringArray = strStringArray + Chr(0)

Call RegCreateKey(HKEY_CURRENT_USER, _
                "Software\MyCompany\MyApp\Settings", hkey)
If RegSetValueEx(hkey, "Colors", 0, REG_MULTI_SZ, _
             ByVal strStringArray, Len(strStringArray)) _
             <> ERROR_SUCCESS Then _
             MsgBox "Error writing registry value"
Call RegCloseKey(hkey)
```

It is not really necessary to add the final terminating null character to the array, since in any case this is handled automatically by VB when *strStringArray* is passed to the *RegSetValueEx* function. In this case, however, the length of the string array should be defined as Len(strStringArray) + 1.

Binary Data: REG_BINARY

Binary data is really a residual category for all data types that are not numeric or string data. This includes structured data types, as well as Boolean data, byte data, and genuine free-form binary data. Given the broad array of data that can be stored as REG_BINARY, we'll focus on storing structured data, as well as on techniques for handling free-form binary data.

Saving a structured data type to the registry is as easy as saving a long integer or a string value: you just initialize the structured variable and pass it by reference to *RegSetValueEx*. For instance, since users expect the application window to appear in the same location as when they last used it, it is generally a good idea to have the main window's *Form_Unload* event procedure save information on its position in the registry. For example, the following data structure, if defined in a code module or in the form's declarations section, provides all of the information necessary to position a normal or maximized window:

```
Type WindowPosition
    x As Long
    y As Long
    width As Long
    height As Long
End Type
```

A *Form_Unload* event procedure can then use a variable of type *WindowPosition* to save the position of the user's window in the registry, as the following code fragment illustrates:

```
Private Sub Form_Unload(Cancel As Integer)

Dim hKey As Long
Dim udtCoordinates As WindowPosition

udtCoordinates.x = Form1.Left
udtCoordinates.y = Form1.Top
udtCoordinates.width = Form1.width
udtCoordinates.height = Form1.height

Call RegCreateKey(HKEY_CURRENT_USER, _
                Software\MyCompany\MyApp\Settings", hKey)
If RegSetValueEx(hKey, "WindowPos", 0, REG_BINARY, udtCoordinates, _
            Len(udtCoordinates)) <> ERROR_SUCCESS Then _
            MsgBox "Unable to write registry value"
```

```
Call RegCloseKey(hKey)

End Sub
```

Although this example uses a structured data type that consists exclusively of numeric values, it is also possible to include strings as elements of a structured data type. If this is the case, though, variable-length VB strings cannot be used; instead, each string element must be defined as having a fixed length. For instance, if we decided to enhance our *WindowPosition* data structure to include the window's caption, we could define a new data type, *WindowInfo*, with the following structure:

```
Private Type WindowInfo
    x As Long
    y As Long
    width As Long
    height As Long
    caption As String * 56
End Type
```

Although the exact interpretation of free-form binary data varies widely, saving this data to the registry usually involves storing the binary data to a character string or a byte array before calling *RegSetValueEx*. To see how this works, let's take a fairly typical example—an application that uses the registry to preserve several user application settings from session to session. The five specific settings to be saved are:

- Whether settings are to be saved when the application closes

- Whether the main window should contain a status bar

- Whether the main window should contain a tool bar to permit single-click access to common menu commands

- Whether the file menu should contain a list of the most recently used files

- Whether the program should periodically make an automatic backup copy of open files

There are, of course, a variety of ways to save these data. One possibility is to store each item as a single-character string whose value can be "0" (indicating "off," "no," or "unchecked") or "1" (indicating "yes," "on," or "checked"); another is to store each item as a long integer whose possible values are 0 or 1, or 0 and any non-zero number. A third, which aims at minimizing the storage space required for this information, is to store a single byte of binary data in the registry, and to use its first five bits as flags indicating the state of these settings. A fourth approach, which we'll use in our example, aims at minimizing storage space while at the same time avoiding the need to manipulate individual bits of data. This involves storing five bytes of binary data in the registry as a single value entry, with each byte reflecting the state of one of these settings. These values can be ordered as shown in Figure 6-10. Each setting corresponds to a menu option, as shown in Table 6-3. Since these are all clearly user settings (another user of the application on the same computer would want to preserve their own application environment), these values should be stored in a subkey of HKCU; in this case, we'll store them in the `Flags` value entry of HKCU\Software\MyCompany\MyApp\Settings.

Table 6-3. Menu items that control user settings

Menu Text	Menu Item Location	Menu Item Name
Toolbar	View	mnuViewToolbar
Status Bar	View	mnuViewStatusbar
File List	Options	mnuOptionsFileList
Automatic Backup	Options	mnuOptionsAutoBack
Save Settings on Exit	Options	mnuOptionsSave

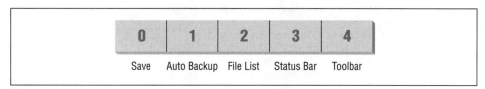

Figure 6-10. The organization of some binary data in the registry

Once we've decided exactly what we want to store in the registry, how we want it to be organized, and where we want to store it, we can include the code to save these settings in the main window's *Form_Unload* event procedure, which is called whenever the program exits. One method of doing this is shown in Example 6-17. This code fragment focuses on maintaining and saving these five user settings only; a working application would include other housekeeping tasks in this module, like maintaining the file MRU list.

Example 6-17. Using a byte array to save binary data

```
Private Sub Form_Unload(Cancel As Integer)

Dim intCtr As Integer              ' loop counter
Dim hKey As Long                   ' handle to Registry key
Dim lngBytes As Long               ' Number of bytes in Flags entry
Dim bytSettings(4) As Byte         ' Array of menu settings
Dim bytCurrentSettings(4) As Byte  ' Array of current flag values
Dim blnSave As Boolean             ' State of "Save Settings" option

' Determine if data is to be saved
If mnuOptionsSave.Checked Then blnSave = True
bytSettings(0) = Abs(mnuOptionsSave.Checked)
```

Example 6-17. Using a byte array to save binary data (continued)

```
' Open/create Registry key
Call RegCreateKey(HKEY_CURRENT_USER, "Software\MyCompany\MyApp\Settings",
hKey)
' Retrieve current settings
lngBytes = UBound(bytCurrentSettings) + 1
If RegQueryValueEx(hKey, "Flags", 0, 0, bytCurrentSettings(0), lngBytes) =
ERROR_SUCCESS Then
   If Not blnSave Then
' Save current settings if they are not to be changed
      For intCtr = 1 To 4
         bytSettings(intCtr) = bytCurrentSettings(intCtr)
      Next
   End If
' If Flags entry does not exist, use default values
Else
   bytSettings(1) = 0       ' automatic backup disabled
   bytSettings(2) = 1       ' file list enabled
   bytSettings(3) = 1       ' status bar displayed
   bytSettings(4) = 1       ' toolbar displayed
End If
' Save current settings if "Save Settings" checked
If blnSave Then
' Save state of automatic backup option
   bytSettings(1) = Abs(mnuOptionsAutoBack.Checked)
' Save state of MRU list
   bytSettings(2) = Abs(mnuOptionsFileList.Checked)
' Save status bar flag
   bytSettings(3) = Abs(mnuViewStatusbar.Checked)
' Save toolbar flag
   bytSettings(4) = Abs(mnuViewToolbar.Checked)
End If
' Write data to Registry
lngBytes = UBound(bytSettings) + 1
'Call RegSetValueEx(hKey, "Flags", 0, REG_BINARY, bytSettings(0), lngBytes)
If RegSetValueEx(hKey, "Flags", 0, REG_BINARY, bytSettings(0), lngBytes)
<> ERROR_SUCCESS Then
   MsgBox "Error writing values"
End If
Call RegCloseKey(hKey)

End Sub
```

Whether or not the user has decided to save his or her application settings, the one setting that always has to be saved is the state of the Save Settings on Exit menu option. However, *RegSetValueEx* does not allow you to replace only a portion of an entry's value; the attempt to write a single byte of binary data to the registry would cause, in the case of our example, five bytes of binary to be replaced by a single byte of data. This need to always write the complete *bytSettings* array to the registry introduces two complications into our code sample.

First, because the application must always write a complete set of values, it has to be careful to preserve the existing registry settings if the user does not want to save his or her current settings. To do this, the procedure uses the *RegQueryValueEx* function to retrieve the current value of the **Flags** entry from the registry. In a working application, though, this detail would most likely be handled by the main window's *Form_Load* event procedure, with the **bytSettings** array initialized as a public variable so that it would be visible to the *Form_Unload* event procedure as well.

Second, if the user is running the application for the first time, the **Flags** value entry will not exist (unless, of course, the application has an installation program that records default values in the registry). So if the user has chosen not to save the application's current settings and the **Flags** value entry cannot be found, the **bytSettings** array must be assigned default values.

In the actual call to *RegSetValueEx*, **bytSettings** is passed by reference to the function. An entire numeric array is passed by reference in VB by passing its first element by reference. This is because the function call passes a pointer to the first element to *RegSetValueEx*, and a pointer to the first element of an array is obviously the same as a pointer to the entire structure.

The sample program in Example 6-17 illustrates how to use an array of byte data to store and retrieve **REG_BINARY** data from the registry. While this is the easiest approach, it is also possible, although in this case considerably more cumbersome, to use a string variable to write **REG_BINARY** data to the registry. This is illustrated in Example 6-18, which is similar to Example 6-17 except that it uses a string rather than a byte array to hold the values of the user's settings.

Example 6-18. Using a string variable to save binary data

```
Private Sub Form_Unload(Cancel As Integer)

Dim hKey As Long                  ' handle to Registry key
Dim lngBytes As Long              ' Number of bytes in Flags entry
Dim strSettings As String         ' Current menu settings
Dim strCurrentSettings As String  ' Value of menu settings in Registry
Dim blnSave As Boolean            ' State of "Save Settings" option

' Determine if data is to be saved
If mnuOptionsSave.Checked Then blnSave = True
' Save "save settings" flag
strSettings = Chr(Abs(mnuOptionsSave.Checked))

' Open/create Registry key
Call RegCreateKey(HKEY_CURRENT_USER, "Software\MyCompany\MyApp\Settings", _
hKey)
' Retrieve current settings
lngBytes = 6
```

Example 6-18. Using a string variable to save binary data (continued)

```
strCurrentSettings = String(lngBytes, 0)
If RegQueryValueEx(hKey, "Flags", 0, 0, ByVal strCurrentSettings,
lngBytes) = ERROR_SUCCESS Then
' Save current settings
   strCurrentSettings = Left(strCurrentSettings, lngBytes)
   strSettings = strSettings & Mid(strCurrentSettings, 2)
' If Flags entry does not exist, use default values: automatic backup
'      disabled, file list enabled, status bar and toolbar displayed
Else
   strSettings = strSettings & Chr(0) & Chr(1) & Chr(1) & Chr(1)
End If
' Save current settings if "Save Settings" checked
If blnSave Then
' Save state of automatic backup option
   strSettings = Mid(strSettings, 1, 1) &
Chr(Abs(mnuOptionsAutoBack.Checked))
' Save state of MRU list
   strSettings = strSettings & Chr(Abs(mnuOptionsFileList.Checked))
' Save status bar flag
   strSettings = strSettings & Chr(Abs(mnuViewStatusbar.Checked))
' Save toolbar flag
   strSettings = strSettings & Chr(Abs(mnuViewToolbar.Checked))
End If
' Write data to Registry
lngBytes = Len(strSettings)
Call RegSetValueEx(hKey, "Flags", 0, REG_BINARY, ByVal strSettings,
lngBytes)
Call RegCloseKey(hKey)

End Sub
```

Perhaps the major difference in this version of the *Form_Unload* event procedure, aside from the need to manipulate individual characters in the **strSettings** and **strCurrentSettings** variables, is that we must be careful to properly initialize the **strSettings** string variable. Since our application requires that the value of each byte be either 0 or 1, we cannot initialize it with an assignment statement such as:

```
strSettings = space(5)
```

since this actually stores a binary value of 20 (&H20, or 32, is the ASCII value for a space) to each character of the string. In addition, the *CHR* function must be used to convert numeric values to string data.

Since in Example 6-18 *RegSetValueEx* writes a string value to the registry, **strSettings** must be passed by reference to the function as a null-terminated C string by explicitly using the BYVAL keyword.

VB Data Types: Boolean, Currency, and Date

So far, we've examined how to store data in the "native" data formats supported by the registry. For the most part, we've assumed that the VB data type that you want to write to the registry is broadly comparable to the data type supported by the registry. VB, however, supports several additional data types that don't readily correspond to data types found in the registry. Very frequently, the value that you really want to store resides in a VB variable. In this section, we'll examine methods for storing it with or without conversion into a "standard" data type.

It's probably worth mentioning that storing VB variant data to the registry is not one of the topics covered here. That's because, with very rare exceptions, we don't recommend the use of variant data types. (In the event that you haven't noticed, they don't appear in any of the VB code fragments presented in this book.) There are two major reasons for this:

- Moving a program's data to a higher level of abstraction and freeing the programmer from the need to pay attention to data types is almost invariably fatal when calling external library routines.

- They are wasteful. Numeric variants require 16 bytes to store their data. String variants require 22 bytes plus the actual length of the string.

If you do prefer to continue using variant data types, though, you'll almost certainly benefit from using the Desaware Registry Control, since it offers seamless support for VB variant data. It's discussed in Chapter 7.

Boolean variables

A VB Boolean variable is really just a special kind of integer (16-bit or 2-byte) data type that has either of two values: 0 for false, and -1 (&FFFF) for true. As a result, you can store it to the registry as a two-byte binary value using a code fragment like the following:

```
Dim hKey As Long
Dim blnFlag As Boolean

blnFlag = True
Call RegOpenKey(HKEY_LOCAL_MACHINE, _
                "Software\MyCompany\MyApp\Settings", hKey)
Call RegSetValueEx(hKey, "Flag", 0, REG_BINARY, blnFlag, len(blnFlag))
Call RegCloseKey(hKey)
```

The following code fragment then successfully retrieves the value of this registry setting:

```
Dim hKey As Long
Dim lngFlag as Long
Dim blnFlag As Boolean
```

```
lngFlag = Len(blnFlag)

Call RegOpenKey(HKEY_LOCAL_MACHINE, _
                "Software\MyCompany\MyApp\Settings", hKey)
Call RegQueryValueEx(hKey, "Flag", 0, 0, blnFlag, lngFlag)
Call RegCloseKey(hKey)
```

Actually, it is possible to store the Boolean value in several ways—as a single binary byte, a 2-byte binary value, a 4-byte binary value, or a long integer. As long as the value of the *lpcbData* parameter to *RegQueryValueEx* indicates that the *lpData* buffer is large enough to retrieve the data without an overflow, the function succeeds, and VB correctly interprets the registry value entry. Boolean data stored in this manner is also portable: using a code fragment like the following, a C program can successfully retrieve this Boolean data:

```
BOOL blnFlag ;
HKEY hKey ;
DWORD lenFlag ;

RegOpenKey(HKEY_LOCAL_MACHINE,
           "Software\\MyCompany\\MyApp\\Settings", hKey) ;
RegQueryValueEx(hKey, "Flag", 0, 0, blnFlag, lenFlag) ;
```

Currency data

Internally, VB stores currency values as signed, 8-byte integers that are scaled (or multiplied) by 10,000. This means that a currency value of $0.0001, for example, is stored by VB as &h0000000000000001. It can be safely and accurately stored to the registry as REG_BINARY data, as shown by the following code fragment:

```
Dim hKey As Long
Dim curValue As Currency

curValue = 167.23

Call RegOpenKey(HKEY_LOCAL_MACHINE, "test", hKey)
Call RegSetValueEx(hKey, "Currency", 0, REG_BINARY, curValue, _
                   len(curValue))
Call RegCloseKey(hKey)
```

Extracting a currency value from the registry is just as easy:

```
Dim hKey As Long
Dim curValue As Currency
Dim lngLenValue As Long

lngLenValue = len(curValue)

Call RegOpenKey(HKEY_LOCAL_MACHINE, _
                "Software\MyCompany\MyApp\Settings", hKey)
Call RegQueryValueEx(hKey, "Currency", 0, 0, curValue, lngLenValue)
Call RegCloseKey(hKey)
If lngLenValue <> Len(curValue) Then MsgBox "Something's wrong!"
```

The major objection to this solution is that it is not portable: it creates data that can be accessed only by code created using Microsoft's Basic programming tools. Programs or code written using other development tools, like Microsoft Visual C++, cannot easily make sense of a VB currency value unless they know how VB stores currency values. If you're certain that VB or VB for Applications will be the only tool used to develop programs that read and modify these values, that may not be a problem. If it is a problem, three major alternatives are available:

- If the currency values are always within the range of long integers, convert them to long integers before storing them as `REG_DWORD` values.

- Use the *CDbl* function to convert the currency values to double values before storing them in the registry as `REG_BINARY` data. When retrieving them from the registry, initialize a variable of type **double** before calling the *RegQuery-ValueEx* function.

- Decide whether the registry is really an appropriate location for storing your currency data. Since currency data is typically not considered state information and typically is sensitive information, it may be more appropriate to store it in a file.

Security and the Registry

As a general rule, sensitive data like monetary information, credit card numbers, or passwords do not belong in the registry, since, under Win95, it is not a secure structure. It is possible, of course, to encrypt this information. But of course encrypted information is not necessarily secure either. Until a better algorithm was implemented, for instance, Microsoft's encrypted password list (.PWL) files for Windows 95 were susceptible to unauthorized decryption.

Date and time data

Internally, VB uses eight bytes to store date variables as floating-point numbers that represent dates ranging from 1 January 100 to 31 December 9999 and the number of seconds from 0:00:00 to 23:59:59. This means that, if you use the registry to store data such as the date your application was installed, the date it was last used, or the date its data files were last backed up, you can store VB date data as `REG_BINARY` data. The following code fragment, for instance, writes the current date and time to an entry named `Date Updated` in HKCU\MyCompany\ MyApp\Settings:

```
Dim hKey As Long
Dim datToday As Date
```

```
datToday = Now

Call RegOpenKey(HKEY_CURRENT_USER, _
                "Software\MyCompany\MyApp\Settings", hKey)
Call RegSetValueEx(hKey, "Date Updated", 0&, REG_BINARY, _
                   datToday, Len(datToday))
Call RegCloseKey(hKey)
```

Once it's stored in the registry, retrieving this date value is just as easy:

```
Dim hKey As Long
Dim lngDataLength As Long
Dim datUpdated As Date

lngDataLength = len(datUpdated)

Call RegOpenKey(HKEY_CURRENT_USER, _
                "Software\MyCompany\MyApp\Settings", hKey)
Call RegQueryValueEx(hKey, "Date Updated", 0&, REG_BINARY, _
           datUpdated, lngDataLength)
If lngDataLength <> Len(datUpdated) Then MsgBox "Something's wrong!"
```

The major objection to this solution is, once again, its limited portability. As long as a date value entry will be accessed only from VB code, it can safely be stored in VB's own date format. If applications written in other languages need to access these data, though, it's far better to avoid VB's proprietary date format. Most date information in the registry is stored as **REG_SZ** data, which suggests that a far better alternative is to use the *CStr* function to convert a date/time value to a string, or to use the *CStr(Int())* function to extract the date component of a date time value before storing it to the registry. The following code fragment does the latter:

```
Dim hKey As Long
Dim strDate As String
Dim strTime As String
Dim datToday As Date

datToday = Now
strDate = CStr(Int(datToday))

Call RegOpenKey(HKEY_CURRENT_USER, _
                "Software\MyCompany\MyApp\Settings", hKey)
Call RegSetValueEx(hKey, "Date Updated", 0&, REG_SZ, _
                   ByVal strDate, Len(strDate) + 1)
Call RegCloseKey(hKey)
```

Summary

In this chapter, we've tried to supplement the basic information on accessing the registry API that was covered in Chapter 4, with information specifically of interest to Visual Basic programmers:

- Visual Basic includes four intrinsic functions that allow you to read from and write to the registry without calling the registry API. Unfortunately, they are implemented to insure compatibility across Windows platforms, rather than to take full advantage of the registry. Nor do they allow you to adhere to Microsoft's software interface guidelines. We don't recommend using them.

- The first step in calling a registry API function involves using the DECLARE statement to define it to Visual Basic. The DECLARE statement names the function as you'll use it in your code and as it appears in the Win32 DLL, specifies the DLL in which it's included, indicates the parameters that are passed to the function and the value it returns. DECLARE statements are typically placed in the declarations section of a code module.

- The second step in accessing the registry API is to declare all necessary constants. Typical Windows or registry constants, like HKEY_CURRENT_USER, REG_SZ, or ERROR_SUCCESS, have no meaning to Visual Basic unless you define them. Like DECLARE statements, these are typically placed in the declarations section of a code module.

- Once you've properly defined a registry function, you can call it in code as if it were an intrinsic VB function. However, if you've used the AS ANY type definition to specify the data type of any parameters, you should be particularly careful to make sure that they are passed correctly by value or by reference.

- The error codes or status codes returned by registry API functions are not recognized by VB and do not generate trappable run-time errors. If you want to integrate them with VB's error handling system, you can define a range of custom error codes and use the Err.Raise method to handle them.

Much of the actual discussion of reading and writing registry data, although it contains VB code examples and focuses on VB-related issues, is of interest to anyone developing registry-enabled applications:

- If you don't know basic information about a registry value entry, like its name, data type, or data length, the best approach is to turn it into a known value type by using the *RegEnumValue* function. To make sure you properly initialize a buffer to store the value name, you can call the *RegQueryInfoKey* function beforehand.

- You can also use the *RegEnumValue* function to retrieve a value entry's data. However, since it returns a byte array, you then have to piece the individual bytes into a recognizable data type. Although this is possible, it's almost never worth the trouble involved.

- If you know all of the basic information about a value entry, or once you've succeeded in transforming an unknown value entry into a known one by using *RegEnumValue*, you can use the *RegQueryValueEx* function to retrieve the data.

7

The Desaware Registry Control

If you're using an OLE-compliant development tool that supports OCX controls, such as Microsoft Visual Basic or Microsoft Access, you can avoid making direct calls to the registry API by adding an OLE custom control (an .OCX control) to your application that interposes itself between your application and *ADVAPI32.DLL*, in the process simplifying registry access. If you're interested in doing this, the diskette included with *Inside the Windows 95 Registry* includes a design-time version of one such OLE custom control, the Desaware Registry Control. "Design-time" means you can use it within Visual Basic's interpreted programming environment, but users can't access it at run-time, i.e., outside the development environment. If you feel that the control will speed your development efforts and you choose to purchase a run-time version, you'll find a coupon at the back of the book that entitles you to a 10% discount off the normal retail price of StorageTools, a product that includes the Desaware Storage Control, an OLE control that allows you to store and retrieve compound documents, in addition to the Desaware Registry Control.

The Desaware Registry Control simplifies registry access for the Visual Basic programmer[*] in several ways:

- *Automatic opening and closing of registry keys.* Although you can override this behavior by changing the value of its KeyLock property, you don't have

---

[*] If you're using Microsoft Visual C++, you can add the Desaware Registry Control to your project. However, its use of the Visual Basic variant data type—which is not native to C or C++—means that you'll have to write a substantial amount of code to massage the data that you pass to and retrieve from the control. For C/C++ programmers, directly accessing the registry API is much more straightforward.

to explicitly open and close registry keys. Instead, this detail is automatically handled by the control.

- *Automatic reporting of registry information.* You don't have to call *RegQuery-InfoKey* to gather such items of information as the number of subkeys or the number of value entries that belong to the current key. These data are immediately stored to the current key's NumOfSubkeys and NumOfValues properties regardless of whether the current key is a top-level key or one of its subkeys.

- *Automatic access to the current key's subkeys and values.* You don't have to enumerate subkeys or values once you access a particular key. The names of all subkeys are stored to the SubkeyArray() property, while the names of all value entries are stored to the ValueNameArray() property.

- *Integrated error handling.* Run-time errors encountered by the registry control are part of Visual Basic's error-handling system. You can define an error handler by using the ON ERROR GOTO statement, and the Visual Basic error object's Number and Description properties are updated to reflect the error.

- *Easy searching of the registry.* You don't have to wade through innumerable registry keys by calling *RegEnumKey* recursively to see if a particular key, value name, or value is stored in the registry. Instead, you can simply search the registry using the FindFirstKey, FindNextKey, FindFirstValue, FindNextValue, FindFirstValueName, and FindNextValueName ·methods.

- *Support for Visual Basic data types.* Ordinarily, in accessing the registry using the registry API, you have to be very aware of the types of data that you're using in your application and that the registry expects to receive. In addition, you frequently have to avoid the use of data types that are unique to Visual Basic. This applies above all to the variant data type, which many Visual Basic programmers find convenient precisely because it frees them from the need to focus on data types. The registry control, on the other hand, not only allows you to use variant data; in many cases, it requires it.

Adding the Desaware Registry Control to Your Project

In the event that you haven't used Visual Basic custom controls, let's quickly review how to add a control to your project, and to a form in your project.

How you add a custom OCX control to your project depends on whether you want to add it to a single project, or to have it added to all projects when you create them. To add it to a single project:

1. After you've opened an existing project or created a new one, select the Custom Controls... option from Visual Basic's Tools menu. Visual Basic opens the Custom Controls dialog shown in Figure 7-1.

2. Make sure that the Controls check box in the Show group box is checked; otherwise, the Available Controls list box won't display the names of any controls.

3. Scroll through the Available Controls list box until you see the custom control you'd like to add to your project. The Desaware Registry Control is listed as "Desaware Registry OLE Demo." When you find it, check its box and click the OK button.

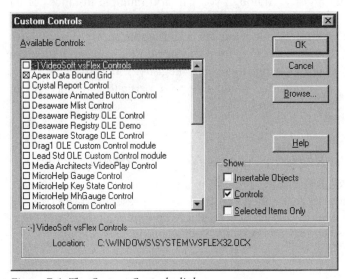

Figure 7-1. The Custom Controls dialog

Sometimes, the control you want may not appear in the Available Controls list box. This usually happens when a custom control doesn't have its own installation procedure; it also happens when a control is not self-registering (i.e., does not enter the information that defines it as an OLE custom control in the registry; for details, see Chapter 8, *What Goes in the Registry: System Settings*). If that's the case, click the Browse button to open the Add Custom Control dialog. This is a standard Win95 file open common control; you can use it to navigate your file system until you locate the custom control you want.

Once you add the control to your project, it appears in the Visual Basic toolbox along with the standard Visual Basic controls and any other custom controls you've added to the project.

You can also have a particular custom control automatically added to any new project that you create. To do this, select the Open Project... option from Visual

Basic's File menu, then open a project named *AUTO32LD.VBP*. (This assumes that you're using the 32-bit version of Visual Basic 4.0; if you're using the 16-bit version, the project file to load is named *AUTO16LD.VBP*.) Then add the custom controls you'd like included by default in every project you create and save the project to disk. *AUTO32LD.VBP* is a project file that serves as a template which configures every new project that you create by selecting the New Project option from Visual Basic's File menu.

Once you've added the Desaware Registry Control to a project, you can add it to a form just like you would any other control. The control has no interface, and is hidden at run-time. It simply serves as an intermediate layer between your application and the Windows 95 registry. Although you can add multiple instances of the control to your project, there is rarely any reason to; because it has no interface, a single instance of the control is sufficient for most applications. Visual Basic assigns the first control that you add to a form the name Registry1, and adds one to the number in each control's name thereafter (Registry2, Registry3, etc.). You can, of course, assign any name that you'd like to a particular instance of the control by modifying its Name property.

Remote Registry Access Not Supported

Since the Desaware Registry Control requires that the value of the CurrentRoot property be one of the six predefined constants that represent top-level keys in the Win95 registry, remote registry access is not supported. You can use the control only to access the registry on which your application is running.

Properties and Methods

The Desaware Registry Control supports a number of properties and methods, which are listed in Tables 7-1 and 7-2; it does not support any custom events.

Table 7-1. Properties supported by the Desaware Registry Control

Property	Description
CurrentKey	The key currently being accessed by the registry control. If it is not set explicitly, it defaults to the root key ("\") specified by the CurrentRoot property. In using this property to change the current key, you should provide the complete path from the top-level key to the key you'd like to access. Note that, unlike a complete registry path that you'd specify using the registry API, the value of the CurrentKey property must begin with an initial backslash. You can also use the `ChangeKey` method, which allows you to specify either a relative or an absolute path to a registry key, to change the value of the CurrentKey property.

Table 7-1. Properties supported by the Desaware Registry Control (continued)

Property	Description

CurrentRoot	The registry tree which the control currently accesses. The control supports the following predefined constants:
	`Hkey_Classes_Root`
	`Hkey_Current_User`
	`Hkey_Local_Machine`
	`Hkey_Users`
	`Hkey_Current_Config`
	`Hkey_Dyn_Data`
	The value of this property defaults to `Hkey_Classes_Root`; because of this, it's very important to explicitly set the value of this property before performing any registry operations; otherwise, all registry operations will have erratic or unintended results unless you actually intend to access `HKEY_CLASSES_ROOT`.
	If you intend to use the registry API along with the registry control, though, these constants duplicate the registry top-level key constants defined in the registry API. In this case, the registry control supports an alternate set of predefined top-level key constants:
	`hkClassesRoot`
	`hkCurrentUser`
	`hkLocalMachine`
	`hkUsers`
	`hkCurrentConfig`
	`hkDynData`

DefaultValue	The default value of the currently accessed key. Its value is empty (`""`) if no default value is assigned to the key.
FindResultKey	A read-only property containing the name of the latest key found with the `FindFirstKey`, `FindNextKey`, `FindFirstValue`, `FindNextValue`, `FindFirstValueName`, or `FindNextValue-Name` methods.
FindResultValue-Name	A read-only property containing the name of the latest value entry found with the `FindFirstValue` or `FindNextValue` methods.
KeyLock	Indicates whether the current key should remain open after the next registry operation completes. By default, its value is False; the control opens and closes a key for each registry operation. To improve performance, it can be set to True to keep the key open if a series of operations are to be performed on a single key.
NumOfSubkeys	A read-only property that indicates the number of subkeys belonging to the current key.
NumOfValues	A read-only property that indicates the number of value entries belonging to the current key.
Subkey-Array *(index%)*	A read-only, zero-based array containing the names of all the subkeys belonging to the current key. The total number of elements in the array is indicated by the value of the NumOfSubkeys property, while the array's upper bound is one less than the value of the NumOfSubkeys property.
ValueName-Array *(index%)*	A read-only, zero-based string array containing the names of all value entries belonging to the current key. It has one less value than the NumOfValues property.

Table 7-2. Methods supported by the Desaware Registry Control

Method	Description
ChangeKey (*ChangeStr$*)	Allows you to access a new registry key, in the process changing the value of the CurrentKey property. *ChangeStr$* supports either absolute or relative navigation of registry keys: If it begins with a backslash, *ChangeStr$* must specify an absolute path from the root key to the key being accessed. If it doesn't begin with a backslash, *ChangeStr$* is interpreted as a relative path from the key designated by the CurrentKey property. The ".." symbol moves from a subkey to its parent key, just like when you're navigating your computer's file system.
CreateKey (*NewKey$*)	Creates a new key in the registry tree designated by the value of the CurrentRoot property. *NewKey$* can specify an absolute path from the root key (in which case it must begin with a backslash) or a relative path from the key designated by the CurrentKey property. Any intermediate keys, if they do not exist, will also be created. Creating a new registry key does not change the value of the CurrentKey property.
DeleteKey(*Key$*, *EraseSubkeys* As Boolean)	Deletes the key specified by *Key$*. If this string begins with a backslash, it is interpreted as a complete path from the root; otherwise, it is interpreted as a path relative to the key designated by the CurrentKey property. If *EraseSubkeys* is True, any subkeys are also deleted. If it is false and *Key$* contains subkeys, it is not deleted.
DeleteValue (*Name$*)	Deletes an existing value entry belonging to the key designated by the CurrentKey property. To delete a key's default value, *Name$* should be an empty string (" ").
FindFirstKey (*Name$*, *Case* As Boolean, *Full-String* As Boolean, *StartAtRoot* As Boolean)	Searches for the first key whose name contains the string designated by *Name$*. If *Case* is True, the string comparison is case sensitive; otherwise, the search ignores case. Since the registry API does not distinguish the case of key names, you'll ordinarily want to set the value of this parameter to False. If *FullString* is True, *Name$* must match the key name exactly; otherwise, *Name$* can be a substring of the key name. If *StartAtRoot* is True, the search begins at the root key designated by the CurrentRoot property; otherwise, it begins with the key specified by the CurrentKey property. If a match is found, **Find-FirstKey** returns True and stores the result to the FindResultKey property; otherwise, it returns False.
FindNextKey()	Used to locate subsequent keys matching the search criteria after **FindFirstKey** succeeds in finding an initial match. As long as there are keys matching the search criteria, **FindNextKey** returns True and stores the key's name to the FindResultKey property; if there are no more matches, **FindNextKey** returns False and clears the FindResultKey property.

Table 7-2. Methods supported by the Desaware Registry Control (continued)

Method	Description
FindFirstValue (*Value* As Variant, *TypeOfValue* As Long, *SizeOfValue* As Long, *FullData* As Boolean, *StartAtRoot* As Boolean)	Searches for the first key that contains a value entry whose value matches *Value*. The data type that the method is to search for in the registry is designated by *TypeOfValue*; it should be a regular registry data type constant, like REG_SZ, REG_DWORD, etc. The size of the Value in bytes is indicated by *SizeOfValue*. If *FullData* is true, *Value* must correspond exactly to the value found in the registry for the search to be successful; otherwise, *Value* can be located anywhere within the full registry value. The *FullData* parameter is ignored if *TypeOfValue* is one of the numeric data types (REG_DWORD or REG_DWORD_BIG_ENDIAN). If *StartAtRoot* is True, the search begins at the root key designated by the value of the CurrentRoot property; otherwise, it begins with the current key designated by the value of the CurrentKey property. If *TypeOfData* is a string (REG_SZ, REG_EXPAND_SZ, or REG_MULTI_SZ), comparisons are not case sensitive. If a match is found, FindFirstValue returns True and stores the result to the FindResultKey and FindResultValueName properties; otherwise, it returns False.
FindFirstValue-Name(*Name$, Case* As Boolean, *Full-String* As Boolean, *StartAtRoot* As Boolean)	Searches for the first key that has an entry whose value name matches *Name$*. If Case is True, the search is case sensitive; otherwise, case is ignored in determining whether the strings match. Since the registry API does not distinguish the case of value names, you'll ordinarily want to set the value of this parameter to False. If *FullString* is true, *Name$* must correspond exactly to the value name found in the registry for the search to be successful; otherwise, *Name$* can be a substring of the full value name. If *StartAtRoot* is True, the search begins at the root key designated by the value of the CurrentRoot property; otherwise, it begins with the current key designated by the value of the CurrentKey property. If a match is found, FindFirstValueName returns True and stores the result to the FindResultKey and FindResultValueName properties; otherwise, it returns False
FindNextValue()	Used to locate subsequent values matching the search criteria after FindFirstValue succeeds in finding an initial match. As long as there are values matching the search criteria, FindNextValue returns True and stores the key's name to the FindResultKey property and the value entry's name to the FindResultValueName property; if there are no more matches, FindNextValue returns False and clears both the FindResultKey and FindResultValueName properties.
FindNextValue-Name()	Used to locate subsequent values names matching the search criteria after FindFirstValueName succeeds in finding an initial match. As long as there are value names matching the search criteria, FindNextValueName returns True and stores the key's name to the FindResultKey property and the value entry's name to the FindResultValueName property; if there are no more matches, FindNextValueName returns False and clears both the FindResultKey and FindResultValueName properties.

Table 7-2. Methods supported by the Desaware Registry Control (continued)

Method	Description
FlushRegistry()	Immediately flushes the registry to disk. The KeyLock property should be set to False before calling this method. Since repeated calls to this method severely degrade an application's performance, it should only be used when you must be absolutely certain that changes to the registry have been committed to disk. Its use, in any case, is not strictly necessary, since changes to the registry are buffered and will be written in a few seconds; the FlushRegistry method only makes that happen sooner.
GetValueData (*Name$, AsString* As Boolean)	Returns a variant containing the data value stored to the value entry whose name is specified by the *Name$* parameter. *Name$* must be a value entry belonging to the key designated by the CurrentKey property. If *AsString* is True, the entry's value is returned as a string; otherwise, it is returned as a variant array. You can use the GetValueSize and GetValueType methods to correctly allocate the right amount of memory before calling the method. If the value entry indicated by *Name$* does not exist in the current key, GetValueData returns a NULL. Test the value returned by GetValueData before using it; otherwise, your application is likely to encounter run-time error 94, "Invalid use of Null." For details, see the sidebar "Handling a GetValueData Error" in the section "Error Handling" later in this chapter.
GetValueSize (*Name$*)	Returns the number of bytes used to store the data value belonging to the *Name$* value entry. *Name$* must be a value entry belonging to the key designated by the value of the CurrentKey property. If the value entry does not exist, GetValueSize returns 0.
GetValueType (*Name$*)	Returns the data type of the *Name$* value entry. *Name$* must be a value entry belonging to the key designated by the value of the CurrentKey property. If the value entry does not exist, GetValueType returns 0 (REG_NONE).
SetValue(*Name$*, *Data* As Variant, *TypeOfValue* As Long, *SizeOfValue* As Long)	Modifies or creates a value entry belonging to the key specified by the CurrentKey property. *Name$* is the name of the value entry; if it does not exist, the method creates it. *Data* provides the data to be stored to the value entry; any existing data is overwritten. *TypeOfValue* indicates the value entry's data type. *SizeOfData* indicates the number of bytes occupied by *Data*.

How the Control Works

Basically, the Desaware Registry Control is triggered to perform an operation when any of the following occur:

- The value of the CurrentRoot property changes. You can change it at design-time, or your program can change it at run-time, as the following line of code illustrates:

```
Registry1.CurrentRoot = Hkey_Current_User
```

When the CurrentRoot property changes, the value of the CurrentKey property automatically changes to "\", and the control immediately updates the DefaultValue, NumOfSubkeys, NumOfValues, SubKeyArray, and ValueNameArray properties.

- The value of the CurrentKey property changes. You can change it at design-time, or your program can change it at run-time, as the following lines of code illustrates

```
Registry1.CurrentRoot = Hkey_Local_Machine
Registry1.CurrentKey = "\Software\Microsoft\Windows\CurrentVersion"
```

When the CurrentKey property changes, the control immediately updates the DefaultValue, NumOfSubkeys, NumOfValues, SubKeyArray, and ValueNameArray properties.

- Any method is invoked.

In each of these cases except for the registry search methods, the registry control opens the necessary key, performs the needed operation, then immediately closes the key. By setting the value of the KeyLock property to True, you can keep the key open for subsequent operations. In the case of the search methods, each method opens and immediately closes each of the keys that it searches, and ignores the state of the KeyLock property.

Because the registry control handles most of the low-level details that you would otherwise have to handle in your own code, accessing the registry using the control requires relatively little coding. For example, Examples 7-1 and 7-2 both contain a routine, *GetTTFonts*, that retrieves the name of a system's TrueType fonts (which Win95 stores as the names of value entries in `HKLM\Software\Microsoft\Windows\CurrentVersion\Fonts`) and displays them in a list box. Example 7-1 uses the registry API to retrieve the registry's font information; Example 7-2, a much smaller piece of code, uses the Desaware Registry Control.

Example 7-1. Retrieving TrueType font names by calling the registry API

```
Public Sub GetTTFonts()

Dim intPos As Integer
Dim lngIndex As Long
Dim hKey As Long, lngValues As Long, lngMaxValueName As Long
Dim lngLenValueName As Long
Dim strKey As String, strValueName As String
Dim udtFiletime As FILETIME
Dim udtOS As OSVERSIONINFO

' Determine platform
udtOS.dwOSVersionInfoSize = Len(udtOS)
If GetVersionEx(udtOS) Then
    Select Case udtOS.dwPlatformId
```

Example 7-1. Retrieving TrueType font names by calling the registry API (continued)

```
        Case VER_PLATFORM_WIN32_WINDOWS
            strKey = "Software\Microsoft\Windows\CurrentVersion\Fonts"
        Case VER_PLATFORM_WIN32_NT
            strKey = "Software\Microsoft\Windows NT\CurrentVersion\Fonts"
        Case Else
            MsgBox "This program does not run under Win32s"
            End
    End Select
Else
    MsgBox "Unable to determine platform..."
    End
End If
' Open TTFont key
Call RegOpenKey(HKEY_LOCAL_MACHINE, strKey, hKey)
' Determine value entry information
Call RegQueryInfoKey(hKey, 0, 0, ByVal 0, 0, 0, 0, lngValues, _
                     lngMaxValueName, 0, 0, udtFiletime)
' Enumerate values
For lngIndex = 0 To lngValues - 1
   lngLenValueName = lngMaxValueName + 1
   strValueName = String(lngLenValueName, 0)
   Call RegEnumValue(hKey, lngIndex, strValueName, _
                     lngLenValueName, ByVal 0, 0, ByVal 0, 0)
   ' Trim string
   strValueName = Left(strValueName, lngLenValueName)
   ' Add only TT fonts to list box and remove '(TrueType)'
   intPos = InStr(1, strValueName, "(TrueType)")
   If intPos > 0 Then
      List1.AddItem Left(strValueName, intPos - 2)
   End If
Next
Call RegCloseKey(hKey)

End Sub
```

Example 7-2. Retrieving font names with Desaware Registry Control

```
Public Sub GetTTFonts()

Dim intCtr As Integer, intPos As Integer
Dim strKey As String, strValueName As String
Dim udtOS As OSVERSIONINFO

' Determine platform
udtOS.dwOSVersionInfoSize = Len(udtOS)
If GetVersionEx(udtOS) Then
   Select Case udtOS.dwPlatformId
      Case VER_PLATFORM_WIN32_WINDOWS
         strKey = "\Software\Microsoft\Windows\CurrentVersion\Fonts"
      Case VER_PLATFORM_WIN32_NT
         strKey = "\Software\Microsoft\Windows\Nt\CurrentVersion\Fonts"
      Case Else
```

Example 7-2. Retrieving font names with Desaware Registry Control (continued)

```
        MsgBox "This program does not run under Win32s."
        End
   End Select
Else
   MsgBox "Unable to determine platform..."
   End
End If
' Set TTFonts key
Registry1.CurrentRoot = Hkey_Local_Machine
Registry1.CurrentKey = StrKey
' Get value names
For intCtr = 0 To Registry1.NumOfValues - 1
   strValueName = Registry1.ValueNameArray(intCtr)
   ' Add only TT fonts to list box (and remove TT description)
   intPos = InStr(1, strValueName, "(TrueType)")
   If intPos > 0 Then
      List1.AddItem Left(strValueName, intPos - 2)
   End If
Next

End Sub
```

Getting Fonts and the Windows Platform

The routines in Examples 7-1 and 7-2 run under both Win95 and WinNT, even though the two operating systems store font information in different registry keys. (WinNT stores font information in `HKLM\Software\Microsoft\Windows NT\CurrentVersion\Fonts`.) The program uses *GetVersionEx* to determine the platform on which it's running; the program then defines the value of the *strKey* variable accordingly. The program also exits if it determines that it's running under Win32s. For details on using *GetVersionEx*, see Appendix A, *Where Am I Running?*

We'll begin by examining how to handle errors when using the registry control, then examine how the control can simplify registry access.

Error Handling

The Desaware Registry Control takes advantage of Visual Basic's normal error handling system. That is, when the control attempts to perform an operation that results in an error, the Visual Basic error object is updated accordingly. Err.Number contains the error code, and Err.Description contains a string describing the error.

The values of the error codes supported by the control are different than those returned by the registry API; consequently, defining the registry API error code constants in your project's code module won't help you handle errors reported by the registry control. Along with returning a unique set of error values, though, the control automatically supports a set of constants. These, along with the error codes themselves, are listed in Table 7-3.

Table 7-3. Error codes returned by the Desaware Registry Control

Error Constant	Error Code	Description
Reg_E_Access_Denied	30005	Either the key or value does not exist, or you do not have the authority to access it.
Reg_E_BadDB	31009	The registry is corrupt.
Reg_E_BadKey	31010	The key has been corrupted or does not exist.
Reg_E_BadRoot	30006	You've specified an invalid top-level key. This error most commonly occurs because of attempts to access a key that exists on one platform but not on others (e.g., HKEY_DYN_DATA on Win95).
Reg_E_Bad_Root_Value	32008	The root key is invalid.
Reg_E_CantOpen	31011	The key cannot be accessed.
Reg_E_CantRead	31012	The key cannot be read. Under Windows NT, this is usually because the user does not have permission to read a particular key or value.
Reg_E_CantWrite	31013	The key cannot be modified. Under WinNT, this might occur because the user does not have write permission to the key. It also might be caused by an attempt to write to a read-only (e.g., volatile or dynamic) key.
Reg_E_Child_Must_Be_ Volatile	31021	The key does not allow the creation of child keys.
Reg_E_Default_Value_Type	32007	The program is attempting to store a data type other than REG_SZ as the default value of a key.
Reg_E_Key_Deleted	31018	The key has been deleted and therefore cannot be accessed.
Reg_E_Local_Machine_Root	30087	The root structure of HKLM cannot be changed; this is a WinNT-specific message.
Reg_E_No_Log_Space	31019	There is not enough free disk space to save the entire registry.
Reg_E_Path_Not_Found	30002	The path to the designated key does not exist.

Table 7-3. Error codes returned by the Desaware Registry Control (continued)

Error Constant	Error Code	Description
Reg_E_Registry_Corrupt	31015	The registry is corrupt.
Reg_E_Registry_IO_Failed	31016	The registry cannot be accessed. One possible reason is that the hard disk is out of free space.

The error codes begin at 30000 to differentiate them from errors returned by Visual Basic. In many cases, the registry control is simply passing on an error code that it received when it called a particular function in the registry API. This is true of error codes with values from 30000 to 31999; they are derived by adding 30000 to the value returned by the control's call to the Registry API function. For instance, `Reg_E_Access_Denied` (whose value is 30005) corresponds to the Win32 API's `ERROR_ACCESS_DENIED` constant (its value is 5). Errors with values above 32000 are unique to the control and do not coincide with any API error.

If you're accustomed to calling the registry API and begin using the Desaware Registry Control as well, you should be aware of an almost philosophical difference between the two regarding what constitutes an error. As we noted in the "Handling Errors" section in Chapter 6, *The Registry and Visual Basic*, the return values of the registry functions are really status codes; whether or not a status code indicates an error depends on how the registry call is used in the context of your program. For example, if your program *needs* to open a key and finds that it's absent, that's an error. But if your program only *checks* to see whether a key is present and finds it absent, that's a piece of information.

Handling a GetValueData Error

The operation of the `GetValueData` method is rather more in the spirit of the registry API if you attempt to retrieve data from a value entry that doesn't exist. If the value entry does exist, the method returns its data; if it doesn't exist, it returns a variant Null[a] rather than invoking the error handler. If you don't test the value of the entry to make sure that it isn't Null, though, you'll encounter Visual Basic run-time error 94, "Invalid use of Null," when you first use the variable. To prevent this error, you should store the value returned by the method to a variant variable (otherwise, you'll have difficulty determining whether the method returned Null or not), and use the *IsNull* function to determine whether `GetValueData` returned a valid value.

[a] A Visual Basic Null, incidentally, is different from a C NULL. In Visual Basic, a Null is a special value that indicates that a variant contains no valid data. It results either from an explicit assignment (e.g., `varData = Null`) or from an operation involving expressions whose value is Null.

Implementing such a status reporting system in a control whose properties are interdependent, as is the case in the Desaware Registry Control, is very difficult, if not impossible, since operations such as failing to find a key would leave the value of a number of properties undefined. Consequently, if registry operations that involve property assignments, like opening a key, fail, the control always generates a "hard" error and invokes the error handler, if one is present.

Reading from and Writing to the Registry

The registry control's major use, of course, is to retrieve and write data to and from the registry. The Desaware Registry Control simplifies this process in several ways. First, rather than requiring strong variable typing, it allows you to use Visual Basic's variant data type when performing registry operations, something that won't work if you're calling the registry API directly. Second, when retrieving data in string form from the registry, with just one exception, you don't have to concern yourself with allocating buffers in advance; the registry control automatically takes care of this detail for you.

It is important to note that the registry control has been developed expressly to work with Visual Basic's variant data type. This means that, when your application retrieves data from the registry, it can assign it to any of several data types, one of which is the variant data type. In these cases, Visual Basic is able automatically to handle the conversion from one data type to another. For instance, if you use the `GetValueData` method to retrieve `REG_SZ` data from the registry, you can assign it to either a variant string or a regular string variable.

On the other hand, when your application writes data to the registry, the variable supplied as the *Data* parameter to the `SetValue` method should be a variant data type, since Visual Basic does not handle data conversion when calling functions derived from external sources. If the data that you want to write to the registry is stored in a variable of a different data type, you should convert it to a variant and then pass that variant data to the `SetValue` method. The registry control then handles the process of converting this variant data into the kind of registry data specified by the `SetValue` method's *TypeOfValue* parameter.

In the following sections, we'll examine how the control can simplify the process of storing and retrieving the most common data types found in the Windows registry.

String (REG_SZ) Data

The Visual Basic project *DWREGOP1.VBP* illustrates the process of retrieving and writing registry string data, in this case a "Most Recently Used" (MRU) list that is added at run-time to the File menu. (For details on how to store most recently used file information, see "Storing MRU Lists" in Chapter 9, *What Goes in the Registry: Application and User Settings.*) To support a most recently used file list, use the Menu Designer to include a single item of a menu control array in your application's File menu and set its Visible property to False. The File menu created with the Menu Designer at design time is shown in Table 7-4.

Table 7-4. The design-time File menu of DWREGOP1.VBP

Caption	Name	Shortcut	Index	Visible
&File	mnuFile			Checked
&New	mnuFile_New	^N		Checked
&Open	mnuFile_Open	^O		Checked
&Close	mnuFile_Close			Checked
-	mnuFile_Sep1			Checked
&Save	mnuFile_Save	^S		Checked
Save &As	mnuFile_SaveAs			Checked
-	mnuFile_Sep2			Checked
<MRU>	mnuFile_MRU		0	Unchecked
-	mnuFile_MRUSep			Unchecked
E&xit	mnuFile_Exit			Checked

At run-time, the name of the first file can be stored to this menu item's Caption property, and its Visible property can be set to True. For each additional file to be listed, a menu item is dynamically added to the menu control array by using the Load statement, its Caption property set to contain the filename, and its Visible property set to True. Example 7-3 displays the application's *Form_Load* event procedure, which constructs the most recently used file list by retrieving the values stored in the `HKCU\Software\MyCompany\RegApp\MRU` key. It also uses two public variables that are defined in the form's declarations section, *varMRUList* and *strMRUarray()*, to insure that they are visible to all of the form's procedures.

Example 7-3. The Form_Load event procedure of DWREGOP1.VBP

```
Private Sub Form_Load()

On Error GoTo ErrorHandler

Dim intCtr As Integer
```

Example 7-3. The Form_Load event procedure of DWREGOP1.VBP (continued)

```
Dim lngMRULen As Long
Dim strSubKey As String
Dim strMRUName As String, strMRUFile As String

strSubKey = "\Software\MyCompany\RegApp\MRU"

' Open MRU key
Registry1.CurrentRoot = Hkey_Current_User
Registry1.CurrentKey = strSubKey
Registry1.KeyLock = True
' Retrieve value of MRUList entry
If Registry1.NumOfValues = 0 Then
    Call Registry1.SetValue("MRUList", "", Reg_SZ, 0)
End If
lngMRULen = Registry1.GetValueSize("MRUList")

If lngMRULen > 0 Then ReDim strMRUarray(lngMRULen - 1)
varMRUList = Registry1.GetValueData("MRUList", True)
' Determine names of MRU values
intCtr = 1
Do While intCtr <= lngMRULen
    strMRUName = Mid(varMRUList, intCtr, 1)
    strMRUFile = Registry1.GetValueData(strMRUName, True)
    If Len(Trim(strMRUFile)) > 0 Then
' Add or show MRU file on menu
        If intCtr = 1 Then
            mnuFile_MRU(0).Visible = True
            mnuFile_MRUSep.Visible = True
        Else
            Load mnuFile_MRU(intCtr - 1)
        End If
        strMRUarray(intCtr - 1) = strMRUFile
        mnuFile_MRU(intCtr - 1).Caption = "&" & Trim(Str(intCtr)) & _
                            " " & strMRUFile
    End If
    intCtr = intCtr + 1
Loop

Registry1.KeyLock = False

Exit Sub

ErrorHandler:

Select Case Err.Number
' key does not exist
    Case Reg_E_Path_Not_Found
        Call Registry1.CreateKey(strSubKey)
        Resume
' Other error
    Case Else
        MsgBox Str(Err.Number) & ": " & Err.Description
```

Example 7-3. The Form_Load event procedure of DWREGOP1.VBP (continued)

```
    If Registry1.KeyLock = True Then Registry1.KeyLock = False
End Select

End Sub
```

This procedure makes no assumptions about the existence of MRU data in the registry. If the attempt to open the MRU subkey fails by assigning its path to the CurrentKey property, the error handler is called and creates the key. If the MRUList value entry does not exist, the value of the NumOfValues property is 0; in that case, the SetValue method creates the value entry and assigns it a null string. In addition, since the module performs an unknown number of operations on the same key, the KeyLock property is set to True to improve the application's performance; it is set back to False at the end of the module.

Since the module retrieves string data from the registry and assigns it to a string variable, very little overhead is involved in calling the GetValueData method in comparison with using the registry API directly. This example uses the DIM statement to declare *strMRUList* and *strMRUName* as strings, although we've done this only because we believe in strong typing and in declaring all variables in advance; they could also be variant data types. Unlike accessing the registry API directly, we don't have to concern ourselves with allocating a sufficiently large buffer to store the registry string or with removing terminating null characters.

Typically, the MRU list on the File menu is updated whenever the user opens an existing file or saves a new file. Frequently, though, those changes are made only to the menu; the registry itself is not updated to reflect the most recent MRU list until the application closes. This can be extremely inconvenient: it means that, if an application crashes or terminates abnormally, its MRU list when the application is next launched reflects the files used two sessions ago. (If you're testing a particularly buggy Visual Basic application, you've probably found this behavior annoying: after your application crashes, its name does not appear on the Visual Basic File menu.) A better approach involves calling a procedure to update the registry whenever an existing file is opened or a new file is saved. Example 7-4 shows such a procedure, *UpdateMRU*. Its single parameter is the name of the file being opened or saved.

Example 7-4. The UpdateMRU subroutine of DWREGOP1.VBP

```
Public Sub UpdateMRU(strFileName As String)

Dim intCtr As Integer, intItems As Integer
Dim intMaxItems As Integer
Dim lngFilenameLen As Long
Dim strTemp As String, strMRUName As String
Dim strMRUFile As String
Dim blnOrdered As Boolean, blnNewFile As Boolean
```

Example 7-4. The UpdateMRU subroutine of DWREGOP1.VBP (continued)

```
Dim blnNewItem As Boolean

If Len(Trim(strFileName)) = 0 Then Exit Sub

' intMaxItems is number of MRU items supported; instead
' of a variable, this could be defined by a registry value
intMaxItems = 4
intItems = Len(varMRUList)     ' Number of actual items
' Is filename already in MRU list?
strTemp = varMRUList
If intItems > 0 Then
    For intCtr = 0 To UBound(strMRUarray)
        If strFileName = strMRUarray(intCtr) Then
            ' Make sure position has changed
            In intCtr = 0 Then
                binOrdered = True
                Exit For
            Else
                varMRUList = Mid(strTemp, intCtr + 1, 1) & _
                             Mid(strTemp, 1, intCtr)
            End If
            ' Check if any of the string is left
            If intCtr + 1 <> Len(strTemp) Then
                varMRUList = varMRUList & Mid(strTemp, intCtr + 2)
            End If
            blnOrdered = True
            Exit For
        End If
    Next
End If
' if filename is new
If Not blnOrdered Then
    ' Add next item to MRU list if it's not full
    If intItems < intMaxItems Then
        varMRUList = Chr(97 + intItems) & varMRUList
        blnNewItem = True
        intItems = intItems + 1
    ' Move last item of MRU list to first
    Else
        varMRUList = Right(varMRUList, 1) & Left(varMRUList, intItems - 1)
    End If
    blnNewFile = True
End If
' Write to Registry
Registry1.CurrentRoot = Hkey_Current_User
Registry1.CurrentKey = "\Software\MyCompany\RegApp\MRU"
Registry1.KeyLock = True
Call Registry1.SetValue("MRUList", varMRUList, Reg_SZ, Len(varMRUList))
If blnNewFile Then
    Call Registry1.SetValue(Left(varMRUList, 1), CVar(strFileName), _
                            REG_SZ, Len(CVar(strFileName)))
End If
```

Example 7-4. The UpdateMRU subroutine of DWREGOP1.VBP (continued)

```
' Add new element to MRU array and new menu item
If blnNewItem Then
   ReDim Preserve strMRUarray(intItems - 1)
   ' Add new menu item
   If intItems > 1 Then
     Load mnuFile_MRU(intItems - 1)
       mnuFile_MRU(intItems - 1).Visible = True
   Else
       mnuFile_MRU(0).Visible = True
       mnuFile_MRUSep.Visible = True
   End If
End If
' Update menu
For intCtr = 1 To Len(varMRUList)
   strMRUName = Mid(varMRUList, intCtr, 1)
   strMRUFile = Registry1.GetValueData(strMRUName, True)
   lngFilenameLen = Registry1.GetValueSize(strMRUName)
   If lngFilenameLen > 0 Then
       strMRUFile = Left(strMRUFile, lngFilenameLen)
       strMRUarray(intCtr - 1) = strMRUFile
       mnuFile_MRU(intCtr - 1).Caption = "&" & Trim(Str(intCtr)) & _
                           " " & strMRUFile
   End If
Next

Registry1.KeyLock = False

End Sub
```

In using the `SetValue` method to write `REG_SZ` data to the registry, it is extremely important that the variable passed to the method be a variant data type; the registry control assumes that it is being passed variant data, and automatically handles its conversion into the string data type specified by the *TypeOfValue* parameter. If it is any other data type, its value may be modified when control returns from the `SetValue` method.

Numeric (REG_DWORD) Data

Reading and writing `REG_DWORD` values with the registry control is straightforward. For instance, ordinarily the Windows shell automatically saves a number of settings, like the position of desktop icons, the state of open windows, and the size and position of the task bar, when Windows exits. This behavior can be controlled by a registry setting, the `NoSaveSettings` entry of the `HKCU\Software\Microsoft\Windows\CurrentVersion\Policies\Explorer` key, which is not accessible through the Windows user interface. `NoSaveSettings` is a `REG_DWORD` value. If it equals 0, settings are saved; if it equals 1, settings are not saved. Knowing this, we can very easily construct a simple utility that allows the user to see whether or not these settings are saved when Windows exits.

Since the utility operates on only one value entry in one registry key, the following are defined as constants in the form's declarations section:

```
Const EXPL_KEY = "\Software\Microsoft\Windows\CurrentVersion\Policies\
Explorer"
Const EXPL_SAVE = "NoSaveSettings"
```

In addition, the following value keeps us from having to remember how many bytes are in a REG_DWORD value:

```
Const LEN_DWORD = 4
```

The *Form_Load* event procedure shown in Example 7-5 retrieves the value of the NoSaveSettings value entry and updates the form's single check box. Since this value entry does not exist in the default Win95 registry, the procedure first calls the GetValueSize method to determine whether or not it is present. If the value entry does not exist, the procedure creates it and assigns it the Windows default value of 0.[*]

Example 7-5. The Form_Load event procedure to retrieve the NoSaveSettings value entry

```
Private Sub Form_Load()

Dim varSaveValue As Variant

Registry1.CurrentRoot = Hkey_Current_User
Registry1.CurrentKey = EXPL_KEY
If Registry1.GetValueSize(EXPL_SAVE) > 0 Then
   If Registry1.GetValueData(EXPL_SAVE, True) = 0 Then
      Check1.Value = 1
   Else
      Check1.Value = 0
   End If
Else
   varSaveValue = 0
   Call Registry1.SetValue(EXPL_SAVE, varSaveValue, Reg_Dword, _
                           LEN_DWORD)
End If

End Sub
```

In retrieving the value of the setting, the procedure compares it to a constant value; instead, it could have stored the value of this setting directly to either a variant or long variable.

To write the NoSaveSettings value entry to theWin95 registry,[†] the Form_Load event procedure passes a variant variable to the SetValue method's *Data*

---

[*] Since this program relies on a registry setting that is ordinarily created and interpreted by the Win95 shell, it does not run under WinNT 3.x.

[†] Once again, this program does not run under WinNT 3.x.

parameter. It is also possible to use a constant, as the check box's Check1_Click event procedure in Example 7-6 does, or even to use a long integer variable. If you do use either a constant or a variant value, it is important that the value of the `SetValue` method's *SizeOfValue* parameter equal 4; otherwise, a corrupted value entry is added to the registry. For instance, a line of code like the following:

```
' Incorrect
Call Registry1.SetValue(EXPL_SAVE, varValue, Reg_Dword, Len(varValue))
```

generates an incorrect value entry in the registry, since the value returned by the *Len* function when used with a variant value is not necessarily 4. To prevent this, it's best to use a constant (like `LEN_DWORD` in the example in Example 7-5) to represent the length of the `REG_DWORD` value.

Example 7-6. The Check1_Click event procedure to save the NoSaveSettings value entry

```
Private Sub Check1_Click()

Registry1.CurrentRoot = Hkey_Current_User
Registry1.CurrentKey = EXPL_KEY
If Check1.Value = 0 Then
    Call Registry1.SetValue(EXPL_SAVE, 1, Reg_Dword, LEN_DWORD)
Else
    Call Registry1.SetValue(EXPL_SAVE, 0, Reg_Dword, LEN_DWORD)
End If

End Sub
```

Binary Data

While reading and writing string and long integer values using the registry control is considerably easier than making direct calls to the registry API, this is not invariably the case when reading or writing binary (`REG_BINARY`) data. There are two reasons for this:

- The registry control uses a variant data type to read data from or write data to the registry. In some cases, Visual Basic can automatically convert variables to and from the variant data type. However, the variant data type is unable to handle user-defined types (i.e., structured data types), which are very common in the Win95 registry.

- Binary data does not correspond to any data type recognized by Visual Basic. Consequently, it is best handled as a collection of individual bytes that are stored either to a string or to an array. These must then be manipulated on a byte-by-byte basis, depending on the format of the binary data.

In using the registry control to retrieve and store binary data, you can use either a variant string or an array of byte data to retrieve binary registry data, or a string or variant byte array to store data in the registry. In general, using a variant string is easiest; you don't have to worry about allocating the size of the string in advance, whereas you do have to dimension either the variant byte array or the array of byte data in advance. But other than this, in reading and writing binary data from the registry, you use the same basic techniques that you use if you access the registry through the registry API; to review these, see the sections on reading and writing binary data in Chapter 6. In fact, if you're not intimidated by assembling individual bytes into a structured data type or disassembling a structured data type into its component bytes, you can even use the registry control to read and write structured data.

Generally, exactly how you handle the binary data stored in the registry depends on the character of the binary data and how it's used in your application. In this section, we'll focus on a single example to illustrate how to read and write a particular kind of REG_BINARY data with the registry control: binary data whose individual bits are used as flags.

The Win95 file system supports an ease-of-use feature called AutoPlay, which is intended predominantly for CD-ROM drives.[*] Whenever Windows 95 detects that a new CD-ROM has been inserted in the drive, it checks for a script file named *AUTORUN.INF*. If it finds the file, it executes the commands contained within it. For developers, this poses a problem: you want to be able to test your *AUTORUN.INF* file before manufacturing the CD-ROM, rather than afterwards. By modifying the registry, however, you can do this.

The kinds of devices Win95 will automatically examine for an *AUTORUN.INF* file is determined by the NoDriveTypeAutoRun value entry in HKCU\Software\ Microsoft\Windows\CurrentVersion\Policies\Explorer. It is a four-byte REG_BINARY value, the last three bytes of which are undefined and must be zero. The eight bits of the first byte each represent a particular kind of drive, as shown in Table 7-5.

Table 7-5. The first byte of the NoDriveTypeAutoRun value entry

Bit	Constant[a]	Explanation
0	DRIVE_UNKNOWN	The drive type cannot be determined
1	DRIVE_NO_ROOT_DIR	The root directory does not exist
2	DRIVE_REMOVABLE	The disk can be removed from the drive
3	DRIVE_FIXED	The disk cannot be removed from the drive
4	DRIVE_REMOTE	The drive resides on a network

---

[*] AutoPlay, however, is not supported by WinNT 3.x; as a result, the sample program does not execute under WinNT.

Table 7-5. The first byte of the NoDriveTypeAutoRun value entry (continued)

Bit	Constant[a]	Explanation
5	DRIVE_CDROM	
6	DRIVE_RAMDISK	The drive is a memory-resident RAM disk
7	Reserved	Reserved for future use

[a] These constants represent the values returned by the *GetDriveType* API function.

If a particular bit in this bit mask is set to 1, AutoPlay does not work with that drive type; conversely, if the bit is "off" (0), AutoPlay is enabled for that drive type. By default, Win95 supports AutoPlay for fixed, CD-ROM, and RAM drives, as well as for drives with no root directory; that is, the value that Win95 ordinarily assigns to this first byte is &h95. In other words, AutoPlay by default is disabled for network drives and floppy (removable) drives. However, by changing the values of individual bits, you can configure AutoPlay to work or not work with particular drive types.

DRIVES.VBP is a Visual Basic project that allows these settings to be modified, in the process illustrating how to retrieve **REG_BINARY** data from the registry. The application's only form contains a control array of eight check boxes, each of which represents a particular drive type. Each check box's Index property directly corresponds to the position of that drive type in the first byte of the **NoDrive-TypeAutoRun** value entry.

In the case of this application, data is written to and retrieved from the registry using a byte array, *bytDrive()*, that, because it is defined in the form's declarations section, is visible throughout the program. The application's *Form_Load* event procedure, which is responsible for displaying the initial value of the AutoPlay bits, is shown in Example 7-7. After the control's CurrentRoot and CurrentKey properties are set, the **GetValueSize** method redimensions the byte array to the proper size. The **GetValueData** method then retrieves the four bytes of data, storing it to the *bytDrive* array.

Example 7-7. The Form_Load event procedure of DRIVES.VBP

```
Private Sub Form_Load()

Dim intCtr As Integer

Registry1.CurrentRoot = Hkey_Current_User
Registry1.CurrentKey = _
        "\Software\Microsoft\Windows\CurrentVersion\Policies\Explorer"
ReDim bytDrives(Registry1.GetValueSize("NoDriveTypeAutoRun"))
bytDrives = Registry1.GetValueData("NoDriveTypeAutoRun", False)

For intCtr = 0 To 7
   If (2 ^ intCtr And bytDrives(0)) = 0 Then _
```

Example 7-7. The Form_Load event procedure of DRIVES.VBP (continued)

```
            chkDrive(intCtr).Value = 1
Next

End Sub
```

Although we've stored four bytes of data to the array, we're only concerned with the first byte. Since Visual Basic lacks a direct bit manipulation function, we can determine if a particular bit is "on" or "off" by ANDing it with the value of that bit when it is "on." If the bit is off, AutoPlay is enabled for that drive type, and we can set the Value property of the check box accordingly. If the bit is on, we need do nothing, since the check box is unchecked by default.

After the user modifies the values and clicks the OK button, the *Command1_Click* event procedure is responsible for writing changes back to the registry. The code to do this is shown in Example 7-8. Since the position of each disk type in the *chkDrive* control array is the same as its bit position in the first byte, we simply examine each check box and enable its bit in *bytDrive(0)* if it is *not* checked.

Example 7-8. The Command1_Click event procedure of DRIVES.VBP

```
Private Sub Command1_Click()

Dim intCtr As Integer
Dim varValue As Variant
Dim objCheckBox As Object

bytDrives(0) = 0

For Each objCheckBox In chkDrive
    If objCheckBox.Value = 0 Then
        bytDrives(0) = bytDrives(0) + 2 ^ objCheckBox.Index
    End If
Next

varValue = Chr(bytDrives(0))
For intCtr = 1 To 3
    varValue = varValue + Chr(0)
Next

Call Registry1.SetValue("NoDriveTypeAutoRun", varValue, _
                        Reg_Binary, Len(varValue))

End Sub
```

While the `GetValueData` method allows you to store a registry value either to a variant string or to a byte array, the `SetValue` method requires that the *Data* parameter be a variant data type. Therefore, the procedure uses the *Chr* function to convert the first element of the *bytDrives* array to a variant string, and adds three more bytes containing *Chr(0)* to it. This value is then written to the registry.

Searching the Registry Using the Registry Control

The area in which the registry control really shines is support for searches. Using the control, you can easily search the registry for a key or a value name that contains a particular string or substring. You can also search a value entry for a particular data value. This eliminates the need to recursively call either or both the *RegEnumKey* and *RegEnumValue* functions, and makes writing code that searches the registry fast and painless. In fact, the search facilities provided by the registry control are far more sophisticated than those provided by *REGEDIT.EXE*, the Registry Editor included with Win95.

Searching for Keys and Value Names

To illustrate the control's searching features, let's construct a utility that lists the shell verbs that applications have registered, and displays additional information about a particular verb when the user clicks on it. (For information on shell verbs and the organization of file association information in the registry, see "Handling Application Data Files" in Chapter 8.) The first step is to include the code in our main window's *Form_Load* event procedure to fill a list box with all registered verbs, as Example 7-9 shows. To do this, we search HKEY_CLASSES_ROOT for all keys named "shell," since the subkeys of each `shell` key should contain one or more verbs. Whenever the program finds a match, it examines each of the subkeys of the shell key. It first checks for the presence of a subkey named "command." If this generates an error, the error handler is called; it simply returns control to the bottom of the `For` loop, which allows the next verb name to be examined. If a `command` subkey is present, the program compares the verb with the verbs already contained in the list box; if the verb does not appear there, it is added to the list box. The result is a unique list of shell verbs. In addition, the list box entry's ItemData property is updated to reflect the number of occurrences of that verb in the registry. (We could use this information to allow the program to display information about each occurrence of the verb, if we chose to.) Note that, after calling the registry control's `FindFirstKey` method, the *Form_Load* event procedure changes several registry properties, including the value of the current key, without affecting the control's ability to continue its search using the original search criteria.

Example 7-9. The Form_Load event procedure of a search routine

```
Private Sub Form_Load()

Dim intctr As Integer, intListCtr As Integer
Dim strVerb As String
Dim blnSearch As Boolean, blnUnique as Boolean
```

Example 7-9. The Form_Load event procedure of a search routine (continued)

```
On Error GoTo ErrorHandler

Registry1.CurrentRoot = Hkey_Classes_Root
blnSearch = Registry1.FindFirstKey("shell", False, True, True)
' search for all keys named "shell"
Do While blnSearch
    Registry1.CurrentKey = Registry1.FindResultKey
' Iterate subkeys of shell key
    For intctr = 0 To Registry1.NumOfSubkeys - 1
        strVerb = Registry1.SubkeyArray(intctr)
' Check that possible verb has a "command" subkey
        Registry1.ChangeKey (strVerb & "\command")
' Iterate listbox elements to make sure verb is unique
        blnUnique = True
        For intListCtr = 0 To List1.ListCount - 1
            If UCase(strVerb) = UCase(List1.List(intListCtr)) Then
                List1.ItemData(intListCtr) = _
                    Val(List1.ItemData(intListCtr)) + 1
                blnUnique = False
                Exit For
            End If
        Next
' Add verb to list box if it is unique
        If blnUnique Then
            List1.AddItem strVerb
            List1.ItemData(List1.NewIndex) = 1
        End If
Error_Recover:
        Registry1.CurrentKey = Registry1.FindResultKey
    Next
' Search for next "shell" key
    blnSearch = Registry1.FindNextKey()
Loop

List1.ListIndex = 0
Load frmSrchDlg

On Error GoTo 0

Exit Sub

' Indicates key is not a verb: it lacks a "command" subkey
ErrorHandler:
    Resume Error_Recover
End Sub
```

When the user selects a verb from the Verbs list box, the program displays the following items of information about the first occurrence of the verb:

- The file types on which the verb operates. To locate these, the program searches for the application identifier in the default values of the file association keys.

- The verb's description. This is the default value of the shell's **verb** subkey.

- The application identifier. This is the name of the shell's parent key.

- The command-line string passed to the Windows shell. This is the default value of the verb's **command** subkey.

The code to do this is located in the list box's *List1.Click* event procedure, and is shown in Example 7-10. We've deliberately resorted to registry searches as much as possible to illustrate the registry control's search capabilities. However, from the viewpoint of application performance, an intensive use of searches when other means are available (like storing registry information to variables and then accessing the relevant registry keys or value entries directly) is far from optimal. Registry searches are, in the best of cases, extremely time-intensive operations that can severely degrade an application's performance. Because of this, it's a good idea to include some type of notification to the user when your application is searching the registry.

Example 7-10. The List1_Click event procedure of a search routine

```
Private Sub List1_Click()

On Error GoTo ErrorHandler

Static intIndex As Integer
Static blnDefined As Boolean
Dim intCurrentSel As Integer, intPos As Integer
Dim strVerb As String, strTemp As String, strFileExt As String
Dim blnSearch As Boolean

If List1.ListIndex <> intIndex Or Not blnDefined Then
    intCurrentSel = List1.ListIndex
' Find first occurrence of key
    strVerb = List1.List(intCurrentSel)
    Label2.Caption = strVerb & ":"
    frmSrchDlg.Show
    Call DoEvents
    Call Registry1.FindFirstKey(strVerb, False, True, True)
' Make result key current
    Registry1.CurrentKey = Registry1.FindResultKey
' Change to its command key
    Registry1.ChangeKey ("command")
    txtCmdLine.Text = Registry1.DefaultValue
' Change back to initial key to retrieve menu item text
    Registry1.ChangeKey ("..")
    If Len(Trim(Registry1.DefaultValue)) = 0 Then
        txtDescription.Text = "< Default: " & strVerb & " >"
    Else
        txtDescription.Text = Registry1.DefaultValue
    End If
' Retrieve value of application identifier from parent of verb's shell key
    Registry1.ChangeKey ("..\..")
    strTemp = Registry1.CurrentKey
```

Example 7-10. The List1_Click event procedure of a search routine (continued)

```
    intPos = InStr(1, strTemp, "\")
    Do While intPos > 0
        strTemp = Mid(strTemp, intPos + 1)
        intPos = InStr(1, strTemp, "\")
    Loop
    txtAppID.Text = strTemp
' Retrieve file associations handled by this verb
    blnSearch = Registry1.FindFirstValue(strTemp, Reg_SZ, Len(strTemp),
True, True)
    Do While blnSearch
        strFileExt = Mid(Registry1.FindResultKey, 2) & "; "
        blnSearch = Registry1.FindNextValue()
    Loop
    txtFileTypes.Text = strFileExt

    frmSrchDlg.Hide
    intIndex = intCurrentSel
    blnDefined = True
End If

On Error GoTo 0

Exit Sub

ErrorHandler:

Select Case Err.Number
' Invalid key for search
    Case Reg_E_Access_Denied
        If Registry1.FindNextKey Then
            Resume
        Else
            If Screen.ActiveForm.Name = "frmSrchDlg" Then frmSrchDlg.Hide
            If MsgBox(strVerb & _
        " does not appear to be a valid verb. Remove it from the list?", _
                    vbYesNoCancel, "Verb Not Found") = vbYes Then
                List1.RemoveItem intCurrentSel
            Else
                txtFileTypes.Text = "< No information available >"
                txtCmdLine.Text = "< No information available >"
                txtAppID.Text = "< No information available >"
                txtDescription.Text = "< No information available >"
            End If
        End If
    Case Else
        MsgBox("Registry error: " & Err.Description
        txtFileTypes.Text = "< No information available >"
        txtCmdLine.Text = "< No information available >"
        txtAppID.Text = "< No information available >"
        txtDescription.Text = "< No information available >"
End Select

End Sub
```

Searching for Registry Data

Along with its ability to search keys and value names, the registry control also allows you to search values independently of their data type. This is a unique and extremely valuable feature; in other words, you can search for binary (REG_BINARY) data as well as strings and other registry data types. In contrast, using RegEdit, you can search value entries of type REG_SZ for particular strings or substrings, but you can't search for any other registry data types.

In using the registry control's FindFirstValue and FindNextValue methods to search for a particular value, you can ordinarily search for a subvalue within the larger registry value by setting the value of its *FullData* parameter to False. This, however, is not true of searches for REG_DWORD or REG_DWORD_BIG_ENDIAN values: when you search these two integer data types, the *FullData* parameter is ignored, and the search value must always correspond exactly to the registry value for a match to be made; you cannot successfully search for particular byte values within a larger REG_DWORD value.

The Registry Value Finder and Windows Platforms

The Registry Value Finder tests for the 32-bit Windows platform on which it is running and exits if it finds that the platform is Win32s. If the platform is Windows NT, it disables the buttons for top-level registry keys not found on WinNT 3.x. In addition, although it identifies the value names of data types not supported by Windows 95, it does not display them; if you want to see what a REG_RESOURCE_LIST looks like, for instance, you'll have to use the WinNT Registry Editor. Finally, if the program is running under Win95, it disables the registry data types not supported by the Win95 registry. For details on testing for version, see Appendix A.

Interestingly, if the variant data passed as the *Value* parameter to the FindFirstValue method is Empty (that is, it hasn't been initialized by assigning it a value), the registry control will attempt to locate every instance of a particular data type regardless of its value. This is a particularly valuable feature if you're interested in exploring the structure and organization of the registry. In order to search for a data type rather than a particular data value, two requirements must be met:

* The value of the *FullData* parameter to the FindFirstValue method must be False.

* When the FindFirstValue method is called, the control must not ignore the value of the *FullData* parameter. This means, in other words, that you

can't search for all instances of REG_DWORD or REG_DWORD_BIG_ENDIAN data in the registry; you can, however, search for all other data types.

The Registry Value Finder, which is shown in Figure 7-2, is a general-purpose registry data search utility developed using the Desaware Registry Control that illustrates how you can use the control's FindFirstValue method to search for a wide range of data values. It also illustrates how to handle individual data types. The utility's main window is shown in Figure 7-1.

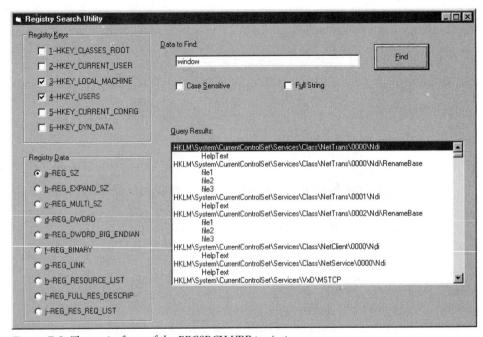

Figure 7-2. The main form of the REGSRCH.VBP project

The program relies on a "trick" to eliminate the need to translate a top-level key's name (e.g., the string "HKEY_CLASSES_ROOT") into a numeric constant in code. The Tag property of each check box in the Registry Keys group box has been assigned the constant value belonging to that top-level key, while the Tag property of each option button in the Registry Data group box has similarly been assigned that data type's constant value. For example, the value &H80000000 has been stored to the Tag property of the *chkTree(0)* check box, since this is the value of the HKEY_CLASSES_ROOT constant.

Example 7-11 contains the Find button's *Click* event procedure, which is responsible for establishing the search criteria, calling the FindFirstValue and FindNextValue methods, and handling the results that they return. A surprisingly small amount of coding is required to conduct the actual registry search;

most of the code in Example 7-11 is concerned with formatting the results of the search so that they can be displayed in a list box.

Example 7-11. The cmdFind_Click event procedure

```
Private Sub cmdFind_Click()

Dim blnCase As Boolean, blnFullString As Boolean, blnFound As Boolean
Dim blnNewKey As Boolean
Dim lngCurrentRoot As Long, lngLastRoot As Long, lngRegTree As Long
Dim lngDataType As Long, lngDataSize As Long
Dim strLastKey As String, strCurrentKey As String, strTemp As String
Dim strValueName As String
Dim varValue As Variant
Dim objTree As Control, objOption As Control

lstSearchResults.Clear

' Initialize search parameters
'
' Determine data type for search
For Each objOption In optData
    If objOption.Value = True Then
        lngDataType = Val(objOption.Tag)
        Exit For
    End If
Next
' Get search string
strTemp = txtDataToFind.Text
If lngDataType = Reg_Binary Then
    varValue = ConvertToBin(strTemp)
Else
    varValue = strTemp
End If
' Determine size of data
If lngDataType = Reg_Dword Or lngDataType = Reg_Dword_Big_Endian Then
    lngDataSize = LEN_DWORD
Else
    lngDataSize = Len(varValue)
End If
' Get case sensitive and exact match settings
blnCase = chkCase.Value
blnFullString = chkFullString.Value

' Cycle through each selected tree for search
For Each objTree In chkTree
    If objTree.Value = 1 Then
        Registry1.CurrentRoot = objTree.Tag
        Registry1.CurrentKey = "\"
        Form1.MousePointer = 11
        blnFound = Registry1.FindFirstValue(varValue, lngDataType, _
                lngDataSize, blnFullString, True)
        Do While blnFound
            lngCurrentRoot = objTree.Tag
```

Example 7-11. The cmdFind_Click event procedure (continued)

```
            strCurrentKey = Registry1.FindResultKey
'Determine if new key is unique
            If lngCurrentRoot = lngLastRoot Then
                If strCurrentKey <> strLastKey Then blnNewKey = True
            Else
                blnNewKey = True
            End If
' Add key if it's unique
            If blnNewKey Then
                Select Case lngCurrentRoot
                    Case Hkey_Classes_Root
                        lstSearchResults.AddItem "HKCR" & strCurrentKey
                    Case Hkey_Current_User
                        lstSearchResults.AddItem "HKCU" & strCurrentKey
                    Case Hkey_Local_Machine
                        lstSearchResults.AddItem "HKLM" & strCurrentKey
                    Case Hkey_Users
                        lstSearchResults.AddItem "HKU" & strCurrentKey
                    Case Hkey_Current_Config
                        lstSearchResults.AddItem "HKCC" & strCurrentKey
                    Case Hkey_Dyn_Data
                        lstSearchResults.AddItem "HKDD" & strCurrentKey
                End Select
                lstSearchResults.ItemData(lstSearchResults.NewIndex) = 1
                strLastKey = strCurrentKey
                lngLastRoot = lngCurrentRoot
                blnNewKey = False
            End If
' Add value name
            strValueName = Registry1.FindResultValueName
            If Len(Trim(strValueName)) = 0 Then
                lstSearchResults.AddItem vbTab & "<Default Value>"
            Else
                lstSearchResults.AddItem vbTab & strValueName
            End If
            lstSearchResults.ItemData(lstSearchResults.NewIndex) = 0
            blnFound = Registry1.FindNextValue
        Loop
    End If
Next
Form1.MousePointer = 0
' Display message if there are no matches
If lstSearchResults.ListCount > 0 Then
    lstSearchResults.ListIndex = 0
Else
    MsgBox "No value entries matched the search criteria."
End If

End Sub
```

The user indicates what kind of data to search for in the registry by selecting one of the *optData* option buttons; the initial *For Each/Next* statement then examines each element of the control array to determine which data type was selected. Once the data type is known, the values that are to be supplied in place of the FindFirstValue method's *Value* and *SizeOfValue* parameters can be determined. If the user is not searching for binary data, the contents of the txtDataToFind text box can simply be assigned to a variant variable, *varValue*. If the user is searching for REG_BINARY data, the program assumes that the user has entered the hexadecimal value to locate in the txtDataToFind text box. In this case, the *CmdFind_Click* event procedure calls the *ConvertToBin* function to convert these hexadecimal characters into a string variant containing the binary search value:

```
Public Function ConvertToBin(strText As String) As Variant

Dim intCtr As Integer, intHexValue As Integer
Dim varHexString As Variant

For intCtr = 1 To Len(strText) - 1 Step 2
    intHexValue = "&h" & Mid(strText, intCtr, 2)
    varHexString = varHexString & Chr(intHexValue)
Next

ConvertToBin = varHexString

End Function
```

ConvertToBin is responsible for parsing the string, extracting every two hexadecimal characters that form a single byte's value, converting them to an integer, and then storing the string equivalent of this numeric value to the *varValue* variant character string.

```
For intCtr = 1 To Len(strTemp) - 1 Step 2
    intHexValue = "&h" & Mid(strTemp, intCtr, 2)
    varValue = varValue & Chr(intHexValue)
Next
```

If the user is searching for either REG_DWORD or REG_DWORD_BIG_ENDIAN data, the value of the *SizeOfValue* parameter must be 4; the LEN_DWORD constant, which is defined in the form's general declarations section, is used for this purpose. Otherwise, *SizeOfValue* is the size (i.e., the number of bytes) in the *varValue* variable, and can be determined by using the *Len* function.[*]

Having assigned values to all of the parameters required by the FindFirstValue method, the program then calls the method itself. Since the program allows the user to search multiple registry keys, this is handled within

---

[*] Visual Basic also has a *LenB* function that returns the number of bytes used to represent a string. When used with variant data, it returns the total number of bytes required to store the variant data structure. This is not what the *SizeOfValue* parameter expects, however; it merely wants to know the total number of bytes of data that it is expected to search for in the registry.

the module's second *For Each/Next* statement, which examines each element of the `chkTree` control array to determine whether its check box is selected. For each match that the program finds, the program adds either one or two items to the lstSearchResults list box:

- If the registry key was not duplicated by the previous search result, it adds the key's complete path (including an abbreviation for the top-level key) to the list box.

- The name of the value entry, preceded by a tab character.

If the user double-clicks on a key in the lstSearchResults list box, a dialog box instructs him or her to select a value entry instead. By double-clicking on a particular value entry, a read-only dialog box opens which allows the user to examine its value. The code that retrieves the registry value and stores it to a text box is contained in the *DisplayValue* procedure, which is shown in Example 7-12.

Example 7-12. The DisplayValue subroutine

```
Public Sub DisplayValue()

Dim intCtr As Integer, intElements As Integer, intCharPos As Integer
Dim intByteCtr As Integer
Dim lngDataType As Long, lngDataLength As Long
Dim strKeyName As String, strValueName As String, strRoot As String
Dim strValue As String, strTemp As String, strHexValue As String
Dim objOption As Object

' Exit if this is a key
If lstSearchResults.ItemData(lstSearchResults.ListIndex) = 1 Then
   MsgBox "This is a registry key. Select a value entry instead."
   Exit Sub
End If


' Determine data type
For Each objOption In optData
   If objOption.Value = True Then
      lngDataType = Val(objOption.Tag)
      Exit For
   End If
Next
' Get key name
For intCtr = lstSearchResults.ListIndex To 0 Step -1
   If lstSearchResults.ItemData(intCtr) = 1 Then
      strKeyName = lstSearchResults.List(intCtr)
      Exit For
   End If
Next
' Remove root keyname
strRoot = Left(strKeyName, InStr(1, strKeyName, "\") - 1)
strKeyName = Mid(strKeyName, InStr(1, strKeyName, "\"))
' Get value name
```

Example 7-12. The DisplayValue subroutine (continued)

```
strValueName = lstSearchResults.List(lstSearchResults.ListIndex)
' Change current key
Select Case strRoot
    Case "HKCR"
        Registry1.CurrentRoot = Hkey_Classes_Root
    Case "HKCU"
        Registry1.CurrentRoot = Hkey_Current_User
    Case "HKLM"
        Registry1.CurrentRoot = Hkey_Local_Machine
    Case "HKU"
        Registry1.CurrentRoot = Hkey_Users
    Case "HKCC"
        Registry1.CurrentRoot = Hkey_Current_Config
    Case "HKDD"
        Registry1.CurrentRoot = Hkey_Dyn_Data
End Select
Registry1.CurrentKey = strKeyName
' Retrieve value name
strValueName = Mid(lstSearchResults.List(lstSearchResults.ListIndex), 2)
If strValueName = "<Default Value>" Then strValueName = ""
' Format value dialog
frmValue.Caption = strValueName
' Retrieve data
Select Case lngDataType
    Case Reg_SZ, Reg_Expand_SZ
        frmValue.Icon = LoadPicture(App.Path & "\string.ico")
        If lngDataType = Reg_SZ Then
            frmValue.lbltype.Caption = "Reg_SZ:"
        Else
            frmValue.lbltype.Caption = "Reg_Expand_SZ:"
        End If
        strValue = Registry1.GetValueData(strValueName, True)
        frmValue.txtSingleLine.Text = strValue
    Case Reg_Multi_SZ
        frmValue.Icon = LoadPicture(App.Path & "\string.ico")
        frmValue.lbltype.Caption = "Reg_Multi_SZ:"
        strValue = Registry1.GetValueData(strValueName, True)
        If Len(strValue) > 0 Then
            strTemp = ""
            For intCharPos = 1 To Len(strValue) - 1
                If Mid(strValue, intCharPos, 1) = Chr(0) Then
                    strTemp = strTemp & Chr(13) & Chr(10)
                Else
                    strTemp = strTemp & Mid(strValue, intCharPos, 1)
                End If
            Next
            strValue = strTemp
        End If
        frmValue.txtSingleLine.Visible = False
        frmValue.txtMultiLine.Visible = True
        frmValue.txtMultiLine.Text = strValue
    Case Reg_Dword
```

Example 7-12. The DisplayValue subroutine (continued)

```
        frmValue.Icon = LoadPicture(App.Path & "\binary.ico")
        frmValue.lbltype.Caption = "Reg_DWord:"
        frmValue.txtSingleLine.Text = Registry1.GetValueData(strValueName, _
                                      True)
    Case Reg_Dword_Big_Endian
        frmValue.Icon = LoadPicture(App.Path & "\binary.ico")
        frmValue.lbltype.Caption = "Reg_DWord_Big_Endian:"
        frmValue.txtSingleLine.Text = Registry1.GetValueData(strValueName, _
                                      True)
    Case Reg_Binary
        frmValue.Icon = LoadPicture(App.Path & "\binary.ico")
        frmValue.lbltype.Caption = "Reg_Binary:"
        lngDataLength = Registry1.GetValueSize(strValueName)
        strValue = Registry1.GetValueData(strValueName, True)
        strTemp = ""
        For intCtr = 1 To lngDataLength
            strHexValue = Hex(Asc(Mid(strValue, intCtr, 1)))
            If Len(Trim(strHexValue)) < 2 Then
                strHexValue = Right("00" & strHexValue, 2)
            End If
            strTemp = strTemp & strHexValue & " "
            intByteCtr = intByteCtr + 1
            If intByteCtr = 8 Then
                intByteCtr = 0
                strTemp = strTemp & Chr(13) & Chr(10)
            End If
        Next
        frmValue.txtSingleLine.Visible = False
        frmValue.txtMultiLine.Visible = True
        frmValue.txtMultiLine.Text = strTemp
    Case Else
        MsgBox "Data type " & lngDataType
        Exit Sub
End Select

frmValue.Show vbModal

End Sub
```

Before calling the `GetValueData` method to retrieve the entry's value, the procedure first retrieves the values needed to access the value entry and to pass as parameters to the method:

- *The top-level key.* The *InStr* function extracts the abbreviation for the top-level key from the key's full path in the lstSearchResults list box, and the `Select Case` statement then stores the top-level key's constant value to the `CurrentRoot` property. Since the list box contains both keys and values, the program is easily able to differentiate the two by examining the value of each item's ItemData property; whenever the *cmdFind_Click* event procedure added an item to the list box, it assigned a value of 1 to its ItemData property if the entry was a key, and a value of 0 if it was a value entry. To locate the key to which a value entry belongs, the module needs only to loop backward from the item selected by the user until it finds an item whose ItemData value is 1.

- *The current key.* The *InStr* function extracts the key name from the complete registry path. This is then assigned to the registry control's CurrentKey property.

- *The value name.* The module removes the leading tab character from the list box item on which the user clicked and assigns it to the *strValueName* variable. This variable is then passed to the *Name* parameter of the GetValueData method.

- *The data type.* Like the *cmdFind_Click* event procedure, the module determines the type of data for which the user searched by cycling through the optData collection until it finds the selected option button. The value of its Tag property is then stored to the *lngDataType* variable. This is used in determining how to handle the value returned by the GetValueData method.

About half of the procedure's code is devoted to handling the results returned by the GetValueData method; it is all contained within the rather large *Select Case* statement in the second half of the routine. In the case of REG_SZ, REG_EXPAND_SZ, REG_DWORD, and REG_DWORD_BIG_ENDIAN data, the module does not have to do any intermediate processing of the data returned by the method; it simply assigns the value directly to the text box's Text property, although it could also have stored the value to a variable of the proper data type. (If desired, the REG_EXPAND_SZ string could also have been expanded by calling the *ExpandEnvironmentStrings* API function.) In the case of REG_MULTI_SZ and REG_BINARY data, though, additional processing is required:

- *String array data (REG_MULTI_SZ).* An application has to be prepared to handle REG_MULTI_SZ value entries that contain no data; several applications, like Microsoft Developer's Studio, use string arrays to handle MRU lists. If the GetValueData method does retrieve real data, each element of the array should be extracted from the string returned by the function. In the case of the DisplayValue routine, which is concerned only with displaying the data, this is accomplished by substituting the carriage return and line feed characters for every occurrence of a null character (Chr(0)) except the final one. If the elements of the string array are to be assigned to an array variable, the string should first be parsed to determine how many elements it contains and the array redimensioned accordingly, as the following code fragment shows:

```
Dim strArray() As String
```

```
For intCtr = 1 To Len(strValue) - 1
    If Mid(strValue, intCtr, 1) = Chr(0) Then
        intElements = intElements + 1
    End If
Next
Redim strArray(intElements - 1)
```

- *Binary data (REG_BINARY)*. For binary data, the `GetValueSize` method should first be called to determine the value's total length. This is less important when the value is stored to a string; it is essential, however, if the value is to be stored to a byte array (i.e., if the value of the `GetValueData` method's *AsString* parameter is False), since the array should first be appropriately redimensioned to hold all of the binary data. The string or byte array must then be parsed and converted into the form required by the application. Since the *DisplayValue* routine merely displays the binary data in hexadecimal format, it extracts each character of the string, converts it to a numeric value using the *Asc* function, and then converts it to a hexadecimal string using the *Hex* function.

If you're interested in exploring the registry, the Registry Search Utility can be a useful tool. If you're interested in programming for the registry, you can easily extend *REGSRCH.VBP* into a professional-quality application. For starters, you can replace lstSearchResults, the list box that displays the keys and values returned by the `FindFirstValue` and `FindNextValue` methods, with a graphical Tree-View control. (This requires either the Professional or Enterprise editions of Visual Basic 4.0.) Second, you can modify the application so that the user can modify, instead of merely view, registry values. Third, you can modify the program so that it runs under both Win95 and WinNT. Doing this requires that you check for the version (see Appendix A for details on how to do this), and that, if the program is running under WinNT, you either disable or hide the option buttons for top-level registry keys that are present in the Win95 registry but absent under WinNT.

Summary

In this chapter, we've shown how you can use the Desaware Registry Control as a substitute for direct calls to the Win32 registry API if you program in Visual Basic. The control handles most of the low-level details of registry access for you, and allows you to focus on getting the data that you want into and out of the registry. The following features are worth noting:

- Like any control, the Desaware Registry Control uses properties and methods to give your application access to the registry.

- Once you successfully access a registry key by setting the values of the CurrentRoot and CurrentKey properties, the control automatically retrieves a variety of information about that key's subkeys and value entries. In contrast, collecting this information using the registry API requires calls to a number of API functions.

- The control offers full support for Visual Basic's variant data type. You can store the values that you retrieve from the registry to a variant. If you write values to the registry, you *must* use a variant variable.

- Registry access errors are automatically integrated into Visual Basic's error handling system. This means, though, that anything other than a successful operation generates an error and invokes the error handler, if one is present. (If one is not present, of course, your application crashes.)

- A major strength of the control is its support for searches. Like RegEdit, it allows you to search for complete strings or substrings in REG_SZ data (although your application can search the other string data types as well). In addition, you can also search for long integer values or for individual bytes within REG_BINARY data.

8

What Goes in the Registry: System Settings

So far, we've focused on using either C or Visual Basic to retrieve values from or store information in the Win95 registry. We've almost completely neglected the most important question of all: What information can you store in the registry? The answer is a fairly simple one: you can store anything that you want to store in the registry, provided that the total size of the value entry is less than about 16K (or, in WinNT, about 1MB).

For example, rather than use separate proprietary-format data files, you could put your application's data into the registry. This may sound like a facetious remark, but in fact if your application's data requirements are small (perhaps up to a few thousand records of perhaps up to 100 bytes each), the registry might turn out to be a *perfect* place to store your application's data. Win95 will take care of swapping your data between disk and memory as required; searching for an entry is as simple as calling *RegQueryValueEx*. The Win95 registry is really a first step toward breaking down the somewhat artificial barrier between memory and the file system. So long as you trust the registry and refrain from using *RegFlushKey,* the registry really can serve as a kind of file system that, from your application's point of view, is always in memory yet always saved to disk too. On the other hand, a word processing program should not keep the user's documents in the registry, nor should a Web browser cache HTML and GIF files in the registry.

Most developers will probably use the registry to store the same kinds of data that under Win3x have been stored in the Windows system and private initialization files. In particular, three distinct kinds of information about your application should be stored in the registry:

- *System-level information.* Any information needed by Windows to integrate your application into the Windows environment must be stored in the registry. This includes such things as the path to your application, file types used by your application, dynamic link libraries that your application calls or that were developed for your application, and the OLE components of your application. These settings are stored in various parts of the registry, and are customarily accessed by the Windows shell, rather than by your application. With a few exceptions, they are written to the registry only once, by your application's installation routine.

- *Application information.* Any information that your application needs to run that is not specific to a particular user should be stored in the registry. This includes such items as licensing information or the path to the application's installation files. These data should be stored in either `HKLM\Software\`*`<CompanyName>\<AppName>\<Version>`* or `HKLM\Software\`*`<CompanyName>\<AppName>`*. Again, you might also consider the registry for an application's *data*, if there's a fairly small amount.

- *User settings.* Win95 supports multiple users sharing a single computer, and uses the registry to store each user's settings. This includes the current position of the application's windows, the state of the application's interface. They should be stored in `HKCU\Software\`*`<CompanyName>\<AppName>\`*`<Version>` or `HKCU\Software\`*`<CompanyName>\<AppName>`*.

It is important to stress that there is nothing "magical" about the registry. Information stored in the registry has no effect on Windows or your application's operation—and instead just lifelessly consumes space on a hard disk—unless it is read, either by your application or by Windows itself, using either the registry API or one of the low-level VMM registry access functions.

The ability to disable editing of the registry provides an excellent example of this. As we mentioned in "Launching RegEdit" in Chapter 2, *Using the Registry Editor*, a system administrator can use the System Policy Editor to disable direct editing of the registry. When this option is selected, the System Policy Editor creates a `HKCU\Software\Microsoft\Windows\CurrentVersion\Policies\System` key if necessary, adds a value entry named `DisableRegistryTools`, and sets its value to 1. Presumably, in this case, if the value of the `DisableRegistryTools` entry in `HKCU\Software\Microsoft\Windows\CurrentVersion\Policies\System` is 1, direct user access to the registry is not allowed; a utility such as RegEdit refuses to execute, and instead displays a warning dialog before terminating. However, for this setting to be meaningful, each utility that allows the user to directly access and modify the registry must include code to explicitly query this setting and act accordingly. If it does not—and many registry utilities in fact don't—the application will naturally permit modification of the registry regardless of this setting.

In the remainder of this chapter, we'll focus on the kinds of system-level information that your application is likely to record in the registry, and provide coding examples in both C and Visual Basic; the next chapter focuses on some of the application and user settings that you might want to store in the registry. For the most part, both this and the following chapter follow Microsoft's guidelines for the kinds of information to be written to the registry.

Ordinarily, when you write your application's data to the registry, you are free to choose key names and value names and to format the data in a way that makes sense to you (see Chapter 9, *What Goes in the Registry: Application and User Settings*). This is because you can assume that these settings are of exclusive or near-exclusive interest to your application. In the case of the system settings that we'll discuss here, however, that isn't the case: once you write the information, usually in your application's installation program, your application will rarely, if ever, read it again. Instead, Win95 itself or the Windows shell will use these settings to integrate your application into the Windows environment. As a result, Windows must know in advance what information is to be retrieved and where it is to be found. This means that in most cases, you must create or access a key with a particular name; the key used to store data must be a subkey of a particular registry key, which is located in a specific registry tree; you must use a value name that is defined in advance by Windows; and you must choose from among predefined values offered by Windows, which Windows is capable of interpreting correctly.

Registering the Application's Path

In some cases, when the user attempts to launch your application, Windows needs to know where to find it. This is true in two major cases:

- *From the Run dialog.* When the user selects the Run option from the Start menu and enters the name of the application without its associated path in the Open drop-down combo box, Windows needs some means of identifying where the application is stored.

- *From a shortcut.* Sometimes, a shortcut on the Start menu or in a program group window does not include path information. (The shortcut's Properties dialog contains only the application name without its path in the Target text box, and the Start In text box is blank.) To launch the application, Windows first must know where find it.

To locate a file, Windows first searches for the application in the Windows directory, followed by the Windows system directory. Finally, it searches the directories specified in the Windows' PATH environment variable. If it is still unable to locate the application, the Windows shell next reads the subkeys of `HKLM\Software\Microsoft\Windows\CurrentVersion\App Paths`. The name of each subkey must contain the complete filename of the executable file; the subkey's default value provides the path and name of the application. For example, Table 8-1 lists some application paths commonly found in the Win95 registry:

Table 8-1. Some common application paths stored in the registry

Subkey Name	Default Value
EXCEL.EXE	C:\MSOffice\Excel\excel.exe
HYPERTRM.EXE	C:\Progra~1\Access~1\Hypert~1\HYPERTRM.EXE
MSPAINT.EXE	C:\Progra~1\Access~1\MSPAINT.EXE
WINWORD.EXE	C:\MSOffice\Winword\winword.exe
WORDPAD.EXE	C:\Progra~1\Access~1\WORDPAD.EXE

The subkey name must contain the complete filename of the application, along with its extension. If the extension is absent, Windows fails to match the application name to the key, and as a result reports that it is unable to locate the application. It is not completely necessary to include the file's extension in the value itself; however, the root filename must be included, or Windows will simply open an Explorer window that depicts the directory's contents.

Incidentally, note that the registry values in Table 8-1 do not use long filenames ("C:\Progra~1\Access~1" is the short alias for "C:\Program Files\Accessories"). At one point during its "Chicago" beta-test period, Win95 could be run without long filenames (LFNs). This feature was turned on by storing a value of 1 to `Win31FileSystem`, a `REG_BINARY` value entry found in `HKLM\System\CurrentControlSet\control\FileSystem`. In the final retail version of Win95, this registry entry has no effect. Win95 requires LFNs, so storing them in the registry is actually safe.

In DOS and Win3x, the operating system sometimes had difficulty locating library and other program files used by a particular application. Under Win3x, the most common solution to this problem was simply to dump all DLLs into the Windows system directory or the top-level Windows directory. Although Win95 continues to search these two directories for DLLs, you can also store libraries developed for your application in any other directory of your choice. If you create a Path value entry in your `HKLM\Software\Microsoft\Windows\CurrentVersion\App Paths` subkey and store the path or paths to your DLLs to it, Windows can

---

Where Should You Store Your Application?

Microsoft recommends that, ultimately, the user should be allowed to choose the drive and directory in which an application is stored. However, the default choice that should be offered to the user is an application subdirectory in the Windows "Program Files" directory. The location of the latter is usually `C:\ Program Files`, although it is, of course, unwise to treat the drive, path, and directory name as "hard-coded" constants. The actual name and location of the Windows program files directory is stored in the `ProgramFilesDir` value entry of `HKLM\Software\Microsoft\Windows\CurrentVersion`.

Although this is the recommended default location for installing an application, some programs offer other default locations. The most notable of these is Microsoft Office, which, unless the user specifies otherwise, installs itself in `C:\ MSOffice`.

---

access the libraries successfully. If you assign multiple paths to the `Path` value entry, they should be separated by semicolons.

Ordinarily, you'd want to store application path information in the registry just once, as a part of your application's installation program. For instance, the C code fragment in Example 8-1 records the location of an application named *MYAPP.EXE* in the registry:

Example 8-1. C code to register an application's path

```
char *AppPath = "C:\\Program Files\\My App\\MYAPP.EXE";
HKEY hKey ;
DWORD dwDisposition ;

RegCreateKeyEx(HKEY_LOCAL_MACHINE,
    "Software\\Microsoft\\Windows\\CurrentVersion\\App Paths\\MYAPP.EXE",
    0, 0, REG_OPTION_NON_VOLATILE, 0, 0, &hKey, &dwDisposition) ;
if (dwDisposition == REG_CREATED_NEW_KEY)
    RegSetValueEx(hKey, "", 0, REG_SZ, AppPath, sizeof(AppPath) );
RegCloseKey( hKey) ;
```

In Visual Basic, if you use the setup toolkit to create your application's installation program, it automatically adds the appropriate entry to the `App Paths` key. If you're creating an installation program from scratch, though, the Visual Basic code fragment in Example 8-2 records the location of an application named *MYAPP.EXE* in the registry.

Example 8-2. Visual Basic code to register an application's path

```
Dim hKey As Long
Dim lngDisposition As Long
```

Example 8-2. Visual Basic code to register an application's path (continued)

```
Dim udfSecure As SECURITY_ATTRIBUTES

Call RegCreateKeyEx(HKEY_LOCAL_MACHINE, _
   "Software\Microsoft\Windows\CurrentVersion\App Paths\MYAPP.EXE", _
   0, 0, REG_OPTION_NON_VOLATILE, 0, udfSecure, hKey, lngDisposition)

If lngDisposition = REG_CREATED_NEW_KEY Then _
     Call RegSetValueEx(hKey, "", 0, REG_SZ, ByVal strAppPath, _
           Len(strAppPath) + 1)
RegCloseKey (hKey)
```

In these code fragments, *AppPath* or *strAppPath* is a string that contains the name of the application, along with the path to the directory in which it is being installed (e.g., "C:\Program Files\MyApp\MYAPP.EXE"). Ordinarily, a default value would be provided, which the user could modify by entering an alternate installation location in a text box or selecting it using a common dialog.

Microsoft's *Windows Interface Guidelines for Software Design* indicates that, if the Explorer (i.e., the Windows shell) moves or renames your application, Windows automatically updates the value of its **App Paths** subkey. However, this is inaccurate: if the user moves or renames your application, information in the registry is *not* updated to reflect its new location or its new filename. If you're concerned about users moving your application and want to insure that the registry always contains the correct path to your application, your application could, at startup, use the Win32 API *GetCurrentDirectory* function to determine its location (or, if you're using Visual Basic, retrieve the value of the App.Path property) and check the registry to see if its present location corresponds to its registered location.

Registering Dynamic Link Libraries

The tendency of applications under Win3x to use the Windows system directory, in particular, to store their dynamic link libraries tended to transform this directory into an enormous dumping ground. While it was easy enough for installation routines to place files in the directory, it was very difficult for users to get rid of unneeded ones. On particularly active systems in which applications were installed and deleted with some regularity, it was not uncommon for the Windows system directory to expand continually until it contained tens of megabytes of unused DLLs.

The registry attempts to bring some order to this chaos through the `HKLM\Software\Microsoft\Windows\CurrentVersion\SharedDLLs` key. The name of each of its value entries corresponds to the path and filename of a particular dynamic link library installed in the system. The value of each entry is a usage

---

Where Do I Store My Application's DLLs?

If a dynamic link library is likely to be used exclusively by your application (which means, presumably, that you've provided no documentation about the functions it exports), Microsoft recommends that it be stored in a subdirectory of your application directory named *SYSTEM*. For instance, if you develop *MYAPP.DLL* to accompany your application, you'd store it in *C:\Program Files\ MyApp\System*. In this case, you don't have to create a usage counter (see below), since you can legitimately expect that no other application will use your library.

If the DLL is to be accessed by other applications as well, it should be stored an application subdirectory in the Windows common files directory. The precise name and location of this directory is stored as a REG_SZ value to the `CommonFilesDir` value entry of `HKLM\Software\Microsoft\Windows\CurrentVersion`. In this case, you definitely should create or increment the DLL's usage counter in the `SharedDLLs` key.

---

counter, a `REG_DWORD` value that reflects the number of applications that use the DLL. An application's installer should increment the usage counter for each DLL that it shares with other applications; the deinstaller should decrement the usage counter. If the counter's value is 0, the deinstallation routine should give the user the option of deleting the DLL, and warn the user that deleting it may actually disable some applications that have not updated the usage counter properly. (Microsoft appears to be adopting the realistic viewpoint that bringing method to the madness of random DLLs will be no easy matter.)

Although the key's purpose is to maintain a count of the dynamic link libraries used that either are or can be shared by several applications, the term "dynamic link libraries" is to be interpreted broadly. The `SharedDLLs` key on most computers actually contains entries for several different kinds of files:

- *"Standard" dynamic link libraries*—i.e., DLLs with a file extension of .DLL.

- *Other dynamic link libraries.* Several other file types (.EXE, .OCX, .VBX, .VXD) sometimes or always are special-purpose dynamic link libraries; there should be an entry for each of those that are DLLs. This means, for instance, that if your application uses an OLE custom control (an .OCX file), it should update the control's value entry in the `SharedDLLs` key.

- *Any other file that might be shared by more than one application.* For instance, Microsoft Office 95 creates entries for individual graphics filters (*.FLT) in this subkey, and Microsoft Visual C++ uses it to store usage counters for an enormous array of non-DLLs, like files with extensions of .BAT, .DAT, .ERR, .H, .HLP, .INI, .LIB, and .XLM.

The intent of the `SharedDLLs` key is that it contain accurate usage counters for shared *application* files. This specifically excludes all of the Windows system library files (like *ADVAPI32.DLL*, *USER32.DLL*, and *GDI32.DLL*), none of which have value entries in this key. This makes a certain amount of sense, since any usage counter that might be applied to a system DLL is necessarily purely artificial; if the DLL were to be deleted once its usage counter reached 0, Windows would be completely disabled. At the same time, though, the distinction between system DLLs and shared DLLs is rather nebulous. The files listed in Table 8-2, for instance, are DLLs bundled with Win95 that have usage counters in the registry. Despite this ambiguity, a useful criterion to differentiate between system and shared files is that, if you have to redistribute a shared file to insure that your application will run on the user's system, you should create or update its usage counter.

Table 8-2. System DLLs with usage counters

File	Description
MFC30.DLL	Standard 32-bit MFC 3.0 DLL
MFCANS32.DLL	MFC OLE unicode-ANSI conversion layer
MFCD30.DLL	MFC 3.0 database classes
MFCN30.DLL	Standard 32-bit MFC 3.0 DLL
MFCO30.DLL	MFC 3.0 OLE library
MFCUIA32.DLL	MFC OLE common dialogs
MSVCRT20.DLL	Microsoft Visual C 2.0 run-time library
OLEPRO32.DLL	OLE standard types library

Examples 8-3 and 8-4 contain the C and VB code for an *IncrDLLUsage* function, which assumes that you're storing your shared DLL in a subdirectory of the Windows common files directory, and updates its usage counter accordingly. (For information on the common files directory, see the sidebar "Where Do I Store My Application's DLLs?" earlier in this section.) The function's single parameter is a string containing the subdirectory in which the DLL is located, along with the DLL's filename. If, for instance, you're incrementing the usage counter for *MYAPP.DLL*, which is stored in the `MyCompany` subdirectory of the Windows common files directory, you'd call the function as follows:

```
dwCtr = IncrDLLUsage("MyCompany\\MYAPP.DLL") ;
```

In VB, of course, you would include only a single backslash to separate the path and filename, and omit the semicolon. Note that, by initializing *dwUsageCount* to 0, we don't care if *RegQueryValueEx* succeeds: if the DLL's value entry does not exist, *RegSetValueEx* creates it and sets its usage counter to 1; if it does exist, the function increments it by one. *IncrDLLUsage* then returns the new value of the usage counter; if it fails, it returns 0.

Example 8-3. A C function to update the SharedDLLs value entry

```c
#include <windows.h>

DWORD IncrDLLUsage(char *lpszFileName)
    {
    char szCommonDir[MAX_PATH], szDLLFile[MAX_PATH] ;
    HKEY hKey ;
    DWORD dwCommonDir = sizeof(szCommonDir) ;
    DWORD dwUsageCount = 0;         // if init to 0, always works
    DWORD dwByteCount = sizeof(dwUsageCount) ;

    // Retrieve location of common files directory
    RegOpenKey(HKEY_LOCAL_MACHINE,
            "Software\\Microsoft\\Windows\\CurrentVersion", &hKey) ;
    RegQueryValueEx(hKey, "CommonFilesDir", 0, 0, szCommonDir,
                &dwCommonDir) ;
    RegCloseKey(hKey) ;
    // Create string containing full path and filename
    strcpy(szDLLFile, szCommonDir) ;
    strcat(szDLLFile, "\\") ;
    strcat(szDLLFile, lpszFileName) ;
    // Open SharedDLLs key
    RegOpenKey(HKEY_LOCAL_MACHINE,
            "Software\\Microsoft\\Windows\\CurrentVersion\\SharedDLLs",
            &hKey) ;
    // Retrieve value of usage counter
    RegQueryValueEx(hKey, (LPTSTR) szDLLFile, 0, 0, &dwUsageCount,
                &dwByteCount) ;

    // Increment and store usage counter
    dwUsageCount++ ;
    if (RegSetValueEx(hKey, (LPTSTR) szDLLFile,0,REG_DWORD,&dwUsageCount,
                sizeof(dwUsageCount)) != ERROR_SUCCESS)
        dwUsageCount = 0 ;
    // Close registry key
    RegCloseKey(hKey) ;

    return dwUsageCount ;
    }
```

Example 8-4. A Visual Basic function to update the SharedDLLs value entry

```vb
Public Function IncrDLLUsage(strDLL As String) As Long

Dim hKey As Long                  ' Handle to registry key
Dim lngCount As Long              ' SharedDLL usage counter
Dim lngLenCount As Long           ' Size of lngCount (should be 4)
Dim lngLenSharedDLL As Long       ' Size of strSharedDLL
Dim strSharedDLL As String        ' Value entry name
```

Example 8-4. A Visual Basic function to update the SharedDLLs value entry (continued)

```
lngCount = 0
lngLenCount = Len(lngCount)
' Retrieve location of common files directory
lngLenSharedDLL = MAX_PATH
strSharedDLL = String(lngLenSharedDLL, 0)
Call RegOpenKey(HKEY_LOCAL_MACHINE, "Software\Microsoft\Windows\
CurrentVersion", hKey)
Call RegQueryValueEx(hKey, "CommonFilesDir", 0, 0, ByVal strSharedDLL,
lngLenSharedDLL)
Call RegCloseKey(hKey)

' Create string containing full path and filename
strSharedDLL = Left(strSharedDLL, lngLenSharedDLL - 1) & "\" & strDLL

' Open SharedDLLs key
Call RegOpenKey(HKEY_LOCAL_MACHINE, "Software\Microsoft\Windows\
CurrentVersion\SharedDLLs", hKey)
' Retrieve value of usage counter
Call RegQueryValueEx(hKey, strSharedDLL, 0, 0, lngCount, lngLenCount)
' Increment and store usage counter
lngCount = lngCount + 1
If RegSetValueEx(hKey, strSharedDLL, 0, REG_DWORD, lngCount, lngLenCount)
   <> ERROR_SUCCESS Then lngCount = 0
' Close registry key
Call RegCloseKey(hKey)

IncrDLLUsage = lngCount

End Function
```

The *IncrDLLUsage* function makes an important assumption: that the location of the DLL or other shared file is known at the point that your application is installed. In the case of our example, we know that *MYAPP.DLL* should be found in the MYAPP subdirectory of the Windows common files directory. Because of this, it is possible to use *RegQueryValueEx* to retrieve the file's usage counter. In cases where the shared file is a proprietary one and you or your development team have developed uniform standards that determine where particular files should be stored, this assumption is warranted. But if you haven't, or if the shared file is a non-proprietary, general-purpose DLL (like *VB40032.DLL*, the Visual Basic run-time library, or *OLEPRO32.DLL*, the OLE standard types library), you can't necessarily make any assumptions about its location. Whereas in Win3x shared DLLs were almost invariably dumped into the Windows system directory, 32-bit applications developed for Win95 can deposit them virtually anywhere. So if your application's installation routine includes shared files that may already be on the user's system and whose location is not known, you should do the following:

- *Determine whether the shared file already exists on the user's system.* The best way to do this is to call the *VerFindFile* function in the Win95 file installation library, *VERSION.DLL*. A less effective solution, since it assumes all shared files have been properly registered, is to use *RegEnumValue* to retrieve each entry's value name, extract each entry's filename without its path, and compare this to the filename of the shared file included with your application's installation routine.

- *Retrieve the existing file's version information.* If the file already exists on the user's system, call the *GetFileVersionInfoSize* function to determine if version information has been stored with the file. (This requires that a version resource was included with the file when it was compiled.) If version information is present, you can retrieve it with the *GetFileVersionInfo* function. If not, you can retrieve its date and time to compare with those of your shared file.

- *Copy your file.* If the installation program establishes that the shared file does not exist on the user's system or that the copy included with your installation routine is a later version, you can copy it to the user's system. In the latter case, you should replace the existing copy with the new one by using the *VerInstallFile* function.

- *Update the file's shared usage counter in the registry.*

Along with incrementing the usage counter in your application's installation program, your uninstall routine should include a routine like the one shown in Examples 8-5 and 8-6 that decrements the DLL's usage counter and, if it reaches zero, asks the user whether or not it should be deleted. If the user does choose to delete the file, it's a good idea to use the Windows shell services to move it to the Recycle Bin, rather than to delete it outright. That way, if the user notices a problem caused by the missing DLL before next emptying the Recycle Bin, he or she can restore it to its original location.

Example 8-5. DecrDLLUsage, a C function to decrement the DLL usage counter

```
#include <windows.h>
#include <shlobj.h>
#include <string.h>

VOID DecrDLLUsage(HWND hWnd, LPSTR szFileName)
    {
    HKEY hKey ;
    signed long dwCounter ;
    DWORD dwLenCounter = 4 ;
    char szMsg[512] ;
    SHFILEOPSTRUCT shFI ;
    BOOL fAborted ;

// Retrieve current value of usage counter
    RegOpenKey(HKEY_LOCAL_MACHINE,
            "Software\\Microsoft\\Windows\\CurrentVersion\\SharedDLLs",
            &hKey) ;
```

Example 8-5. DecrDLLUsage, a C function to decrement the DLL usage counter (continued)

```
    if (RegQueryValueEx(hKey, szFileName, 0, 0,
                        &dwCounter, &dwLenCounter) == ERROR_SUCCESS)
// Decrement counter
        {
        dwCounter-- ;
// Write positive counter to registry
        if (dwCounter > 0)
            RegSetValueEx(hKey,szFileName,0,REG_DWORD,&dwCounter,4) ;
// Prompt user if DLL with 0 counter is to be deleted
        else
            {
            strcpy(szMsg,"Windows reports that file ") ;
            strcat(szMsg, szFileName) ;
            strcat(szMsg, " is no longer needed by applications. "
                        "If this is not accurate, applications that "
                        "use it may not function properly.\n\n"
                        "Do you want to move ") ;
            strcat(szMsg, szFileName) ;
            strcat(szMsg, " to the Recycle Bin?") ;
            if (MessageBox(hWnd, szMsg, "File No Longer in Use",
                        MB_APPLMODAL | MB_ICONQUESTION | MB_YESNO) == IDYES)
                {
// Move File to Recycle Bin
                shFI.hwnd = hWnd ;
                shFI.wFunc = FO_DELETE ;
                shFI.pFrom = szFileName ;
                shFI.pTo = NULL ;
                shFI.lpszProgressTitle = "Moving to Recycle Bin..." ;
                shFI.fFlags = FOF_ALLOWUNDO |
                            FOF_NOCONFIRMATION | FOF_SILENT ;
                shFI.fAnyOperationsAborted = fAborted ;
                shFI.hNameMappings = NULL ;
// If successful, delete value entry
                if(SHFileOperation(&shFI) == 0)
                    RegDeleteValue(hKey, szFileName) ;
                }
            else
                if (dwCounter == 0)
                    RegSetValueEx(hKey,szFileName,0,REG_DWORD,&dwCounter,4) ;
            }
        }
// Close registry key
    RegCloseKey(hKey) ;

    return ;
    }
```

Example 8-6. Visual Basic function to decrement the usage counter

```
Public Sub DecrUsageCounter(strFileName As String)

Dim hKey As Long                    ' SharedDLLs handle
```

Example 8-6. Visual Basic function to decrement the usage counter (continued)

```
Dim lngCounter As Long           ' DLL usage counter
Dim lngLenCounter As Long        ' Length of DWORD
Dim strKey As String             ' SharedDLLs path
Dim strMsg As String             ' Deletion warning message
Dim udtFI As SHFILEOPSTRUCT      ' udtFIleOpStruct for udtFIleOperation

lngLenCounter = 4
strKey = "Software\Microsoft\Windows\CurrentVersion\SharedDLLs"
strMsg = "Windows reports that file " & strFileName & " is no longer "
strMsg = strMsg & "needed by applications. If this is not accurate, "
strMsg = strMsg & "applications that use it may not function properly."
strMsg = strMsg & vbCrLf & vbCrLf & "Do you want to move "
strMsg = strMsg & strFileName & " to the Recycle Bin?"

' Retrieve current value of usage counter
Call RegOpenKey(HKEY_LOCAL_MACHINE, strKey, hKey)
If RegQueryValueEx(hKey, strFileName, 0, 0, lngCounter, _
                   lngLenCounter) = ERROR_SUCCESS Then
' Decrement counter
  lngCounter = lngCounter - 1
' Write positive counter to registry
  If lngCounter > 0 Then
     Call RegSetValueEx(hKey, strFileName, 0, REG_DWORD, lngCounter, 4)
' Prompt user if DLL with 0 counter is to be deleted
  Else
     If MsgBox(strMsg, vbYesNo Or vbQuestion, _
               "File No Longer in Use") = vbYes Then
' Move file to Recycle Bin
        udtFI.hwnd = 0&
        udtFI.wFunc = FO_DELETE
        udtFI.pFrom = strFileName
        udtFI.lpszProgressTitle = "Moving to Recycle Bin..."
        udtFI.fFlags = FOF_ALLOWUNDO Or _
                       FOF_NOCONFIRMATION Or FOF_SILENT
' If successful, delete value entry
        If (SHFileOperation(udtFI) = 0) Then _
           Call RegDeleteValue(hKey, strFileName)
     Else
        If lngCounter = 0 Then
           Call RegSetValueEx(hKey, strFileName, 0, REG_DWORD, _
                              lngCounter, 4)
        End If
     End If
  End If
' Close registry key
  Call RegCloseKey(hKey)
End If

End Sub
```

If you're using the Visual Basic Setup Wizard to develop your application's installation routine, it automatically performs version checking and updates the usage counter for each OLE custom control, OLE in-process server, and major dynamic link library (like *STKIT432*, the Visual Basic 4.0 Setup Toolkit's dynamic link library, or *VB40032.DLL*, the Visual Basic 4.0 32-bit run-time DLL) used by your application. However, it does not parse your application's DECLARE statements to determine whether your application includes proprietary dynamic link libraries that should be distributed with your application. And although it allows you to add these to your installation routine, it does not register them or increment their usage counters. To do this, you must modify your setup script to directly call the registry API.

Recording an Uninstall Program

Along with recommending that applications increment the usage counter for each application DLL they use, Microsoft recommends that applications include uninstall programs to end the anarchy and the proliferation of unnecessary files that characterized Win3x. When your application's installation routine registers an uninstall program, it is listed in the Install/Uninstall property sheet of the Control Panel's Add/Remove Programs Properties dialog. By selecting it, the user can automatically launch the uninstall program that removes your application and all of its associated files from their computer.

To register an application's uninstall program, add a subkey for the application to the HKLM\Software\Microsoft\Windows\CurrentVersion\Uninstall key. The key's name is arbitrary: since it is used by Win95 only to enumerate uninstall programs to fill the "Remove Programs" list box, you can name it anything you'd like, as long as it doesn't duplicate an existing key name. To avoid duplication, though, it's best to give it a name that corresponds at least roughly to your application's name; the best choice is probably the name of your application's main executable file. Your application's uninstall key in turn must have two REG_SZ value entries:

- DisplayName. This is a user-friendly name that Win95 displays in the remove programs list box. It should allow the user to unambiguously identify your program.

- UninstallString. The command line needed to launch your uninstall program. This should include the program's complete path and filename, along with any command line switches or other parameters needed to successfully execute the uninstall.

If you're using the Visual Basic Setup Wizard or the Setup Toolkit to develop your application's installation routine, a properly registered uninstall routine is automatically included when the user installs your application. The Setup Toolkit includes a generic uninstall engine, *ST4UNST.EXE*, which the setup routine copies to the

What Goes in the Uninstall Routine?

Your application's uninstall routine should remove your application's executable files, along with any supplementary files and data files that it uses. In addition, it should delete any user, application, and system or application entries that it made in the registry. These include its application path key and its uninstall key. Finally, it should decrement the usage counter for any shared files that it used. If this results in the usage counter reaching 0, the program should warn the user that the DLL appears to be unused, but that if other applications use the DLL, they will no longer work; it should also prompt the user whether the shared file should be deleted or not. If the user does choose to delete the file, it's a good idea to move it to the Recycle Bin using the *SHFileOperation* function as shown in Examples 8-5 and 8-6, rather than deleting it outright. This at least allows the user to recover it until the Recycle Bin is next emptied.

Windows directory. When the uninstall program is launched from the Win95 Add/Remove Programs applet, it reads a log file, *ST4UNST.LOG*, that was created during installation and is stored in the application's directory. It then "undoes" each of the action items listed in the log file.

Handling Application Data Files

Windows is increasingly moving toward a data-centric model of computing, which allows users to focus on their data and documents rather than on the applications used to create them. The conventional application-centric model in which an application loads a data file, and the user then works with that file, is meant to become a thing of the past. Many users expect that Win95 will behave in a fairly predictable manner when handling their data files. This means that:

- The Explorer uses a unique icon to represent particular kinds of data files.

- When the user drags a data file from the Explorer to the desktop, Windows uses the proper icon to represent the link.

- When the user double-clicks on a desktop link or on the file in an Explorer window, Windows launches the application and loads the file.

- If the user uses the Explorer to drag and drop a file onto a system object like the printer, the file is printed. But this isn't automatic: it requires that your application respond appropriately.

- If the user right-clicks the mouse button on your application's data file in the Explorer window, a context menu should appear.

All of these behaviors, though, depend on applications using the registry to provide Win95 with the information that it needs to handle their data files. In this section, we'll examine the kinds of information that you need to store in the registry to insure that your application and its data files take full advantage of the Windows interface.

Registering a File Association

In Win3x, handling file associations was a responsibility shared by *WIN.INI* and the registration database, *REG.DAT*. In Win95, the registry is the central location which stores information on file associations—on what to do when the user does such things as double-clicking on a file. In fact, all of this information is contained within the subkeys of `HKEY_CLASSES_ROOT` (which is just an alias for `HKEY_LOCAL_MACHINE\SOFTWARE\Classes`).

Information on file associations in the registry follows a regular format. A *file association key*—a key whose name corresponds to a particular file extension—identifies a file type. Its default value is an *application identifier*—a medium-length string used to identify the application capable of handling that data type. To retrieve information about a file association, an application searches the `HKCR` branch for a particular file association key. If it finds the key, it retrieves the application identifier. It then uses the application identifier to retrieve the *application identifier key*—the key whose subkeys contain information about how an application should handle its associated files.

For example, suppose the user double-clicks on a file with a .BMP extension in the Explorer window, and Explorer needs to know what application to launch to display it. The Explorer begins by searching for the `HKCR\.bmp` file association key and retrieving its default value, which is the application identifier `Paint.Picture`. It then searches for `HKCR\Paint.Picture`, the application identifier key. The value of one of its subkeys then provides the application path of the program (in this case, Microsoft Paint) that knows how to open and read the file. Using the *REGDUMP* program from Chapter 5, *Win95 Registry Access from Win16, DOS, and VxDs,*, here is what the `.bmp` and `Paint.Picture` entries look like in a typical registry:

```
HKEY_CLASSES_ROOT
  .bmp -> "Paint.Picture"
    ShellNew
      NullFile=""
  Paint.Picture -> "Bitmap Image"
    shell
      open
        command -> '"C:\PROGRA~1\ACCESS~1\MSPAINT.EXE" "%1"'
      print
        command -> '"C:\PROGRA~1\ACCESS~1\MSPAINT.EXE" /p "%1"'
```

```
printto
   command -> '"C:\PROGRA~1\ACCESS~1\MSPAINT.EXE" /pt "%1" "%2" "%3" "%4"'
DefaultIcon -> "C:\Progra~1\Access~1\MSPAINT.EXE,1"
Insertable -> ""
protocol
   StdFileEditing
      verb
         0 -> "&Edit"
      server -> "C:\Progra~1\Access~1\MSPAINT.EXE"
CLSID -> {Bitmap Image}
```

Although this indirection—the use of a file association key's value (such as `.bmp`) as a pointer to an application identifier key (such as `Paint.Picture`)—may seem awkward, it allows multiple file types to be handled by a common set of registry keys. Rather than storing identical information about multiple file types handled by your application to multiple registry keys, sometimes you can just create a single application identifier:

- If your application works with a single type of data file that can have more than one file extension. This is primarily a result of Win95's support for long file names: a file extension no longer is limited to three letters. For instance, HTML documents can be stored either as .HTM or .HTML files; if Microsoft Plus or the Microsoft Internet Explorer is installed, it assigns the application identifier label "`htmlfile`" to both file extensions. As a result, the potentially hazardous duplication of application information in the registry is minimized.

- Your application may be responsible for handling more than one file type. For instance, WinZip, a utility for creating, manipulating, and browsing compressed and archived files, works with six different file formats: .ARC, .ARJ, .LZH, .TAR, .Z, and .ZIP. The WinZip installation program registers each of these file types and assigns them a single application extension, WinZip. This means that, if the location of the WinZip program changes or information about the way it handles data files needs to be modified, these changes can be made in a single place in the registry rather than in six different places.

- You can change the handler for a particular type of file by changing a single value in the registry, rather than by adding or modifying a complete set of keys and values about the application that is to handle the file.

Because of this indirection, file associations can be handled by a *many-to-one relationship*; that is, more than one kind of file can be handled by a single application. It is important to recognize, though, that Win95's use of file associations does not readily support a *one-to-many relationship*; that is, multiple applications cannot handle a single file type. For instance, even though both WordPad and Microsoft Word for Windows are capable of handling .DOC files, only one of these applications can at any given time be designated as the "official" handler of .DOC files. Similarly, you must choose whether Netscape Navigator or Microsoft

Internet Explorer will at any given time handle HTML files. This means that, unless you're developing an application to work with some well known or well established file type, you should make sure that the file extensions used by your application are unique—i.e., that they don't duplicate the file extensions that are in conventional use (like .GIF or .JPG) or that are used by Windows (like .386 or .DRV) or by well known applications (like .WK4 or .DOC).

Launching Your Application

Typically, when a user double-clicks on a data file on the desktop or in an Explorer window, he or she expects to launch the application that created it, which in turn is expected to load the data file. Not surprisingly, the exact way in which Windows responds to a user double-click is defined by the Win95 registry.

When the user double-clicks on a file object in the Windows shell, the shell calls the *ShellExecute* function, passing it the name of the file on which the user has clicked. (The same thing happens when you use the Run option on the Start menu or run *START.EXE* from the Win95 command prompt.) The function then performs the following steps to open the document:

1. It searches HKCR to find a subkey whose name is the same as the file's extension. For instance, if the user clicks on a file named *INTERNET.TXT*, *ShellExecute* searches for a subkey named HKCR\.txt.

2. If the subkey is not present, *ShellExecute* reports that it is unable to find the file association (ordinarily it returns SE_ERR_NOASSOC) and terminates. Otherwise, *ShellExecute* checks whether a default value, the application identifier, has been assigned to the key. The default value of HKCR\.txt, for instance, is "txtfile".

3. If the key does have a default value, *ShellExecute* treats it as a label and looks for a key with that name in HKCR. In our example, *ShellExecute* searches for an application identifier key named HKCR\txtfile.

4. *ShellExecute* next looks for a subkey of the application identifier key named shell\open\command. If our example, *ShellExecute* searches for HKCR\ txtfile\shell\open\command.

5. Finally, *ShellExecute* retrieves the default value of the command subkey, which tells it how to handle the data file. Usually, this value consists of an optional path and filename, followed by a single parameter. For instance, the default value of HKCR\txtfile\shell\open\command is "notepad.exe %1". In this case, the single parameter is the name of the file on which the user clicked. So *ShellExecute* finally calls *WinExec* to launch Notepad, passing to it the filename of the file on which the user has double-clicked.

To make this clearer, here is how `.txt` and `txtfile` appear in a typical registry, as displayed by *REGDUMP* from Chapter 5:

```
HKEY_CLASSES_ROOT
  .txt -> "txtfile"
    Content Type="text/plain"
    ShellNew
      NullFile=""
  txtfile -> "Text Document"
    DefaultIcon -> "C:\WINDOWS\SYSTEM\shell32.dll,-152"
    shell
      open
        command -> "C:\WINDOWS\NOTEPAD.EXE %1"
      print
        command -> "C:\WINDOWS\NOTEPAD.EXE /p %1"
```

Typically, when the user double-clicks on a file, Windows launches its associated application, which opens and displays the file. This means, of course, that your application must be able to load a data file by handling the command-line string that Windows passes to it. But you can define that command-line string, as well as the way your application behaves when passed a file or a command-line string as a parameter, in any way that is appropriate for your application.

Actually, even if "open" is the default action taken by the Explorer when the user double-clicks on a file system object, its precise meaning is governed by the program itself, rather than by Windows. Win95 simply calls the *ShellExecute* function and passes it whatever parameters and command-line switches that are indicated in the `HKCR\<label>\shell\open\command` subkey. It is these parameters and switches, however the program chooses to interpret them, that determine the behavior of the program.

The operation of RegEdit, the Registry Editor, illustrates this. Ordinarily, if the user double-clicks on the RegEdit program icon, Win95 opens the Registry Editor window, which in turns displays the six top-level registry keys. But when the user double-clicks on a .REG file, Win95 retrieves the default value of `HKCR\.REG`, which is `regfile`. It then retrieves the following value from `HKCR\regfile\shell\open`:

```
regedit.exe %1
```

But as we saw in Chapter 2, when RegEdit is passed a command-line parameter when it is launched, it doesn't display the file or the registry: instead, it imports/merges the specified .REG file as a background process. This is a good example of how "open" is interpreted in an application-specific manner. Here is how this is represented in a typical registry, as displayed by *REGDUMP*:

```
HKEY_CLASSES_ROOT
  .reg -> "regfile"
  regfile -> "Registration Entries"
```

```
DefaultIcon -> "C:\WINDOWS\regedit.exe,1"
shell -> ""
  open -> "Mer&ge"
    command -> "regedit.exe %1"
  print -> ""
    command -> "C:\WINDOWS\NOTEPAD.EXE /p %1"
  edit -> "&Edit"
    command -> "C:\WINDOWS\NOTEPAD.EXE %1"
```

Earlier, we mentioned that, if *ShellExecute* is unable to find the extension of the file on which the user has double-clicked in the registry, the function returns an error message like SE_ERR_NOASSOC. This doesn't complete the shell's handling of a user double-click, though. The Explorer next retrieves the default value of HKCR\Unknown\shell\openas\command, which is *C:\WINDOWS\ rundll32.exe shell32.dll,OpenAs_RunDLL %1*, and passes it, along with the name of the file on which the user double-clicked, once more to *ShellExecute*. HKCR\ Unknown is used in handling user double-clicks when the file type doesn't have a shell\open\command subkey; it's what produces the Open With dialog.

The result is that, if you fail to register a file association and the user double-clicks on your unregistered file, Win95 launches the Open With dialog shown in Figure 8-1, which allows the user to select the application that the shell uses to open the file. Since this behavior, by leaving inexperienced users in particular free to use possibly inappropriate tools to modify files inadvertently, can have extremely undesirable consequences, it is important to instruct Windows how to handle user double-clicks.

Figure 8-1. The Open With dialog

Ordinarily, then, Windows executes the command string stored to the default value of an application identifier's shell\open\command subkey when the user clicks on an associated file. It is possible, though, to override this default behavior by assigning something other than a null value or the verb "open" to the application identifier's `shell` subkey. Consider the registry's handling of batch (.BAT) files as an example:

```
HKEY_CLASSES_ROOT
  .bat -> "batfile"
  batfile -> "MS-DOS Batch File"
    EditFlags=BIN (4 bytes) [4D0h]
    shell -> ""
      open -> ""
        EditFlags=BIN (4 bytes) [0]
        command -> '"%1" %*'
      print -> ""
        command -> "C:\WINDOWS\NOTEPAD.EXE /p %1"
      edit -> "&Edit"
        command -> "C:\WINDOWS\NOTEPAD.EXE %1"
    shellex
      PropertySheetHandlers
        {86F19A00-42A0-1069-A2E9-08002B30309D} -> ""
    DefaultIcon -> "C:\WINDOWS\SYSTEM\shell32.dll,-153"
```

The registry's `batfile` application identifier key defines three verbs for dealing with batch files:

- They can be opened (or executed), an action that is defined by the default value of the `HKCR\batfile\shell\open\command` key

- They can be edited, an action defined by the default value of the `HKCR\batfile\shell\edit\command` key

- They can be printed, an action defined by the default value of the `HKCR\batfile\shell\print\command` key

Now, if the string "edit" is stored as the default value of `HKCR\batfile\shell`, the Explorer retrieves the default value of the `HKCR\batfile\shell\edit\command` key when the user double-clicks on a batch file. Since its value is `C:\WINDOWS\NOTEPAD.EXE %1`, Windows doesn't execute the file; instead, it opens it for browsing or editing using Notepad.

Displaying Data File Icons

To create a well-behaved application for Win3x, you had to supply a single 32x32-pixel icon for your application that could be displayed in a Program Manager group window or on the desktop when your application was minimized. Generally, this involved creating an icon (.ICO) file and using the resource compiler to include it in your application. Each .ICO file, in any case, could contain a single 32x32 icon.

Preventing Your Application from Appearing in the "Open With" Dialog

You may prefer that your application not appear in the "Open With..." dialog that appears when the user double-clicks on an unknown file type. Since Win95 derives the names of the programs listed in the dialog from the registry, it's possible to do that. For the most part, Windows assembles the names of programs that can handle an unknown file type by enumerating the subkeys of HKCR, opening all subkeys named `<app identifier>\shell\open\command`, retrieving the key's default value, and extracting the filename.

This means that, to keep your program out of the dialog, you can simply name what would otherwise be the **open** subkey something other than "open." You can still make it define Windows' handling of a user double-click, though; just store its name to the default value of the shell subkey. And you can still have it read "Open" if you store the string "&Open" to the key's default value. The only thing that you lose by doing this is the automatic localization of the verb "open" if you develop your application to support another language.

For example, suppose that your application, *MYAPP.EXE*, reads garbage files that have a .GRB file extension (for garbage, of course). Ordinarily, you'd define this file association as shown by the following fragments from a .REG file:

```
[HKEY_CLASSES_ROOT\.GRB]
@="garbagefile"

[HKEY_CLASSES_ROOT\garbagefile]
@="Garbage Files"

[HKEY_CLASSES_ROOT\garbagefile\shell]
[HKEY_CLASSES_ROOT\garbagefile\shell\open]
[HKEY_CLASSES_ROOT\garbagefile\shell\open\command]
@="c:\\Program Files\\MyCompany\\MyApp.exe %1"
```

To keep your application from appearing in the "Open With..." dialog, you can define a "collect" verb instead of the open verb, make the default value of its subkey "&Open" so that open is displayed in context menus, and make the default value of the **shell** subkey "collect" so that collect, and not open, becomes the default behavior when the user double-clicks on a .GRB file. The **garbagefile** application identifier key and its subkeys then appear as follows:

```
[HKEY_CLASSES_ROOT\garbagefile]
@="Garbage Files"
[HKEY_CLASSES_ROOT\garbagefile\shell]
@="collect"
[HKEY_CLASSES_ROOT\garbagefile\shell\collect]
@="&Open"
[HKEY_CLASSES_ROOT\garbagefile\shell\collect\command]
@="c:\\windows\\notepad.exe %1"
```

Win95 presents the user with a more iconic interface than did previous versions of Windows. Unlike Win3x and the Win3x File Manager, which relied on a few graphical elements to supplement its basic emphasis on text to depict a file system, Win95 attempts to use a meaningful (at least in theory) icon to depict every object or file known to the system. And icons are displayed to represent particular objects in the computer system in a much larger number of cases:

- In an Explorer window in either its Large Icon or Small Icon view

- On the task bar, once an application is open

- On the desktop, to represent a link

- On the application window's or MDI window's caption bar, in place of the system menu bar

To accommodate this shift to a more graphical environment, Win95 requires, at a minimum, that you provide both a large (32x32) and a small (16x16) version of each icon. To support this, the meaning and format of the icon file have changed. A single icon resource (usually an .ICO file) can now contain multiple icons. Generally, these are a single set of icons, each of which contains essentially the same image at a different resolution. When Win95 needs a particular icon, it automatically attempts to extract an icon of the proper resolution from the icon resource. If your application uses particular kinds of data files, in addition to providing multiple versions of a single icon, you also should provide multiple icons, one to represent your application and one or more to represent each type of data file that it uses. Typically, if you use a resource compiler to include icons in your executable file, the icon resource that represents your application icon should be the first icon included in the resource file, followed by the data-specific icon resource or resources.

Information on the icon resource to display for an application's associated files is stored as the default value of an application identification key's `DefaultIcon` subkey. For example, the icon resource used to display bitmap (.BMP) files is indicated by the default value of the `HKCR\Paint.Picture\DefaultIcon` key. The default value of the `DefaultIcon` subkey can contain any one of four kinds of string values:

- The path and filename of any valid standalone image file that Win95 is capable of depicting as an icon. This includes any of the file types listed in Table 8-3. So if you haven't compiled the necessary icon resources into your executable file, you can still use any of several different kinds of external image files to supply icons for your application and its data files. In cases where the file format does not support multiple resolutions of the same image (e.g., .SCR files) or where only a single image is included in the file (e.g., .ICO files for Win3x), though, the result may not be particularly attractive, since Win95 will automatically scale any image to reduce it to the necessary size.

Table 8-3. Valid icon file formats

File Extension	Description	Remarks
.ICO	An icon file	
.BMP	A Windows bitmap file	Not supported by Win3x
.RLE	A Windows run-length encoded bitmap	Not supported by Win3x
.CUR	A cursor file	Not supported by Win3x
.ANI	An animated cursor file	Not supported by Win3x
.SCR	A screen saver file	Not supported by Win3x

- The path and filename of an executable file (.EXE) or a dynamic link library (.DLL) containing an icon, along with the icon resource's position in the file (i.e., its offset from zero). This is the most common form of icon definition used in the Win95 registry. For instance, the default value of HKCR\comfile\DefaultIcon, which defines the icon resource to display for a .COM file, is:

```
C:\WINDOWS\SYSTEM\shell32.dll,2
```

which is the icon resource stored in the third ordinal position of *SHELL32.DLL*. If multiple icons are present, Win95 will automatically extract the one whose resolution is nearest to that needed. If an ordinal position is not specified, the Explorer will use the first icon (i.e., the icon at ordinal position zero) in the file.

- The path and filename of an executable file (.EXE) or a dynamic link library (.DLL) containing an icon resource, along with the icon resource's resource identifier preceded by a minus sign. (The resource ID is generated at the time an icon resource is stored in a resource file.) Once again, if the icon resource contains multiple icons, Win95 automatically extracts the one whose resolution is closest to that needed. The Win95 registry contains the following value entry, for example, that defines the icon resource used to represent dynamic link libraries:

```
C:\WINDOWS\SYSTEM\shell32.dll,-154
```

This indicates that Windows should use the icon resource in *SHELL32.DLL* whose resource ID is 154. You can find resource IDs with a tool such as Microsoft Developer Studio, the integrated development environment that ships with a number of Microsoft language products, including Microsoft Visual C++.*

- The string %1, which indicates that the application relies on an icon handler to supply a different icon for each instance of that file type. %1 indicates that the filename is passed as a parameter to the icon handler.

An icon handler is a particular kind of shell extension—that is, a special-purpose registered OLE in-process server that provides services to the Windows shell. (For information on registering OLE components in the registry, see "Registering OLE Components" later in this chapter.) When the Explorer encounters the string %1 as the default value of the `DefaultIcon` key, it looks for the icon handler's class ID (CLSID), which should be stored as the default value of the `shellex\Icon-Handler` subkey of the application identifier key. With a valid class ID, the Explorer can then identify the OLE in-process server by looking up its subkey in the `HKCR\CLSID` key. However, if an `IconHandler` subkey is absent, the Windows shell uses the default icon handler contained in *SHELL32.DLL*. The default icon handler assumes that one or more resources that can be represented as icons are contained in the file whose name is passed to it as a parameter, and simply displays an appropriate image from the first icon resource that it can find in the file.

.EXE files are the best example of this. Ordinarily, Windows assigns icons on the basis of file extension; all files of a particular type share an icon. If this were how icons for .EXE files were assigned, though, all executable files would display the same icon! Instead, each Windows application is expected to have its own distinctive icon. So rather than identifying an icon resource to be used for all .EXE files, the default value of `HKCR\exefile\DefaultIcon`, the key that determines a file's default icon, is "%1". Since the `exefile` application identifier key lacks an `IconHandler` subkey, the Windows shell's default icon handler assigns the first icon resource that it finds in an .EXE file as its icon. Along with executable files, the Windows shell ordinarily uses its default icon handler to display icons on a per-instance basis for icon (.ICO), cursor (.CUR), and animated cursor (.ANI) files as well. And in fact, any of the file types listed earlier in Table 8-3 can have their icons displayed on a per-instance basis by changing the value of their application identifier's `DefaultIcon` subkey to "%1".

This in fact is how the fairly well-known registry "trick" of displaying the image in a bitmap (.BMP) file as its own icon works: you simply change the value from "C:\Progra~1\Access~1\MSPAINT.EXE,1" to "%1". Doing an AltaVista search on the

---

* To view a .DLL or .EXE's resources, select the Open option from the File menu, select "Executable Files" in the Files of Type drop-down list box, and select "Resources" in the Open As drop-down list box. You can then select the file whose resources you'd like to examine.

World Wide Web for the string "Paint.Picture" turned up literally dozens of sites with this Win95 trick. One site (*http://kaos.deepcove.com/computerist/regedit-macros.html*) that presents a whole collection of .REG files, cleverly describes these as "REGEDIT macros"; for example:

```
bitmap_thumbnails.reg
    REGEDIT4
    [HKEY_CLASSES_ROOT\Paint.Picture\DefaultIcon]
    @="%1"
```

If you fail to register the file types of your data files, or if you register them but fail to add a `DefaultIcon` subkey to the application identifier key, Win95 automatically uses the icon shown in Figure 8-2, which is the first icon found in *SHELL32.DLL*, to represent the file.

Figure 8-2. The default Windows icon

We've noted that the registry supports a one-to-many relationship between an application and data files. That means, if your application uses multiple data file types and you want to define a distinct set of icons for each of them, you must assign a separate application identifier, and include a separate application identifier key and `DefaultIcon` subkey, for each file type to which you'd like to assign an icon. Technically, this is mandated by the requirements for the Win95 logo. It also negates many of the advantages of the one-to-many relationship used by the registry to handle file associations.

Context Menus

An interesting end-user feature of Win95 is its support for context menus—on menus whose options are unique to the kind of file that the user selects. When the user selects a particular object in the Explorer window or an icon on the desktop and clicks the right mouse button, Win95 displays a pop-up menu offering options that are tailored to that type of object. Support for context menus is a feature that you can add to your application almost "for free," since it's handled by the registry and requires little or no coding.

Figure 8-3 shows a more or less typical context-sensitive menu that is displayed when the user selects a file (in this case, a text file named *C:\WINDOWS\ TIPS.TXT*) and clicks the right mouse button. If you compare this context menu with the one that appears when you click the right mouse button on other files or objects in the Explorer window, you'll find that, although the context menu remains broadly similar, the options available above the first menu separator are customized to reflect the kind of file selected.

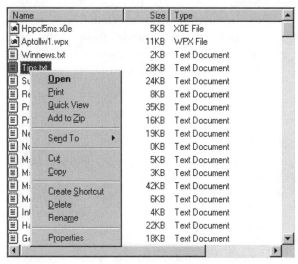

Figure 8-3. A context-sensitive menu

Windows assembles its context menus from three different sources, in the following order:

- *Static menu items*, which are defined in the registry. In Figure 8-3, for example, the Open, Print, and Quick View menu options are all static items. These items are extensible by the end-user; by selecting the Options option from the Explorer's View menu, an end-user can access a dialog that allows him or her to customize, modify, or add to these. If you want to prevent users from doing this, see the section "Preventing the User from Changing File Association Information" later in this chapter.

- *Dynamic menu items*, which are provided by a context menu handler. In Figure 8-3, the Add to Zip option is a dynamic menu item.

- *Program-defined menu items*, which reside as resources within the Explorer itself and are not subject to modification. In Figure 8-3, for instance, all menu items after the first menu separator are program-defined.

When Windows is about to display a context menu, it first looks for any *static menu items*, which are defined entirely based on file associations. To do this, it begins by looking for subkeys of the HKCR*\shell key; each subkey defines a menu item that is to be displayed for every file regardless of extension. (Ordinarily, the registry includes no definitions of menu items in this key, though.) Next, it retrieves a particular file's application identifier, and then searches the application identifier's shell subkey for subkeys that indicate what items are to be represented on the menu. For instance, in building the context menu for *TIPS.TXT*, the file that's highlighted in Figure 8-3, it opens HKCR\txtfile\shell and finds two subkeys: open and print.

The subkeys of the `shell` key are known as *verbs*; that is, each subkey defines an action that is to be carried out when the menu item is selected. Win95 recognizes several *canonical verbs*; that is, Windows "understands" these verbs, and automatically adds a localized option to the context menu. The canonical verbs supported by Win95, as well as their English language descriptions and their meanings, are shown in Table 8-4.

Table 8-4. Canonical verbs supported by Win95

Verb	Menu Description	Explanation
explore	Explore	Opens an object to display its component objects in an Explorer window
find	Find...	Opens the Find dialog, allowing the user to search for files or objects
open	Open	Executes a program, or launches an associated application to load a data file
openas	Open With...	Opens the Open With dialog, allowing the user to select an application to handle the selected file
print	Print	Prints the file
printto		Prints the file; `printto` is used for drag-and-drop operations, and is not used in building context menus

Canonical verbs have two major advantages: first, when Windows encounters them it automatically assigns the appropriate localized text string to a menu item. Second, Windows also automatically assigns an *access key* (a key that, if it is pressed when the menu is open, automatically selects that item) to the menu item. In some cases, however, either this default description or the default access key may be inappropriate. In this case, it is possible to change either one by assigning a string as the default value of the verb key. For example, HKCR\regfile\shell\open, which defines one of the menu options for .REG files, contains the default value "Mer&ge," which explains why Merge appears as the first option when you click the right mouse button on a .REG file, and why its access key is "g."

In addition to these canonical verbs, *any* verb can define a context menu item. In this case, though, the default value of the key defining the verb must contain the string that is to appear on the context menu. If a string is not supplied, Windows will use the verb itself for the text of the menu item, and will make its first character the item's access key. Win95 contains several examples of these non-canonical verbs, as shown in Table 8-5. Note that, if the menu option is to include an access key, it should be preceded by the ampersand (&) character.

Besides establishing the presence of a particular context menu item and defining its text, Windows needs to do something if that menu item is selected: it takes the

Table 8-5. Non-canonical verbs used in a typical Win95 registry

Verb	Menu Description	Explanation
AutoRun	Auto&Play	Automatically executes an *AUTORUN.INF* file
config	C&onfigure	Configures a screen saver
connect	&Connect	Opens a communications session using a file's terminal settings
cplopen	Open with Control Panel	Opens a Control Panel (.CPL) file
edit	&Edit	Opens a file for editing
install	&Install	Runs an installation routine using .INF file settings
play	&Play	Uses a multimedia software program to play a Sound file or an audio CD
show	S&how	Executes a PowerPoint presentation file

string that is stored as the default value of the verb's `command` subkey, and executes it.

Once Windows retrieves all of the available static menu items, it retrieves *dynamic menu items*. These are menu items that are defined by a *context menu handler*, which is a special OLE in-process server that is responsible for adding items to the context menu of particular kinds of files. In Figure 8-3, for example, "Add to Zip" is a menu item added by a context menu handler. Like static menu items, dynamic ones are based on the type of object for which a context menu is being displayed. Unlike static menus, though, dynamic menus can be displayed based on conditional logic. For instance, the context menu of drives and directories might have a Share menu item that is displayed only for drives and directories on networked computers; or all files might have a Backup menu item that appears only for files whose archive flags are set, indicating that they have been modified since the last backup.

Context menu handlers are defined by a particular application identifier's `shellex\ContextMenuHandlers` key; it is possible to use multiple context menu handlers to create a single context menu. For each context menu handler, there should be an arbitrarily named subkey whose default value is the class ID of the dynamic link library that contains the context menu handler, or whose name corresponds to the class ID of the context menu handler. The name and location of this DLL can then be determined by looking up its class ID in the `HKCR\CLSID` subkey and retrieving its default value from the class ID key's `InProcServer32` subkey.

For instance, if you select a directory in an Explorer window and open its context menu, a Sharing... option is included on the menu. Its appears because a context menu handler is defined by the default value of the `HKCR\Folder\shellex\` `ContextMenuHandlers\SharingMenu` subkey.

If the object on which the user has clicked the right mouse button is a file, Windows begins its search for context menu handlers by looking at the subkeys of `HKCR\*\shellex\ContextMenuHandlers`. If you've installed the Briefcase application, for example, you'll find that its generalized context menu handler is defined by the `HKCR\*\shellex\ContextMenuHandlers\BriefcaseMenu` key. The Windows shell then looks for subkeys of the application identifier's `shellex\ContextMenuHandler` key, if any are present. Incidentally, `HKCR\*` is sort of a global file association key that applies to all files regardless of their extension. It's used in particular to define shell extensions— context menu handlers and property sheet handlers—which typically apply to a group of files or to certain files based on some conditional logic.

Once it has called any context menu handlers defined for a particular file type, the Windows shell then proceeds to add those menu items defined by its internal resources.

The New Submenu

Along with using the registry so that users can manipulate existing data files created by your application, you can use the registry to allow users to easily create new data files. When the user opens the Explorer's File menu, right-clicks within an Explorer pane without selecting a file or other object, or right-clicks anywhere on the desktop, Windows opens a menu that contains a New option. Selecting it in turn opens a submenu that allows the user to create a variety of objects, as illustrated in Figure 8-4. If you'd like, you can use the registry to add your data file to the options listed below the menu separator.

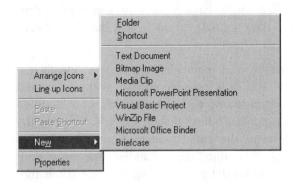

Figure 8-4. The New submenu

When the user selects the New menu item, Windows scans the subkeys of the file association keys in `HKCR` for a `ShellNew` key to identify file types to be listed on the New submenu. Ordinarily, `ShellNew` is a direct subkey of the file association key (e.g., `HKCR\.bmp\ShellNew`). The file association key, rather than the application identifier key, is a sensible place to locate the `ShellNew` subkey, since a single application frequently can handle multiple file types.

By itself, the presence of the `ShellNew` subkey does not guarantee that the menu item will be displayed. Two pieces of information are required:

- *The text of the menu item.* To describe the new file, Windows uses the text stored as the default value of the application identifier key. To retrieve it, the default value of the file association key must include an accurate application identifier. For example, the default value of the `HKCR\.bmp` key is "Paint.Picture", and the default value of `HKCR\Paint.Picture` is "Bitmap Image". Therefore, Windows uses "Bitmap Image" as the menu item's text.

- *How to create the file.* Windows requires that the `ShellNew` key contain a value entry that indicates how the file should be created; if there is none, the option will not appear on the New submenu. The entry's value name must be one of the four listed in Table 8-6, which also shows the kind of data that Windows expects to find for each value name.

Table 8-6. Value names for the ShellNew key

Value Name	Data Type	Value	Description
NullFile	REG_SZ	""	Creates an empty, zero-length file
Data	REG_BIN	<< binary value >>	Creates a file with the byte pattern specified by << *binary value* >>
FileName	REG_SZ	<< filename >>	Copies << *filename* >> to create the file
Command	REG_SZ	<< command >>	Executes a command that creates the file

Two of these value entries require additional explanation:

- The `FileName` entry can include the complete path and name of a file. More common, however, is to simply specify the filename. In that case, Windows will look for the file in the directory indicated by the value of the `Templates` entry in `HKCU\Software\Microsoft\Windows\CurrentVersion\Explorer\Shell Folders`; on most machines, its value is *C:\WINDOWS\SHELLNEW*. If the file does not exist or if Windows is unable to locate it, Windows will still display the menu item, but it will not be able to create the file if the user selects the menu item.

- The string stored to the `Command` value entry can include any valid command that creates a file. The following, for instance, is the value of the `Command` entry of the `HKCR\.lnk\ShellNew` key, which is executed when you select the Shortcut option from the New submenu:

```
C:\WINDOWS\rundll32.exe AppWiz.Cpl,NewLinkHere %1
```

In this case, Windows uses *RUNDLL32.EXE* to call the *NewLinkHere* function in the AppWiz Control Panel applet (a Control Panel applet, or .CPL file, is just a special form of dynamic link library), passing to it the path and name of the file (represented by the %1 parameter). *RUNDLL32.EXE*, incidentally, is a small program which uses Windows run-time dynamic linking to do string invocation, more or less like this:

```
int rundll32(char *arg1, char *arg2, char *arg3)
{
    HANDLE mod = LoadLibrary(arg1);
    int (*func)(char *) = GetProcAddress(mod, arg2);
    int retval = (*func)(arg3);
    FreeLibrary(mod);
    return retval;
}
main(int argc, char *argv[])
{
    return rundll32(argv[1], argv[2], argv[3]);
}
```

Controlling What the User Sees

For each file system object, Win95 displays, in addition to its icon, a variable amount of textual information, depending on the context in which the file is displayed. For instance, a file displayed on the desktop or in an Explorer window in its Large Icons, Small Icons, and List views includes a filename. It also includes a document type in the Explorer's Details view and in the File Types property sheet of the Options dialog shown in Figure 8-5. When you register a file association, you should also provide a user-friendly description of your data file format, and define whether your data file's file extension is displayed or not.

In determining what label is to describe a particular file type, the Explorer simply uses the *application identifier label*, which is the default value of a particular file extension's application identifier key. For example, an Excel spreadsheet (.XLS) file is described as a "Microsoft Excel Worksheet." That's because the default value of the file association key HKCR\.xls is Excel.Sheet.5, and the default value of the application identifier key HKCR\Excel.Sheet.5 is the string "Microsoft Excel Worksheet." The application identifier label can be up to 40 characters long.

If you fail to register a file association, or if you register a file association but fail to include an application identifier label, the Explorer in Details view simply displays a string that includes the file extension along with the text "File." *DRVS-PACE.BIN*, for instance, is described as a "BIN File."

Despite their significance in defining Windows' behavior, Win95 aims at hiding file extensions from the user to the greatest degree possible. The Win95 logo

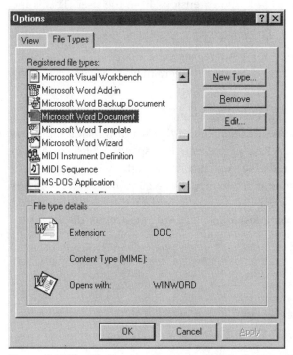

Figure 8-5. The File Types property sheet of the Options dialog

requirements also "strongly recommend" that the file extension be hidden. In its default configuration, the Explorer displays file extensions only for unregistered file types, although it provides an option that allows the user to decide whether he or she would like to have the extensions of registered files displayed. So in most cases, whether or not the Explorer displays file extensions is a detail that the Explorer itself handles automatically.

"Levels" of File Associations

If your application uses one or more distinct file types, it's not necessary to provide each of them with an icon, a description, and one or more shell verbs. Instead, you should differentiate between files based on how they're used in your application. Basic data or document files that are accessible to the user should be assigned an icon, a description, and a set of shell verbs; above all, it's important to support the "open" verb, so that the application is launched when the user double-clicks on one of its files. Temporary files, and permanent files that aren't intended to be accessed by the user, should be assigned an icon and a description, but not shell verbs.

It is not always desirable, though, to hide file extensions from the user. This is the case, for instance, if your application automatically generates multiple files, all with the same root filename but with different extensions. Particularly if you've defined only a single icon resource for your registered file types, this can easily confuse a user, who may respond by deleting the seemingly duplicate files or by reporting a bug in Win95.

You can determine the way that Win95 handles your file extensions by adding a single value entry to the application identifier key. If the Windows shell finds that a value entry named `AlwaysShowExt` is present, it displays a file's extension even if the display of registered file extensions is otherwise suppressed. Conversely, if the shell finds a value entry named `NeverShowExt`, it suppresses the display of a file's extension, even if it is configured to display all registered file extensions. Here are some examples from a typical registry, as displayed by *REGDUMP*:

```
lnkfile -> "Shortcut"
  IsShortcut=""
  NeverShowExt=""

piffile -> "Shortcut to MS-DOS Program"
  IsShortcut=""
  NeverShowExt=""

Directory -> "File Folder"
  AlwaysShowExt=""
```

`AlwaysShowExt` and `NeverShowExt` are examples of *registry flags*: when the Explorer reads these value entries, it does not care what value has been assigned to them. (In most cases, these entries are stored as `REG_SZ` values with a null string.) Instead, it is their presence or absence, rather than their value, that defines how the Explorer should behave. In the example just shown, `IsShortcut` is another registry flag. Another typical one is `URL Protocol`; for details on its use, see the discussion of URL processing later in this chapter.

Preventing the User from Changing File Association Information

Unfortunately, once you've gone to the trouble of associating your application with one or more data files, of defining icons for your data files, or of building a context menu, any user can change that basic information, possibly in the process even partially or wholly crippling your application. This is surprisingly easy to do. A great thing about Win95 is that it is highly reconfigurable by end-users; a potential big problem with Win95 is that it is highly reconfigurable by end-users. In this case, when the user selects the Options item from the View menu of the Explorer or any other window that displays computer system objects in a listview control, the Windows shell opens the Options dialog; its File Types property sheet, which displays basic file association information, was shown earlier in Figure 8-5. The Remove button allows the user to completely delete a file association. In addition, if the user clicks the Edit button, the Windows shell opens the Edit File Type dialog shown in Figure 8-6, which gives the user free reign to change each item of information that you've used to define a file association. Using this dialog, it is possible to change a data file's icon, its MIME category (see the discussion of MIME later in this chapter), or the verbs it supports and the commands invoked by those verbs.

By adding an `EditFlags` value entry to your application identifier key, you can prevent users from making changes to your application's file association information through the Options dialog. (Changes can, of course, still be made by editing the registry directly with RegEdit.) `EditFlags` is a four-byte `REG_BINARY` value, each bit of which, if enabled, turns off some editing feature in the options dialog. Table 8-7 shows the settings controlled by each of these bits.

Table 8-7. Individual flags in the EditFlags value entry

Byte	Bit	If Bit Is Enabled...
0	0	Does not display any of that file type's association information in the File Types property sheet; prevents the user from changing or removing *any* file association information
	1	Disables the Content Type (MIME) drop-down list box on the Edit File Type dialog; prevents the user from changing MIME information
	2	Reserved
	3	Disables the Edit button on the File Types property sheet; prevents the user from editing any file association information
	4	Disables the Remove button on the File Types property sheet; prevents the user from deleting the file association
	5	Disables the New button on the Edit File Type dialog; prevents the user from adding a new verb
	6	Disables the Edit button on the Edit File Type dialog; prevents the user from editing information about an existing verb
	7	Disables the Remove button on the Edit File Type dialog; prevents the user from removing a verb
1	0	Disables the Description of Type text box on the Edit FileType dialog
	1	Disables the Change Icon button on the Edit File Type dialog
	2	Disables the Set Default button on the Edit File Type dialog
	3-7	Reserved
2	0	Suppresses the Open/Save dialog so that remote files selected using Microsoft Internet Explorer are always opened
	1-7	Reserved
3	0-7	Reserved

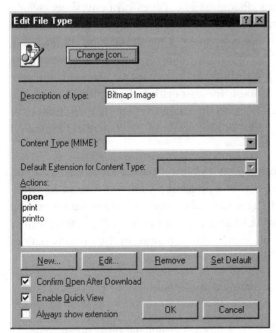

Figure 8-6. The Edit File Type dialog

More than one flag can be set at a single type by using the bitwise OR operator. In some cases, setting multiple flags is unnecessary. For instance, the value

```
EditFlags=hex:01,00,00,00
```

renders every other flag superfluous, since it prevents the file type from appearing in the Options dialog in the first place; similarly, disabling the Edit button on the File Types property sheet (that is, setting bit 3 of byte 0) eliminates the need to set bits 1 and 5 through 7 of byte 0 and bits 0 through 2 of byte 2.

Once you know what the individual bits in the **EditFlags** value entry are used for, it's quite easy to decide on how you'd like to partially protect your file association information and to add a routine to your installation procedure that implements that level of protection. For example, Example 8-7 contains the C code for a function named *NoEditAssn*, which prevents information on a file type from appearing in the Options dialog. The function takes a single parameter, a pointer to a string that contains the file extension, and returns a Boolean that indicates whether or not the function succeeded. Its Visual Basic equivalent is shown in Example 8-8.

Example 8-7. Disabling Explorer editing of file associations, using C

```
#include <windows.h>

BOOL NoEditAssn(LPSTR szFileType)
```

Example 8-7. Disabling Explorer editing of file associations, using C

```
{
BOOL fFlagWritten ;
HKEY hKey ;
DWORD lenAppId, dwFlag = 1 ;       // Disable all editing
char szAppId[80] ;

if (RegOpenKey(HKEY_CLASSES_ROOT, szFileType, &hKey) == ERROR_SUCCESS )
    {
    // Get application identifier
    lenAppId = sizeof(szAppId) ;
    RegQueryValueEx(hKey, "", NULL, NULL, szAppId, &lenAppId) ;
    RegCloseKey(hKey) ;
    // Open applicaton identifier key
    if (RegOpenKey(HKEY_CLASSES_ROOT, szAppId, &hKey) ==
                    ERROR_SUCCESS)
        {
        if (RegSetValueEx(hKey, "EditFlags", 0, REG_BINARY, &dwFlag,
                        sizeof(dwFlag)) == ERROR_SUCCESS)
            fFlagWritten = TRUE ;
        RegCloseKey(hKey) ;
        }
    }
return (fFlagWritten) ;
}
```

Example 8-8. Disabling Explorer editing of file associations, using VB

```
Public Function NoEditAssn(strFileType As String) As Boolean

Dim hKey As Long, lngLenAppId As Long, lngFlag As Long
Dim strAppId As String
Dim blnSuccess As Boolean

lngFlag = 1

' Open registry key
If RegOpenKey(HKEY_CLASSES_ROOT, strFileType, hKey) = ERROR_SUCCESS Then
   ' Retrieve application identifier
   lngLenAppId = 80
   strAppId = String(lngLenAppId, 0)
   Call RegQueryValueEx(hKey, "", 0, 0, ByVal strAppId, lngLenAppId)
   strAppId = Left(strAppId, lngLenAppId - 1)
   Call RegCloseKey(hKey)
   ' Open application identifier key
   If RegOpenKey(HKEY_CLASSES_ROOT, strAppId, hKey) = ERROR_SUCCESS Then
      If RegSetValueEx(hKey, "EditFlags", 0, REG_BINARY, lngFlag, _
                       Len(lngFlag)) = ERROR_SUCCESS Then _
         blnSuccess = True
      RegCloseKey (hKey)
   End If
End If
```

Example 8-8. Disabling Explorer editing of file associations, using VB (continued)

```
NoEditAssn = blnSuccess

End Function
```

MIME

Most Internet applications can handle one or at most several kinds of files in their data streams. Most email applications, for instance, allow you to compose and in turn will display only plain ASCII text. Although you can send any possible kind of file to a recipient, the mailer itself is able to display only those files that consist of text. Similarly, although Web browsers are capable of displaying a wider range of file types, including HTML (or hypertext markup language, which creates ASCII files with embedded tags), plain ASCII text, .GIF, and .XBM files, they are unable to display the full range of file types that are encountered on the Web or in the other Internet services supported by the Web. To allow the user to view or otherwise manipulate unsupported file types, Internet applications typically rely on helper applications, or external browsers.

For this system to work, Internet applications need some means of identifying a file type and determining which helper application is to handle it. For this purpose, the MIME (Multipurpose Internet Mail Extensions) standard was developed (see *http://ds.internic.net/rfc/rfc1521.txt*). MIME works very much like the traditional file associations under Windows: MIME uses a content type that consists of a major type and a subtype. Some content types, for instance, are:

- `text/plain`. Text is the major type, and plain is the subtype. This indicates a normal ASCII file.

- `image/jpeg`, which indicates a JPEG graphics image.

- `video/mpeg`, which represents an MPEG video file.

- `application/x-zip-compressed`, which indicates a compressed UNIX ZIP file and, in some cases, a compressed MS-DOS file using the PKZIP format.

Each file's content type is embedded in a header that is sent when the file is transmitted. The client receiving the file then looks up its content type to determine which helper application to launch and pass the filename to. The major practical difference between MIME and file associations is that the latter requires that a file extension reflect the file's type, whereas the former, by embedding the content type in the header, imposes no restrictions on a filename. This is particularly important in a multiplatform environment like the Internet, where filenaming conventions do not follow the Windows model.

Unlike Internet software for Win31, which was able to recognize file types based solely on their extension, Win95 offers MIME support to Internet applications. It is able to do this, of course, because of the enormously expanded capability of the registry under Win95 in comparison with Win31.

By default, the Windows registry contains no MIME information. Typically, MIME information is entered into the registry on systems that allow Internet access by the installation program of a MIME-enabled Internet software application that uses the registry, such as Microsoft Exchange or Microsoft Internet Explorer. Notably (since it commands about 85% of the Web-browser market), Netscape Navigator does not use Microsoft's MIME registry settings. Instead, it uses `HKEY_CURRENT_USER\Software\Netscape\Netscape Navigator\Viewers`, which contains values such as `"application/x-gocserve"="C:\\cis\\Gocserve.exe"`.

Regardless of whether the Internet application is sending or receiving a file, MIME is actually integrated into Win95's system of file associations. We'll see how this works for incoming files first, and then examine how MIME content types are handled for outgoing files.

MIME Content Types as System-Level Information

A number of Internet applications don't use the registry to support MIME content types. It is also possible to store information on MIME content types in an application's subkeys (as just noted, `HKEY_CURRENT_USER\Software\Netscape\Netscape Navigator\Viewers` is the perfect example). However, if you intend to implement MIME in your Internet applications, we recommend using this basic scheme established by Microsoft. This allows all MIME-enabled applications to share the same set of information on helper applications, and saves the user from having to configure and reconfigure each Internet application individually.

Content Types of Incoming Files

To handle a particular incoming file type correctly, an email program or a Web browser that supports MIME ultimately depends on its ability to handle a MIME type as a standard Windows file type, even if that file's extension does not conform to the standard Windows file type. It does this, basically, by converting the MIME content type into a recognized file extension.

MIME file types for incoming files are defined in the registry by *content type keys*, which are subkeys of `HKCR\MIME\Database\Content Type`. The name of each subkey corresponds to a MIME type. Table 8-8, for instance, shows a representative sampling of MIME content types. Each content type key has a `REG_SZ` entry named `Extension` whose value is a file extension. In other words, this system allows the Internet application to ignore an incoming file's extension, but still to treat it as a file of a particular type defined by the file association keys in the Win95 registry. Once the MIME content type is converted to a standard Windows file extension, the file's helper application can be identified by retrieving the default value of the file association key, then using its value to look up the default value of the application identifier's `shell\open\command` subkey.

Table 8-8. Some MIME content types defined in the Win95 registry

MIME Type (Subkey Name)	Extension value entry
`application/mac-binhex40`	.hqx
`application/postscript`	.ps
`application/x-zip-compressed`	.zip
`audio/wav`	.wav
`image/gif`	.gif
`image/jpeg`	.jpeg
`image/tiff`	.tiff
`text/html`	.html
`text/plain`	.txt
`video/mpeg`	.mpeg
`video/quicktime`	.qt

Obviously, if an Internet application offers native support for a particular content type such as HTML or GIF, there's no need to access the registry at all to find a helper application. When you do look in the registry to find a helper application, though, it's also possible that you won't be able to find one. This is most likely to happen in two cases:

- When a MIME content type is not registered. This can happen whenever a non-standard MIME type is used to describe a file.

- When no helper application is defined for a particular file type. This is in fact very common. For instance, in a registry whose MIME information is organized as shown in Table 8-8, if the user attempts to open a QuickTime file but no QuickTime viewer is available on his or her system, `HKCR\.qt` lacks a default value, indicating that no helper application has been assigned to that file type.

Example 8-9, generated by *RegSpy95*, shows how Microsoft Internet Explorer 2.0 uses the Win95 registry when information on a helper application has not been

---

Installation and MIME Content Types

Since the registry does not automatically contain MIME information, the installation program for your Internet application should be prepared to create it. If any of the standard MIME content types aren't registered, it should also create keys for them, create an `Extensions` value entry, and assign it a file extension. If this file extension is not registered in HKCR, your application should also create its file association key, and add a `Content Type` value entry whose REG_SZ value is the MIME content type. However, if your installation program is unable to identify a helper application for that content type, you should not assign a default value to the file association key.

---

assigned to the default value of the file association key that corresponds to a MIME content type. To identify a helper application, Microsoft Internet Explorer performs the following steps:

- Retrieves a file extension from the content type's `Extension` entry, uses its value to open a file association key, and attempts to retrieve the file association key's default value. In this case, the call to the *RegQueryValueEx* function shows that the default value is unassigned, indicating that no helper application is available.

- In lines 7 through 9, opens the file association key that corresponds to the incoming file's file association and retrieves its default value, which is unassigned. This appears to simply duplicate the previous three registry accesses. But Internet Explorer opened HKCR\\.hqx initially based on the content type of the incoming file, and opened the same key the second time based on its file extension. We can see that the intent of the registry accesses are different, even if the keys accessed are the same, by examining the following fragment from *RegSpy95*, which shows how the Internet Explorer accesses the registry when it is unable to find a particular MIME content type, in this case "application/zip", which a Web server assigned to a compressed MS-DOS .ZIP file:

```
_RegOpenKey        Iexplore  HKCR       0042ED40   NOFILE
                   'MIME\Database\Content Type\application/zip'
_RegOpenKey        Iexplore  HKCR       C33F7DD0          '.zip'
_RegQueryValueEx   Iexplore  C33F7DD0   SZ   7      ''     'WinZip'
_RegCloseKey       Iexplore  C33F7DD0
```

- Once again opens the content type key to determine if the file is encoded. The `Encoding` value entry is typically present for ASCII files to indicate whether they are plain text (`Encoding` is a REG_BIN entry whose value is 7) or make use of the high bit (`Encoding` is a REG_BIN entry whose value is 8).

- Once again opens the file association key, this time to check for a `Content Type` value entry. Internet Explorer then uses the content type to open the content type key, extract the value of its `Extension` entry, open the corresponding file association key, and extract its default value. Once again, much of this duplicates previous registry accesses. But once again, a definite intent underlines this duplication: the `Content Type` value entry, as we'll see shortly, reflects the MIME content type of *outgoing* files that have a particular file extension. In this case, the two content types are identical (Internet Explorer did not do a string comparison to avoid duplicate registry accesses), although they needn't be the same.

Example 8-9. RegSpy95 shows Internet Explorer's search for a helper application

```
_RegOpenKey            Iexplore  HKCR       C33F8628
                       'MIME\Database\Content Type\application/mac-binhex40'
_RegQueryValueEx       Iexplore  C33F8628   SZ    5    'Extension'  '.hqx'
_RegCloseKey           Iexplore  C33F8628
_RegOpenKey            Iexplore  HKCR       C33F8628            '.hqx'
_RegQueryValueEx       Iexplore  C33F8628   SZ    1              ''    ''
_RegCloseKey           Iexplore  C33F8628
_RegOpenKey            Iexplore  HKCR       C33F8628            '.hqx'
_RegQueryValueEx       Iexplore  C33F8628   SZ    1              ''    ''
_RegCloseKey           Iexplore  C33F8628
_RegOpenKey            Iexplore  HKCR       C33F8628
                       'MIME\Database\Content Type\application/mac-binhex40'
_RegQueryValueEx       Iexplore  C33F8628   0     NOFILE   'Encoding'  ''
_RegCloseKey           Iexplore  C33F8628
_RegOpenKey            Iexplore  HKCR       C33F8628            '.hqx'
_RegQueryValueEx       Iexplore  C33F8628   SZ    25
                       'Content Type'  'application/mac-binhex40'
_RegCloseKey           Iexplore  C33F8628
_RegOpenKey            Iexplore  HKCR       C33F8628
                       'MIME\Database\Content Type\application/mac-binhex40'
_RegQueryValueEx       Iexplore  C33F8628   SZ    5    'Extension'  '.hqx'
_RegCloseKey           Iexplore  C33F8628
_RegOpenKey            Iexplore  HKCR       C33F8628            '.hqx'
_RegQueryValueEx       Iexplore  C33F8628   SZ    1              ''    ''
_RegCloseKey           Iexplore  C33F8628
```

At this point, when its admirable persistence in attempting to locate a helper application fails, Internet Explorer displays the Unknown File Type dialog shown in Figure 8-7, the equivalent of the Explorer's Open With... dialog, and allows the user either to download the file (a standard option that requires no helper application) or to select an application that can handle it.

Content Types of Outgoing Files

`HKCR\MIME\Database\Content Type` is used primarily to define the MIME types of incoming files. Web servers and MIME-enabled mail applications in partic-

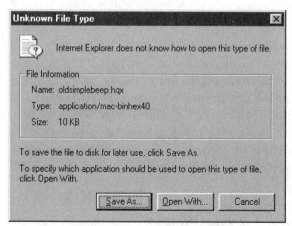

Figure 8-7. The "Unknown File Type" dialog

ular, though, need to know the content type to attach to outgoing files. At least in principle, the scheme used to do this can be much more straightforward: since the files are located on a Windows system, it's safe to assume that, in most cases, they adhere to Windows filenaming conventions. Consequently, the MIME content type of an outgoing file is defined by the `Content Type` value entry in its file association key. For instance, a mail application that's used to attach *MYPICT.GIF* to a message might assign it the MIME content type "image/gif", since that's the value of the `Content Type` entry in `HKCR\.gif`.

Browsing Your Files

Although the most common use of file associations is to identify the application that created a particular data file so that the application can be launched to open the file, there are several situations in which it is either not desirable or not possible to launch the application. Frequently, a user wants to open a data file not to edit or modify it, but simply to view it. In that case, launching the program that created the file, particularly if it is a resource-intensive application like a word processor, spreadsheet, or desktop publishing program, takes far too long and consumes far too many system resources for a relatively simple operation. In other cases, the user may have been given a data file whose associated application is not even installed on their computer.

To handle situations such as these, Win95 provides Quick View, which lets users select a file in the Explorer window and view it, without having to load the application that created it. When the user selects a file type for which a quick viewer is defined and either opens the File menu or right-clicks the mouse to open a context menu, a Quick View option appears on the menu. The Windows shell relies on the registry both to determine whether a file viewer is available for a particular file type and to load the file viewer itself.

If your application registers its own file extensions, you may be able to use an existing file viewer to allow the user to display it in read-only mode. This is particularly true if your file type is some variation on the plain ASCII (.txt) file. Since a file viewer is simply an OLE in-process server that implements the IPersistFile and IFileViewer interfaces, you can also develop your own file viewer. In this section, we'll first focus on the registry modifications required to associate a particular file type with an existing file viewer. Then, for those who are creating file viewers as additional components of their application, we'll discuss how to define the file viewer itself.

Associating a File Type with a File Viewer

"Quick View" is an optional component in Win95 that is installed only if the user, administrator, or OEM explicitly chooses to include it. Therefore, the first step in enabling a file viewer for a particular kind of file is to determine whether or not Quick View is installed. Determining whether Quick View is present is quite simple: the HKCR\QuickView key serves as a flag. The following code fragment tests for the key and, if it exists, continues with the file viewer definition:

```
if (RegOpenKey(HKEY_CLASSES_ROOT, "QuickView", &hKey) == ERROR_SUCCESS)
    {
    << code to define file association follows >>
    }
```

The second step is to define a particular file type as Quick View-enabled. To do this, you add a file identification key to HKCR\QuickView; when the user uses the Explorer to open a file's context menu, the Explorer automatically scans these subkeys to determine whether a file viewer is available for that file extension. In addition, a human-readable description of the file type is usually stored as the key's default value. This is shown in the following fragment produced by *REGDUMP*, which lists the Quick View file identification key for dynamic link library (.DLL) files:

```
HKEY_CLASSES_ROOT
    QuickView -> "Quick View File"
        .DLL -> "Dynamic Link Libraries"
```

The final step is to define the file viewer to be used if the Quick View menu option is selected by adding one or more keys to HKCR\QuickView\<*file association key*> whose names correspond to the class identifier (CLSID) of the file viewer. (For more information on class identifiers, see the following section, "Registering OLE Components.") The following output from *REGDUMP*, for example, completes the definition of .DLL files for Quick View:

```
HKEY_CLASSES_ROOT
   QuickView -> "Quick View File"
      .DLL -> "Dynamic Link Libraries"
         {F0F08735-0C36-101B-B086-0020AF07D0F4} -> "SCC Quick Viewer"
```

This step is required not only to launch the file viewer, but also to cause the Quick View item to appear on the File or context menu. If the user selects a file of this type and opens either of these menus, the Windows shell attempts to enumerate the file association key's subkeys. If it finds that there are none, it automatically deletes the file association key; it does not, however, attempt to determine whether any of the subkeys define a valid file viewer.

If the Quick View option is selected, the Windows shell launches *QUIKVIEW.EXE*, which is responsible for loading the appropriate file viewer. It does this, of course, by enumerating the subkeys of the Quick View file association key. If more than one key is present—indicating that more than one file viewer has been defined for a particular document type—it attempts to load the viewers in reverse order; that is, Quick View first attempts to display the file by using the viewer that was defined most recently.

Since our emphasis here is on reusing an existing file viewer, you simply need to retrieve its class identifier from the subkey of another file type that it supports. Two examples below illustrate how to do this. The first defines a file viewer for header (.H) files; the second defines a file viewer for Visual Basic form (.FRM) files. Although both are ASCII files, neither is automatically Quick View-enabled. Example 8-10 displays a program written in C that defines a file viewer for header files, while Example 8-11 contains a Visual Basic subroutine that defines a viewer for Visual Basic form (.FRM) files. Notice that these two programs extract the file viewer's CLSID by enumerating a single subkey whose index is *dwSubkeys*-1 (or, in the Visual Basic program, *lngSubkeys*-1). If there are multiple ASCII file viewers, this key designates the viewer whose key was added most recently, and therefore that is the last viewer to be defined. (*RegEnumKey* and *RegEnumKeyEx*, remember, enumerate keys in the order in which they were created.) These programs' only real error handling occurs when the `QuickView` key is opened; they assume that, if Quick View is enabled on a system, a viewer for text files will be available. Given this, it is possible, but very, very unlikely, that the value of *dwSubkeys* (or *lngSubkeys*) could be 0.

Example 8-10. Defining a file viewer for .H files

```
#include <windows.h>

int APIENTRY WinMain(HANDLE hInstance, HANDLE hPrevInstance,
                     LPSTR lpszCmdLine, int nCmdShow)
   {
   HKEY hKey, hFileKey, hCLSIDKey ;
   DWORD dwDisposition, dwSubkeys;
```

Example 8-10. Defining a file viewer for .H files (continued)

```
LPCTSTR lpCLSID[40], lpViewDesc[60] ;
DWORD dwSubkeyNameLen = 40 ;
LONG lenViewDesc = 60 ;

// Determine if Quick View is installed
if (RegOpenKey(HKEY_CLASSES_ROOT, "QuickView", &hKey) ==
             ERROR_SUCCESS)
   {
   // Create or open file association key
   RegCreateKeyEx(hKey,".H", 0, NULL, NULL, NULL, NULL,
                 &hFileKey, &dwDisposition) ;
   RegCloseKey(hKey) ;
   // Execute only if file viewing is not enabled
   if (dwDisposition == REG_CREATED_NEW_KEY)
      {
      // Add file type description
      RegSetValueEx(hFileKey, "", 0, REG_SZ,
                   "C Header File", 14) ;
      // Get CLSID of latest text viewer
      RegOpenKey(HKEY_CLASSES_ROOT, "QuickView\\.txt", &hKey) ;
      RegQueryInfoKey(hKey, NULL, NULL, NULL, &dwSubkeys, NULL,
                     NULL, NULL, NULL, NULL, NULL, NULL) ;
      // dwSubkeys - 1: get last one
      RegEnumKeyEx(hKey, dwSubkeys-1, lpCLSID, &dwSubkeyNameLen,
                  NULL, NULL, NULL, NULL) ;
      RegQueryValue(hKey, lpCLSID, lpViewDesc, &lenViewDesc) ;
      RegCloseKey(hKey) ;
      // Define Viewer
      RegCreateKey(hFileKey, lpCLSID, &hCLSIDKey) ;
      RegCloseKey(hFileKey) ;
      RegSetValueEx(hCLSIDKey, "", 0, REG_SZ, lpViewDesc,
                   lenViewDesc) ;
      RegCloseKey(hCLSIDKey) ;
      }
   }
return 0 ;
}
```

Example 8-11. Defining a file viewer for .frm Files

```
Public Sub AddViewer()

Dim hKey As Long, hFileKey As Long, hCLSIDkey As Long
Dim lngDisposition As Long, lngSubkeys As Long
Dim lngSubkeyNameLen As Long, lngLenViewDesc As Long
Dim strCLSID As String, strViewDesc As String
Dim udtSecurity As SECURITY_ATTRIBUTES
Dim udtFiletime As FILETIME

lngSubkeyNameLen = 40
lngLenViewDesc = 60

' Determine if Quick View is installed
```

Example 8-11. Defining a file viewer for .frm Files (continued)

```
If RegOpenKey(HKEY_CLASSES_ROOT, "QuickView", hKey) = _
                ERROR_SUCCESS Then
   ' Create or open file association key
   Call RegCreateKeyEx(hKey, ".frm", 0, 0, 0, 0, _
                        udtSecurity, hFileKey, lngDisposition)
   Call RegCloseKey(hKey)
   ' Execute only if file viewing is not enabled
   If lngDisposition = REG_CREATED_NEW_KEY Then
      ' Add file type description
      Call RegSetValueEx(hFileKey, "", 0, REG_SZ, _
                        ByVal "Visual Basic form file", 23)
      ' Get CLSID of latest text viewer
      Call RegOpenKey(HKEY_CLASSES_ROOT, "QuickView\.txt", hKey)
      Call RegQueryInfoKey(hKey, 0, 0, 0, lngSubkeys, 0, _
                        0, 0, 0, 0, 0, 0)
      strCLSID = String(lngSubkeyNameLen, 0)
      ' lngSubkeys - 1 : use last one
      Call RegEnumKeyEx(hKey, lngSubkeys - 1, strCLSID, _
                        lngSubkeyNameLen, 0, 0, 0, udtFiletime)
      strCLSID = Left(strCLSID, lngSubkeyNameLen)
      strViewDesc = String(lngLenViewDesc, 0)
      Call RegQueryValue(hKey, strCLSID, strViewDesc, lngLenViewDesc)
      Call RegCloseKey(hKey)
      strViewDesc = Left(strViewDesc, lngLenViewDesc)
      ' Define Viewer
      Call RegCreateKey(hFileKey, strCLSID, hCLSIDkey)
      Call RegCloseKey(hFileKey)
      Call RegSetValueEx(hCLSIDkey, "", 0, REG_SZ, ByVal strViewDesc, _
                        lngLenViewDesc)
      Call RegCloseKey(hCLSIDkey)
   End If
End If

End Sub
```

Defining a New File Viewer

It is also possible to extend Quick View either by adding a new file viewer or by replacing an existing viewer with a more full-featured one. (File viewers, for example, can allow you to print a document, and can also offer Clipboard support so that you can select and copy parts of a document, two enhancements not offered by the file viewers that ship with Win95.) A file viewer is an in-process OLE server that implements the IFileViewer interface.

Defining a new file viewer is a straightforward extension of associating a new file type with an existing file viewer. For each file type that your file viewer is capable of displaying, you must create a file extension subkey whose name corresponds to the file extension your viewer supports. This file association key then contains a subkey whose name corresponds to your viewer's class identifier (CLSID); for details on class identifiers, see "The Class Identifier, or CLSID" later in this chapter. As the default value of the Quick View file association key, you can include a string that describes the file type; as the default value of the class identifier subkey, you can include a description of the file viewer.

In addition, your file viewer must be registered as an OLE server by creating a subkey for it in `HKCR\CLSID`. The subkey's name should be the class identifier of your file viewer; its default value should be a description of your file viewer. Most file viewers use the same string for the default values of both this key and the `HKCR\QuickView\<file association>\<CLSID>` key. This key should contain one subkey, named `InProcServer32`, whose default value provides the complete path and filename of your file viewer. If the file viewer is multithreaded, an additional value entry, named `ThreadingModel`, is also required; since multi-threaded file viewers must support the apartment threading model, its value must be either `Apartment` or `Both`. For example, the following fragment from a *REGDUMP* listing shows the definition of the SCC Quick View file viewer in the Win95 registry:

```
HKEY_CLASSES_ROOT
  CLSID -> "OLE (Part 1 of 5)"
    {F0F08735-0C36-101B-B086-0020AF07D0F4} -> "SCC Quick Viewer"
      InProcServer32 -> "C:\WINDOWS\SYSTEM\VIEWERS\sccview.dll"
        ThreadingModel="Apartment"
```

Supporting DDE

In the section "Handling Application Data Files," we saw how a lot of the "object-oriented" behavior of Win95 really just results from the Windows Explorer using the registry to look up an application and then passing a command line to it. So when you double-click on a file, Windows "knows" how to handle it, typically, by retrieving the value of its application identifier's `shell\open\command` subkey and passing this to *ShellExecute*, which in turn launches the application and passes it the path and name of the file on which you've clicked as a parameter. But Windows also has another method of conveying user actions to applications: Dynamic Data Exchange (DDE). If your application supports or will support DDE, you may prefer to use DDE for such tasks as loading and printing files or handling the user's selection on a context menu. Since your application already is capable of functioning as a DDE server, this eliminates the overhead of having to parse command-line parameters to call particular services within your application.

Although Microsoft has de-emphasized DDE in favor of OLE, the role of DDE as an interface between the Windows shell and your application is actually somewhat expanded in Win32 applications. In Win16 applications, DDE could be used to load a file (i.e., handle the "open" verb) or print a file (the "print" verb). In Win95, on the other hand, DDE can handle *any* context menu selection.

Dynamic Data Exchange (DDE) has two distinctive components. The first, which is better known, is a form of interprocess communication that uses the Windows messaging system to establish a conversation between a client (which is either an application that requests a service or, in a peer-to-peer conversation, the application that initiates the conversation) and a server application, usually to exchange data. The registry is not used to define or support this form of DDE.

In the second form, which is called *DDE execute*, the Windows messaging system is used to send one or more command strings from a client application to a server. Here, the goal is not so much data exchange as driving and controlling the behavior of a server by issuing commands to it. The Win95 registry supports this second type of DDE. The client application—the application that initiates the "conversation"—is the Windows shell on behalf of the file that the user has selected. The server application is the application associated with that file extension.

The Windows shell selects the client and initiates a DDE conversation based purely on file associations and verbs located in the registry. The Windows shell identifies the application that can handle the file—which in this case is the DDE server—by examining the default value of a verb's `command` subkey. Windows knows that DDE is to be used in performing the operation indicated by a particular verb by the presence of a `shell\<verb>\ddeexec` subkey. Here's an example from a typical registry, as displayed by *REGDUMP*:

```
HKEY_CLASSES_ROOT
   Word.Document.6
      "Microsoft Word 6.0 Document"
      shell
         open
            command
               "C:\WINWORD\WINWORD.EXE /w"
            ddeexec
               '[FileOpen("%1")]'
         print
            command
               "C:\WINWORD\WINWORD.EXE /w"
            ddeexec
               '[FileOpen("%1")][FilePrint()][DocClose(2)]'
               ifexec
                  '[FileOpen("%1")][FilePrint .Background =
                  0][FileExit(2)]'
```

Like any DDE conversation, DDE execute has two phases:

- The client initiates the conversation by sending an *application* string and a *topic* string. The application string identifies the server application, and is usually—but not always—the server application's root filename, without its file extension. The topic string lets the server know what the conversation is about, so that the server can determine whether or not it supports it. For *DDE execute*, typical values of the topic string are "System", "AppProperties", and "AssocSupport". The values of these strings are defined in the registry by the default values of the `ddeexec\application` and `ddeexec\topic` subkeys. In both cases, the Windows shell substitutes a default value if a key or a default value entry is not present. If the `application` subkey is absent or has no default value entry, Windows uses the application's root filename; if the `topic` subkey is absent or lacks a default value entry, Windows uses the string "system."

- If the server application responds to the DDE connection, the Windows shell sends the command string, which is stored as the default value of the `ddeexec` subkey. It is the responsibility of the server to decide which topics it supports, as well as to define the syntax used for DDE command strings.

DDE requires that both client and server applications be open for a conversation to occur. In most cases when the Windows shell initiates a DDE conversation, the server application probably is not open. Therefore, the Windows shell performs the following steps in trying to open a DDE conversation:

- It attempts to initiate the conversation by sending the application and topic strings.

- If a server does not respond, the Windows shell calls the *ShellExecute* function, using the default value of the `command` subkey as a parameter. Typically, this launches the server application.

- It attempts to initiate the conversation once again, and, if successful, sends the string specified by the `ifexec` subkey. If the `ifexec` subkey is not present, the command string stored to the `ddeexec` key is resent.

Table 8-9 provides a concise summary of the organization of the registry to support DDE. (Notice how it corresponds to the output from *REGDUMP* shown above.)

Table 8-9. The format of registry entries for DDE execute

Key	Default Value
HKCR	
<AppID>	Human-readable application description
shell	Default verb
<verb>	Menu item
command	Path and name of application
ddeexec	DDE command string
application	DDE application name
topic	DDE topic name
ifexec	DDE command if attempt to open conversation fails

Although the format of DDE command strings tends to vary widely from application to application, they take the general format:

```
<Action> [<fileName>] [<options>]
```

where *action* uniquely identifies an operation, *filename* indicates the file that the user has selected, and *options* consists of one or more optional parameters. Typically, DDE execute strings are enclosed in brackets. For example, Table 8-10 lists some DDE command strings used by Microsoft Word 6.0 and Excel for Windows 5.0 that are commonly found in the Win95 registry. Notice that, as the values for `print` and `printto` show, multiple commands can be grouped into a single DDE exec string.

Table 8-10. Some ddeexec command strings in the Win95 registry

Application Identifier	Verb	ddeexec string
Excel.Sheet.5	new	`[new("%1")]`
Excel.Sheet.5	open	`[open("%1")]`
Excel.Sheet.5	print	`[open("%1")][print?()][close()]`
word.document.6	new	`[FileNew("%1")]`
word.document.6	open	`[FileOpen("%1")]`
word.document.6	print	`[REM _DDE_Minimize][FileOpen("%1")][File-Print 0][DocClose 2]`
word.document.6	printto	`[REM _DDE_Minimize][FileOpen("%1")][File-Print 0][DocClose 2]`

The Windows shell uses %1 as a replaceable parameter to represent the name of the file selected by the user when sending a DDE command string.

Registering OLE Components

In Chapter 1, *The Registry, or, What Was So Bad About .INI Files?*, we saw that the Win31 registration database, *REG.DAT*, was introduced in large measure to support OLE. It is not surprising, then, that OLE components depend on the Win95 registry. In fact, one can argue that support for OLE is the driving force behind the movement away from initialization files and toward a centralized registry. With the registry, client applications are easily able to identify OLE server and OLE object applications.

Much as the Windows shell uses file associations as the means of uniquely identifying a particular file type, an OLE client application requires some means of identifying the server object that is to provide a particular service. For instance, if a user double-clicks on an embedded object within a document, the container application needs some way of knowing which server application can handle that object. Similarly, if the Windows shell is to display a property sheet for an object, it requires some method of identifying a custom property sheet handler, if there is one. In both of these as well as in other cases, the class identifier, or CLSID, provides the means of identifying a particular OLE component. If you've browsed the registry, you've probably come across these {a-b-c-d-e} things. These are CLSIDs: they are what let clients locate servers.

The Class Identifier, or CLSID

When it is created, every OLE server is assigned a 16-byte *globally unique identifier* (GUID) that is guaranteed to be unique not only on a single machine, but in space and time as well. (Since this range includes over 11 quintillion possible values, the probability of an overlap, given an algorithm capable of generating even a fairly unique number, is very small.) This GUID, which is called a *class identifier* or CLSID when it belongs to a component object class, is calculated based on an algorithm defined by the Open Software Foundation's Distributed Computing Environment (DCE), and is computed from the current date and time, a clock sequence, a forcibly incremented counter, and an IEEE machine identification number that is taken from the system's network card or synthesized, if one is absent. It is then embedded within the object's file.[*]

Ordinarily, there are several ways to generate a class identifier for an OLE component:

• By using the command-line *UUIDGen* utility (*UUIDGEN.EXE*), which is included in Visual C++ and the OLE 2.0 SDK.

• By using the graphical version of *UUIDGen*, *GUIDGEN.EXE*, which is shown in Figure 8-8. It is a utility developed using MFC that is included with Microsoft Visual C++.

• By calling the Component Object Model's *CoCreateGuid* function.

Despite their apparent diversity, each of these utilities or functions is ultimately a wrapper that calls the DCE Remote Procedure Call function *UuidCreate* in *RPCRT4.DLL*, one of the RPC run-time libraries. (Yes, RPC: if you think about it, OLE is really a local, non-network form of RPC.) *CoCreateGuid*, however, generates a dynamic CLSID at run-time, which makes it unsuitable for defining an OLE server application, where you want to have a single, static class identifier that can be assigned to all copies of a particular OLE component, regardless of the machine on which they run. So to generate a class identifier that you can enter

---

[*] For a discussion of DCE and UUIDs, see Ward Rosenberry and Jim Teague, *Distributing Applications Across DCE and Windows NT*, published by O'Reilly & Associates.

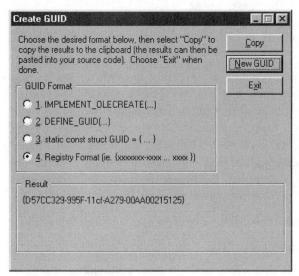

Figure 8-8. The GUIDGen utility

into the user's registry, you should use either of the first two utilities to generate a static CLSID. If you're developing a single server that implements several OLE interfaces or several different OLE classes, you can also assign it multiple CLSIDs using *UUIDGen*; the syntax for doing this is:

```
uuidgen /n<number>
```

where *<number>* is the number of consecutive CLSIDs that are to be generated.

Interestingly, the registry is used to generate a CLSID. Example 8-12 contains a fragment of the output from a *RegSpy95* session that traps registry accesses made by *UUIDGen*. Notice that *UUIDGen* uses the **NetworkAddress** value from HKLM\ **Software\Description\Microsoft\Rpc\UuidTemporaryData** (this corresponds exactly to the final six bytes of the CLSID), as well as the **ClockSequence** and **LastTimeAllocated** values from HKLM\Software\ **Description\Microsoft\Rpc\UuidPersistentData**.

Example 8-12. Registry accesses by UUIDGen

```
_RegOpenKey       Uuidgen  HKLM     C23A0D18
           'Software\Description\Microsoft\Rpc\UuidPersistentData'
_RegOpenKey       Uuidgen  HKLM     C271BEB0
           'Software\Description\Microsoft\Rpc\UuidTemporaryData'
_RegQueryValueEx  Uuidgen  C271BEB0 0   6  'NetworkAddress'  ''
_RegQueryValueEx  Uuidgen  C271BEB0 0   4  'NetworkAddressLocal'  ''
_RegQueryValueEx  Uuidgen  C23A0D18 0   4  'ClockSequence'  ''
_RegQueryValueEx  Uuidgen  C23A0D18 0   8  'LastTimeAllocated'  ''
_RegSetValueEx    Uuidgen  C23A0D18 DW  4  'ClockSequence'  '00002279'
_RegSetValueEx    Uuidgen  C23A0D18 BIN 8
```

Example 8-12. Registry accesses by UUIDGen (continued)

```
                    'LastTimeAllocated'  '80 67 16 FB 24 BB CF 01 '
_RegCloseKey        Uuidgen   C23A0D18
_RegCloseKey        Uuidgen   C271BEB0
```

Although the CLSID is a 16-byte integer, it is stored in the registry as a string value. Its standard string representation consists of eight hexadecimal digits (or four bytes), a hyphen, three groups of four hexadecimal digits (two bytes each, for a total of six bytes) separated from each other by hyphens, followed by the final 12 hexadecimal digits (the final six bytes). This string value is then delimited by braces. For example, the following are some of the CLSIDs assigned to the Windows shell, in this case to handle the desktop namespace, shortcuts (.LNK files), and Control Panel applets, respectively:

```
{00021400-0000-0000-C000-000000000046}
{00021401-0000-0000-C000-000000000046}
{21B22460-3AEA-1069-A2DC-08002B30309D}
```

The standard CLSIDs are defined in several header files, including *COGUID.H*, *OLEGUID.H*, and *SHLGUID.H*.

This string representation of the class identifier then serves to identify the OLE server's key in the registry. All OLE components present in a Win95 system are defined by subkeys belonging to one of three keys:

- `HKCR\CLSID`. Its subkeys define the OLE classes that are available on the system.

- `HKCR\Interface`. These subkeys contain the interface identifiers, or IIDs,[*] that define both the standard OLE interfaces (like *IUnknown* and *IClassFactory*) as well as custom ones. All *remotable interfaces* (that is, interfaces that can cross process boundaries, and therefore that can be implemented either in out-of-process servers or in remote servers) must be defined here.

- `HKCR\TypeLib`. These subkeys contain the CLSIDs of *type libraries*, which are OLE compound documents that are used to store information on OLE classes, interfaces, and data structures. (The Visual Basic Object Browser, for instance, is a type library.)

For each OLE component, there is a single subkey whose name corresponds to the component's class identifier. The subkey's default value is a name that you want to associate with the class identifier. Since this value is generally not displayed, it is not uncommon to find OLE components whose CLSID keys have no assigned default value.

---

[*] An *interface* is a group of methods that belong to a particular class; a class can (and invariably does) have multiple interfaces. Very much like the CLSID is a unique identifier of a class, an IID is a unique identifier of an interface.

The major purpose of an OLE component's CLSID key is to identify the location and filename of the OLE server component. Usually, if there are separate 16- and 32-bit versions of a single component, they share a single CLSID. So the registry also must allow Windows and individual applications to determine the platform a particular component serves. The subkeys of the class identifier key that are listed in Table 8-11 are used both to indicate the name and location of the component as well as its "bitness;" at least one of these six subkeys is required for a CLSID key. In each case, the path must be the full path to the file; if it is not, the OLE libraries refuse to load it.

Table 8-11. Subkeys that indicate the name, location, and platform of an OLE component

Subkey Name	Default Value	Explanation
LocalServer	Path and name of a 16- or 32-bit .EXE, along with any command-line arguments	Local (i.e., on the same computer) out-of-process server
LocalServer32	Path and name of a 32-bit .EXE, along with any command-line arguments	Local (i.e., on the same computer) 32-bit out-of-process server
InprocServer	Path and name of a 16-bit DLL	Local 16-bit in-process server
InprocServer32	Path and name of a 32-bit DLL	Local 32-bit in-process server
InprocHandler	Path and name of a 16-bit DLL	16-bit object handler for this object type; if no custom handler is specified, it defaults to *OLE2.DLL.*
InprocHandler32	Path and name of a 32-bit DLL	32-bit object handler for this object type; if no custom handler is specified, it defaults to *OLE32.DLL.*

Of these entries, HKCR\CLSID\<*CLSID*>\LocalServer is the only key that ignores "bitness" in defining the location of its OLE server. That's because objects created by 32-bit OLE applications can be inserted into 16-bit container applications. 16-bit container applications, however, identify OLE servers that support embedded objects by the presence of two keys:

- HKCR\CLSID\<*CLSID*>\Insertable, which indicates that the OLE server supports embedded objects
- HKCR\CLSID\<*CLSID*>\LocalServer, which indicates the path and filename of the executable OLE server

So if there are not separate 16- and 32-bit OLE server applications, the CLSID key that defines the 32-bit server should include both a LocalServer and a LocalServer32 subkey.

16- and 32-Bit Custom Handlers

If you assign a single CLSID to a 16-bit and a 32-bit custom handler and define them using the `InProcHandler` subkey (for 16-bit applications) and the `InProcHandler32` subkey (for 32-bit applications), 16-bit applications may not be able to load the 16-bit handler. One workaround is to delete the `InProcHandler32` subkey; but this means that 32-bit applications can't load a custom handler. The second is to delete the `InProcHandler` and `InProcHandler32` keys and replace them with `InProcServer` and `InProcServer32` keys.

In addition to its default value that defines the path and filename of a 32-bit OLE in-process server, the `InProcServer32` subkey typically has a value entry named `ThreadingModel`, which defines the server's multithreading model. Since by default in-process servers are single-threaded, no value entry is present for a single-threaded server. For multithreaded servers, the following values are recognized:

- `Apartment`. The server supports the "apartment-threading" model. Although multiple objects can be created, every object created by the server can exist in only one thread (apartment). Each thread containing objects must have its own message queue.

- `Both`. The server supports both apartment-threading and free-threading. In "free threading," a single COM object can be accessible from multiple threads of a single process.

A major design goal of OLE is support of versioning—that is, a new version of a server component should be able to replace an existing version of that component without breaking applications that used the older component. Although this support of versioning is largely due to the design of COM, the registry is also involved in its implementation. If the CLSID key belonging to the old version of the OLE server contains a subkey named either `TreatAs` or `AutoTreatAs`, the COM API instead uses the OLE server whose CLSID is indicated by the subkey's default value. `AutoTreatAs` indicates that the substitution of the new component for the older component is permanent, and is typically used when a new version of a component is installed over a previous version. `TreatAs`, on the other hand, indicates a temporary replacement, and is usually used by a component that emulates an original component without being directly related to it.

For the most part, the particular registry entries needed to properly register an OLE object depend on the services that object provides. Let's briefly survey the registry entries required for the more common OLE services.

OLE automation objects

OLE automation objects are software components that expose their functionality through interfaces that a scripting tool (called an *automation controller*) can access. To make this possible, the name and location of the server should be defined by the **InProcServer** or **InProcServer32** subkeys of the automation object's CLSID key if the automation object is a DLL, or by the **LocalServer** or **LocalServer32** subkeys if the automation object is an executable. The subkey's default value should take the general form:

```
<path and filename of OLE automation object> /Automation
```

In addition, the automation object's CLSID key should include the subkeys listed in Table 8-12.

Table 8-12. Additional subkeys to define an OLE automation controller

Subkey Name	Subkey's Default Value
InProcHandler or InProcHandler32	<path and filename of object handler>. This is an optional subkey; if absent, it defaults to *OLE2.DLL* for 16-bit automation objects or *OLE32.DLL* for 32-bit objects
ProgID	<programmatic identifier>
VersionIndependentProgID	<version-independent programmatic identifier>
TypeLib	<CLSID of type library>

The **ProgID** and **VersionIndependentProgID** subkeys, which are discussed below in the section "The Programmatic Identifier, or ProgID," allow scripting languages, which ordinarily don't work with CLSIDs, to create and manipulate objects based on something resembling a recognizable name. This makes it possible, for instance to embed a Word document in a Visual Basic form with a code fragment like the following:

```
OLE1.Class = "word.document.6"
OLE1.DisplayType = 1
OLE1.CreateEmbed ("C:\My Documents\My Letter of Today.doc")
```

A *type library* is a resource or a standalone file (usually with a .TLB or .OLB extension) that describes a particular collection of objects, as well as their data structures, properties, and member functions. In Visual Basic, for instance, the Object Browser is simply a front-end tool that allows you to browse a type library. Type libraries are required when implementing OLE automation objects and OLE custom controls. The default value of the **TypeLib** subkey contains the type library's CLSID, which allows OLE to access a particular OLE automation object's type library. The registry information needed to define the type library itself is discussed in a later section, "Type Libraries."

OCX custom controls

Unlike most OLE components, whose registry entries can usually be created by including a .REG file along with the control and launching it during installation, a custom control is supposed to be self-registering. In other words, the control is supposed to make the necessary entries in the registry that allow it to be properly defined the first time that it is used. This is done using the *DllRegisterServer* function.

The registry entries needed to define a control are stored as subkeys of the control's CLSID in `HKCR\CLSID\`*`<clsid>`*; they are listed in Table 8-13.

Table 8-13. Subkeys needed to define an OLE custom control

Subkey Name	Explanation	Subkey's Default Value
`Control`	Although optional, this subkey provides a convenient method of allowing client applications to differentiate controls from other OLE components when building list boxes.	< none >
`InProcServer` or `InProcServer32`		<control's path and filename>
`Insertable`	Optional; indicates that the control can be inserted into an OLE document as an embedded object (most OCX controls can't).	< none >
`MiscStatus\1`	Miscellaneous status flags allow a container to determine an object's properties without actually creating an instance of it. Although possible names of subkeys of the `Misc-Status` key are 1 (for flags that define an embedded object's content), 2 (an object's thumbnail representation), 3 (its iconic representation), and 4 (its printed representation), only 1 (which corresponds to the control's content) is relevant.	<value of status flags>
`ProgID`	See "The Programmatic Identifier, or ProgID" later in this chapter.	*<ProgID>*
`ToolboxBitmap` or `ToolboxBitmap32`	Defines a 16x15 image that can depict the control in a toolbox. Along with indicating the path and filename, its default value can be either a zero-based integer indicating the ordinal position of the image in the file or the image's resource identifier.	<filename, resource ID>
`TypeLib`	See the next section, "Type libraries."	*<type library's CLSID>*
`Version`		<major version.minor version>

For example, the Desaware registry control (see Chapter 7, *The Desaware Registry Control*) is defined as follows in the Win95 registry:

```
HKEY_CLASSES_ROOT
    CLSID -> "OLE (Part 1 of 5)"
        {9638694A-DA15-101B-8F41-00AA00517888} -> "Desaware Registry Demo"
            ProgID -> "REGISTRYD.RegistryCtrl.1"
            InprocServer32 -> "C:\WINDOWS\SYSTEM\DWREG32D.OCX"
            ToolboxBitmap32 -> "C:\WINDOWS\SYSTEM\DWREG32D.OCX, 1"
            MiscStatus -> "0"
                1 -> "132497"
            Control -> ""
            TypeLib -> {Desaware Registry OLE Demo}
            Version -> "1.0"
```

Type libraries

Type libraries, which are typically used to describe the objects, properties, structures, and methods of one or more OLE automation objects or OLE custom controls, are usually standalone files that, in all cases, are assigned their own class identifier. Type libraries are registered by including a subkey whose name is their CLSID in HKCR\TypeLib. (Actually, in this case the CLSID is referred to as LIBID, or *library identifier*.) The default value of the type library's CLSID key is a full descriptive string that indicates the name of the type library; the registry entries for most type libraries, though, do not assign a value for this descriptive string.

The subkeys of the type libraries CLSID key are shown in Table 8-14.

Table 8-14. Subkeys of HKCR\TypeLib

Subkey Name	Explanation	Subkey's Default Value
<version>	Version number of the library in <major version>.<minor version> format. This allows multiple versions of the same type library to share a common CLSID.	Description of the type library
<LangID>	Language identifier (the lower 2 bytes of a locale identifier) or primary language identifier (the lower 9 bits of a locale identifier) of the type library.	None
Win16		Path and filename of the 16-bit version of the type library, if one exists
Win32		Path and filename of the 32-bit version of the type library, if one exists

Table 8-14. Subkeys of HKCR\TypeLib (continued)

Subkey Name	Explanation	Subkey's Default Value
FLAGS	The combined value of bit flags indicating restrictions on the type library's use; LIBFLAG constants and their literal values are shown in Table 8-15.	< ORed value of flags >
HELPDIR	Optional	Path to the type library's help files

Table 8-15. Constants used by the type library's Flags subkey

Constant	Value	Description
	0	No restrictions.
LIBFLAG_FCONTROL	1	The type library describes controls; it should not be displayed in type browsers for non-visual objects.
LIBFLAG_ FRESTRICTED	2	The type library is restricted and should not be displayed to users.
LIBFLAG_FHIDDEN	4	The type library should not be displayed to users, although its use is not restricted. To be used by controls, hosts should create a new type library that wraps the control with extended properties.

Typically, the `Flags` and `HelpDir` subkeys are direct children of the type library's version key. However, they can also be direct subkeys of a particular language identifier subkey. For example, the type library for Visual Basic's IDE is defined as follows in the registry:

```
HKEY_CLASSES_ROOT
   CLSID -> "OLE (Part 1 of 5)"
      {EF404E00-EDA6-101A-8DAF-00DD010F7EBB}
         4.0 -> "Microsoft Visual Basic 4.0 Development Environment"
            FLAGS -> "0"
            0
               win32 -> "C:\VB\vbext32.olb"
               win16 -> "C:\VB16\vbext.olb"
            HELPDIR -> "C:\VB16"
```

Once the type library's CLSID has been defined, it can be associated with one or more OLE classes or interfaces by adding a `TypeLib` subkey to each class's `CLSID` key (or each interface's `IID` key) and assigning it a default value equal to the type library's CLSID. For example, Table 8-16 lists some of the OLE interfaces that include a `TypeLib` subkey whose default value is "{EF404E00-EDA6-101A-8DAF-00DD010F7EBB}", the CLSID of the type library for the Visual Basic IDE.

Table 8-16. OLE interfaces that use the VB IDE type library

CLSID	Interface
{2F3304A0-1602-11CE-BFDC-08002B2B8CDA}	Components
{31DE1170-1602-11CE-BFDC-08002B2B8CDA}	ProjectTemplateEvents
{79B1F921-EC2C-101A-B1F9-08002B2B8CDA}	FormTemplate
{79B1F922-EC2C-101A-B1F9-08002B2B8CDA}	ControlTemplate
{79B1F923-EC2C-101A-B1F9-08002B2B8CDA}	Property
{79B1F924-EC2C-101A-B1F9-08002B2B8CDA}	ControlTemplates

OLE documents

In its original version, OLE 1.0, OLE was an acronym for Object Linking and Embedding, and focused exclusively on ways of sharing data created by individual applications. Although OLE 2.0 has been expanded to provide a complete object-oriented run-time environment, compound documents remain an important part of OLE. OLE documents require two OLE components: a client application capable of creating and managing a compound document container, and an OLE server application, which manages individual components within the container. Both are identified by their CLSID, as well as by a programmatic identifier, or ProgID, which is discussed in the following section. In addition, the registry entries for OLE document client and server applications typically include the subkeys of the CLSID key that are shown in Table 8-17.

Table 8-17. Class identifier subkeys for OLE document clients and servers

Subkey Name	Explanation	Subkey's Default Value

`AuxUserType`
`2`
`3`
	The Auxiliary user type—an alternate set of names for the object besides the name stored as the default value of the object's CLSID. The name assigned as the default value of key 2 is typically a short name of under 10 characters; the name assigned as the default value of key 3 is a longer, more descriptive name that appears in the Paste Special dialog. The names of the subkeys (i.e., 2 and 3) is arbitrary and cannot be changed.	The default value of subkey 2 is a short name; of subkey 3, a longer name.

`Conversion`
`Readable`
`Main`
`Readwritable`
`Main`
	Identifies other data formats that the object can either convert to its own format (identified by the `Readable` subkey) or emulate (the `Readwritable` subkey). The default value of the Main subkey identifies the formats.	Only the Main subkey has a default value. It consists of one or more formats, separated by commas. Each format is either a clipboard format string or an OLE ProgID.

Table 8-17. Class identifier subkeys for OLE document clients and servers (continued)

Subkey Name	Explanation	Subkey's Default Value
DefaultIcon	Identifies the icon to use to display an inserted object if the user chooses to represent it with an icon. Its format is identical to that of the DefaultIcon subkey of an application identifier key.	Path and filename of the file containing the icon resource, along with an index identifying the particular icon resource.
DataFormats DefaultFile GetSet *\<int\>*	Identifies the data formats supported by the object. Each subkey of GetSet identifies additional supported formats. The name of each subkey is a sequential, zero-based integer. Each subkey's default value identifies one supported format.	The default value of the DefaultFile subkey indicates the object's "native" data format. The default values of the subkeys of GetSet identify additional formats. They take the form *\<format\>,\<aspect\>,\<medium\>,\<direction\>*. *\<format\>* identifies a Clipboard format, *\<aspect\>* is a literal DVASPECT value (-1 indicates all views), *\<medium\>* is the sum of TYMED values, and *\<direction\>* is a DATADIR value.
InProcHandler	The default in-process handler; if the key is absent, it defaults to *OLE2.DLL*.	Path and filename of the default OLE in-process handler.
InProcHandler32	The default 32-bit in-process handler; if the key is absent, it defaults to *OLE32.DLL*.	Path and filename of the 32-bit default OLE in-process handler.
InprocServer	Identifies a 16- or 32-bit OLE in-process server. This entry is relatively rare for OLE documents.	Path and filename of the 16- or 32-bit OLE in-process server.
InprocServer32	Identifies a 32-bit OLE in-process server. This entry is relatively rare for OLE documents.	Path and filename of the 32-bit OLE in-process server.
Insertable	Identifies an application as an OLE server that can manage an object within an OLE document container. Since the Insertable subkey has no subkeys, no value entries, and no default value, it serves as an example of a flag to signal the presence or absence of some feature.	None.
LocalServer	Identifies the 16- or 32-bit server application (i.e., an executable file on the same machine).	Path and filename of a 16- or 32-bit local server.

Table 8-17. Class identifier subkeys for OLE document clients and servers (continued)

Subkey Name	Explanation	Subkey's Default Value
`LocalServer32`	Identifies the 32-bit server application (i.e., an executable file on the same machine).	Path and filename of a 32-bit local server.

`MiscStatus`
`<DVASPECT`
`value>`
	Defines the attributes of the object overall (the `MiscStatus` key's default value) and in individual views (the default value of its subkeys).	The default value of the `MiscStatus` key is the sum of the object's miscellaneous status bits. Each subkey's name corresponds to the literal value of a DVASPECT constant; its default value is the literal value of the flags set for that particular view.

`ProgID`	The OLE component's programmatic identifier, which provides an alternative way to refer to it other than by its CLSID. For a more detailed explanation of the programmatic identifier, see the following section.	The programmatic identifier (e.g., Word.Document.6).
`verb` `<int>`	Each subkey of the `verb` key identifies verbs that can be passed to the `IOleObject::DoVerb` method. Frequently, they also represent items on the container's pop-up menu. Each subkey is assigned an arbitrary unique integer: the primary verb is indicated by subkey 0; subkeys with positive integers are displayable on pop-up menus; and subkeys with negative integers indicate non-menu items. The subkey's default value defines the verb.	The general format of each subkey's default value is `<text>,<menu flags>,<verb flags>`. `<text>` is the text of the verb, along with an ampersand if the verb appears in a menu. `<menu flags>` is the literal value of the `MF_` constants that are used to define menu items for the *AppendMenu* and *InsertMenu* API functions. `<verb flags>` is the literal value of the `OLEVERBATTRIB` constants that apply to this verb.
`VersionIndepen-` `dentProgID`	The OLE component's version-independent programmatic identifier. For details, see the following section.	The version-independent programmatic identifier (e.g., Excel.Sheet).

For example, Microsoft Word is both an OLE container and an OLE server application. It is defined in the Win95 registry as follows:

```
HKEY_CLASSES_ROOT
   CLSID
      {00020900-0000-0000-C000-000000000046} -> "Microsoft Word Document"
         Conversion
```

```
Readwritable
  Main -> "MSWordDoc"
Readable
  Main -> "MSWordDoc,WordDocument,1"
MiscStatus -> "0"
  1 -> "1"
DataFormats
  GetSet
    3 -> "Rich Text Format,1,1,3"
    2 -> "3,1,32,1"
    1 -> "1,1,1,3"
    0 -> "Embed_Source,1,8,1"
    4 -> "NoteshNote,-1,1,1"
  DefaultFile -> "MSWordDoc"
  PriorityCacheFormats
    0 -> "Rich Text Format"
  DelayRenderFormats
    0 -> "Woozle"
DefaultIcon -> "C:\MSOFFICE\WINWORD\WINWORD.EXE,0"
AuxUserType
  3 -> "Microsoft Word 7.0"
  2 -> "Document"
Insertable -> ""
DocObject -> ""
Verb
  0 -> "&Edit,0,2"
  1 -> "&Open,0,2"
LocalServer32 -> "C:\MSOFFICE\WINWORD\WINWORD.EXE"
InprocHandler32 -> "ole32.dll"
ProgID -> "Word.Document.6"
AutoConvertTo -> ""
Printable -> ""
DefaultExtension -> ".doc,Word Document (.doc)"
RTFClassName -> "MSWord6"
```

The Programmatic Identifier, or ProgID

Many OLE components have an additional means of identification, known as their *programmatic identifier* or ProgID. This is really the same thing as the application identifier, which was discussed earlier in this chapter in "Registering a File Association," except that it identifies an OLE component rather than a standalone application. (In some cases, when an application is capable of serving both as an OLE client and an OLE server, the programmatic identifier is in fact the same as the application identifier.) The ProgID is used in two major instances:

* When the component is an object application or an insertable class that the user can select from a dialog. For instance, the Visual Basic programmer, by selecting the Custom Controls option from the Tools menu, can use the Custom Controls dialog shown in Figure 8-9 to add a custom .OCX control to a project. To be meaningful, though, the programmer must be able to identify

the control. The programmatic identifier allows an object to be associated with a longer, more comprehensible description.

- When a particular development environment does not allow the developer to define static class identifiers. This is true, for example, of Visual Basic; developers creating Visual Basic class modules assign them ProgIDs rather than CLSIDs.

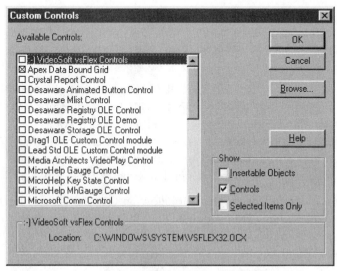

Figure 8-9. Visual Basic's Custom Control dialog

Like the application identifier, the programmatic identifier is stored as the name of a direct child key of HKCR. The programmatic identifier must have fewer than 40 characters. Its first letter cannot be a number, and it cannot contain any punctuation or other non-alphanumeric characters other than periods.

The ProgID itself is not supposed to be displayed to the user in a dialog or similar interface element. Instead, its default value should contain a string that accurately describes the object. For instance, MSGraph.Chart.5 is the programmatic identifier of a Microsoft Chart object, as defined by the HKCR\MSGraph.Chart.5 key. If the user attempts to use Word for Windows to insert a chart object into their document, though, the Object dialog describes this object as Microsoft Graph 5.0, since that is the key's default value.

Actually, ProgIDs come in two forms: the *version-dependent* programmatic identifier, and the *version-independent* programmatic identifier. The version-dependent ProgID takes the form `<Vendor>.<Component>.<Version>`. For example, Excel.Sheet.5 is a version-dependent ProgID. The version-independent ProgID takes the form `<Vendor>.<Component>`, but does not specify a version. It enhances portability by allowing macro languages and client application code to use a constant name when referring to the instance of an object, rather than having to concern themselves with the component's version. `Excel.Sheet`, for instance, is a version-independent ProgID. If both a version-dependent and a version-independent ProgID are defined, the version-independent ProgID should also include a subkey named `CurVer` whose default value specifies the component's version-dependent programmatic identifier; this allows the version-independent ProgID to be mapped to a version-dependent one. For instance, the value of `HKCR\Excel.Sheet\CurVer` is `Excel.Sheet.5`. In addition, both the version-independent and the version-dependent ProgIDs should have a subkey named `CLSID` whose default value is the CLSID of the OLE object application.

Along with using its `CLSID` subkey to map the OLE component application's ProgID to its CLSID, the registry is also used to map a CLSID to its corresponding version-dependent or version-independent ProgID. Where a particular component application has programmatic identifier keys, its class identifier key should have subkeys named `ProgID` and `VersionIndependentProgId` whose default values are the version-dependent and version-independent ProgIDs, respectively.

One major use of the version-dependent ProgID is to allow an OLE 2.0 class to be inserted into an OLE 1.0 container. This requires that the version-dependent ProgID have a subkey named `Protocol`, which has a subkey named `StdFileEditing`. The `StdFileEditing` key in turn should have two subkeys:

- `Server`, whose default value is the path and filename of the OLE 2.0 object application.

- `Verb`, whose subkeys indicate the commands that the container is to display in its own menus to activate the object. Subkeys are numbered consecutively from 0. The default value of each subkey is a verb. The verb stored to `Protocol\StdFileEditing\Verb\0` is the primary verb; this defines the action to execute when the user clicks on the object. Typically, the verb stored to this key is `&Edit`; if the key is absent or has no assigned value, its value is defined on a system-wide basis by the default value of `HKCR\Software\Microsoft\Ole2\UnregisteredVerb`.

If the object application should also be listed in the Insert Object dialog of an OLE 2.0 container application, it should have an `Insertable` subkey immediately under the `ProgID` key; the subkey should have no value assigned to it.

For example, Visual Basic supports the creation of OLE in-process servers, which are assigned a CLSID when they are registered. Visual Basic, however, does not allow objects to be referenced using their CLSIDs. So to use the OLE in-process server created by Visual Basic within a Visual Basic project, you must instead use its assigned ProgID. For instance, the following code fragment creates an instance of the `InterfaceDateClass`:

```
Dim objInt As Object
Set objInt = New InterfaceProj.InterfaceDateClass
```

`InterfaceProj.InterfaceDateClass` is the server's ProgID, as shown from its definition in the Win95 registry:

```
HKEY_CLASSES_ROOT
InterfaceProj.Interface.DateClass -> ""
      CLSID -> {8F0E48DA-8A1A-11CE-B781-00AA006EC3D4}
```

Launching Local Applications Using OLE

In "Launching Your Application" earlier in this chapter, we emphasized that the Windows shell uses file associations as the basis for interpreting user actions, particularly the meaning of a user double-click. Although that's true, it's only a partial explanation. Using file associations defined in the registry is only one of the ways that the Windows shell "knows" how to launch an application that's associated with a particular data file.

To see an alternate method in action, if Microsoft Word is available on your computer, rename a Word document so that it has no file extension. Then double-click on it in an Explorer window. Even though the file no longer has an extension, Win95 still recognizes it as a Word document, launches Word, and loads the file. If file associations provided the only way that the Windows shell linked data files to the applications capable of handling them, this should not be happening. OLE is the reason why it does happen correctly.

In fact, OLE and the OLE components of the Windows shell provide three methods for identifying and launching the application associated with a document and then opening that document:

- By identifying a file extension with a ProgID. This is actually a straightforward extension of standard file associations, since it continues to rely on a file's extension to determine the application that handles it. Instead of an application identifier, the file association key's default value is a programmatic identifier. The `ProgID` key contains a `CLSID` subkey whose default value indicates the CLSID of the OLE component that handles the file. For instance, Word uses both the standard file association and the OLE file association. The latter appears in the registry as follows:

```
HKEY_CLASSES_ROOT
    .doc -> "Word.Document.6"
    word.document.6 -> "Microsoft Word Document"
      CLSID -> {00020900-0000-0000-C000-000000000046}
```

- By identifying a byte pattern within the data file (similar to what is called "magic" in UNIX) and identifying it with an OLE component through the subkeys of the `HKCR\FileType` key. The immediate child key of `HKCR\File-Type` contains the `CLSID` of an OLE server that is capable of handling a particular file type; generally, it has no default value. The `CLSID` key in turn has one or more subkeys, each of which identifies a particular byte pattern in the file. The name of each of these subkeys, referred to as the *type ID*, is simply a unique zero-based sequential integer. Each type ID key's default value takes the following form:

```
offset, cb, mask, value
```

where *offset* is the position in the file at which the comparison begins, *cb* is the number of bytes to match, *mask* is an optional byte sequence that is used to perform a bitwise AND operation on the contents of the file starting at position *offset*, and *value* is the byte pattern that must occur in the file or result from the bitwise AND operation in order for the match to be successful. For example, the following registry entries identify four particular byte patterns as various older versions of Excel spreadsheets (for example, an Excel 2.1 spreadsheet might begin with the byte pattern 09 00 04 00 07 00 10 00; this only applies to older versions because the newer ones will use the OLE mechanism described below):

```
HKEY_CLASSES_ROOT
    FileType -> "OLE (Part 5 of 5)"
        {00020810-0000-0000-C000-000000000046}
            0 -> "0,8,FF00F9FF0000FFFF,0900000000001000"
            1 -> "0,8,FF00F9FF0000FFFF,0900000000004000"
            2 -> "0,8,FF00F9FF0000FFFF,0900000000000001"
            3 -> "0,8,FF00F9FF0000FFFF,0900000000002000"
```

- If the data file is an OLE compound object or an OLE container, by embedding the CLSID of its OLE server application within it by calling the *WriteClassStg* or *WriteClassStm* function at the time the file is created. When the user double-clicks on the file, the Windows shell only has to look up its CLSID among the subkeys of `HKCR\CLSID`. This is precisely what happened in the example above, when we double-clicked on a Word document with no file extension, as the following *RegSpy95* output shows:

```
_RegOpenKey     Explorer  HKCR      C33ECBE4
                'CLSID\{00020900-0000-0000-C000-000000000046}'
_RegQueryValue  Explorer  C33ECBE4  16      11840000 'ProgID'  ''
_RegCloseKey    Explorer  C33ECBE4
```

URL Processing with OLE

It's clear from the preceding discussion that Win95 lends a lot of importance to file extensions. They can be more than three characters now (for example, .html), but much of what users take for granted as built-in Win95 behavior is really a reflection of registry settings keyed to file extensions. Type "foo.doc" into the Start | Run dialog, and Win95 launches WordPad or Word. Type "foo.html" into Start | Run and, if the HTML file exists on a local hard disk, the Explorer launches your Web browser to view it. If a file doesn't have a "proper" extension, then (with the important exception noted in the previous section) you get the Open With dialog box.

But even as dependent as Win95—or, really, the Win95 Explorer—is on file extensions, it is a bit more sophisticated than that. Type "http://www.ora.com/index.html" into Start | Run, and your Web browser is launched to browse the O'Reilly & Associates home page. Well, that sort of makes sense given the .HTML extension: files with extensions of .HTM or .HTML are assigned an application identifier of "htmlfile",[*] and the default value of the `HKCR\htmlfile\shell\open\command` key is

```
"C:\MICROS~1\iexplore.exe" -nohome %1
```

But type plain "http://www.ora.com" and the same thing happens! Even though the "filename" ends in ".com", Win95 does *not* look for an old DOS .COM file; it somehow "knows" (which of course means that the registry somehow stores this information) to browse the Web. Win95 must know what do because of the "http://" protocol at the beginning, right? But check this out: typing plain "www.ora.com", with no "http://" prefix, produces the same correct result! As another twist, consider a URL that points to a Win-CGI program on another machine (for more on Win-CGI, see the book *CGI for Windows* by Bob Denny and Linda Mui, published by O'Reilly & Associates, available late 1996). For example, "http://pc168.west.ora.com/cgi-win/wregcgi.exe". Note the .exe extension. Now, if you type this into Start | Run without the http:// prefix, sure enough Win95 will screw up and look for *wregcgi.exe* on the local hard disk, in some path it can't quite get. But give it the http:// prefix, and it does the right thing.

---

[*] Actually, this isn't true on the vast majority of Windows systems running Netscape Navigator. There, files with the extensions .html and .htm have the type "NetscapeMarkup", as shown in the following output from *REGDUMP* (though the "htmlfile" type still points to "iexplore.exe"):

```
HKEY_CLASSES_ROOT
  .html -> "NetscapeMarkup"
    Content Type="text/html"
  .htm -> "NetscapeMarkup"
    Content Type="text/html"
  NetscapeMarkup -> "Netscape Hypertext Document"
    shell
      open
        command -> 'C:\NAVGOLD3\PROGRAM\PROGRAM\NETSCAPE.EXE "%1"'
  ...
```

There's something really interesting going on here, but what? Let's use *RegSpy95* to figure it out. If we use the Run dialog to enter "www.ora.com" while *RegSpy95* is trapping the Explorer's calls to the Registry, *RegSpy95* produces the output shown in Example 8-13.

Example 8-13. Registry accesses when "running" a URL

```
_RegOpenKey       Explorer  HKCU      C33EBC80
                            'Software\Microsoft\Windows\CurrentVersion\Policies'
_RegOpenKey       Explorer  C33EBC80  C3411000          'Explorer'
_RegQueryValueEx  Explorer  C3411000  0           NOFILE   'NoRun'   ''
_RegCloseKey      Explorer  C3411000
_RegCloseKey      Explorer  C33EBC80
_RegOpenKey       Explorer  HKLM      C33EBC80
  'Software\Microsoft\Windows\CurrentVersion\Explorer\ShellExecuteHooks'
_RegEnumValue     Explorer  C33EBC80  0     0     0
                            '{FBF23B40-E3F0-101B-8488-00AA003E56F8}'  ''
_RegOpenKey       Explorer  HKCR      C3411000
            'CLSID\{FBF23B40-E3F0-101B-8488-00AA003E56F8}\InProcServer32'
_RegQueryValue    Explorer  C3411000  8     8F90C10A ''  ''
_RegQueryValueEx  Explorer  C3411000  SZ    10    'ThreadingModel'
                            'Apartment'
_RegQueryValueEx  Explorer  C119F470  0           NOFILE   'URL'   ''
```

When we selected the Run menu item, the Explorer first checked whether the Run dialog should be disabled. (Like "DisableRegistryTools" discussed at the end of this chapter, "NoRun" is a policy that can be set with the Policy Editor.) Then, when we entered "www.ora.com" into the Run dialog, the Explorer immediately opened `HKLM\Software\Microsoft\Windows\CurrentVersion\Shell-ExecuteHooks`, and proceeded to enumerate its values. What are ShellExecuteHooks? They're a special form of shell extension that intercepts requests to launch processes from the Windows shell and provides special handling for selected processes. *RegEnumValue* returns the CLSID of an OLE in-process server, {FBF23B40-E3F0-101B-8488-00AA003E56F8}. This is the Internet shortcut handler, *URL.DLL*. Ordinarily, if the user double-clicks on an Internet shortcut (.URL) file, it causes the Explorer to pass the following command line to *ShellExecute*:

```
rundll32.exe url.dll,OpenURL %1
```

But in this case, when the user enters a URL in the Run dialog, it is invoked as well. It then passes control to the system's Web browser.

System Printers and the Default Printer

Interestingly, if your application needs to retrieve or to change information about the default printer, you use the initialization file functions rather than the registry API. This is the recommended method, in fact, on all Windows platforms. In the case of WinNT, this works because calls to initialization file functions in this case have been remapped to the registry. Since Win3x lacks a registry and Win95 does not support initialization file mapping, however, the initialization file functions on those platforms must read data from and write data to *WIN.INI*.

This is not to say that printer information is not stored in the registry. They are. (And we'll see in a moment that Win95 "migrates" printer information from *WIN.INI* to the registry.) The names of all printers available in the system's current configuration are stored as separate subkeys of `HKCC\System\CurrentControlSet\Control\Print\Printers`; the default printer is indicated by the `Default` value entry in `HKCC\System\CurrentControlSet\Control\Print\Printers`. The printer driver for each printer is stored in the `Driver` value entry of each printer's key, which is a subkey of `HKLM\System\CurrentControlSet\control\Print\Environments\Windows 4.0\Drivers`. Each printer's port is indicated by the `Port` value entry of each printer's subkey in `HKLM\System\CurrentControlSet\ control\Print\Printers`.

Whereas printer information in the registry is somewhat dispersed, it is more centralized in *WIN.INI*. Information on the default printer is stored as a formatted string (*<printer name>, <device driver name>, <port>*) assigned to the `device=` entry in the `[Windows]` section of *WIN.INI*. These three items of information for each of the system's printers are also found as formatted strings in the `[Devices]` section of *WIN.INI*; their general format is *<printer name>=<device driver name>, <port>*.

To retrieve information on the default printer, you use the *GetProfileString* function, which retrieves a string value from *WIN.INI*. Its general syntax is:[*]

```
DWORD GetProfileString(lpAppName, lpKeyName, lpDefault, lpReturnedString,
nSize) ;
```

where the parameters are:

LPCTSTR	*lpAppName*	A pointer to the string containing the name of the section of *WIN.INI*.
LPCTSTR	*lpKeyName*	A pointer to the string containing the name of the key within section *lpAppName*.
LPCTSTR	*lpDefault*	A pointer to the string that will be used as the default value if the key name cannot be found in *WIN.INI*. This parameter cannot be NULL.

---

[*] There are a number of syntactical variations of *GetProfileString* that allow the function to retrieve all section names and all key names in a section. However, we won't discuss them, since our focus is on *GetProfileString* within the restricted context of reading a particular setting from *WIN.INI* rather than from the registry.

LPTSTR   *lpReturnedString*   Pointer to a buffer to which the function is to store the key's value. If the key cannot be found, the function copies the contents of *lpDefault* to the buffer.

DWORD   *nSize*   Size in bytes of the *lpReturnedString* buffer. Note that this is a value, not a pointer.

The function returns the number of characters written to *lpReturnedString*. If the function fails because the buffer is too small, its return value is *nSize* - *1*, and it writes *nSize* - *1* characters plus a terminating null character to *lpReturnedString*.

This function call, then, retrieves the name, device driver, and port of the default printer:

```
dwChars = GetProfileString("windows", "device","",lpBuffer,
                           sizeof(lpBuffer)) ;
```

Since it writes all three values as a single string, you then have to parse the string. The following code fragment, for instance, uses the C *strtok* function to display information on the default printer in a message box:

```
if ((dwChars > 1) && (dwChars < sizeof(szBuffer) - 2))
   {
   char *szPrinter = strtok(szBuffer, cDelim) ;
   char *szDriver = strtok(NULL, cDelim) ;
   char *szPort = strtok(NULL, cDelim) ;

   sprintf(szMsg, "Printer %s on port %s uses driver %s.",
           szPrinter, szPort, szDriver) ;
   MessageBox(NULL, szMsg, "Default Printer", MB_OK) ;
   }
```

To change the default printer, of course, you have to know what printers are available on the system. To retrieve this information, it's best to use the *GetProfileSection* function, which retrieves all of the key names and their associated values within an entire section of *WIN.INI*. This function, incidentally, is one of the enhanced initialization file functions added to the Win32 API (and also to the Win16 API under Windows 95) that is not found in the Win31 API. Its syntax is:

```
DWORD GetProfileSection(lpAppName, lpReturnedString, nSize) ;
```

where the parameters are:

LPCTSTR   *lpAppName*   A pointer to the string containing the name of the section of *WIN.INI*.

LPTSTR	*lpReturnedString*	Pointer to a buffer to which the function is to store the key's value. When the function returns, the buffer should contain each keyword/value entry in the section along with a terminating null character. To mark the end of the string, a second null character is appended to the end of the final keyword/value entry.
DWORD	*nSize*	Size in bytes of the *lpReturnedString* buffer.

Like *GetProfileString*, *GetProfileSection* returns the number of characters written to *lpStringReturned*. If the buffer is too small, the function returns *nSize - 2*.

To retrieve the names of all system printers, you call the function as follows:

```
int size = GetProfileSection("devices", NULL, 0) ;
char *lpBuffer = malloc(size+2) ;
dwChars = GetProfileSection("devices", lpBuffer, size+2) ;
```

Each keyword/value combination written to *lpReturnedString* takes the form *<keyname>=<value>*, followed by a null character. In addition, a null terminates the section as a whole, so that the final keyword/value combination is followed by two null characters. (Its format is very much like that of REG_MULTI_SZ data.) So once you call the function, you have to parse *lpReturnedString* to extract each null-terminated string. The string containing the name of the new default printer also must be reformatted. Then the new default printer name can be written to *WIN.INI* using the *WriteProfileString* function, whose syntax and parameters are:

```
BOOL WriteProfileString (lpAppName, lpKeyName, lpString) ;
```

LPCTSTR	*lpAppName*	A pointer to the string containing the name of the section of *WIN.INI* to which the string should be written; if the section does not exist in *WIN.INI*, it is added.
LPCTSTR	*lpKeyName*	A pointer to the string containing the name of the key whose value the function is writing. If the key name cannot be found within the section, the function creates it.
LPCTSTR	*lpString*	A pointer to the string value to be assigned to the key.

WriteProfileString returns True if it succeeds and False if it fails.

The call to the function would resemble the following:

```
WriteProfileString("windows", "device", szPrinter) ;
```

The final step in modifying the default printer involves sending a WM_WININICHANGE message:

```
SendMessage(HWND_BROADCAST, WM_WININICHANGE, 0, "windows")
```

The *SendMessage* function is particularly important: without it, Win95 modifies *WIN.INI* but does not migrate information on the new printer to the registry. It's also important that you exactly follow this method for changing the default printer. For example, if you call *RegSetValueEx* to modify the default printer in the Win95 registry and then send the `WM_WININICHANGE` message, Windows changes the name of the default printer in the registry and then copies the original value back from *WIN.INI*, in the process overwriting your modification.

Automatically Launching Your Application

In some cases, you might want to have Windows launch your application automatically whenever Windows itself starts. For example, those using Win95 primarily for word processing might prefer to automatically launch their favorite word processor whenever they log on to Win95. Those using Win95 primarily as a Solitaire engine might want to have Win95 automatically launch *SOL.EXE* and *FREECELL.EXE* whenever they log on (we've even seen one person put `shell=sol.exe` in the `[boot]` section of their *SYSTEM.INI*, but that's another story).

Win95 provides two methods to automatically launch an application on a per-user basis:

- *As a link.* Whenever a new user logs on to Win95, the Windows shell retrieves the value of the user's startup directory (such as "C:\WINDOWS\ Start Menu\Programs\StartUp") from the registry; it is stored as a `REG_SZ` string in the `Startup` value entry of `HKCU\Software\Microsoft\Win-dows\CurrentVersion\Explorer\Shell Folders`. Windows then launches each of the applications whose links are stored in this folder. By placing a link to your application in this directory, you can have Windows launch your application whenever the user logs on.

- *As a registry entry.* If you store the path and name of your application to a value entry in `HKCU\Software\Microsoft\Windows\CurrentVer-sion\Run`, Windows will launch it automatically whenever the user logs on. The name of the value entry is arbitrary—you can name it anything, as long as you do not attempt to duplicate an existing value entry name; this is usually not a concern, since the key, if it exists, rarely contains any entries. The entry's value, however, should include the complete path and filename of your application. If you use this method, it's best to use *RegCreateKey* or *RegCreateKeyEx* to open the `Run` subkey, since it does not exist by default on Win95 systems.

Of these two methods, the first is far preferable, since it gives users more control over their Windows environment. If the user at some point prefers that the application no longer be launched automatically, he or she can simply remove it from the Start Menu program group. On the other hand, the user cannot access the Run subkey without using RegEdit or a similar editing tool. The fact that this setting is buried in the registry and is transparent to the user makes it unclear how and why your application is launched and makes it difficult for the casual user to stop running it automatically.

Along with launching an application at start up on a per-user basis, it is also possible to launch an application at start up on a per-machine basis. Many system-wide utilities, like the Windows System Tray (*SYSTRAY.EXE*), are run in this manner; the application is launched automatically regardless of which user is currently logged on to a particular system. To do this, you add a value entry to the `HKLM\Software\Microsoft\Windows\CurrentVersion\Run` key (note: HKLM, *not* HKCU) that contains the complete path and filename of the application that you'd like to have Windows launch at start up. The value entry's name is arbitrary—you can assign it any unique name that you'd like.

In addition to having Windows launch your application every time a Win95 session begins or a particular user logs on, you can also have Windows automatically launch your application at start up just one time. Several Windows applications take advantage of this feature. For example, Windows automatically reopens each Explorer window that was open on the desktop when the previous session terminated. The Windows setup program also uses takes advantage of this registry entry to relaunch itself when Windows is started for the very first time. This works just like the Run keys in HKLM and HKCU, except the key is called RunOnce, and after Windows launches your application, it automatically deletes the value entry. (This is all taken care of by a program called *RUNONCE.EXE*.)

The major use for this feature is to reopen your application if it was closed when Windows was last open. If you're developing with C/C++, you can respond to the WM_QUERYENDSESSION message in your main window procedure by writing a value entry to either the RunOnce subkeys, as the code fragment in Example 8-14 shows. If you're using Visual Basic, you can examine the value of the *UnloadMode* parameter in the *QueryUnload* event procedure of your main form. A value of vbAppWindows indicates that the request to unload the Window has come from Windows itself; in this case, a value can be written to the RunOnce subkey, as shown in Example 8-15.

Example 8-14. Writing to the RunOnce subkey using C

```
case WM_QUERYENDSESSION:
    RegCreateKey(HKEY_CURRENT_USER,
                "Software\\Microsoft\\Windows\\CurrentVersion\\RunOnce",
                &hKey) ;
    RegSetValueEx(hKey,"MyApp",0,REG_SZ, szAppPath,
                strlen(szAppPath)+1)) ;
```

Example 8-14. Writing to the RunOnce subkey using C (continued)

```
    RegCloseKey(hKey) ;
    return TRUE ;
    break ;
```

Example 8-15. Writing to the RunOnce subkey using Visual Basic

```
Private Sub Form_QueryUnload(Cancel As Integer, UnloadMode As Integer)

Dim hKey As Long
Dim strRunCmd As String

If UnloadMode = vbAppWindows Then
    strRunCmd = App.Path & "\" & App.EXEName & ".EXE"

    Call RegCreateKey(HKEY_CURRENT_USER, _
            "Software\Microsoft\Windows\CurrentVersion\RunOnce", hKey)
    Call RegSetValueEx(hKey, "MyApp", 0&, REG_SZ, ByVal strRunCmd, _
                    Len(strRunCmd) + 1)
    Call RegCloseKey(hKey)
End If

End Sub
```

Automatically Launching a Service

Whether they are located in HKLM or HKCU, the Run and RunOnce subkeys both automatically run applications at the point that a user logs on. In some cases, though, what's really needed is what is called a *service* on the WinNT platform: a program that runs whenever the operating system is running, independently of whether a user is logged on or not. Although Win95 doesn't support NT services in the strict sense, it does allow processes to be started when Windows boots, rather than when a user logs in.

To begin a process when Windows boots, rather than when a user logs in, you add a value entry to HKLM\Software\Microsoft\Windows\CurrentVersion\RunServices. (If you want to start the application only once at boot time, you can instead add the value entry to to HKLM\Software\Microsoft\Windows\CurrentVersion\RunServicesOnce.)[*] The value entry name is arbitrary; it can be any name, as long as it is unique to that key. Its value is the optional path and filename of the program to be launched, along with any required parameters. At system boot time, Win95 uses the *CreateProcess* function to launch the program.

---

[*] Since services are tied to computers rather than users, there are no RunServices or RunServicesOnce keys in HKCU. (Or, to put it another way, if an application creates these keys in HKCU, they won't be read by Windows at start up.)

This feature is particularly valuable for starting background server applications, which are expected to be accessible as long as a computer is turned on, whether or not a user is currently logged on to it. For example, system administrators naturally expect that their ability to access a remote registry should not depend on whether someone is using it at the same time; in many ways, in fact, it's preferable to access a registry remotely and modify its settings when no one is using it. Microsoft Remote Registry Services, in fact, is a particularly good example, since its installation routine creates a `regserv` entry in `HKLM\Software\ Microsoft\Windows\CurrentVersion\RunServices` that launches the remote registry RPC server, *REGSERV.EXE*, automatically whenever Win95 boots.

A major problem with applications started in this way, though, is that they are automatically closed when the user logs off. If any user ends his or her session by selecting the "Close all programs and log on as a different user" option, the application will not be restarted when the next user logs on. Certainly that's highly undesirable; if a Win95 system is responsible for running a Web server, for instance, it means that access to the computer's (or even the company's) Web documents is suddenly disabled, possibly for a protracted period, even though the computer itself continues to run. It also means that user intervention is required to restore a process that should, in most cases, be transparent to the user.

There is, however, a workaround that uses an undocumented Win32 API function, *RegisterServiceProcess*, to prevent an application from being closed. Its syntax is:

```
DWORD RegisterServiceProcess( DWORD dwProcessID, DWORD dwServiceType) ;
```

DWORD   *dwProcessID*   Identifier of the process to register as a server. This parameter is intended primarily to allow one process to register another process as a server; if the current process is being registered, this parameter can be NULL.

DWORD   *dwServiceType*   One of the values shown in Table 8-18.

Table 8-18. Values of the RegisterServiceProcess dwServiceType parameter

Constant	Value	Explanation
RSP_SIMPLE_SERVICE	0x00000001	Registers the process as a simple service
RSP_UNREGISTER_ SERVICE	0x00000000	Unregisters the process as a simple service

Typically, the function is called in response to the user's attempt to end his or her Windows session. For C programmers, the program's message processing loop should examine the *lParam* parameter of either the `WM_QUERYENDSESSION` or `WM_ENDSESSION` messages. It its value is NULL, Windows is being shut down, and there is no need to register the process as a service. If its value is `EWX_REAL-LYLOGOFF`, the user is merely logging off, and *RegisterServiceProcess* should be called. Before calling it, however, a pointer to its address should be retrieved using the *GetProcAddress* function. In addition, `EWX_REALLYLOGOFF` is not defined in any header file; it can be defined as follows:

```
#define EWX_REALLYLOGOFF 0x80000000
```

Example 8-16 illustrates a call to the *RegisterServiceProcess* function from a C **switch** statement responsible for handling the WM_QUERYENDSESSION message.

Example 8-16. Calling the RegisterServiceProcess function

```
static LONG (APIENTRY *pRegisterServiceProcess) (DWORD dwProcessID,
                                                 DWORD dwServiceType) = 0;

case WM_QUERYENDSESSION:
   #define EWX_REALLYLOGOFF 0x80000000
   #define RSP_SIMPLE_SERVICE 0x00000001
   #define RSP_UNREGISTER_SERVICE 0x00000000
   if (!pRegisterServiceProcess)
      pRegisterServiceProcess =
                  GetProcAddress(GetModuleHandle("Kernel32.dll"),
                  "RegisterServiceProcess") ;
   if (lParam == EWX_REALLYLOGOFF)
      if((*pRegisterServiceProcess)(NULL, RSP_SIMPLE_SERVICE) == 0)
         MessageBox(NULL, "Unable to Continue Service",
                        "Failure", MB_OK) ;
   return (TRUE);
```

Unless you have a subclassing control,[*] Visual Basic does not allow you to differentiate between a system shutting down to reboot or one shutting down to permit a new user to log on. Actually, this makes it extremely easy to insure that a server continues to run even if a new user logs on: *RegisterServiceProcess* must be called once from anywhere within a program. There is no need to intercept the WM_QUERYENDSESSION or WM_ENDSESSION messages. In VB, there is no need to call *GetProcAddress*. It is only important that the function be correctly declared:

```
Declare Function RegisterServiceProcess Lib "kernel32.dll" _
   (ByVal dwProcessID As Long, ByVal dwServiceType As Long) As Long
```

Supporting Plug and Play

For the most part, developers view Plug and Play (PnP), which supports dynamic changes in a computer system's physical configuration and allows system and application software to respond to those changes, as a matter of hardware and

---

[*] A *subclassing control* is an OCX custom control that allows you to intercept messages to Windows objects and either supplement or replace their own message handlers. The most robust subclassing control that we've found is the Generic Subclass control included in SpyWorks, OCX Edition, from Desaware. It gives your Visual Basic application full access to all Windows messages directed to your application windows, and allows you to determine precisely how those messages are handled.

device driver implementation. Whether because of the lack of useful code samples, the absence of a focused, detailed, practical discussion on how to respond to changes in hardware configuration, the newness of PnP and the relative paucity of PnP devices, or the fact that Win95 is the only operating system (at least at the time this book was written) that offers PnP support, the software side of PnP has been almost completely ignored. Since most developers are not particularly well versed in how PnP works at an application level, and because the information on PnP in the Win32 SDK—which is where the bulk of information on PnP for application developers is found—is not a model of clarity, we'll provide an overview of how PnP is implemented in the Win32 API before discussing some registry applications.

The basics of PnP support in application software are fairly simple: your application learns of a dynamic change to the system's hardware configuration by processing one of three messages in its window procedure:

WM_DEVICECHANGE

> The main PnP message, it indicates that the system's hardware configuration either has changed, is about to change, or that a pending change has been canceled. The message's *wParam* parameter indicates the *event*, or the type of change that either has occurred or will occur, while *lParam* is either 0 or a pointer to a structure that contains specific information about the change.
>
> If it is a pointer to a structure, that structure is a superset of the DEV_ BROADCAST_HDR structure shown in Table 8-19. In other words, DEV_ BROADCAST_HDR forms the header of every DEV_BROADCAST structure (incredibly, the documentation never really mentions this, and implies that *lParam* points to a DEV_BROADCAST_HDR structure *only*).
>
> For all events but DBT_USERDEFINED (DBT stands for "Device Broadcast Type"), you can determine which particular DEV_BROADCAST structure *lParam* points to by examining the value of the DEV_BROADCAST_HDR *dbch_devicetype* member. A value of DBT_DEVTYP_OEM indicates that *lParam* points to a DEV_BROADCAST_OEM structure; DBT_DEVTYP_ VOLUME, a DEV_BROADCAST_VOLUME structure; and DBT_DEVTYP_PORT, a DEV_BROADCAST_PORT structure.
>
> The sole exception to this is the DBT_USERDEFINED event, in which *lParam* should always point to a DBT_BROADCAST_USERDEFINED structure.
>
> If the event indicates a request to change the system's hardware configuration, it can be approved by returning True and canceled by returning

`BROADCAST_QUERY_DENY;`[*] otherwise, True should always be returned when processing the message.

WM_DISPLAYCHANGE

The message indicates that the display resolution has changed, usually because Win95 or an application has called the *ChangeDisplaySettings* function.[†] *wParam* indicates the new image depth of the display in bits per pixel; *LOWORD(lParam)* indicates the new horizontal resolution of the screen, while *HIWORD(lParam)* indicates the new vertical resolution of the screen. These are the same values that are returned by calling *GetSystemMetrics(SM_CXSCREEN)* and *GetSystemMetrics(SM_CYSCREEN)*, respectively.

WM_POWERBROADCAST

This message is sent on systems with an advanced power management BIOS to signal a change in the system's power system or its battery status that may affect its operation. Generally, the window procedure should not return a value after processing the message. But in cases where the message indicates a request to change the system's power state, the window procedure can return True to grant the request and `BROADCAST_QUERY_DENY` to refuse it.

Table 8-19. wParam constants for the WM_DEVICECHANGE message

wParam	Description	lParam
DBT_CONFIG-CHANGECANCELED	A docking or undocking request has been canceled.	0
DBT_CONFIG-CHANGED	A docking or undocking has changed the current configuration.	0
DBT_DEVICE-ARRIVAL	A new device has been inserted and is available.	Pointer to a **DEV_BROADCAST_HDR** structure identifying the inserted device.
DBT_DEVICE-QUERYREMOVE	Requests permission to remove a device; an application can deny this request by returning BROADCAST_QUERY_DENY.	Pointer to a **DEV_BROADCAST_HDR** structure identifying the device to be removed.
DBT_DEVICEQUE-RYREMOVEFAILED	Indicates that a request to remove a device has been canceled.	Pointer to a **DEV_BROADCAST_HDR** structure identifying the device.

---

[*] The documentation for `WM_DEVICE_CHANGE` mistakenly uses the constant `QUERY_BROADCAST_DENY` for this return value. This constant is not defined in any of the header files included in the Win32 SDK.

[†] Evidently, a preliminary version of the Win32 SDK for Windows 95 included a function, *ResetChange*, that sent the `WM_DISPLAYCHANGE` message twice, the first time with *wParam* set to False to indicate a pending display change, the second time to signal the change. The basic idea was that an application should modify the display settings in the registry, then call *ResetChange*. However, the function is no longer implemented in the Win32 API. If you use Spy++ to spy on messages, though, it mistakenly interprets *wParam* as a Boolean value.

Table 8-19. wParam constants for the WM_DEVICECHANGE message (continued)

wParam	Description	lParam
DBT_DEVICERE-MOVECOMPLETE	A device has been removed. This message can be preceded by the DBT_DEVICEQUERYREMOVE and DBT_DEVICEREMOVEPENDING messages for devices whose removal or ejection is under software control, although it can also be sent alone to signal a *fait accompli.*	Pointer to a DEV_ BROADCAST_HDR structure identifying the device.
DBT_DEVICERE-MOVEPENDING	A device is about to be removed. The application cannot halt the removal; the message provides an application with its last chance to prepare for the removal of the device.	Pointer to a DEV_ BROADCAST_HDR structure identifying the device.
DBT_DEVICE-TYPESPECIFIC	A device-specific event has occurred.	0, or a pointer to a DEV_ BROADCAST_HDR structure identifying the device.
DBT_QUERY-CHANGECONFIG	Requests permission to change the current configuration by docking or undocking; an application can deny this request by returning BROADCAST_QUERY_DENY.	0
DBT_USERDE-FINED	A user-defined message sent by an application or driver, rather than the system.	0, or a pointer to a appli-cation-defined data.

Table 8-20. The DEV_BROADCAST_HDR data structure

Type	Member	Description
ULONG	*dbch_size*	Size of the structure.
ULONG	*dbch_devicetype*	Type of the device; its value can be one of the following constants: DBT_DEVTYP_OEM. OEM- or IHV-defined device DBT_DEVTYP_VOLUME. Logical volume DBT_DEVTYP_PORT. Serial or parallel port device For all events except for DBT_USERDEFINED, this value indicates the complete data structure to which *lParam* points. If its value is DBT_DEVTYP_OEM, *lParam* points to a DEV_BROADCAST_OEM structure (see Table 8-21); if DBT_DEVTYP_VOLUME, to a DEV_ BROADCAST_VOLUME structure (see Table 8-23); and if DBT_DEVTYP_PORT, to a DEV_BROADCAST_PORT structure (see Table 8-22).
ULONG	*dbch_reserved*	Unused.

Table 8-21. The DEV_BROADCAST_OEM data structure

Type	Member	Description
ULONG	*dbco_size*	Size of the structure.
ULONG	*dbco_devicetype*	Type of the device; its value must be **DBT_DEVTYP_ OEM**, indicating an OEM- or IHV-defined device.
ULONG	*dbco_reserved*	Unused.
ULONG	*dbco_identifier*	The device's globally unique identifier (GUID).
USHORT	*dbco_suppfunc*	An OEM-specific function value.

Table 8-22. The DEV_BROADCAST_PORT data structure

Type	Member	Description
ULONG	*dbcp_size*	Size of the structure.
ULONG	*dbcp_devicetype*	Type of the device; its value must be **DBT_DEVTYP_ PORT**, indicating a serial or parallel port or device.
ULONG	*dbcp_reserved*	Unused.
char	*dbcp_name[1]*	A null-terminated string specifying the friendly name of the port (such as COM1") or the device connected to the port (such as "Hayes 2400 Smartmodem").

Table 8-23. The DEV_BROADCAST_VOLUME data structure

Type	Member	Description
ULONG	*dbcv_size*	Size of the structure.
ULONG	*dbcv_devicetype*	Type of the device; its value must be **DBT_DEVTYP_ VOLUME**, indicating a logical volume.
ULONG	*dbcv_reserved*	Unused.
ULONG	*dbcv_unitmask*	A mask identifying one or more logical units. Each bit in the mask represents one logical drive. Bit 0 represents drive A, bit 1, drive B, etc.
USHORT	*dbvc_flags*	A flag indicating the type of volume. A value of DBTF_MEDIA indicates a change of the media in a drive; a value of DBTF_NET indicates a network drive; any other value indicates a change to a physical drive or device.

In most cases, responding to PnP messages does not require registry access. We'll examine some of the cases in which it does, as well as look at some of the potential "gotchas" that you might encounter in responding to PnP messages.

Responding to WM_DEVICECHANGE

The set of messages that provide the least amount of information about the change in a device's status concern docking and undocking. Part of the reason is that the system also sends individual `DBT_DEVICEREMOVECOMPLETE` and `DBT_DEVICEARRIVAL` messages for each PnP device that the computer accesses through the docking station. In any case, for the most part, registry access is not required to respond to the docking or undocking of a computer.

Visual Basic and WM_DEVICECHANGE

When you program in C, you process Windows messages through a *window procedure*, which is a function in your application that Windows itself invokes whenever it sends a message. Visual Basic, on the other hand, hides Windows messages from its applications, and instead translates selected messages into the events supported by VB forms and controls. Visual Basic, though, does not translate the `WM_DEVICECHANGE` message into a VB event. So if you want to respond to dynamic changes in screen resolution, you'll have to add a subclassing control such as Desaware's to your project and have your control trap the `WM_DEVICECHANGE` message.

Docking or undocking a computer, however, does have one non-obvious side effect that you should be aware of, and that may require registry access. The *DBT_QUERYCHANGECONFIG* event indicates that, if the request to change the current configuration is approved, the subkey of `HKEY_LOCAL_MACHINE\Config` that `HKEY_CURRENT_CONFIG` points to is about to change. *DBT_CONFIGCHANGED* indicates that it has changed, while *DBT_CONFIGCHANGEDCANCELED* indicates that the possible change signaled by *DBT_QUERYCHANGECONFIG* will not occur.

Since `HKEY_CURRENT_CONFIG` is primarily a hardware branch maintained by the system, application software should probably never write to it. It's even fairly rare for application software to retrieve settings from it. But if your application has written to HKCC and depends on a particular value being set, you cannot assume that it will continue to be set in the new configuration.

For instance, imagine that you've developed a small desktop utility that allows the user to control mouse trails. Typically, mouse trails are enabled on some laptops to improve mouse visibility on LCD displays, but disabled on docked systems that use standalone monitors. If your utility is active, though, it should insure that the mouse trails setting remains the same regardless of the system's current configuration. So you might handle the configuration change messages as follows:

```
static BOOL fConfigToChange ;
case WM_DEVICECHANGE:
   switch(wParam)
      {
      case DBT_QUERYCHANGECONFIG:
```

```
        // We shouldn't need to retrieve the current setting from
        // the registry (it should be a global variable), but let's do
        // it anyway
        RegOpenKey(HKEY_CURRENT_CONFIG, "Display\\Settings", &hKey) ;
        if (RegQueryValueEx(hKey, "MouseTrails", NULL, NULL, szMTrails,
                            &cbszMTrails) == ERROR_SUCCESS)
            RegCloseKey(hKey) ;
        else
            // since MouseTrails isn't present by default, supply a
            // value
            strcpy(szMTrails, "2" ;
        // indicate that change of configuration requested; write later
        fConfigToChange = TRUE ;
        return TRUE ;
    case DBT_CONFIGCHANGECANCELED:
        // modify flag to indicate no notification of change
        fConfigToChange = FALSE ;
        return TRUE ;
    case DBT_CONFIGCHANGED:
        // write current setting to registry
        RegOpenKey(HKEY_CURRENT_CONFIG, "Display\\Settings", &hKey) ;
        // provide a default value if no notification
        if (!fConfigToChange) strcpy(szMTrails, "2") ;
        RegSetValueEx(hKey, "MouseTrails", 0, REG_SZ, szMTrails,
                      strlen(szMTrails) ;
        RegCloseKey(hKey) ;
        fConfigToChange = FALSE ;
        return TRUE ;
    default:
        return TRUE ;
    }
```

In a small special-purpose utility that relies on one or a few registry settings, our application would probably store the current values of those settings in memory at all times as global variables. General-purpose applications, though, are unlikely to. This presents a difficulty, since an application can't assume that Win95 will send messages signaling both the *DBT_QUERYCONFIGCHANGE* and *DBT_CONFIGCHANGED* events during the undocking process; a user can simply undock the system, so that only notification of the *DBT_CONFIGCHANGED* event is sent. To handle that possibility, a static flag, `fConfigToChange` in the case of our example, can be used to indicate whether the application has been able to retrieve the current value of the registry setting, or whether it has to substitute a default.

In addition to setting values in the new HKCC, if your application relies on settings in HKCC, you should reread their values when you process the *DBT_CONFIGCHANGED* notification. If your application depends on having the current value of the default printer, for instance, you should determine if the default printer has changed when you handle the *DBT_CONFIGCHANGED* event. For details on how to do this, see "System Printers and the Default Printer" earlier in this chapter.

Handling the *DBT_DEVICEXXX* events is broadly similar regardless of the device type. For the most part, registry access is not required here, either. It may, however, be useful to clear up a potential area of confusion that's likely to arise between device notification and autoplay. (For a discussion of autoplay, see the section "Reading from and Writing to the Registry," in Chapter 7.) For example, you may have an application that stores its data files on a local hard drive, but relies on a CD-ROM drive to access supplementary files, such as help files. Naturally, your application needs to know when the CD-ROM in the drive changes, making its help files unavailable. You may think that, to insure that you receive notification of a *DBT_DEVICEXXX* event, you should make sure that autoplay is enabled for that drive type. This, however, is not the case: autoplay specifically controls whether Win95 responds to the presence of a file named *AUTORUN.INF* when it detects a medium change; it does not control Win95's sensitivity to medium or drive changes. Provided that the driver supports it, Win95 will automatically detect a change in medium or the availability of a drive whether or not autoplay is enabled.

This is confusing, so let's look at it again: autoplay is really a plug and play feature that's based on Win95's ability to sense device changes. (A media change generates a WM_DEVICECHANGE message, as does a drive change.) You can enable and disable autoplay for particular drives. By default, autoplay is disabled on network and floppy drives. So in creating the sample program, we thought that we first had to autoplay-enable network drives in order to see if they were being disconnected, added, etc. But in spying on messages, we discovered that we didn't. So PnP provides automatic detection of all drive and media changes; that feature (as far as we know) can't be disabled. Autoplay is a feature built on top of PnP's autosense feature that executes an *AUTORUN.INF* script file when it detects a drive change.

Responding to WM_DISPLAYCHANGE

When your application receives a WM_DISPLAYCHANGE message, you should resize your main window, resize any child windows, and resize and reposition any interface objects within those windows. Given the ease with which users can change screen resolution on the fly, this is an important detail to implement in your application. It is also one that most applications currently implement poorly, if at all.

To respond to a WM_DISPLAYCHANGE message appropriately, of course, your application needs to know what the screen resolution was before the change. Once the message is sent, however, it's too late to retrieve this information; WM_DISPLAYCHANGE only provides information about the new screen resolution. So

---

Visual Basic and WM_DISPLAYCHANGE

As the earlier sidebar, "Visual Basic and WM_DEVICECHANGE," mentions, Visual Basic automatically translates selected Windows messages into events. The WM_DISPLAYCHANGE message, though, is not one of these. So if you want to control the way that your application responds to dynamic changes in screen resolution, you'll have to add a subclassing control to your project and have your control trap the WM_DISPLAYCHANGE message.

---

to handle changes in screen resolution effectively, your application needs to store the current screen resolution.

One of the ways of doing this is by using two global variables to represent the screen's horizontal and vertical resolution. In your application's initialization code, you can initialize these two variables by making calls to the *GetSystemMetrics* function. Then, in your window procedure, you can use them to determine how to resize application objects before updating them with the new values provided by WM_DISPLAYCHANGE. Although this approach allows you to respond to the WM_DISPLAYCHANGE message adequately, it does have a major drawback: it does not guarantee that your application windows are positioned correctly (or at least conveniently, from the user's viewpoint) when your application first loads.

Ordinarily, when your application loads, you'll want to place your windows at the same position as when the user last saved them. To do this, you should use the registry to save window coordinates when the user exits your application. However, those coordinates are only meaningful in relation to the screen resolution at the time the window was saved. When you later retrieve these coordinates from the registry, it's nearly impossible to determine whether the system's resolution has changed since the user last ran your application.[*] In other words, your application should not only respond to a WM_DISPLAYCHANGE message while it is running, but it should also be prepared to respond to a change in screen resolution that occurred since the last time that it ran. The best way of doing this is by writing the screen resolution along with your main window's coordinates to the registry. You can do this efficiently by using something like the WPOSITION data structure which is discussed in "Positioning Application Windows" in Chapter 9.

In handling the WM_DISPLAYCHANGE message, you can use the value of *lParam* to determine the new screen resolution. There is, however, a discussion in an

---

[*] The only real indication, which occurs *only* when a given screen resolution is changed to a lower resolution, is that some portion of the main application window is positioned off the screen. But even then, you can't be sure that that isn't how the user deliberately positioned the window.

early background paper from Microsoft, written by Lee Fisher, "Win32 Application Support for Plug and Play," that urges not to do this; it argues that since `WM_DISPLAYCHANGE` is sent asynchronously, screen resolution can change multiple times before an application processes the first `WM_DISPLAYCHANGE` message. Our experience suggests that the value of *lParam* is accurate, so in most cases it provides an accurate indication of display mode. However, if you want to be absolutely sure of the new screen resolution, you can call *GetSystemMetrics(SM_CXSCREEN)* and *GetSystemMetrics(SM_CYSCREEN)*.

There's also a potential "gotcha" involved in responding to the `WM_DISPLAY-CHANGE` message if you decide for some reason that, instead of using *lParam* or calling *GetSystemMetrics*, you'd like to access the registry directly. Ordinarily, the screen resolution is provided by the `Resolution` value entry in `HKCC\Display\Settings`. Although this value is usually accurate, and in fact is used by Win95 at system start up to initialize the display, it is possible to change the screen resolution dynamically *without* updating the registry. The first call to the *ChangeDisplaySettings* function shown below dynamically changes the screen resolution and updates the registry, while the second only changes the screen resolution:

```
nDisplay = ChangeDisplaySettings(&dm, CDS_UPDATEREGISTRY) ;
```

```
nDisplay = ChangeDisplaySettings(&dm, 0) ;
```

So while you do want to store screen resolution along with window position information in the registry, you don't want to depend on the registry API to provide you with the current screen resolution.

Coping with Changes (or, How to Respond When They Pull the Rug Out from Under Your Program)

Optimally, the plug and play messages always give you advance notice whenever some catastophic event—like the removal of a device on which your application depends—is about to occur. In that case, you can process the notification of the *DBT_QUERYCHANGECONFIG* or *DBT_DEVICEQUERYREMOVE* event, warn the user of the consequences of his or her action, and, if the user indicates that they still want to remove the device or change the system's configuration, close any open files and perform whatever cleanup is necessary for your application to respond gracefully to the user's action. Unfortunately, it isn't an optimal world, and more often than not, the only notification you'll receive is that some event has already occurred. This is particularly true of events that signal changes in drives and media: the *DBT_DEVICEQUERYREMOVE* and *DBT_DEVICEREMOVE-PENDING* event messages are almost never sent, and instead your window procedure is left to process a *DBT_DEVICEREMOVECOMPLETE* notification.

Obviously, once you're notified of a completed event, it frequently is too late to do anything about it. For instance, if your application is a word processor that loads only portions of its documents into memory at any particular time, a WM_DEVICECHANGE message informing your application that the remote drive that housed several open document files has disappeared usually means that the memory-resident portions of the files must be abandoned.

In less extreme cases, though, the registry is an excellent place to store information about the state of the application at the time that it was terminated, and that can be used to restore its state either the next time that the same user logs in or the next time that the application is launched. Whether this is done when the same user logs in or the next time the application is run depends on the character of the application: if the application accesses centralized files that are the same regardless of the user, the restoration procedure should occur the next time the application is launched. An accounting system, for instance, would be restored in this way. On the other hand, if the application allows the user to choose the files that the application creates or modifies, the restore procedure should execute the next time the same user launches the application. (For a discussion of the difference between application settings and user settings, see Chapter 9.)

For instance, Example 8-17 contains the portion of a window procedure that processes the WM_DEVICECHANGE message to determine if a drive used by the application is no longer available, and stores file information in the registry. To determine whether a drive is the subject of the message, the procedure examines the message parameters in the following sequence:

- It compares the value of *wParam* with *DBT_DEVICEREMOVECOMPLETE*, since this procedure is only concerned with devices in general (and drives in particular) that are no longer available.

- *lParam* is a pointer to a data structure that begins with a DEV_BROADCAST_HDR header. The routine compares the value of its *dbch_devicetype* member with *DBT_DEVTYP_VOLUME*. A successful test indicates two things: that the message concerns the removal of a drive, rather than the removal of some port device or other device, and that DEV_BROADCAST_VOLUME is the complete data structure to which *lParam* points.

- Assign the value of *pdbh*, the pointer to the DEV_BROADCAST_HDR data structure header, to *pdbv*, the pointer to the DEV_BROADCAST_VOLUME data structure. This makes the members of DEV_BROADCAST_VOLUME that are not included in DEV_BROADCAST_HDR accessible.

Example 8-17. Handling WM_DEVICECHANGE in the window procedure

```
case WM_DEVICECHANGE:
    // handle devices removed without notification
```

Example 8-17. Handling WM_DEVICECHANGE in the window procedure (continued)

```
if ((wParam == DBT_DEVICEREMOVECOMPLETE) && (!fNotif))
    {
    char szFileName[MAX_PATH+1] ;

    // determine if device is a disk
    pdbh = (PDEV_BROADCAST_HDR) lParam ;
    if (pdbh->dbch_devicetype == DBT_DEVTYP_VOLUME)
        {
        // determine if drive(s) was in use
        pdbv = (PDEV_BROADCAST_VOLUME) pdbh ;
        strcpy(szFileName, fn) ;
        if (IsBadDrive(szFileName, (LPARAM) pdbv->dbcv_unitmask))
            {
            char *tmpPath, szTempFN[MAX_PATH+1] ;
            long dwFileCtr = 1 ;
            // Display message to user
            MessageBox(NULL, "A drive the application was using "
                             "is no longer available.",
                             "Disconnected Drive", MB_OK) ;
            // Create "Terminated" subkey
            RegCreateKey(HKEY_LOCAL_MACHINE,
                        "Software\\MyCompany\\MyApp\\Settings\\Terminated",
                        &hKey) ;
            // Write path and name of file
            RegSetValueEx(hKey, "Filename", 0, REG_SZ, fn, strlen(fn)) ;
            // Determine Temporary FileName
            tmpPath = getenv("TEMP") ;
            sprintf(szTempFN, "%s\\temp%-ld.tmp", tmpPath, dwFileCtr++);
            RegSetValueEx(hKey, "TempFilename", 0, REG_SZ, szTempFN,
                          strlen(szTempFN)) ;
            RegCloseKey(hKey) ;
            // Code to save file comes here
            }
        }
    }
else
    // if notification, just modify flag
    fNotif = FALSE ;

return TRUE ;
break ;
```

The window procedure then calls the *IsBadDrive* function to determine whether the application's single file is located on a drive that is now unavailable. The code for *IsBadDrive* is shown in Example 8-18. It takes two parameters: the path and name of the open file, and the value of the DEV_BROADCAST_VOLUME structure's *dbcv_unitmask* member, which indicates which drives are unavailable, is a bit mask, with each bit representing a single drive. (Bit 0 represents drive A, bit 1 represents drive B, etc.) More than one bit can be (and frequently is) set. In addition, *dbcv_unitmask* depicts the status of all the system's drives, and not only those that have caused this message to be sent. For instance, if a system has two

floppy drives, both without diskettes, these are included in the value of *dbcv_*
unitmask when Windows sends a WM_DEVICECHANGE message to notify applications that a network drive has been disconnected. This makes it important to
examine each bit of the bit mask and compare it with the drives on which the
application files are stored. If there is only a single application file, the procedure
can simply examine each bit mask from bit 0 (for drive A) to bit 25 (for drive Z)
until it finds a match.

Example 8-18. The IsBadDrive function

```
#include <windows.h>
#include <dbt.h>
#include <string.h>

BOOL IsBadDrive(char szFileName[], unsigned long dwDrives)
    {
    char *drive, *tmpPath ;
    char szTempFN[MAX_PATH+1], delim[] = ":" ;
    LPTSTR szPossDrive = " " ;
    BOOL fTemp, fBadDr ;

    // get drive that has open file
    if ((drive = strtok(szFileName, delim)) == NULL)
        {
        char cd[MAX_PATH+1] ;
        GetCurrentDirectory(sizeof(cd), cd) ;
        drive = strtok(cd, ":") ;
        }
    // get removed drive
    for (*szPossDrive = 'a'; *szPossDrive <= 'z'; (*szPossDrive)++)
        {
        fTemp = dwDrives & 1 ;
        dwDrives >>= 1 ;
        // Is disconnected  drive current drive?
        if (fTemp)
            if (memcmp(szPossDrive, drive, 1) == 0)
                fBadDr = TRUE ;
        }
    return (fBadDr) ;
    }
```

If the application file was stored on a drive that is no longer available, the procedure creates an HKLM\Software\MyCompany\MyApp\Settings\Termi-
nated key and adds two REG_SZ value entries: Filename, which indicates the
original path and name of the file, and TempFilename, which indicates its
temporary filename and path. The next time the application is run, it should
check for the existence of a Terminated key, which serves as a flag indicating
an abnormal termination; then it should check for the availability of the drive and,
if it is available, copy the file from the location indicated by TempFilename to
that indicated by Filename. Finally, it should delete the Terminated subkey.

Allowing Registry Access

If you're developing a registry utility, you should attempt to respect the wishes of system administrators who *thought* that they disabled registry access for particular users by using the System Policy Editor. The intent of the System Policy Editor in imposing this restriction is that, although the registry can be accessed and its keys and values modified programmatically, editing tools that give the user access to the registry to modify its contents should refuse to run.

Rather than implementing this restriction at a system level, so that Win95 or the Windows shell decides whether to allow or to deny access to the registry to particular classes or kinds of applications, the designers of Windows placed the responsibility for enforcing this restriction on the applications themselves. To determine whether directly editing the registry is permitted, they are to read a registry setting and, if editing of the registry is disabled, refuse to load. Security resting on voluntary compliance is risky enough. It becomes even more risky when no one is told that they should voluntarily comply. And this is in fact the case with the restriction on registry editing tools: it is undocumented. Really!

Whether direct user access to the registry through editing tools is allowed or disallowed is controlled by the `DisableRegistryTools` value entry of the `HKCU\Software\Microsoft\Windows\CurrentVersion\Policies\System` key. `DisableRegistryTools` is a REG_DWORD value. If its value is 1, direct editing of the registry is not allowed; if it is 0, direct access to the registry is permitted. In the "default" Win95 registry, the `DisableRegistryTools` value entry does not exist, nor does the `System` subkey.

Example 8-19 displays the C language code and Example 8-20 displays the Visual Basic code for a function, *IsRegEditingDisabled*, that checks the registry to determine whether direct access with editing tools is allowed. The function returns True if access is allowed; if it is not, the function displays a warning dialog to the user and returns False, which allows the application to perform any needed cleanup operations before exiting.

Example 8-19. C language version of the IsRegEditingDisabled function

```
BOOL IsRegEditingDisabled()
    {
    HKEY hKey ;
    LONG dwDisableAccess, dwValueLen = sizeof(dwDisableAccess);

if (RegOpenKey(HKEY_CURRENT_USER,
        "Software\\Microsoft\\Windows\\CurrentVersion\\Policies\\System",
                    &hKey) != ERROR_SUCCESS)
        return FALSE ;
if (RegQueryValueEx(hKey, "DisableRegistryTools", NULL,
                    NULL, &dwDisableAccess,
```

Example 8-19. C language version of the IsRegEditingDisabled function (continued)

```
                            &dwValueLen) != ERROR_SUCCESS)
      {
      RegCloseKey(hKey) ;
      return FALSE ;
      }
   RegCloseKey(hKey) ;
   if (dwDisableAccess == 1)
      {
      MessageBox( NULL, "Direct access to the registry is not allowed.",
                 "Access Denied", MB_OK | MB_ICONSTOP) ;
      return TRUE ;
      }
   else
      return FALSE ;
   }
```

Example 8-20. Visual Basic version of the IsRegEditingDisabled Function

```
Public Function IsRegEditingDisabled() As Boolean

Dim hKey As Long
Dim lngDisableAccess As Long, lngValueLen As Long

lngValueLen = 4

' Test if key exists
If RegOpenKey(HKEY_CURRENT_USER, _
   "Software\Microsoft\Windows\CurrentVersion\Policies\System", _
              hKey) <> ERROR_SUCCESS Then
   IsRegEditingDisabled = False
   Exit Function
End If

' Test if value entry exists
If RegQueryValueEx(hKey, "DisableRegistryTools", 0, _
                   0, lngDisableAccess, lngValueLen) _
                   <> ERROR_SUCCESS Then
   IsRegEditingDisabled = False
Else
   If lngDisableAccess = 1 Then
      Call MsgBox("Direct access to the registry is not allowed.", _
                  vbOKOnly Or vbCritical, "Access Denied")
      IsRegEditingDisabled = True
   Else
      IsRegEditingDisabled = False
   End If
End If
Call RegCloseKey(hKey)

End Function
```

Summary

Chapter 4, *The Win32 Registry API*, focused on the *mechanism* for getting information in and out of the Win95 registry; this and the following chapter focus on the *policy*—on what information needs to go in what places for Windows to access it, and on how you might organize and store your own application-specific information. In this chapter, we've seen that:

- The information that you store in the registry can be divided into three broad categories: system-level information, application information, and user information.

- System-level information is used by Windows itself to integrate your application into the Windows environment. In order for Windows to successfully locate and process system information about your application and its files, the information that you store in the registry must follow a fixed format required by Win95 and the Windows shell.

- For the most part, system-level information needs to be written to the registry just once, by the installation routine that accompanies your application.

- You should always register your application path, as well as any shared DLLs or other shared files used by your application. If any of the shared files may already be installed on the user's system, you should use the Win95 file installation library, *VERSION.DLL*, to locate them and insure that your copy does not replace a later version of the file.

- You should always develop an uninstall routine for your application, and record its location in the registry.

- If your application makes use of data files with unique extensions, you should register these in HKEY_CLASSES_ROOT. You should provide an icon and a description for temporary files that the user does not access; you should also provide shell verbs for files that end users manipulate directly with your application.

- You can use the registry to automatically launch your application every time any user or a particular user logs in (although using the registry for this purpose is often confusing to users). You can also arrange to have Win95 load your application when a user logs in just once; this latter feature is most useful if the application was open when Windows was last closed. If you've developed a server application, you can also use the registry to have Windows load it automatically whenever Windows boots.

- In order for other applications to access OLE components, they must be assigned CLSIDs and registered in the registry.

- Plug and Play requires applications—even ones that seemingly have nothing to do with hardware—to respond properly to the WM_DEVICECHANGE, WM_DISPLAYCHANGE, and WM_POWERBROADCAST messages.

9

What Goes in the Registry: Application and User Settings

The previous chapter discussed Win95 system registry settings, which have a fixed structure determined by Win95 itself. You can of course also use the registry to store application settings (assorted items of information needed by your application, independent of who is using it) and user settings (settings that the user can configure directly or that can vary depending on who is using the application). Aside from following some general guidelines, particularly in selecting and naming the higher-level keys used to store these data, you control what goes into the registry, as well as when and how your application retrieves data from the registry.

Since in this case you have almost absolute control over the use of the registry, this is your opportunity to exercise your creativity, and to use the registry in novel and unique—but also in consistent and non-haphazard—ways. In this chapter, we'll take a look at some of the application and user settings that are commonly written to the registry, and suggest the best ways of handling them.

Application Settings

Application settings are software configuration settings that apply to a program as a whole or to the computer that it's running on, independent of who is using it. Consequently, while each user who works at a machine can have individual user settings, it makes sense to have only a single set of application settings, since they are the same regardless of the user.

While your application should create a registry application key when it's installed, its exact content is really up to you, and depends on the character and needs of your application. Since there are no real guidelines or clear standards for storing application information, we'll focus on the general format of the application key, as well as on some of the individual items of data that might be stored in it.

Setting Standards and Following Them...

Although we urge you to be creative in your use of the registry, such creativity is not the same as carelessness. Initialization files became dumping grounds for all sorts of incongruous data that were stored in a chaotic fashion. This could easily happen to the registry as well. If you're working in a multiprogrammer environment, or if you're developing more than one application that uses the registry, you should develop and adhere to a set of standards for registry usage.

To see what these standards should include, you just have to take a look at the current Win95 registry to find examples of the disorganization that results from a failure to develop—or adequately communicate—standards. Not surprisingly, perhaps, the worst transgressor turns out to be Microsoft. For instance, while most Microsoft software programs quite appropriately store their application settings in `HKLM\Software\Microsoft`, the Win95 Device Driver Kit (DDK) uses `HKLM\Software\Microsoft Corporation`.

Even more interesting is Microsoft RPC, which stores its settings in `HKLM\ Software\Description\Microsoft\RPC`. "Description"? What's that do- ing there? Well, the published guidelines for registry storage mention that ap- plication settings be stored in the "`Hkey_Local_Machine\Software\ Description` subkeys." Obviously, the RPC programmer stopped reading at that point, for the following paragraph goes on to define a "description sub- key" as `CompanyName\ProductName\Version`.

To Version or Not To Version

Although Microsoft recommends that you store application settings in the subkeys of `HKLM\Software\<CompanyName>\<ApplicationName>\<Version>`, you should decide whether that organization really suits the needs of your applica- tion. In creating their registry application key, various applications seem to have adopted three solutions:

- *No version information.* Instead of creating a key that indicates the current ver- sion of the application, many applications simply store application settings in `HKLM\Software\<CompanyName>\<ApplicationName>`, and com- pletely dispense with defining a separate version key. Microsoft's own Inter- net Explorer for Win95 does this; it stores its application settings in the subkeys of `HKLM\Software\Microsoft\Internet Explorer`.

- *Generic version information.* Rather than distinguishing the particular version of an application that's being installed, many applications simply name the version subkey "CurrentVersion." Win95 itself, in fact, follows this convention: Windows stores its major application settings in the subkeys of `HKLM\Software\Microsoft\Windows\CurrentVersion` and `HKLM\Software\Microsoft\Windows NT\CurrentVersion`.

- *Specific version information.* Other applications comply with Microsoft's guidelines to the letter by including a registry key that indicates the specific version of the installed software. For instance, one of the many Microsoft Office 95 application keys is `HKLM\Software\Microsoft\Microsoft Office\95`.

Your application should store its version number *somewhere*; the only issue here is whether it's stored as the name of a subkey or as the value of a value entry. Even where applications store no version information or generic version information in their application subkey, they still create value entries indicating the current version of the software. In the case of one of our examples, Internet Explorer creates the following two value entries in `HKLM\Microsoft\Internet Explorer`:

```
Build      REG_SZ  "516"
IVer       REG_SZ  "102"
```

Microsoft Windows also creates three version-related value entries in `HKLM\Software\Microsoft\Windows\CurrentVersion`:

```
Version            REG_SZ  "Windows 95"
Version Number     REG_SZ  "4.00.950"
SubVersionNumber REG_SZ  ""
```

If it's likely that users will have more than one version of your application installed at a single time (consider, for example, beta testers using a new version of your product while continuing to rely primarily on the older retail version), you'll definitely want to segregate application settings by version in the registry. Otherwise, you can organize your application settings in any of the three ways with which you feel most comfortable.

In many cases, applications create an application key and a version subkey, but don't populate them with any additional subkeys or value entries. So if you don't quite know what else belongs in the application key, take comfort in the fact that your situation is not unique. Resist the temptation to add values and subkeys just because you feel you have to.

The possibility that you might add an otherwise empty application key, of course, raises another question: why bother with the application key, and with storing version information at all, if the application key is otherwise empty? But storing version information, and having your installation program check the registry for an existing version number, is invaluable in handling three very common occurrences:

- *The user is attempting to install a previous version of your application over the current one.* Ordinarily, this is something that users do by accident—they've deleted some files accidentally, need to reinstall your application, and have found the wrong diskette or CD-ROM. Depending on how your application is structured and how the current version differs from the previous one, this can be catastrophic. Your installation program should check version numbers and, at a bare minimum, warn users that they're attempting to replace the current version with an older one. If the two versions are partially or wholly incompatible, you might require that the user uninstall the current version before proceeding with the installation.

- *The user is installing a new version over an older one.* In a new installation, you can simply write whatever default values that you want to the registry to configure the application in whatever way you see fit. In an upgrade, however, you want to be very careful to retrieve all of the old version's settings from the registry and preserve those that are still applicable to the new version. You also may want to delete settings that are no longer used, or modify existing settings whose usage has changed, or correct erroneous registry entries that were discovered in the last version.

- *The user is reinstalling the present version of your application.* A reinstallation is very different from a new installation or an upgrade. In particular, you want to be sure that your installation program preserves your application's existing configuration to the greatest degree possible.

Notice that, even though the application key is unused except for its version information, version information can still be sufficiently important that it determines how other registry settings, including both system settings and individual user settings, are handled.

While version information should always be present, the remaining items of information that can be stored to the application key (if in fact there are any) are widely variable. Given this diversity, we'll briefly survey some of the kinds of information that existing applications store in their application keys.

Installation and Licensing Information

Depending on the kind of installation program your application uses, placing some kind of application installation information in the registry may help to improve the user's overall perception of your application. At an early stage of the installation procedure, most applications begin a rather slow and time-consuming search for "installed components." Instead of scouring the user's hard disk for traces of a previous or current version of the application being installed, it's much more efficient to record some information about those "installed components" in the registry.

Some of the particular items of information related to installation that programs place in the registry include:

- The date and time the application was last installed.

- The target directory for the installation. Particularly if the user has overridden the application's default directory during installation, this can be very useful for an installation program to identify whether an application still resides on the system. However, adding a separate value entry for this information is usually unnecessary if you've added a key for your application in `HKLM\Software\Microsoft\Windows\CurrentVersion\App Paths`.

- The source directory for the installation.

- The name of the registered user and organization. The name of the registered user is not a user setting, since multiple users should not be registered owners of the same piece of software. If your installation program displays a dialog containing the registered user's name, it's best to retrieve this information from the registry. Frequently, an application's About dialog also includes the name of its registered user.

Other Application Information

Given the enormous diversity of applications themselves and of the kinds of application state information they need to store, it is difficult to generalize about the additional items of data that might go into the registry. Although the point seems obvious, it is important that this application state information in fact be application state information, and not something else masquerading as application state information. In particular:

- It should not be used as a convenient way of storing Windows system information that can be accessed with slightly greater effort through the Windows API. For instance, while the registry may be used to store the name of an application's current font, it should not be used to store an extensive collection of font information. The major dilemma here is one of data redundancy and concurrency of updates: font information is maintained by Windows at a system level. At the time that this information was gathered, it was accurate, although it duplicated Windows' own information. System fonts, however, can be dynamic: the Win95 user interface makes it easy to add new fonts and to remove installed ones, and Windows automatically records this information in the registry. However, Windows cannot update an application's font information, since it is unaware of its existence. And the application is unlikely to gather updated information on a sufficiently regular basis, since it's gone to considerable lengths to circumvent Windows services in the first place.

- It should not be used to store settings that are unique to a particular user; these should instead be stored in the subkeys of an application's user key. For instance, a word processing application might use its application key to store information about the paths and filenames of additional components, like dictionaries, spelling checkers, grammar checkers, and thesauruses. These are all basic components that remain the same regardless of who is using the application. It should not include the path and filename of a personal dictionary, though, since these dictionaries tend to be highly customized by their users. User settings should be stored in the user branch of the registry; for details, see "User Settings" later in this chapter.

Some of the more common items that existing applications store in their application keys are:

- Central special-purpose directories used by an application. For instance, if an application stores templates in a templates directory and its subdirectories, the registry can be used to indicate the path to this directory.

- The paths and filenames of any optional components or add-on tools used by an application. (These should not be shared system-level components like OLE servers, though.)

- The paths and names of application help files.

- The hardware devices for which an application has been configured. But this should avoid duplicating configuration settings maintained by Windows as a system.

- Information on application caches, assuming that an application uses its own data cache. This might include such items as the number of documents cached, the number of images cached, or the amount of memory or of local disk space devoted to a data cache.

- The number of items in the history list of hypertext and hypermedia applications. (This could also be a per-user setting. In all cases, though, the history list itself should be a per-user setting.)

- The number of items in an application's MRU list. (Once again, this could be a per-user setting as well. The MRU list itself, though, should always be a user setting.)

- Whether (and where) the application makes automatic backup copies of data files.

- Page setup information for printed documents.

- Application file filters for Win95 common dialogs.

These are just some of the kinds of application settings that can go in the registry. Since there are no real "standards" for what application settings should be stored in the registry, and since the registry is an excellent storage and retrieval (database) system for small and medium amounts of relatively static data, don't be afraid to be creative. In Chapter 11, *Migrating from .INI Files to the Registry*, for instance, you'll see that we use the registry to store frequency information about the users accessing a Web site, as well as about the Web browsers they use. If you're a database programmer, you may frequently need to assign a record number to multiple records in a relational database. The registry is, once again, an excellent place to store the next available record number. Think of the registry as a handy, in-memory file system.

User Settings

Unlike Win3x, Win95 allows multiple users to share a single computer system, and can save each user's computing environment. Each user can customize such features as system sounds, colors, and desktop patterns and wallpaper. Users will also expect that any customizable features supported by your application will be preserved from session to session.

In its default state, Win95 assumes that there is only a single user per system, and will not save individual user settings. The HKEY_USERS key of the Win95 registry contains a single subkey, .Default, in which all user settings are stored. HKEY_CURRENT_USER, the registry tree that contains the current user's settings, by default merely points to HKU\.Default.

On systems that have been configured to support multiple users, though, the construction of the registry user keys is somewhat more complicated. The key HKLM\Software\Microsoft\Windows\CurrentVersion\ProfileList contains subkeys for each user of a system. The name of each subkey reflects the name of a particular user. In addition, there is a subkey, NewUser, that contains default user settings for new users who log on to the system for the first time. Each subkey contains a single value entry, ProfileImagePath, whose value is the full path to the directory that contains the user's settings. When a particular user logs on to the system, Windows uses this value to read the appropriate *USER.DAT* file to form the user component of the registry. In a Win95 system configured for multiple users, HKEY_USERS is an amalgam of the *USER.DAT* file found in the location indicated by the NewUser subkey and the *USER.DAT* file stored in the directory indicated by the subkey belonging to the user who logs on to the system. HKCU then points to the subkey of HKEY_USERS that belongs to the user who is currently logged on. So when recording and accessing user settings in the registry, you write to and read from the subkeys of HKEY_CURRENT_USER. You can determine the name of the current user, and therefore the subkey of HKU that HKCU points to, by retrieving the value of `the Current User` entry from `HKLM\System\CurrentControlSet\control`.

To save your user-specific application settings, Microsoft's interface guidelines recommend that you create a registry key named `HKCU\Software\<Company Name>\<Application Name>\<Version Number>`. This allows users to maintain more than one version of your application, and insures that the settings from one version won't trample on the settings from another version. Most applications that record user information in the registry, though, don't differentiate between individual versions of the application. So if you aren't concerned about maintaining version-specific information for your applications, you can simply create a key named `HKCU\Software\<Company Name>\<Application Name>` to store individual user settings.

Exactly what user settings you choose to store, of course, is dependent on your application, and is completely up to you. In the following sections, we'll examine some of the more common settings that are stored in the user portion of the registry, and suggest efficient ways to store and retrieve these data. This is not meant to be an exhaustive list; you should feel free to add any per-user setting that makes your application easier and more intuitive for your users.

For example, the Win32 version of the FreeCell solitaire game stores its game statistics in `HKEY_CURRENT_USER\Software\Microsoft\Windows\Current-Version\Applets\FreeCell`. The Win16 version uses an *ENTPACK.INI* file ("Entertainment Pack"), which sounds like a good equivalent, but isn't: on a machine with multiple users playing FreeCell, the Win16 version will keep just one set of statistics for everyone, as if it were a team effort. The Win32 version will maintain separate game statistics for each player, which is much more appropriate.

Before examining what specific user settings you might store in the registry, though, we'll examine some of the complications that result from Win95's support for multiple users.

Handling Multiple Users

In retrieving individual user settings from the registry, be careful that your code does not require that a particular setting exist, and that some sensible default value is supplied in the event that a setting cannot be found. This is a particular concern here because per-user information on your application may not be available to a particular user who is running your application for the first time.

Imagine that a Win95 system has five users (or, more precisely, five user profiles): Jack, Jane, Jill, John, and New User. Jane runs your application's installation

program, which installs your application and writes default user settings to `HKCU\`
`Software\WidgetCo\WidgInv`. An initialization module in your application
assumes that these values have been properly stored in the registry, and will
retrieve them whenever the application is run. Jane runs the application, custom-
izes it, and closes it. The next time that Jane runs your application, all of her
settings are preserved. So far, so good.

Next, John attempts to run your application, but is not successful. Why not?
Because while you've written to `HKCU\Software\WidgetCo\WidgInv`, that's
really just a pseudonym for `HKU\Jane\Software\WidgetCo\WidgInv`.
When John launched your application, it attempted to retrieve the settings from
`HKCU\Software\WidgetCo\WidgInv`, just like before, but that now is a
pseudonym for `HKU\John\Software\WidgetCo\WidgInv`. Since you assumed
that user information was properly created by your installation program and failed
to provide adequate error handling or to substitute default values, your application failed when John attempted to run it. In other words:

```
HKCU\Software\WidgetCo\WidgInv != HKCU\Software\WidgetCo\WidgInv
```

That's because in one session `HKCU\Software` means `HKU\Jane\Software`
and in another session it means `HKU\John\Software`.

In trying to resolve the problem, you revise your installation program. Now,
instead of writing user settings to `HKCU\Software\WidgetCo\WidgInv`, you
use the *RegEnumKeyEx* function to enumerate the subkeys of `HKEY_USERS` and
then create a `Software\WidgetCo\WidgInv` subkey in each user's key.

This sounds good, but involves a basic misunderstanding of how the `HKEY_`
`USERS` tree is formed. Barring some anomaly (like a user loading a .REG file that
contains some other user's preferences), the `HKEY_USERS` key on a Win95
system configured to support multiple users *contains only two subkeys at any
particular time*:

- `HKU\.Default`, which contains the default settings to be assigned to a new
  user

- `HKU\<user name>`, which contains the current user's settings

The registry settings for other users not currently using the system are *not*
included in the registry; this prevents one user from accidentally or deliberately
modifying or even viewing the settings of another user. So the *RegEnumKeyEx*
function allowed the installation program to add user settings to `HKU\.Default`
and `HKU\Jane`. The key `HKU\John` *was not present in the registry* when the
application was installed, and therefore user settings could not be stored there.

There are several ways in which this and similar problems that arise from multiple users running an application can be handled:

- Always write a complete set of user settings to HKU\.Default. When a user launches your application, check HKCU to determine if user settings for your application are present. If not, copy them from HKU\.Default.

- To make sure that user keys exist, always use the *RegCreateKey* or *RegCreateKeyEx* functions, or examine the error code returned by *RegOpenKey* or *RegOpenKeyEx*.

- Always examine the error code returned by *RegQueryValueEx* and, if you use it to retrieve registry values, *RegEnumValue*. If it does not equal ERROR_SUCCESS, indicating that the value entry does not exist, have your application substitute some sensible default value for the missing setting.

Positioning Application Windows

Users typically expect that an application window be opened in the same position in which it was last saved. In some cases, they also expect that applications that were either minimized or maximized when they were last closed should also be reopened in the same state. The registry is the perfect place to store this per-user information.

There are several ways to store the position of application windows. One of the more common ways involves storing them as a value entry consisting of string (REG_SZ) data, similar to the following:

```
WindowPos ->"200, 150, 320, 200"
```

This method, however, is a legacy of initialization files, which were only capable of storing string data. It requires that the string be parsed and each of the four window coordinates be extracted from it.

A better approach stores the window coordinates as long integer (REG_DWORD) values. In that case, the WindowPos value entry shown above becomes four different value entries:

```
Left        200
Top         150
Width       320
Height      200
```

But to correctly position the screen, the program must now retrieve what is essentially a single set of values by making four separate calls to *RegQueryValueEx*.

The best approach involves storing all of these values as members of a single structure. In this case, we can store them as a value entry of REG_BINARY data and retrieve them with a single call to *RegQueryValueEx*. One way of doing this is by adapting an existing structure from the Win32 API (like RECT, WINDOWPLACE-MENT, STARTUPINFO, or WINDOWPOS); of these, WINDOWPOS is probably the most suitable. But we can also define our own structure, which allows us to store precisely the data that we want in our function, and to determine precisely what the function should do.

The first step, if we're going to define our own data structure, is to decide what's in it (duh!). Obviously, we want to include the standard information needed to position any window: the coordinate of its left edge, the coordinate of its top edge, the window's width, and the window's height. It's also useful to be able to restore the window to its previous desktop state (minimized, maximized, or restored). Finally, it's best to include the screen's width and height as part of our structure.

Why include the screen's width and height? This isn't immediately obvious. As part of its support for Plug and Play, Win95 makes it very easy to change screen resolution on the fly; and the *Windows 95 Resource Kit* includes a small System Tray utility, Microsoft QuickRes, that makes it easier still. As a result, it's unwise to treat the system's screen resolution as a constant, or to make any assumptions about screen resolution.* The current screen dimensions can be retrieved by calling *GetSystemMetrics*. But even if your application does that, it's frequently difficult to determine whether a monitor's current resolution is different from its resolution when the window coordinates were last saved. The seemingly best indi-cation—that some portion of the window is positioned off the screen—may well be the result of a deliberate action by the user; and if this is the case, the window should be restored to its previous position, with only part of it visible on the desktop. All this points to the need to include the screen's width and height as part of our structure.

Having decided on what information our data structure should contain, we can proceed to define it and store it in a header file, *WPOS.H*:

```
typedef struct _WPOSITION {    // window position structure
    int x;                      // left edge of window
    int y;                      // top of window
    int cx;                     // width of window
    int cy;                     // height of window
    int state;                  // window state (iconized, etc.)
    int lastX;                  // width of screen
    int lastY;                  // height of screen
} WPOSITION, *LPWPOSITION;
```

---

* Although it's clearly important that an application handle changes in screen resolution elegantly, this is something that very few applications do well. The sample code shown here illustrates how to resize an application window when screen resolution has changed between application sessions. In addition, though, your application should be prepared to resize the window when screen resolution changes *during* a session by processing the WM_DISPLAYCHANGE message. See the discussion of Plug and Play in Chapter 8, *What Goes in the Registry: System Settings*.

The next step is to decide where we'll store window position information in the registry. Since we want to make sure the window is restored to the position it was last in when each user of the application closed it, we'll clearly want to store this value entry in the one of our application's subkeys in HKCU. A good choice is to store it to a value entry named `WindowPos` in `HKCU\Software\MyCompany\MyApp\Settings`.

The final issue is how the window's position should be initialized—that is, how the window coordinates should be determined when a particular user runs the application for the first time. In developing an application, you can choose from between two equally acceptable options:

- On systems configured to support multiple users, write the `WindowPos` value entry to the current user's key and to `HKU\.Default`. The application's initialization code can then check for the presence of the value entry in its application subkeys in HKCU and, if it is absent, copy the entry from `HKU\.Default`.

- Provide a new set of values in the application's initialization code whenever the `WindowPos` value entry cannot be found in HKCU. This is the approach that we'll adopt in developing our sample application.

Example 9-1 illustrates how an application written in C might retrieve and save the main application window's position. The program's initialization code uses the *RegCreateKey* function to open `HKEY_CURRENT_USER\Software\MyCompany\MyApp1\Settings`; if the key doesn't exist (although presumably it should have been created by the application's installation routine), it is created. Then *RegQueryValueEx* is called to retrieve the `WINDOWPOS` structure from the `WindowPos` value entry. If the function returns `ERROR_SUCCESS` and the current screen resolution is the same as the screen resolution when the window was last saved, the four window coordinates are passed to the *CreateWindow* function.

Example 9-1. Positioning an application's main window

```
#include <windows.h>
#include <dbt.h>
#include "wpos.h"

LRESULT CALLBACK WndProc(HWND hWnd, UINT uMsg, WPARAM wParam,
                         LPARAM lParam) ;

VOID InitWindowPos(HKEY hKey, int cxScrn, int cyScrn,
                   LPWPOSITION lpWinPos, DWORD dwWinPos,
                   BOOL fNew) ;

int APIENTRY WinMain(HANDLE hInstance, HANDLE hPrevInstance,
                     LPSTR lpszCmdLine, int nCmdShow)
    {
```

Example 9-1. Positioning an application's main window (continued)

```c
char szClassName[] = "WindowPos" ;
int cxScrn, cyScrn ;
MSG msg ;
WNDCLASS wndclass ;
HWND hWnd ;
HKEY hKey ;
WPOSITION wPos ;
DWORD dwWndPos = sizeof(wPos) ;

// Define window class
wndclass.style = CS_HREDRAW | CS_VREDRAW ;
wndclass.lpfnWndProc = WndProc ;
wndclass.cbClsExtra = 0 ;
wndclass.cbWndExtra = 0 ;
wndclass.hInstance = hInstance ;
wndclass.hIcon = LoadIcon (NULL, IDI_APPLICATION) ;
wndclass.hCursor = LoadCursor (NULL, IDC_ARROW) ;
wndclass.hbrBackground = (HBRUSH)(COLOR_WINDOW + 1) ;
wndclass.lpszMenuName = NULL ;
wndclass.lpszClassName = szClassName ;
RegisterClass(&wndclass) ;

// Get current screen resolution
cxScrn = GetSystemMetrics(SM_CXSCREEN) ;
cyScrn = GetSystemMetrics(SM_CYSCREEN) ;
// Open application's settings key
RegCreateKey(HKEY_CURRENT_USER, "Software\\MyCompany\\MyApp1\\Settings",
             &hKey) ;
// Retrieve window position
if (RegQueryValueEx(hKey, "WindowPos", NULL, NULL, (LPBYTE)&wPos,
                    &dwWndPos) != ERROR_SUCCESS)
   // if entry is absent, call initialization routine
   InitWindowPos(hKey, cxScrn, cyScrn, &wPos, sizeof(wPos), TRUE) ;
else
   // only if screen size changed, call initialization routine
   if ((wPos.lastX != cxScrn) || (wPos.lastY != cyScrn))
      InitWindowPos(hKey, cxScrn, cyScrn, &wPos, sizeof(wPos),FALSE);

// Create and display window at designated position
RegCloseKey(hKey) ;
hWnd = CreateWindow(szClassName,
                    "Positioning the Application Window",
                    WS_OVERLAPPEDWINDOW, wPos.x, wPos.y, wPos.cx,
                    wPos.cy, NULL, NULL, hInstance, NULL) ;

ShowWindow(hWnd, wPos.state) ;
UpdateWindow(hWnd) ;
// Message processing loop
while (GetMessage(&msg, NULL, 0, 0))
   {
   TranslateMessage (&msg) ;
   DispatchMessage (&msg) ;
```

Example 9-1. Positioning an application's main window (continued)

```
        }
    return msg.wParam ;
    }

// Window procedure
LRESULT CALLBACK WndProc (HWND hWnd, UINT uMsg, WPARAM wParam ,
                         LPARAM lParam)

    {
    HKEY hKey ;
    RECT winRect ;
    WPOSITION winPos ;
    WINDOWPLACEMENT wpl ;
    PDEV_BROADCAST_HDR pdbh ;
    PDEV_BROADCAST_VOLUME pdbv ;
    char szBuffer[50] ;
    static BOOL fNotif ;
    DWORD dwWndPos = sizeof(winPos) ;

    switch (uMsg)
        {
        case WM_CREATE:      break ;
        case WM_SETFOCUS:    SetFocus (hWnd) ; break ;
        case WM_DESTROY:     PostQuitMessage (0) ; break ;
        case WM_CLOSE:
            // Get current window coordinates
            GetWindowRect(hWnd, &winRect) ;
            winPos.x = winRect.left ;
            winPos.y = winRect.top ;
            winPos.cx = winRect.right - winRect.left ;
            winPos.cy = winRect.bottom - winRect.top ;
            // Get current screen size
            winPos.lastX = GetSystemMetrics(SM_CXSCREEN) ;
            winPos.lastY = GetSystemMetrics(SM_CYSCREEN) ;
            // Determine if window is iconized, maximized, normal
            winPos.state = (IsIconic(hWnd)) ? SW_MINIMIZE:
                           (IsZoomed(hWnd)) ? SW_MAXIMIZE :
                           /* default */     SW_RESTORE ;
            // Write new value to Registry
            RegOpenKey(HKEY_CURRENT_USER,
                    "Software\\MyCompany\\MyApp1\\Settings",
                    &hKey) ;
            RegSetValueEx(hKey, "WindowPos", 0, REG_BINARY,
                        (LPBYTE)&winPos, sizeof(winPos)) ;
            RegCloseKey(hKey) ;
            break ;
        case WM_DISPLAYCHANGE:
            // open registry key
            RegOpenKey(HKEY_CURRENT_USER,
                    "Software\\MyCompany\\MyApp1\\Settings", &hKey) ;
            RegQueryValueEx(hKey, "WindowPos", NULL, NULL, (LPBYTE) &winPos,
&dwWndPos) ;
            // get window's current coordinates
```

Example 9-1. Positioning an application's main window (continued)

```
            wpl.length = sizeof(wpl) ;
            GetWindowPlacement(hWnd, &wpl) ;
            winPos.x = wpl.rcNormalPosition.left ;
            winPos.y = wpl.rcNormalPosition.top ;
            winPos.cx = wpl.rcNormalPosition.right ;
            winPos.cy = wpl.rcNormalPosition.bottom ;
            winPos.state = wpl.showCmd ;
            // Reposition window
            InitWindowPos(hKey, LOWORD(lParam), HIWORD(lParam), &winPos,
                          sizeof(winPos), FALSE) ;
            RegCloseKey(hKey) ;
            wpl.rcNormalPosition.left = winPos.x ;
            wpl.rcNormalPosition.top = winPos.y ;
            wpl.rcNormalPosition.right = winPos.cx ;
            wpl.rcNormalPosition.bottom = winPos.cy ;
            SetWindowPlacement(hWnd, &wpl) ;
            break ;
        case WM_DEVICECHANGE:
            // handle devices removed without notification: see Chapter XXX
            break ;
        }
    return DefWindowProc (hWnd, uMsg, wParam, lParam) ;
    }
```

If the `WindowPos` value entry cannot be found, or if the screen resolution (as determined by the earlier calls to the *GetSystemMetrics* function) has changed since the window position information was last saved—and this includes "on the fly" changes which the program learns about through `WM_DISPLAYCHANGE` (see the discussion of Plug and Play in Chapter 8)—the program calls the *InitWindowPos* function shown in Example 9-2, and passes it several parameters, the most important of which is a pointer to *wndPos*, the `WINDOWPOS` structure. If the value of *fNew* is True, the registry contains no information on the window's position, so the function assigns some default values based on the current screen's resolution. If its value is False, indicating that the screen resolution has changed, the function modifies the values of the data structure's individual elements so that the window appears in the same relative position on the screen. In either case, *InitWindowPos* writes the new coordinates to the registry.

Example 9-2. The InitWindowPos function

```
#include <windows.h>
#include "wpos.h"

VOID InitWindowPos(HKEY hKey, int cxScrn, int cyScrn,
                   LPWPOSITION lpWinPos, DWORD dwWinPos,
                   BOOL fNew)
    {
    if (fNew)
        {
```

Example 9-2. The InitWindowPos function (continued)

```
        lpWinPos->x = cxScrn/5 ; lpWinPos->y = cyScrn/5 ;
        lpWinPos->cx = cxScrn/5 * 3 ; lpWinPos->cy = cyScrn/5 * 3 ;
        lpWinPos->state = SW_SHOWNORMAL ;
        lpWinPos->lastX = cxScrn ; lpWinPos->lastY = cyScrn ;
        }
    else
        {
        // determine new scale
        long xMultiplier = (cxScrn * 10)/lpWinPos->lastX ;
        long yMultiplier = (cyScrn * 10)/lpWinPos->lastY ;
        // Recalculate values of structure elements
        lpWinPos->x = (lpWinPos->x * xMultiplier)/10 ;
        lpWinPos->y = (lpWinPos->y * yMultiplier)/10 ;
        lpWinPos->cx = (lpWinPos->cx * xMultiplier)/10 ;
        lpWinPos->cy = (lpWinPos->cy * yMultiplier)/10 ;
        lpWinPos->lastX = cxScrn ;
        lpWinPos->lastY = cyScrn ;
        }
    // Write new settings to registry
    RegSetValueEx(hKey, "WindowPos", 0, REG_BINARY, (LPBYTE) lpWinPos,
                    dwWinPos) ;

    return ;
    }
```

If you're not experienced using C, the call to *RegSetValueEx* in the *InitWindowPos* function in Example 9-2 is worth noting. Ordinarily, to write a structured data type to the registry, you pass a pointer to the structure, so the call takes the following form:

```
RegSetValueEx(hKey, "WindowPos", 0, REG_BINARY, &winPos, dwWinPos) ;
```

When we called the *InitWindowPos* function, though, we passed it a pointer to *wndPos*. In other words, *lpWinPos* is a four-byte pointer to the starting address of the *winPos* structure, rather than the structure itself. So *lpWinPos* must be passed by value to *RegSetValueEx*; otherwise, we'll be passing the function a pointer to a pointer, which it is not expecting. It is also important to pass *RegSetValueEx* a correct value for the size of the *wndPos* data structure. Since *lpWinPos* is a pointer to a structure, the value of the *dwWinPos* argument cannot equal `sizeof(lpWinPos)`, since this simply returns the length of the pointer (which is 4), and not of the data structure. Instead, *dwWinPos* must be equal to `sizeof(WinPos)`, which is why that value was passed as a parameter to the *InitWindowPos* function.

Finally, the application's window procedure in Example 9-1 is responsible for writing the current position of the user's application window to the registry when the application closes. This is done when the procedure processes the WM_CLOSE message, which indicates that an application should terminate either because of the actions of the user or because Windows itself is closing. The message handler calls the *GetWindowRect* API function to retrieve the application window's rectangular coordinates; these are then converted to values that are compatible with the WINDOWPOS structure before the call to *RegSetValueEx*.

Although the Visual Basic code responsible for positioning the application window, which is shown in Example 9-3, is broadly similar to the C code, there are three important differences:

- The definition of the WPOSITION structure is somewhat different, since the size of a Visual Basic integer is only two bytes, while the size of a C integer is four bytes. Consequently, the WPOSITION structure is defined as follows:

```
Private Type WPOSITION
    x As Long           ' left edge of window
    y As Long           ' top of window
    cx As Long          ' width of window
    cy As Long          ' height of window
    state As Long       ' window state (iconized, etc.)
    lastX As Long       ' width of screen
    lastY As Long       ' height of screen
End Type
```

- Other than the calls to the registry functions, positioning the application window does not require any explicit calls to the Win32 API. Such items of information as the window state and the screen resolution are readily available by accessing a form's properties, in the first case, and the properties of the screen object, in the second.

- Typically, the Win32 API measures screen coordinates in units of pixels; the default unit of measure in Visual Basic, on the other hand, is the *twip*.[*] While twips can safely be used with the WPOSITION data structure, this limits the portability of the application and its data. Consequently, the application uses the Screen.TwipsPerPixelX and Screen.TwipsPerPixelY properties to convert the application's screen coordinates to units of pixels for storage in the registry.

Example 9-3. Positioning the main window in a Visual Basic application

```
Private Sub Form_Load()

Dim lngXTwips As Long, lngYTwips As Long
Dim hKey As Long, lngWinPos As Long
Dim udtWinPos As WPOSITION

' Initialize public variables for twip/pixel ratio
sngTwipsX = Screen.TwipsPerPixelX
```

---

[*] A *twip* is a device-independent unit of measure that equals 1/20 of a printer's point. It expresses the size of an object when printed; sizes on the video monitor vary according to monitor resolution.

Example 9-3. Positioning the main window in a Visual Basic application (continued)

```
sngTwipsY = Screen.TwipsPerPixelY


' Get dimensions of screen in twips
lngXTwips = Screen.Width
lngYTwips = Screen.Height
lngWinPos = Len(udtWinPos)
' Get window coordinates from Registry
Call RegCreateKey(HKEY_CURRENT_USER, _
                  "Software\MyCompany\MyApp\Settings", hKey)
If RegQueryValueEx(hKey, "WindowPos", 0, ByVal 0, udtWinPos, _
                   lngWinPos) <> ERROR_SUCCESS Then
   Call InitWindowPos(hKey, udtWinPos, True)
Else
   ' Assign window coordinates
   Form1.Left = udtWinPos.x * sngTwipsX
   Form1.Top = udtWinPos.y * sngTwipsY
   Form1.Width = udtWinPos.cx * sngTwipsX
   Form1.Height = udtWinPos.cy * sngTwipsY
   Form1.WindowState = udtWinPos.state
   ' Check if screen resolution has changed
   If udtWinPos.lastX <> lngXTwips / sngTwipsX Or _
                       udtWinPos.lastY <> lngYTwips / sngTwipsY Then
      Call InitWindowPos(hKey, udtWinPos, False)
   End If
End If


Form1.Show


End Sub


Private Sub Form_Unload(Cancel As Integer)


Dim hKey As Long
Dim udtWinPos As WPOSITION


udtWinPos.x = Form1.Left / Screen.TwipsPerPixelX
udtWinPos.y = Form1.Top / Screen.TwipsPerPixelY
udtWinPos.cx = Form1.Width / Screen.TwipsPerPixelX
udtWinPos.cy = Form1.Height / Screen.TwipsPerPixelY
udtWinPos.state = Form1.WindowState
udtWinPos.lastX = Screen.Width / Screen.TwipsPerPixelX
udtWinPos.lastY = Screen.Height / Screen.TwipsPerPixelY


Call RegOpenKey(HKEY_CURRENT_USER, _
                "Software\MyCompany\MyApp\Settings", _
                hKey)
Call RegSetValueEx(hKey, "WindowPos", 0, REG_BINARY, _
                   udtWinPos, Len(udtWinPos))
Call RegCloseKey(hKey)


End Sub
```

Example 9-3. Positioning the main window in a Visual Basic application (continued)

```
Private Sub InitWindowPos(ByVal hKey As Long, udtWPos As WPOSITION, _
                          ByVal blnNew As Boolean)

Dim maxX As Long, maxY As Long
Dim sngMultX As Single, sngMultY As Single

maxX = Screen.Width
maxY = Screen.Height
sngTwipsX = Screen.TwipsPerPixelX
sngTwipsY = Screen.TwipsPerPixelY
' Use default values for new entry
If blnNew = True Then
   Form1.Left = maxX / 5
   Form1.Top = maxY / 5
   Form1.Width = maxX / 5 * 3
   Form1.Height = maxY / 5 * 3
   Form1.WindowState = 0
Else
   ' Determine new scale
   sngMultX = (maxX / sngTwipsX) / udtWPos.lastX
   sngMultY = (maxY / sngTwipsY) / udtWPos.lastY
   ' Recalculate screen coordinates
   Form1.Left = Form1.Left * sngMultX
   Form1.Top = Form1.Top * sngMultX
   Form1.Width = Form1.Width * sngMultX
   Form1.Height = Form1.Height * sngMultX
   Form1.WindowState = udtWPos.state
End If

End Sub
```

If your application supports the multiple document interface (MDI), you can also place child windows in the same position as when the user last closed them. This only makes sense, however, for applications that have defined special-purpose window classes. For instance, in a utility application that devotes one child window to a particular category of system information (like memory or disk drives), the user may legitimately expect individual child windows to appear in the same position when the application is opened. In a text processing application, though, repositioning a particular document's window is likely to provide little or no utility to the user. Your application should be able to dynamically reposition child windows in response to changes in screen resolution, though. Most existing applications do a *terrible* job of this! (Try it and see for yourself.)

Storing MRU Lists

It has become fairly standard for applications that allow users to create or open files to display a list of the most recently used (MRU) files at the bottom of the File menu, before the application's Exit menu option. This, in fact, is an extremely popular end-user feature, since it enormously simplifies access to commonly used files. It is also easy to implement using the registry.

One of the ways to do this is to create an MRU list key, and then to add one value entry for each item to be listed on the menu. These can be assigned names with consecutive numbers, like File1, File2, File3, etc. The value of each entry is the complete path and name of the file that the user last used. This approach has the advantage of portability across the 16-bit and 32-bit applications of Windows; with only slight modifications of code, an application can construct its MRU list from initialization files if it runs under Win3x, and from the registry if it runs under Win95. Microsoft Visual C/C++ 4.0, for instance, implements its file and projects MRU lists in this manner. At the same time, this is a very traditional, awkward approach to constructing an MRU list. In particular, it requires that the values assigned to each entry be continually parsed and moved to reflect a given file's position in the MRU list.

In contrast, the Windows Explorer offers a vastly superior method for implementing MRU lists. A subkey (like `HKCU\Software\Microsoft\ Windows\ CurrentVersion\Explorer\RunMRU`) contains several value entries, each of which has a single character name (a, b, c, etc.). The value of each entry is the name of a recently used file. In addition, the string stored to an entry named `MRUList` orders the names of the value entries whose filenames are to be displayed from first to last. Each character of the string serves as a pointer to the value entry containing the filename. For instance, an `MRUList` value of "dcabf" indicates that the most recently used file is stored in the value entry named `d`, while the next most recently used file is stored in the value entry named `c`, etc. The chief advantage of this scheme is that it minimizes the amount of string manipulation and the number of registry accesses required to maintain an MRU list. Although you still have to check whether a particular file already appears on the list, you can simply change the position of individual files by modifying the sequence of characters in `MRUList`, rather than by moving one or more string values from one key to another.

For example, adding a new file (i.e., one created with the File New menu option) to an MRU list that contains five items involves the following steps when using the traditional approach:

- Retrieving the filenames stored to each of the entries File1 through File4. This requires four registry accesses.

- Moving each filename from its current value entry to the next sequential value entry. (For example, the value stored in File1 must be moved to File2, etc.) This requires four more registry accesses.

- Writing the new filename to the File1 value entry.

In all, adding a new file to the MRU list using this technique requires nine registry read and write operations.

In contrast, the steps involved in the "new" approach require only three registry accesses:

- Extracting the last character of the `MRUList` value entry, moving it to the first character position, and writing the new `MRUList` value back to the registry. This requires one read and one write operation.

- Writing the new filename to the value entry whose name is the same as the first character of the `MRUList` value. This requires one write operation.

When we think of an MRU list, we typically think of files: a list of most recently used files is appended to the bottom of an application's File menu, and offers easy access to the file with either keyboard or mouse. However, the MRU list can consist of any related computer system objects. For example, the Explorer stores the following MRU lists in the registry:

- Document files regardless of the application that created them
- Windows previously open in the Explorer's desktop namespace
- Filename search criteria entered into the Explorer's Find dialog
- Source directories for software installation
- Recent network connections
- Commands entered into the Start Menu's Run dialog
- Printer ports

Nor do MRU lists have to be implemented as menu items; drop-down list boxes and drop-down combo boxes are also suitable interface elements.

Example 4-9 in Chapter 4, *The Win32 Registry API*, illustrated one way to build an application's File menu from the MRU information stored in the registry. Along with using the registry's MRU information to build a File menu, though, your application must maintain the MRU list while the application is running and, at one or more intervals, must write it back to the registry.

In developing your application, you can decide exactly what "maintaining the MRU list" means. In particular, you must decide when the application's File menu (or the interface object responsible for displaying the list) is to be updated, and when the registry is to be updated to reflect the current order of most recently used objects. By focusing on the example of a text editor and its File menu, we can explore these two issues in greater depth.

In most applications, once MRU data is retrieved from the registry, it maintains a separate existence in memory (and on the application's File menu) for some or all of the application's lifetime. When prompted by some event, like the notification that either the application or Windows is closing, the application copies the current version of its MRU list from memory to the registry. (It's also possible to implement an MRU list in a completely opposite fashion, so that the most current version of the MRU list is stored by the registry, but the application's File menu is updated periodically to reflect the MRU list in the registry. This approach tends to minimize memory consumption at the expense of increased registry access.) To update the memory-resident MRU list and the File menu, applications can focus on one of two events:

- The user opens an existing file or saves (and in the process assigns a name to) a new file. This is the way that most applications implement the MRU list: as soon as the name of an open document is known, the File menu's MRU list is updated to reflect it. Ironically, especially in applications that support a multiple document interface, its effect is to diminish the utility of the MRU list from the user's viewpoint. For instance, if the File menu displays the four most recently used files and the application has four existing documents open in MDI child windows, all of the files shown in the MRU list are currently open; as a result, the MRU list ceases to offer the user easy access to any files at all.

- The user closes a document. Although this method offers the user the greatest utility, almost no applications implement it (unless, of course, the user closes a new document at the same time that he or she assigns a name to it). It means that, at any given point, the entire contents of the MRU list displayed on the File menu consists of documents that the user can open.

For most applications, updating the MRU list in the registry occurs independently of maintaining it in memory or as an interface element. Usually, the registry's MRU value entries are updated either when a document closes or when the user closes the application. This, however, has a significant drawback: if the application terminates abnormally (which sometimes happens to even the most robust of applications), the registry is not updated to reflect the most recent set of open files. When the user next runs the application, the MRU list reflects the most recently used files from two sessions ago.

This suggests that the way that most applications implement an MRU list is actually the very opposite of an optimal implementation. Optimally, the application's MRU list in the registry should be updated whenever the user opens an existing document or names a new document. The memory-resident MRU list (and the list that appears on the File menu or in drop-down list boxes and combo boxes) should then be updated from the registry whenever the user closes the file.

Saving User Settings

Typically, applications that offer configurable options to the end-user allow users to save or not save these configurable settings. This allows a user to establish whether the application's interface should always be the same when it is loaded as when it was last closed, or whether changes made to the interface remain in effect only for the duration of a Windows session. Most frequently, this is implemented as an independent setting on the main window's Options menu. Whether or not the user chooses to save his or her settings, the state of *this* should-settings-be-saved option must of course always be saved (think about it).

The particular settings to be saved, of course, vary so widely from application to application that it is difficult to generalize about them. Nevertheless, many applications use the registry to handle the following:

- Displaying the application's status bar.

- Displaying the application's toolbar.

- Determining which buttons are to be included in the application's toolbar.

- Storing the default directory for saving data files.

- The status of toolbar buttons that serve as toggles. Typically, this is implemented using a bit mask or a byte mask.

- Colors to be used for particular interface elements. These settings should not duplicate Windows' color scheme, though.

- The number of files displayed in an MRU list.

- The names, positions, and states (maximized, minimized, restored) of open child windows.

Sound Events

For many users, the difference between a great application and an ordinary application is their ability to customize it. Frequently, the kinds of customization that users particularly enjoy—and that make them enjoy an operating system or an application that much more—have little to do with the core functionality of the application itself. Some of Windows' enormous popularity, for instance, is almost certainly attributable to the fact that users can easily add innumerous custom fonts, can readily select and change their screen saver, and can define custom wallpaper for the Windows desktop. It all sounds quite silly, but it's extremely important. Adding sound support is another way that an application can allow users to customize their environment, in the process making the user's experience with the application enjoyable. In this section, we'll examine the support for sound that Windows automatically provides your application, and then explore how you can add some extra sparkle to your application by taking advantage of custom sound events.

Like Win3x, Win95 allows sounds to be attached to particular system events, like opening a help window or displaying an application error dialog. Using the Control Panel's Sound applet, the user can determine which sounds are attached to particular system events. Information on these events and their related sounds are all stored in the subkeys of HKCU\AppEvents. The sound events automatically supported by Win95 are listed in Table 9-1.

Table 9-1. System sound events supported by Win95

System Event	Description
.Default	The sound played if a predefined sound file cannot be found
AppGPFFault	A program error occurs
Close	A window closes
MailBeep	Acknowledges receipt of a mail message (on mail-enabled systems only)
Maximize	A window expands to fill the screen or MDI form
MenuCommand	The user selects a menu command
MenuPopup	The user opens a menu
Minimize	A window is minimized or iconized
Open	A window opens
RestoreDown	A window is restored from full-screen
RestoreUp	A window is restored from an icon
SystemAsterisk	An informational dialog opens
SystemExclamation	A dialog with a warning message opens
SystemExit	Windows exits
SystemHand	A critical error dialog opens
SystemQuestion	A dialog with a warning query opens
SystemStart	Windows first loads

Since these sound events are supported at a system level, they are automatically added to your application "for free," without your having to do any coding to take advantage of them; in fact, you don't even have to be aware of their existence. This means, for example, that when the user minimizes your application, the sound assigned to the *Minimize* event is played automatically.

Defining application sound events

However, it is also possible to define your own application sound events in the Win95 registry, and several applications have taken advantage of this feature. For example, the Explorer defines an *EmptyRecycleBin* event that is triggered, and its associated sound played, whenever the user empties the Win95 Recycle Bin. Similarly, Microsoft Developer Studio adds support for several sounds that are triggered by events, like *BuildComplete* and *BuildWarning*, which are unique to a compiler's development environment. But largely because of poor documentation, the number of applications that have taken advantage of custom sound events is quite small.

Ordinarily, when you allow the user to customize some feature of your application, you incur the overhead of developing a maintenance routine that allows the user to configure these customization settings. This isn't true, though, of adding support for custom sound events. When you use the registry to define custom sound events, Windows automatically incorporates them into its Control Panel Sound applet, which allows the user to review the sounds that are assigned to particular events and to modify them. Provided that you've defined your registry keys properly, the details of reviewing and assigning sounds to particular events are handled entirely by Windows; you don't have to do any additional coding to give the user the ability to control your application's sound events.

Windows uses a group of labels to define all of the sound events that are available on a system, regardless of whether they are system sound events (i.e., defined by Windows itself) or application sound events. These labels are stored as the names of subkeys of HKCU\AppEvents\EventLabels. In addition, the default value of each subkey furnishes the text that the Control Panel's Sound applet uses to describe that sound. For instance, *AppGPFFault* is the name of a system sound event, while "Program Error" is the text that Control Panel uses to describe that event in the Sounds Properties dialog.

The presence of a subkey of HKCU\AppEvents\Eventlabels, however, doesn't define a sound event; it only provides the Control Panel with the information that it needs to maintain, display, and update information about that sound event.

Each application that supports its own sound events has its own subkey in the HKCU\EventLabels\Schemes\Apps key. The key belonging to Windows as a system, for instance, is HKCU\EventLabels\Schemes\Apps\.Default, while the Explorer's key is HKCU\EventLabels\Schemes\Apps\Explorer. The default value of the application key defines the text that describes the application in the Sound Properties dialog. For instance, instead of the Sound Properties dialog displaying the string ".Default" when it lists the Windows system sound properties, it lists the string "Windows," since this is the default value of the .Default subkey. The application subkey should in turn contain one key for each sound event that it supports. The name of the subkey should correspond to the sound event's corresponding key in HKCU\AppEvents\Eventlabels.

Given this general organization, it's tempting to conclude, if you want to add support for a custom sound event to your application, that all you have to do is add a subkey for your sound event to HKCU\EventLabels\Schemes\Apps\ .Default (which is where Windows system sound events are stored). Then, since it's a system sound event, Windows will support it, and you'll have expended minimal effort in adding a sound event to your application. Unfortunately, this won't work. While it is possible to add additional system events to the registry and to assign sounds to them (or for a user to assign sounds to them), Win95 and Windows applications do not fully support them. In fact, although the sound events are duly recorded in the registry, Windows won't read them automatically, since it's not expecting them to be there; nor does it know what particular event (or Windows message, generally) your application sound event translates into. So for your added sound events to be meaningful, *your application must be specifically written to call that sound event*; you not only have to define them as custom sound events, but also have the sound assigned to them played whenever the event is fired.

Attaching sound to sound events

Windows support for sound events is somewhat complicated by the fact that the Sound Properties dialog allows the user to define entire sets of sounds, called *schemes*. Consequently, the subkeys of HKCU\AppEvents presume that the user assigns sounds to events as a group, rather than on an individual basis. Out of the box, Windows recognizes two sound schemes: Windows Default and No Sounds. The names of all available schemes are stored in subkeys of HKCU\AppEvents\ Schemes\Names. The name of each subkey is a label by which Win95 refers to the scheme internally; the subkey's default value is the descriptive name that the user assigns to the scheme, and the name that the Sounds applet uses to describe the scheme. For example, the subkey .Default contains the default value "Windows Default", while the default value of the .None subkey is "No Sounds".

To allow the user to choose entire schemes or to include individual sounds that are not part of an existing scheme, the registry's HKCU\Appevents\Schemes subkeys are structured as follows:

- HKCU\AppEvents\Schemes\App has one subkey for each application (including Windows itself) that supports its own sound events; we'll refer to this as the *application event subkey*. For example, HKCU\AppEvents\ Schemes\App\MPlayer is an application event key.

- Each application event subkey has one subkey for each sound event that it supports. (These are the keys whose names are duplicated in HKCU\App-Events\EventLabels.) We'll refer to this as the *event subkey*. For example, HKCU\AppEvents\Schemes\App\MPlayer has two event subkeys, Close and Open.

- Each event subkey can have as many subkeys as there are schemes.[*] We'll refer to this as the *scheme subkey*. In fact, for each scheme named in HKCU\ AppEvents\Schemes\Names except for .None, there is a corresponding subkey in HKCU\AppEvents\Schemes\App\<AppName>\<Event>. In place of a .None key, there is a .Current key.

- The default value of each scheme subkey is the complete path and filename of the .WAV file assigned to the sound event reflected by its parent key.

- HKCU\AppEvents\Schemes\Apps\<<AppName>>\<<EventLabel>>\ .Current always contains the name of the *.WAV* file that is currently assigned to the << *EventLabel* >> system event. When a sound scheme is selected, the value of each .Current subkey is the same as that scheme's subkey. But when the user selects a sound that is not part of a sound scheme, this organization allows Win95 to preserve the user's settings.

- The name of the current sound scheme is stored as the default value of HKCU\AppEvents\Schemes. When the current set of .WAV files are not all part of a sound scheme, the default value of the key is .Current. This allows the Control Panel to display the current scheme, if there is one, whenever the Sounds applet is opened.

This organization of the registry to support sound is depicted in Figure 9-1, which focuses on the subkeys of a single system sound event, *SystemAsterisk*, as an example.

If you want to assign a sound to your application sound event, you have to make several choices. First, your installation program should definitely assign a sound to each custom sound event; otherwise, the user won't notice them, and you'll have wasted some of your development time. You can do this in either of two ways: you can provide a sound file to attach to each of your custom sound events in your installation routine, or you can select a similar Windows system event and use its sound for your sound event as well. The sample program below adopts this second approach.

The second choice concerns the number of sound schemes for which you define a sound. At a minimum, you want to attach a sound to your sound event's .Current subkey. But it's probably a good idea to assign sounds to the other schemes as well, if they are present. That means that, if the user changes sound schemes on a regular basis, your sound event won't fall by the wayside.

---

[*] Windows automatically handles the creation of these subkeys on an as-needed basis. As a result, how many subkeys each event key actually has depends on when the schemes were created in relationship to the event key, when the user changed schemes or defined new ones, and how the installation routine handled creating the event.

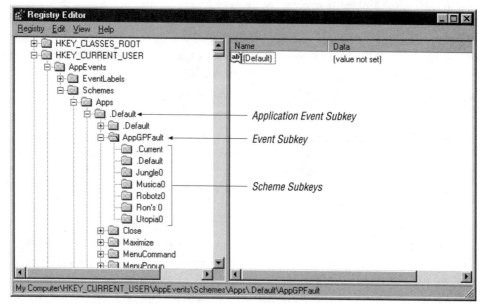

Figure 9-1. The organization of sound event information in the registry

Example 9-4 shows one possible implementation of this procedure. *AssignApp-Sound* is a C function that accepts five string parameters: the name of the application for which a sound event is being defined (*lpAppName*), the name of the sound event (*lpEventName*), the name of a comparable system sound event whose sounds are to be copied (*lpSysEventName*), and both the application description (*lpAppDescr*) and the event description *(lpEventDescr)*. The function then retrieves the name of each scheme and the sound assigned to that scheme for a particular system event. It then assigns a sound to the new application sound event for that scheme. When the function finishes enumerating all of the schemes (and substituting the `.Current` scheme for the `.None` scheme), it adds the event label key and writes the event and application description strings. The result is a fully initialized sound event that appears in the Control Panel's Sound Properties dialog and that can be modified by the user.

Example 9-4. AssignAppSound, a C function to define an application sound event

```
#include <windows.h>
#include <string.h>

VOID AssignAppSound(LPCTSTR lpAppName, LPCTSTR lpEventName,
                    LPCTSTR lpSysEventName, LPCTSTR lpAppDescr,
                    LPCTSTR lpEventDescr)
    {
    HANDLE hHeap ;
    HKEY hNamesKey, hSysKey, hAppKey ;
    DWORD cSubkeys, cbMaxSubkeyLen, nCounter ;
```

Example 9-4. AssignAppSound, a C function to define an application sound event (continued)

```
     DWORD cbNameBuffer, cbSysSound, dwDisposition ;
     char lpSysEvent[MAX_PATH], lpAppEvent[MAX_PATH] ;
     char lpSysSound[MAX_PATH], lpSysKey[MAX_PATH], lpAppKey[MAX_PATH];
     char lpAppPath[MAX_PATH], lpEventPath[MAX_PATH] ;
     LPTSTR lpNameBuffer ;
     BOOL fHasSound ;

// Define path to System Event
     strcpy(lpSysEvent, "AppEvents\\Schemes\\Apps\\.Default\\") ;
     strcat(lpSysEvent, lpSysEventName) ;
     strcat(lpSysEvent, "\\") ;
// Define path to App Event
     strcpy(lpAppEvent, "AppEvents\\Schemes\\Apps\\") ;
     strcat(lpAppEvent, lpAppName) ;
     strcat(lpAppEvent, "\\") ;
     strcat(lpAppEvent, lpEventName) ;
     strcat(lpAppEvent, "\\") ;
// Enumerate schemes
     RegOpenKey(HKEY_CURRENT_USER, "AppEvents\\Schemes\\Names",
                &hNamesKey) ;
     RegQueryInfoKey(hNamesKey, NULL, NULL, NULL, &cSubkeys,
                     &cbMaxSubkeyLen, NULL, NULL, NULL, NULL,
                     NULL, NULL) ;
// Allocate memory for scheme names
     hHeap = GetProcessHeap() ;
     lpNameBuffer = HeapAlloc(hHeap, 0, ++cbMaxSubkeyLen) ;
// Retrieve each scheme name
     for (nCounter = 0; nCounter < cSubkeys; nCounter++)
         {
         fHasSound = FALSE ;
         cbNameBuffer = cbMaxSubkeyLen ;
         RegEnumKeyEx(hNamesKey, nCounter, lpNameBuffer,
                      &cbNameBuffer, NULL, NULL, NULL, NULL) ;
// Change name of .None to ".Current"
         strcpy(lpSysKey, lpSysEvent) ;
         if(strcmp(lpNameBuffer, ".None")== 0)
            strcpy(lpNameBuffer, ".Current") ;
         strcat(lpSysKey, lpNameBuffer) ;
// Get sound assigned to scheme's SystemExclamation event
         if(RegOpenKey(HKEY_CURRENT_USER, lpSysKey, &hSysKey) ==
                       ERROR_SUCCESS)
            {
            cbSysSound = MAX_PATH ;
            if (RegQueryValueEx(hSysKey, "", NULL, NULL, lpSysSound,
                          &cbSysSound) == ERROR_SUCCESS)
               fHasSound = TRUE ;
            RegCloseKey(hSysKey) ;
            }
// Store sound to Timer scheme
         strcpy(lpAppKey, lpAppEvent) ;
         strcat(lpAppKey, lpNameBuffer) ;
         RegCreateKeyEx(HKEY_CURRENT_USER, lpAppKey, 0, 0,
```

Example 9-4. AssignAppSound, a C function to define an application sound event (continued)

```
                           REG_OPTION_NON_VOLATILE, 0, 0, &hAppKey,
                           &dwDisposition) ;
        if ((dwDisposition == REG_CREATED_NEW_KEY) && fHasSound)
            RegSetValueEx(hAppKey, "", 0, REG_SZ, lpSysSound,
            sizeof(lpSysSound)) ;
        RegCloseKey(hAppKey) ;
        }
    RegCloseKey(hNamesKey) ;
// Store application description
    strcpy(lpAppPath, "AppEvents\\Schemes\\Apps\\") ;
    strcat(lpAppPath, lpAppName) ;
    if (RegOpenKey(HKEY_CURRENT_USER, lpAppPath, &hAppKey)
                   == ERROR_SUCCESS)
        {
        RegSetValueEx(hAppKey, "", 0, REG_SZ, lpAppDescr,
                      sizeof(lpAppDescr)) ;
        RegCloseKey(hAppKey) ;
        }
// Store event description
    strcpy(lpEventPath, "AppEvents\\EventLabels\\") ;
    strcat(lpEventPath, lpEventName) ;
    RegCreateKeyEx(HKEY_CURRENT_USER, lpEventPath, 0, 0,
                      REG_OPTION_NON_VOLATILE, 0, 0, &hAppKey,
                      &dwDisposition ) ;
    if (dwDisposition == REG_CREATED_NEW_KEY)
        RegSetValueEx(hAppKey, "", 0, REG_SZ, lpEventDescr,
                      sizeof(lpEventDescr)) ;
    RegCloseKey(hAppKey) ;

    return ;
    }
```

Supporting sound events

If you defined your custom events as system events, you can call a single function, *PlaySound*. Its syntax is:

```
BOOL PlaySound(LPCSTR pszSound, HMODULE hmod, DWORD fdwSound);
```

LPCSTR	*pszSound*	Depending on one of the *fdwSound* flags, the name of the .WAV file to be played, a .WAV sound resource, or a registry event label that identifies a .WAV file. If NULL, it indicates the system is to stop playing the current sound.
HMODULE	*hmod*	If one of the *fdwSound* flags is SND_RESOURCE, specifies the handle of the executable file containing the resource; otherwise, its value is NULL.
DWORD	*fdwSound*	A set of flags that define the meaning of *pszSound* and determine how the sound is played. Their values are shown in Table 9-2.

Table 9-2. Values of the PlaySound fdwSound parameter

Constant	Explanation
SND_APPLI-CATION	The name of an application event defined in the registry. *pszSound* defines the application event; the application's root file-name defines which subkey of HKCU\AppEvents\Schemes\Apps the function queries to retrieve the name of the sound file. For example, if your application is named *MYAPP*, Windows will look for the custom sound event in HKCU\AppEvents\Schemes\Apps\MYAPP. If the key name and application filename don't correspond, *PlaySound* will be unable to locate the custom sound event or its attached sound.
SND_ALIAS	The sound belongs to a system event defined in the registry; the Win32 SDK documentation incorrectly indicates that this flag is not supported in Win95.
SND_ASYNC	The sound is played asynchronously; the function returns immediately after beginning to play the sound.
SND_FILENAME	*pszSound* is a filename.
SND_LOOP	The sound is played repeatedly until the function is called again with *pszSound* set to NULL.
SND_MEMORY	The sound is memory resident; *pszSound* points to the location of the sound in memory.
SND_NODEFAULT	No default sound event is used. If *pszSound* cannot be found, the function returns without playing the default sound; otherwise, by default, it plays the default system sound.
SND_NOSTOP	If another sound is playing, the function returns FALSE immediately and does not play *pszSound*; otherwise, it attempts to stop playing the current sound so *pszSound* can be played.
SND_NOWAIT	Returns immediately without playing the sound if the driver is busy.
SND_PURGE	Sounds started by the calling task are to be stopped.
SND_RESOURCE	*pszSound* is a resource identifier; in that case, *hmod* must identify the instance that contains the resource.
SND_SYNC	The sound plays synchronously; the function returns only after *pszSound* finishes playing.

If you include the *SND_ALIAS* flag, Windows will play the file whose name is stored as the default value of HKCU\AppEvents\Schemes\Apps\.Default\ <pszSound>\.Current; if you include the *SND_APPLICATION* flag, Windows plays the file whose name is stored as the default value of the HKCU\ AppEvents\Schemes\Apps\<root application name>\<pszSound>\ .Current key.

For instance, if you've used the *AssignAppSound* function shown earlier in Example 9-4 to define a sound event named *Timer* that belongs to an application

---

Determining if Sound Is Enabled on a System

Before calling the *PlaySound* function, you might want to determine whether the system on which your application is running supports sound. You can do this by calling the *waveOutGetNumDevs* function; it takes no parameters, and returns the number of installed devices that support sound. If its return value is 0, the system does not support sound.

---

named *MYAPP*, and your application is named *MYAPP.EXE*, the following code fragment plays the sound assigned to the event:

```
if (waveOutGetNumDevs > 1)
    PlaySound("Timer", NULL, SND_APPLICATION | SND_ASYNC | SND_NODEFAULT) ;
```

Summary

Along with system settings, you should use the registry to store both application settings and user settings. In this chapter, we've tried to provide some guidelines and suggestions for doing that:

- *Application settings* apply to your application regardless of who is using it. Typically, you should store application settings in the subkeys of HKLM\ Software\<CompanyName>\<AppName>.

- Saving separate *user settings* allows each user to configure your application in a way that makes sense to them. Typically, you should write settings for the current user to the subkeys of HKCU\Software\<CompanyName>\<App-Name>.

- If your application supports user settings, it is important to recognize that, if a particular user installs your application on a system configured to support multiple users, user settings many not be available to other users. You should decide how you want to handle this possibility when you design your installation program.

- Whenever possible, take advantage of the registry's support for diverse data types in order to minimize coding. For instance, rather than storing window settings as string data that your application must parse, use a structured data type that can be passed almost without additional processing to a Win32 API routine.

- In deciding what data to store in the registry, feel free to be creative. The registry is a very efficient structure for storing and retrieving data. Along with automagically committing your data to disk, it also offers a registry-wide locking scheme to safeguard the integrity of your data. (On the other hand, note that there is no built-in support for *sorting* registry values, and hence no built-in support for performing binary searches.)

- At the same time, be consistent in your use of the registry. Follow Microsoft's guidelines when writing to the registry (even though Microsoft itself often strays from these guidelines), and, if your application is just one of many produced by your company, make sure that your company has developed uniform standards for registry storage.

10

Spying on the Registry

When we first began work on *Inside the Windows 95 Registry*, we intended to write a book that thoroughly documented the minimally documented registry: not just the registry API, but the actual registry itself. We wanted to explore the value entries belonging to thousands of keys, show what values they might take, and discuss how the Win95 registry used them. We wanted to do this, moreover, in a way that, instead of focusing on individual registry tips and tricks that you could use (and that might get you into serious trouble) located this information within the broader context of how Win95 works.

However, the whole idea of a "complete" registry reference was really based on some fundamental misconceptions: since any application can put anything it wants (and users can put anything they want) into the registry, there is a way in which a "complete" registry reference is as impossible as a "complete" list of prime numbers. Even if we limit ourselves to some sort of "standard" Win95 registry—the registry found in a newly-installed copy of Win95 with no applications running—we soon realize that a "standard" Win95 registry is also a mythical being. Is this "standard" copy of Win95 connected to a network? Which one? Is there a Plug and Play (PnP) BIOS? Does the user have Win95 Plus! installed? How about a Web browser? Microsoft's or Netscape's? And, surely, they are running some application, such as Microsoft Office. But which version? Is the system enabled for multiple users? Has a system administrator established policies? There are a million questions like this confronting anyone who wants to assemble a "complete" registry reference, or even to describe a single "standard" Win95 registry. It's not possible. At least, it's not possible to do a good job.

So instead, we ended up writing a book for developers that focuses on how to use the registry API and how to use the registry. For the most part, this has been a book about using the registry safely, and not about exploring it. Except for admittedly many occasional asides, we haven't really explained how actual applications use—or misuse, or fail to use, as the case may be—the registry.

However, we have included on the disk accompanying this book two utilities—*RegSpy95* and *ApiSpy32*—that you can use to explore the registry. Rather than give you some fish, in other words, we have given you two fishing poles, and in this chapter we'll teach you how to fish.

RegSpy95 is a console mode Win32 application that was developed especially for this book by Alex Shmidt. It intercepts programs' requests for registry services from the Win95 Virtual Machine Manager (VMM), as well as their calls to the *SYSTEM.INI* initialization file during system start up. It also shows registry accesses coming from Win95 itself.

APISpy32 was developed by Matt Pietrek; a version of it originally appeared in his book, *Windows 95 System Programming Secrets*, published by IDG Books. We heartily recommend this book; for a brief excerpt, "Dirty Little Secrets about Windows 95," and online ordering information, see *http://www.ora.com/pub/examples/windows/win95.update/dirty.html.*

The Win95 Registry Monitor (RegMon)

The diskette accompanying *Inside the Windows 95 Registry* contains an additional registry spying utility, the *Win95 Registry Monitor*, or *RegMon*, which was written by Mark Russinovich and Bryce Cogswell. Like *RegSpy95*, *RegMon* consists of two components: *REGVXD.VXD*, a dynamic VxD; and *REG-MON.EXE*, the shell program that communicates with *RegVxD*. Since *RegVxD* is a dynamic rather that a static VxD, it's loaded automatically when you launch *RegMon*. (This means, though, that you can't use it to spy on Win95 during system initialization.) *REGMON.EXE* itself is a Windows application; that is, it collects information from *RegVxD* and displays it in a window. For NTRegMon, a registry monitor for Windows NT, see *http://www.ora.com/pub/examples/windows/win95.update/registry.html.*

RegSpy95

RegSpy95 spies on a system's interactions with the Win95 registry as a background process, and therefore doesn't require any user interaction or intervention at runtime. Instead, the software accepts command-line parameters that control its operation, reads settings from a configuration file, or does both. When it executes, *RegSpy95* intercepts all calls to the registry that are handled by the VMM and stores information about the calls in a buffer; when you execute the *RegSpy95* program, it displays this information to the console. However, because Win95 programs use the registry extensively, a single *RegSpy95* session can easily spit out an overwhelming amount of information. For this reason, it's usually best to redirect *RegSpy95*'s output to a file that can be viewed later with a standard text editor.

In documenting *RegSpy95*, we'll begin by showing you how to configure and run *RegSpy95*. Then we'll provide a few examples that show how you might go about using it to explore the registry. Finally, we'll examine the architecture of *RegSpy95* and its accompanying virtual device driver (VxD), *FOOTPRNT.386*, and discuss how the program can intercept calls to the registry.

Running RegSpy95

RegSpy95 consists of two components: a virtual device driver (VxD) named *FOOT-PRNT.386*, and an executable file, *REGSPY95.EXE*. *REGSPY95.EXE* is really just a shell that organizes, formats, displays, and deletes the information collected by the VxD, and in some cases controls its operation; the actual spying, though, is done by the VxD. *FOOTPRNT.386* is a static VxD; this means that it must be loaded when Win95 boots. To do this, copy *FOOTPRNT.386* to a directory of your choice, and insert the following line in the [386Enh] section of your *SYSTEM.INI* file:

```
device=c:\Windows\System\footprnt.386
```

(assuming, of course, that *C:\WINDOWS\SYSTEM* is the path to the directory in which you've chosen to store *FOOTPRNT.386*).

RegSpy95 Source Code

Along with its executable components, the *Inside the Windows 95 Registry* diskette includes the complete source code for *REGSPY95.EXE* (although not for *FOOTPRNT.386*). For information on building *REGSPY95.EXE*, see "Rebuilding RegSpy95" later in this chapter.

If you prefer, you can use the registry instead of *SYSTEM.INI* to load *FOOT-PRNT.386*. Using RegEdit, do the following:

1. Create a new subkey of HKLM\System\CurrentControlSet\Services\ VxD and name it FOOTPRNT. The subkeys of HKLM\System\CurrentCon- trolSet\Services\VxD define the static VxDs that are to be loaded at system start up.

2. Add a `REG_BINARY` value entry to the `HKLM\System\CurrentControlSet\Services\VxD\FOOTPRNT` key. Name it `Start`, and assign it a value of 00. This defines `FOOTPRNT`'s load order.

3. Add a second value entry, this one to contain `REG_SZ` data. Name it `StaticVxD`. Like the device= line in *SYSTEM.INI*, its value should be the complete path and filename of *FOOTPRNT.386*.

Or, assuming that *FOOTPRNT.386* is located in *C:\BOOKS\REGISTRY* for example, just run the following RegEdit "macro," *FOOTPRNT.REG*:

```
REGEDIT4
[HKEY_LOCAL_MACHINE\System\CurrentControlSet\Services\VxD\FOOTPRNT]
"Start"=hex:00
"StaticVxD"="c:\\books\\registry\\footprnt.386"
```

Be Careful not to Double-Load VxDs!

You may have surmised that you can use the registry, rather than *SYSTEM.INI*, to load any static VxD; this is in fact true. However, if you choose to "migrate" the definition of a static VxD from *SYSTEM.INI* to the registry, be sure to delete or to comment out the VxD's `DEVICE=` line in *SYSTEM.INI*. (The comment character is a semi-colon.) Otherwise, you'll end up double loading the VxD. *FOOTPRNT* can handle this; it checks to see if an instance of itself is already loaded, and if it is, refuses to load the new instance. Most or all other VxDs, however, do not; the result is inevitably a system crash during start up.

Why did we choose to spy on the registry using a VxD? Because as we saw in Chapter 5, *Win95 Registry Access from Win16, DOS, and VxDs*, all Win95 access to the local registry eventually winds up down at the VMM/VxD layer. By intercepting registry calls at that layer, *RegSpy95* sees *all local registry accesses*. By trapping the VMM *_RegOpenKey* service, for example, we see all Win32 calls to *RegOpenKey*, all Win16 calls, even any DOS-based registry calls, and of course the many registry accesses which come from the VMM/VxD layer itself.

RegSpy95 and Win95

RegSpy95 was developed to run exclusively under Win95; it does not run under either WinNT or Win32s. When it is launched, *RegSpy32* tests its current environment; if it finds that it is running under either of these two platforms, it refuses to continue, and displays an error message. Again, for a registry monitor for Windows NT, see *http://www.ora.com/pub/examples/windows/win95.update/registry.html*.

Command-Line Options

RegSpy95 is a configurable Win95 console (Win32 character mode) program that accepts several one-character command-line switches and reads settings from a configuration file that also is specified at the command line. The command-line switches can be preceded either by the dash ("-") or the slash ("/") character. Its general syntax is:

```
REGSPY95 <filename> -h -a -d -f -g
```

The meaning of each parameter or switch is shown in Table 10-1:

Table 10-1. RegSpy95 command-line parameters and switches

Parameter or Switch	Explanation
`<filename>`	Uses a configuration file either to control what information on registry calls *RegSpy95* displays, or to determine which registry calls FOOTPRNT traps. `<filename>` represents the filename, along with an optional path, of a valid *RegSpy95* configuration file. The contents of configuration files are discussed in the section "Reconfiguring RegSpy95 Dynamically: Configuration Files."
`-h, -?`	Displays *RegSpy95* help information.
`-g`	Displays *RegSpy95* version information, as well as the status of *FOOTPRNT.386*. In particular, at any given time it indicates which system calls and which calling applications are *not* being spied upon.
`-f`	Clears/flushes the contents of FOOTPRNT's buffer.
`-a`	Displays the output in chronological order; a fragment of *RegSpy95* output formatted in this way is shown below.
`-d`	Displays the output by function call; a fragment of *Regspy95* output formatted in this way is shown below. This is the default value: if *RegSpy95* is executed from the command line with no switches or parameters, it displays output from FOOTPRNT's buffer arranged by function.

Since you're no doubt eager to see what *RegSpy95* tells you about registry accesses, we'll begin by examining *RegSpy95*'s output first. Then we'll discuss how you can configure *RegSpy95* so that it spies on the registry accesses that you want to intercept.

RegSpy95's Output

By default, when *RegSpy95* is invoked from the command line with either the -a switch, the -d switch, or no switch, the program displays the registry access information that *FOOTPRNT.386* has collected to the screen. If there's more than a screenful of information (and even in a brief session, *RegSpy95* frequently manages to accumulate several megabytes of information), it quickly scrolls out of sight. In almost all cases, then, you'll want to redirect *RegSpy95*'s output to a file using the standard redirection character, >. For example, the following command creates a file in the console's current directory named *RegEditByOrder.txt* that contains information on registry accesses in chronological order:

```
RegSpy95 -a > RegEditByOrder.txt
```

You have to be careful about overwriting existing files, though: Win95 won't ask you whether you want to overwrite an existing file if one exists.

RegSpy95 produces two kinds of formatted output. If the *RegSpy95* program is launched either with no command-line switch or with the -d switch, it produces output ordered on a function-by-function basis. Within a particular function group, calls are listed in chronological order. In addition, within a function group, calls that occurred as part of Win95 system initialization are differentiated from those that occurred afterward. For example, the following output shows calls to the *_RegCreateKey* and *_RegOpenKey* functions that were made while *RegSpy95* was trapping registry accesses made by System Monitor:[*]

```
===== _RegCreateKey =====
Caller  hKey   hSubKey    Error   SubKey Name
----    ----   ----       ----    ----

********  Initialization completed  ********

Sysmon  HKCU  C239F3BC   'Software\Microsoft\Windows\CurrentVersion\Applets\
System Monitor'
Sysmon  HKCU  C239F3BC   'Software\Microsoft\Windows\CurrentVersion\Applets\
System Monitor'
Sysmon  HKCU  C239F3D8   'Software\Microsoft\Windows\CurrentVersion\Applets\
System Monitor'
Sysmon  HKCU  C239F3D8   'Software\Microsoft\Windows\CurrentVersion\Applets\
System Monitor'

===== _RegOpenKey =====
Caller   hKey     hSubKey    Error   SubKey Name
----     ----     ----       ----    ----

********  Initialization completed  ********

Sysmon  HKLM     C239F3BC    'Software\Microsoft\Windows\CurrentVersion\
Network'
Sysmon  HKDD     C1147A38    'PerfStats\StatData'
Sysmon  C239F3BC C239F3E8    'STATS'
Sysmon  HKDD     C1147B10    'PerfStats\StartSrv'
Sysmon  HKDD     C1147B58    'PerfStats\StopSrv'
Sysmon  HKDD     C1147B10    'PerfStats\StartSrv'
Sysmon  HKDD     C1147B58    'PerfStats\StopSrv'
```

---

[*] System Monitor, or *SYSMON.EXE*, is a system performance reporting tool included with Windows 95 that gathers its data by querying value entries in the subkeys of **HKEY_DYN_DATA\PerfStats**.

```
Sysmon   HKLM      C11485FC    'System\CurrentControlSet\Control\PerfStats\
Enum'
Sysmon   C11485FC  C1148628    'KERNEL'
Sysmon   C11485FC  C11AAEE8    'Nwlink'
Sysmon   C11485FC  C11B46F8    'SMBRedir'
Sysmon   C11485FC  C11CA2D4    'VMM'
Sysmon   C11485FC  C1174268    'VFAT'
Sysmon   C11485FC  C11C9C48    'NWREDIR'
Sysmon   C11485FC  C11478BC    'MSNServer'
Sysmon   HKLM      C1174268    'System\CurrentControlSet\Control\
PerfStats\Enum\VFAT'
Sysmon   C1174268  C119AD58    'WritesSec'
Sysmon   C1174268  C119AD84    'ReadsSec'
Sysmon   C1174268  C119ADB0    'BWritesSec'
Sysmon   C1174268  C119ADDC    'BReadsSec'
Sysmon   C1174268  C11C9BFC    'DirtyData'
```

Ordinarily, registry accesses that occur during system initialization occur before the line that reads "**Initialization completed**", while registry accesses that occur after initialization appear, not surprisingly, after it. But because we configured *RegSpy95* to not spy on Windows during system initialization for this session (for details on how to do this, see "Reconfiguring RegSpy95 Statically: SYSTEM.INI," later in this chapter), *RegSpy95* has no information to report on registry accesses during initialization.

Notice that, in the sample output shown above, System Monitor uses *RegCreateKey* to open its own key in HKCR\Software\Microsoft\Windows\CurrentVersion\Applets, but uses *RegOpenKey* otherwise; since System Monitor does not have its own installation routine, that allows it to create its own registry keys "on the fly" the first time that it's loaded. The registry accesses shown in this output occur mostly during System Monitor's initialization, and while the user is choosing the particular statistics that the monitor is to display. Hence, the program opens the network subkey (HKLM\Software\Microsoft\Windows\CurrentVersion\Network) to check whether a network is installed, opens its own STATS subkey to retrieve the names of the statistics it's already been configured to monitor, and opens the keys necessary to retrieve information to populate its Add Item dialog, which allows the user to select the precise statistics that System Monitor is to gather during its current session.

Aside from listing the function, each group includes a header that indicates what items of information are displayed for the function. Different information is displayed for each function, depending on its parameters. Recalling the syntax of each high-level registry function from *ADVAPI32.DLL* also helps interpret this listing, since they correspond very closely. For instance, the syntax of *RegOpenKey* (and of *RegOpenKeyEx*, once unused parameters are eliminated) is:

```
LONG RegOpenKey( hKey, lpszSubkey, phKResult ) ;
```

while the syntax of *_RegOpenKey* is

```
LONG _RegOpenKey( hKey, lpszSubkey, phKResult ) ;
```

In the case of the calls to the *RegOpenKey* function displayed in the listing, *RegSpy95* displays the following items of information:

- The handle of the open key or, if it is a top-level key, the abbreviated constant (like HKCR, etc.) that represents its predefined handle.

- The name of the subkey that the function attempted to open.

- The handle assigned to the newly opened key. Whether or not it is non-zero, this is a valid handle only if the function succeeds.

- The result of the function call if it was something other than ERROR_SUCCESS. For example, the following call failed because an application identifier did not have a `shell` subkey:

  ```
  _RegOpenKey     Explorer C117C5B0  00000000  NOFILE  'Shell'
  ```
- The name of the calling program.

For example, the fourth call to *RegOpenKey* in the listing above attempted to open the key `HKDD\PerfStats\StartSrv`. It succeeded, returning the handle 0xC1147B10. The same key was opened in the sixth call, and it returned the same handle. The eighth call to *RegOpenKey* attempts to open `HKLM\System\CurrentControlSet\Control\PerfStats\Enum`, probably in order to find out what performance statistics the system is collecting. The function again succeeds, returning handle 0xC11485FC. And so on.

The second kind of output, which *RegSpy95* displays if it is invoked with the -a command-line switch, lists calls to registry services *chronologically*, in the order in which they occurred. This means that calls to dissimilar functions are interspersed, which makes it more difficult to understand what values are passed as parameters to and from the functions. But it also provides a more accurate indication of how the registry is being used. For example, the following is the chronological output from the same System Monitor session that contains the *_RegOpenKey* calls that we examined in the function-by-function listing:

```
_RegQueryValueEx   Sysmon      C1147A38  0      4            'VFAT\BReadsSec'    ' '
_RegQueryValueEx   Sysmon      C1147A38  0      4            'VFAT\BWritesSec'   ' '
_RegQueryValueEx   Sysmon      C1147A38  0      4            'VFAT\DirtyData'    ' '
_RegQueryValueEx   Sysmon      C1147A38  0      4            'VFAT\ReadsSec'     ' '
_RegQueryValueEx   Sysmon      C1147A38  0      4            'VFAT\WritesSec'    ' '
_RegQueryValueEx   Sysmon      C119AD0C  0          NOFILE
                   'C:\PROGRAM FILES\PLUS!\THEMES\Mystery menu popup.wav'       ' '
_RegQueryValueEx   Sysmon      C1147A38  0      4            'VFAT\BReadsSec'    ' '
_RegQueryValueEx   Sysmon      C1147A38  0      4            'VFAT\BWritesSec'
' '
_RegQueryValueEx   Sysmon      C1147A38  0      4            'VFAT\DirtyData'    ' '
_RegQueryValueEx   Sysmon      C1147A38  0      4            'VFAT\ReadsSec'     ' '
```

```
_RegQueryValueEx    Sysmon    C1147A38  0    4            'VFAT\WritesSec'  ''
_RegQueryValueEx    Sysmon    C119AD0C  0         NOFILE
                    'C:\PROGRAM FILES\PLUS!\THEMES\Mystery menu command.wav'  ''
```

Here, the program repeatedly queries key 0xC1147A38 to retrieve the file system performance data selected by the user. After each complete set of information is retrieved, the program queries key 0xC119AD0C to retrieve information on a sound event, but finds that the value entry does not exist. These failed calls to *RegQueryValueEx*, incidentally, are made by Windows on behalf of System Monitor; they are not made from direct calls to *RegQueryValueEx* in System Monitor's source code, but rather are made from within a Windows API function that System Monitor called. If you scan the output by function for this System Monitor session, you wouldn't be able to find a call to *RegCreateKey* or *RegOpenKey*, nor will you be able to find out what key handle 0xC119AD0C corresponds to, since Windows itself opened the key and retrieved the handle value.

Once *RegSpy95* finishes listing calls to the Windows registry and profile APIs, it displays the module-to-filename lookup table and the legend of literal contractions used in the listing. The module table lists the module name of every process that accessed the registry while *FOOTPRNT* was resident in memory; it can be used to look up module names for use in configuration files. For example, a portion of the module table from our Explorer session appears as follows:

```
Module Table:

KERNEL32   C:\WINDOWS\SYSTEM\KRNL386.EXE
MSGSRV32   C:\WINDOWS\SYSTEM\MSGSRV32.EXE
Mprexe     C:\WINDOWS\SYSTEM\MPREXE.EXE
Regserv    C:\WINDOWS\REGSERV.EXE
Vshwin32   C:\PROGRAM FILES\MCAFEE\VSHWIN32.EXE
Explorer   C:\WINDOWS\EXPLORER.EXE
Curves a   C:\WINDOWS\SYSTEM\CURVES AND COLORS.SCR
Infoview   C:\MSDN\INFOVIEW.EXE
Regedit    C:\WINDOWS\REGEDIT.EXE
Regspy95   C:\REGISTRY.95\REGSPY\REGSPY95.EXE
Notepad    C:\WINDOWS\NOTEPAD.EXE
```

Regardless of the format you choose, *RegSpy95* displays one registry call per line (although sometimes it's a rather long line) in its output. The only exceptions are calls to the *_RegCreateDynKey* service, since they generate too much data to fit on a single line. The following, for example, is an excerpt from *RegSpy95*'s function-by-function output that shows the Configuration Manager adding the Direct Memory Access controller's key to HKDD\Config Manager\Enum:

```
===== _RegCreateDynKey =====
Caller    KContext  KHandle  Error   Key Name
----      --------  -------  ----    --------


CONFIGMG  C11657D4  C11CA670          'Config Manager\Enum\C11657D4'
    PROVIDER  pi_R0_1val  pi_R0_allvals  pi_R3_1val  pi_R3_allvals
```

```
                pi_flags C024608A  0  0  0  1
  PVALUE  pv_valuelen  pv_value_context  pv_type    pv_valuename
  0                 0  C0245FFA          00000001   'HardWareKey'
  1                 0  C0246016          00000003   'Problem'
  2                 0  C0246029          00000003   'Status'
  3                 0  C024604C          00000003   'Allocation'
```

_RegCreateDynKey

You're probably wondering how you missed _RegCreateDynKey when you were reading Chapter 4, *The Win32 Registry API*. But you didn't miss anything; it's not discussed there, since it's a Win95 VxD function, not a Win32 API function. _RegCreateDynKey, which is the sole function capable of creating dynamic keys in Win95, can be called only from a VxD. It is documented in the Win95 Device Driver Kit (DDK), which also provides a sample program.

Flushing RegSpy95's Buffers

Because the virtual device driver continues to intercept registry accesses throughout a Win95 session, the amount of memory allocated to it can become quite large. This, in turn, degrades system performance and threatens to exhaust your system's resources. Consequently, it's best to reduce *RegSpy95*'s memory consumption periodically if you're planning on running a lengthy Win95 session in which you've loaded *FOOTPRNT.386*. To do this, once you've run *RegSpy95* and redirected its output to a file, the contents of all buffers can be safely discarded (or flushed) to make more memory available for future registry calls (and for other applications as well) by periodically issuing the command:

```
regspy95 -f
```

Because its expanding buffers can exhaust your system's memory and effectively bring your system to a grinding halt, *FOOTPRNT* displays the dialog shown in Figure 10-1 when it detects that the size of its buffers has exceeded 1.5 megabytes. This is a system modal dialog; when it appears, you must respond to it before you can give any other window the input focus.

In its default mode of operation, *RegSpy95* traps all registry calls for the entire Windows session. If you save the output from even a relatively brief session to a file, you'll find that its size is well in excess of a megabyte. This is, in short, information overload: without some user intervention, *RegSpy95* provides far too much detail for anyone to meaningfully interpret it or to make sense of it. Fortunately, *RegSpy95* is a customizable spying tool: you can configure it either statically, by using *SYSTEM.INI*, or dynamically, by using a configuration file, so that you can

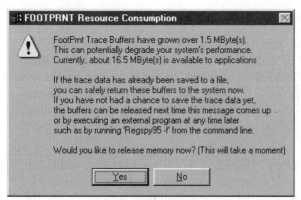

Figure 10-1 . The FOOTPRNT Resource Consumption dialog

control when and how *RegSpy95* does its spying. By configuring *RegSpy95* in SYSTEM.INI, as well as by executing one or more simple configuration files, you can precisely determine exactly which registry interactions *RegSpy95* will record.

Reconfiguring RegSpy95 Statically: SYSTEM.INI

As discussed in greater detail in the section "Spying on Registry Calls at the System Level," *RegSpy95* traps all calls to the registry from Ring 0 and Ring 3 for the entire Windows session, including its initialization portion. This severely degrades system performance, and also means that *RegSpy95* expends a good deal of time and system resources gathering the same basic information that occurs during each system initialization. The *SYSTEM.INI* file, though, can be used to configure *RegSpy95* to improve its performance and to save you from having to wade through this redundant information.

To successfully modify *FOOTPRNT*'s behavior, all profile strings must be placed in the `[Footprnt]` section of *SYSTEM.INI*. If you choose to statically configure *FOOTPRNT* in this way, you can choose from the following methods of controlling *FOOTPRNT*:

- *Disable trapping of all registry calls during initialization.* Unless you've added new devices or device drivers to your system, or deliberately or accidentally removed them, or unless your system is experiencing some configuration problem, Windows makes the same calls to the registry from the time *FOOTPRNT* begins intercepting calls until all VxDs have processed the `INIT_COMPLETE` message. In most cases, you won't have any use for this repetitive information. Therefore, *FOOTPRNT* allows you to disable all spying during system initialization by adding the following line to the `[FootPrnt]` section of *SYSTEM.INI*:

```
InitCalls=off
```

FOOTPRNT.386 and SYSTEM.INI

You may be wondering why static configuration settings for *RegSpy95* are stored in *SYSTEM.INI* instead of in the registry. The answer is that, although it *spies* on the registry, *FOOTPRNT.386* does not really *support* the registry. *FOOTPRNT* is a general-purpose VxD for spying and debugging operations that originally was developed for Windows 3.x. To allow it to remain a general purpose tool, as well as to allow it to run under 16-bit Windows, it continues to use initialization files.

You can use the registry to define *FOOTPRNT* as a static VxD (for details, see "Running RegSpy95" earlier in this chapter); any static VxD can be loaded in this way, whether or not it supports the registry. You cannot, though, use the registry to store the values of any settings that you'd otherwise place in the [FootPrnt] section of *SYSTEM.INI*. For *FOOTPRNT* to access these, it would itself have to call the VMM's registry services—and this would keep *FOOTPRNT.386* from running under Win31.

This setting affects *FOOTPRNT*'s behavior only during system initialization; once initialization has completed, *FOOTPRNT* will begin trapping registry calls regardless of this setting.

*   *Disable trapping of selected registry calls during initialization.* In addition to letting you disable spying on system initialization entirely, *FOOTPRNT* allows you to configure startup calls individually for each registry function; that is, you can determine whether *FOOTPRNT* collects information about calls to registry functions at start up on a function-by-function basis. For instance, to disable trapping of the *_RegCloseKey* function until all VxDs have processed the INIT_COMPLETE message, you would add the following profile string to *SYSTEM.INI*:

```
_RegCloseKey=off
```

(It is also possible to specify which calls are to be trapped by using the "on" switch, but this merely duplicates *FOOTPRNT*'s default behavior.) Of course, setting the value of each VMM registry service to "off" has the same effect as including the InitCalls=off statement.

Table 10-2 lists the keywords supported by *FOOTPRNT* to disable its trapping of selected functions. This set of settings governs the behavior of *FOOTPRNT* only during its initialization phase; once Win95 has completed its initialization, *FOOTPRNT* begins trapping registry accesses regardless of the values assigned to these keywords.

- *Disable trapping of all registry calls at run-time.* It is also possible to disable trapping of all "run-time" calls (i.e., post-initialization calls, after *FOOTPRNT* detects that all VxDs have processed an `INIT_COMPLETE` message) by including the following profile string in the `[footprnt]` section of *SYS-TEM.INI*:

```
RunTimeCalls=off
```

This may seem at first like a silly thing to do: Win95 loads *FOOTPRNT* so that it resides in memory but disables it so that it does no useful work other than record the same repetitive registry calls at start up. And if you combine this setting with `InitCalls=off`, *FOOTPRNT* will do absolutely nothing but consume memory. However, it is possible to override this idle state on the fly, which allows you to specify precisely when *RegSpy95* should begin trapping calls to the registry API; for details on how to do this, see "Reconfiguring RegSpy95 Dynamically: Configuration Files" below. (It is also possible to specify `RuntimeCalls=on`, although this once again is unnecessary, since it is *FOOTPRNT*'s default behavior.)

Table 10-2. Registry function keywords supported by FOOTPRNT

Keyword	Corresponds to	Explanation
GetRegistryKey	N/A	Returns the handle to a registry key containing a particular device name.
GetRegistryPath	N/A	Retrieves the path to the registry key where information about a VxD is stored; can be called during initialization only.
RegCloseKey	*RegCloseKey*	
RegCreateDynKey	N/A	Creates a key in the `HKEY_DYN_DATA` tree of the Win95 registry.
RegCreateKey	*RegCreateKey, RegCreateKeyEx*	
RegDeleteKey	*RegDeleteKey*	
RegDeleteValue	*RegDeleteValue*	
RegEnumKey	*RegEnumKey, RegEnumKeyEx*	
RegEnumValue	*RegEnumValue*	
RegFlushKey	*RegFlushKey*	
RegLoadKey	*RegLoadKey*	
RegOpenKey	*RegOpenKey, RegOpenKeyEx*	
RegQueryInfoKey	*RegQueryInfoKey*	
RegQueryMultipleValues	*RegQueryMultipleValues*	

Table 10-2. Registry function keywords supported by FOOTPRNT (continued)

Keyword	Corresponds to	Explanation
RegQueryValue	*RegQueryValue*	
RegQueryValueEx	*RegQueryValueEx*	
RegRemapPreDefKey	*RegRemapPreDefKey*	Changes the key to which the top level key HKCU or HKCC points; reserved for system use, rather than use by device drivers, but surprisingly implemented in *ADVAPI32.DLL*.
RegReplaceKey	*RegReplaceKey*	
RegSaveKey	*RegSaveKey*	
RegSetValue	*RegSetValue*	
RegSetValueEx	*RegSetValueEx*	
RegUnloadKey	*RegUnloadKey*	
Get_Next_Profile_String	N/A	Returns the next profile string from *SYSTEM.INI*; available during initialization only.
Get_Profile_Boolean	N/A	Returns Boolean value from *SYSTEM.INI*; initialization only.
Get_Profile_Decimal_Int	N/A	Returns decimal value from *SYSTEM.INI*; initialization only.
Get_Profile_Fixed_Point	N/A	Returns fixed-point value from *SYSTEM.INI*; initialization only.
Get_Profile_Hex_Int	N/A	Returns hexadecimal value from *SYSTEM.INI*; initialization only.
Get_Profile_String	N/A	Returns string value from *SYSTEM.INI*; initialization only.

What's Missing From Table 10-2?

You may notice that several high-level functions found in *ADVAPI32.DLL* are missing from Table 10-2. *RegConnectRegistry* is absent, since attempts to connect to a remote registry are handled by *WINREG.DLL* and Remote Procedure Calls to *REGSERV.EXE*, rather than by the Win95 VMM. If you run *RegSpy95* on the remote machine, however, you will see *REGSERV.EXE*'s calls down to the VMM registry services. More interesting is the absence of *RegCreateKeyEx*, *RegEnumKeyEx*, and *RegOpenKeyEx* and the presence of their corresponding "compatibility" functions. Ordinarily, the "compatibility" functions are described as "wrappers" that add a few default values and call the corresponding Win32 version of the function. Certainly, this is true of the registry API under WinNT. These omissions, however, suggest that in these three cases, the new Win32 functions are wrappers that call the old "compatibility" functions.

Reconfiguring RegSpy95 Dynamically: Configuration Files

You can also configure *RegSpy95* at run-time, once Win95 has completed its initialization, by creating a configuration file. Pass the name of this configuration file to *RegSpy95* as a command-line parameter. A valid instruction inside the configuration file takes the form of a switch (the "-" or "/" characters, along with a single letter) followed by a string that represents either of the following:

- A VxD name or Win32 module name. For example, the line:

   ```
   -vKERNEL32
   ```

   is a valid instruction because the module name of the Win32 kernel (*KERNEL32.DLL*) is preceded by the -v switch (which instructs *RegSpy95* to display all registry calls made by the specified module; see below).[*] The module name is defined by the module definition (.DEF) file at the time the application was created, and is *usually* the same as an application's root filename.

How Do I Find the Module Name?

An application's module name is not always the same as its filename without the extension. If you want to be sure about an application's module name, you can find it using Microsoft Spy++, which is included with the 32-bit versions of Microsoft Visual C++, or a similar utility. First, launch the application. Then, using Spy++, select the Processes option from the Spy menu to open a process window, which is shown in Figure 10-2. The string to the right of the process ID is the module name.

If you don't have a utility like Spy++, or if the module name does not appear in the Spy++ process window because it is a VxD (VxDs are not processes), simply use *FOOTPRNT* to trap registry calls when you run the application, then use *RegSpy95* to view the output. *RegSpy95* displays a module table near the end of its listing that contains an application's module name and its corresponding path and filename. For example, the following excerpt from a *RegSpy95* module table shows that the module names of *WINWORD.EXE* and *REGEDIT.EXE* are Winword and Regedit, respectively:

```
Module Table:

Winword   C:\MSOFFICE\WINWORD\WINWORD.EXE
Regedit   C:\WINDOWS\REGEDIT.EXE
```

---

[*] Note that although *KERNEL32.DLL* is a dynamic link library, it also includes a module, Kernel32, that executes as a process.

- A VxD registry function name or service number. Valid function names and
  their corresponding service codes are listed in Table 10-3. For example, the
  lines:

```
-x_RegCreateKey
-x#1014A
```

are equivalent; both enable trapping of calls to *_RegCreateKey*. Note that, if
you choose to use service codes, these must be preceded by the "#" symbol;
in addition, the code's hexadecimal (and not its decimal) value must be used.
Service codes can appear with or without leading zeros.

Table 10-3. VMM Service Codes for registry functions

VMM Registry Function	Service Code
GetRegistryKey	0x0001016F
GetRegistryPath	0x0001016E
RegCloseKey	0x00010149
RegCreateDynKey	0x00010176
RegCreateKey	0x0001014A
RegDeleteKey	0x0001014B
RegDeleteValue	0x0001014F
RegEnumKey	0x0001014C
RegEnumValue	0x00010150
RegFlushKey	0x00010155
RegOpenKey	0x00010148
RegQueryInfoKey	0x0001015E
RegQueryMultipleValues	0x00010177
RegQueryValue	0x0001014D
RegQueryValueEx	0x00010151
RegReMapPreDefKey	0x00010171
RegSetValue	0x0001014E
RegSetValueEx	0x00010152
Get_Next_Profile_String	0x000100B4
Get_Profile_Boolean	0x000100B1
Get_Profile_Decimal_Int	0x000100AB
Get_Profile_Fixed_Point	0x000100AD
Get_Profile_Hex_Int	0x000100AF
Get_Profile_String	0x000100B3

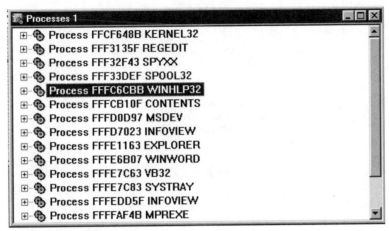

Figure 10-2. The Spy++ Process window

Any other line is interpreted as a comment. (It's a good idea, though, to begin comment lines with a semicolon.) Broadly, configuration switches or instructions can control *RegSpy95* in two different ways:

- *Modifying RegSpy95's default output format.* This group of three switches, which are shown in Table 10-4, can control what kinds of information *RegSpy95* reports and how it presents it.

Table 10-4. Output format switches supported by RegSpy95

Switch	Description
-v\<module>	Only lists calls made by the designated module. For example, the following two instructions instruct *RegSpy95* to report only the calls made by VCOMM (a communications VxD) and the Explorer, and to filter out those made by any other module: -vVCOMM -vExplorer If there is no line containing a -v switch in the configuration file, *RegSpy95*'s default behavior is to show the calls of all programs.
-s\<function> or -s#\<service#>	Only displays the designated function calls. The functions to display can be designated either by their name (e.g., *_RegCloseKey*) or their VMM service number. For example, the following three lines instruct *RegSpy95* to display output for only three functions: -s_RegSetValue -s_RegSetValueEx -s#10148 ; VMM service # for _RegOpenKey If no line in the configuration file contains an -s switch, *RegSpy95*'s default behavior is to display the calls to all registry functions.

Table 10-4. Output format switches supported by RegSpy95 (continued)

Switch	Description

-n
or
-n#
	Renames functions in the output file, usually to condense output lines or to reduce the total amount of output. Its precise syntax is either:
	`-n<function name>=<output name>`
	or
	`-n#<VMM service number>=<output name>`
	For example, the following line instructs *RegSpy95* to use the string "QValueEx" to describe calls to the *_RegQueryValueEx* function.
	`-n_RegQueryValueEx=QValueEx`

- *Controlling FOOTPRNT's run-time behavior.* This second group of two switches shown in Table 10-5 controls *FOOTPRNT* through calls to *DeviceIO-Control.* Each switch has two variations: a switch with an *uppercase* letter indicates that a particular behavior is to be disabled, while a switch with a *lowercase* letter re-enables that behavior. (There is no need for this switch to define *FOOTPRNT's* initial operation, since by default all behaviors are enabled.)

Table 10-5. FOOTPRNT run-time control switches supported by RegSpy95

Switch	Description

-X<function>
or
-X#<service#>
or
-x<function>
or
-x#<service#>
	Instructs *FOOTPRNT* to disable and enable, respectively, trapping calls to a particular registry function. For example, the following statements tell *FOOTPRNT* to stop trapping calls to *_RegOpenKey* and *_RegCloseKey*, and to re-enable trapping of calls to *_RegCreateDynKey*:
	`;=== Disable trapping of these services ===`
	`-X_RegOpenKey`
	`-X_RegCloseKey`
	`;=== Enable trapping of these services ===`
	`-x#10176                    ;_RegCreateDynKey`

-C<module>
or
-c<module>
	Instructs *FOOTPRNT* to stop and to restart, respectively, trapping calls made by a particular module. For example, the following statements tell *FOOTPRNT* to stop registering calls from the Configuration Manager (CONFIGMG) and the Explorer and to begin spying on VCOMM and RegEdit:
	`;=== Disable trapping all calls by these modules ===`
	`-CCONFIGMG`
	`-CExplorer`
	`;=== Enable trapping all calls by these modules ===`
	`-cVCOMM`
	`-cRegedit`

Any number of statements from either category can be included in the file. Their order is not important.

If the `RuntimeCalls=off` setting was included in *SYSTEM.INI*, the only way to reactivate *FOOTPRNT* is by including at least one statement with the -x switch and

> ## *Module and Function Names Are Case Sensitive*
>
> All module and registry function names in *RegSpy95* configuration file state-
> ments are case sensitive. If you're unsure how to spell module names, run the
> application, then have *RegSpy95* send its output to either the screen or a file.
> Finally, look for the module name or names in which you're interested at the
> end of the output, under the section "Module Table."

designating at least one registry API call to trap in your configuration file.
(Including at least one statement with the -c switch to trap calls made by a particular module won't succeed in reactivating *FOOTPRNT*, since *RegSpy95* still won't
know which registry API functions to trap.) Incidentally, you can tell which VMM
registry services are *not* being trapped at any particular time by using the -g
switch on the command line.

The correct use of the -c switch, which resumes spying on registry calls made by
a particular program module, requires some further explanation. It is only meaningful to enable spying if previously spying on that module (and presumably on
other modules as well) has been disabled.

For example, imagine that you plan to trap only calls from the Registry Editor,
RegEdit. Therefore, you include the `RuntimeCalls=off` and `InitCalls=off`
statements in *SYSTEM.INI*. Then, right before running RegEdit, you run *RegSpy95*
with the command line pointing to the following configuration file:

```
; resume spying on all high-level registry services
-x_RegFlushKey
-x_RegQueryValue
-x_RegRemapPreDefKey
-x_RegDeleteValue
-x_RegCreateDynKey
-x_RegEnumValue
-x_RegEnumKey
-x_RegQueryValueEx
-x_RegSetValueEx
-x_RegSetValue
-x_RegCloseKey
-x_RegOpenKey
-x_RegCreateKey
-x_RegDeleteKey
-x_RegQueryInfoKey
-x_RegQueryMultipleValues
; resume spying on Reg, but only for RegEdit
-cRegedit
```

When you inspect the output, you find that, although the Registry Editor's calls to the registry API are included, they are intermixed with calls made by program modules like VCOMM, CONFIGMG, and Explorer. This happens because you did not disable spying on calls from these program modules; you only enabled (unnecessarily, by the way, since it was already enabled) spying on calls from RegEdit.

To produce output that lists only the calls made by the Registry Editor, you'd have to do either of the following:

- Before running the configuration file that resumes spying on all registry services and intercepts registry calls made by RegEdit, execute a configuration file that looks something like the following:

```
-CKERNEL32
-CMSGSRV32
-CMprexe
-CVshwin32
-CMMTASK
-CExplorer
-CSystray
-CFastboot
-CFindfast
-CRegedit
-CWINOLDAP
-CVCOMM
-CCONFIGMG
```

    This explicitly disables spying on all of the designated VxDs and program modules so that, when you have *RegSpy95* read your next configuration file, you can re-enable spying by RegEdit. The exact programs that appear on your list will vary, depending on the software that you ordinarily run. To see precisely what module names you need to include, take a look at the module table near the end of *RegSpy95*'s output just before you're ready to create and execute the script.

- Instead of using the -C option, run a configuration file with the following statement, which instructs *RegSpy95* to filter any calls not made by the Registry Editor out of the output:

```
-vRegedit
```

    In this case, *RegSpy95* will continue to spy on other programs, information about their registry calls will continue to be stored in *RegSpy95*'s buffer (and therefore you should be sure to flush the buffer regularly), but the program's output will reflect only those calls that RegEdit made to the registry API.

Why Bother?

At this point, you may be asking yourself why you'd want to bother with *RegSpy95* in the first place. After all, it's much easier to simply open the Windows registry with the Microsoft-supplied Registry Editor utility and navigate through it in search of interesting keys and entries.

This is not to deny, of course, that RegEdit is an extremely valuable utility for exploring the registry, and one that you should frequently use. But at the same time, RegEdit offers a fundamentally static view of the registry: it shows us what is in a particular registry at a specific point in time. It offers us, in other words, a view of what information *is stored* (the passive voice here is deliberate) in the registry. It doesn't show us *who* stored the registry entries, or who *uses* them. Nor—and this is particularly important, even if obvious-sounding—does it show what *isn't* stored.

In the introduction to Chapter 8, *What Goes in the Registry: System Settings*, we somewhat facetiously argued that you could use the registry to store anything, including sounds and large graphic images. But in fact, whatever is put in the registry has meaning only if it is read and properly interpreted either by Windows or by an application. To put this another way, what is important is not so much what is in the registry as what applications *think* is in the registry.

How well do the available registry tools let us see what applications think is in the registry? Since it depicts the registry in a static way, RegEdit necessarily shows us things in the registry that *would* lead to successful registry API calls. Some of these, of course, are the things that an application thinks are in the registry because they actually are in the registry. But others are "dead" data—information that has made its way into the registry for a variety of reasons, but that programs either no longer access or never accessed in the first place; these settings are unused, but because we can see them present in the registry, and because RegEdit presents them with the same emphasis as those settings that applications actually use in the registry, it becomes very tempting to draw erroneous conclusions about how they are used. These "dead" settings are trees that fall in the forest, so to speak, with no one around to hear them.

RegSpy95, on the other hand, focuses precisely on what applications *think* is in the registry, rather than on what actually *is* in the registry. This means, of course, that it doesn't draw your attention to registry data that no application uses. But it also means that *RegSpy95* shows you data that applications look for or expect to find in the registry, but that turns out not to be present in the registry. RegEdit, on the other hand, is completely unable to show you things that applications expect to find, but don't succeed in finding, in the registry. This relationship is summarized by the simple matrix shown in Table 10-6.

Table 10-6. Comparing RegSpy95 and RegEdit

	Data Programs Look For	Data No Program Looks For
Data present in registry	RegEdit and *RegSpy95*	RegEdit
Data not present in registry	*RegSpy95*	?!

The registry, in other words, is not a passive or static structure, but an active and dynamic one. What is important is not what is in the registry, but how the contents of the registry are used and how the Windows environment interacts with the registry. Sometimes what's *not* in the registry, but what an application or Win95 itself is looking for, is just as important as what's in the registry. Consider, for example, the following listing from *RegSpy95*:

```
_RegOpenKey        Explorer  HKCU       C117C5DC
                   'Software\Microsoft\Windows\CurrentVersion\Policies'
_RegOpenKey        Explorer  C117C5DC  C117FA98              'Explorer'
_RegQueryValueEx   Explorer  C117FA98  0             NOFILE    'NoFind'   ''
_RegCloseKey       Explorer  C117FA98
```

Here, the Explorer is looking for a value entry named `NoFind` in `HKCU\Software\Microsoft\Windows\CurrentVersion\Policies\Explorer`, but fails to find it. If a `REG_DWORD` entry with a value of 1 had existed, the Find option would not have appeared on the Explorer's tools menu; instead, it opens its Find dialog. RegEdit at times provides glimpses of this dynamic registry, but in the end they are only glimpses. From the snapshot of the registry provided by RegEdit, you may make some assumptions about the character of the dynamic registry. But in the end, without other registry access tools, they are only assumptions.

RegSpy95 records what applications ask for in the registry, what data they put in the registry, and what data, if any, the registry supplies them with. With *RegSpy95*, you see registry accesses that fail, as well as those that succeed. This is the essence of the dynamic registry. In the remainder of this section, we'll look at a few of the ways that *RegSpy95* can uncover this dynamic registry.

Some Data Are More Equal Than Others...

For many experienced users and developers, the registry is a daunting structure because of its enormity and seeming unmanageability. With tens of thousands of keys and value entries, it is very difficult to focus on what is important and what is not. In many cases, there's no real way of knowing whether the data stored to the subkeys of `HKCU\KillerAppCompany\BuggySoftware\OnlyVersion\0` are unaccessed subkeys resulting from an accident or are the settings that are responsible for integrating the company's two near-killer applications.

Using Registry Editor, it's impossible to answer that kind of question. Registry Editor graphically depicts keys and values, all of which appear to be equally important. In other words, they're all there. From using Registry Editor, you get absolutely no sense of the "weight" to be assigned to particular subkeys. You don't know whether a subkey or a value entry is actually read by Windows or another application, or whether it merely occupies space in the registry.

For example, many of the OLE-related keys in HKCR\CLSID have a subkey, InProcServer32, that contains a value entry named ThreadingModel. Each occurrence of ThreadingModel in the registry always has the same value: Apartment. This seems like a value entry that can be safely ignored or perhaps even discarded: after all, why bother with the value entry if its value is always the same?

Without *RegSpy95*, you'd never know that, in anything other than a very short Explorer session, the Win95 Explorer makes literally dozens of calls to retrieve the value of the ThreadingModel entry, and even queries the same value entries again and again. So ThreadingModel is a far more important entry than appears from a casual inspection of the registry with Registry Editor.

The *threading model* defines the method used by an OLE server to insure that its objects are thread-safe. Single-threading is one such model: there can only be a single process per thread. Starting with Win95 and Windows NT 3.51, though, OLE supports multithreaded applications: OLE client applications can make OLE calls from multiple threads, and create COM objects in multiple threads. The "apartment" model is one method of making OLE thread-safe. It means that every apartment (i.e., every thread) that creates one or more objects must have its own message queue. It also means that, while objects can be created in multiple threads and multiple objects can be created within a single thread, a particular object can live in only one thread, and all calls to an object must come from that thread. With OLE servers indicating their support for apartment threading in the registry, the system OLE components know, when a multithreaded OLE client attempts to create instances of an object in multiple threads, to instantiate it in the client's main thread.

Our original conclusion about the ThreadingModel value entry was incorrect because it was based on the static character of the registry. We concluded that Apartment was the only valid value because it was the only one that we could find in the registry. In fact, however, a particular OLE in-process server can support any of four threading models: none (i.e., single-threading), apartment, free, or both apartment and free-threading. Only one value representing a single model appears in the registry, though, for two very good reasons. First, until the implementation of the Distributed Component Object Model (DCOM), Win95 and OLE do not support free-threading. That means that the values Free and Both will appear in the near future, but (at least of this writing) the apartment model is the sole multithreaded model available for OLE. Second, single-threaded OLE servers can hardly be expected to define their threading model in the registry, since many were developed at a point when multithreading was not supported. So an OLE in-process server indicates that it is single threaded by *not* adding the `ThreadingModel` value entry and *not* specifying a value. In other words, the absence of the value is significant.

It's Not What's Up Front That Counts

Aside from allowing you to gauge the importance of a key or value entry by evaluating the frequency with which it is used, the previous example also hints at another way in which *RegSpy95* differs from RegEdit: while RegEdit focuses on what's in the registry, *RegSpy95* also allows you to find keys and value entries that could have been in the registry but weren't. And frequently what isn't in the registry matters as much as what is.

One of the most useful ways to read *RegSpy95*'s output is to search for calls that return `ERROR_FILE_NOT_FOUND` (abbreviated to `NOFILE` in the *RegSpy95* output), which indicates that the key or value entry does not exist. Generally, this failure to find a key or a value entry is not the result of an error on the part of the calling application; instead, it usually indicates that a key that might be present is merely absent.

For example, one of the most dramatic instances of this inability to find keys and values occurs during the initialization of the Win95 kernel, *KERNEL32.DLL*, as the following output from *RegSpy95* shows:

```
_RegOpenKey             KERNEL32  HKCU      C116F1C0         'Control
                                                   Panel\International'
_RegQueryValueEx        KERNEL32  C116F1C0  SZ    9    'Locale'  '00000409'
_RegCloseKey            KERNEL32  C116F1C0

... several function calls omitted...

_RegOpenKey             KERNEL32  HKCU      C116F1C0         'Control
                                               Panel\desktop\ResourceLocale'
_RegQueryValueEx        KERNEL32  C116F1C0  SZ    9        ''  '00000409'
_RegCloseKey            KERNEL32  C116F1C0
_RegOpenKey             KERNEL32  HKLM      C116F1C0         'SYSTEM\
                                    CurrentControlSet\Control\nls\codepage'
_RegQueryValueEx        KERNEL32  C116F1C0  SZ    12   '1252' 'cp_1252.nls'
_RegCloseKey            KERNEL32  C116F1C0
_RegOpenKey             KERNEL32  HKLM      C116F1C0         'SYSTEM\
                                    CurrentControlSet\Control\nls\codepage'
_RegQueryValueEx        KERNEL32  C116F1C0  SZ    11   '437'  'cp_437.nls'
_RegCloseKey            KERNEL32  C116F1C0
_RegOpenKey             KERNEL32  HKCU      C116F1C0         'Control
                                                   Panel\International'
_RegQueryValueEx        KERNEL32  C116F1C0  0     NOFILE    'sLanguage'  ''
_RegQueryValueEx        KERNEL32  C116F1C0  0     NOFILE    'iCountry'   ''
```

_RegQueryValueEx	KERNEL32	C116F1C0	0	NOFILE	'sCountry'	' '
_RegQueryValueEx	KERNEL32	C116F1C0	0	NOFILE	'sList'	' '
_RegQueryValueEx	KERNEL32	C116F1C0	0	NOFILE	'iMeasure'	' '
_RegQueryValueEx	KERNEL32	C116F1C0	0	NOFILE	'sDecimal'	' '
_RegQueryValueEx	KERNEL32	C116F1C0	0	NOFILE	'sThousand'	' '
_RegQueryValueEx	KERNEL32	C116F1C0	0	NOFILE	'sGrouping'	' '
_RegQueryValueEx	KERNEL32	C116F1C0	0	NOFILE	'iDigits'	' '
_RegQueryValueEx	KERNEL32	C116F1C0	0	NOFILE	'iLZero'	' '
_RegQueryValueEx	KERNEL32	C116F1C0	0	NOFILE	'iNegNumber'	' '
_RegQueryValueEx	KERNEL32	C116F1C0	0	NOFILE	'sCurrency'	' '
_RegQueryValueEx	KERNEL32	C116F1C0	0	NOFILE	'sMonDecimalSep'	' '
_RegQueryValueEx	KERNEL32	C116F1C0	0	NOFILE	'sMonThousandSep'	' '

… 20 more _RegQueryValueEx calls that returned NOFILE omitted…

_RegCloseKey   KERNEL32   C116F1C0

First, the kernel opens the Control Panel\International key, queries the Locale entry, and retrieves its data: nine bytes of REG_SZ data whose value is "00000409." Then it closes the key. Several registry calls later, it opens the same key in search of an entire array of values that, in this instance, are entirely absent ("NOFILE"), since no default locale values have been overridden.

In this case, the value stored to the Locale value entry defines the locale ID, or LCID. For example, in computers in the United States, the customary value of Locale is "00000409"; since the LCID is a 32-bit numeric value, Windows converts it into the hexadecimal value 0x00000409. A single LCID both enables one or more values for such local settings as the currency symbol, the decimal symbol, or the time and date separators, and establishes a default value for each of these settings. However, any default value can be overridden. If a default value is overridden, that value is stored to one of the value entries that the Win95 kernel attempts to read—and in the case of our example, fails to find—from HKCU\Control Panel\International.

Locale and WIN.INI

You may have discovered that all of the locale value entries that the kernel tries to read, but fails to find, in this example are stored in *WIN.INI*. It's tempting to conclude from this that initialization files are the primary source of locale information, but that isn't the case. Windows 3.1 did not support the locale ID, and most 16-bit applications don't. So to make sure that the proper locale information is available to 16-bit applications, Win95 updates *WIN.INI* to reflect the proper value for each element defined by the LCID.

Who Said .INI Files Aren't Important?

It's been commonly argued that Win95 really doesn't need initialization files—that it uses them primarily or exclusively to make 16-bit applications compatible with Win95. RegEdit is of no help in exploring the validity of this assertion—it displays the state of the registry, and nothing else. *RegSpy95*, on the other hand, spies on calls to *SYSTEM.INI* while the Win95 VMM/VxD layer initializes itself.

The following, for example, is a fragment of *RegSpy95*'s function-by-function output that lists calls to the low-level profile API made by Win95 during initialization:

```
===== Get_Profile_Boolean =====
Caller    Section       Key Name              Default
------    -------       --------              -------
VPICD     386Enh        IRQ9GLOBAL            00000000
VTD       386Enh        TimerAutoEOI          FFFFFFFF
VTD       386Enh        AutoDateUpdate        FFFFFFFF
IOS       386Enh        VirtualHDIRQ          00000000
VCD       386Enh        COMMDRV30             00000000

…Numerous function calls omitted…

SHELL     386Enh        Paging                FFFFFFFF
SHELL     386Enh        ConservativeSwapfileUsageFFFFFFFF
SHELL     386Enh        EnableIOAliasTrap     00000000
DOSMGR    386Enh        MODIFYDOSINT2A        00000000
SHELL     386Enh        TRANSLATESCANS        00000000

********  Initialization completed  ********

===== Get_Profile_Decimal_Int =====
Caller    Section       Key Name              Default
------    -------       --------              -------
VCACHE    VCache        minfilecache          00000000
VCACHE    VCache        maxfilecache          00000000
VCACHE    VCache        CacheBufRRT           00000000
IOS       386Enh        HardDiskDMABuffer     00000000
IOS       386Enh        IOSHeapSize           00000002

…Numerous function calls omitted…

SHELL     386Enh        WindowKBRequired      00000100
SHELL     386Enh        MinPagingFileSize     00000000
SHELL     386Enh        MinUserDiskSpace      00000200
SHELL     386Enh        MaxPagingFileSize     00200000
VDD       Display       RefreshRate           00000000

********  Initialization completed  ********
```

```
===== Get_Profile_Hex_Int =====
Caller     Section            Key Name                 Default
------     -------            --------                 -------
VDMAD      386Enh             MAXDMAPGADDRESS          00100000
ENABLE     Enable             WarnOnFeature           000000FF
ENABLE     Enable             UpSirenDuration         00000028
ENABLE     Enable             UpSirenStartTone        00000520
ENABLE     Enable             DownSirenDuration       00000028

...Numerous function calls omitted...

ENABLE     Enable             ClickTone               000006C0
ENABLE     Enable             BellDuration            000000FA
ENABLE     Enable             BellTone                00000538
SHELL      386Enh             MessageBackColor        00000001
SHELL      386Enh             MessageTextColor        FFFFFFFF

********   Initialization completed   ********

===== Get_Profile_String =====
Caller     Section            Key Name                 Default
------     -------            --------                 -------
VKD        386Enh             8042READCMD             00004463
VKD        386Enh             8042WRITECMD            00004463
VNETBIOS   386Enh             V86ModeLanas            0000032C
SHELL      386Enh             WinTimeSlice            00000000

...Numerous function calls omitted...

NWREDIR    NWREDIR            PREFERREDSERVER         00000000
SHELL      386Enh             SHELLNAME               C0380565
SHELL      386Enh             PagingFile              00000AEC
SHELL      386Enh             PagingDrive             00000AEC

********   Initialization completed   ********

===== Get_Next_Profile_String =====
Caller     String             Key Name                 Default
------     -------            --------                 -------

********   Initialization completed   ********

===== Get_Profile_Fixed_Point =====
Caller     Section            Key Name                 Default
------     -------            --------                 -------
VKD        386Enh             KeyBoostTime            00000001
VKD        386Enh             KEYIDLEDELAY            000001F4
COMBUFF    386Enh             COM1AUTOASSIGN          FFFFFFFE
COMBUFF    386Enh             COM2AUTOASSIGN          FFFFFFFE
VPD        386Enh             LPT1AUTOASSIGN          0000EA60
VPD        386Enh             LPT2AUTOASSIGN          0000EA60
VPD        386Enh             LPT3AUTOASSIGN          0000EA60
********   Initialization completed   ********
```

Of course, the isolated fact that Win95 makes a multitude of calls to the profile API doesn't necessarily indicate that Win95 "needs" initialization files—you have to figure out, in each instance, why Win95 is looking for a particular setting in *SYSTEM.INI*. Many of the calls are made to insure that Win95 remains compatible with 16-bit drivers, which for the most part store their configuration information in *SYSTEM.INI* and not in the registry. But particular calls may well reflect attempts to retrieve information that could have been—but was not—stored in the Win95 registry.

It's also important to recognize that *RegSpy95* does not furnish a complete record of Win95's interactions with system initialization files. It spies only on calls to *SYSTEM.INI*, and only during Windows system initialization. It does not intercept *WIN.INI* accesses at all.

How Do I Do It?

In some cases, you may be confronted with a registry-related programming problem that you're not quite sure how to solve. In this case, using *RegSpy95* to see how other applications approach the problem can save you a good deal of time and speed your application development.

For example, you've probably noticed that RegEdit allows you to rename keys. If you're developing a registry utility, you might want to allow users to rename keys as well. There isn't a "RegRenameKey" API. You suspect that doing this involves enumerating all subkeys and values of the key to be renamed, copying them to a new key, and then deleting the original. But you're hoping that there's an easier solution.

In this case, while you're using *RegSpy95* to intercept RegEdit's calls to the registry, you can run RegEdit twice. The first time, you can just load RegEdit, navigate to a key that you'd like to rename, and immediately exit. The second time, you run RegEdit, navigate to the key to be renamed, and actually rename it. You can then use a utility such as *diff* or *WinDiff* to compare the two files to determine what registry calls RegEdit makes to rename a file.

The following, for instance, is a chronological listing of RegEdit's calls to the registry API when we renamed the key HKCU\Software\MyCompany\MyApp to HKCU\Software\MyCompany\MyApp1:

```
_RegOpenKey          Regedit   HKCU      00100000  NOFILE   'Software\
MyCompany\MyApp1'
_RegCreateKey        Regedit   HKCU      C11CCA54           'Software\
MyCompany\MyApp1'
_RegEnumValue        Regedit   C11CCFB8  0                  NOMORE   ''  ''
_RegEnumKey          Regedit   C11CCFB8  0                  'Settings'
_RegOpenKey          Regedit   C11CCFB8  C11CCA80           'Settings'
```

Windows 95 and Initialization Files

In general, Win95's use of initialization files is a complex issue requiring that each initialization file access be examined carefully, since Windows uses initialization files in a number of different ways:

- To store settings, like the value of the `shell` and `scrnsave.exe` keywords in the `[boot]` section of *SYSTEM.INI*, that could (should?) have been stored in the registry but, for one reason or another, were not.

- To store settings needed by 16-bit Windows drivers and applications that, because they were developed for Windows 3.x, have no knowledge of the registry. These entries, like many of the names of device drivers and VxDs in *SYSTEM.INI* and of application settings in *WIN.INI*, are either totally ignored by Win95 itself or, in the case of device drivers, are read only to load the driver.

- To provide registry settings to 16-bit applications. Since 16-bit applications cannot be expected to access the registry, the values of some system-level settings are copied from the registry to system initialization files so that 16-bit applications will be "in synch" with Windows itself and with 32-bit applications. Localization information, which was discussed in the preceding section, "It's Not What's Up Front That Counts," is an example of this use of initialization files.

- To store information needed by 16-bit applications that is then copied to the registry. This is somewhat different than providing settings to 16-bit applications, since this involves moving information from the initialization file to the registry. It also means, though, that the initialization file setting is "live"—that is, it determines the value of the registry setting, and not vice versa. For instance, in Chapter 8, we saw that the name of the default printer is stored in *WIN.INI* and the registry. If you change the registry setting, Win95 is likely to change it back to the default printer defined in *WIN.INI*.

- To migrate information to the registry. Some of the contents of *WIN.INI* and *SYSTEM.INI* are moved to the registry during installation or when Win95 boots. The settings remain in *WIN.INI* or *SYSTEM.INI*, but they are never updated if their corresponding registry entries are modified, since Windows doesn't use the information they provide.

```
_RegCreateKey          Regedit   C11CCA54  C11CCAAC              'Settings'
_RegEnumValue          Regedit   C11CCA80  0      16     BIN
        'WindowPos'    'EB 05 00 00 92 04 00 00 9A 1A 00 00 C9 18 00 00 '
_RegSetValueEx         Regedit   C11CCAAC  BIN    16
```

480   *Chapter 10: Spying on the Registry*

```
            'WindowPos'    'EB 05 00 00 92 04 00 00 9A 1A 00 00 C9 18 00 00 '
_RegEnumValue            Regedit   C11CCA80  1            BIN    NOMORE
                                                            'WindowPos'    ' '
_RegEnumKey              Regedit   C11CCA80  0     NOMORE  'Settings'
_RegCloseKey             Regedit   C11CCAAC
_RegCloseKey             Regedit   C11CCA80
_RegEnumKey              Regedit   C11CCFB8  1     NOMORE  'Settings'
_RegCloseKey             Regedit   C11CCFB8
_RegCloseKey             Regedit   C11CCA54
_RegDeleteKey            Regedit   HKCU            'Software\MyCompany\MyApp'
```

Notice that, when you rename a key, RegEdit first attempts to open the newly renamed key. Of course, since two keys that share a common parent key can't have the same name, it should find that the key does not exist. If it can open the key, presumably it displays an error dialog. If it can't open the key (as happened here: NOFILE), the error is in this case a *good* thing: the user is not attempting to duplicate an existing key name and therefore the rename operation is legal, so *_RegCreateKey* creates the "renamed" key. RegEdit then enumerates the original key's subkeys and value entries, and adds a copy of each to the renamed key. It then closes both keys and deletes the original. So our original suspicion—that renaming in Win95 involves using the registry enumeration functions to copy existing keys and values to a new key, and then deleting the old key—is correct. You could now go and write this missing "RegRenameKey" API.

Testing and Debugging

Along with its utility as a tool for exploring the role of the registry in Win95, *RegSpy95* can be invaluable as a tool for testing and debugging your applications. RegEdit is also a valuable debugging tool, except that, unless you use a debugger to step through your program, it only shows you the results of executing your program on the registry. If those results are not quite what you had in mind, you're left to figure out why that is and to identify which particular function calls are the offenders.

Since in most cases *RegSpy95* allows you to see the values that are being passed as parameters to the registry API, the values that the registry API writes to buffers, and the return value of each function, it becomes easy to locate the exact line of code where your program is being derailed and to identify exactly what the problem is. Quite simply, *RegSpy95* speeds up the debugging process for registry-related operations.

A real-world example helps to illustrate one of the many ways in which RegEdit can be used in the debugging process. When working on the section "Supporting sound events" in Chapter 9, *What Goes in the Registry: Application and User Settings*, we were trying to use the SND_APPLICATION constant as an argument to the *PlaySound* function to automatically play an application's sound event. We had defined an application sound event, HKCU\AppEvents\Schemes\Apps\ MyApp\Timer, in the registry, assigned a .WAV file to the event, and a created a simple alarm clock application, *SNDEVENT.EXE*, that used the *PlaySound* function to play that sound. Since Windows 95 does a good deal of scanning of subkeys of the registry independently of the names of their parent keys,[*] it seemed natural to assume that the only requirement for the *PlaySound* function to work is that the function's *pszSound* parameter be the name of a valid application event. We assumed, in other words, that Windows would scan the subkeys of each application that had defined custom application events to find the subkey whose name corresponded to *pszSound*. Unfortunately, though, this didn't work, and no alarm sounded.

In looking through the documentation, we found a note that the *PlaySound* function does not support the SND_ALIAS constant under Windows 95. (This turns out to be untrue, by the way.) It seems likely, then, that if the SND_ALIAS constant is not supported, the SND_APPLICATION constant is not supported as well.

At this point, it occurred to us that, if we used *RegSpy95* to trap the registry calls made by *SNDEVENT.EXE*, we might be able to see whether calling the *PlaySound* function with the SND_APPLICATION constant actually translated into a registry call. If it didn't, we could establish once and for all that the SND_APPLICATION constant is not supported; if it did, we could see exactly how Windows was attempting to identify the sound event, and in the process determine what was wrong with our application. *RegSpy95*'s output identified two registry calls that were relevant:

```
_RegQueryValue        Sndevent  HKCU     260   9BA00000
                  'AppEvents\Schemes\Apps\SNDEVENT\Timer\.Current'   ''
_RegQueryValue        Sndevent  HKCU     260   E4DC0000
                  'AppEvents\Schemes\Apps\.Default\Timer\.Current'   ''
```

So in response to the SND_APPLICATION constant, Windows first attempted to retrieve the filename stored to HKCU\AppEvents\Schemes\Apps\SNDEVENT\ Timer\.Current. When it was unable to find that key, it attempted to retrieve the name of the sound file stored to the system sound event HKCU\AppEvents\ Schemes\Apps\.Default\Timer\.Current. Since neither of those keys existed, no sound was played.

This in turn called into question the original assumption that Windows would scan the subkeys of the subkeys of HKCR\AppEvents\Schemes\Apps in order to find one whose name corresponded to the custom sound event. In this case, Windows does not scan; instead, it attempts to directly access a particular key's

---

[*] For instance, in constructing the contents of its New submenu, the Explorer scans HKCR for every file association key that has a ShellNew subkey.

default value. In order for the function to succeed, then, the name of the executable program must be the same as the name of the application for which the custom event is defined. In other words, our custom sound was defined by a subkey of `HKCU\AppEvents\Schemes\Apps\MyApp`. Windows couldn't find it, though, because it was looking for a subkey of `HKCU\AppEvents\Schemes\Apps\SNDEVENT`. So, when we renamed our application from *SNDEVENT.EXE* to *MYAPP.EXE*, the program worked as expected, in the process establishing that the *PlaySound* function directly supports application sound events.

Inside RegSpy95

This section on the implementation of RegSpy95 was written by Alex Shmidt (73302.60@compuserve.com), the developer of FootPrnt.386 and RegSpy95.

Unlike spying tools (such as *APISpy32*; see below) that are designed to monitor calls made by a specific program for the duration of the spying session, *RegSpy95* belongs to a second category of spy utility that collects information on registry calls made by all programs. In addition, *RegSpy95* monitors registry and initialization file calls made by the operating system itself, including those that it makes at system initialization time, a time when no application program is running.

To make this possible, *RegSpy95* uses a Virtual Device Driver (VxD). This, of course, immediately destroys any possibility of compatibility with Microsoft Windows NT, since VxDs are not supported by WinNT. The number 95 was deliberately included in the program's name to stress that *RegSpy95* is exclusively a Win95 program; it has no functionality when it runs under either WinNT or Win32s. Bye, bye, Windows logo!

RegSpy95 Source Code

For your programming enjoyment, the *Inside the Windows 95 Registry* diskette includes the complete source code, along with a complete set of header files, for *RegSpy95*. You can use it to make modifications and enhancements to *RegSpy95*. Or you can even use the header files, along with the insight that the source code provides into the organization of *FOOTPRNT*'s buffers, to build your own applications and shells that retrieve information from *FOOT-PRNT.386*. Source code for *FOOTPRNT.386*, though, is *not* included.

What RegSpy95 Spies On

There are two distinct groups of registry services in Win95. The first, well-known group consists of such functions such as *RegCloseKey*, *RegConnectRegistry*, and so on. These are the APIs that are, for the most part, compatible across the different Win32 platforms, that are documented in the Win32 SDK, that are exported from *ADVAPI32.DLL,* and that you can read about at length in Chapter 4.

The second group of registry APIs is not well known and makes its first appearance in Win95. This group contains functions with similar but not exactly identical names, such as *_RegCloseKey* and *_RegCreateDynKey.* These API services are provided by the Win95 Virtual Machine Manager (VMM) and can only be called from a VxD or from VMM itself. Particularly at system initialization time, many VxDs take advantage of this opportunity to configure themselves or to query the registry about the configuration of other VxDs.

How can *RegSpy95* both monitor registry calls from any other Win32 program and see activities at the operating system level? Building mechanisms that would provide this kind of functionality seem to present a major technical challenge. First of all, like Windows NT, Win95 runs each Win32 process in its own linear address space by remapping different sets of physical memory pages called Address Contexts into a unique range of linear addresses. Among other things, this means that when *RegSpy95* receives its time-slice from the Win95 process scheduler, no other Win32 process is supposed to be accessible in memory; for all practical purposes, *RegSpy95* doesn't have anything to spy on. But this is not all. The Virtual Machine Manager, which together with the other VxDs that comprise the Win95 operating system, works at Ring 0 (the privileged supervisor level), while Win32 programs (including *RegSpy95* itself, by the way) operate at Ring 3 (the user level).

While solving these problems may seem technically challenging, two factors make them fairly easy to overcome. First, all registry APIs in Win95 that are exported by *ADVAPI32.DLL* are implemented as really thin wrappers around calls through the thunking layer down to their Ring 0 counterparts in VMM. Thus, by spying on the Ring 0 registry services, *RegSpy95* can see everybody's calls regardless of their privilege level. This tells us *where* to spy, but not *how.* Secondly, and decisively, *RegSpy95* itself is not really a spying program, but rather a utility program that conveniently dumps data collected elsewhere, namely by the VxD called *FOOTPRNT.386.*

Spying on Registry Calls at the System Level

Although *FOOTPRNT.386* is the heart and brain of *RegSpy95*'s functionality, this VxD was not designed with the registry in mind and, in fact, was not even developed specifically for Win95. It was developed a few years ago, probably at a time when Win95 was not even in its early beta. Instead, *FOOTPRNT* was intended to be as generic as possible to work on any Windows platform that supports the

VxD-based kernel model. *FOOTPRNT* is a regular static virtual device that is defined by the "device=" line in *SYSTEM.INI*, but it also *pretends* to be a debugger.

Although not exactly a debugger, *FOOTPRNT* provides lots of functionality on which to build various debugging and exploring tools. Some of these tools have already been created, while others are still under development or are waiting to be written in the future. Over the years, the VxD system kept growing in both size and complexity, and so did *FOOTPRNT*. Because it is under perpetual construction, *FOOTPRNT* is not marketed separately (at least, not at the source code level) at the time of this writing. For more information on *FOOTPRNT* availability, contact Alex Shmidt at *73302.60@compuserve.com*.

FOOTPRNT is the spying engine that monitors and records various operating system activities at system initialization time. It does this by intercepting calls to operating system services. (Actually, *FOOTPRNT* does more than just record calls, but this extra functionality is irrelevant to spying on registry calls.) Why at initialization time? Because the most important aspects of any VxD's run-time behavior can be (or, at least, was in Windows 3.x) discovered by examining its initialization. The VMM broadcasts startup messages to all VxDs registered in the VxD chain. In response to these messages, VxDs invoke code responsible for setting them up for the entire Windows session. Whether a VxD hooks an interrupt, replaces another VxD service, patches the real-mode code with breakpoints, or simply configures itself using settings in the *SYSTEM.INI* file, it does so in response to one of the startup system control messages. In addition, some VMM and VxD services are available only at initialization time. Usually, VxD startup code resides in discardable code segments, so that when the system is fully initialized, this code no longer resides in memory. (That's why startup code is not easy to explore and to debug, and even commercial disassemblers sometimes have problems with it.)

In Windows, the boundaries of the initialization time frame are drawn by the system broadcast messages `SYS_CRITICAL_INIT` and `INIT_COMPLETE` (Win95 and WfW 3.11 also support dynamic VxDs). Because it has an "init order" of 0, *FOOTPRNT.386* is loaded in front of other VxDs, usually right after the VMM. Therefore, *FOOTPRNT.386* is the first in line to receive the `SYS_CRITICAL_INIT` message. It responds to the message by hooking into every possible VMM or VxD service, and begins to store information about calls to these services in a single linked list of data structures called FPLIST.

In other words, every time some VxD calls a service that *FOOTPRNT* is configured to monitor, it triggers *FOOTPRNT*'s corresponding hook handler, which allocates a new list node, decodes parameters passed to the service being trapped, fills the node with this information (along with the calling VxD's name and the stage of initialization on which the call occurred), and appends the list node to the tail of

FPLIST. The result is that call trace data is stored in the same chronological order as the calls themselves were made.

FOOTPRNT uses VMM list services for its linked list machinations, which makes it easy for an external program (like *REGSPY95.EXE*, in our case) to traverse the list later on. All *RegSpy95* needs for this is the list handle; *FOOTPRNT* provides a facility (discussed in the next section) for obtaining this list handle.

Because *FOOTPRNT* itself uses VMM services that it could be instructed to monitor, every effort has been taken to make *FOOTPRNT*'s code reenterable and safe. *FOOTPRNT.386* also arranges to be the last VxD to receive the `INIT_COMPLETE` message, after all VxDs that have device description blocks (DDBs) in the VxD chain have completed their initialization. In response to the message, *FOOTPRNT* releases all the services that it has intercepted and discards most of its code, leaving resident only a relatively small stub of code and, of course, FPLIST (which *RegSpy95* uses as one of the output buffers to dump).

Everything I've just described is what *FOOTPRNT.386* has been doing for a couple of years without knowing anything about the registry, but the framework turned out to be good enough for tracing registry calls that VxDs make at system startup. All that was required was to add new services into a table of calls to hook, plus some knowledge about decoding the call parameters. However, one of *RegSpy95*'s major design goals was to log registry calls issued by or on behalf of Ring 3 applications at any time during a Win95 session. Because of the implementation of registry services at the VMM level, this seemed to be easy, so I simply added code to extend the functionality of *FOOTPRNT*'s existing interception mechanism for registry APIs beyond the scope of the system boot-up.

This modification, however, immediately presented an unpleasant surprise: severe performance degradation. While it's always been okay to append new nodes to the end of FPLIST for calls during initialization, doing so at run-time led to a significant system-wide slowdown. The obvious reason for this is that to append a new node to the list's tail, the VMM's Linked List Manager has to walk the entire list in the first place. The link list services provided by VMM, however, allows for a really simple solution. First of all, *FOOTPRNT* creates a second list, called REGLIST, to store information about registry calls made after all VxDs finish processing `INIT_COMPLETE`. Second, instead of appending nodes to the tail of the list, *FOOTPRNT* attaches them to the head, which in effect makes call traces appear in REGLIST in reverse chronological order. The only difference in the way that *RegSpy95* has to handle this list from the way it handles FPLIST is that it has to reverse the order in which nodes are stored in REGLIST before it actually starts traversing the linked list. We'll discuss this reversal in greater detail a bit later, in the section "Linked Lists Everywhere."

Another new piece of the code in *FOOTPRNT* that traps the registry APIs figures out the names of calling processes and constructs yet another linked list, MODLIST. As can be seen in the header file *FPREG.H*, the *FOOTPRNT* union of structures, which reflects the data layout of the FPLIST and REGLIST nodes, contains a pointer to the name of the calling VxD or Windows module. While module names are convenient in making sense of *RegSpy95* trace listings, frequently they make it difficult to identify the calling program. MODLIST was implemented for this reason; it's nothing more than a lookup table that contains module names and their corresponding filenames. The contents of MODLIST can be found near the end of every *RegSpy95* trace file.

When it comes to saving string parameters from the registry calls, *FOOTPRNT* allocates chunks of the system heap for string storage and inserts the block pointers inside list nodes. As you can imagine, *FOOTPRNT*'s hook handlers encounter identical registry key and value names many times within a single Windows session. This is the case not only because the registry is a system-wide facility, but also because some programs stubbornly make exactly the same calls again and again. *FOOTPRNT*'s initial memory consumption is high even without these repeated calls, so it contains code that avoids storing duplicate strings.

FOOTPRNT and Memory

Even though every effort has been taken to make Win95 perform as efficiently as possible when running *FOOTPRNT*, the basic fact is that *FOOTPRNT* is an avid consumer of system resources, and particularly of system memory. By default, *FOOTPRNT* installs hook handlers for all services of which it has knowledge. However, this approach is wasteful in several ways. First, system performance and available memory vary in inverse relation to the actual number of calls that *FOOT-PRNT* traps by the time the Windows GUI is completely initialized. Second, if system configuration doesn't change from session to session, the initial content of *FOOTPRNT*'s lists will not change across sessions either. Thus, there is little point in running *FOOTPRNT* in full capacity each time Win95 starts up. As discussed earlier, however, you can reduce *FOOTPRNT*'s memory usage with settings in *SYSTEM.INI* or with a *FOOTPRNT* configuration file.

Interfacing with FOOTPRNT and Win95's Dangerous Memory Model

FOOTPRNT excels at collecting call trace information, but VxDs have no viable way of presenting it to users in a humanly readable form; that's what *RegSpy95* is for. For *RegSpy95* to access *FOOTPRNT*'s data externally, an interface of some sort is required. While there are plenty of ways to communicate with a VxD these days (both Microsoft-sanctioned and not), one of them looks just right for the job in this case: *DeviceIOControl.* Implemented for Windows NT, *DeviceIOControl* has always been an interface for Win32 processes to talk to device drivers, but in Win95 it makes its debut as a communication channel between user programs (i.e., programs in Ring 3) and VxDs. Not only is *DeviceIOControl* suitable because *RegSpy95* is a Win32 application, but it also doesn't require that a VxD have a Device ID (and *FOOTPRNT* doesn't have one); instead, *DeviceIOControl* is name-based.

The Ring 0 side of *DeviceIOControl,* which is newly introduced with Win95, requires that a VxD respond to the newly added system control message W32_DEVICEIOCONTROL. According to the interface specifications, an application program is supposed to pass a control code in one of the function's parameters. For the device side, these codes, which are usually just sequential numbers starting at 1, are interpreted as subfunction identifiers. The following excerpt from the *RegSpy95* header file *FPREG.H* lists *FOOTPRNT*'s IOControl interfaces:

```
/* Footprnt IOCONTROL codes  */
typedef enum {
  FP_GETVERSION=1,        // get Footprnt version
  FP_GETFPLIST=2,         // get init list handle
  FP_GETLISTNODE=3,       // get next node (for list walkers)
  FP_GETMODLIST=4,        // get win32 module lookup list handle
  FP_GETREGLIST=5,        // get run-time list handle
  FP_EMPTYLIST=6,         // delete registry entries from all lists
  FP_ENABLESERVICE=7,     // enable/disable service trap
  FP_ENABLECALLER=8,      // enable/disable trapping calls made by the caller
  FP_GETDISABLEDSERVICE=9,// retrieve list of disabled service hooks
  FP_GETDISABLEDCALLER=10,// retrieve list of disabled caller hooks
  FP_COPYMEMORY=11,       // copy bytes from Ring 0 memblock to Ring3 memblock
}FOOTPRNT_IOCTL;
```

Note particularly the following three constants (or subfunctions):

FP_GETFPLIST=2	Returns the list handle for FPLIST
FP_GETREGLIST=5	Returns the list handle for REGLIST
FP_GETLISTNODE=3	Returns the next node pointer for any given linked list

These three constants are all that *RegSpy95* needs to access the entire call trace. For example, to dump all records chronologically, *RegSpy95* first acquires the FPLIST handle by calling *DeviceIOControl* with the FP_GETFPLIST constant. Armed with the handle, *RegSpy95* enters a loop in which it repeatedly calls *Device-IOControl* with the FP_GETLISTNODE constant until the function returns 0, indicating that there are no more list nodes. On each iteration of the loop, *RegSpy95* takes the next node pointer and displays the node content. The *FOOT-PRNT* union from *FPREG.H* lays out the structure for all types of nodes so that *RegSpy95* knows exactly how to interpret the data. After it's done with FPLIST, the initialization-time list, *RegSpy95* repeats this procedure for REGLIST, in the process reversing the list (remember that, unlike FPLIST, REGLIST stores all records in reverse chronological order).

Although this *RegSpy95*-to-*FOOTPRNT* conversation appears simple, there is a serious architectural problem. All list nodes that *RegSpy95* manipulates directly are allocated by *FOOTPRNT* (which is, don't forget, a piece of the supervisor-level code) from the VMM memory heap. Likewise, some *FOOTPRNT* union members are also pointers to chunks of the system heap. An application accessing system memory is a dubious technique that can lead to two serious problems. Both are related to the CPU's protection facilities and how the operating system utilizes (or how it doesn't utilize) them.

First, all the pointers that *FOOTPRNT.386* provides to *RegSpy95* are not necessarily valid in the *RegSpy95* context. It's very feasible that, when used within a Win32 process, a linear pointer will point to a totally different memory location than when the same pointer is used by a VxD. Although both the VxD system and Win32 programs use flat-model code and data pointers, the flat-memory model does not imply the equality of linear and virtual pointers. Even though flat-model programs usually do not need to explicitly use the CPU segment registers (which in protected mode contain selectors), the selectors are still with us at all times. Selectors (or, more precisely, Descriptor Table entries that selectors point to) are what determines memory model "flatness," and the truth is that flat-model selectors are not necessarily zero-based. But in Win95, both Ring 0 and Ring 3 flat data (and code) selectors are based at the linear address 0 and thus map to the same virtual address space. That is why direct access to system memory using a pointer from a Win32 process is acceptable.[*] In any case, *RegSpy95* doesn't have the pointer mapping problem in Win95 because the system abandons selector isolation as its first-level protection.

The second problem concerns protection at the page level. In the Intel architecture, every page table entry (which references a 4Kb block of physical memory called a *page*) contains an array of property bits that control access to that page. This includes a User/Supervisor bit that allows an operating system to decide whether non-privileged, user-level programs can touch physical memory within a given page. In the case of *RegSpy95*, these pages consist of the system's heap memory, from which *FOOTPRNT* allocates linked list nodes and small blocks of

---

[*] To see that this virtual-to-linear pointer correspondence is not written in stone, look no further than the implementation of the Win32s subsystem, where Win32 processes receive flat selectors whose base addresses are somewhere above the two-gigabyte line. Because of such memory management in Win32s, a program that dereferences linear pointers obtained from a VxD would destabilize the system. There are relatively simple ways to convert pointers between two distinct flat-memory models, but *RegSpy95* in any case refuses to run when it detects Win32s.

heap. If the system memory manager within the VMM marked these memory blocks with the Supervisor attribute, *RegSpy95*'s attempt to access them would raise an exception. This doesn't happen, though, because Win95, just like Windows 3.x, does not protect memory allocated by VxDs at the page level.* It is ironic that in Win95, while Win32 processes have no way of seeing each other, they can access almost anything else, including memory belonging to the system itself, the DOS region of the system VM, and static copies of all running virtual machines.

Incidentally, Win95 memory scheme is sometimes called the DMM (Dangerous Memory Model; for a collection of programs illustrating the Win95 DMM, see *http:/ /www.ora.com/pub/examples/windows/win95.update/unauthor.html*). Since *RegSpy95* works as implemented, that phrase would seem to be more than justified. And in fact, *RegSpy95* could have gone (but didn't go) much further in taking advantage of the DMM. Consider the following: the transparency of Ring 0 and Ring 3 data selector mappings apply as well to code selectors. Thus, a Win32 program can call any VMM or VxD service! In most cases, of course, this totally crashes Win95. However, simple VMM services can be accessed in a relatively safe manner (please note that I don't advocate doing this; I'm just saying it's certainly possible). Don't believe it? Then look at the following VMM code for the *List_Get_First* and *List_Get_Next* functions that *FOOTPRNT.386* invokes when *RegSpy95* calls the *DeviceIOControl* function with the FP_GETLISTNODE constant:

```
List_Get_First:
    mov     eax, [esi]
    cmp     eax, 0
    ret

List_Get_Next:
    mov     eax, [eax-4]
    cmp     eax, 0
    ret
```

There's no need to be an assembly language expert to understand this code. When each of these functions is called from within a VxD, it's entered with the flat zero-based Ring 0 code and data selectors. When the code is called directly by a Win32 process, it's entered with the flat zero-based Ring 3 code and data selectors. Both pairs of selectors are mapped to the same memory range, which is not page-protected. If *RegSpy95* somehow located these 2 services and called

---

* In fact, even if the designers of Win95 had contemplated this type of page protection, it could hardly have been implemented because of the need to maintain compatibility with Windows 3.x, where it was almost habitual for programmers to allocate memory within a VxD, and then access that memory from Ring 3 programs. Nevertheless, to access "foreign" memory from 16-bit code, a program has to specifically arrange for it by manipulating such system objects as selectors, linear and segmented addresses, etc. In contrast, a Win32 program gets such access for free whether its creators intended this or not.

them directly,[*] nothing would indicate to the operating system that a non-privileged program is executing the operating system's code. Some people might even advocate this to dramatically increase *RegSpy95*'s performance, since it eliminates a lot of ring transitions. However, I'll gladly take credit for not using this kind of hack!

RegSpy95 also uses several other *DeviceIOControl* subfunctions that allow *RegSpy95* to control individual aspects of *FOOTPRNT.386*'s run-time behavior and to retrieve current settings. One subfunction that *RegSpy95* does not use is *FP_COPYMEMORY*, which lets you copy several bytes from a Ring 0 buffer to a Ring 3 buffer in a manner that is independent of the internal system implementation, since this makes it difficult to exploit holes in the Win95 VMM. But developers who feel insecure about taking advantage of the absence of protection in Win95 can make *RegSpy95* slower but "safer" by modifying the program to use *FP_COPYMEMORY* when making code modifications.

Linked Lists Everywhere

Although not the most perfect data collection structure, linked lists are among the easiest to understand and use. Ultimately, every resourceful programmer ends up writing his or her own linked list manager of some sort. We have already seen the usefulness of the VMM linked list services, which let *FOOTPRNT.386* organize its call trace storage in a kind of "object-oriented" fashion. *RegSpy32*'s linked list management is reflected in the static run-time library called *LIST32.LIB*. I also considered encapsulating my list manager into a DLL like I did when programming for Win16, but then decided not to. After all, with Win32 processes running in separate address spaces, the main purpose of dynamic link libraries—sharing code and data between applications—is inapplicable to *RegSpy95*.

For the most part, the functionality of LIST32 mimics that of the VMM's List Manager. For a description of what is available, look at *LIST32.H*, which defines such functions as *ListCreate* and *ListGetFirst* that are functionally identical to VMM's *List_Create* and *List_Get_First*. Every list that is created is uniquely identified by its handle; it can be referenced by the handle until the list is explicitly destroyed. The major difference between the VMM list manager and List32 is that, unlike VMM's lists, LIST32's lists can manage nodes of variable size. To create a list like this, you'd pass the LIST_VARIABLE flag to the *ListCreate* function. The link pointers are managed automatically for both fixed and variable sized lists;

---

[*] There *are* ways to do this; see the *VXDCHAIN* program, particularly the *Get_VxD_Proc_Address* function, at O'Reilly & Associates' Web site: *http://www.ora.com/pub/examples/windows/win95.update/vxdchain.html*. This is a Win32 program containing a direct call into VMM. Another Win32 program that directly calls VMM is available at *http://www.ora.com/pub/examples/windows/win95.update/vm.html*.

however, unlike fixed lists, it's the responsibility of the caller to specify the new node size when calling *ListAllocate* for a variable sized list.

Another LIST32 novelty is very clearly a matter of programming convenience. One of the basic properties of linked lists is that they are easily traversed. In fact, all *RegSpy95* does is to methodically traverse several linked lists; everything else that you'll find in *RegSpy95*'s code is just utility functions. A new function in *LIST32.LIB*, *ListWalk32*, automates this process. The function is prototyped in *LIST32.H* like this:

```
LPVOID ListWalk32 (LISTFILTER32 filterproc, HLIST hlist, DWORD refdata);
```

As you can see, *ListWalk32* takes three parameters: a list handle, a DWORD of reference data, and a pointer to a callback function of type LISTFILTER32. The callback function is prototyped in the header file as:

```
typedef BOOL (*LISTFILTER32)(LPVOID,DWORD);
```

ListWalk32 knows nothing about the linked list whose handle is *hlist*; it simply traverses it, one node at a time, within a loop. On each iteration of the loop, ListWalk32 obtains a pointer to the next list node and passes it along with the reference data to the filter function. The filter function can do whatever it wants with the node, like testing the node against certain conditions defined by the reference data. When it has finished with the node, the filter function returns a Boolean value, which indicates to *ListWalk32* whether or not to continue traversing the list. If the filter function returns True, *ListWalk32* exits the walking loop and returns the current node pointer to its caller; if the filter function returns False, *ListWalk32* obtains the next node pointer and calls the filter again. The main purpose of *ListWalk32* is to provide a convenient way to find a node in the list that satisfies a condition presented by the reference data. However, most *RegSpy95* filter functions that traverse FPLIST and REGLIST unconditionally return False because their goal is to squeeze as much as possible out of the lists rather than to find any specific node.

RegSpy95's major goal, of course, is to format and output the contents of its lists, a job that's handled by calling the *LogDump* function. But while it's easy to manipulate the linked list created at Ring 0, *RegSpy95* first has to reverse the run-time list from Ring 3. One way of doing this is to simply reverse REGLIST. That solution, however, is impractical: it means that calls that have already been logged appear in the list in chronological order, while *FOOTPRNT* continues registering new calls in reverse chronological order. As a result, the second attempt to use *RegSpy95* to output registry access information during the same Win95 session would produce totally distorted output.

Since *RegSpy95* has to leave REGLIST intact, it instead reverses a copy of REGLIST (identified by the list handle *hReversedList* in the source code) that this time is stored in *RegSpy95*'s own address space; this is done in the function *CopyReversedList*. This function copies nodes from the *FOOTPRNT*'s Ring 0 list to LIST32's Ring 3 list, reversing the order of the nodes on the fly. As you can see by looking at *REGSPY95.C*, this function is nothing more than a very thin wrapper around yet another linked list walking function, *Ring0ListWalk*. This latter function has exactly the same functionality as its Win32 counterpart, *ListWalk32*, with the "minor" exception that it works with VMM linked lists. While *ListWalk32* goes through lists using the *ListGetFirst/ListGetNext* pair of functions, *Ring0ListWalk* calls the *DeviceIOControl* wrapper, *ListGetNode*, within a loop.

The list filter function for *CopyReversedList* is *CopyNode*. (Remember that a filter function is called for each list node in order. The function simply allocates a new node for **hReversedList**, copies the current REGLIST node into it, and then attaches the new node at the head of **hReversedList**. Repeating this operation for all REGLIST nodes produces a copy that is the reverse of the original in the application's address space.

With REGLIST effectively reversed, *RegSpy95* has everything it needs to call the *LogDump* function.

LogDump (in *RSUTIL.C*) is both table-driven and linked list-driven; it takes three list handles as parameters (**PFLIST**, **hReversedList**, and **MODLIST**) and uses an internal array of structures of type REGDUMP (which are defined in *DUMP.H*). Each element of the array of type REGDUMP contains the name of one of the VMM registry services that *RegSpy95* spies on, and a pointer to a "dumper" procedure that interprets and displays information about that VMM service.

LogDump iterates both **FPLIST** and **hReversedList** once if it's to display registry access information in chronological view, or once for each entry in the **REGDUMP** array if it's to produce the function-by-function view. Naturally, the function traverses these lists using the *Ring0ListWalk* and *ListWalk32* functions. The filter functions for *LogDump* are *FunctionGroups* for the function-by-function view and *Chrono* for the chronological view. However, these functions just test whether, given *RegSpy95*'s current configuration, it's appropriate to dump a particular list node. If it is, they call the actual "dumper" function that corresponds to the current node's service number. Otherwise the filter functions simply skip the node. Notice that both *FunctionGroups* and *Chrono* unconditionally return False. This causes *Ring0ListWalk* and *ListWalk32* to continue their loops until they reach the end of each list.

When *LogDump* finishes iterating the lists, it displays the module-to-filename table by calling the *ShowModulesAndFiles* function, which (as you no doubt guessed) is also a list walker for MODLIST. Finally, *LogDump* prints a legend of abbreviations used in the main dump.

If you are going to use *LIST32.LIB* a lot in your own programs, it is important to remember that, because LIST32 is a static library, your program must explicitly initialize it before making the first list management call, and then it must shut it down at the end. The functions *ListStartup* and *ListCleanup* serve this purpose.

DeviceIOControl Wrapper Functions

A Win32 program can communicate with a virtual device through input and output buffers. A program allocates one buffer to hold input parameters and another buffer for the return values. Both buffers should be large enough to accommodate the number of DWORD values defined by the interface of the specific *IOControl* subfunction. A program then stuffs DWORDs into the input buffer, passes buffer pointers along with their sizes to a VxD, and parses the content of the output buffer when *IOControl* returns. If a program uses *DeviceIO-Control* many times, it would be better off having a less cumbersome interface. For this reason I've written simple wrapper functions, one for each of the *FOOT-PRNT DeviceIOControl* codes. This makes it possible to write compact code, like:

```
node = ListGetNode (hlist, node);
```

Other *DeviceIOControl* wrappers include *ExcludeService, ExcludeCaller,* and *ListEmpty,* which are used to stop *FOOTPRNT* from monitoring calls to selected functions, to disable spying on particular modules, and to clear *FOOTPRNT's* buffers, respectively. All *DeviceIOControl* wrappers reside in a single source module, *RSDIOC.C.*

Spying on SYSTEM.INI Profile Settings

When coding and debugging of *RegSpy95* was virtually finished, I received a request to add the ability to spy on *SYSTEM.INI* as well. This proved to be fairly easy to do, since the Virtual Machine Manager has been providing a set of *profile* (or initialization file) services for VxDs to configure themselves since the release of Windows 3.0; these include the *Get_Profile_Boolean, Get_Profile_Decimal_Int, Get_Profile_Hex_Int, Get_Profile_String, Get_Next_Profile_String,* and *Get_ Profile_Fixed_Point* functions, along with a few other complementary functions that convert data from one type to another but are not of much interest to spy on. These functions all provide initialization time services; that is, virtual devices can no longer call them after receiving the `INIT_COMPLETE` system message.

But why do we need to spy on *SYSTEM.INI* at all? Presumably, the registry was introduced to supplant *SYSTEM.INI* and other system and private initialization files. And in any case, it is easy enough just to load *SYSTEM.INI* using any text editor and inspect the entries it contains. In fact, though, *SYSTEM.INI* continues to be used for more than reasons of compatibility: it contains several settings (like the identity of the Windows shell) of critical interest to 32-bit Windows that are not duplicated in the Win95 registry. Simply inspecting *SYSTEM.INI*, though, doesn't necessarily tell us what those entries are, or to what degree *SYSTEM.INI* continues to be important. In many cases, what is important is not so much the contents of *SYSTEM.INI*, but what Windows and other applications look for (but don't necessarily find) in it. By spying on the profile service calls, it is possible to discover entries that are undocumented or barely documented, and which might otherwise remain completely unknown.

If you're both adventurous and somewhat skeptical about this persistence of initialization files, you might want to try the following. If you've already custom-ized your display driver and Windows desktop, enter the following line in the [Display] section of *SYSTEM.INI* and then reboot Win95:

```
IgnoreRegistry=on
```

Regardless of how your computer was configured, you'll notice some major changes to your current Windows desktop. You'll also notice, in some cases, error messages about your system using incorrect display drivers. The reason for this is that, for the most part, your display settings and desktop settings are stored in the registry, and Win95 commonly executes a sequence of registry accesses like the following during initialization:

```
_RegOpenKey        VDD     HKCC               C1175DC4            'display\settings'
_RegQueryValueEx   VDD     C1175DC4    SZ     3      'BitsPerPixel'    '16'
_RegQueryValueEx   VDD     C1175DC4    SZ     8      'Resolution'      '800,600'
_RegQueryValueEx   VDD     C1175DC4    SZ     3      'DPILogicalX'     '96'
_RegCloseKey       VDD     C1175DC4
```

The `IgnoreRegistry` entry, though, told the Virtual Display Device (VDD) to ignore them.

In any case, adding this new functionality to *RegSpy95* was not hard at all. As a driver originally written for Windows 3.x, when the registry was not available but initialization files were, *FOOTPRNT* already handled the profile services. Most of the modifications to support profile services occurred to *RegSpy95*, which in any case is structured to support such enhancements. All that was required to have *RegSpy95* interpret and display profile information in FPLIST was a few new entries in the array of REGDUMP structures, an additional "dumper" function, *DumpProfiles*, and one new data structure, PROFILE, that was added to the *FPREG.H* header file.

Rebuilding RegSpy95

Along with *RegSpy95*'s executable components, the diskette accompanying *Inside the Windows 95 Registry* contains the complete source code for *RegSpy95*. (It does not, though, include source code for *FOOTPRNT.386*.) *RegSpy95*'s source code consists of the following five modules:

REGSPY95.C	The main loop
REGSCRPT.C	Configuration file parser
RSDIOC.C	Wrapper functions for *FOOTPRNT*'s *DeviceIOControl* interface
RSDUMP.C	*Filter* function and service "dumpers"
RSUTIL.C	*LogDump* and various other utility functions

The source code in turns depends on various definitions that can be found in the following header files:

DDK.H	Some VxD system definitions
DUMP.H	*RegSpy95* general definitions
FPREG.H	*FOOTPRNT.386* structures and interfaces
LIST32.H	Interface to *LIST32.LIB*
REGCONST.H	Important registry constants
RSDIOC.H	Prototypes for the *DeviceIOControl* wrapper functions

If you have Microsoft Visual C++ version 2.0 or higher, you can rebuild *RegSpy95* using the supplied make file, *REGSPY95.MAK*. I'm not a great fan of IDEs, so run *REGSPY95.MAK* from the command line. If you're using a non-Microsoft compiler, you should have no problem building the program, since no vendor-specific language extensions have been used in *RegSpy95*'s code. You will, however, have to construct your own make file.

If you want, though, you can go well beyond making modifications to *RegSpy95*. The accompanying diskette contains a complete set of header files needed to interface *RegSpy95* or any other application to *FOOTPRNT.386*. That, along with an understanding of how *FOOTPRNT*'s buffers are organized, is all that you need to develop your own applications to replace *RegSpy95*.

APISpy32

Since they are both spying programs, *APISpy32* has a great deal in common with *RegSpy95*: both intercept calls to the Windows API, in the process recording information about which functions were called, what parameters were passed to them, and what values they returned. At the same time, *APISpy32* is different from *RegSpy95* in several respects:

- *APISpy32* intercepts calls to high-level API functions, like *CreateWindow* or *RegOpenKey*. In contrast, *RegSpy95* is a low-level spying utility that intercepts an application's requests for registry services. If you're interested in the registry API, for instance, a call to the high-level API does not always translate into a call to the low-level API. (*APISpy32*, for instance, detects calls to *RegConnectRegistry* to connect to a remote computer; *RegSpy95* does not.) Conversely, a call to a non-registry API often translates into a request for registry services, and sometimes even translates into multiple registry accesses. *RegSpy95* detects these requests, but *APISpy32* does not. (*APISpy32*, for instance, would detect an application's call to the *FindExecutable* function. The function itself uses file association information in the registry to retrieve the name and handle of an executable file associated with a file; *RegSpy95* would detect each of the function's requests for registry services, something that *APISpy32* was not intended to do.) To put this another way, *APISpy32* intercepts calls to registry services that occur from a program's code. *RegSpy95* also intercepts *most* of these, but intercepts calls made by Windows itself to registry services on behalf of the application.

- *APISpy95* is a general-purpose spying utility. Although you can configure it to spy on only the registry API, it was developed to spy on the entire Win32 API. In contrast, *RegSpy95* is a special-purpose registry (and system initialization file) spying utility.

- *APISpy95* can only spy on a single program at a time. In contrast, *RegSpy95* by default intercepts all requests for registry services, regardless of whether the request comes from an application, a virtual device driver (VxD), or the system itself. *RegSpy95* can also be configured to spy on none, one, or multiple designated programs.

Inside APISpy32

If you're interested in learning how *APISpy32* works, and more generally in how to go about writing a spying utility, see Chapter 10, *Writing a Win32 API Spy*, in Matt Pietrek's outstanding book, *Windows 95 System Programming Secrets*, published by IDG Books. See *http://www.ora.com/pub/examples/windows/win95.update/dirty.html* for an excerpt from the book and online ordering information.

These differences, and the way in which *RegSpy95* and *APISpy32* can provide complementary information, will become clear as you read the documentation for *APISpy32*.

Running APISpy32

APISpy32 consists of three components:

- A shell, *APISPYLD.EXE*, that is responsible for loading the application whose API calls are to be intercepted

- A dynamic link library, *APISPY32.DLL*, that does the actual spying

- A text configuration file, *APISPY32.API*, that indicates the precise API functions that *APISpy32* is to intercept

You begin spying on an application by running *APISPYLD.EXE*. *APISPYLD.EXE* displays the window shown in Figure 10-3, which allows you to designate the program that you'd like to spy on. Enter the path and filename of the program whose API calls you want to intercept in the text box; if you're not quite sure of its path or its filename, you can click on the File button to bring up the Open dialog; this is the standard Open common dialog that allows you to navigate your local file system to find the file.

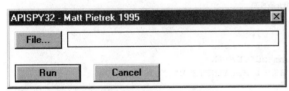

Figure 10-3. APISPYLD.EXE

Once *APISpy32* launches the program, you continue to use it as you would normally. When you close the program, you'll find that *APISpy32* has created a log file containing the application's API calls in the same directory as the executable file you spied on. Its filename is the same as the application's root filename (i.e., without its file extension), but with an .OUT file extension. A fragment from the registry-related functions calls from *MSPAINT.OUT*, an output file generated when *APISpy32* was spying on MS Paint, is shown in Example 10-1.

Example 10-1. A fragment from the .OUT file produced by MSPAINT.EXE

```
RegCreateKeyA(HND: HKCU,"Software",)
RegCreateKeyA ret 0
RegCreateKeyA(HND:C23A0FF0h,"Microsoft\Windows\CurrentVersion\Applets",)
RegCreateKeyA ret 0
RegCreateKeyA(HND:C23A101Ch,"Paint",)
RegCreateKeyA ret 0
RegOpenKeyA(HND:C23A1048h,"View",)
RegOpenKeyA ret 0
RegCloseKey(HND:C23A1048h)
RegCloseKey ret 0
RegCloseKey(HND:C23A101Ch)
RegCloseKey ret 0
```

Example 10-1. A fragment from the .OUT file produced by MSPAINT.EXE (continued)

```
RegCloseKey(HND:C23A0FF0h)
RegCloseKey ret 0
RegQueryValueExA(HND:C23A1074h,"WindowPlacement")
RegQueryValueExA ret 0
RegCloseKey(HND:C23A1074h)
RegCloseKey ret 0
CreateBitmap(DW:8h,DW:8h,DW:1h,DW:1h,)
CreateBitmap ret 20BE
CreatePatternBrush(HND:20BEh)
CreatePatternBrush ret 1C9E
CreateBitmap(DW:8h,DW:8h,DW:1h,DW:1h,)
CreateBitmap ret 8AA
CreatePatternBrush(HND:8AAh)
CreatePatternBrush ret D52
SetErrorMode(DW:1h)
SetErrorMode ret 8000
RegCreateKeyA(HND: HKCU,"Paint.Picture\shell",)
RegCreateKeyA ret 0
GetModuleFileNameA(HND:400000h,"",DW:104h)
GetModuleFileNameA ret 28
RegCreateKeyA(HND:C23A0FF0h,"Open",)
RegCreateKeyA ret 0
wsprintfA("",""%s" "%%1"")
wsprintfA ret 27
RegSetValueA(HND:C23A101Ch,"command",DW:1h,
             ""C:\PROGRA~1\ACCESS~1\MSPAINT.EXE" "%1"",DW:0h)
RegSetValueA ret 0
RegCloseKey(HND:C23A101Ch)
RegCloseKey ret 0
RegCreateKeyA(HND:C23A0FF0h,"Print",)
RegCreateKeyA ret 0
wsprintfA(""C:\PROGRA~1\ACCESS~1\MSPAINT.EXE" "%1"",""%s" /p "%%1"")
wsprintfA ret 2A
RegSetValueA(HND:C23A101Ch,"command",DW:1h,
             ""C:\PROGRA~1\ACCESS~1\MSPAINT.EXE" /p "%1"",DW:0h)
RegSetValueA ret 0
RegCloseKey(HND:C23A101Ch)
RegCloseKey ret 0
```

This example contains an excerpt from MS Paint's initialization portion. In this
fragment, MSPaint retrieves the value of the `WindowPlacement` entry from
`HKCU\Software\Microsoft\Windows\CurrentVersion\Applets\Paint\`
`View`. It does this by opening the Applets, Paint, and View keys separately, even
though the former two keys are not accessed otherwise. It then begins to register
a complete set of shell verbs without testing to see whether they've already been
registered or determining whether they're still accurate.

Configuring APISpy32

By default, *APISpy32* spies on the bulk of Win32 API functions that are exported by the system libraries listed below. It does this because it automatically reads an ASCII file, *APISPY32.API*, that lists the functions exported by these libraries; you can, however, modify this configuration file to list only those functions that you'd like to intercept.

ADVAPI32.DLL

COMDLG32.DLL

GDI32.DLL

KERNEL32.DLL

USER32.DLL

Checking APISPY32.API

Before using *APISpy32*, you should always check *APISPY32.API* to make sure that it contains the functions in which you're interested. It contains definitions for most, but not all, of the functions exported by the five libraries listed above.

Figure 10-4 shows the definitions of some of the Win32 registry functions in the *APISPY32.API* file. To define a function that you'd like to have *APISpy32* intercept, *APISPY32.API* requires the following syntax:

```
API:<Filename>:<FunctionName>
   <ParameterList...>
```

Parameter	Explanation
`<Filename>`	The name of the dynamic link library. A path is not required if the file is located in the Windows' system directory, but the file's extension is.
`<FunctionName>`	The name of the function as it is exported from the DLL. `<FunctionName>` must correspond exactly to a function that appears in the DLL's export table. This means that case must be the same, and that the ANSI or unicode version of a function must be specified if the library includes both.
`<ParameterList...>`	The function's parameter list. Each item of `<Parameter-List...>` appears on a separate line and indicates the simple data type of the parameter, as defined in Microsoft's *Win32 Programmer's Reference*. Where the function requires a structured data type as a parameter, you can specify *LPDATA* as its parameter.

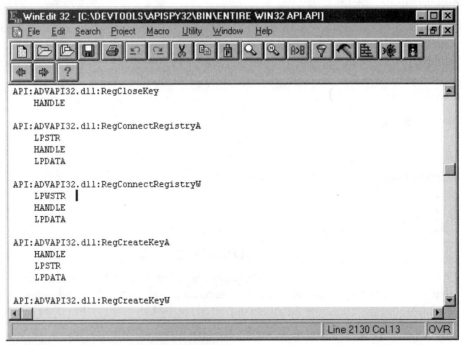

Figure 10-4. A portion of an APISPY32.API file

Aside from spying on a subset of the Win32 API (like the registry API), you can also expand *APISPY32.API* to spy on calls to other system libraries (like the multimedia library, *MMSYSTEM.DLL*, for example) and possibly on calls to private DLLs as well, provided that you know what parameters they require. To successfully spy on a particular function, though, it must be called *directly* in the source code of the application you're running. In other words, *APISpy32* won't intercept calls by system libraries to functions that they import from other libraries or to other functions in the same library (*RegSpy95 would* intercept such calls).

APISpy32's output

Example 10-2 shows an excerpt from *APISpy32*'s output for the initialization portion of a WordPad session, when WordPad was querying the registry. In most cases, a pair of lines are devoted to each API call. The first lists the parameters passed to the API function, while the second displays the function's return value. For example, in the first line, *RegQueryValueEx* is used to retrieve the value of the FrameRect entry belonging to the key whose handle ("HND" in the *APISpy32* output) is 0xC11CCF7C. (If we search the for the string "FrameRect" in the registry, we'd discover that the key's name is HKCU\Software\Microsoft\ Windows\CurrentVersion\Applets\WordPad\Options.) The second line indicates that the function returned 0, or ERROR_SUCCESS. Unfortunately, no further information about the `FrameRect` value entry is provided. The third line successfully closes this open key, as witnessed by the return value shown in the fourth line. In the next four lines, the *GetSystemMetrics* function, which retrieves system-level information about the dimensions of Windows display elements, is called twice. In the first call to the function, the index value of 1 (or SM_CYSCREEN) indicates that the function is to retrieve the number of vertical pixels on the screen; in the second, the 0 (or SM_CXSCREEN) indicates that it's to retrieve the number of horizontal pixels. The function returns the relative metric; in this case, the screen's dimensions are 800 (or 0x320) by 600 (or 0x258). *GetSystemMetrics* is interesting because it in turn is implemented as a call to *RegQueryValueEx*; the screen dimensions are stored as a single string value entry named `Resolution` in HKCC\\`Display`\\`Settings`. But because this API call is not made directly by WordPad itself, it does not appear in *APISpy32*'s output.

Example 10-2. An excerpt from the API calls made by WordPad during initialization

```
RegQueryValueExA(HND:C11CCF7Ch,"FrameRect",,,,)
RegQueryValueExA ret 0
RegCloseKey(HND:C11CCF7Ch)
RegCloseKey ret 0
GetSystemMetrics(DW:1h)
GetSystemMetrics ret 258
GetSystemMetrics(DW:0h)
GetSystemMetrics ret 320
IntersectRect(,,)
IntersectRect ret 201
SetRect(,DW:708h,DW:5A0h,DW:708h,DW:5A0h)
SetRect ret FFFFFFFF
RegQueryValueExA(HND:C11CCF7Ch,"PageMargin",,,,)
RegQueryValueExA ret 0
RegCloseKey(HND:C11CCF7Ch)
RegCloseKey ret 0
RegQueryValueExA(HND:C11CCF7Ch,"Layout",,,,)
RegQueryValueExA ret 0
RegCloseKey(HND:C11CCF7Ch)
RegCloseKey ret 0
RegQueryValueExA(HND:C11CCF7Ch,"Layout",,,,)
RegQueryValueExA ret 0
RegCloseKey(HND:C11CCF7Ch)
RegCloseKey ret 0
```

Take a look at the calls to *RegQueryValueEx* in Example 10-2 again. In each case, *APISpy32* lists two parameters passed to the function: *hKey*, the handle of the open registry key; and *lpValueName*, the name of the value entry. It does not, however, list the values of the *lpType*, *lpData*, and *lpcbData* parameters. That's because in each of these cases a pointer is passed to the function, and the function supplies the appropriate data value. We've modified *APISpy32* to not display the values of data passed by reference, except in the case of string buffers. A partial display of the contents of what a function wrote to a string buffer is shown only on the next call to the function, and only if a pointer to the same buffer was passed to the function.

In the function calls shown in Example 10-2, program flow proceeds on a function-by-function basis: a function is called, it does something and returns a value, then the next function is called. In other cases, though, a function does not return a value immediately after it is called, and some additional functions execute between the time the function is called and the time that it finishes executing. These cases are indicated in *APISpy32*'s output by various levels of indentation.

This is illustrated by the *UpdateWindow* function in Example 10-3. *UpdateWindow* causes a **WM_PAINT** message to be sent to a window whose client area needs to be updated. The window whose client area needs repainting is identified by its window handle; in this case, the handle 0x0E5C is WordPad's own window handle. The function returns a Boolean value that indicates whether or not the window has been updated. However, in the case of our example, this value can be returned only after WordPad's window procedure has processed the **WM_PAINT** message; and of course, processing the message involves making additional calls to the Win32 API. To delineate these, *APISpy32* indents them: the indented API calls from *GetClientRect* to *BitBlt* are actually executed by WordPad's window procedure in response to the **WM_PAINT** message.

Example 10-3. Indented output from WORDPAD.OUT

```
ShowWindow(HWND:E5Ch,DW:5h)
ShowWindow ret 0
UpdateWindow(HWND:E5Ch)
  GetClientRect(HWND:E58h,)
  GetClientRect ret 39
  GetStockObject(DW:7h)
  GetStockObject ret 5CA
  Rectangle(HND:5EEh,DW:0h,DW:0h,DW:32h,DW:34h)
  Rectangle ret 1
  GetStockObject(DW:3h)
  GetStockObject ret 5BA
  SetRect(,DW:32h,DW:4h,DW:36h,DW:38h)
  SetRect ret FFFFFFFF
  FillRect(HND:5EEh,,HND:5BAh)
  FillRect ret 5BA
  SetRect(,DW:4h,DW:34h,DW:36h,DW:38h)
  SetRect ret FFFFFFFF
  FillRect(HND:5EEh,,HND:5BAh)
  FillRect ret 5BA
  CreateCompatibleDC(HND:5EEh)
  CreateCompatibleDC ret 10DA

BitBlt(HND:5EEh,DW:2h,DW:2h,DW:2Eh,DW:30h,HND:10DAh,DW:0h,DW:0h,DW
:CC0020h)
  BitBlt ret 1
UpdateWindow ret 1
```

Spying on the Explorer

Because of its reliance on OLE, its dependence on the registry, and its central role in the operation of Windows, the Explorer is a very attractive target for spying programs. If you simply try typing "explorer.exe" in *APISpy32*'s File text box to launch the Explorer, though, you'll be disappointed: the Explorer will load, but *APISpy32* will trap a totally insignificant number of API calls. And if you've included the calls to registry functions in your .API file, you'll find that not a single registry call appears in *EXPLORER.OUT*!

The reason is actually quite simple: at the same time that the Explorer is a utility for browsing your computer system, it is also the Windows shell. So when you use *APISpy32* to spy on the Explorer in this way, you're really just launching a second copy of the Explorer, which in its turn is invoking the first copy.

This doesn't mean that you can't use *APISpy32* to spy on the Explorer; it just means that you'll have to resort to a workaround: you'll have to replace the Explorer with an alternate temporary Windows shell. This isn't quite enough, though: when the Explorer is launched, it determines whether or not it's the Windows shell. If it is, it loads the complete object-oriented Explorer, which organizes the Win95 desktop as a hierarchy of namespaces; it it's not, it loads the Explorer file manager. So to use *APISpy32* to intercept the Explorer's calls to the registry API, you have to define an alternate shell at the same time that you trick the Explorer into thinking that it's the shell.

To spy on the Explorer, do the following:

1. Use Notepad or another text editor to define a new Windows shell. The best way to do this is by opening the *SYSTEM.INI* file and changing the `shell=` line in the `[boot]` section of *SYSTEM.INI* to:

   `shell=c:\command.com`

   Then reboot Win95.

2. When Win95 comes back up (with a very rudimentary-looking but perfectly functional—some might even argue, *more* functional—`C:\>` shell), edit *SYSTEM.INI* again to change the value of the `shell=` line in the `[boot]` section of *SYSTEM.INI* back to its original value (which is "EXPLORER.EXE"). When you load the Explorer, this fools it into thinking that it's the Win95 shell (yes, the Explorer really does read *SYSTEM.INI* to discover whether it's the shell).

3. Run *APISPYLD.EXE* from the DOS window.

4. Launch the Explorer by typing "EXPLORER.EXE" into *APISpy32*'s File text box.

When you end your Windows session either by selecting any of the options available on the Shut Down Windows dialog, Windows will close the *EXPLORER.OUT* file; you can examine it when you next log in to Windows. For example, the fragment from an Explorer session shown in Example 10-4 shows why you have to resort to this workaround when you spy on Win32 API calls to the Explorer. The Explorer calls the *GetModuleFileName* function to determine its own filename, retrieves the name of the Windows shell from *SYSTEM.INI* by calling the *GetPrivateProfileString* function, and then performs a case-insensitive comparison on the two strings with the *lstrcmpi* function. If the Explorer finds that it is the shell, as it does in Example 10-4, its behavior is very different than if it is not defined as the shell.

Example 10-4. The Explorer determining if it's the Win95 shell

```
GetModuleFileNameA(HND:0h,"?",DW:104h)
GetModuleFileNameA ret 17
GetPrivateProfileStringA("Boot","Shell","EXPLORER.EXE","",92",DW:104h,
                        "system.ini")
GetPrivateProfileStringA ret C
CharPrevA("Explorer.exe","")
CharPrevA ret 66FCAF
lstrcmpiA("Explorer.exe","EXPLORER.EXE")
lstrcmpiA ret 0
DdeNameService()
DdeNameService ret 1
DdeNameService()
DdeNameService ret 1
PeekMessageA(,HWND:0h,DW:12h,DW:12h,DW:0h)
PeekMessageA ret 0
RegOpenKeyA(HND: HKLM,
           "Software\Microsoft\Windows\CurrentVersion\RunOnce",)
RegOpenKeyA ret 0
```

Using APISpy32

Like *RegSpy95*, *APISpy32* is a flexible, configurable program that you can use in an almost unlimited number of ways to focus on those particular areas that are of greatest interest to you. At the same time, *APISpy32* frequently tends to generate an enormous amount of output when it spies on Windows API calls. Its volume is not quite as overwhelming as *RegSpy95*'s, but it is still sufficiently large to become unmanageable.

One of *APISpy32*'s real strengths is the ability to look at particular API calls within the broader context in which they occur. For instance, it is possible not only to see an application retrieve particular items of data from the registry, but also, if this involves subsequent API calls, to see how an application uses them.

This suggests that, for applications that make a particularly large number of API calls, you might want to run *APISpy32* twice to have it spy on two identical application sessions. In the first run, you can spy on a discrete subset of the Win32 API (like the registry API, for example) by including only those functions in your *APISPY32.API* file. Before the second run, you can copy back the full version of *APISPY32.API* so that you can spy on all APIs. You can then use the first .OUT file containing only the subset of the API to identify function calls that interest you, and the second .OUT file to investigate them more fully.

In other cases, you may be interested in exploring a particular question that *APISpy32* is especially well suited to investigate. For instance, in Chapter 3, *Backing Up and Restoring the Registry*, we mentioned that the Configuration Backup Utility, the registry backup program included in the `Microsoft Windows 95 Resource Kit`, appears to save files in a compressed proprietary format. By including only calls to the registry API in our *APISPY32.API* file, we can configure *APISpy32* to spy only on calls to the registry API. By using *APISpy32* to run Microsoft Configuration Backup and examining the resulting .OUT file, which is shown in Example 10-5, we can see how Microsoft Configuration Backup goes about backing up the registry.

Example 10-5. Calls to the registry API by Microsoft Configuration Backup

```
RegEnumKeyExA(HND: HKLM,DW:0h,"oP",,,"",,)
RegEnumKeyExA ret 0
RegEnumKeyExA(HND: HKLM,DW:1h,"Network",,,"",,)
RegEnumKeyExA ret 0
RegEnumKeyExA(HND: HKLM,DW:2h,"Config",,,"",,)
RegEnumKeyExA ret 0
RegEnumKeyExA(HND: HKLM,DW:3h,"Security",,,"",,)
RegEnumKeyExA ret 0
RegEnumKeyExA(HND: HKLM,DW:4h,"hardware",,,"",,)
RegEnumKeyExA ret 0
RegEnumKeyExA(HND: HKLM,DW:5h,"Enum",,,"",,)
RegEnumKeyExA ret 0
RegEnumKeyExA(HND: HKLM,DW:6h,"System",,,"",,)
RegEnumKeyExA ret 0
RegEnumKeyExA(HND: HKLM,DW:7h,"SOFTWARE",,,"",,)
RegEnumKeyExA ret 103
RegEnumKeyExA(HND: HKU,DW:8h,"SOFTWARE",,,"",,)
RegEnumKeyExA ret 103
RegOpenKeyExA(HND: HKLM,"SOFTWARE",DW:0h,DW:20019h,)
RegOpenKeyExA ret 0
RegSaveKeyA(HND:C2FFFE10h,"C:\WINDOWS\REGBACKA",)
RegSaveKeyA ret 0
RegCloseKey(HND:C2FFFE10h)
RegCloseKey ret 0
RegOpenKeyExA(HND: HKLM,"System",DW:0h,DW:20019h,)
RegOpenKeyExA ret 0
RegSaveKeyA(HND:C2C7E584h,"C:\WINDOWS\REGBACKA",)
RegSaveKeyA ret 0
RegCloseKey(HND:C2C7E584h)
RegCloseKey ret 0
```

Example 10-5. Calls to the registry API by Microsoft Configuration Backup (continued)

```
RegOpenKeyExA(HND: HKLM,"Enum",DW:0h,DW:20019h,)
RegOpenKeyExA ret 0
RegSaveKeyA(HND:C2C7E584h,"C:\WINDOWS\REGBACKA",)
RegSaveKeyA ret 0
RegCloseKey(HND:C2C7E584h)
RegCloseKey ret 0
RegOpenKeyExA(HND: HKLM,"hardware",DW:0h,DW:20019h,)
RegOpenKeyExA ret 0
RegSaveKeyA(HND:C2C7E584h,"C:\WINDOWS\REGBACKA",)
RegSaveKeyA ret 0
RegCloseKey(HND:C2C7E584h)
RegCloseKey ret 0
RegOpenKeyExA(HND: HKLM,"Security",DW:0h,DW:20019h,)
RegOpenKeyExA ret 0
RegSaveKeyA(HND:C2C7E584h,"C:\WINDOWS\REGBACKA",)
RegSaveKeyA ret 0
RegCloseKey(HND:C2C7E584h)
RegCloseKey ret 0
RegOpenKeyExA(HND: HKLM,"Config",DW:0h,DW:20019h,)
RegOpenKeyExA ret 0
RegSaveKeyA(HND:C2C7E584h,"C:\WINDOWS\REGBACKA",)
RegSaveKeyA ret 0
RegCloseKey(HND:C2C7E584h)
RegCloseKey ret 0
RegOpenKeyExA(HND: HKLM,"Network",DW:0h,DW:20019h,)
RegOpenKeyExA ret 0
RegSaveKeyA(HND:C2C7E584h,"C:\WINDOWS\REGBACKA",)
RegSaveKeyA ret 0
RegCloseKey(HND:C2C7E584h)
RegCloseKey ret 0
```

Certainly this tells us why the format of .RBK files are proprietary; it also hints at why Microsoft Configuration Backup has difficulty with saving user configurations. The program begins by determining how many subkeys it needs to back up. First, it enumerates the subkeys of HKLM. Next, it evidently tries to enumerate the subkeys of HKU. Unfortunately, though, the same variable used in the enumeration of HKLM was supplied as an argument to the *dwIndex* parameter, and someone forgot to reinitialize it to 0. As a result, *RegEnumKeyEx* attempts to enumerate the ninth ordinal subkey (*dwIndex* = 8) of HKU. Not surprisingly, the function fails and returns ERROR_NO_MORE_ITEMS (error code 259, or 0x103). The utility then proceeds to use *RegSaveKey* to save each subkey of HKLM as a detached registry hive. Since its attempt to enumerate HKU failed, though, no user information is included in the .RBK file.

Summary

In this chapter, we've shown you how to use two powerful spying utilities, *RegSpy95* and *APISpy32*:

- *RegSpy95*'s operative component is *FOOTPRNT.386*, a virtual device driver (VxD) that intercepts all requests for registry services that are handled by the Win95 Virtual Machine Manager (VMM). This allows you to see a program's own registry accesses, as well as the calls made to registry services on its behalf, particularly by Windows DLLs.

- Because it is a static VxD, *FOOTPRNT* can be loaded either by including a `device=` statement in *SYSTEM.INI* or by defining it as a static VxD in the registry.

- The behavior of *FOOTPRNT* can be customized by including statements in the `[FootPrnt]` section of *SYSTEM.INI*. *RegSpy95* and *FOOTPRNT* also allow you to create configuration files which *RegSpy95* reads if their names are passed to it as a parameter on the command line.

- Since *FOOTPRNT* by default logs all registry accesses, the amount of memory consumed by *FOOTPRNT* can quickly begin to cripple your Windows session. As a result, it's a good idea to flush *FOOTPRNT*'s buffer once you've redirected its output to disk.

- *RegSpy95* reports not only what information programs retrieve from the registry, but also what information they attempt to retrieve, but are unable to find.

- The diskette includes the source code for *RegSpy95*, which allows you to modify and enhance the program.

- In comparison to *RegSpy95*, *APISpy32* is a high-level spying utility that intercepts an application's direct calls to the Win32 API. Basically, *APISpy32* intercepts the function calls that appear in an application's source code.

- *APISpy32* can be configured by modifying its .API file, which lists the functions that it is to intercept.

- Like *RegSpy95*, *APISpy32* reports not only what information applications succeed in retrieving from the registry, but also what information they attempt but fail to retrieve.

Although there is a certain degree of overlap in the information that they report, *RegSpy95* and *APISpy32* are really complementary tools, rather than mutually exclusive ones. Together, they allow you to explore the dynamic Windows 95 registry.

11

Migrating from .INI Files to the Registry

In the course of working on this book, our own thinking about the registry has evolved. We were interested in the registry initially largely because it's a badly underdocumented structure that plays a critical role in the operation of Microsoft's 32-bit operating systems; quite simply, we wanted to know more. Gradually, the notion of the registry as a centralizing agent that promised to end (or at least to minimize) the anarchy introduced by Windows 3.x, with its use of system and private initialization files, became more and more appealing to us. Finally, we began to appreciate the registry not only as a centralized place to store configuration information, but also as an extremely efficient structure for storing and retrieving any kind of small-to-medium amount of application information.

As a result, we believe that, wherever possible, developers should rely on the registry rather than on initialization files to store application information. In fact, beyond using the registry simply to store application state information, we've found that the registry is a suitable repository for any application with small-to-medium-sized database needs. Quite simply, using the registry makes good sense. As the performance benchmark presented in Chapter 1, *The Registry, or, What Was So Bad About .INI Files?*, as well as all the other benchmarks we ran, suggest, the registry offers superior performance almost without exception. Its flexibility and its support for a diversity of data types makes it easy to get data into and out of the registry, and minimizes the coding that developers must do to handle data stored in the registry. And the fact that it is mostly hidden from the view of overly inquisitive users makes it a much more reliable structure for storing data.

Collecting User Information

One of our Web servers includes a Win-CGI program called *CGIHELLO.EXE*, the CGI equivalent of a "hello world" program (see *http://dev1.ora.com/andcgi/*

> ## *The Registry as an Application Database*
>
> Beyond using the registry to store application state information, we also recommend the registry as a repository for small and medium amounts of persistent data generated by an application. In that case, the registry becomes a sort of database that can be used in place of small databases or individual data files. For instance, in *CGIHELLO*, the application whose migration to the registry forms the focus of this chapter, we use the registry to store counter data that shows the number of times particular browsers and particular users have launched the *CGIHELLO* program.
>
> Many developers are still using .INI files, and continue to rely on them for 32-bit applications. To encourage you to use the registry, we've developed a small Windows 95 console mode utility, *INI2REG.EXE*, that allows you to migrate your initialization files to the registry. Before we actually show you how to use it, let's begin by seeing how it came into being.

cgihello.exe). CGI stands for *Common Gateway Interface*, a standard interface that permits a Web server to produce dynamic, "on the fly" hypertext pages that are displayed on a Web browser, as well as to do background processing and validation when the user requests a particular service. Win-CGI is a standard for writing Windows applications that produce dynamic Web pages.* When the user clicks on a link, the server launches *CGIHELLO.EXE*. The result is shown in Figure 11-1.

Whenever the user accesses the Web site, the server generates a temporary initialization file that contains a variety of information, including the user's fully qualified domain name such as "pc229.west.ora.com" and the name of his or her Web browser such as "Mozilla/2.01Gold (Win95; I)" for the Win95 version of Netscape Navigator Gold 2.01. When the user clicks on a link to *CGIHELLO.EXE*, the server launches the program and passes it the initialization filename as a parameter.

CGIHELLO itself is actually more than a simple "hello world" program. Behind the scenes, it maintains a count of the browsers used by users who launch the program, and also counts the number of accesses by each user. Over time, this could be turned into a Web-browser survey program.

This initial version of *CGIHELLO.EXE* relied exclusively on initialization files. The use of a temporary private initialization file is handled by the server; it just happens to be the way that Win-CGI is currently implemented. But *CGIHELLO*

---

* If you're interested in learning more about CGI, see *CGI Programming on the World Wide Web*, by Shishir Gundavaarm, and *CGI for Windows*, by Bob Denny and Linda Mui (available late 1996), both published by O'Reilly & Associates. Also see *http://dev1.ora.com/andrew/wincgi*.

version of the program is shown in Example 11-2. The program retrieves the name of the browser and the client from the Web server's temporary initialization file. But instead of using *WEBTRACK.INI*, it uses *RegCreateKey* to open the application's browser key, `HKLM\Software\O'Reilly\Win-CGI\CGIHello\Browsers`, and its client's key, `HKLM\Software\O'Reilly\Win-CGI\CGIHello\Clients`; if these keys don't exist, they're created. The program then calls a *RegIncrDword* function, passing it as arguments a registry handle and the name of either the browser or the client.

Example 11-2. A code fragment from the revised version of the CGIHELLO program

```
DWORD count;
char client_name[256], user_agent[256];

// ... get client_name from Win-CGI, do reverse lookup ...
// ... get user_agent (i.e., browser type) from Win-CGI

// use registry instead of INI file
HKEY hkey;
char *browsers_str = "SOFTWARE\\O'Reilly\\Win-CGI\\CGIHello\\Browsers";
char *clients_str = "SOFTWARE\\O'Reilly\\Win-CGI\\CGIHello\\Clients";

// keep track of browsers
if (RegCreateKey(HKEY_LOCAL_MACHINE, browsers_str, &hkey) != 0)
    return 0;  // don't fail Win-CGI output?
count = RegIncrDword(hkey, user_agent);
RegCloseKey(hkey);

// keep track of who we've said hello to
if (RegCreateKey(HKEY_LOCAL_MACHINE, clients_str, &hkey) != 0)
    return 0;
count = RegIncrDword(hkey, client_name);
RegCloseKey(hkey);

// show stats on browsers seen so far with registry --
// this is easy: just enumerate!
```

RegIncrDword is a general-purpose utility function shown in Example 11-3. It retrieves the `REG_DWORD` entry for the value entry whose name is *lpValue-Name*, increments it by one, writes the new value back to the registry, and returns the new value. If an entry named *lpValueName* does not exist, it initializes its value to one and creates the entry in the registry.

Example 11-3. The RegIncrDword function

```
// Note: if valuename doesn't already exist, this function will create
// it, with a count of 1
DWORD RegIncrDword(HKEY hKey, LPCSTR lpValueName)
{
    DWORD dw = 0;
    int size = sizeof(DWORD);
    DWORD type = REG_DWORD;
```

Example 11-3. The RegIncrDword function (continued)

```
    RegQueryValueEx(hKey, lpValueName, 0, &type, &dw, &size);
    // if (type != REG_DWORD) something wrong
    dw++;
    RegSetValueEx(hKey, lpValueName, 0, REG_DWORD, &dw, size);
    return dw;
}
```

The new version of *CGIHELLO* as it appears on the user's browser is shown in Figure 11-2. Now, instead of simply echoing back the fully qualified domain name of the user's computer, it also presents information on the frequency of browsers that launched the program.

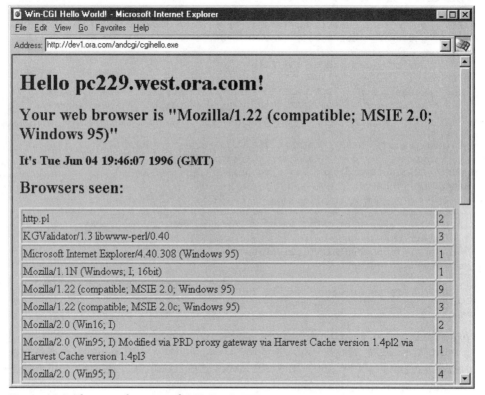

Figure 11-2. The revised version of CGIHELLO.EXE

Migrating Data to the Registry: *INI2REG.EXE*

A major problem with this new version of *CGIHELLO.EXE*, though, is that we already had valid data in *WEBTRACK.INI*. Now, with our new registry-enabled version of *CGIHELLO.EXE*, we presumably must start all over from scratch, and in the process lose all of the information that we've accumulated. Or must we?

Instead, we decided to migrate our data to the registry. One way of doing this is by hand: we could load our .INI file into any text editor and convert it into a .REG file, and then use RegEdit to load it into the registry. This involves adding a .REG file header (REGEDIT4) to the beginning of the file, changing our section names to key names, and changing each *x=y* keyword/value combination to a value entry in the format:

x=dword:HEX*y*

This is possible, but not particularly appealing. In fact, this is precisely the kind of routine chore that we have computers for. So instead, we wrote the C program shown in Example 11-4.

Example 11-4. The C source code for INI2REG.EXE

```
// ini2reg.c -- convert Windows .INI files to Win95 .REG files
// Andrew Schulman, May 1996

#include <stdlib.h>
#include <stdio.h>
#include <string.h>
#include <ctype.h>

void fail(const char *s) { puts(s); exit(1); }

int isnumber(char *s)
{
    char *s2;
    for (s2=s; *s2; s2++)
        if (! isdigit(*s2))
            return 0;
    // still here
    return 1;
}

main(int argc, char *argv[])
{
    char buf[1024];
    char branch2[1024];
    char *branch, *s, *s2;

    if (argc < 2)
        fail("Usage: ini2reg [branch] < ini_file > reg_file\n"
            "Example:\n"
"ini2reg HKEY_LOCAL_MACHINE\\SOFTWARE\\MyCompany\\MyApp < app.ini >
app.reg\n"
            "To merge into registry, run regedit app.reg");
    branch = argv[1];

    printf("REGEDIT4\n\n");
```

Example 11-4. The C source code for INI2REG.EXE (continued)

```c
strcpy(branch2, branch);
for (s=branch2; *s; s++)
{
    if (*s == '\\')
    {
        *s = '\0';
        printf("[%s]\n\n", branch2);
        *s = '\\';
        s2 = s+1;
    }
}
printf("[%s]\n", branch);

while (s = gets(buf))  // for each line of input
{
    if (! *s)  // ignore blank lines
    {
        printf("\n");
        continue;
    }
    else if (buf[0] == ';') // print comments as is
        printf("%s\n", buf);
    else if ((*s == '[') && strchr(s+1, ']')) // lines with [x]
    {
        char *s3;
        if (s3 = strstr(s+1, "\\\\"))
        {
            printf(";;; ***ERROR!! ***\n");
            *s3 = '!'; s3[1] = '!';
        }
        printf("\n[%s\\%s\n", branch, s+1);
    }
    else if (s = strchr(buf, '=')) // lines with x=y
    {
        char *name = buf;
        char *val = s+1;
        *s = '\0';
        printf("\"%s\"=", name);
        if (isnumber(val))
        {
            unsigned long dw;
            sscanf(val, "%lu", &dw);
            printf("dword:%08lx\n", dw);
        }
        else
        {
            char *comment = (char *) 0;
            char *s;
            putchar('\"');
            // Escape chars within quote must be escaped!!
            for (s=val; *s; s++)
```

Example 11-4. The C source code for INI2REG.EXE (continued)

```
                    if (*s == '\\') // escape backslash
                        printf("\\\\");
                    else if (*s == '\"') // escape quote
                        printf("\\\"");
                    else if (*s == ';') // comment
                    {
                        // todo: remove trailing spaces from value!!
                        comment = s;
                        break;
                    }
                    else
                        putchar(*s);
                putchar('\"');
                if (comment) printf(" %s", comment);
                putchar('\n');
            }
        }
        else  // put anything else out as a comment
            printf("; %s\n", buf);
    }
}
```

Ini2Reg is a general-purpose conversion utility; it will generate a .REG file for any .INI file. Its syntax is:

```
Ini2Reg RegistryPath < INIFileName > RegFileName
```

RegistryPath	The complete registry path to the parent key for which the initialization file sections will become subkeys. It should include the name of the top-level registry key (e.g., **HKEY_LOCAL_MACHINE**).
INIFileName	The path and name of the initialization file, including its (.INI) file extension.
RegFileName	The path and name of the .REG file, including its .REG file extension.

So to generate a .REG file that contains the settings in *MYAPP.INI*, you could use the following command line:

```
Ini2Reg HKEY_CURRENT_USER\Software\MyCompany\MyApp < MYAPP.INI > MYAPP.REG
```

Note the use of the two DOS redirection symbols, < and >, so that the program gets its input from a file (in this case, the initialization file) and outputs it to a .REG file rather than to the screen. Once the .REG file is generated, you can merge it into the registry by double-clicking on it in an Explorer window or by selecting the Run option on the file menu. You can also store the file in your desktop directory, so that you just have to double-click its icon on the desktop so that RegEdit merges it into your registry in the background.

All values in initialization files are necessarily stored as strings; the sole API functions that allow you to retrieve a value from an initialization file are *GetProfileString* and *GetPrivateProfileString*. *Ini2Reg*, on the other hand, examines each string value to determine whether it is best stored as a string or as a numeric (DWORD) value, and converts it accordingly. It also handles comments by transferring them to the .REG file. However, *Ini2Reg* does not evaluate initialization file data to determine if its format is optimal for the registry. This means that entries such as:

```
windowpos=124 162 132 146
```

are written to the registry as string data. If you're considering a major revision of your application, it's worthwhile to review Chapter 9, *What Goes in the Registry: Application and User Settings*, to see if some alternate type of data, like a structured data type, offers greater flexibility and ease of access to a particular kind of data. This is not the kind of thing, in any case, that can be handled by a porting or migration tool.

RegEdit's "Cannot import xxx.reg" Message

Given the enormous diversity (and occasional bizarre format) of the data stored in initialization files, RegEdit may sometimes have difficulty merging a .REG file. If it displays the "Cannot import xxx.reg: error accessing the registry" message, it usually indicates that RegEdit was unable to import part—but not all—of a .REG file. To find what caused RegEdit to choke, export the newly added branch of the registry back to a .REG file, then run *WinDiff* (or a similar file comparison utility) and compare the two files. Those entries present in your original .REG file that are not present in the exported copy are the culprits. You might try repairing them, deleting the newly imported branch of the registry, and reimporting the .REG file.

Also remember that the registry requires that the names of all values and keys belonging to a single key be unique. So if you for some reason use *Ini2Reg* to import your system's *SYSTEM.INI* file into the registry, you'll find that the multiple `device=` lines in the [`386Enh`] section have been merged as a single line whose value is that of the last `device=` entry in *SYSTEM.INI*. Unless you've been using low-level file functions to access data in your initialization files, though, this is usually only a problem with *SYSTEM.INI*, which is read by device drivers using a special set of low-level initialization file functions.

Enhancing CGIHELLO

It's sometimes the case that making one modification to a program suggests several other improvements and new features. This was certainly true of *CGIHELLO*, and will probably be true of applications that you migrate to the registry as well. We've found that, once we became comfortable with the registry

API, data in the registry became far more accessible than comparable data in initialization files. We also became more inclined to think of creative uses for the registry (storing browser counters in the registry is itself one such example), and for additional ways that we could put its data to good use.

As you can see by comparing the original version of *CGIHELLO* in Figure 11-1 with the revised version in Figure 11-2, the original version did not include the portion of the page from "Browsers seen:" on. Although certainly the use of initialization files did not preclude this modification, neither did they encourage it. In order for the old version of the file to display the names of browsers that ran the *CGIHELLO* program along with their usage count, it would have been necessary to use the *GetPrivateProfileSection* function to retrieve all of the [Browsers] section's data at once. The program then would have had to parse it to separate each entry from one another, and to separate each browser from its counter. Although not an impossible programming task by any means, it involves just enough extra coding, and threatens to worsen the application's performance just enough, that we didn't want to do it. It remained a comment in our code—an item on a wish list that we may well never have gotten around to implementing.

Once the data was migrated to the registry, though, it seemed like an automatic enhancement. Each browser name and its counter can be retrieved with a single call to *RegEnumValue*. The name and counter can then be used as is by our application; no further parsing or processing of the data is necessary. The ease of implementing this change made it seem silly not to do it.

Basically, the newer version of *CGIHELLO* just enumerates the registry values into an HTML table. HTML tables are especially pleasant to work with because the user's Web browser will take care of all details like column widths, scrolling, and so on. It's a much nicer interface, at a much higher level, than anything in the Windows API:

```
char *browsers_str = "SOFTWARE\\O'Reilly\\Win-CGI\\CGIHello\\Browsers";
// do RegEnumValue of all browsers into HTML table
void list_browsers(void)
{
    HKEY hkey;
    int i;

    if (RegOpenKey(HKEY_LOCAL_MACHINE, browsers_str, &hkey) != 0)
        return 0;
    write_tag("H2", "Browsers seen:");
    write_html("<TABLE BORDER>");
    for (i=0; ; i++)
    {
        char str[256];
        DWORD len, type, count, size;
        len = sizeof(str);
        size = sizeof(count);
        if (RegEnumValue(hkey, i, str, &len, 0, &type, &count, &size) != 0)
```

```
            break;
        if (type != REG_DWORD) break;
        if (size != sizeof(DWORD)) break;
        write_html("<TR><TD>%s<TD> %u </TR>\n", str, count);
    }
    write_html("</TABLE>");
    RegCloseKey(hkey);
}
```

Well, this is interesting. Basically we've got a mini-registry browser. With only a small amount of extra work, we can create a remote registry browser. Actually, in a way it's less work: we just remove the program's knowledge of the specific `HKLM\Software\O'Reilly\Win-CGI\CGIHello\Browsers` key, and let it show anything in the registry. The resulting program, *WREGCGI* (*http://dev1.ora.com/andcgi/wregcgi.exe*), is an interesting contrast to Microsoft's own remote registry access facility in RegEdit. It uses a standard tool—a Web browser—rather than a custom tool like RegEdit. Anyone can browse (though not change) the registry of anyone running *WREGCGI*. Whether this is a good or bad thing, depends.

Summary

We recognize that initialization files generate a certain inertia of their own: because developers have been using them to hold application data, they are reluctant to abandon them in favor of the registry. In this chapter, we've tried to make a case for migrating that data to the registry:

- The registry has several advantages over initialization files, including better performance and more efficient and easier access to data. Think of the registry as a big file that's always present in memory, and that is very easy to find things in, put things in, and remove things from. It is, unfortunately, not easy to sort; this in turn implies that searches are linear rather than binary.

- Where initialization files contain application data that you don't want to lose, you can use *Ini2Reg* to migrate it to the registry.

- Storing data in the registry, because it makes data more accessible, often suggests further enhancements at the same time as it makes implementing them easier.

- Since it is a flexible data repository, the registry can be used to store not only application state information, but also any small or medium amount of persistent application data.

Where Am I Running?

Such a seemingly simple task as determining the version of the operating system on which an application is running has been surprisingly difficult for many programmers. In the past, the enormous prevalence of errors in version checking in both DOS and Windows applications led Microsoft to various forms of DOS and Windows version "spoofing" simply to compensate for the fact that developers didn't quite get it right.[*] The introduction of Microsoft's 32-bit platforms in many ways has made a confusing situation even more confusing. In this appendix, we'll review how you determine the platform on which your application is running.

What does this have to do with the registry? Since the registry API—and, more important, the registries themselves—are so different in Windows 3.1, Windows 95, and Windows NT, it's important to know which platform your registry-enabled application is running on. Notice that the distinction here is Win31 vs. Win95 vs. WinNT, and *not* Win16 vs. Win32. The key is the operating system the application is running under, *not* what sort of application it is.

---

[*] Under DOS, the version table that was activated by including the command `DEVICE=SETVER.EXE` in *CONFIG.SYS* listed applications that incorrectly queried the version number. Each entry in the table consisted of the application's filename and the version of DOS it *thought* it required in order to run. When the application queried the DOS version, it was given this number, rather than the actual DOS version number. Windows 3.1 supported *compatibility bits*, a variety of hexadecimal bit settings stored in the `[Compatibility]` section of *WIN.INI* that instructed Windows to provide special handling so that a Win30 application could run under Win31; the bulk of these settings were added to *WIN.INI* during installation.

Windows 95 continues to use these compatibility bits defined in the `[Compatibility]` section of *WIN.INI* (and not in the registry). But it goes a bit further, indicating the pervasiveness of these problems: Win95 includes a special utility, *MKCOMPAT.EXE*, that allows any user to modify the compatibility bits for a particular application. One of its standard options is to (in the program's own words) "lie about Windows' version number"! Surely it says something about the real world of software development when the two major operating systems must provide options to lie about something simple like the operating-system version number on an application-by-application basis.

It would be nice, of course, if there were a single function that determined the platform and version of the operating system that worked uniformly and consistently across all of Microsoft's graphical systems software. This, unfortunately, isn't the case. The way that you determine the platform on which your application is running depends above all on whether your application was developed using the Win16 or the Win32 API.

32-Bit Applications

32-bit applications, of course, can only run on 32-bit operating systems. This means, as you're no doubt aware, that your application may be running under Windows 95 or Windows NT. But it also means, remember, that your application may be running on Windows 3.1 under Win32s.

Traditionally, the *GetVersion* function is used to retrieve version information. The 16-bit version of *GetVersion*, as we mentioned in Chapter 5, *Win95 Registry Access from Win16, DOS, and VxDs*), returns a long (four-byte) integer. Its lower-order word contains the version of Windows: the low-order byte contains the major version number, while the high-order byte contains the minor version number. The high-order word reports the MS-DOS version: its major version is stored in the high-order byte, and its minor version is in the low-order byte. This seems clear enough, but many developers still had difficulty with it. Two problems were particularly common:

- *Confusing the major and minor version numbers.* Probably because the bytes used to store the major and minor version numbers are the reverse of one another for DOS and Windows, it was very common to retrieve Windows' minor version number and treat it as the major version, and to retrieve the major version and interpret it as the minor version. When this happened, 3.10—the official version number reported by Win31—became transmogrified into Windows version 10.3.

- *Testing for a particular version, rather than a baseline version.* Almost all applications are written to take advantage of a particular API or some feature that is new to the underlying operating system. In these cases, the application has to require that it run on the new version of that operating system, and not on earlier versions. One would think that developers would remember, though, that particularly in the software industry, nothing is immutable, and new versions inevitably give rise to even newer versions. In numerous instances, however, someone forgot this, and checked the version in a way similar to the following code fragment:

```
if (!(nMajorVersion == 3) && (nMinorVersion == 10))
    {
    MessageBox(NULL, "You might think about upgrading!",
```

```
                        "Wrong O/S", MB_OK) ;
        return FALSE ;
      }
```

Except in the rare case that the programmer's intention was really to run *only* under Windows 3.1, the program should check for version 3.1 *or greater*; instead, it checks for version 3.1 and refuses to run if it finds anything else.

GetVersion is still present under Win32. However, in large measure to prevent silly mistakes like this, the Win32 API includes a new function, *GetVersionEx*, that also happens to provide the best way to determine the platform and version of the entire family of Microsoft's 32-bit systems software. Its syntax is:

```
BOOL GetVersionEx( LPOSVERSIONINFO lpVersionInformation ) ;
```

The function returns True if it succeeds and False if it fails. Its single parameter is an OSVERSIONINFO data structure that is defined as shown in Table A-1. The only requirement in calling the function is that the OSVERSIONINFO's *dwOSVersionInfoSize* member be assigned an accurate value beforehand.

Table A-1. The OSVERSIONINFO structure

Member	Type	Description
dwOSVersionInfoSize	DWORD	The size of the OSVERSIONINFO structure. It should be set to *sizeof(OSVERSIONINFO)* before the *GetVersionEx* function is called.
dwMajorVersion	DWORD	The major version of the operating system.
dwMinorVersion	DWORD	The minor version of the operating system.
dwBuildNumber	DWORD	The low-order word contains the operating system's build number; the high-order word identifies the operating system's major and minor versions.
dwPlatformId	DWORD	The platform supported by the operating system. It can have any of the following values: VER_PLATFORM_WIN32S = 0 VER_PLATFORM_WIN32_WINDOWS = 1 VER_PLATFORM_WIN32_NT = 2
szCSDVersion[128]	TCHAR	A zero-terminated string containing additional information about the operating system.

This makes it very easy to determine the platform on which your application is running. The *GetPlatform* function in Example A-1, for example, returns the value of the OSVERSIONINFO structure's *dwPlatformId* member. You can then use it at run-time to define a flag that determines if a particular version is present.

GetVersion and the Win32 API

Although we prefer *GetVersionEx*, you can, if you like, continue to use *GetVersion*. If you want to do this because you're developing both 16- and 32-bit applications and want to minimize platform differences, you should note that the Win32 version differs from the Win16 version. Both variations of the function return the version number of Windows in the same way. They differ in their use of the high-order word. In the 16-bit version, it is used to hold the major and minor version of MS-DOS. The 32-bit version, on the other hand, uses the high-order bit of the high-order byte to indicate the platform: if the bit is on, the platform is either Windows 95 or Win32s; if it is off, the platform is Windows NT. For platforms other than Windows 95 (where it is not supported), the remaining bits of the high-order byte indicate the build.

Since they both set the high-order bit of the high-order byte on, you have to also examine the major version number to differentiate between Windows 95 and Win32s. Windows 95 has a version number of 4 (and presumably forthcoming versions of 32-bit Windows will have a version number of greater than 4); Win32s has a version number of 3. So you could define a Boolean variable to indicate the presence or absence of each operating system as follows:

```
dwVer = GetVersion() ;
fWin95 = (dwVer && 0x80000000) && (LOBYTE(LOWORD(dwVer)) == 4) ;
fWin32s = (dwVer && 0x80000000) && (LOBYTE(LOWORD(dwVer)) == 3) ;
```

Example A-1. The GetPlatform function

```
BOOL fWin95 = (VER_PLATFORM_WIN32_WINDOWS == GetPlatform()) ;
#include <windows.h>

DWORD GetPlatform(VOID)
{
   OSVERSIONINFO osVer ;
   osVer.dwOSVersionInfoSize = sizeof(osVer) ;
   return (GetVersionEx(&osVer)) ? osVer.dwPlatformId : 0;
}
```

If you're using Visual Basic, you first have to declare the *GetVersionEx* function and define its constants and data structure, as shown in Example A-2. Note that the *lpVersionInformation* data structure is passed by reference to the function, and that its *szCSDVersion* member is defined as a fixed-length string. The *GetPlatform* function is shown in Example A-3.

Example A-2. The Visual Basic code module defining GetVersionEx

```
Public Declare Function GetVersionEx Lib "kernel32" _
      Alias "GetVersionExA" _
      (lpVersionInformation As OSVERSIONINFO) As Boolean
```

Example A-2. The Visual Basic code module defining GetVersionEx (continued)

```
Type OSVERSIONINFO
    dwOSVersionInfoSize As Long
    dwMajorVersion As Long
    dwMinorVersion As Long
    dwBuildNumber As Long
    dwPlatformId As Long
    szCSDVersion As String * 128
End Type

Public Const VER_PLATFORM_WIN32s = 0
Public Const VER_PLATFORM_WIN32_WINDOWS = 1
Public Const VER_PLATFORM_WIN32_NT = 2
```

Example A-3. The Visual Basic GetPlatform function

```
Public Function GetPlatform() As Long

Dim udtVer As OSVERSIONINFO

udtVer.dwOSVersionInfoSize = Len(udtVer)

If (GetVersionEx(udtVer)) Then
    GetPlatform = udtVer.dwPlatformId
Else
    GetPlatform = 0   ' returns Win32 as lowest common denominator
End If

End Function
```

GetVersionEx does have one relatively small limitation as far as determining the operating system platform is concerned: it doesn't allow you to distinguish between Windows NT Workstation and Windows NT Server, the two varieties of Windows NT. If you want to do that, you'll have to check the Windows NT registry; one of the string values shown in Table A-2 that indicates the type of Windows NT is stored as the default value of `HKLM\SYSTEM\CurrentControlSet\Control\ProductOptions`.

Table A-2. Values of the ProductOptions subkey

REG_SZ String	Description	Windows NT Versions
WINNT	Windows NT Workstation	all
SERVERNT	Windows NT Server	3.5+
LANMANNT	Windows NT Advanced Server	3.1

In addition to making it easy to determine the platform on which your application is running, *GetVersionEx* makes determining the operating system's version number very simple: you just have to evaluate the `OSVERSIONINFO`'s *dwMajorVersion* and *dwMinorVersion* members. Table A-3 indicates the version number returned by calling *GetVersionEx* under existing 32-bit Windows operating systems. Note that, when reporting the version number of Win32s, *GetVersionEx* returns the version number of Win32s itself; *GetVersion,* on the other hand, returns 3.10 as the Windows version.

Table A-3. Version numbers of 32-bit operating systems reported by GetVersionEx

Operating System	Major Version	Minor Version
Win32s	1	0
	1	10
	1	15
	1	20
	1	25
	1	30
Windows 95	4	0
Windows NT	3	10
	3	50
	3	51

If you do need to retrieve the version number to make sure that your application is running on an operating system with the appropriate feature set, it's important, unless there's a pressing reason to do otherwise (like the feature that you need is present in one release but discontinued in later releases), to make sure that the operating system version *is greater than or equal to* some base version. In the case of Windows 95 (or the .0 release of any operating system), you don't even have to bother with the minor version:

```
if (osVer.dwMajorVersion >= 4)
//  version is OK
```

In other cases, for example if you require that your program run under Windows NT 3.51 or greater, you do have to look at the minor version:

```
if (osVer.dwMajorVersion == 3 && osVer.dwMinorVersion >= 51) ||
             (osVer.dwMajorVersion >= 4))
//  version is OK
```

16-Bit Applications

For the most part, retrieving version and platform information for 16-bit applications relies almost completely on the *GetVersion* function. The sole possible exception is a 16-bit application running under Windows 95, which can still use *GetVersionEx*; like the registry API discussed in Chapter 5, *Win95 Registry Access from Win16, DOS, and VxDs,* it is an undocumented function exported by

KRNL386.EXE.[*] This makes determining the platform or operating system on which an application is running somewhat more complicated, since 16-bit applications can run not only on 16-bit operating systems (Windows 3.x and Windows for Workgroups), but on 32-bit ones as well.

Once again, *GetVersion* returns a DWORD value in which the low-order byte of the low-order word contains the major version of the operating system, while the high-order byte of the low-order word contains the operating system's minor version. So you can retrieve the major and minor version as follows:

```
dwVersion = GetVersion() ;
dwMajorVersion = LOBYTE(LOWORD(dwVersion)) ;
dwMinorVersion = HIBYTE(LOWORD(dwVersion)) ;
```

Relying on the *GetVersion* function to identify a platform means that you have to be able to determine the platform on which your application is running based on its version number. Table A-4 lists the current and past versions of Microsoft's major graphical operating systems, environments, and operating system extensions.

Table A-4. Major and minor versions returned by GetVersion

Operating System	Type	Versions
Windows	16-bit	3.0, 3.10[a]
Windows for Workgroups	16-bit	3.10[*]
Win32s	32-bit	3.10
Windows	32-bit	3.95
Windows NT	32-bit	3.10, 3.50, 3.51

[a] Although Microsoft released version 3.11 of both Windows for Workgroups and plain-vanilla Windows, both operating systems return 3.10 as their major and minor version. We might conjecture that one of the considerations involved in the decision to use the same version number for two different versions of the operating system was the reluctance to deal with all of the broken applications caused by developers thinking that their applications would be forever running happily under Win31.

This introduces a complication. Notice that the *GetVersion* function returns the same version for a variety of 16-bit (Windows and Windows for Workgroups) and 32-bit (Win32s and Windows NT) operating systems. In addition, the major and minor version numbers reported by future versions of Windows and Windows NT may also be identical. So *GetVersion* alone is unable to indicate the platform whose version it reports.

---

[*] This raises a chicken and egg problem: On the one hand, to successfully call the API, you need to know the version number, since *GetVersionEx* is implemented on 16-bit platforms only under Win95. On the other hand, you're calling the function in the first place because you don't know the version. So how do you check the platform or version using a function that presupposes a particular platform (Windows 95) and version (Windows 4.0)? The solution is *GetProcAddress*, which returns a function's address if it is present and NULL if it is not. See Chapter 5 for examples that use this remarkably useful function.

The Two Faces of Windows 95

Windows 95 reports two different version numbers to applications, depending on whether they are 16-bit or 32-bit. If a 16-bit application uses *GetVersion* to determine the version number of Windows 95, the major version is reported as 3 and the minor version as 95. But if a 32-bit application uses *GetVersion* or *GetVersionEx* to retrieve the version number, the major version is reported as 4 and the minor version as 0.

From the viewpoint of accessing the registry API from 16-bit code, there are really just two distinct cases in which it may be difficult to deduce the underlying platform from its version number:

- *Windows NT 3.1 versus Windows 3.1, Windows for Workgroups 3.1, and Win32s.* Although it may be important for other reasons to determine whether your 16-bit application is running under Windows 3.1, Windows for Workgroups 3.1, or Win32s, all use the same limited registration database. Windows 3.1 and Windows for Workgroups 3.1 both support the "compatibility functions" in the registry API, while Win32s supports a number of Win32 functions as well,[*] although these can only operate on the limited registration database. So practically, you don't really need to distinguish between them. You do, however, have to differentiate these three platforms from Windows NT 3.1.

- *Future versions of Windows NT and Windows.* Since they haven't been released yet, we of course don't know what version numbers future versions of these two 32-bit operating systems will report to 16-bit applications.

In both cases, what is really important to detect is the presence of Windows NT. To do this, you just have to call the *GetWinFlags* function and test for the *WF_WINNT* flag; if it's set, your application is running under Windows NT; if not, it's running under Windows 3.x, Windows for Workgroups, Win32s, or Windows 95. Before calling the function, you'll also have to define the flag's value, since it's not included in the Win16 SDK:

```
#define WF_WINNT(0x4000)
```

For example, the *IsWinNT* function shown in Example A-4 returns a True if the platform at run-time is Windows NT, and returns False if it is anything else. Its Visual Basic equivalent is shown in Example A-5.

---

[*] Win32s also supports *RegCreateKeyEx, RegEnumValue, RegOpenKeyEx, RegQueryValueEx, RegSetValueEx,* and *RegUnloadKey.*

Example A-4. The IsWinNT function

```
#include <windows.h>

#define WF_WINNT        (0x4000)

BOOL IsWinNT(VOID)
{
   return (WF_WINNT & GetWinFlags()) ;
}
```

Example A-5. The Visual Basic version of IsWinNt, including its code module

```
Public Declare Function GetWinFlags Lib "kernel" _
        () As Long

Public Const WF_WINNT = &H4000

Public Function IsWinNT() As Boolean

#If Win16 Then
    IsWinNT = False
    If GetWinFlags() And WF_WINNT Then IsWinNT = True
#End If

End Function
```

You can then distinguish between 32-bit Windows and Windows NT with a code snippet like the following:

```
if (dwVerMajor > 3 || (dwVerMajor == 3 && dwVerMinor >= 50)))
//   32-bit O/S version 3.5 or greater is present
   if IsWinNT()
//   Windows NT 3.50+ is present
   else
//   Windows 3.95+ is present
```

The point may seem silly, but it's worth emphasizing that this fragment avoids a common error. If we simply checked the version with the code fragment

```
if   (dwVerMajor == 3 && dwVerMinor >= 50)
```

our `if` statement would be true only for versions with numbers between 3.5 and 3.99. Instead, we want to check for versions greater than or equal to 3.5, and then differentiate Win95 (and future versions of the Windows platform) from WinNT.

B

The Inside the Windows 95 Registry Diskette

In this appendix, we'll survey the contents and organization of the diskette accompanying *Inside the Windows 95 Registry*. Broadly, it consists of two major components: software products, like RegSpy95 and APISpy32, that are immediately usable in exploring and developing for the Win95 registry; and code samples that appear in the book, accompanied, in cases where it's appropriate, by shell programs that allow you to call the book's sample functions.

We haven't provided an installation program for the diskette's contents. That leaves you free to simply copy the software or code samples to a directory or directories of your choice. We do, however, give you complete directions for installing the software, and compiling the programs, when it's necessary. All software has been compressed into .ZIP files; however, we haven't provided a decompression program. We assume that one—particularly the DOS PKUNZIP.EXE or the Windows WINZIP32.EXE—is already available to you.

For last-minute changes, additional comments, or a discussion of such things as differences in source code between the book's program examples and the disk, be sure to read the README.TXT file in the diskette's root directory. And check our Web page, at *http://www.ora.com/pub/examples/windows/win95.update/ registry.html*.

Software

All usable software programs and development tools are stored in subdirectories of \SOFTWARE on the accompanying diskette. The files in each directory are compressed into a single .ZIP file.

RegSpy95

RegSpy95, a configurable low-level spying utility developed by Alex Shmidt that allows you to intercept registry calls to the Virtual Machine Manager by some or all applications and by Windows 95 itself, is found in the \SOFTWARE\REGSPY95 directory. RegSpy95 consists of two components: *FOOTPRNT.386*, a 32-bit static virtual device driver (VxD) for Windows 95; and *REGSPY95.EXE*, the shell program that interfaces with *FOOTPRNT*. In addition, the directory contains the complete source code for *REGSPY95.EXE*. For installation instructions, see "Running RegSpy95" in Chapter 10, *Spying on the Registry*. In addition, the diskette contains the following batch files and sample configuration files that you can use to help you configure or control the behavior of RegSpy95:

File	Parameters	Description
SYSINI		A sample [FootPrnt] section that you can add to *SYSTEM.INI* to control FootPrnt's behavior at system startup.
RS95.CFG		A sample configuration file that you can adapt to control RegSpy95's behavior interactively.
RSBYFUNC.BAT	`<filename>`	Dumps the contents of FootPrnt's buffers arranged by function call to a file; `<filename>` is the name of the file you'd like to write the output to, along with an optional path. Note that, if `<filename>` exists, it is overwritten without warning.
RSCHRON.BAT	`<filename>`	Dumps the contents of FootPrnt's buffers arranged chronologically to a file; `<filename>` is the name of the file you'd like to write the output to, along with an optional path. Note that, if `<filename>` exists, it is overwritten without warning.
RSFLUSH.BAT		Flushes FootPrnt's buffers.
RSHELP.BAT		Displays RegSpy95's help information.
RSINFO.BAT		Displays information on RegSpy95's current configuration.

All batch (.BAT) files should be stored in the same directory as RegSpy95 itself.

Finally, you can use *FOOTPRNT.REG* to make the necessary registry entries if you want to have *FOOTPRNT.386* loaded from the registry, rather than from *SYSTEM.INI*. Before double-clicking on *FOOTPRNT.REG* to have RegEdit automatically merge its contents into the registry, you should use a text editor to modify the path to *FOOTPRNT.386* to reflect the location where you've installed it on your system. Be sure to use double backslashes, rather than a single backslash, as the path separator.

APISpy32

APISpy32, which was developed by Matt Pietrek, is a high-level spying utility for 32-bit Windows platforms that intercepts a particular application's calls to designated Win32 API functions. It differs from RegSpy95 in three major ways: first, it spies only on a single application's API calls, rather than on calls made by a wide range of applications and by Windows itself. Second, it traps all API calls, and not only calls to the registry API. Finally, as a high-level spying program, it intercepts only calls to API functions that are made from the application's code; in contrast, RegSpy95, as a low-level spying utility, detects not only registry calls made by the application, but also registry calls made by Windows on the application's behalf. This means that RegSpy95 and APISpy32 are complementary, rather than competing, tools.

APISpy32 is found in the \SOFTWARE\APISPY32 subdirectory. It consists of *APISPY32.DLL*, a dynamic link library whose routines do the actual spying, *APISPYLD.EXE*, a shell application used to launch the application whose API calls are to be intercepted, and two .API files. These are text files that define the API functions that APISpy32 intercepts. The first of these, *APISPY32.API*, is the default file used by APISpy32, and contains definitions of the bulk of the Win32 API. We've also included *REGAPI.API*, a text file containing information only on the registry API. Since APISpy retrieves the names of the functions it should trap from a text file whose name must be *APISPY32.API*, you can rename *REGAPI.API* to *APISPY32.API* if you want to trap only registry calls. Be sure, though, to make a backup copy of *APISPY32.API* with the complete Win32 API first.

For details on installing and using APISpy32, see "APISpy32" in Chapter 10. If you'd like source code for APISpy, it's available in Matt Pietrek's excellent book, *Windows 95 System Programming Secrets*, published by IDG Books.

RegMon

The Win95 Registry Monitor (RegMon), which is found in the \SOFTWARE\REGMON subdirectory, is a low-level spying program that was written by Mark Russinovich and Bryce Cogswell. It is similar to RegSpy95 in two major respects:

- Like RegSpy95, RegMon consists of two components: a virtual device driver, *REGVXD.VXD*, that spies on registry calls, and a shell program, *REGMON.EXE*, that presents the information gathered by the VxD.

- Because it's implemented as a VxD, RegMon, like RegSpy95, can operate by intercepting requests for registry services at the Virtual Machine Manager (VMM) level.

However, RegMon differs from RegSpy95 in equally significant ways:

- RegMon (or, more precisely, *REGVXD.VXD*) is a *dynamic* virtual device driver. (RegSpy95, as you may recall from Chapter 10, uses a static VxD.) That means that you load the VxD, and begin spying on the registry, simply by launching *REGMON.EXE* at any point during your Windows session. The downside is that, as a dynamic VxD, RegVxD cannot access VMM services during initialization time; hence, RegMon, unlike RegSpy95, cannot spy on registry access or initialization file access during system initialization.

- *REGMON.EXE* is a GUI application that presents information on registry accesses in a window. In Figure B-1, for instance, RegMon is displaying the registry calls made by the Windows shell when the user double clicks on the Recycle Bin.

- The operation of RegMon is controlled through its graphical interface. You turn spying on and off by enabling or disabling the Capture Events option on the Events menu.

- RegMon provides less detail about each registry access than RegSpy95. For instance, it does not indicate the program that requests a particular VMM registry service, nor does it generally display the parameters passed to the registry function or the values returned by it.

#	Request	Path	Result	Other
1074	OpenKey	ROOT\CLSID\{645FF040-5081-101B-9F0...	SUCCESS	hKey: 0xC33F420C
1075	OpenKey	ROOT\CLSID\{645FF040-5081-101B-9F0...	SUCCESS	hKey: 0xC33F3E24
1076	QueryValueEx	ROOT\CLSID\{645FF040-5081-101B-9F0...	SUCCESS	
1077	CloseKey	ROOT\CLSID\{645FF040-5081-101B-9F0...	SUCCESS	
1078	OpenKey	ROOT\Folder	SUCCESS	hKey: 0xC3328FB8
1079	OpenKey	ROOT\CLSID\{645FF040-5081-101B-9F0...	SUCCESS	hKey: 0xC33F420C
1080	OpenKey	ROOT\Folder	SUCCESS	hKey: 0xC3328FB8
1081	CloseKey	ROOT\CLSID\{645FF040-5081-101B-9F0...	SUCCESS	
1082	CloseKey	ROOT\Folder	SUCCESS	
1083	OpenKey	ROOT\CLSID\{645FF040-5081-101B-9F0...	SUCCESS	hKey: 0xC33F3E24
1084	QueryValueEx	ROOT\CLSID\{645FF040-5081-101B-9F0...	SUCCESS	
1085	CloseKey	ROOT\CLSID\{645FF040-5081-101B-9F0...	SUCCESS	
1086	QueryValue	0xC3328E8C\{645FF040-5081-101B-9F08-...	SUCCESS	
1087	OpenKey	ROOT\CLSID\{645FF040-5081-101B-9F0...	SUCCESS	hKey: 0xC33F3E24
1088	QueryValue	ROOT\CLSID\{645FF040-5081-101B-9F0...	SUCCESS	
1089	QueryValueEx	ROOT\CLSID\{645FF040-5081-101B-9F0...	SUCCESS	
1090	CloseKey	ROOT\CLSID\{645FF040-5081-101B-9F0...	SUCCESS	
1091	OpenKey	ROOT\CLSID\{645FF040-5081-101B-9F0...	SUCCESS	hKey: 0xC33F3E24
1092	QueryValue	ROOT\CLSID\{645FF040-5081-101B-9F0...	SUCCESS	
1093	EnumKey	ROOT\CLSID\{645FF040-5081-101B-9F0...	SUCCESS	{645FF040-5081-101B-9F0..
1094	EnumKey	ROOT\CLSID\{645FF040-5081-101B-9F0...	NOMORE	
1095	CloseKey	ROOT\CLSID\{645FF040-5081-101B-9F0...	SUCCESS	
1096	OpenKey	ROOT\Folder\shellex\ContextMenuHandlers	SUCCESS	hKey: 0xC33F3E24
1097	QueryValue	ROOT\Folder\shellex\ContextMenuHandlers	SUCCESS	

Figure B-1. The Win95 Registry Monitor window

To install RegMon, simply copy *REGVXD.VXD* and *REGMON.EXE* to a directory of your choice. The sole requirement is that the two files be stored in the same directory, so that *REGMON.EXE* can dynamically load *REGVXD.VXD*.

OREGLIB.DLL

OREGLIB.DLL is a Win32 dynamic link library containing a variety of "convenience" functions that save you from having to call the registry API directly from your C or Visual Basic programs to gather information about registry keys and values or to perform some simple operations. For the most part, they eliminate the need to call *RegQueryInfoKey*, with its myriad of parameters, when all that you really want to retrieve is one or two simple items of information about an open key. (*RegQueryInfoKey*, we've found, is a function whose 12 parameters are difficult to commit to memory, so it can safely be included in code only if you have a some online or written reference available while you're coding.)

With the exception of a few functions that rely on Win95-specific features, like *RegIsMultiConfig*, *RegImportFile*, and *RegMakeFile*, *OREGLIB.DLL* works under both Win95 and WinNT 3.x. One function, *RegHasDefaultValue*, also works under Win32s; for the most part, though, functions that return a Boolean value return FALSE when run under Win32s, while those that return a long integer return ERROR_CALL_NOT_IMPLEMENTED.

Besides the source code (*OREGLIB.C* and *OREGLIB.DEF*) and the library file (*OREGLIB.LIB*), the DLL is accompanied by two additional files: *OREGLIB.H*, a standard C header file that allows you to call *OREGLIB.DLL* from your C programs, and *OREGLIB.BAS*, a Visual Basic code module containing DECLARE statements for the DLL, to allow both C and Visual Basic programmers to call the library's routines from their code.

To install *OREGLIB.DLL*, copy the file to your Windows system directory; you also might want to use RegEdit to create a shared DLLs key for it in the registry. (For details, see "Registering Dynamic Link Libraries," in Chapter 8, *What Goes in the Registry: System Settings*.) If you're programming in C, copy *OREGLIB.LIB* to the directory indicated by your LIB environment variable, and copy *OREGLIB.H* to the directory indicated by your INCLUDE environment variable. If you're programming in Visual Basic, you'll also need *OREGLIB.BAS*, which contains the DECLARE statements that allow Visual Basic to identify the routines in OREGLIB.DLL; store it in a directory of your choice.[*]

---

[*] Note, though, that if you store *OREGLIB.DLL* in a directory other than one which Windows automatically searches, you'll have to modify the LIB argument of the DECLARE statement for each function in *OREGLIB.BAS* to indicate the full path to *OREGLIB.DLL*.

To call the functions in *OREGLIB.DLL* from your C programs, use the **#include** preprocessor directive to include *OREGLIB.H* in each of the source code modules that call the library's functions. Then, when you link your program, designate *OREGLIB.LIB* as one of the libraries whose references are to be linked in to your program. To call *OREGLIB.DLL* from your VB programs, add *OREGLIB.BAS* to each project that uses the library. You can then call the library's routines just as you would call any intrinsic Visual Basic function.

OREGLIB.DLL contains the functions described below.

RegDecrDword   *Win95, WinNT*

Decrements a REG_DWORD value entry in the registry. If the entry's value is 0, it is left unchanged.

SYNTAX	`LONG RegDecrDword(HKEY hKey, LPCSTR lpValueName) ;`
PARAMETERS	*hKey* Handle of the open key containing the value entry.
	lpValueName Name of the entry whose value is to be decremented.
RETURNS	The new **REG_DWORD** value. If the function fails, or if it is executed under Win32s, it returns -1.
SEE ALSO	*RegIncrDword*

RegGetMaxSubkeyLen   *Win95, WinNT*

Indicates the length of the longest subkey name belonging to the open key. If used to retrieve the size of the longest subkey name of a remote key under Win95, the function returns the correct value.

SYNTAX	`LONG RegGetMaxSubkeyLen(HKEY hKey,` `                        LPDWORD lpcchMaxSubkey) ;`
PARAMETERS	*hKey* Handle of the open key whose subkey count is requested.
	lpcchMaxSubkey Pointer to a long integer value to receive the number of characters of the subkey with the longest name, excluding its terminating null character. If the open key has no subkeys, the value of *lpcchMaxSubkey* is 0 when the function returns.
RETURNS	**ERROR_SUCCESS** if the function succeeds; otherwise, a standard registry error code. Under Win32s, the function returns **ERROR_CALL_NOT_ IMPLEMENTED**.
SEE ALSO	*RegGetSubkeyInfo, RegGetSubkeyLen*

RegGetMaxValueLen   *Win95, WinNT*

Indicates the length of the longest data value belonging to a value entry of the open key.

SYNTAX	LONG RegGetMaxValueLen(HKEY hKey, LPDWORD lpcchMaxValueData) ;	
PARAMETERS	*hKey*	Handle of the open key whose longest data value length is requested.
	lpcchMaxValueData	Pointer to a long integer value to receive the number of bytes in the longest data value. In cases where the longest data value is string data, this count includes the final terminating null. If *hKey* has no values, its value is 0 when the function returns.
RETURNS	ERROR_SUCCESS if the function succeeds; otherwise, a standard registry error code. Under Win32s, the function returns ERROR_CALL_NOT_IMPLEMENTED.	
SEE ALSO	*RegGetMaxValueNameLen, RegGetNumValues, RegGetValueInfo*	

RegGetMaxValueNameLen   *Win95, WinNT*

Indicates the length of the longest name belonging to a value entry of the open key. If the function runs under Win95 and *hKey* is the handle to a remote registry key, the function accurately computes the length of the open key's longest value name.

SYNTAX	LONG RegGetMaxValueNameLen(HKEY hKey, LPDWORD lpcchMaxValueName) ;	
PARAMETERS	*hKey*	Handle of the open key whose longest value name length is requested.
	lpcchMaxValueName	Pointer to a long integer value to receive the number of characters in the longest value entry name. This value does not include the name's final terminating null character. If the *hKey* has no *named* value entries, its value is 0 when the function returns.
RETURNS	ERROR_SUCCESS if the function succeeds; otherwise, a standard registry error code. Under Win32s, the function returns ERROR_CALL_NOT_IMPLEMENTED.	
SEE ALSO	*RegGetNumValues, RegGetMaxValueLen, RegGetValueInfo*	

RegGetNumSubkeys   *Win95, WinNT*

Indicates how many subkeys the open key has.

SYNTAX	LONG RegGetNumSubkeys(HKEY hKey, LPDWORD lpcSubkeys) ;
PARAMETERS	*hKey* — Handle of the open key whose subkey count is requested.
	lpcSubkeys — Pointer to a long integer value to receive the number of subkeys belonging to *hKey*. If the open key has no subkeys, its value is 0 when the function returns.
RETURNS	ERROR_SUCCESS if the function succeeds; otherwise, a standard registry error code. Under Win32s, the function returns ERROR_CALL_NOT_ IMPLEMENTED.
SEE ALSO	*RegGetSubkeyLen, RegGetSubkeyInfo*

RegGetNumValues   *Win95, WinNT*

Indicates how many value entries belong to the open key.

SYNTAX	LONG RegGetNumValues(HKEY hKey, LPDWORD lpcValues) ;
PARAMETERS	*hKey* — Handle of the open key whose value entries are to be counted.
	lpcValues — Pointer to a long integer value to receive the number of value entries belonging to *hKey*.
RETURNS	ERROR_SUCCESS if the function succeeds; otherwise, a standard registry error code. Under Win32s, the function returns ERROR_CALL_NOT_ IMPLEMENTED.
SEE ALSO	*RegGetMaxValueLen, RegGetMaxValueNameLen, RegGetValueInfo*

RegGetSubkeyInfo   *Win95, WinNT*

Indicates the number of subkeys belonging to the open key and the number of characters in the longest subkey name. If used for remote registry access under Win95, the function accurately counts the number of characters in the longest subkey name.

SYNTAX	LONG RegGetSubkeyInfo(HKEY hKey, LPDWORD lpcSubkeys, LPDWORD lpcchMaxSubkey) ;
PARAMETERS	*hKey* — Handle of the open key whose subkey information is requested.
	lpcSubkeys — Pointer to a long integer value to receive the number of subkeys belonging to *hKey*. After the function returns, its value is 0 if the *hKey* has no subkeys.
	LpcchMaxSubkey — Pointer to a long integer value to receive the length of the open key's longest subkey name. After the function returns, its value is 0 if the *hKey* has no subkeys.

| RETURNS | ERROR_SUCCESS if the function succeeds; otherwise, a standard registry error code. Under Win32s, the function returns ERROR_CALL_NOT_ IMPLEMENTED. |
| SEE ALSO | *RegGetMaxSubkeyLen, RegGetNumSubkeys* |

RegGetValueInfo   *Win95, WinNT*

Indicates the number of value entries belonging to the open key, as well as the number of characters in the longest value entry name and the number of bytes in the largest value. If the function executes under Win95 and *hKey* is the handle of a remote registry key, the function correctly calculates the number of characters in the key's longest value entry name.

SYNTAX	LONG RegGetValueInfo(HKEY hKey, LPDWORD lpcValues, LPDWORD lpcchMaxValueName, LPDWORD lpcchMaxValueData) ;
PARAMETERS	*hKey*	Handle of the open key about which subkey information is requested.
	lpcValues	Pointer to a long integer value to receive the number of value entries belonging to *hKey*.
	lpcchMaxValueName	Pointer to a long integer value to receive the number of characters in the longest name of a value entry belonging to *hKey*.
	lpcchMaxValueData	Pointer to a long integer value to receive the number of bytes in the open key's largest data value.
RETURNS	ERROR_SUCCESS if the function succeeds; otherwise, a standard registry error code. Under Win32s, the function returns ERROR_CALL_NOT_ IMPLEMENTED.
SEE ALSO	*RegGetMaxValueLen, RegGetMaxValueNameLen, RegGetNumValues*

RegHasDefaultValue   *Win95, WinNT, Win32s*

Indicates whether the open key has a default or unnamed value.

SYNTAX	BOOL RegHasDefaultValue(HKEY hKey) ;
PARAMETERS	*hKey* Handle of an open key.
RETURNS	TRUE if the open key has a default value; FALSE otherwise.
SEE ALSO	*RegOnlyHasDefaultValue*

RegImportFile   *Win95, WinNT*

Imports a .REG file into the registry. The function checks whether the filename that is passed to it as a parameter designates an existing file. If it does, the function uses *ShellExecute* to launch RegEdit as a background process. The function can be used to import a .REG file on the local computer only; importing to a remote registry is not supported.

SYNTAX	BOOL RegImportFile(LPCTSTR lpFilename) ;
PARAMETERS	*lpFilename* The complete path and filename, including the file extension, of the .REG file to be imported by the function.
RETURNS	TRUE if the .REG file is successfully imported; FALSE otherwise. If the function succeeds in launching RegEdit, it also may generate its own error messages.
SEE ALSO	*RegMakeFile*

RegIncrDword   *Win95, WinNT*

Increments a REG_DWORD value entry in the registry. If the value entry does not exist, the function creates it and sets its value to 1.

SYNTAX	LONG RegIncrDword(HKEY hKey, LPCSTR lpValueName) ;
PARAMETERS	*hKey* Handle of the open key containing the value entry.
	lpValueName Name of the entry whose value is to be incremented.
RETURNS	The new REG_DWORD value. If the function fails, or if it is executed under Win32s, it returns 0.
SEE ALSO	*RegDecrDword*

RegIsEditingDisabled   *Win95*

Determines whether a system administrator has used a tool like Policy Editor to disable user access to the local computer's registry with registry editing tools. If direct registry access is disabled, the function displays a message box and returns FALSE, which permits the application to perform whatever cleanup is necessary before exiting. This function executes on the local computer only; it cannot determine whether direct access to the registry with editing tools has been disabled on a remote computer.

SYNTAX	BOOL RegIsEditingDisabled() ;
PARAMETERS	None
RETURNS	TRUE if the system is configured to disallow registry editing tools; FALSE otherwise. Under Windows NT and Win32s, the function always returns FALSE.

RegIsHKeyRemote   *Win95*

Determines whether the handle of an open registry key is local or remote.

SYNTAX	BOOL RegIsHKeyRemote(HKEY hKey) ;
PARAMETERS	*hKey* Handle of an open key returned by *RegOpenKey, RegOpen-KeyEx, RegCreateKey, RegCreateKeyEx,* or *RegConnectRegistry.*
RETURNS	TRUE if the handle belongs to a remote registry key; FALSE otherwise. Under Win32s, the function always returns FALSE; under WinNT, its return value is undefined.

RegIsMultiConfig   *Win95, WinNT 4.0*

Determines whether a system is configured to support multiple hardware configurations. The function executes on the local computer only; it does not determine whether a remote registry contains multiple configurations.

SYNTAX	BOOL RegIsMultiConfig() ;
PARAMETERS	None
RETURNS	TRUE if the system is configured to support multiple configurations; FALSE otherwise. If run under Win32s or WinNT 3.x, the function also returns FALSE.

RegIsMultiUser   *Win95, WinNT*

Determines whether a system is configured to support multiple users or a single default user. The function executes on the local computer only; it does not determine whether a remote registry is configured to support multiple users.

SYNTAX	BOOL RegIsMultiUser() ;
PARAMETERS	None
RETURNS	TRUE if the system is configured to support multiple users; FALSE otherwise. If run under Win32s, the function also returns FALSE.

RegIsRemoteClient   *Win95*

Determines whether a system is configured to serve as a client for remote registry access. It checks for the presence of *WINREG.DLL*, and can be used before an application attempts to connect to a remote registry, as the following code fragment illustrates:

```
if (RegIsRemoteClient())
   RegConnectRegistry(lpMachineName, hKey, &phkResult) ;
```

The function executes under Win95 only; under both WinNT and Win32s, it returns FALSE.

SYNTAX	BOOL RegIsRemoteClient() ;
PARAMETERS	None
RETURNS	TRUE if the system is configured for remote registry access; FALSE otherwise. Under WinNT and Win32s, the function also returns FALSE.

RegMakeFile   *Win95, WinNT*

Creates a .REG file. The function checks whether the registry path that is passed to it as a parameter designates a valid registry key. If it does, the function uses the Win32 API *ShellExecute* function to launch RegEdit as a background process. The function can be used to generate a .REG file on the local computer only; generating registration files containing information from remote registries is not supported.

SYNTAX	BOOL RegMakeFile(LPCTSTR lpFilename, LPCTSTR lpRegPath) ;	
PARAMETERS	*lpFilename*	The complete path and filename, including the file extension, of the .REG file to be created by the function. If *lpFilename* already exists, it will be over-written without warning.
	lpRegPath	A fully qualified registry path to the topmost key that is to be included in the .REG file.
RETURNS	TRUE if the .REG file is created; FALSE otherwise. If the function invokes RegEdit, it also may generate its own error messages. The most common reason for the function to fail is that *lpszRegPath* specifies an invalid registry path.	
SEE ALSO	*RegImportFile*	

RegOnlyHasDefaultValue   *Win95, WinNT, Win32s*

Indicates whether the open key's only value is its default value (i.e., it has no named value entries).

SYNTAX	BOOL RegOnlyHasDefaultValue(HKEY hKey) ;	
PARAMETERS	*hKey*	Handle of an open key.
RETURNS	TRUE if the open key has a default value and no named values; FALSE if it has no default value or has a default value in addition to one or more named values.	
SEE ALSO	*RegHasDefaultValue*	

The Desaware Registry Control

The Desaware Registry Control, *DWREG32D.OCX*, is a 32-bit design-time only OCX custom control for Visual Basic that allows you to read from and write to the registry by accessing the control's properties and methods, rather than by calling the registry API directly. It is stored in the \SOFTWARE\DESAWARE directory.

Like most OCX controls, the Desaware Registry Control is self-registering. This means that, the first time that it is used, the control itself makes the necessary registry entries that Windows requires to identify the control. (If you're interested in the registry entries that are required to define an OLE control, see "OCX custom controls" in Chapter 8.) So to install the control, simply copy it to a directory of your choice. When you want to use it for the first time, do the following:

1. Select the Custom Controls option from the Tools menu. Visual Basic opens the Custom Control dialog. However, because it is not registered yet, the Desaware Registry Control does not appear in the Available Controls list box.

2. Click on the Browse button. VB opens the Add Custom Control dialog, which is a standard Windows common dialog.

3. Navigate to the drive and directory in which you've stored the control, then select the control. In the course of adding it to the Available Controls list box, the control will also be registered.

WINREG.BAS

WINREG.BAS is a Visual Basic code module that includes definitions of the DECLARE statements, data structures, and constants needed to access the registry API from Visual Basic applications. *WINREG.BAS* is used in most of the Visual Basic code examples that appear in *Inside the Windows 95 Registry*. You can also add it to your own projects when you want to call the registry API.

For the most part, the DECLARE statements contained in *WINREG.BAS* are identical to those provided by *WIN32API.TXT* or *WIN32API.MDB*, the files containing 32-bit declarations, structures, and constants that are used by the API Viewer. There are, however, some differences:

- Both *RegQueryInfoKey* and *RegEnumKeyEx* include a parameter named *lpftLastWriteTime* whose data type is FILETIME. Since the Win95 registry does not save the date and time that the last write to a key occurred, this parameter is usually a major annoyance: it requires that you define a dummy variable of type FILETIME just to call these functions. To avoid this, *WINREG.BAS* defines the data type of *lpftLastWriteTime* as Any, thus allowing you to pass a null in place of a FILETIME data structure. This means, though, that you have to explicitly pass the null by value if you're using the

DECLARE statement on Windows NT, as the final `ByVal` 0 in the following call to *RegEnumKeyEx* shows:

```
if RegEnumKeyEx(hKey, lngIndex, strSubkey, lngLenSubkey, _
    0, "", ByVal 0, ByVal 0)
```

Since Win95 doesn't perform any validity checking on the parameter and doesn't use it, it doesn't care whether it's correctly passed a null or not.

- A number of functions have an `lpReserved` parameter that is supposed to be a pointer to a long integer. *ADVAPI32.DLL* and the Win95 VMM perform no error checking on the parameter and don't use it. For remote registry access and under WinNT, though, a validity check is performed on the parameter, even though it isn't used; if `lpReserved` is not a null, these functions fail and return `ERROR_INVALID_PARAMETER`. Consequently, the DECLARE statements for each of these functions have been modified to pass `lpReserved` by value; this allows you to pass a null (a zero value) in place of the parameter without having to pay any attention to it. The functions whose DECLARE statements have been modified are *RegEnumKeyEx*, *RegEnum-Value*, *RegQueryInfoKey*, and *RegQueryValueEx.*

- The most common error in using *RegSetValueEx* occurs when the programmer is writing a string value to the registry and forgets that the data type of `lpData` is defined as `As Any` in the function's standard DECLARE statement; as a result, he or she forgets to add the ByVal keyword when passing the parameter. To save you from having to continually pay attention to this small detail, *WINREG.BAS* includes the definition for a function named *RegSetStringValue* that writes a string value to the registry; it is simply an aliased version of *RegSetValueEx.*

Along with its definition of all registry functions, constants, and data structures, *WINREG.BAS* also contains definitions for a number of registry related functions (like *ExpandEnvironmentStrings*, *GetVersionEx*, and *RegisterServiceProcess*), data structures (like `OSVERSIONINFO`), and constants (like `RSP_SIMPLE_SERVICE`).

RegDump

RegDump, developed by Andrew Schulman, is presented in Chapter 5, *Win95 Registry Access from Win16, DOS, and VxDs*, to show how to access the Win95 registry from a Win16 or a DOS application. It also is a standalone utility that can be used to output the contents of the registry to a file. Its output differs from the .REG files and the printed output created by RegEdit in a number of respects:

- *Condensed output.* For instance, .REG files generated by RegEdit consume a good deal of space to depict `HKCR\exefile` and its subkeys:

```
[HKEY_CLASSES_ROOT\.exe]
@="exefile"
```

```
[HKEY_CLASSES_ROOT\exefile]
@="Application"
"EditFlags"=hex:d8,07,00,00

[HKEY_CLASSES_ROOT\exefile\shell]
@=""

[HKEY_CLASSES_ROOT\exefile\shell\open]
@=""
"EditFlags"=hex:00,00,00,00

[HKEY_CLASSES_ROOT\exefile\shell\open\command]
@="\"%1\" %*"

[HKEY_CLASSES_ROOT\exefile\shellex]

[HKEY_CLASSES_ROOT\exefile\shellex\PropertySheetHandlers]

[HKEY_CLASSES_ROOT\exefile\shellex\PropertySheetHandlers\{86F19A00-
42A0-1069-A2E9-08002B30309D}]
@=""

[HKEY_CLASSES_ROOT\exefile\DefaultIcon]
@="%1"
```

RegDump, on the other hand, presents the same information in a much more condensed and readable manner:

```
exefile -> "Application"
  EditFlags=BIN (4 bytes) [7D8h]
  shell -> ""
   open -> ""
    EditFlags=BIN (4 bytes) [0]
    command -> '"%1" %*'
  shellex
   PropertySheetHandlers
    {86F19A00-42A0-1069-A2E9-08002B30309D} -> ""
  DefaultIcon -> "%1"
```

- *Substitution of OLE class names for CLSIDs.* Where an OLE CLSID is used as an entry's value, RegDump automatically substitutes the name corresponding to that CLSID. For instance, the registry typically contains the definition of a ProgID named Word.Document.6. The output from RegEdit links it to an OLE class as follows:

```
[HKEY_CLASSES_ROOT\Word.Document.6\CLSID]
@="{00020900-0000-0000-C000-000000000046}"
```

In contrast, RegDump presents this information in a way that makes it easy to see just what {00020900-0000-0000-C000-000000000046} represents:

```
  CLSID -> {Microsoft Word Document}
```

RegDump is found in the \SOFTWARE\REGDUMP directory, and consists of the following files:

REGDMP16.EXE	A Win16 version of RegDump
REGDUMP.EXE	A Win32 version of RegDump
REGDUMPD.EXE	A DOS version of RegDump
DOSREG.H	Header file for registry access under Win95 from DOS
WINREG16.H	Header file for registry access under Win95 from Win16
REGDUMP.C	The multi-platform source code for RegDump
DOSREG.C	Source code for registry access under Win95 from DOS
WIN16REG.C	Source code for registry access under Win95 from Win16

Registry File System Device

The Registry File System Device, or RegFSD, is a virtual device driver that offers an alternate view of—and therefore provides an alternate means of accessing—the Win95 registry. RegFSD, which is stored in the \SOFTWARE\REGFSD directory, was developed by Fred Hewett of Vireo Software, and is included as a sample VxD in Vireo's VToolsD VxD development toolkit (see *http://www.vireo.com*). RegFSD locates the registry within the shell namespace, and allows you to access it just like you would any file system.

RegFSD is intended to illustrate a concept—namely, that any computer system object can be located within the shell's namespace, and can be handled using a familiar metaphor and a set of API functions appropriate to that metaphor. Because of this, RegFSD is not really intended as a practical replacement for the registry API. Nevertheless, we found this particular implementation of the registry as a conventional file system sufficiently interesting (and fun to explore as well) that we chose to include it on the accompanying diskette. The diskette also includes source code so that, if you want to enhance RegFSD and have a copy of VToolsD available, you can write a robust replacement for the registry API that you can incorporate into your applications.

To install RegFSD, do the following:

1. Extract the files in *REGFSD.ZIP* to a temporary directory.

2. Open Control Panel and select the Add New Hardware option. When the Add New Hardware wizard appears, select the No option so that Win95 does not scan for new hardware.

3. When Win95 displays a dialog containing the Hardware Types list box, which asks you to select the particular hardware device you'd like to install, select the Hard Disk controllers option.

4. When the dialog asking you to indicate the hardware's model and manufacturer appears, click the Have Disk button.

5. When Win95 opens the Install From Disk dialog, type the full path to your temporary directory in the text box, or click on the browse button to navigate to the directory.

6. When an Add New Hardware wizard dialog reappears, click on the Next button. When the next dialog appears, click on the Finish button.

As Figure B-2 shows, once RegFSD is installed, the registry appears in the Explorer window as a logical device within the Win95 file system: registry keys correspond to directories, and registry value entries correspond to files. With RegFSD installed, you can access the registry from an application just as you would any other file system object: you can treat the registry as a folder within the desktop's namespace, or you can use the standard file operation functions in place of the registry API. For example:

- *SetCurrentDirectory* can be used instead of *RegOpenKey* and *RegOpenKeyEx*

- *FindFirstFile, FindNextFile,* and *FileClose* can be used instead of *RegEnumKey, RegEnumKeyEx,* and *RegEnumValue*

- *ReadFile* can be used instead of *RegQueryValue* and *RegQueryValueEx*

- *WriteFile* can be used instead of *RegSetValue* and *RegSetValueEx*

At the same time, this implementation of the registry as a file system has several limitations:

- Some keys, like `HKEY_CLASSES_ROOT\.txt` or `HKLM\Enum\Root\ *PNP0000)`, are not accessible because they use what the file system considers to be invalid characters

- A key's default value, because it has no name, cannot be opened using RegFSD

- The contents of a registry file system "file" consists of an individual value entry's data; when retrieving the data using the *ReadFile* function, there is no indication of the type of data stored to that value entry

Along with the VxD and its source code, the diskette includes a sample program, *RFSPROG.C,* that illustrates how RegFSD is used. It can be compiled using the following command line syntax:

```
CL RFSPROG.C PUTFS.C USER32.LIB GDI32.LIB
```

The program first retrieves the names of all available system drives, and examines the volume name of each to determine which drive name represents the Win95 registry. The program then opens (or, more precisely, changes the current direc-

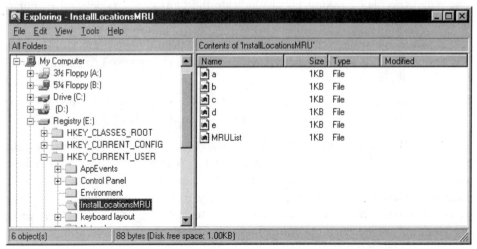

Figure B-2. The registry as a part of the Win95 file system

tory to) the `HKLM\Software\Microsoft\Windows\CurrentVersion` key. The *FindFirstFile/FindNextFile* API functions are then used to enumerate the objects stored in the directory. Each call to the function updates a `WIN32_FIND_DATA` structure whose pointer is passed to it; based on the value of its *dwFileAttributes* member, the names of subdirectories (or keys) are added to a Subkeys list box, while the names of files (or value entries) are added to a Value Entries list box.

Ini2Reg

Ini2Reg, the initialization file to the registry migration utility, is documented in Chapter 11, *Migrating from .INI Files to the Registry*; both the source code (INI2REG.C) and executable (INI2REG.EXE) versions of the file are stored in the \SOFTWARE\INI2REG subdirectory. The command line syntax to recompile Ini2Reg is:

```
CL INI2REG.C ADVAPI32.LIB
```

Code Samples

Sample programs and functions from *Inside the Windows 95 Registry* are stored in the subdirectories of the \SAMPLE directory, with one subdirectory for each chapter of the book in which a code example appears. In most cases, both source code and an executable file are included on the disk.

For the examples in C, the easiest way to rebuild the executables yourself is to use Win95's console mode. Each table includes the command line syntax necessary to compile and link the sample source code if you're using Microsoft Visual C++. The C language examples don't include a make file or a project file. So if you prefer to use an IDE like Microsoft Developer Studio to generate your executables, you can simply create a new project, then add the necessary source code file or files to it.

Running the sample Visual Basic executables requires that the files listed in Table B-1 be present on your hard disk. If you have a working copy of Visual Basic on your computer, all of the files should have been copied to your hard disk when you installed Visual Basic 4.0. If you program in C, and don't have a copy of Visual Basic on your computer, you can still run the executables. All files but VB40032.DLL, the Visual Basic 4.0 32-bit run-time library, should have been installed on your computer by Windows itself, by your C language product, or by some other application. If you don't have the VB run-time library, you'll find it on the Inside the Windows 95 Registry diskette in \SAMPLES\VB; you can simply uncompress it and copy it to the Windows system directory.

Table B-1. Files required by Visual Basic

Filename	Description
CTL3D32.DLL	3-D control library
MSVCRT20.DLL	Visual C++ 2.0 run-time library
MSVCRT40.DLL	Visual C++ 4.0 run-time library
OLEPRO32.DLL	32-bit standard OLE library
VB40032.DLL	Visual Basic 32-bit run-time library

To examine the source code for the Visual Basic examples, or to generate a new executable using the Visual Basic compiler, you can simply open the Visual Basic Project (.VBP) file for that example. If you don't have Visual Basic installed on your computer, you can still examine the Visual Basic source code files by using any text editor.

Almost all the sample Visual Basic programs rely on *WINREG.BAS*, which is included in the \SOFTWARE\WINREG directory of the *Inside the Windows 95 Registry* diskette; this is the VB code module that contains the definitions of all Registry API functions, data structures, and constants. Since we've left you free to decide exactly where you want to store the individual components contained on the diskette, you're almost certain to see the error dialog shown in Figure B-3 when you use Visual Basic to load a project. This occurs because each VB project (.VBP) file must contain a hard-coded path to the code module; in each case, the project file indicates that it's found in the directory in which your project and its source code files are stored. So in order to get the sample programs to work in the Visual Basic design-time environment, you'll have to add *WINREG.BAS* to your project. You can do this as follows:

- Select the Add File option from VB's File menu. Visual Basic opens the Add File common dialog.

- Navigate to the directory in which you've chosen to store *WINREG.BAS*, and select the file.

Once you've added the code module to a project, you should be able to run the program normally.

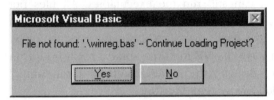

Figure B-3. Visual Basic's file not found error dialog

Chapter 1: The Registry, or, What Was So Bad About .INI Files?

Of the numerous benchmarks that we ran to compare the performance of registry access with initialization file access, the diskette includes *INREG.C*, which is discussed in Chapter 1. *INIREG.C* was written by Andrew Schulman.

Example	Filename	Description, Compiler Command Line
1-1	*INIREG.C*	.INI file-registry performance benchmark
		`CL INIREG.C ADVAPI32.LIB`

Chapter 2: Using the Registry Editor

For the most part, all components needed to run the Visual Basic sample executables are either included on the diskette or are present on any system on which either Visual Basic or a C language product is installed. The source code for the Registry Editor clone discussed in Chapter 2, however, is a notable exception. Since we have not included the TreeView, ListView, or ImageList controls on the accompanying diskette, this program requires that you have either the Professional Edition or the Enterprise Edition of Visual Basic 4.0 installed on your system.

The Registry Editor clone is not a complete working replacement for the RegEdit, and does not implement the entire feature set of RegEdit. Instead, it's a "proof of concept" to show that it's fairly easy to create your own Registry Editor.

Example	Filename	Description
2-3 and 2-4	*REGCLONE.VBP*[a]	RegEdit clone

[a] Project requires the *WINREG.BAS* code module.

Chapter 4: The Win32 Registry API

C programs illustrating calls to the registry API are found in \SAMPLES\CHAP04.

Example	Filename	Description, Compiler Command Line
4-1	*OPENKEY1.C*	Illustrates enumerating and opening the subkeys of a root key. `CL OPENKEY1.C ADVAPI32.LIB USER32.LIB`
4-2	*OPENKYX1.C*	Uses *RegOpenKeyEx* to launch a program and open its associated data file. `CL OPENKYX1.C ADVAPI32.LIB USER32.LIB`
4-3	*REGCREAX.C*	Uses *RegCreateKeyEx* to create an application identifier key along with and its subkeys. `CL REGCREAX.C ADVAPI32.LIB`
4-4	*REGCONN.C*	Assessing the performance of *RegConnectRegistry*, written by Andrew Schulman. `CL -DUSE_THREAD REGCONN.C ADVAPI32.LIB`

4-5	*COMPNAME.C*
	ISLOCAL.C
		Determines whether a particular computer is local or remote. *COMPNAME.C* is a shell program that allows you to call the *IsLocal* function.
		`CL COMPNAME.C ISLOCAL.C ADVAPI32.LIB`
		`USER32.LIB`

4-6	*BROWNET.C* *GETREM.C*	Retrieves the name of a local computer using the Win95 shell namespace. *BROWNET.C* is a shell program that calls the *GetRemoteComputer* function. `CL BROWNET.C GETREM.C USER32.LIB SHELL32.LIB`

4-7	*ENUMLIST.C*
	FILLLIST.C
		Enumerates registry keys to fill a list box. *ENUMLIST.C* is a shell program that calls the *FillList* function.
		`CL ENUMLIST.C FILLLIST.C ADVAPI32.LIB`
		`USER32.LIB`

4-8	*UNION.C*	Using a union as the `lpByte` parameter to *RegEnumValue* to retrieve unknown data types. `CL UNION.C ADVAPI32.LIB USER32.LIB`
4-9	*MRUMENU.C*	Using *RegQueryValueEx* to build an MRU menu. `CL MRUMENU.C ADVAPI32.LIB USER32.LIB`

Example	Filename	Description, Compiler Command Line
-----	*MRUMENU2.C* *MRUMENU.H*	Making *RegQueryValueEx* self-correcting. `CL MRUMENU2.C ADVAPI32.LIB USER32.LIB`
4-10	*QMULTI.C*	Using *RegQueryMultipleValues* `CL QMULTI.C ADVAPI32.LIB USER32.LIB`

Chapter 5: Win95 Registry Access from Win16, DOS, and VxDs

Sample 16-bit code for accessing the Win95 registry is stored in \SAMPLES\ CHAP05.

Example	Filename	Description
5-1	*CHKWIN95.C* *ISWIN95.C*	The *IsWindows95* function. Note that the function tests for Windows 95 *only*, and not for any version of the 32-bit Windows platform. *CHKWIN95.C* is a shell program that calls *IsWindows95*.
5-2	*ISWIN95.VBP* *ISWIN95.BAS*	Testing for the presence of Windows 95 with a 16-bit Visual Basic application. This is a console mode program in which the *Main* procedure calls *IsWindows95*.
5-3 and 5-4	*DOSREG.C* *DOSREG.H*	These code fragments are included in the \SOFTWARE\ REGDUMP subdirectory.
5-5	*REGDUMP.C*	Source code for RegDump is included in the \SOFTWARE\ REGDUMP subdirectory.

Chapter 6: The Registry and Visual Basic

Each sample program listed in the following table includes not only a Visual Basic project (.VBP) file, but also a Visual Basic form (.FRM) file with the same root filename; the latter, though, is not listed in the table. In addition, projects denoted with asterisks require *WINREG.BAS*.

Example	Filename	Description
6-1	*VBAFUNC.VBP*[a]	Coding for 16- and 32-bit versions of Windows
6-2	*GETSET.VBP*	Using *GetSetting* to position an application window
6-3	*GETALLS.VBP*	Using *GetAllSettings* to build an MRU list
		Before testing the program, use RegEdit to create a key named HKCU\Software\VB and VBA Program Settings\VBRegF\MRU. Add a REG_SZ value entry named MRU, and assign it a value of "3124". Finally, add four REG_SZ value entries named 1, 2, 3, and 4, and assign each of them an arbitrary filename.
6-4	*SAVESET.VBP*	Using *SaveSetting* to save application state information

Example	Filename	Description
6-5	*INLINE1.VBP*[a]	In-line error handling
6-6 to 6-8	*RAISEERR.VBP*[a]	Enabling an error handler User-defined error codes for the **Err.Raise** method are included in *WINREG.BAS*
6-9	*TOKNOWN.VBP*[a]	Determining the data type of a value entry
6-10	*STRBUFF1.VBP*[a]	Retrieving string data from the registry
6-11	*GETDWORD.VBP*[a]	Retrieving long integer data from the registry
6-12	*BINSTR2.VBP*[a]	Retrieving structured data from the registry
6-13	*BINSTR3.VBP*[a]	Retrieving structured data containing a string
6-14 and 6-15	*HKDDRPT.VBP*[a]	Storing REG_BINARY data to a long integer
6-16	*MULTISZ1.VBP*[a]	Writing REG_MULTI_SZ data to the registry
6-17	*SAVEFR1.VBP*[a]	Writing byte data to the registry using a byte array
6-18	*SAVEFR2.VBP*[a]	Writing byte data to the registry using a string

[a] Project requires the *WINREG.BA*S code module.

Chapter 7: The Desaware Registry Control

All but the first sample program contained in Chapter 7 require that you've installed the Desaware Registry Control; for details, see "The Desaware Registry Control" in the Software section earlier in this appendix, as well as the Desaware web site at *http://www.desaware.com*. Since the diskette contains a design-time only version of the control, executables of sample programs that use the control are not included on the *Inside the Windows 95 Registry* diskette. Finally, each project consists of a Visual Basic Project (.VBP) file, along with a Visual Basic form (.FRM) file with the same root filename; to save space, the latter file is not listed in the table. Any additional files required by each project, though, are listed.

Example	Filename	Description
7-1	*FONTS.VBP*[a]	Retrieving font information using the registry API
7-2	*TTFONTS2.VBP*	Retrieving font information using the Desaware registry control
7-3 and 7-4	*DWREGOP1.VBP*	Retrieving string data from the registry The lower portion of the application window includes a command button and a text box that you can use to add test MRU data to the registry; just enter a filename in the text box, then click on the Add MRU File button.

Example	Filename	Description
7-5 and 7-6	SAVESET.VBP	Retrieving REG_DWORD data from the registry
		This program can modify the `NoSaveSettings` value entry of `HKCU\Software\Microsoft\Windows\CurrentVersion\Policies\Explorer`. You might want to make sure that you change its value back to the original if you modify it. The entry's default value is 0.
7-7 and 7-8	DRIVES.VBP	Retrieving byte (REG_BINARY) data from the registry
		This program can modify the `NoDriveTypeAutoRun` value entry in `HKCU\Software\Microsoft\Windows\CurrentVersion\Policies\Explorer`. You might want to make sure that you restore its original value if you do modify it. The entry's default value is 95h.
7-9 and 7-10	DWSRCH3.VBP DWSRCH3.FRX SRCHDLG.FRM	Searching for registry keys
7-11 and 7-12	VALSRCH1.VBP VALSRCH1.FRX STATUS.FRM FRMVALUE.FRM FRMVALUE.FRX REGVFIND.BAS FRMVALUE.FRX	Searching for registry values

[a] Project requires the WINREG.BAS code module.

Chapter 8: What Goes in the Registry: System Settings

Because they use the same basic filenames, C programs are stored in \SAMPLES\CHAP08\C, while Visual Basic programs are stored in \SAMPLES\CHAP08.VB.

Example	Filename	Description, Compiler Command Line
8-1	APP_PATH.C	Registering an application path
		`CL APP_PATH.C ADVAPI32.LIB`
8-2	APPPATH.VBP[a] APPPATH.BAS	Registering an application path
		This is a console mode application; APPPATH.BAS is used instead of APPPATH.FRM.
8-3	SHARETST.C SHAREDLL.C	Increments the shared DLL counter. SHARETST.C is a shell program that calls the IncrDLLUsage function.
		`CL SHARETST.C SHAREDLL.C ADVAPI32.LIB USER32.LIB`
8-4	SHAREDLL.VBP SHAREDLL.BAS	Increments the shared DLL counter.
		This is a console mode application; SHAREDLL.BAS is used instead of SHAREDLL.FRM.

Example	Filename	Description, Compiler Command Line
8-5	*DECRTEST.C* *DECRUSE.C*	Decrements the shared DLL counter. *DECRTEST.C* is a shell program that allows you to call the *DecrDLLUsage* function. `CL DECRTEST.C DECRUSE.C ADVAPI32.LIB` `SHELL32.LIB USER32.LIB` Before running the application, you should do the following: 1. Create a test file in C:\WINDOWS\SYSTEM called *MYOWNDLL.DLL*. 2. Add a REG_DWORD value entry named `C:\Windows\` `System\MyOwnDLL.DLL` to `HKLM\Software\` `Microsoft\Windows\CurrentVersion\Shared-` `DLLs`, and set its value to 2. Then run the program twice.
8-6	*DECRUSE.VBP* *DECRUSE.BAS*	Decrements the shared DLL counter. This is a console mode application; *DECRUSE.BAS* is used instead of *SHAREDLL.FRM*. Before running the program, follow the same directions as for Example 8-5.
8-7	*EFLAGTST.C* *NOEDASSN.C*	Prevents the user from editing file association information. *EFLAGTST.C* is a shell program that allows you to call the *NoEditAssn* function. `CL EFLAGTST.C NOEDASSN.C ADVAPI32.LIB` `USER32.LIB` The program disables the ability to edit the .H file association, if it's defined in your registry. You might want to modify the string passed to *NoEditAssn* to disable editing of another file type. And, after running the program, you also might want to use RegEdit to delete the `EditFlags` value entry.
8-8	*EDITFLG.VBP*[a] *EDITFLG.BAS*	Prevents the user from editing file association information. This is a console mode application; *EDITFLG.BAS* is used instead of *EDITFLG.FRM*. The program disables the ability to edit file association information for .VBP files. You might want to modify the string passed to *NoEditAssn* to disable editing of another file type. And, after running the program, you also might want to use RegEdit to delete the `EditFlags` value entry.
8-10	*QV.C*	Defines a Quick View file viewer for C header (.H) files `CL QV.C ADVAPI32.LIB`
8-11	*VBQV.VBP*[a] *VBQV.BAS*	Defines a Quick View file viewer for Visual Basic Form (.FRM) files This is a console mode application; *VBQV.BAS* is used instead of *VBQV.FRM*.
8-14	*RUNONCE.C*	Writes to the `RunOnce` subkey when processing WM_QUERYENDSESSION `CL RUNONCE.C ADVAPI32.LIB USER32.LIB` To test *RUNONCE.EXE*, run the program, then end your Windows session while the RunOnce window is still open.

Example	Filename	Description, Compiler Command Line
8-15	*RUNONCE.VBP*[a]	Writes to the RunOnce subkey from the Form_QueryUn-load event procedure
		See the comments above for *RUNONCE.C*.
8-16	*RUNSRV.C*	Preventing a service from being closed when a user logs off
		`CL RUNSRV.C ADVAPI32.LIB USER32.LIB` `KERNEL32.LIB`
		To test RUNSRV.EXE, run the program, then end your Win95 session by closing all programs and logging on as a different user. After testing it, you'll want to delete the `HKLM\Software\Microsoft\Windows\Current-``Version\RunServices\RunSrv` key.

8-17 and 8-18	*PNPTST1.C*
	ISBADDR.C
	INITWP.C
	WPOS.H
		Handling a WM_DEVICECHANGE message
		
		`CL PNPTST1.C ISBADDR.C INITWP.C ADVAPI32.LIB`
		`USER32.LIB`

8-19	*EDITTST.C* *NOEDIT.C*	Determining if direct Registry access is disabled. *EDITTST.C* is a console mode shell program that calls the *IsRegEditingDisabled* function.
		`CL EDITTST.C NOEDIT.C ADVAPI32.LIB USER32.LIB`
8-20	*VBISEDIT.VBP*[a] *VBISEDIT.BAS*	Determining if direct Registry access is disabled.
		This is a console mode application; *VBISEDIT.BAS* is used instead of *VBISEDIT.FRM*.

[a] Project requires the *WINREG.BAS* code module.

Chapter 9: What Goes in the Registry: Application and User Settings

All code samples are stored in the \SAMPLES\CHAP09 subdirectory.

Example	Filename	Description

9-1 and 9-2	*WINPOS.C*
	INITWPOS.C
	WPOS.H
		Positioning an application window
		
		`CL WINPOS.C INITWPOS.C ADVAPI32.LIB`
		`USER32.LIB`

9-3	*VBWINPOS.VBP*[a]	Positioning an application window

9-4	*DEFSND.C*
	ASSGNSND.C
		Defining application sound events. *DEFSND.C* is a console mode shell program that calls the *AssignApp-Sound* function.
		
		`CL DEFSND.C ASSGNSND.C ADVAPI32.LIB`
		`USER32.LIB`

[a] Project requires the *WINREG.BAS* code module.

Chapter 11: Migrating from .INI Files to the Registry

INI2REG.C, the source code for *INI2REG.EXE*, is stored in \SOFTWARE\INI2REG. A slightly different version of the source code for the *RegIncrDword* function can be found in *OREGLIB.C*, which is stored in the \SOFTWARE\OREGLIB subdirectory.

Appendix A: Where Am I Running?

All code samples are stored in \SAMPLES\APP_A.

Example	Filename	Description

A-1	*GETPLATF.C*
	PLATFORM.C
		The 32-bit *GetPlatform* function; *PLATFORM.C* is a shell program that calls the *GetPlatform* function.
		
		`CL PLATFORM.C GETPLATF.C KERNEL32.LIB`
		`USER32.LIB`

A-2 and A-3	*GETPLATF.VBP* *GETPLATF.BAS*	The 32-bit *GetPlatform* function for Visual Basic.
A-4	*ISWINNT.C* *PLATF16.C*	The 16-bit *IsWinNT* function. *PLATF16.C* is a shell program that calls the *IsWinNT* function.
A-5	*ISWINNT.VBP* *ISWINNT.BAS*	The IsWinNT function for the 16-bit version of VB.

Index

& (ampersand)
   in menu options, 350
   as type specifier, 224
* (asterisk) in registry key names, 111
\ (backslash)
   escaping, 107
   in registry key names, 111
= (equal sign) in registry key names, 111
- (minus sign) in key pane, 38
% character in variable names, 140
. (period) in registry key names, 111
+ (plus sign) in key pane, 38

16-bit applications, 526–529
32-bit applications, 522–526

A

access
   keys for canonical verbs, 350
   to particular key values, 145–153
   to registry, 413–414
      from DOS, 191–195
      from Win16, 183–190
   to registry keys, 52
   remote, 203
      Desaware Control and, 286
      to registry, 60
      requirements for, 117
   VBA functions and, 211
   to Win32 registry, 201–204
      via VB, 217–232
   to Win95 registry, 11
   (*see also* security)
Access Control property sheet, 60
AccessCheck function, 104
adding
   keys to registry, 50
   new file viewer, 369
   OCX controls to project, 284–286
   values to keys, 54–56
administration, remote, 60
ADVAPI32.DLL library, 96, 222
ALIAS clause, 221, 223
   type checking and, 230
aliases for DLL routines, 223–224
ampersand (&)
   in menu options, 350
   as type specifier, 224
ANSI version of functions, 97
API (*see* Win32 registry API)
API Viewer, 218
APISpy32 utility, 62, 495–506, 533
   versus RegSpy95, 495
APISPYLD.EXE shell, 497
AppendMenu function, 151
application keys, sound events subkeys
   and, 441
application strings, 371

C

calling convention, 224
calling registry API, 232–249
Cannot Import... message, 518
canonical verbs, 350
cascading delete, 162
case sensitivity
    DLL routine names, 221
    key names, 102
    RegSpy95 and, 469
    searches, 41
cbName parameter, 132
CD-ROM drives and Win95, 304
CFGBACK.EXE utility, 74–75
CGIHELLO.EXE program, 509–520
ChangeKey method, 288
checking
    APISPY32.API, 499
    if sound is enabled, 448
chronological RegSpy95 output, 458
class identifier (CLSID), 374–386
class names, 113
client-server communication, 371
Clipboard, 41
closing
    applications after logging off, 399
    files, and MRU lists, 438
    keys, 170, 283
CLSIDs, OLE class names for, 545
cmdFind_Click event procedure, 313
CoCreateGuid function, 374
code, 548–557
    RegSpy95, 482
command line
    importing .REG files via, 46
    running RegEdit from, 36, 48–50
Command1_Click event procedure, 306
commands, RegSpy95, 455
Common Gateway Interface (CGI), 509
    for Windows (*see* Win-CGI)
comparing .REG files with WinDiff, 73
compatibility
    lack of error handling, 244
    RegCreateKey function, 110
    RegOpenKey function, 104
    VB date and time, 280
    VBA functions, 210–212
    Win95 and WinNT registries, 12, 31

compressing backup files, 75
computers
    docking and undocking, 404
    local, 22, 25
    remote
        accessing registry from, 60
        listing, 123
CONFIG.POL file, 19
Configuration Backup utility, 74–75, 86,
    505
configuring
    APISpy32, 499
    ERU.EXE and, 76
    hardware, 24
    RegSpy95
        dynamically, 465–470
        statically, 461–464
    users, data for, 11
    Win95 for multiple users, 18
    (*see also* initialization files; settings)
conformance, initialization files and, 5
Connect Network Registry option, 60
Constant expression required error, 232
constants, 231, 238
content types, MIME, 360
    incoming files, 361–364
    outgoing files, 364–365
context menus, 348–352
    handler, 351
Control Panel, 58
    Mouse applet, 58
    Network applet, 60
    Sound applet, 440
CONTROL.INI file (*see* initialization files)
controls (*see* OCX controls)
ConvertToBin function, 315
CopyNode function, 492
CopyReversedList function, 492
corrupted registry (*see* restoring the
    registry)
CreateKey method, 288
creating
    detached registry hive, 164
    key values, 156–159
    .REG files, 44
    registry keys, 50, 109–115
currency data type, 278
current user, determining, 169
CurrentKey property, 286

About the Author

Ron Petrusha began working with computers in the mid 1970s, programming in SPSS (a programmable statistical package) and FORTRAN on the IBM 370 family. Since then, he has been a computer book buyer, editor of a number of books on Windows and UNIX, and a consultant on projects written in dBASE, Clipper, and Visual Basic. Ron also has a background in quantitative labor history, specializing in Russian labor history, and holds degrees from the University of Michigan and Columbia University.

Colophon

Our look is the result of reader comments, our own experimentation, and distribution channels. Distinctive covers complement our distinctive approach to technical topics, breathing personality and life into potentially dry subjects. UNIX and its attendant programs can be unruly beasts. Nutshell Handbooks help you tame them.

The animal featured on the cover of *Inside the Windows 95 Registry* is a dog. Often referred to as "[hu]man's best friend," dogs (canis familaris) are believed to be among the first animals domesticated by humans. Dogs most likely lived with cave dwellers to assist in hunting and to protect the clan. It is possible that scavenger dogs adopted humans, rather than the other way around, as potential providers of food, i.e., table scraps. (Think of those historical ties the next time Rex looks up at you at the dinner table.)

Dogs are probably descendants of wolf-like creatures. Thousands of years of breeding dogs has led to hundreds of varieties. Dogs have been bred and trained for many purposes, including hunting, herding, sports, security, and life-saving. They have been proven to have a positive effect on the well-being of people and to contribute to the quality of human life. Humans have also bred dogs for less benevolent uses, such as fighting, causing a loss of anti-aggression blockers in otherwise tame and nonviolent breeds. However, most breeds of dogs make excellent companions for humans. Puppies have a great capacity and eagerness to learn and to please, and the more they are exposed to people in their first year the more comfortable they will be when they grow up.

Edie Freedman designed this cover and the entire UNIX bestiary that appears on Nutshell Handbooks, using a 19th-century engraving from the Dover Pictorial

Archive. The cover layout was produced with Quark XPress 3.3 using the ITC Garamond font. Whenever possible, our books use RepKover™, a durable and flexible lay-flat binding. If the page count exceeds RepKover's limit, perfect binding is used.

The inside layout was designed by Jennifer Niederst and Nancy Priest and implemented in FrameMaker 5.0 by Mike Sierra. The text and heading fonts are ITC Garamond Light and Garamond Book. The illustrations that appear in the book were created in Macromedia Freehand 5.0 by Chris Reilley.

 # *More Titles from O'Reilly*

Windows

Developing Windows Error Messages

By Ben Ezzell
1st Edition November 1997 (est.)
300 pages (est.), Includes diskette
ISBN 1-56592-356-1

This book teaches C, C++, and Visual Basic programmers how to write effective error messages that notify the user of an error, clearly explain the error, and most importantly offer a solution to the error.

Win32 Multithreaded Programming

By Aaron Cohen & Mike Woodring
1st Edition November 1997 (est.), 700 pages (est.), Includes diskette, ISBN 1-56592-296-4

This book clearly explains the concepts of multithreaded programs and shows developers how to construct efficient and complex applications. An important book for any developer, it illustrates all aspects of Win32 multithreaded programming, including what has previously been undocumented or poorly explained.

Windows NT File System Internals

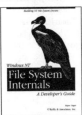

By Rajeev Nagar
1st Edition September 1997, 794 pages, Includes diskette, ISBN 1-56592-249-2

Windows NT File System Internals presents the details of the NT I/O Manager, the Cache Manager, and the Memory Manager from the perspective of a software developer writing a file system driver or implementing a kernel-mode filter driver. The book provides numerous code examples included on diskette, as well as the source for a complete, usable filter driver.

Access Database Design & Programming

By Steven Roman
1st Edition June 1997, 270 pages, ISBN 1-56592-297-2

This book provides experienced Access users who are novice programers with frequently overlooked concepts and techniques necessary to create effective database applications. It focuses on designing effective tables in a multi-table application; using the Access interface or Access SQL to construct queries; and programming using the Data Access Object (DAO) and Microsoft Access object models.

Inside the Windows 95 File System

By Stan Mitchell
1st Edition May 1997
378 pages, Includes diskette
ISBN 1-56592-200-X

In this book, Stan Mitchell describes the Windows 95 File System, as well as the new opportunities and challenges it brings for developers. Its "hands-on" approach will help developers become better equipped to make design decisions using the new Win95 File System features. Includes a diskette containing MULTIMON, a general-purpose monitor for examining Windows internals.

Dictionary of PC Hardware and Data Communications Terms

By Mitchell Shnier
1st Edition April 1996
532 pages, ISBN 1-56592-158-5

This comprehensive dictionary provides complete descriptions of complex terms in two of the most volatile and interesting areas of computer development: personal computers and networks. It contains up-to-date information about everything from a common item like "batteries" to an obscure font technology called "Speedo." Also available online. See *http://www.ora.com/reference/dictionary/* for details.

Inside the Windows 95 Registry

By Ron Petrusha
1st Edition August 1996
594 pages, ISBN 1-56592-170-4

An in-depth examination of remote registry access, differences between the Win95 and NT registries, registry backup, undocumented registry services, and the role the registry plays in OLE. Shows programmers how to access the Win95 registry from Win32, Win16, and DOS programs in C and Visual Basic. VxD sample code is also included. Includes diskette.

O'REILLY™

Developing Web Content

WebMaster in a Nutshell, Deluxe Edition

By O'Reilly & Associates, Inc.
1st Edition September 1997 (est.)
356 pages (est.), includes CD-ROM
ISBN 1-56592-305-7

The Deluxe Edition of *WebMaster in a Nutshell* is a complete library for web programmers. The main resource is the Web Developer's Library, a CD-ROM, containing the electronic text of five popular O'Reilly titles: *HTML: The Definitive Guide, 2nd Edition*; *JavaScript: The Definitive Guide, 2nd Edition*; *CGI Programming on the World Wide Web*; *Programming Perl, 2nd Edition*—the classic "camel book," written by Larry Wall (the inventor of Perl) with Tom Christiansen and Randal Schwartz; and *WebMaster in a Nutshell*. The Deluxe Edition also includes a printed copy of *WebMaster in a Nutshell*.

WebMaster in a Nutshell, Deluxe Edition, makes it easy to find the information you need with all of the convenience you'd expect from the Web. You'll have access to information webmasters and programmers use most for development—complete with global searching and a master index to all five volumes—all on a single CD-ROM. It's incredibly portable. Just slip it into your laptop case as you commute or take off on your next trip and you'll find everything at your fingertips with no books to carry.

The CD-ROM is readable on all hardware platforms. All files except Java code example files are in 8.3 file format and, therefore, are readable by older systems. A web browser that supports HTML 3.2 (such as Netscape 3.0 or Internet Explorer 3.0) is required to view the text. The browser must support Java if searching is desired.

The Web Developer's Library is also available by subscription on the World Wide Web. See http://www.ora.com/catalog/webrlw for details.

WebMaster in a Nutshell

By Stephen Spainhour & Valerie Quercia
1st Edition October 1996
374 pages, ISBN 1-56592-229-8

Web content providers and administrators have many sources for information, both in print and online. *WebMaster in a Nutshell* puts it all together in one slim volume for easy desktop access. This quick reference covers HTML, CGI, JavaScript, Perl, HTTP, and server configuration.

HTML: The Definitive Guide, 2nd Edition

By Chuck Musciano & Bill Kennedy
2nd Edition May 1997
552 pages, ISBN 1-56592-235-2

This complete guide is chock full of examples, sample code, and practical, hands-on advice to help you create truly effective web pages and master advanced features. Learn how to insert images and other multimedia elements, create useful links and searchable documents, use Netscape extensions, design great forms, and lots more. The second edition covers the most up-to-date version of the HTML standard (HTML version 3.2), Netscape 4.0 and Internet Explorer 3.0, plus all the common extensions.

JavaScript: The Definitive Guide, 2nd Edition

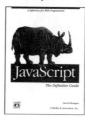

By David Flanagan
2nd Edition January 1997
664 pages, ISBN 1-56592-234-4

This second edition of the definitive reference guide to JavaScript, the HTML extension that gives web pages programming language capabilities, covers JavaScript as it is used in Netscape 3.0 and 2.0 and in Microsoft Internet Explorer 3.0. Learn how JavaScript really works (and when it doesn't). Use JavaScript to control web browser behavior, add dynamically created text to web pages, interact with users through HTML forms, and even control and interact with Java applets and Navigator plugins. By the author of the bestselling *Java in a Nutshell*.

CGI Programming on the World Wide Web

By Shishir Gundavaram
1st Edition March 1996
450 pages, ISBN: 1-56592-168-2

This book offers a comprehensive explanation of CGI and related techniques for people who hold on to the dream of providing their own information servers on the Web. It starts at the beginning, explaining the value of CGI and how it works, then moves swiftly into the subtle details of programming.

Developing Web Content *continued*

Information Architecture for the World Wide Web

By Louis Rosenfeld & Peter Morville
1st Edition November 1997 (est.)
200 pages (est.), ISBN 1-56592-282-4

Information Architecture for the World Wide Web is about applying the principles of architecture and library science to web site design. With this book, you learn how to design web sites and intranets that support growth, management, and ease of use. This book is for webmasters, designers, and anyone else involved in building a web site.

Learning VBScript

By Paul Lomax
1st Edition July 1997
616 pages, includes CD-ROM
ISBN 1-56592-247-6

This definitive guide shows web developers how to take full advantage of client-side scripting with the VBScript language. In addition to basic language features, it covers the Internet Explorer object model and discusses techniques for client-side scripting, like adding ActiveX controls to a web page or validating data before sending it to the server. Includes CD-ROM with over 170 code samples.

Web Client Programming with Perl

By Clinton Wong
1st Edition March 1997
228 pages, ISBN 1-56592-214-X

Web Client Programming with Perl shows you how to extend scripting skills to the Web. This book teaches you the basics of how browsers communicate with servers and how to write your own customized web clients to automate common tasks. It is intended for those who are motivated to develop software that offers a more flexible and dynamic response than a standard web browser.

Building Your Own WebSite

By Susan B. Peck & Stephen Arrants
1st Edition July 1996
514 pages, ISBN 1-56592-232-8

This is a hands-on reference for Windows® 95 and Windows NT™ users who want to host a site on the Web or on a corporate intranet. This step-by-step guide will have you creating live web pages in minutes. You'll also learn how to connect your web to information in other Windows applications, such as word processing documents and databases. The book is packed with examples and tutorials on every aspect of web management, and it includes the highly acclaimed WebSite™ 1.1 server software on CD-ROM.

Designing for the Web: Getting Started in a New Medium

By Jennifer Niederst
with Edie Freedman
1st Edition April 1996
180 pages, ISBN 1-56592-165-8

Designing for the Web gives you the basics you need to hit the ground running. Although geared toward designers, it covers information and techniques useful to anyone who wants to put graphics online. It explains how to work with HTML documents from a designer's point of view, outlines special problems with presenting information online, and walks through incorporating images into web pages, with emphasis on resolution and improving efficienc

How to stay in touch with O'Reilly

1. Visit Our Award-Winning Web Site

http://www.oreilly.com/

★"Top 100 Sites on the Web" —*PC Magazine*
★"Top 5% Web sites" —*Point Communications*
★"3-Star site" —*The McKinley Group*

Our web site contains a library of comprehensive product information (including book excerpts and tables of contents), downloadable software, background articles, interviews with technology leaders, links to relevant sites, book cover art, and more. File us in your Bookmarks or Hotlist!

2. Join Our Email Mailing Lists

New Product Releases

To receive automatic email with brief descriptions of all new O'Reilly products as they are released, send email to:
listproc@online.oreilly.com
Put the following information in the first line of your message (*not* in the Subject field):
subscribe oreilly-news "Your Name" of "Your Organization" (for example: subscribe oreilly-news Kris Webber of Fine Enterprises)

O'Reilly Events

If you'd also like us to send information about trade show events, special promotions, and other O'Reilly events, send email to: **listproc@online.oreilly.com**
Put the following information in the first line of your message (*not* in the Subject field):
subscribe oreilly-events "Your Name" of "Your Organization"

3. Get Examples from Our Books via FTP

There are two ways to access an archive of example files from our books:

Regular FTP
- ftp to:
  ftp.oreilly.com
  (login: anonymous
  password: your email address)
- Point your web browser to:
  ftp://ftp.oreilly.com/

FTPMAIL
- Send an email message to:
  ftpmail@online.oreilly.com
  (Write "help" in the message body)

4. Visit Our Gopher Site

- Connect your gopher to:
  gopher.oreilly.com

- Point your web browser to:
  gopher://gopher.oreilly.com/

- Telnet to:
  gopher.oreilly.com
  login: gopher

5. Contact Us via Email

order@oreilly.com
To place a book or software order online. Good for North American and international customers.

subscriptions@oreilly.com
To place an order for any of our newsletters or periodicals.

books@oreilly.com
General questions about any of our books.

software@oreilly.com
For general questions and product information about our software. Check out O'Reilly Software Online at **http://software.oreilly.com/** for software and technical support information. Registered O'Reilly software users send your questions to: **website-support@oreilly.com**

cs@oreilly.com
For answers to problems regarding your order or our products.

booktech@oreilly.com
For book content technical questions or corrections.

proposals@oreilly.com
To submit new book or software proposals to our editors and product managers.

international@oreilly.com
For information about our international distributors or translation queries. For a list of our distributors outside of North America check out:
http://www.oreilly.com/www/order/country.html

O'Reilly & Associates, Inc.
101 Morris Street, Sebastopol, CA 95472 USA
TEL   707-829-0515 or 800-998-9938
          (6am to 5pm PST)
FAX   707-829-0104

Titles from O'Reilly

Please note that upcoming titles are displayed in italic.

WEB PROGRAMMING

Apache: The Definitive Guide
Building Your Own Web Conferences
Building Your Own Website
CGI Programming for the World Wide Web
Designing for the Web
HTML: The Definitive Guide, 2nd Ed.
JavaScript: The Definitive Guide, 2nd Ed.
Learning Perl
Programming Perl, 2nd Ed.
Mastering Regular Expressions
WebMaster in a Nutshell
Web Security & Commerce
Web Client Programming with Perl
World Wide Web Journal

USING THE INTERNET

Smileys
The Future Does Not Compute
The Whole Internet User's Guide & Catalog
The Whole Internet for Win 95
Using Email Effectively
Bandits on the Information Superhighway

JAVA SERIES

Exploring Java
Java AWT Reference
Java Fundamental Classes Reference
Java in a Nutshell
Java Language Reference, 2nd Edition
Java Network Programming
Java Threads
Java Virtual Machine

SOFTWARE

WebSite™ 1.1
WebSite Professional™
Building Your Own Web Conferences
WebBoard™
PolyForm™
Statisphere™

SONGLINE GUIDES

NetActivism   NetResearch
Net Law   NetSuccess
NetLearning   NetTravel
Net Lessons

SYSTEM ADMINISTRATION

Building Internet Firewalls
Computer Crime: A Crimefighter's Handbook
Computer Security Basics
DNS and BIND, 2nd Ed.
Essential System Administration, 2nd Ed.
Getting Connected: The Internet at 56K and Up
Linux Network Administrator's Guide
Managing Internet Information Services
Managing NFS and NIS
Networking Personal Computers with TCP/IP
Practical UNIX & Internet Security, 2nd Ed.
PGP: Pretty Good Privacy
sendmail, 2nd Ed.
sendmail Desktop Reference
System Performance Tuning
TCP/IP Network Administration
termcap & terminfo
Using & Managing UUCP
Volume 8: X Window System Administrator's Guide
Web Security & Commerce

UNIX

Exploring Expect
Learning VBScript
Learning GNU Emacs, 2nd Ed.
Learning the bash Shell
Learning the Korn Shell
Learning the UNIX Operating System
Learning the vi Editor
Linux in a Nutshell
Making TeX Work
Linux Multimedia Guide
Running Linux, 2nd Ed.
SCO UNIX in a Nutshell
sed & awk, 2nd Edition
Tcl/Tk Tools
UNIX in a Nutshell: System V Edition
UNIX Power Tools
Using csh & tsch
When You Can't Find Your UNIX System Administrator
Writing GNU Emacs Extensions

WEB REVIEW STUDIO SERIES

Gif Animation Studio
Shockwave Studio

WINDOWS

Dictionary of PC Hardware and Data Communications Terms
Inside the Windows 95 Registry
Inside the Windows 95 File System
Windows Annoyances
Windows NT File System Internals
Windows NT in a Nutshell

PROGRAMMING

Advanced Oracle PL/SQL Programming
Applying RCS and SCCS
C++: The Core Language
Checking C Programs with lint
DCE Security Programming
Distributing Applications Across DCE & Windows NT
Encyclopedia of Graphics File Formats, 2nd Ed.
Guide to Writing DCE Applications
lex & yacc
Managing Projects with make
Mastering Oracle Power Objects
Oracle Design: The Definitive Guide
Oracle Performance Tuning, 2nd Ed.
Oracle PL/SQL Programming
Porting UNIX Software
POSIX Programmer's Guide
POSIX.4: Programming for the Real World
Power Programming with RPC
Practical C Programming
Practical C++ Programming
Programming Python
Programming with curses
Programming with GNU Software
Pthreads Programming
Software Portability with imake, 2nd Ed.
Understanding DCE
Understanding Japanese Information Processing
UNIX Systems Programming for SVR4

BERKELEY 4.4 SOFTWARE DISTRIBUTION

4.4BSD System Manager's Manual
4.4BSD User's Reference Manual
4.4BSD User's Supplementary Documents
4.4BSD Programmer's Reference Manual
4.4BSD Programmer's Supplementary Documents
X Programming
Vol. 0: X Protocol Reference Manual
Vol. 1: Xlib Programming Manual
Vol. 2: Xlib Reference Manual
Vol. 3M: X Window System User's Guide, Motif Edition
Vol. 4M: X Toolkit Intrinsics Programming Manual, Motif Edition
Vol. 5: X Toolkit Intrinsics Reference Manual
Vol. 6A: Motif Programming Manual
Vol. 6B: Motif Reference Manual
Vol. 6C: Motif Tools
Vol. 8 : X Window System Administrator's Guide
Programmer's Supplement for Release 6
X User Tools
The X Window System in a Nutshell

CAREER & BUSINESS

Building a Successful Software Business
The Computer User's Survival Guide
Love Your Job!
Electronic Publishing on CD-ROM

TRAVEL

Travelers' Tales: Brazil
Travelers' Tales: Food
Travelers' Tales: France
Travelers' Tales: Gutsy Women
Travelers' Tales: India
Travelers' Tales: Mexico
Travelers' Tales: Paris
Travelers' Tales: San Francisco
Travelers' Tales: Spain
Travelers' Tales: Thailand
Travelers' Tales: A Woman's World

O'REILLY™

TO ORDER: **800-998-9938** • **order@oreilly.com** • **http://www.oreilly.com/**
OUR PRODUCTS ARE AVAILABLE AT A BOOKSTORE OR SOFTWARE STORE NEAR YOU.
FOR INFORMATION: **800-998-9938** • **707-829-0515** • **info@oreilly.com**

International Distributors

UK, Europe, Middle East and Northern Africa (except France, Germany, Switzerland, & Austria)

INQUIRIES
International Thomson Publishing
Europe
Berkshire House
168-173 High Holborn
London WC1V 7AA, United Kingdom
Telephone: 44-171-497-1422
Fax: 44-171-497-1426
Email: itpint@itps.co.uk

ORDERS
International Thomson Publishing
Services, Ltd.
Cheriton House, North Way
Andover, Hampshire SP10 5BE,
United Kingdom
Telephone: 44-264-342-832
 (UK orders)
Telephone: 44-264-342-806
 (outside UK)
Fax: 44-264-364418 (UK orders)
Fax: 44-264-342761 (outside UK)
UK & Eire orders: itpuk@itps.co.uk
International orders: itpint@itps.co.uk

France

Editions Eyrolles
61 bd Saint-Germain
75240 Paris Cedex 05
France
Fax: 33-01-44-41-11-44

FRENCH LANGUAGE BOOKS
All countries except Canada
Phone: 33-01-44-41-46-16
Email: geodif@eyrolles.com

ENGLISH LANGUAGE BOOKS
Phone: 33-01-44-41-11-87
Email: distribution@eyrolles.com

Australia

WoodsLane Pty. Ltd.
7/5 Vuko Place, Warriewood NSW 2102
P.O. Box 935, Mona Vale NSW 2103
Australia
Telephone: 61-2-9970-5111
Fax: 61-2-9970-5002
Email: info@woodslane.com.au

Germany, Switzerland, and Austria

INQUIRIES
O'Reilly Verlag
Balthasarstr. 81
D-50670 Köln
Germany
Telephone: 49-221-97-31-60-0
Fax: 49-221-97-31-60-8
Email: anfragen@oreilly.de

ORDERS
International Thomson Publishing
Königswinterer Straße 418
53227 Bonn, Germany
Telephone: 49-228-97024 0
Fax: 49-228-441342
Email: order@oreilly.de

Asia (except Japan & India)

INQUIRIES
International Thomson Publishing Asia
60 Albert Street #15-01
Albert Complex
Singapore 189969
Telephone: 65-336-6411
Fax: 65-336-7411

ORDERS
Telephone: 65-336-6411
Fax: 65-334-1617
thomson@signet.com.sg

New Zealand

WoodsLane New Zealand Ltd.
21 Cooks Street (P.O. Box 575)
Wanganui, New Zealand
Telephone: 64-6-347-6543
Fax: 64-6-345-4840
Email: info@woodslane.com.au

Japan

O'Reilly Japan, Inc.
Kiyoshige Building 2F
12-Banchi, Sanei-cho
Shinjuku-ku
Tokyo 160 Japan
Telephone: 81-3-3356-5227
Fax: 81-3-3356-5261
Email: kenji@oreilly.com

India

Computer Bookshop (India) PVT. LTD.
190 Dr. D.N. Road, Fort
Bombay 400 001
India
Telephone: 91-22-207-0989
Fax: 91-22-262-3551
Email: cbsbom@giasbm01.vsnl.net.in

The Americas

O'Reilly & Associates, Inc.
101 Morris Street
Sebastopol, CA 95472 U.S.A.
Telephone: 707-829-0515
Telephone: 800-998-9938 (U.S. & Canada)
Fax: 707-829-0104
Email: order@oreilly.com

Southern Africa

International Thomson Publishing
Southern Africa
Building 18, Constantia Park
138 Sixteenth Road
P.O. Box 2459
Halfway House, 1685 South Africa
Telephone: 27-11-805-4819
Fax: 27-11-805-3648